Prai~~se~~

This collection offers a thought-provoking opportunity to parse multiplicities and recent directions in global justice organizing. Sen's framing in this book sets us up to take stock of two decades of social and political movement in terms of dynamic motion: Not only as strategy and organization, but as kinaesthetic experience, embodied transformation through space and time. The nuanced, critical emphases on indigeneity, spirituality, gender, and ecology, rich with specificity and insight, locate us unmistakably in our present moment with its lessons gleaned of recent history and praxis, even while bringing us full circle to the themes introduced an unbelievable twenty years ago. We shall not be moved. We shall move. We shall keep moving.

 —Maia Ramnath, teacher, writer, activist, and dancer/aerialist;
  author of *Decolonizing Anarchism*

An important contribution to a developing internationalism that doesn't assume that the North Atlantic left has all the answers for the rest of the world and which recognizes that emancipatory ideas and practices are often forged from below. Refreshingly free of tired dogmas, non-sectarian, taking internationalism seriously, and reaching back to 1968, the book provides a bracing window into some of the central ideas to have emerged from within movements in the sequence of struggle that unfolded from 2006 to 2010. This book will be useful for activists and intellectuals in movement—be they in universities, parties, trade unions, social movements, or religious organisations—around the world.

 —Richard Pithouse, researcher and lecturer in politics, Rhodes
  University, Grahamstown, South Africa

Someone once suggested that movement cannot be thought, it has to be lived. In other words, social movements—the coming together in processes that build the power to bring about change—stem not from any kind of blueprint that can set out an ideal for the world we ought to live in, nor can there be a simple step-by-step guide on how to get there. At the same time, there can't be movement without a collective effort to understand the shared and embodied experiences that constitute it, along with the problems, concerns, and trajectories that arise in struggle. It's this kind of critical reflection that the authors assembled in this volume undertake, providing intelligent and engaged analyses that avoid any stifling dichotomies, whether between theory and practice, activism and academia, or indeed between thinking and feeling. Possible futures, right now in the making, become legible in how *The Movements of Movements* doesn't shy away from the complex and unsettling issues that shape our time, while thinking through struggles for social and ecological justice in the wider contexts of their past and present.

—Emma Dowling, Senior Researcher in Political Sociology at the Institute for Sociology, Friedrich-Schiller-University Jena, Germany

The Movements
of Movements

Part 2

Rethinking Our Dance

Jai Sen, editor

Volume 5 in OpenWord's
Challenging Empires series

OpenWord is about open publication, and sees itself as a contribution to the wider struggle for making knowledges open for people across cultures and languages and on as many and as wide platforms as possible.

In this book, there are two broad categories of essays: Open and Restricted. You are free to re-use—for non-commercial purposes only—all those essays that have the **OpenWord** logo OpenWord on their opening page. For all other essays, check endnote 1 in each essay.

In all cases, please make your work available to others just as we are doing for you, and please acknowledge your source and the respective authors.

The Movements of Movements, Part 2: Rethinking Our Dance
© 2018 This collection as a whole, Jai Sen
© 2018 The individual essays, the respective authors
© 2018 This edition, OpenWord and PM Press

The Work is published and made available on a Creative Commons License, Attribution-NonCommercial-ShareAlike 4.0 International (CC BY-NC-SA 4.0).

Volume 5 in the OpenWord's *Challenging Empires* series

ISBN: 978-1-62963-380-0
Library of Congress Control Number: 2016959567

Editor: Jai Sen
Contributing Editor: Peter Waterman
Associate Editor: Madhuresh
Content Editors: Parvati Sharma, Vipul Rikhi, and Jai Sen
Text Compilation: Jim Coflin
Cover: John Yates/stealworks.com
Layout: Jonathan Rowland
Wordle Illustrations: Jai Sen

PM Press   OpenWord
P.O. Box 23912   R-21 South Extension Part II - Ground floor
Oakland, CA 94623, USA   New Delhi 110 049, India
www.pmpress.org   www.openword.net.in

10 9 8 7 6 5 4 3 2 1

Printed in the USA by the Employee Owners of Thomson-Shore in Dexter, Michigan
www.thomsonshore.com

To the dance of life
And the dance of movement
And to the warriors among us, past, present, and future;

And

To my Elainita (or Nina, as she is coming to be known), for the dance in her life,
and towards her becoming a warrior too

*

Life moves on. Things have happened.

As was its companion volume, this book is dedicated to

Peter Waterman
(January 26 1936—June 17 2017)

Friend, compañer@, and fellow birthday bearer
for the past thirty-five years,
and co-editor for the past fifteen;

Labour internationalist, cyberian, feminist, and feisty and fearless, always.
And to Peter's indomitable spirit and infectious
humour—and to the optimism of his will.
May those live on forever!

**Also to the many other warriors who have walked
on during these months and years,**
including contributors to these books

**And to all those who are being arrested, tortured,
and assassinated in our times**

in these increasingly grim days across the world,

in the struggle for social and ecological justice across Mother Earth,

as the storms rise

as our dances rise

Contents

4

REFLECTIONS ON POSSIBLE FUTURES

Acknowledgements and Credits
Jai Sen

This book is the companion volume to its predecessor in the *Challenging Empires* series, *The Movements of Movements, Part 1: What Makes Us Move?*, and so much of what I say here will—and must—be similar. But this volume is also likely to be the last book I will compile and edit, after a decade and more (and eight or nine books). I have learned a lot in this time, and not only about compiling books, and so this is also a good time and a good place for me to bring things and thoughts together.

I want to start these acknowledgements by drawing on the work of someone who I now consider to be one of my mentors, Taiaiake Alfred, who has in turn also drawn on others—which is as it should be:

> We gather together and see that the cycle of life continues. As human beings, we have been given the responsibility to live in balance and harmony with each other and with all of creation. So now, we bring our minds together as one as we give greetings and thanks to each other as People.
>
> Now our minds are one.
>
> We are thankful for our mother, the earth, for she gives us all that we need for life. She sustains and supports us as our feet move upon her. We are joyful in knowing that she continues to care for us as she has from the beginning of time. To our Mother, we send greetings and thanks.
>
> Now our minds are one.
>
> We give thanks to the waters for quenching our thirst and providing us with strength. Water is life, and we are thankful for its purity. We know its power in many forms—waterfalls and rain, mists and streams, rivers and oceans. With one mind, we send greetings and thanks to the spirit of the Water.
>
> Now our minds are one.
>
> . . .
>
> Now we turn our thoughts to the Creator and to the life-force of the universe. We send greetings and thanks for all the gifts of creation. Everything we need to live a good life is here in our natural world. For all of the love that is still around us, we gather our minds together as one and send our choicest words of greetings for the power of love, life, and creation.
>
> Now our minds are one.
>
> We have now arrived at the place where we end our words. In thanking and acknowledging all of the things we have named we did not intend to leave

anything out. If something was forgotten, we leave it to each of you to send such greetings as we have spoken, and to offer gratitude in your own way.

Onen enska neiokwanikonra. Now our minds are one.[1]

Many people, and many spirits, have helped to make this book and its companion and predecessor.

First, and again following Taiaiake Alfred, I want to thank and send my greetings to all "the true warriors, of all nations and ages who in sharing their thoughts and teachings have shown me the way and have made this book what it is".[2] I am not a writer nor an editor, let alone an academic; I was brought to this path in 2002 by my good friend and fellow spirit Jeremy Brecher in the course of the studies and reflections I was then doing on the dynamics of movement. Having shown me the path, he then left me to follow it, as I have since then.

There is no question that I am most indebted for what I have managed to draw together here and in its companion volume to the contributors to these two books—who are listed by name in the 'Notes on the Contributors' in this volume and in its companion—and to all my colleagues at CACIM and at OpenWord, whom I list below. It has been an extraordinary privilege to have walked this part of my life's journey with you, and I thank you all. My words cannot begin to repay my debts.

I also want to take this opportunity to remember, acknowledge, and honour here, in this last compilation, all those who I have met and worked with in the course of my journeys over these past forty years and more, in India and elsewhere, in activism and in research, sometimes together with others and sometimes alone, and who I have drawn on in innumerable ways in this book and in the others that I have done:

• in the course of our work at Unnayan, the social action group I was first with, and then through the NCHR (the National Campaign for Housing Rights), in India, which we at Unnayan helped form—both the members of the group and the members of the many communities of struggling, labouring people we worked with, many through the Chhinnamul Sramajibi Adhikar Samiti ('Organisation for the Rights of Uprooted Labouring People'), the experience of which re-educated and radicalised me and literally changed my life;
• in the course of the work I then did with others in building the Habitat International Coalition in the late 1980s;
• in the course of the research I did through the 1990s on movement and on the globalisation of movement, in India and Brazil and in many other parts of the world, and especially for the trust that all those I met and interviewed—and, again, especially those in 'communities'—placed in me;
• in the course of all the gatherings of the World Social Forum that I have taken part in; and—

• in the course of the work we have done over the past decade and more at and through CACIM: for the hope that we have sipped on together, for the fires we have lit, for the barriers we have taken down, for the spaces we have opened, for the moments we have shared.

My words cannot begin to repay my debts.

I also want here to acknowledge my teachers and mentors over the years: among them, and in particular, the late Peter Gutkind, the late Ray Affleck, John F C Turner, the late Rajni Kothari, the late John Berger, Jeremy Brecher, John Brown Childs, and, more recently, Taiaiake Alfred.

My words cannot begin to repay my debts.

And finally, in dealing with my past and as I start a new journey, I want also to honour and acknowledge here my debt to my family: first, to my late first wife Munni (Anita) Sen, for her love and for her support to me through my early years as an organiser when I came to be moved and to learn how to dance, and then through my years as a wandering student of movement, till her sudden death in 2002. I want also to honour her here for all that she did in her life and for the love and purpose she gave me and our children and that she brought to so many; and in remembering her, I remember also her parents and the unstinting love and support that they gave us as a family through those many, quite difficult years. I want also to thank and honour my daughters Jayita and Diya for bearing with me through all these years, including all the years when I was so lost in my work that I was never really with them; and also my partner and my wife till recently, Julia Sánchez, for her love and support and her always critical encouragement. And I remember and honour too my father Buddha Sen and my mother Nita Sen, who brought me into this world but who I never really knew.

My words cannot begin to repay my debts.

Content Editors

Beyond the features discussed in the Introduction, an important background feature of this book has been the intensive and extensive background work that has gone into the preparation and finalisation of the essays we are publishing (as is the case with the companion volume to this book, *The Movements of Movements, Part 1: What Makes Us Move?* and with all the books in the *Challenging Empires* series to which this book belongs). The Content Editors for this book—and I as editor—have tried hard to work closely with our authors in helping them more fully develop and articulate their ideas, and I have therefore of course been very happy indeed that so many of our authors have openly appreciated this and said that they have rarely experienced this degree of attention. Most of the credit for this goes to our Content Editors Parvati Sharma and Vipul Rikhi, and I want to warmly thank them for their contribution to making this book what it is.

Since this book is being published in two Parts—see the Introduction—I here list acknowledgements and credits only for the material in Part 2. The chapters are listed here in alphabetical order by the author's surname:

Parvati Sharma, for:
David Graeber—The Shock of Victory
Michael Löwy—Negativity and Utopia in the Global Justice Movement
Michal Osterweil—"Becoming-Woman"? Between Theory, Practice, and Potentiality

Parvati Sharma and Jai Sen, for:
Samir Amin—Towards a Fifth International?
Massimo De Angelis—PR Like PRocess! Strategy from the Bottom Up
Jeffrey S Juris and Geoffrey Pleyers—Incorporating Youth or Transforming Politics? Alter-Activism as an Emerging Mode of Praxis among Young Global Justice Activists
Rodrigo Nunes—Nothing Is What Democracy Looks Like: Openness, Horizontality, and the Movement of Movements

Vipul Rikhi, for:
Ezequiel Adamovsky—Autonomous Politics and its Problems: Thinking the Passage from the Social to the Political
John Brown Childs—Boundary as Bridge
John Holloway—The Asymmetry of Revolution

Vipul Rikhi and Jai Sen, for:
Kolya Abramsky—Gathering Our Dignified Rage: Building New Autonomous Global Relations of Production, Livelihood, and Exchange
Anila Daulatzai—Believing in Exclusion: The Problem of Secularism in Progressive Politics
Chris Carlsson—Effective Politics or Feeling Effective?
Tomás Mac Sheoin and Nicola Yeates—The Antiglobalisation Movement: Coalition and Division
Muto Ichiyo—Towards the Autonomy of the People of the World: Need for a New Movement of Movements to Animate People's Alliance Processes
Stephanie Ross—The Strategic Implications of Anti-Statism in the Global Justice Movement
Jai Sen—Break Free! Engaging Critically with the Concept and Reality of Civil Society (Parts 1 and 2)

Jai Sen, for:
Lee Cormie—Another World Is Inevitable . . . but which Other World?

The Free Association—Worlds in Motion: Movements, Problematics, and the Creation of New Worlds
Josephine Ho—Is Global Governance Bad for East Asian Queers?
François Houtart—'We Still Exist'
Matt Meyer and Ousseina Alidou—The Power of Words: Reclaiming and Reimagining Revolution and Non-Violence
Rodrigo Nunes—The Global Moment: Seattle, Ten Years On
Rodrigo Nunes—The Lessons of 2011: Three Theses on Organisation.

Concept, Design, and Production

As discussed in the Introduction to Part 1 (and therefore not repeated here),[3] working with OpenWord has been an integral part of the conceptualisation and reality of this book—as a book and as an ebook—and as in the case of the immediately previous book in the *Challenging Empires* series (*World Social Forum: Critical Explorations*),[4] much of the credit for this goes to *Nishant*, my former Co-Coordinator at OpenWord. My warm thanks to him once again for accompanying me down this road for several years.

In the case of this book and its companion volume, however, I have had the great privilege of also having the partnership of new volunteers and fellow travellers: *Giulio Maffini*, an old friend I have had the privilege of rediscovering recently nudged me into using diagrams to unpack and open up the meanings of the sometimes dense content of this book (and of my writing!); *Yih Lerh Huang*, a new friend and colleague joined Giulio Maffini in nudging me into using diagrams in the book and infused fresh energy and professionalism into our work at OpenWord; and *Christina Sanchez* generated the Wordle diagrams that we used in Part 1 and showed me the path to the ones generated in this book—and, more generally has been enthusiastically, creatively, and critically involved with my work. Most recently, I have also received the generous help of another new friend, *Jim Coflin*, in dealing with the many technical issues of compiling all the texts into the one file required by our co-publishers PM Press, thereby helping ease the pain of giving birth to these two books. My warm appreciation to all four for their ideas, their contributions, and their critical engagement and encouragement.

Rights and Permissions

In addition to the mentions that we have made in the first endnote of the respective essays, I am happy to also warmly acknowledge here the permission we have got from the following publishers for republishing the following essays in this book:

- The journal *ephemera* for Massimo De Angelis's essay 'PR Like PRocess! Strategy from the Bottom Up';

- The journal *Labour, Capital, and Society* for Stephanie Ross's essay 'The Strategic Implications of Anti-Statism in the Global Justice Movement';
- The journal *Radical Philosophy* for Rodrigo Nunes's essay 'The Global Moment'.

As readers will notice, we have used Wordle diagrams (http://www.wordle.net/) in both this book and its companion volume. I would like to also warmly acknowledge here the open permission on which the designer of Wordle diagrams, Jonathan Feinberg, has made available the results of using his software.

Material Resources

I would like to express my special gratitude to the following for the generous support and solidarity they extended to this book and its companion volume, *The Movements of Movements, Part 1: What Makes Us Move ?*, and to the educational project that some of us have launched around the two books—MOMBOP, the Movements of Movements Book Organising Project:

- The *A J Muste Memorial Institute*, in New York;
- *Ecosocialist Horizons*, in New York;
- The *Resistance Studies Initiative* at the University of Massachusetts, Amherst, USA;
- *Matt Meyer*; and—
- *Two anonymous contributors.*

As with our previous book, *World Social Forum: Critical Explorations*, I would like to acknowledge the support we at CACIM received back in 2007–2009 from Oxfam-Novib, based in The Netherlands, to cover professional editorial expenses in the early stages of the preparation of what became this book—part of a grant titled 'The World Social Forum: A Critical Engagement' (Project No BORX-505275-4713). As discussed in the Introductions to both this book and in its predecessor, these books have in many ways come out of our experience during that period.

I would also like to thank InterPares, Canada, for its supplementary support in 2009 for our work around the World Social Forum; even if the grant was small and not meant to support our books, this act of solidarity when we needed support was very important for what we were trying to do with respect to the WSF and, more generally, for work with movements worldwide. As such, this support also helped this project move forward.

Networking as Resource: The CACIM Community as Cloud

Finally, as editor I again also want to acknowledge that as was the case with its predecessor, this book is the product of an immense amount of almost global networking among a handful of people in different permutations and combinations over several years; indeed, a book like this is perhaps only possible through such a cloud-like process. Aside from a certain amount of professional support for which we were initially able to raise funds, the bulk of the conceptualisation of this book (and also of the book project outlined in the Introduction) and its preparation has involved intense voluntary input from countless individuals over these many years:

- My *colleagues and companer@s in an initiative named Critical Action*, active from 2001 to 2005, for the idea back in 2002 to critically engage with the World Social Forum then taking shape—which also led to the formation in 2005 of CACIM (India Institute for Critical Action: Centre in Movement), the organisation I have worked with since then;
- My good friend *Jeremy Brecher*, a member of Critical Action, for the idea in early 2003 of compiling a book that critically engaged with emerging world movement, at that time the World Social Forum, leading to the books that I have compiled since then, as well as for suggesting that I collaborate with my old compa Peter Waterman in doing this;
- *All the contributors* to this book, without whom it would not have been possible;
- *All the members of a loose, amorphous, and constantly evolving 'Challenging Empires editorial collective'* formed when these two volumes were first taking shape—including Michal Osterweil, Lee Cormie, and the late Peter Waterman, my co-editor of the *Challenging Empires* series;
- *All members of the original OpenWord Working Group* and, subsequently, of the now dormant OpenWord Editorial Collective;
- *Adityan M*, of New Delhi, our former graphic designer at CACIM, with whom it was always both fun and thought-provoking to discuss ways to represent what we are trying to do and the ideas and worlds we are trying to engage with, including early drafts of the cover of this book;
- *Matt Meyer*, of Brooklyn, in the US, who has more recently come on board this project and journey and with whom I am collaborating in our ongoing work at CACIM to conceive and formulate a larger book project around the material in these books; he has also played the vital role in this project of introducing me and our original publisher OpenWord to PM Press, with whom we are now co-publishing the two volumes of *The Movements of Movements*; and—

• *T B Dinesh and his colleagues at Servelots*, in Bangalore, India, for designing and uploading the 'MOMBOP [Movements of Movements Book Organising Project] Advance Pre-final Movement Edition' of all the material in this book, with the agreement of PM Press.

All of these people—many of whom were or became members of the CACIM Community—have made key contributions to the crystallisation of this book and of this book project over these years, in different ways and at different levels. I warmly thank them all!

Ottawa, on unceded Anishinaabe territory in Canada /
on Turtle Island, October 2017

References

Taiaiake Alfred, 2005—*Wasáse: Indigenous Pathways of Action and Freedom*. Peterborough: Broadview Press

Jai Sen, 2017a—'The Movements of Movements: An Introduction and an Exploration'. Introduction to Jai Sen, ed, 2017a—*The Movements of Movements, Part 1: What Makes Us Move?*. Volume 4 in the *Challenging Empires* series. New Delhi: OpenWord, and Oakland, CA: PM Press

Jai Sen and Peter Waterman, eds, 2012—*World Social Forum: Critical Explorations*. Volume 3 in the *Challenging Empires* series. New Delhi: OpenWord

Notes

1. I have drawn here on the invocation at the beginning of the Acknowledgements in Taiaiake Alfred's book *Wasáse: Indigenous Pathways of Action and Freedom* (2005, pp 15–16), which is his adaptation of a version of the Haudenosaunee Environmental Task Force's 'Greetings to the Natural World', published in *Haudenosaunee Environmental Restoration: An Indigenous Strategy for Human Sustainability* (Cambridge, England: Indigenous Development International, 1995). I encourage all readers to read Taiaiake Alfred's book.

2. Ibid, p 16.

3. Sen 2017a.

4. Sen and Waterman, eds, 2012.

0
INVOCATIONS

Offering[1]
Shailja Patel

you wake in the night
lips shaped
around a word that has not
yet
arrived

you close your eyes
wait
for it to grow into a poem
a poem that might breathe itself
into heat, form
into a body merged with yours
and if you entered that body
with every sense
ferocious, tender
nothing withheld

it would become a doorway
you could walk through
clear-eyed
find your country

see it truly
for the first time

and if you stood
in the sticky churning
red mud of your country
naked to the wind

refused to shut
your eyes refused
to shut
your eyes

the word would arrive
cymbal in your mouth
sing history
back onto itself, sing tearing
whole again, sing altered
tally sheets clean, blood
back into bodies, blades
back to the forge

sing women
unviolated, infernos
downward to soil, crops
greenly skyward, sing it all
back to the beginning

in a language
none of us
has ever heard

have you ever woken
in the night? Reached
for the body beside you
as if its living warmth
could teach your hands
a new language?

in the dark
it is your own bare skin
the holy innocence of belly
unslashed
the fearless softness of breast
unraped
that whispers back to you

beloved

history is a million terrors
tides that have engulfed your country
you were never going to arrive
in time

it began before you
will not suck itself
back through the doorway
of your longing

and a doorway
is not a body
to wrap you
in the night

a body
is not a poem
that will teach
the language you yearn for

the poem you seek
will never
fit
grape-round, grape-sweet
into the shape your mouth makes
when you wake in the night
lips open, crying
for all we once believed
we knew

all we once imagined
our struggles had made safe

crying
for all those
choked, drowned
in the quicksands of history
the history we did not arrive
in time to drain

beloved

what remains
blossoms out of the skin
of your belly
nudges into your palm

on your breast
a pulse you fit words to
one by one

breathe
see
choose

truth
work
love

you will wake with your fingers
wrapped around them

breathe
see
choose

wake with them salty
under your tongue

truth
work
love

they hold your right of return
to the country of childhood
they map where you will stand
in the scorched erupting soil

breathe
see
choose

they are your passport
to morning

Notes

1.   Shailja Patel (2008) © All rights reserved.

On Rethinking Our Dance:
Some Thoughts, Some Moves
Jai Sen

It is time for our people to live again. This book is a journey on the path made for us by those who have found a way to live as *Onkwehonwe*, original people. The journey is a living commitment to meaningful change in our lives and to transforming society by recreating our existences, regenerating our cultures, and surging against the forces that keep us bound to our colonial past. It is the path of struggle laid out by those who have come before us; now it is our turn, we who choose to turn away from the legacies of colonialism and take on the challenge of creating a new reality for ourselves and for our people.

The journey and this warrior's path is a kind of *Wasáse*, a ceremony of unity, strength, and commitment to action. *Wasáse* is an ancient *Rotinoshonni* war ritual, the Thunder Dance. The new warrior's path, the spirit of *Wasáse*, this *Onkwehonwe* attitude, this courageous way of being in the world—all come together to form a new politics in which many identities and strategies for making change are fused together in a movement to challenge white society's control over *Onkwehonwe* and our lands. *Wasáse*, as I am speaking of it here, is symbolic of the social and cultural force alive among *Onkwehonwe* dedicated to altering the balance of political and economic power to recreate some social and physical space for freedom to re-emerge. *Wasáse* is an ethical and political vision, the real demonstration of our resolve to survive as *Onkwehonwe* and to do what we must do to force the Settlers to acknowledge our existence and the integrity of our connection to the land.[1]

Although these words are evidently written speaking to other *Onkwehonwe*, the original people (or 'Indigenous Peoples'), I believe that they are today, in the times we live in and are moving into, equally relevant to all those of us who might or might not be Indigenous but who are concerned with justice and peace in this world. They are words that all of us can draw on: all of us are suffering colonialism and imperialism; all of us are experiencing the effects of discrimination, marginalisation, precarity, exclusion, exploitation, and oppression, and consequent alienation, and of the absence of justice and peace—in our bodies and our lives and in the worlds around us.

It is time, as Alfred says, to turn away from these effects and to recover justice and peace—in our lives and on Mother Earth; it is time, as Kolya Abramsky says in his essay in this book, as the Zapatistas said before him, to gather our dignified rage.[2]

This book, dedicated to the dance of life, is the second part of a two-volume book titled *The Movements of Movements*.[3] These two books—which are in turn a part of a series titled *Challenging Empires*[4] and of a longer-term project that my colleagues at CACIM and I have undertaken of critical engagement with and intervention in the local, 'national', and 'world' movement—are a conscious intervention in and contribution to contemporary world movement.

As we see it, our world today is not only a world in profound crisis but also a world in profound movement. We live in times when major and sometimes dramatic movements are irrupting all over the world and sometimes seeming to sweep history aside, with increasingly large numbers of people joining or forming movements precisely because of the crises we are facing: local, national, transnational, and global.[5] Sometimes, however, just what is happening in our times and why it is suddenly happening is bewildering—even to seasoned activists and to seasoned students, teachers, and observers of movement; all that we can sense is that something is different, that we are at a very special moment. There is a great deal of hope in the air, but there is also some considerable confusion and some despondence—perhaps because the odds sometimes seem so great and the losses so huge (the march of the right across the world; the march of neoliberalism; the relentless emergence both of fundamentalisms, on the one hand, and of climate change, on the other), and also, perhaps, because so many things are bursting forth so widely and so rapidly, like sudden storms.

With this as a background and with a strong belief in the transformative power of critical reflection and engagement, we at CACIM have chosen to undertake a project of trying to strengthen movement worldwide by making what is happening more comprehensible, even at the very basic level, for all those we hope to reach, by creating spaces for critical reflection, and thereby helping movements and activists become more critically and fully engaged in the larger movement/s that are unfolding in our time.

At this juncture in the world and the life and death on Mother Earth, this book—and this book project—is an attempt to go beyond individual movements. Together, they are an attempt to present—and to see, hear, feel, and critically explore and engage with—the larger picture that is coming into view: the extraordinary drama of the flow of movement taking place across the world in our times. We are, all of us, and perhaps more than ever before in history, a part of or witness to a unique series of interconnected efforts. The project we have undertaken is an ambitious attempt both to sense movement and also to describe, analyse, interact with, and help bring together these movements, efforts, and their 'authors' in word and in deed. By doing this, the project seeks both to make more comprehensible movements and the praxis *of* movements and to contribute to learning and the spread of ideas *between and across* movements, including in terms of the language, grammar, and syntax of movement. We believe this project can help activists and movements to gain clarity and strength.

This is the companion volume to *The Movements of Movements, Part 1: What Makes Us Move?* While the two books stand independently, it may—I suggest—be of considerable value to see them as two parts of a whole, especially since the two books were conceived as such and 'composed' as such.

Keeping this in mind, as explained in the Introduction to the first book,[6] the overall structure of the two-part book is as follows:

The Movements of Movements

Part 1: What Makes Us Move?	Part 2: Rethinking Our Dance
0: Invocations	0: Invocations
1: Movementscapes	3: Interrogating Movement
2: The Movements of Movements	4: Reflections on Possible Futures
Afterword	Afterword
References	References

Basically, both books have three Sections. The first book opens with a Section 0 titled 'Invocations', containing a Proem by Shailja Patel on 'What Moves Us' and an introductory essay, and then goes on to sketch out, in Section 1, certain key features of the landscape of contemporary movement in the world from 1968 till about 2010. The sketches are by people from different parts of the world and intentionally include essays by both Indigenous Peoples and by settlers,[7] thereby offering fundamentally—and structurally—different views of the landscape they inhabit and see. The same world seen through different eyes and different experiences.

In Section 2 (of Part 1), we present a wide range of sensitive and reflective portraits of movement, several of which are critical discussions of how different movements move (and / or have moved) in different contexts. The essays are by authors—both activists and researchers—from many parts of the world, North and South, and from many different persuasions,[8] broadly speaking, over the past fifty years. This book ends with a major, specially commissioned Afterword by Laurence Cox, activist, teacher extraordinaire, editor, and co-author of *We Make Our Own History: Marxism and Social Movements in the Twilight of Neoliberalism*,[9] that reads across all the essays in this book and critically engages with several in subtle and sensitive ways.[10]

The present volume carries this discussion forward. It too has three sections. As editor, and drawing on and inspired by the lives and cosmologies of aboriginal peoples across the world and in particular on the magnificent body of work by Taiaiake Alfred, a contributor to the book,[11] I invite you to look at movements as the dances of warriors, with this book then posing the question: *How can and should we rethink our dance?*

Here too, following another beautiful, moving poem by Shailja Patel, Section 3 brings together a wide range of essays—again, by both activists and researchers from different parts of the world—but in this case critically reflecting on movement and drawing out some of the fundamental issues that those in movement are concerned with. The book closes with Section 4, composed of several rich and provocative reflections on movement and on possible futures by several outstanding thinkers and doers in movement, followed by a major Afterword by Lee Cormie that reads across both parts of this book and paints an extraordinarily vivid mindscape of the world unfolding around us, reflecting on the meanings of the essays in these two volumes and this collection as a whole.[12] As contributor to the first volume, Cormie is a researcher, teacher, writer, and sometime activist concerning social justice movements and coalitions, as well as a professor emeritus of theology and interdisciplinary studies who has published many articles on liberation theologies and social movements and has been involved in major church-based social justice initiatives over the entire span of movement covered by these books.[13]

This Book / These Books, at This Juncture in History

These books, therefore, seek to speak to the world as it is unfolding and to strengthen the dance of movements for justice and peace. At the time of writing this Introduction, however, in March 2016, when there is a palpable intensification of crisis in the world, I think it is only fair to say that it sometimes feels increasingly difficult to understand what 'the world' is going to be like, not over the next five or ten years, but even by the time this book appears in public[14]—and therefore, and in short, if the crises do indeed take full force, an obvious question that comes to mind is just how 'relevant' this book will be and in what ways it will be relevant.

One of the contributors to these books, Kolya Abramsky, wrote to me recently to ask precisely this question, referring both to his essay in this book[15] and to the book as a whole:

> The political crisis that I talked about in my article has massively intensified, with the US and the EU now in complete political crisis. The US stands a very strong chance of electing a fascist, and a moderate chance of electing a moderate socialist. The former head of the CIA and US national security agency has said that much of Trump's agenda would not command the respect or loyalty of the army if he is elected to be president. The EU is unravelling at the borders and the far right is becoming a significant force both at the level of street politics and electoral politics. One of the major members, UK, is very likely to vote to leave the EU, triggering much more of a crisis for the EU. Even Germany, the rock of political stability in the EU, seems to be teetering on the verge of political

instability, with the far right making major gains. Meanwhile, in Latin America, the left is in great danger throughout the continent. Major oil producing countries will soon face political crises due to the falling price of oil and revenues. Saudi Arabia and Russia are both talking about selling off major state assets to make up for falling revenue.[16]

Reflecting on this, what strikes me is that not only are these things happening *simultaneously*, but each of these currents has potentially enormous consequences for the entire world—beyond this, each is very likely to feed into the others and to synergise in myriad vicious ways. As Kolya said in his quick sketch, these include the great world-historical 'project Europe' looking as if it is going to violently implode, and the polity of the militarily most powerful nation in the world— and in particular the intensity of alienation among its people—being in such an acute state that it has thrown up a candidate for president who is not just from 'the right' but a rabid populist, nationalist, and neo-fascist (and who, if elected, will among other things have his unimpeded finger on the nuclear button to Armageddon). Beyond this, we are also living at a time when there are continuing and intensifying violent actions by cells of ISIS, al-Qaeda, and other factions of fundamentalist Islam in different parts of the world. Also, and in some countries as a direct reaction to all of this, we are seeing a marked rise of the hard right in societies across the world. Looming over all of this are the dark gathering clouds of climate change that most of us are hardly talking about any more—perhaps because we are mesmerised and paralysed by everything else that is happening.

I would like to take this a little further and dwell for a moment not only on the reality that all this—these storms that are today sweeping the world—is raging concurrently but to consider the possibility that these storms are taking shape not independently but are interrelated and to ponder the implications of the possibility that that they could well increasingly intertwine in the years ahead—quite possibly, even more viciously than is the case already.

In particular, I venture the thought that some of us discussed at a meeting some years ago: that there is much reason to expect that the changes that are already taking place in the world's climate (for example, last year being the hottest in history, and this year set to beat that, with unbearable temperatures already the case in some parts of the world and increasing outbreaks of forest fires across the world) are going to fundamentally challenge and change politics and movement at all levels—local, national, regional, and world—and that this may well only contribute to intensifying the whirlwind of reactionary politics that we are already seeing in many parts of the world.[17] What I say here does not take into consideration the distinct possibility of a flash nuclear war in some part of the world, given the huge proliferation of nuclear weapons over the past couple of decades and the directions in which world politics seem to be going.

One scenario is that as a consequence of the pressures that climate change is bringing about (and that too in historically unprecedented, non-linear ways that linear governance systems are as yet incapable of planning for), not only are all kinds of old conflicts—interstate conflicts, intercommunity conflicts, and people vs. state conflicts—going to intensify over the coming decades, but new forces are also going to rise (indeed, are already rising) in this process. In a context of increasingly unstable and weakening state and interstate systems across the world, however, this admittedly extreme reading of possibilities is that aside from rising interstate conflict over resources, the new forces are likely to include local warlords rising in different parts of the world and the exercise of the military power that transnational corporations have, reports suggest, already organised to protect the vast swathes of land, sea, and other resources that they have grabbed across the world over the past decades, whether against local community opposition or against attempted state regulation. This is likely to at first take place sporadically, and then as rising storms as conflicts intensify and as the stakes grow greater.

This is of course only a possible scenario, but at a time like this—at a world historical juncture like this—I believe that we all need (if we are not already there) to most seriously focus on such possibilities and, taking this into account, rethink what we are doing and how we are doing it, individually and collectively. Recalling Taiaiake Alfred's words in the opening quote, we need today to urgently begin to rethink our dance as warriors at the most fundamental levels.

These are things that I am sure that many of us are already thinking about and are likely to be even more seriously debating by the time that this book is published; for this gathering storm seems to be the new reality, even if this is very disturbing: the new permanent. If this is so, then how are we to relate to it?

Without any suggestion that I have a clear and comprehensive picture of what is unfolding, I feel that these questions—and this questioning—is, in fact, *precisely what these books are all about* (and that, in many senses, is the whole idea behind the *Challenging Empires* series), which is why I would like to think that they are and will remain relevant, at least for a good time to come: simply because they may help us address the current moment and the unfolding future.

I of course do not mean this in a literal sense—that the essays in these books anticipate and discuss precisely what is happening at the moment (even though I myself believe that some of the essays are profoundly prescient) and provide 'answers'. I mean it in the sense that the essays in these books, by virtue of being essays in intense critical engagement and reflection—with the past and with the present (and some, with the unfolding future), with the personal and the political, and coming from a wide range of cultures, contexts, and persuasions—can serve as superb material for engaging with our immediate and dramatically unfolding present.

Without doubt, we will of course want and need to also draw on other material, but I would like to think that the range of essays in these books can make a powerful and meaningful contribution.

It is with this in mind that we at CACIM, along with some associates, are presently discussing and formulating a larger book project, tentatively nicknamed the 'Movements of Movements Book Organising Project', where we are planning to invite all the contributors to these books (and perhaps also the contributors to the earlier books in the *Challenging Empires* series)[18] and other interested people to collaborate in a major process of autonomously organising study circles, workshops, and / or conferences (a) around the material in these books, (b) to address the political tasks of the world as it is unfolding, and (c) to loosely associate in a networked process to do this. I would in fact like to use this Introduction to invite readers to also consider doing this.[19]

Towards this, and by agreement between our co-publishers (OpenWord and PM Press), I am happy that the books are being brought out in both hard copy and in ebook form. In addition, most of the essays will also be available in pre-publication form on our organisational website and possibly some other websites to enable and stimulate discussion as early as possible. The published versions of most of the essays will be posted once the respective books are out. As editor, I am of course very happy that our original publisher OpenWord has been able to find a co-publisher like PM Press; they have agreed to make all or most of the material in these books available as widely as possible in these various ways.

In addition, the books are also being published on a Creative Commons license, which makes it possible for everyone, within the limits of the license, to further reproduce the material in these books.

In relation to this turbulent, emerging backdrop the goal of the books and of the book project is to try and contribute—by looking widely and deeply and across history—a deeper and more organic comprehension of what is happening in our times, one that can help us all forge the tools to cope with the changes that are taking place and to deepen the struggle for justice, peace, and social transformation.

The Movements of Movements

Before presenting this book itself, I would like to take a step back and broadly sketch out the content, character, and flow of the two volumes.[20]

Many excellent books that have come out over the past decade or so on movement, and in particular many that have presented, celebrated, and in some cases critically engaged with the emergence of what has variously been called the 'antiglobalisation movement', the 'alter-globalisation movement', the 'global justice movement', or what writer Naomi Klein at one point famously referred to as "the movement of movements"[21]—a phrase that several authors in this book also use. This present collection, however, titled and focused on *the movements* (plural) *of movements*, takes a somewhat different approach: it firstly focuses on the verb 'movement' and not the noun. This radical shift of focus opens up whole new worlds.[22]

Second, it does not focus on the so-called 'alter-globalisation movement' alone, which is often used as a synonym for the so-called 'movement of movements', but rather opens windows to the much wider range of movements that are taking place in the world. Third, rather than suggesting that there is one larger, encompassing 'movement' in our world, it accepts that there are many (different) movements taking place, as well as differing perceptions of justice and many ways of moving, all of which we can learn from. By making visible a wide range of the many movements of movements and their multiple praxes, it tries to enable us— readers, activists, and editors alike—to see the larger picture, to see movements comparatively, and to draw our own lessons.[23]

While reaching back to the great sweeps and swells of movement that have taken place across the world since the 1960s (see, for instance, the essays in Part 1 by Fouad Kalouche and Eric Mielants, by David McNally, and by Lee Cormie),[24] specifically to some of the more iconic movements that have taken place during this period—the student-led revolt in France in 1968, the feminist movements since the 1970s, the Zapatista movement in Mexico since 1994, the 'Battle of Seattle' in 1999, and also the emergence during this period of what some today call 'political Islam'[25]—as well as reaching forward in time to look at, for instance, the Occupy movement from 2011 on, most of the essays in these books focus on the period 2006–2010. They range from discussions and retheorisations of struggle at and from the margins through essays on feminisms, queerdom, struggles of faith, and the struggles of workers reimagining the world and 'forward dreaming'. They also include reflections on issues of division, marginalisation, and exclusion within progressive movement, and more. By juxtaposing essays by a range of people that discuss how movements move in different ways and from different points of view—each with its own cultural and political cadence and rhythm—this book seeks to make more visible, audible, and comprehensible the movements and praxis *of* movements, as well as the larger world of movement *within which* individual movements take place, and thereby to learnings and movements *between and across* movements, including in terms of the language, grammar, and syntax of movement.

Conscious of difference and multiplicity and committed to engaging across standpoints, the two books together are an attempt at sketching out not a single, grand, metanarrative of movement but rather a landscape that begins to reveal the many intersectionalities of movements and their organic nature—where each of us, from our positions in relation to what we are seeing, will have our own perceptions—and through this to contribute to readers developing their own meta-analyses of movement, and in that sense becoming a part of movement and not only a spectator.

Along with other volumes in the series,[26] these books aim to make contemporary movement/s more meaningful to the observer—and perhaps also, in some ways, to those who take part in movement. They hope to be spaces where multidirectional and transcommunal conversations can open up, both between and across movements and between movements and readers; where movements and their ideas speak to each other, and perhaps even begin to move together; and where it also perhaps becomes possible for all to perceive and sense both the vastness of the universe of movement and also, at the same time, the extraordinary range of tactics and rhythms in movement—and, just possibly, some of the fundamental characteristics of movement as life force. Through this and by building on the diverse politico-cultural compositions that the essays represent, it is hoped that these books will make audible / visible / comprehensible the dance and the music of movement—and of a world in movement.

In particular, for me it is a very special privilege that we have been able to include in this collection several essays by women and men who come from and work on the structural margins of society, and who—as will be evident from their essays, and even from their titles—offer perspectives that are at many levels radically different: in Part 1, Anand Teltumbde (on 'Anti-Imperialism, Dalits, and the Annihilation of Caste'), Andrea Smith (on 'Indigenous Feminism and the Heteropatriachal State'), Taiaiake Alfred and Jeff Corntassel (on 'Being Indigenous: Resurgences against Contemporary Colonialism'), Jeff Corntassel alone (on 'Rethinking Self-Determination: Lessons from the Indigenous-Rights Discourse'), and Xochitl Leyva Solano (on 'Geopolitics of Knowledge and the Neo-Zapatista Social Movement Networks'), and with Christopher Gunderson (on 'The Tapestry of Neo-Zapatismo: Origins and Development'); in this volume, among others, Anila Daulatzai (on 'Believing in Exclusion: The Problem of Secularism in Progressive Politics') and Josephine Ho ('Is Global Governance Bad for East Asian Queers?').

In addition, and because of who they have written about, I also mention here the essays in Part 1 by François Houtart ('Mahmoud Mohamed Taha: Islamic Witness in the Contemporary World') and by Roel Meijer ('Fighting for Another World: Yusuf al-'Uyairi's Conceptualisation of Praxis and the Permanent Salafi Revolution'). Each of these authors and / or actors bring to us substantially different points of view, and therefore different lenses through which to comprehend the worlds we live in and different headphones—as it were—to hear the languages and the music of movement.

For me, it is not a minor issue that in Taiaiake Alfred and Jeff Corntassel's essays almost all their citations and references are to works by Indigenous Peoples, which only serves to make their essays that much more outstanding. This fact itself is all too unusual and constitutes a loud reminder to all of us, Indigenous or settler, 'marginal' or mainstream, that there is a lot of excellent work out there by Indigenous Peoples—and crucially, by both women and men at the margins—and so reading, internalising, and citing this 'knowledge from below' is indeed now possible, if we are only willing to make this our priority. Depending on where one is located socially, this is a question of pride in ourselves and / or respect for such peoples and their knowledges. Although seemingly only a small step, this practice has profound epistemological and political meanings and is therefore a vital contribution to building other politics and other worlds: because it has the possibility of changing where one locates oneself and how one sees things, and because it demands that we make this shift consciously, as a political act.

I have also found it particularly fascinating and instructive to read certain essays in relation to each other, such as the ones by Taiaiake Alfred and Jeff Corntassel and the one by Andrea Smith, together with the essays by, say, André Drainville or Roel Meijer, François Houtart, and Roma and Ashok Choudhary, as well as those by Xochitl Leyva Solano (on the Zapatista movement), Virginia Vargas (on international feminisms), James Toth (on the rise of the Muslim Brotherhood), Peter Waterman (on 'labour's others'), Cho Hee-Yeon (on the transformation of the perspective of movements in South Korea), Guillermo Delgado-P (on the idea of a social movement state, in this case in Bolivia), and Alex Khasnabish (on the resonance of the Zapatista movement)—among others. In short, as I see it, Alfred, Corntassel, and Smith very consciously and skilfully use the power of the positions that they have by virtue of their identities in relation to the movements they write on and to larger society, and there is much to be learned from how they have done this. They move, and they dance—not merely as researchers and activists but as warriors—in a dance that is much larger and that has far wider ramifications than the immediately apparent.

As an aspect of this diversity and plurality, I think it is also worth pointing out that we also have—among the contributors to these books—five streetfighting activists and strategists: Tariq Ali, the late Daniel Bensaïd, Ashok Choudhary, Roma, and the late Yusuf al-'Uyairi (whose life and struggles are presented and discussed by Roel Meijer); and also, at a different level the late Mahmoud Mohamed Taha (whose life struggle is presented by François Houtart). I single these essays out for the obvious reason that the location of these individuals—the authors or the individuals written about, respectively—in movement is structurally different from those of scholars and observers, and therefore also the perspectives that they offer us on movement and on the world in movement. Each of these activists draws on his or her wide experience under different conditions and in different parts of the world, North and South, and—crucially—each engages in deep and intense polemical struggle through their writings, but even more so by the conduct of their lives.

The essay by Tariq Ali in Part 1, for instance, thinks back to 1968 and raises angry questions about contemporary movement. In some ways, this essay and the questions it puts forward are strongly complemented by the essay, also in Part 1, by the late Daniel Bensaïd—another veteran of 1968—who also challenges contemporary approaches to movement strategy. I have therefore found it provocative to read these essays in comparison with the ones in Part 1 by, say, André Drainville and by Roma and Ashok Choudhary, and in this book, Part 2, by David Graeber, John Holloway, Rodrigo Nunes, and Michal Osterweil, as well as to read all these essays on strategy against the essay by Roel Meijer on the late Yusuf al-'Uyairi, who as a strategist of a movement (al-Qaeda) had an understanding of modernity that differed radically from today's dominant Western liberal understanding of the word. These essays all challenge each other, but they also jam with each other and dance with each other. In a way, it becomes a fascinating display that reminds me of *capoeira*, "[the] Brazilian martial art and popular street dance that combines elements of dance, acrobatics, and music, and that is sometimes also referred to as a game".[27]

While the collection focuses on movement during the period 2006–2010, we also have essays on movement at different time periods and—crucially—set in different cultural-political contexts. Mentioning here only those essays that deal with more specific places and time periods, we have essays ranging from the rise of an articulation of an alternative interpretation of Islam from the 1930s through to the 1980s in Sudan (by François Houtart), to '1968' and after in France and Britain (Tariq Ali), to a discussion of movement strategy in Europe and Latin America from the 1970s through to the 2000s (the late Daniel Bensaïd), to sweeps across the world from 1968 right through to 1989 (by Fouad Kalouche and Eric Mielants) and from 1994 through to the 2000s (David McNally), to the rise of the Muslim Brotherhood in Egypt during the 1970s through to the 2000s as an aspect of a renewed rise of a global Islam (James Toth), to the jungles of Chiapas, Mexico, during the 1980s and '90s (Xochitl Leyva Solano and Christopher Gunderson), to critical readings of—and reflections on—feminist movement/s during the 1980s through to the 2000s in Canada (Emilie Hayes) and in Latin America and globally (Virginia Vargas), to a discussion of the rise of Indigenous Peoples' social movements during the 1980s through to the 2000s in Bolivia (Guillermo Delgado-P), to the 1990s and 2000s in the forests of India (Roma and Ashok Choudhary), in rural and urban South Korea (Cho Hee-Yeon), and in the 'clash of civilisations' emerging in West Asia (Roel Meijer), to the new movements against neoliberalism in Latin America during the 2000s (Emir Sader) and through to the 2010s, looking at the politics and dialectics of anti-capitalist movements (Ezequiel Adamovsky, André Drainville, Michael Löwy, Tomás Mac Sheoin and Nicola Yeates, Rodrigo Nunes, and Stephanie Ross), the rise of new movements around labour (Peter Waterman), and—in the context of climate change—the emergence of new movements for radical localisation (Peter North and David Featherstone).

And then there are some timeless essays, such as those by John Brown Childs, John Holloway, and Michal Osterweil.

Why 2006–2010?

I should perhaps explain why we have chosen to focus in these books on the period 2006–2010—and not earlier, as well as why we decided not to bring it right up to date. On the one hand, the start date 2006 came out of the simple fact that this book is a part of the *Challenging Empires* series, which was conceived in 2006–2007 by Contributing Editor Peter Waterman and myself, together with my then colleague at OpenWord, Nishant.[28] Beyond this, during the years before this (2003–2007), Peter and I had also intensively collected and edited material for essays up to 2006–2007 for our first two books in the series, two editions of *World Social Forum: Challenging Empires*,[29] and so we somewhat naturally chose at that point both to move on from that earlier period and to focus on the contemporary and the emerging.

On the other hand, the end date for the material in this book came to be defined by two coincidental and conjunctural events: first, I as lead editor, after working and reworking the material we had collected through 2007–2010 (during which time our book project burgeoned from one to two and then three books), finally took a call in December 2010 on how we would organise and bring out the material we had; second, '2011' irrupted on the world (and on us!) precisely at that time, from the start of the Tunisian revolution in December 2010[30] and leading directly on to Tahrir Square and the beginning of the Egyptian uprising in January 2011.[31] This was followed by the amazing irruptions in Spain and Greece, and then by the Occupy movement in North America and Europe, which in turn was followed by huge swells of movement in Brazil, Turkey, India, Hong Kong, and elsewhere.

Even as we at CACIM—along with millions of others across the world—were swept up in the swirling spirals of tumult and hope that progressively unfolded across so much of the world during that year and the next, and however tempted we were to try to also embrace in our books what was happening, it became clear to me that attempting to do this would further delay books that already taken a long time to put together. I therefore elected at that point—December 2010—to organise the material we already had in hand into three books: one as a direct sequel to our previous two books, focussing exclusively on the World Social Forum,[32] and the other two on movements in the world beyond the WSF (but also, at points, impinging on and including it), with a broad concept that we would put most of the non-WSF material we had till then collected into the second volume in the informal trilogy we had conceived of and would collect fresh material for the third book on the period 2011 on.

I subsequently added two essays that look at and draw lessons from the Occupy movement. In the belief that there is much to be learned by focussing on 2006–2010 as a kind of crucible, however, I have kept away from also trying to embrace and explore the subsequent and more contemporary and the entirely new landscape it has created.

The actual experience of editing the material we had in hand—along with trying to engage with the movements sweeping the world in those years (primarily through a listserv I moderated, WSFDiscuss), as well as dealing with some major issues that emerged in my personal life—led to a further major decision: to postpone the 'third' volume and bring out what I had earlier seen as the 'second' volume in two parts—the present two books.

Although the focus of these two books remains the period 2006–2010, it has all along been our approach in the *Challenging Empires* series to locate movement within a historical and cross-cultural perspective, and so I decided to include three essays in Part 1 that specifically took broad sweeps across movements over the past forty to fifty years; the essays by David McNally, Fouad Kalouche and Eric Mielants, and Lee Cormie. All these essays go back to the 1960s, but each provides a unique perspective.

Aside from these three essays, however, I decided that I would also commission and / or harvest material that specifically related to major movements of the past whose resonance carried through to the period we were looking at, including movements that had 'anniversaries' falling during 2006–2010. Therefore, we have essays on '1968', with its fortieth anniversary in 2008 (in Part 1 by Tariq Ali and Daniel Bensaïd); the Zapatista uprising in 1994, with its fifteenth anniversary in 2009 and twentieth anniversary in 2014 (in Part 1 by Xochitl Leyva Solano, by Xochitl Leyva Solano with Christopher Gunderson, and by Alex Khasnabish and in this volume by François Houtart and also by Kolya Abramsky); and the Battle of Seattle in 1999, with its tenth anniversary in 2009 (in this volume, by Rodrigo Nunes).

(It is perhaps worth also mentioning here that there were some significant other movements from the past that I also tried unsuccessfully to commission and / or collect material on, in large part because of our very limited human resources. These included the great Naxalite uprising of 1967, in India,[33] the resonances of which continue to reverberate widely in the country and region forty years and more later,[34] and PGA [People's Global Action], founded in 1998 as an outcome of the Zapatista *Encuentros* in 1995–1996, which strongly impacted 'the battle of Seattle' in 1999 and the anti-capitalist and alter-globalisation movements that subsequently emerged in the 2000s.)

Rethinking Our Dance

Let me now come to this book itself. The objective of this book is to contribute—against the unfolding backdrop of history—to rethinking our dance.

By 'dance', however, and in relation to social and political movement, while I am more generally signalling the interplay that takes place between those in movement, between movements, and between movements and the context they are addressing and / or taking place in, I am in particular here referring to *a warrior's dance* in the sense that is so beautifully conveyed by Taiaiake Alfred, both in the opening quote to this Introduction and in the following, first citing another author, and then in his own words:

> A Warrior is the one who can use words so that everyone knows they are part of the same family. A Warrior says what is in the people's hearts, talks about what the land means to them, brings them together to fight for it.
> —Bighorse, Diné [35]

> To remain true to a struggle within Onkwehonwe values, the end goal of our Wasáse—our warrior's dance—must be formulated as a spiritual revolution, a culturally rooted *social* movement that transforms the whole of society and a *political* action that seeks to remake the entire landscape of power and relationship to reflect truly a liberated post-imperial wisdom. [36]

As I understand them, several of the essays in Section 3 and John Holloway's and Michal Osterweil's essays in Part 4 [37]—speak directly to this invocation. They do so, however, in their many different ways—just as is the case in the accompanying book, *What Makes Us Move?*—and since the authors are from across the world, from a wide range of persuasions and experiences, and are speaking in their own voices, we also see them move in different ways. Ranging from deeply critical reflections on the global justice movement and the World Social Forum to other essays asking questions about the problematics of movement—and interrogating the language and concepts that we use and their power—they all suggest that it is time that we rethink *how* we do what we do and explore the possibilities of moves that we can, and that we perhaps should make.

At the risk of repetition, I think it bears mentioning that readers will find it useful to also look at the essays in Part 1, which in many ways lay the ground for the reflection and interrogation that characterises the essays in this book, and which, for me anyway, dance with those in the other volume. One example among many is the first essay by Rodrigo Nunes in this book, provocatively titled 'Nothing Is What Democracy Looks Like: Openness, Horizontality, and the Movement of Movements', which plays off several essays in Book 1, including, and most directly, David McNally's 'From the Mountains of Chiapas to the Streets of Seattle: This is What Democracy Looks Like'.

I urge you therefore not to read these essays in isolation—great as they individually are—but together with others in the books; you will find meaning in each, but I think you will find even greater meaning in how they interact and jam. Although I tried saying this in some reflections I once sketched out on the experience of compiling the books that were meant to appear in Part 1,[38] I think that Lee Cormie has put it much better than I have, or can, in his Afterword to this book:

> The collection of essays in these two books faithfully reproduces—and also it-self embodies—the complex and chaotic character and multiple dimensions of these dialogues, in their diverse expressions in different places, their increasingly dynamic, frequently jagged, at times conflicting, always incomplete character, the ever-expanding and ever more complex dynamics of producing culture and knowledge, the proliferating challenges to conversion arising from the 'new' voices of so many 'others' on so many fronts, the scope and pace of changes transforming the world.
>
> . . . Taken together in various combinations of two or three or more, these essays often converge and overlap, suggesting new synergies; at other points they diverge on important issues, pointing to many differences and to possible tensions and clashes. At the same time, though, they reflect an increasingly shared awareness that, as Nunes says, "the capacity to exchange and cooperate" with others around the world is expanding.[39] And, beyond purely abstract and false universalisms, these contributions push me, and I trust you readers too, to read across contexts and movements, looking for cross-cutting experiences and insights, points of reference, wider solidarities, and expanding horizons on possible futures.[40]

To me, reading this comment on the books is not only music to my ears as an editor, but this—both the comment and what it is talking about—also itself *sounds* like music and dance: Like Ahmad Jamal in his track 'Ahmad's Blues',[41] and even perhaps like the great Thelonious Monk's composition 'Epistrophe'.[42] But in any case, whatever your own mode of reading is, I suspect that you will find material—individual essays, and especially reading across essays—that will spark arcs across your mind and your imagination, illuminating the reality that surrounds us and that is emerging around us. Material that moves you.

For me the fundamental challenge that arises from all that is happening in the times we are living through—from the incredible pace that things are evolving, from the seriousness of the multiple crises that we are simultaneously facing (and that are only heating up from year to year), and from the distortions that this 'perfect storm' is producing—is that we must rethink who we are, that we must be sure of who we are, and that as a part of this we need to open ourselves to what others are doing and rethink our dance. The times we are living through demand this; the ways we have so far moved are, perhaps, not enough. We need focus and resolve, but we also need, urgently perhaps, to invent new steps and new moves.

Let me try to illustrate what I mean with two examples. I think that per-haps most of us would agree that one of the most profound challenges facing humankind today is the crisis of climate change. While it is true that people all over the world have grasped this and are engaging with it, and while there have been some victories, I think many of us are feeling that time is rapidly slipping away and that we have not been able as yet to muster sufficient force to arrest governments and corporations from the massive damage that they are inflicting.

In this context, I want to point to the argument put forward by Jeremy Brecher since 2013 that what we are seeing today is a "global nonviolent constitutional insurgency" taking shape, where coalitions of ordinary people in countries across the world, appalled by the climate crisis, outraged by government complicity and inaction, and informed by legal opinion are using the constitutional obligations of nation-states as trustees of the environment to arrest their inaction and to force them, using non-violent civil disobedience and the courts, to meet their obligations.[43] In the US, for example, what presently calls itself the 'Break Free Public Trust' and / or the 'Climate Action Public Trust'—a convergence of people with long experience in the labour movement, in climate movement, and in direct action—is using the doctrine of 'Public Trust' (or 'Nature Trust'), drawing on US law and ancient law to bring to bear the force of their will.[44] They in the US are now working with others across the world with similar moves. The move of civil disobedience, of course, is now known and well-established, but the fusion of this with Public (or Nature) Trust is new, and, I believe, is today powerfully relevant, arguably more relevant in our times than ever before in history.[45]

At a different level, my own contribution to this book is to argue that we need to critically engage with the term 'civil society', and in particular with the word 'civil', and that doing this and recognising the power of incivility has radical implications and potential—including empowering us to break free to achieve our full creative powers.[46]

The essays in this book and its companion volume offer us many moves— some old, some new, but *moves*, moves that can inspire us, moves that can help us find our way, moves that will move us—moves of insurgence, moves of resurgence, moves of introspection, moves of meditation, moves of resistance, moves of celebration. The questions we still have to ask ourselves though—which Shailja Patel asks so powerfully in her Proems in both Part 1[47] and this volume[48]—and that ultimately only we as individuals can answer for ourselves, are: Can we hear the music? Can we focus in on the enormous and powerful and positive energies that are surging all around us and allow them to course through us? Are we going to allow our minds, bodies, and souls to dance the Thunder Dance?

The Afterwords

As mentioned in the opening section of this Introduction, both volumes have major Afterwords, by Laurence Cox in Part 1 and by Lee Cormie in this volume.[49]

There are a few things I feel I should say about them, not least because of the scale and ambition of their essays and what they contribute to this collection.

First, some background.[50] Once I had started to become aware of the scale of the two volumes—scale in terms of scope, complexity, and intensity—and increasingly as I thought about the world-historical context in which they were going to appear, I realised that these books would be a unique opportunity for someone to step back and engage with the collections as a whole and that for such a review or reflection to appear *within* the books would make the collections more meaningful, more accessible, and more enjoyable. In more particular terms, the idea of an Afterword came out of the intense discussions I was having with Lee Cormie in 2013 about collaborating on the sequel to these two books—looking more at movements from 2011 on in the emerging world context. As things turned out, Lee and I finally decided to not move ahead with that idea, but stimulated as I was by the conversations and especially by his inputs, I turned the idea around and invited him to instead explore the thoughts we had been discussing through a critical engagement with the material in the two books, what I called an Afterword to the books. Happily, Lee accepted.

I then decided that because of the scale of the two volumes I was putting together, that it would really much preferable to have a commentary with each volume, rather than just one: that we would all gain from the hopefully different takes that the two commentators would have and the dance that may take place between their essays. Again, primarily because of my great respect for what he does and for his extraordinary facility in writing, I approached Laurence Cox to do this—and it was my great privilege that he readily accepted (though, and as is clear from the opening words to his essay, he also suffered heavily as a result of accepting!).[51]

More recently, as the Book Organising Project has started taking shape, I have also come to realise what a valuable asset these two essays will be for this larger project.

It is of course entirely up to you as a reader to decide whether you agree with me or not, but in my understanding at least, they succeed magnificently in doing so, each in their own very particular—and different—way. I think that this is the case even though the Afterword to this book by Lee Cormie has turned out differently to what I had imagined it might be. I had assumed—without ever spelling it out—that 'the way to do an Afterword' was to sculpt the essay out of the material of the essays in the books. Lee however has taken a different approach, and instead composed what I think is an extraordinary piece of music that is at times inspired by the material he has found in the books but that at other times simply resonates and jives with it. As a result he has—I know I am mixing my metaphors here—painted an even larger landscape, *against which* we can read, view, and comprehend the essays in the two books, individually and collectively. Lee was of course always free to do as he wanted, and as it has turned out I have learned much from what he has written—perhaps precisely because it is not what I had expected. Thank you for opening my mind to this, Lee.

Laurence's Afterword, on the other hand, is an exquisite and painstaking sculpture—sculpted out of meditation on the clay that I gave him and crafted as an exercise of critical but patient and respectful engagement. His Afterword is a model of what we at CACIM try to practise as critical engagement and is in many ways also an exemplar of the ethic that my friend and teacher John Brown Childs has urged: moving in movement from a politics of conversion to an ethics of respect.[52] Thank you too, Laurence.

This said, I think I have to also make some further observations on this little subproject.

My first observation—which is something that I came to see only well after we started—was that both authors have the initials LC. How on earth did I manage this, with all the permutations and combinations that are available in the world around me?!

Second, though, and this I came to know only much more recently (and well after we had embarked on this project), is that both are students—and practitioners—of religion. I already knew this of Lee Cormie, who I know well, but I had not known this of Laurence Cox (just as a matter of record, he and I have not yet met in person). I only got to know this when I read the first draft of his Afterword. I can only say that realising this further coincidence has left me wondering whether there is not something similar in their respective work—in the way, perhaps, that they see the world and / or relate to it—that comes from this background and that has drawn me to them and to developing a very special respect for each of them? Perhaps as students and practitioners of religion, they engage with the world and with life in ways that are just a little different: at a different register.

Third, and especially given my own struggle over the past ten years and more of compiling and editing books to ensure diversity and balance, I feel I have no option but to engage here with the reality that both Lee and Laurence are white males living in the North. (Another commonality is that they are both also scholar-activists, but that is of course a characteristic that was almost a given in terms of my search for people who could relatively quickly write Afterwords of the nature I was looking for.) Given my background, and given my declared aim and practice (of plurality), how and why did I manage to do this?

I can only venture two answers to this. One is that though I know / am privileged to be in touch with a wide range of scholar-activists located in many parts of the world, from my fair experience now of commissioning essays over the past decade and more, Lee and Laurence were among the few who in my estimation had the experience and overview to be able to write something of the order that I wanted *and* who would realistically consider and accept my request and produce essays within the relatively short period of time I was requesting. They have also, as in the case of all the commissioned essays in these books, written their essays on the basis of voluntary labour—of the labour of love and solidarity, and perhaps even out of the love of labour. Both essays are great acts of this love and labour.

Working as we all have on this project purely on the labour of love and solidarity, this was a huge consideration. I of course do not mean any disrespect at all the other people I know—of other races and different genders living elsewhere in the world—who I could have approached; but working as I personally have been over these past some years, in a situation of considerable personal flux, I simply had to be realistic and take my best shot, as they say. Within these limitations, and although I accept the contradiction of this choice with what I otherwise try to practice, I personally think that the result has been very successful and that we are all gainers.

My second and more personal answer though, especially now when I look back, is simply that I was overwhelmed by massive flux I was then going through, and that all said and done, this represents a failure on my part to engage sufficiently critically with the requirements of what was after all my decision alone.

(There is however, also one other way of looking at this, which I have jokingly referred to with both Lee and Laurence: that they should consider the servitude they have done—as white males located in the privileged North working for an initiative coming from the South—as small instalments in the huge historical payback of the North's debt . . . and therefore as their duty to humanity and to the struggle and dance for justice, peace, and social transformation!)

Jokes aside, I want to underline what an extraordinary privilege it has been for me to work with both Laurence Cox and Lee Cormie in this project and to be able to include and publish their work in these books. I cannot thank them enough.

Some More Personal Acknowledgements and Thanks

In addition to what I've said above and in the Acknowledgements and Credits section, I want to offer some more personal acknowledgements. First, I would like to especially thank Ramsey Kanaan and Craig O'Hara at PM Press for agreeing to collaborate in this project and Matt Meyer—who is also a contributor to this book[53]—for introducing me to PM and for playing such an important role throughout the negotiations. Given PM's repertoire of work, I am delighted that these books have now joined the insurrection that they have built and are continuing to build. As Ramsey never fails to say, rock on!

Second, I also want to warmly remember my good friend, compa, and contributing editor for these books, the late Peter Waterman, who walked on on June 17 2017, and his enormous contributions to these books and to my life. Peter, aside from being contributing editor, was a close collaborator of mine for a decade and more, including as co-editor of the *Challenging Empires* series and two earlier books, *World Social Forum: Challenging Empires* (2004; second edition

2009) and *World Social Forum: Critical Explorations* (2012), and was, among many other things, a vigorous and critical member of the World Social Movement Discuss listserv, which I administer, and of its predecessor WSFDiscuss; he made an enormous contribution to all these initiatives. He was always razor sharp in his analysis and repartee—and not always easy to work with!—but looking back, it has been one of the great privileges of my life to have met him back in the early 1980s, in The Hague, where he lived, and that twenty years later, in 2002, we decided to collaborate in bringing out the 'big orange book', as he came to call the first edition of *World Social Forum: Challenging Empires*. Building on how much we both enjoyed that experience, we brought out the *Challenging Empires* book series, of which this is the fifth and perhaps last volume.

My only regret is that Peter did not get to see this book and its companion volume in their final printed form (though, thankfully, he did at least get to see the 'Advance Pre-final Movement Edition' of the first volume posted in December 2016, containing all the material for the book).[54] I have to confess that there is a deep irony in this: these books have taken a long time to bring out, but—and in part given this—Peter was always in favour of bringing them out as fast as possible, if necessary in what he called 'the quick and dirty' way—a quick edit and then posting everything online as an ebook. This was part of both his belief in the wonders of the Internet and a desire to move on to other things. It was me who resisted this and insisted on maturing the collection and bringing out these books 'properly'. Doing this has taken so long that sadly the books came just a little too late. I miss him sorely, and I also miss what surely would have been his witty, cutting comments on these books—and the nicknames he would likely have given them.

Third, I also wish to remember and honour three other contributors to these two volumes who have walked on even as these books were being finalised: the late *Daniel Bensaïd* (a contributor to Part 1, whom I also remembered there); the late *François Houtart*, who contributed to both books and walked on, like Peter Waterman, in June 2017; and the late *Fouad Kalouche*, a contributor to Part 1 (who walked on in 2016 but whose death I only learned of in late 2017, and so could not honour in that book, which was by then already in printing). In all three cases, it was my great privilege to work with them in the preparation and finalisation of their essays, and I feel honoured to be able to include their work in these books. My only regret is that the books have come out too late for them to see them.

Since I knew François Houtart personally, I want to add what an enormous privilege it was for me to have gotten to know him quite well since I first met him in India in the early 1990s, and to then work with him in the course of the World Social Forum process during the 2000s; and to enjoy his warmth and affection throughout. I would therefore like to especially honour here his great contribution to the rise and sustenance of the movements of the spirit throughout the world, and especially in the South over the past many decades.

Finally, I want to end this Introduction by acknowledging what is already perhaps obvious, or will become so, as you move through this book:[55] my profound personal debt to Taiaiake Alfred, Mohawk Nation and Indigenous scholar-activist, teacher, and warrior, for the inspiration and guidance he has given me, in my work and in my life since I learned of his work about ten years ago. Given that I understand myself to have been an activist for some forty years and something of a fighter in my time, he has opened new spaces for me. He has inspired me to reflect on what I have done and can still do towards becoming a warrior and how I can and should rethink my path and my dance. In its own way, this book—these two books—is / are a testament to that.

Let me therefore pay my respect to Taiaiake Alfred by also ending with something by him:

We are each facing modernity's attempt to conquer our souls. The conquest is happening as weak, cowardly, stupid, petty, and greedy ways worm their themselves into our lives and take the place of the beauty, sharing, and harmony that defined life in our communities for previous generations. Territorial loses and political disempowerment are secondary conquests compared to the first, spiritual cause of discontent. The challenge is to find a way to regenerate ourselves and take back our dignity. Then, meaningful change will be possible, and it will be a new existence, one of possibility, where Onkwehonwe will have the ability to make the kinds of choices we need to make concerning the quality of our lives and begin to recover a truly human way of life.[56]

Jai Sen

Ottawa, Canada, on unceded Anishnaabe territory in
Canada / on Turtle Island, and New Delhi, India
October 2017

References

Kolya Abramsky, 2018—'Gathering Our Dignified Rage: Building New Autonomous Global Relations of Production, Livelihood, and Exchange', in Jai Sen, ed, 2018—*The Movements of Movements, Part 2: Rethinking Our Dance*. Volume 5 in the *Challenging Empires* series. New Delhi: OpenWord, and Oakland, CA: PM Press

Taiaiake Alfred—2005. *Wasáse: Indigenous Pathways of Action and Freedom*. Peterborough, ON: Broadview Press

Taiaiake Alfred and Jeff Corntassel, 2017—'Being Indigenous: Resurgences against Contemporary Colonialism', in Jai Sen, ed, 2017—*The Movements of Movements, Part 1: What Makes Us Move?*. Volume 4 in the *Challenging Empires* series. New Delhi: OpenWord, and Oakland, CA: PM Press

John Berger, 1977 [1972]—*Ways of Seeing*. London: British Broadcasting Corporation

Tiana Bighorse, 1990—*Bighorse the Warrior*. Edited by Noel Bennett. Tucson, AZ: University of Arizona Press

Break Free Public Trust Work Group, February 2016—'Using the "Public Trust" to frame "Break Free From Fossil Fuels" Actions: A backgrounder for organizers and participants in "Break Free from Fossil Fuels"', at http://www.labor4sustainability. org/articles/using-the-public-trust-to-frame-break-free-from-fossil-fuels-actions/ (Accessed August 10 2017)

Jeremy Brecher, December 2013b—'Climate Protection: The New Insurgency', on *Truth-Out*, December 28, 2013, at http://truth-out.org/opinion/item/20897-climate-protection-the-new-insurgency (Accessed August 10 2017)

Jeremy Brecher, 2015—*Climate Insurgency: A Strategy for Survival*. Boulder, CO, and London: Paradigm Publishers

Michelle Chihara, September 2002—'Naomi Klein Gets Global', on *AlterNet*, September 24 2002, at http://www.alternet.org/story/14175/naomi_klein_gets_global (Accessed August 10 2017)

John Brown Childs, 2003a—*Transcommunality: From the Politics of Conversion to the Ethics of Respect*. Philadelphia: Temple University Press

John Brown Childs, 2018—'Boundary as Bridge', in Jai Sen, ed, 2018—*The Movements of Movements, Part 2: Rethinking Our Dance*. Volume 5 in the *Challenging Empires* series. New Delhi: OpenWord, and Oakland, CA: PM Press

Climate Action Public Trust, nd [*c.*April 2016]—'Break Free Proclamation: We Are Here to Defend the Climate, the Constitution, and the Public Trust', in Jeremy Brecher—*Against Doom* Oakland, CA: PM Press, p iv

Lee Cormie, 2017—'Re-Creating The World: Communities of Faith in the Struggles For Other Possible Worlds', in Jai Sen, ed, 2017—*The Movements of Movements, Part 1: What Makes Us Move?*. Volume 4 in the *Challenging Empires* series. New Delhi: OpenWord, and Oakland, CA: PM Press

Lee Cormie, 2018—'Another World Is Inevitable . . . but which Other World?'. Afterword for Jai Sen, ed, 2018—*The Movements of Movements, Part 2: Rethinking Our Dance*. Volume 5 in the *Challenging Empires* series. New Delhi: OpenWord, and Oakland, CA: PM Press

Laurence Cox, 2017—'"Learning to Be Loyal to Each Other": Conversations, Alliances, and Arguments in the Movements of Movements'. Afterword for Jai Sen, ed, 2017—*The Movements of Movements, Part 1: What Makes Us Move?*. Volume 4 in the *Challenging Empires* series. New Delhi: OpenWord, and Oakland, CA: PM Press

Laurence Cox and Alf Gunvald Nilsen, 2014—*We Make Our Own History: Marxism and Social Movements in the Twilight of Neoliberalism*. London: Pluto

André C Drainville, 2012—*A History of World Order and Resistance: The making and unmaking of global subjects*. London and New York: Routledge

André C Drainville, 2017—'Beyond *Altermondialisme*: Anti-Capitalist Dialectic of Presence', in Jai Sen, ed, 2017—*The Movements of Movements, Part 1: What Makes Us Move?*. Volume 4 in the *Challenging Empires* series. New Delhi: OpenWord, and Oakland, CA: PM Press

John Holloway, 2018—'The Asymmetry of Revolution', in Jai Sen, ed, 2018—*The Movements of Movements, Part 2: Rethinking Our Dance*. Volume 5 in the *Challenging Empires* series. New Delhi: OpenWord, and Oakland, CA: PM Press

David Harvie, Keir Milburn, Ben Trott, and David Watts, eds, 2005—*Shut Them Down! The G8, Gleneagles 2005 and the Movement of Movements*. Leeds: Dissent, and Brooklyn, NY: Autonomedia

Ahmad Jamal, 1958—'Ahmad's Blues', at https://www.youtube.com/watch?v=l7RIDZu-lyHA (Accessed August 10 2017)

Naomi Klein, 2004—'Reclaiming the Commons', in Tom Mertes, ed, 2004—*A Movement of Movements: Is Another World Really Possible?* London: Verso, pp 219–229

Tomás Mac Sheoin and Nicola Yeates. 'The Antiglobalisation Movement: Coalition and Division', in Jai Sen, ed, 2018—*The Movements of Movements, Part 2: Rethinking Our Dance*. Volume 5 in the *Challenging Empires* series. New Delhi: OpenWord, and Oakland, CA: PM Press

Roel Meijer, 2017—'Fighting for Another World: Yusuf al-'Uyairi's Conceptualisation of Praxis and Permanent Revolution', in Jai Sen, ed, 2017—*The Movements of Movements, Part 1: What Makes Us Move?*. Volume 4 in the *Challenging Empires* series. New Delhi: OpenWord, and Oakland, CA: PM Press

Tom Mertes, ed, 2004—*A Movement of Movements: Is Another World Really Possible?*. London: Verso

Matt Meyer and Ousseina Alidou, 2018—'The Power of Words: Reclaiming and Reimagining Revolution and Nonviolence', in Jai Sen, ed, 2018—*The Movements of Movements, Part 2: Rethinking Our Dance*. Volume 5 in the *Challenging Empires* series. New Delhi: OpenWord, and Oakland, CA: PM Press

Thelonious Monk, with John Coltrane, 1957 [1942]—'Epistrophy', on *Thelonious Monk Trio and John Coltrane at Carnegie Hall*, at https://www.youtube.com/watch?v=K_h1geOaLvY (Accessed August 10 2017)

Notes from Nowhere, eds, 2003—*We Are Everywhere: The Irresistible Rise of Global Anti-Capitalism*. London and New York: Verso, at http://artactivism.members.gn.apc.org/stories.htm (Accessed August 10 2017)

Michal Osterweil, 2018—'"Becoming-Woman"? Between Theory, Practice, and Potentiality', in Jai Sen, ed, 2018—*The Movements of Movements, Part 2: Rethinking Our Dance*. Volume 5 in the *Challenging Empires* series. New Delhi: OpenWord, and Oakland, CA: PM Press

Shailja Patel, 2017—'What Moves Us'. Proem to Jai Sen, ed, 2017—*The Movements of Movements, Part 1: What Makes Us Move?*. Volume 4 in the *Challenging Empires* series. New Delhi: OpenWord, and Oakland, CA: PM Press

Shailja Patel, 2018—'Offerings'. Proem to Jai Sen, ed, 2018—*The Movements of Movements, Part 2: Rethinking Our Dance*. Volume 5 in the *Challenging Empires* series. New Delhi: OpenWord, and Oakland, CA: PM Press

Geoffrey Pleyers, 2010—*Alter-Globalization: Becoming Actors in the Global Age*. Foreword by Alain Touraine. London: Polity Press

Roma and Ashok Choudhary, 2017—'Ecological Justice and the Forest Rights Movements in India: State and Militancy—New Challenges—*The Movements of Movements, Part 1, What Makes Us Move?*. Volume 4 in the *Challenging Empires* series. New Delhi: OpenWord, and Oakland CA: PM Press

Jai Sen, ed, 2017a—*The Movements of Movements, Part 1: What Makes Us Move?*, *Advance Pre-final Online Movement Edition*, at http://www.cacim.net/twiki/tiki-index.php?page=CACIMHome (Accessed August 10 2017)

Jai Sen, 2017a—'The Movements of Movements: An Introduction and an Exploration'. Introduction to Jai Sen, ed, 2017—*The Movements of Movements, Part 1: What Makes Us Move?*. Volume 4 in the *Challenging Empires* series. New Delhi: Open-Word, and Oakland, CA: PM Press

Jai Sen, 2018b—'Break Free! The Power of Incivility (Part 1)', in Jai Sen, ed, 2018—*The Movements of Movements, Part 2: Rethinking Our Dance*. Volume 5 in the *Challenging Empires* series. New Delhi: OpenWord, and Oakland, CA: PM Press

Jai Sen, 2018c—'Break Free! The Power of Incivility (Part 2)', in Jai Sen, ed, 2018—*The Movements of Movements, Part 2: Rethinking Our Dance*. Volume 5 in the *Challenging Empires* series. New Delhi: OpenWord, and Oakland, CA: PM Press

Jai Sen, ed, 2017—*The Movements of Movements, Part 1: What Makes Us Move?*. Volume 4 in the *Challenging Empires* series. New Delhi: OpenWord, and Oakland, CA: PM Press

Jai Sen, Anita Anand, Arturo Escobar, and Peter Waterman, eds, 2004—*World Social Forum: Challenging Empires*. New Delhi: Viveka. Slightly edited version at http://www.openspaceforum.net/twiki/tiki-index.php?page=WSFChallengingEm-pires2004 and at http://www.choike.org/nuevo_eng/informes/1557.html (Both accessed August 10 2017)

Jai Sen and Peter Waterman, eds, 2009—*World Social Forum: Challenging Empires*, updated second edition, Montreal: Black Rose Books

Jai Sen and Peter Waterman, eds, 2012—*World Social Forum: Critical Explorations*. Volume 3 in the *Challenging Empires* series. New Delhi: OpenWord

James Toth, 2017—'Local Islam Gone Global: The Roots of Religious Militancy in Egypt and its Transnational Transformation', in Jai Sen, ed, 2017—*The Movements of Movements, Part 1: What Makes Us Move?*. Volume 4 in the *Challenging Empires* series. New Delhi: OpenWord, and Oakland, CA: PM Press

John F C Turner, 1970—'Housing as a Verb', in John F C Turner and Robert Fichter, eds, 1970—*Freedom to Build*. New York: Macmillan

Notes

1. Alfred 2005, 'first words', p 19.
2. Abramsky 2018.
3. The first volume is titled *The Movements of Movements, Part 1: What Makes Us Move?* and was published in 2017 (Sen, ed, 2017).
4. See the 'Note on the *Challenging Empires* series', in this book.
5. The text in these two paragraphs is based on another document that some of us at CACIM and people associated with it are preparing. I would like to especially acknowledge Matt Meyer, a friend and comrade in struggle and also a contributor to this book (Meyer and Alidou 2018), for his contributions to thoughts and projects we are trying to develop and articulate at CACIM.
6. Sen 2017a.
7. As in the first book, I use the term 'settler' here as it is used in certain but not all contexts of colonisation, as referring to those who come later to a land and 'settle' in and on it, usually in the first waves displacing and sometimes decimating the indigenous populations that had lived there for hundreds and sometimes thousands of years

prior. See http://en.wikipedia.org/wiki/Settler. This historical situation has however become a lot more complicated over the past century or so in structural terms, and all the more during the postcolonial period from the 1950s onwards, and then since the 1980s and the ravages of neoliberalism, where structurally oppressed and often internally colonised peoples from other parts of the world, such as refugees, have in certain contexts become the major immigrants. The second generation—the children—of such immigrants are today asking themselves, can and should they also be categorised—together with the original colonisers—as 'settlers'? Is that how they see themselves? And most importantly: How should they relate with the Indigenous peoples of their new home? For an example of such reflection, see 'South Asians in Solidarity with Idle No More', at https://www.facebook.com/nishant.upadhyay.18/posts/10100389033191971?notif_t=like.

8.   For details on the contributors to this ebook, see 'Notes on the Contributors'.

9.   Cox and Nilsen 2014.

10. Cox 2017. For the teacher that Laurence is, see ceesa-ma.blogspot.com, and for the open-access, activist/academic social movements journal *Interface* that he is one of the guiding sprits for, see http://interfacejournal.net (Both accessed August 10 2017).

11. Alfred and Corntassel 2017; for his larger body of work, see Alfred 2005.

12. Cormie 2017, but with a minor note: "across both parts of this book", except my essay (appearing in this book as Sen 2018b and 2018c), where he had access only to a rough prefinal draft.

13. Cormie 2017.

14. And with Part 1, *What Makes Us Move?*, due out in 2017.

15. Abramsky 2018.

16. Kolya Abramsky, personal correspondence, March 1 2016.

17. See CACIM, with ABN—African Biodiversity Network, Climate SOS, GGJ—Grassroots Global Justice Alliance, IEN—Indigenous Environmental Network, and NFFPFW—National Forum of Forest People and Forest Workers, January 2011.

18. For a list of titles, see 'A Note on the *Challenging Empires* Series' in this book.

19. If you are interested in doing so, please get in touch with me at jai.sen@cacim.net along with an outline of what you would like to do and with details of what you do and of where you are located (place and movements / organisations / institutions, if any). We already—at the time of writing—have some initial commitments for some conferences, and we are looking forward to this number increasing as the word spreads. As the project materialises, and events and processes are defined, we will be posting information on our website at CACIM.

20. This section is an edited extract from Sections IV and V of my Introduction to Part 1 (Sen 2017a). While the two books are companion volumes, they are being published independently, so it makes sense to also have here what is common and fundamental to both. If you have read the previous Introduction, then you can afford to skip this section.

21. Naomi Klein perhaps first used this term in 2002; see Chihara, September 2002. For more discussion of the movement as it emerged and / or the use of the term, see Harvie, Milburn, Trott, and Watts, eds, 2005; Klein 2004; Mertes, ed, 2004; Notes from Nowhere, eds, 2003; Pleyers 2010; and for a very different take on the

phenomenon, Drainville 2012 and André Drainville's essay in the first volume of this book (Drainville 2017).

22.   I would like to warmly acknowledge here my introduction to this conceptual shift, first by reading the seminal work of John Turner on housing back in the 1970s, and then by the great privilege of getting to know John and of working closely with him through to the early 80s. In particular, see Turner 1970.

The shift that I made in how to see things was also greatly liberated and further inspired by the equally seminal work of John Berger, for instance his book *Ways of Seeing* (Berger 1977 [1972]).

23.   Indeed, if we look at the essay in this book by Tomás Mac Sheoin and Nicola Yeates, they argue that "Overall, then, there is no one unitary AGM to be described, diversity is the essence of the AGM. It is highly diverse in composition, organisational features, targets, and tactics; it expresses itself at local, national, regional, and global levels in very different ways"; and that even in the case of the 'AGM' itself, "the AGM has been able to maintain its unity through inclusiveness" and that "the development of what della Porta calls 'tolerant identities': "The self-definition as a 'movement of movements' . . . emphasises the positive aspects of heterogen[eity]'" (Mac Sheoin and Yeates 2018).

24.   Kalouche and Mielants 2017; McNally 2017; Cormie 2017, in Jai Sen, ed, 2017— *The Movements of Movements, Part 1: What Makes Us Move?*. Volume 4 in the *Challenging Empires* series (New Delhi: OpenWord, and Oakland, CA: PM Press).

25.   Though I use this phrase in this Introduction, I remain uncomfortable with it for obvious enough reasons; see the opening sections of the essay in the companion volume to this book by Roel Meijer for a rich discussion of this world of movement (Meijer 2017) and the essay by James Toth on the rise and globalisation of the Muslim Brotherhood (Toth 2017).

26.   As above, for information on the *Challenging Empires* series see the Note in this book from the original publisher, OpenWord, 'A Note on the *Challenging Empires* Series'.

27.   https://en.wikipedia.org/wiki/Capoeira (Accessed September 10 2017).

28.   I discuss our book project in more detail in my Introduction to the book before this in the *Challenging Empires* series, *World Social Forum: Critical Explorations*. See Sen 2012b. This section again draws on that material.

29.   Sen, Anand, Escobar, and Waterman, eds, 2004, and Sen and Waterman, eds, 2009.

30.   "The Tunisian Revolution, also known as the Jasmine Revolution, was an intensive campaign of civil resistance, including a series of street demonstrations. The events began on December 18 2010 and led to the ousting of longtime President Zine El Abidine Ben Ali in January 2011". For one summary, see http://en.wikipedia.org/wiki/Tunisian_Revolution (Accessed September 10 2017).

31.   http://en.wikipedia.org/wiki/Egyptian_Revolution_of_2011 (Accessed September 10 2017).

32.   As mentioned above, this came out in 2012 as *World Social Forum: Critical Explorations* (Sen and Waterman, eds, 2012).

33.   http://en.wikipedia.org/wiki/Naxalite (Accessed September 10 2017).

34.   Even though we didn't manage to include an essay specifically on this movement, we are privileged to have an essay that gives some of that history and comments on its

contemporary form. For a critical view on current resonance of the Naxalite movement, see the essay by Roma and Ashok Choudhary (Roma and Choudhary 2017).

35. Bighorse 1990, as cited in Alfred 2005, p 39.

36. Alfred 2005, p 27. Emphases in original.

37. Holloway 2018; Osterweil 2018.

38. Sen 2017b.

39. Provisionally titled "A Book In and On Movement: Some Reflections on the Idea and Composition of this Book", I finally decided to not include this in the book as published.

40. Cormie 2018.

41. Jamal 1958.

42. Monk1957 [1941].

43. Brecher 2013b, 2015.

44. Climate Action Public Trust nd [c.April 2016]; Break Free Public Trust Work Group, February 2016.

45. For a rich discussion of the principles underlying the new formulation, see Brecher 2015.

46. Sen 2018b, 2018c.

47. Patel 2017.

48. Patel 2018.

49. Cormie 2018, Cox 2017.

50. For those interested in having a full background to these books, please take a look at the Introduction to Part 1 (Sen 2017a).

51. Cox 2017.

52. Childs 2003a. See also his related essay in this book (Childs 2018).

53. Meyer and Alidou 2018.

54. Jai Sen, ed, 2016a.

55. In the subtitle of this book, in the Acknowledgements and Credits, in this Introduction, and in my own essay in this book.

56. Alfred 2005, p 38.

3
INTERROGATING MOVEMENT, PROBLEMATISING MOVEMENT

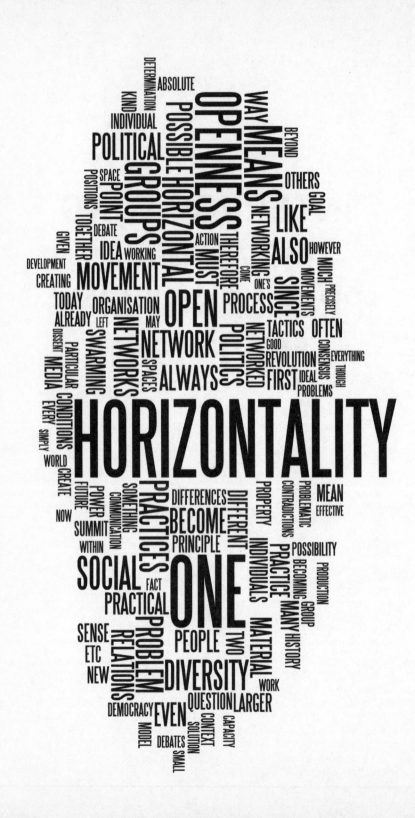

Nothing Is What Democracy Looks Like
Openness, Horizontality, and the Movement of Movements[1]
Rodrigo Nunes

Networked, horizontal forms of movement have been at the centre of many political debates in the last decade and have often been treated alternately as the 'limit' (by their enemies) and the 'solution' (by their proponents) to the problems of organising resistance to global capitalism. This however has unfortunately meant that critiques 'from the inside'—ie, by those who have experienced and share a general belief in them—have been much rarer than those articulated by partisans of other forms of organisation, resulting in much backpatting and triumphalism but few discussions of widely shared anxieties and frustrations; a problem that is only enhanced by the fact that it is often felt that horizontality must be 'defended' from its detractors.[2]

It is this kind of internal critique that this paper attempts by envisaging a demystification of openness and horizontality, showing how they are often presented in complete absence of context, and pointing to their inherent limitations, contradictions, and dead-ends. The point is not to open another debate on 'less' or 'more' horizontality, or horizontality versus verticality, but rather to problematise these very notions; and by opening up their problematic nature to argue for a practice that tackles their ambiguities head on.

Before Openness and Horizontality, There Was Openness and Horizontality

Why have openness and horizontality become so central recently? Two answers seem possible. The first concerns the growing disappointment that erupted in 1968 with the real existing socialism. This was very present (and increasingly outspoken) in progressive movements all over the world, culminating in a strange aftertaste of consternation and indifference when those regimes crumbled circa 1989. In this narrative we encounter a learning process where the lessons of Eastern Europe—whose mistakes were universalised, practically or theoretically, to almost everywhere by communist and socialist parties of all shades—made subsequent waves of people struggling for social transformation wise enough to know what not to do, though still in the dark, and in some cases disillusioned, about what could be done. While this process is undeniable, it is clear that it alone cannot account for the move towards the open and horizontal organisation of struggles in recent years; in fact, one could argue it is more capable of explaining the rise of identity politics, single-issue campaigns, NGOs, and / or the sheer surrender of many people to the inevitability of the world as it is / was, and the neoliberal stance taken by many left parties and trade unions.

What is relevant about the 'rise' of openness and horizontality is not that it substitutes one total theory of organisation with another, but the fact that something like 'network' has a place today in the vocabulary and practices of organisations that remain hierarchical or that it is integral to the practices of companies and highly valued in business and management circles. In other words, what is relevant is not that these ideas have become important but that they have become *practiced*. Even if we say that openness and horizontality are the new ideology—an across the board one at that—the ideology as such can only exist because it has become (or is perceived as being in the process of becoming) materially possible on a large scale.

The bulk of the answer must, therefore, lie in a material process. One current narrative of this process identifies it with a restructuring in the most advanced sectors of capitalism (which, it is argued, exerts a hegemony that restructures all other sectors), commonly called the passage from the Fordist to the post-Fordist model of production. This can be characterised by the transformation of the relations between production and what is 'outside' it, consumption: gathering information about and circulating information that 'constructs' the market, the quantitative and qualitative increase of 'consumer relations' in relation to the productive process, hand in hand with a 'singularisation' of the product.

> We are witnessing today not really a growth of services, but rather a development of the 'relations of service'. The move beyond the Taylorist organization of services is characterized by the integration of the relationship between production and consumption, where in fact the consumer intervenes in an active way in the composition of the product. The product 'service' becomes a social construction and a social process of 'conception' and innovation. . . . The change in this relationship between production and consumption has direct consequences for the organization of the Taylorist labor of production of services, because it draws into question both the contents of labour and the division of labor (and thus the relationship between conception and execution loses its unilateral character).[3]

This transformation is only possible through the socialisation of the material means through which these new relations can be established—ie, the means of communication. The Internet adds another layer to this process, since it is a multipolar (many-to-many) means of production and circulation, as opposed to a one-to-many like television (even though television channels establish their own many-to-one media through surveys, polls, etc). The large-scale massification of these media, and a multipolar one in particular, is thus the chief material cause behind the 'renaissance' of openness and horizontality. It is only within the horizon of a social life that has become networked that a politics of networking as such can appear; and it is only in a politics of networking that openness and horizontality can appear as goals.

'Networks' and 'open spaces' are, therefore, ambiguous: on the one hand, they are what we perceive as the conditions of the possibility of horizontality and the means by which it can be achieved; on the other, they are only partial actualisations of the idea they make possible—not only as instantiation but also as idea, since it is only within a politics of networks and open spaces that horizontality becomes both means and goal.[4]

This is not to deny that many earlier social and political groups practiced open and horizontal ways of organising. While this is obvious, they were always faced with the practical impossibility of extending this internal relation to all of society or even to large numbers of people, because they lacked the material means—they could only propose it as a desirable future by means of some kind of eschatological argumentative device, such as an 'end of history' in the classless society of communism. Faced with material limits, horizontality had to 'stay small' and could only 'think big' in a 'march of history'.

What is important about horizontality today is that the material conditions for its existence are now perceived as given, at least in potential, *in the present*. This explains the emphasis that we see today on horizontality both as means and as goal: by working horizontally, we are developing horizontal forms of cooperation; developing the very social fabric we want to produce, and the means for its production. Organisation and politics coincide. In the past, the non-separation of means and ends was a point of principle or ideology. Now it is a simple matter of practice. And since large-scale media of communication seem to provide the conditions under which this process is possible, it is no wonder that the models of networking, openness, and horizontality we use are largely derived from them. It is today common, for instance, to point to the practices of free and open-source software communities as the 'vanguard' of this democracy to come.[5]

Openness and Horizontality—and Their Contradictions

This however, it must also be said, is the *ideology* of openness and horizontality. It is a way of charting the present and perceiving lines along which the future can be constructed. The ideology is thus secondary to existing practices of horizontality and openness and their condition now. The distinction is important to highlight the fact that it is concrete practices that create the conditions of possibility in which the ideology is produced, and therefore the latter can only be a theoretical production sharing the situation and limits of the practices.

> Foucault: In this sense theory does not express, translate, or serve to apply practice: it is practice. But it is local and regional . . . and not totalising.

Deleuze: Precisely. A theory is exactly like a box of tools. It has nothing to do with the signifier. It must be useful. It must function. And not for itself.[6]

First contradiction: one or many horizontalities? Dependence on material context
Again, the point here is not that 'horizontality is something that happens to people with Internet access' but to highlight the difference between a model that springs from certain practices and models that spring from others.[7] In other words, there can be many horizontalities.

Thus the universalisation of certain ideas of openness and horizontality suffers precisely from the problem of abstracting these ideas from their material contexts. What kind of 'horizontality' do we speak of, for instance, when referring to a social movement such as the MST (Movimento dos Trabalhadores Rurais Sem Terra; 'Brazilian Landless Workers' Movement'), with over a million members, many illiterate and with little access to any means of communication, with no territorial autonomy, constantly criminalised by the media, and facing attacks from landowners' henchmen? It is true that this is a movement with a strong Marxist-Leninist influence, but that does not stop one from asking what form of horizontality it does or could have. If we look at the five "ways in which the kind of openness identified" in free and open-source software communities "practically correspond to specific moments of organisation in the social movement" listed by Jamie King (the organisation of meetings and discussions; their documentation; decision-making; the organisation of demonstrations; the organisation of actions),[8] the problems of applying a model become clear.

The MST as a 'movement' does take part in global networking, through Via Campesina and the World Social Forum (WSF). Many of the material conditions that make networked politics possible in Europe, however, are unavailable to the vast majority of their membership: time-flexibility; high mobility; language skills; technological literacy; access to means of communication, particularly the Internet. Inversely, the frustration many people sense in attending something like a Social Forum is the realisation of the existence of a restricted number of 'hyper-activists' who can attend all these networking spaces. (Of course, as soon as one has this first-hand realisation, one is part of this group.) This is when real-existing networking runs against the real-existing differences in material conditions of its "wider environment".[9] And by fetishising one model of horizontality, it becomes necessary to make the same distinction that is made in liberal democracy between 'formal' and 'material' democracy or access.

Second contradiction: supernodality
A ghost haunts networked politics: the ghost of the supernode. If networked politics is based on communication flows, the supernode can be seen as "not only routing more than their 'fair share' of traffic, but actively determining the

'content' that traverses them".[10] The definition already points to one attribute of the supernode: hyperconnectivity. In other words, some individuals are 'more networked' than others, a quality that can be derived from material conditions such as those described above, and others that are more contingent, such as knowing the relevant people, 'having been around longer', being friends with particular individuals, and personal attributes such as being a good speaker, charisma, etc.

Since in all networks these characteristics—'external' to the network itself—will apply in different ways to different individuals and contingence will distribute others in an equally random fashion, it is safe to say there is no given way of preventing the emergence of supernodes. Also, it is clear that this is not necessarily a matter of "a malicious will to power";[11] supernodality is an emergent function of the way networks (and groups generally) work. For example, one may become a supernode as a result of a temporary group or task-related need or by being active in periods of hypoconnectivity. And, since there are no visible formal structures, the possibility of these informal hierarchies becoming sedimented is high.

Of course, this is only the network age variation of the process described in Jo Freeman's classic text about informal structures within the US American feminist movement: "the tyranny of structurelessness".[12] One must note that her final conclusion is not (unlike that of many who use her arguments today) that the way to counter these tendencies is a return to democratic centralism or the Leninist party. She proposes instead "a few principles we can keep in mind that are essential to democratic structuring and are politically effective also", such as "diffusion of information to everyone as frequently as possible", "equal access to resources needed by the group", and "rotation of tasks among individuals".[13] These are common practices among groups that profess openness and horizontality today. One could say, then, that she does not have anything to say to those who, even when abiding by these principles, keep encountering the problems she identifies. But maybe we are asking the wrong question.

Third and fourth contradictions: no such thing as an open space; determination and indetermination

If networks are the 'permanent' structures of our model of horizontality, 'open spaces' are the temporary coming together of these structures. But how open is an open space? Many are based on hallmarks (People's Global Action, Dissent!) or charters of principles (WSF) that define an inside and an outside; they work, therefore, by exclusion. Others (such as the *Caracol Intergaláctica*) allow the identity of the groups organising them or the process by which they are organised to exercise a 'soft power' of exclusion. In this case, in a chat discussion before the *Caracol Intergaláctica* in 2005, one participant raised the question of the possibility of the youth of a Communist Party wishing to take part in it; there was consensus, however, that there was no need to create a distinction, because the identity of the space itself created it. The very idea of an 'open space' is therefore contradictory—for it must be opened by someone, for some purpose, and with some people in mind; no matter how open this first determination is, it always already creates an exclusion.

This leads to a larger problem: every determination is a closure—every statement like 'this is the problem', 'this is where we stand', 'this is what we have to do now' narrows the terms of debate, and therefore (at least in principle) excludes people who think differently in the same way that hallmarks do. As a consequence, any determination of a goal, position, analysis beyond the constitutive terms of the open space is perceived as negative because it reduces diversity. Discussions of this kind are considered only possible within smaller affinity groups, which means that more defined positions and strategies belong to small groups and / or individuals and not in the debates of larger networks or spaces. In this way, horizontality always posits its own limits: while it can produce decisions in small groups, the possibility of doing so in larger groups is much reduced, and even— since having overarching goals, positions, etc potentially threatens diversity—to be avoided.

Fifth and sixth contradictions: dependence on practical context; diversity of tactics versus consensus decision-making
The movement that first became visible globally in Seattle has since found various solutions to the problem of how it relates internally when networks come together. Seattle was a surprise not only because of the 'coming together', but also because of the latter's very nature: a broad coalition of very loosely related groups, some with interests considered contradictory, coming together through open, horizontal networking—without a previous conference, debates on ten-point programmes, or anything of the kind. That was not only this movement's first show of strength, it was also the first time a networked politics was affirmed loud and clear on such a scale.

This capacity to come together in an ad hoc fashion, with few other determinations besides a common objective, has been described as 'swarming':

> Swarming occurs when the dispersed units of a network of small (and perhaps some large) forces converge on a target from multiple directions. The overall aim is *sustainable pulsing*—swarm networks must be able to coalesce rapidly and stealthily on a target, then dissever and redisperse, immediately ready to recombine for a new pulse.[14]

While activists widely celebrated this definition—overlooking the irony of a think tank specialising in military studies being the first to spell this out—one phrase in it is often overlooked: "on a target". At a summit protest, of course, the target is given—the whole point of the summit protest is precisely finding something that, for a few days, physically represents capitalism. Once the summit is over, however, the question of what being 'anti-capitalist' means opens up again.

The lynchpin of swarming is the implicit principle of a diversity of tactics. The goal (or target) being given in advance, the most effective way to arrive at it, and the only way of also respecting the diversity of approaches of the groups involved, is agreeing that each group follow its own approach. The problem is that this principle was arrived at as a solution to the particular question of swarming—in relation to situations where the objective is already given, such as summit protests. But in situations where a commonality still has to be defined or produced and where some sort of agreement is necessary, diversity of tactics can achieve very little. That most of the swarming moments of this movement have been summit protests cannot obscure this; in fact, to the opposite, it could be that it is the automatism of the ready-made solution that explains the persistence of the summit protest as *the* tactic by which this movement is recognised.

One could even go as far as saying that a too automatic application of the principle of diversity of tactics contradicts the principle of consensus decision-making. It is always possible not to come to any conclusion by applying the former, simply 'agreeing to disagree'; the latter implies that differences cannot be approached as absolutes, consensus being precisely the method of working through them and coming up with new syntheses. Perhaps this contradiction is simply the practical extension of the fourth, between determination and indetermination.

Antiglobalisation and Its Discontents

The first three contradictions show that horizontality is a practical and logical failure: the opening of spaces proceeds by closure and exclusion; all external factors, including but not reduced to material conditions, distort horizontal networks from the outside, creating differences between nodes; and these differences reintroduce the hierarchies and informal structures that one desired to be free of.

The last three contradictions indicate the possibility that if swarming and the principle of diversity of tactics was the great victory of networked politics, it may have been a self-defeating one, because a diversity of tactics reveals a larger contradiction between decision-making and diversity: every time something is decided, diversity is reduced.

These points probably give an idea of people's frustrations with openness and horizontality in their practical experience of it. On the one hand, horizontality in practice does not live up to itself as an ideal, and always ends up creating exclusions and / or informal structures and hierarchies. In email discussions on the future of Dissent! after the G8 summit, for instance, some participants expressed the feeling that Dissent! should not go on because it had served its purpose (creating the conditions for the swarming in Scotland) and that any attempt to move beyond that is bound to degenerate into some sort of proto-Leninist group, a small clique moving it behind the scenes and defining its agendas, or that it had served the purpose of facilitating the summit mobilisation but had failed the purpose of being horizontal, and therefore should not go on.

On the other hand (potentially both opposed and complementary to the first point), horizontality also does not seem effective; it is impossible to make decisions, impossible to see the whole picture, and the only purpose it serves is facilitating moments of swarming, where lots of single-issue (or single-minded) groups can come together without any problems, precisely because there is very little to be decided. This attitude could be seen in the same email debate: some people supported the idea of taking Dissent! forward and made proposals about the next things to focus on; others replied that this would be precisely the problem with continuing to use Dissent!, because everyone would try to impose their pet issues on everyone else as soon as there was no G8 summit to unify peoples' attention.

Two great sources of frustration and dissatisfaction are two of the oldest practical debates—probably because these are the two great non-debates that always occur but never really happen: relations with the media and the use of physical force. The two issues, though always discussed at length, are almost invariably solved by some form of application of the principle of diversity of tactics (in practice this means that the 'pacifists' are defeated, since their goal was to stop 'violence' from happening) or some sort of interpretation of consensus decision-making ('since we have no consensus on talking to the media, we cannot talk to the media', which in turn facilitates the emergence of groups and individuals who, by being alone in talking to the media, become de facto representatives). But since the whole point is couched in terms of diversity of *positions*, this fetishises what positions *are*—ie, general maxims of behaviour that compose some kind of overarching theory of politics, social change, 'revolution', etc—hardly ever debating what positions are possible in a situation or how general maxims can be applied to a particular, practical context. This is where the feeling of the debate never actually happening comes from: from the start, positions are taken to be absolutes, unaffected by any inflection of practical, situational contexts—impervious to debate and unchangeable. Therefore, it becomes a question of one position winning and the other losing; and making such decisions like this is also bad practice, because it reduces diversity.

In the wake of Seattle, debates around tactics often took on an abstract tone. The question of what constitutes 'violence' was posed, and while dogmatic pacifists moralistically condemned property destruction, others imbued it with a veneer of liberatory significance. As the ACME Collective argued in their communiqué on the Seattle Black Bloc, "When we smash a window, we aim to destroy the thin veneer of legitimacy that surrounds private property rights. At the same time, we exercise that set of violent and destructive social relationships which has been imbued in almost everything around us".

Insofar as these debates proceeded on a terrain of absolutes, discussions skirted the context. Those arguing for the enforcement of non-violent guidelines were faced with a context in which non-violent discipline could no longer be enforced and reacted with condemnation and differentiation. "The revolution we are trying to create didn't and doesn't need these parasites" argued one activist in a *Seattle Weekly* article. On the other hand, property destruction was often conflated with revolutionary anti-capitalism. It provided a way to distinguish 'reformist' from 'revolutionary' tactics. The strategic question of when and where property destruction could be effectively utilised was often left unanswered.[15]

In such processes, opinions and grand theories become defined as the private property of individuals and small affinity groups, undesirable on larger levels. This means that groups and individuals hardly ever get a chance to challenge and be challenged in a debate on what it means to be doing something there and then. At best, a debate actually takes place (often because something really must be decided), and some wonder: 'Why can't we have this more often?' At worst, it feels like a convention of tiny communist groupuscules (each with their theories of revolution, manifestos, literature) who differ only because they are capable of working together once a year under the one agreement that they all 'be different together'.

These two internal problems—the feeling that horizontality always fails in practice and that it promotes immobility of ideas and decisions—can be added to an external problem: how horizontal groups relate to those viewed as 'non-horizontal'. This is the horizontal dilemma: If I place horizontality and openness as political means and end, how can I relate to those who do not? If I reject them, I am closed and sectarian? If I work with them, I am indirectly supporting hierarchical, vertical practices?

Like every false problem, this only exists in absolute terms. If you turn 'political parties' or 'universities' or anything else into a concept defined by certain features, one of which is a hierarchical structure, and this feature excludes that concept from participating in horizontality—defined in opposition to 'verticality' and hierarchy—you create a conceptual problem that is difficult to resolve. If these things are not fetishised and turned into concepts, but treated in the particular context in which the relationship may or may not happen (What kinds of relationships can be established in this situation? What is the work they are doing? With what people? What can be achieved? What are the strings attached?), the question ceases being about an idea and becomes a practical problem that requires more information (rather than a theory of organisation and revolution) and, eventually, a practical solution.

Fetishisation works both ways: it is possible to fetishise horizontality. The problem with that is it becomes a word—like 'anarchism', 'socialism', etc—with a normative value abstracted from all the actual practices and social contexts it is drawn from. The problem of this 'identification with oneself'—turning a self-image into a norm—is that it restricts one's capacity to transform oneself, congealing into an ideal that, for a social movement, not only restricts the capacity to act and relate to what is different, but also blinds it to its own cultural, class, gender, etc context.

The reverse of this 'self-identification' is that once one realises oneself as a minority against a majority that is either non-mobilised or identifies with control or against other minorities that propose alternatives of control (such as communist parties), one sees that there is very little in the immediate environment to relate to. The concrete, immediate other is substituted by an abstract other, either absent by definition ('this is a middle-class movement; if we had the working class with us . . . ') or by distance (the 'beautiful resistance' of movements in the Global South, even though they are often hierarchical). What is immediate and near is devalued in favour of an ideal.[16]

Beneath the Network There Is a Network

The source of this idea was a natural reaction against the overstructured society in which most of us found ourselves, the inevitable control this gave others over our lives, and the continual elitism of the Left. . . . The idea of *structurelessness*, however, has moved from a healthy counter to these tendencies to becoming a goddess in its own right.[17]

Hopefully the point of painting this disheartening picture will now become clear. If horizontality as concept is, as shown above, contradictory and unworkable, there is only one way to go: decide this is a false problem and ditch the concept. Nothing is what democracy is like—horizontality is not a model (or a property that can be predicated) but a practice; as such, it remains permanently open to the future and to difference. Saying 'this is what it looks like' closes the door to all future and different things that might come. The point is not that horizontality is problematic but that democracy as such is problematic. And problematic means just that: permanently open.

By deciding upon an 'ideal' model, all we are doing is creating a transcendent image that hovers above actual practices. Because it is cleansed of the 'impurities' of this world, it will serve all sorts of purposes—ideological propaganda; eschatological argument ('when everyone is horizontal, horizontality will reign');

rhetorical device (when a group accuses another of not being horizontal); absolute indeterminacy—and become that in comparison to which everything always falls short. Meanwhile, back in the immanence of the only world that actually exists, we keep suffering within its limits. By becoming this transcendent ideal, horizontality and openness—themselves not unfamiliar to business and management discourses—can become very similar to liberalism. The dream of 'absolute openness' means that openness is only possible if we abstract all concrete differences. Also, nothing can be affirmed, for that would contradict openness.

Jo Freeman criticised structurelessness on two counts: it informally allowed for the differences it formally excluded and it made feminist groups less effective. We have seen that what she had to propose tells us little about our impasses, since her proposals are all more or less incorporated in the current repertoire of horizontal practices. If the other models available today—liberal, representative democracy, different shades of Leninism—do not solve any of these problems (and create others of their own) and are rejected in principle, what are we left with?

Freeman cannot answer because she is looking for principles, for mechanisms. Since we more or less have those and are still unhappy with them, we should seek something else. If horizontality and democracy are problematic by nature because they refer to practices and not mechanisms, what we need is an ethos—a 'becoming open'.

Taking this path does not mean the absolute indeterminacy of never producing any principles or mechanisms. On the contrary, they have to be produced, reproduced, and deconstructed according to needs. Dissent!,[18] for example, came up with a very good solution to the eternal non-debate on media. The Counterspin Collective was, perhaps, another contradictory application of the principle of diversity of tactics (as already mentioned, 'if there's no consensus on not talking to the media, then it is possible to talk to the media'), but it was a workable, practical solution that did not place anyone in charge of 'representing' the network, yet created a channel for people who wanted to give interviews, or simply distribute press releases.[19]

What it also does not mean is the fetishisation of diversity and differences. In fact, the whole attitude that constrains debates because 'diversity must be left alone'—which so often squanders good opportunities for better understandings of positions, collective development of syntheses, and overcoming of contradictions dealt with as insurmountable—smacks of liberalism. Not only because it takes differences as givens, but also because it reduces them to individual property of a person or a group.

This attitude accepts two tenets of liberalism: one, an irresolvable distinction between individual and collective good; two, the liberal concept of individuality. It ignores the reality that beneath and before every political network or group, individuals are always already part of a larger network of communication, meaning, narratives, and power relations. In reality therefore, there cannot be a private opinion, just as there cannot be a private individual. Michelangelo's David is only a particular actualisation of a web of themes, models, techniques, materials, tools, etc that stretches far beyond its sculptor. This also puts the lie to any ideas of 'individual revolution'; 'revolution in one person' is an impossibility, because there is no action that is not always already social. 'Localism' has to mean more than living up to one's ideal of communal living in a house with friends while the world outside, along with the neighbours, goes up in flames.

Nothing here calls for an ethics of sacrifice or normalisation. On the contrary, an ethos of openness would be one of plasticity; ceasing to be an individual does not mean becoming like everyone else but maximising one's capacity to perceive how one has become what one is and what is contingent in that—and therefore one's capacity to adapt and change: abandoning ideas of authorship and ownership of collective processes, giving up one's proper name (in a deeper sense than just by having a web persona), while being unafraid to affirm things, and then revise them again; sensing when is the right moment for an intervention and when it is time to let things go, even if one disagrees; being able to deal with supernodality by bypassing it without burning anyone out. Nothing can be either absolute indetermination or total determination; the art lies in learning how to move between the two. It is between absolute openness and total closure that a political practice of openness as a problematic may happen.

> [S]uch intentions demand constant development of new organisational models adaptable to constantly changing situations. The issue is no longer to express a common way of struggle, nor a unified picture or one-dimensional solidarity, neither an ostentatious unity nor a secretly unifying sub-culture, but the profound understanding and the absolute will, to recognise the internal differences and create flexible groups, where different approaches connect with each other reasonably and for mutual benefit.
>
> It's about political communication in the best sense: networking understood as situational negotiations that are based on the possibility of changing one's own standpoint as well as the standpoint of the other. Rather than being based on some spurious qualifications of good versus evil, this approach instead seeks out the basics of a reasonable and practical temporal togetherness.[20]

The work of networking social movements and groups has been going on for a while. If we keep returning to the same discussions and they make no progress, this is cause for thought. The first step in movement building is believing one is in a movement, in something that moves with a movement of its own. This means that the individual sense of time must be relativised in favour of the larger time of this movement, which stretches indefinitely between past and future, and the individual sense of space must be relativised in favour of all the different positions that are or can be occupied in the movement's larger spatiality. An ethos of the networked individual—simultaneously aware of and transformed by everything that happens in this larger network and ready to sense what spaces in the network could and should be occupied—is necessary.

The problem with traditional Marxist groups is the transformation of an analysis into a philosophy of history that grounds a practice; everything will always have to be absorbed within the theory's larger totality. There are objective laws of the development of history, and the task is to interpret them correctly so as to identify the right practice for the moment. It is no wonder that with such a regime of truth, all political applications of Marxism became known by proper names: Leninism, Stalinism, Trotskyism, etc; the oracular task of correct interpretation cannot be shared. Surely networking moves beyond that, but it cannot be simply to 'devolve' the power of 'correct interpretation' to individuals by banning any large-scale agreements while fostering a fetishised 'diversity'. A networked sensibility demands both the openness to sense the non-totalisable whole of the network and be transformed by it and the determination to act upon that whole in the way that seems most effective for the network. It is like becoming a Lenin *and* a proletarian all at once.

This Revolution, and the Next One

> A black balloon drifts across the dusty cement floor, pushed by an invisible draught. Printed on it in small, white letters are the words, "Everything is connected to everything else".[21]

But beneath the network there is always a network.[22] And before the Internet, mobile phones, radio, and digital TV there was one already. To say that is both to put the lie to a transcendent ideal of absolute openness, where all relations of power are dissolved and to refer to perhaps the largest impasse of all the open, horizontal political networks today: that of effectivity.

The point of these networks cannot be simply their enlargement, even though there is a lot of work to be done globally in bringing more groups together. Achieving that—itself a utopian goal—would only ensure that all mobilised groups of the world know more about each other and become more capable of working together, supporting each other, and swarming every now and then. The network that exists 'underneath' these political networks is the web of social relations that at once reproduce and also transform themselves slightly every day. This is a web of power relations, in the sense of 'actions upon actions', of creating fields of possible actions by excluding the possibility of others; 'domination' is just a species in the larger genus of 'power relations'.[23] Neighbours, parents, workmates, employers, bus drivers, policemen—everyone belongs in it, including political networks. All work for its reproduction in some way, and no one is necessarily good or bad for doing so.

This reinforces the above point about individuality. If every power relation is an 'action upon an action', there is no individuality in the classic sense; an individual is the plastic reconfiguration of her outside. The difference between networked politics and previous forms of political organisation is that it places *nonlinear connection* above *linear accumulation*; and two things never connect, never enter into a relation, without becoming a third thing.

A politics of linear accumulation has much simpler goals: to expand until there are members enough to storm the Winter Palace. Swarming has played in the past and will in the years to come play an important role, but it seems highly unlikely that it will ever achieve its 'anti-capitalist' objective of . . . well . . . ending 'capitalism'. Even if it did, the immediate results might not differ much from what came after the Winter Palace. It is crucial to notice that when the authors of *Networks and Netwars* described the "war of the future", the political organisations they saw as most successful were single-issue campaigns that could have great achievements through networking and swarming.[24] Anti-capitalist counter-summits are obviously not campaigns in the same sense, as they in and of themselves have no deliverable goal, such as getting a law passed, storming a palace, or winning elections. The conclusion is that there is only so much that swarming can do and much still to be invented.[25]

What was given up along with the idea of linear accumulation was the idea that there is a goal. Once you have a goal that can be identified with achieving an action, and this goal is identified as the completion of the entire process, you enter the realm of linearity: history marches towards an end, and the role of the 'revolutionary' is to speed it up. One of the central problems of Western thought from the Enlightenment onwards has been that of the 'next revolution'. The first was that which created the conditions for today's nation-state, property relations, and liberal democracy. Identifying the point of the next one, the one that will change this particular configuration, has been the problem ever since. During this period, however, the linear solution has been largely discredited because all 'ends of history' always had to be enforced, and history stubbornly went on.

This is why the problematic nature of horizontality is its openness towards the future and why its nonlinearity will always move beyond any closure of the 'this is what it looks like' kind. If horizontal movements try to produce this closure, they will be left behind. Even though we call the moment where the configurations of power came to be as they are now the 'first revolution', this cannot be identified with any single point in history. What happened was the result of an open development that went through the Enlightenment and the bourgeois revolutions and has not stopped transforming itself since. This is the problem with the term 'capitalism': it is a name given a posteriori to a historical development that is still in motion, not—like 'communism' or 'anarchism'—the description of a desirable place where history ends.

But if we do not even know what capitalism is, how can we know what its overcoming is? This is why any particular understanding of what openness and horizontality are cannot be allowed to simply become the new dogma. It is clear that enlarging the political networks that already exist is not an end in itself. These can only be effective—beyond swarming effectiveness—by grounding themselves in a thorough politicisation of social relations. This might entail employing ('going back to' and 'reinventing') other, older forms of political action—house visits, neighbourhood organising, community projects—which will in turn entail practices that might be looked down upon by 'horizontal' activists, such as campaigning for laws, lobbying councils, collaborating with religious groups and trade unions, etc. Examples of this in, for instance, the preparations for the G8 in Scotland can be found in the Trapese Collective working within and across academic institutions or the negotiations with local councils in Stirling and Edinburgh, which made possible the rural convergence space and the camping area respectively. It is in the network inhabited by parents, neighbours, bus drivers, migrants, mental patients—even policemen, who are people with employers, parents, and neighbours—and, of course, 'activists', in all the different subject-positions they may occupy that horizontal movements may find the *transversalities* that cut across it and can bring change.

While the question of what this can mean has to remain a practical, problematic (and therefore open) one, it is possible to say here what this does *not* mean.

This does not mean a mystical appeal to 'a working-class politics'. As argued above, this kind of reification of 'the workers' is not only the reverse side of a lack of clarity in the politics of horizontal movements ("the rage of Caliban seeing his face in a glass")[26] but also empirically inaccurate, given that these movements are not deprived of a social base (chiefly the new productive subjects created by the processes of restructuring described at the start). What it means is that issues that are very much at stake in both the productive and political practices of these individuals—such as the struggle against intellectual property—are relevant for a myriad other areas (genetically modified organisms, pharmaceutics, education), and commonalities must be built between these struggles that go beyond the automatic, 'rent-a-swarm' model of 'solidarity action'. In creating concrete relations, subjectivities are produced that are much more than a reified idea of 'worker' or 'activist'.

This does not only mean 'localism', if that is understood as creating local spaces by and for 'activists', be they social centres, newspapers, etc. While these initiatives have undeniable value, they are tools not ends and must be considered in their capacity to create interfaces between struggles and subjectivities—not in a quantifiable capacity of making people 'join the club'.[27]

Finally, this does not mean abandoning any of the horizontal practices that exist today but pushing them forward, exposing them to new situations, creating and recreating them, even if by making mistakes. It is in the word 'transversality' that we find the reason why resorting to practices that are 'older' does not necessarily mean returning to old, Marxist-type linearity. The point is finding the contexts in which horizontal practices can enter or open new spaces, encounter new situations, and establish different relations by identifying, in present lines of conflict, points of leverage and conjunctural possibilities that link different struggles and create commonalities between what is different. If horizontality means putting connectivity above accumulation, there is one answer to the age-old 'What is to be done?': *connect*.

References

John Arquilla and David Ronfeldt, eds, 2001—*Networks and Netwars: The Future of Terror, Crime, and Militancy*. Santa Monica, Ca: RAND Publications, at http://www.rand.org/publications/MR/MR1382/MR1382.ch1.pdf (Accessed August 11 2017)

Giles Deleuze and Michel Foucault, 2001—'*Les intellectuels et le pouvoir*' ('The Intellectuals and Power', in French), in Michel Foucault, ed, 2001—*Dits et écrits* ('Sayings and Writings', in French), Volume 1. Paris: Gallimard, at http://1libertaire.free.fr/MFoucault110.html (Accessed August 11, 2017)

Michel Foucault, 2001—'*Le sujet et le pouvoir*' ('The Subject and Power', in French), in Michel Foucault, ed, 2001—*Dits et ecrits* ['Sayings and Writings', in French], Volume 2. Paris: Gallimard

Jo Freeman (aka Joreen), nd [*c*.May 1970/1971]—'The Tyranny of Structurelessness', at http://www.jofreeman.com/joreen/tyranny.htm (Accessed August 11 2017)

David Harvie, Keir Milburn, Ben Trott, and David Watts, eds, 2005—*Shut Them Down! The G8, Gleneagles 2005 and the Movement of Movements*. Leeds: Dissent, and Brooklyn, New York: Autonomedia

Chris Hurl, 2006—'Anti-Globalization and "Diversity of Tactics"', in *Upping the Anti*, vol 1, pp 53–66, at http://uppingtheanti.org/journal/article/01-anti-globalization-and-diversity-of-tactics/ (Accessed August 11 2017)

Jamie King, 2004—'The Packet Gang', in *Mute Magazine*, Winter / Spring, at http://www.metamute.org/editorial/articles/packet-gang (Accessed August 11 2017)

Susanne Lang and Florian Schneider, September 2003—'The dark side of Camping', at http://www.tacticalmediafiles.net/articles/3338/The-dark-side-of-Camping (Accessed August 11 2017)

Maurizio Lazzarato, 1996—'Immaterial Labour', at http://www.generation-online.org/c/fcimmateriallabour3.htm (Accessed August 11, 2017)

Notes from Nowhere, 2003—*We Are Everywhere: The Irresistible Rise of Global Anticapitalism*, London: Verso

Rodrigo Nunes, May 2005—'Networks, open spaces, horizontality: Instantiations', in *ephemera*, special edition on the World Social Forum, at http://www.ephemerajournal.org/sites/default/files/5-2nunes2.pdf (August 11 2017)

Paul Ormerod and Andrew Roach, June 2003a—'The Medieval Inquisition: Scale-free Networks and the Suppression of Heresy', at http://arxiv.org/abs/cond-mat/0306031 (Accessed August 11 2017)

Paul Ormerod and Andrew Roach, June 2003b—'Go medieval with Al-Qaida', on *Times Higher Education*, at http://www.timeshighereducation.co.uk/177422.article (Accessed August 11 2017)

Ben Trott, 2005—'Gleneagles, Activism, and Ordinary Rebelliousness', in David Harvie, Keir Milburn, Ben Trott, and David Watts, eds, 2005—*Shut Them Down! The G8, Gleneagles 2005, and the Movement of Movements*. Leeds: Dissent, Brooklyn, NY: Autonomedia

Oscar Wilde, 1997 [1890]—*The Picture of Dorian Gray*, at http://www.planetpublish. com/wp-content/uploads/2011/11/The_Picture_of_Dorian_Gray_NT.pdf (Accessed August 11 2017)

Andrew X, 2001—'Give up activism!', in *Do or Die: Voices from the Ecological Resistance*, issue 9, 2001, pp 160–66, at http://eco-action.org/dod/no9/activism.htm (Accessed August 11 2017)

Notes

1. Ed: This is an edited version of an article posted on Interactivist Info Exchange—Collaborative Authorship, Collective Intelligence http://info.interactivist.net, at http://info.interactivist.net/article.pl?sid=06/11/21/2032250 (Both inactive August 11, 2017). It was first published in this form in David Harvie, Keir Milburn, Ben Trott, and David Watts, eds, 2005, but has been further edited. I, and we at OpenWord, thank the author and the editors for publishing this book under a Creative Commons Attribution Non-commercial Share Alike License—thereby empowering and licensing us to freely publish it here in this form.

2. Four 'insider' critiques I have referred to throughout this article are: Hurl 2006; King 2004; Lang and Schneider, September 2003; and Nunes 2005.

3. Lazzarato 1996.

4. Cf Nunes 2005.

5. The fact that openness and horizontality are present in management techniques and even some strains of liberal democratic thought shows even more clearly how these ideologies are all derived from the existence of the material conditions found on the Internet above all.

6. Deleuze and Foucault 2001, p 1177.

7. For example, the Zapatistas' way of organising is often attributed to Indigenous practices, which do not seem to see the coexistence of horizontal organising and a hierarchical structure in the form of the Ejército Zapatista de Liberación Nacional ('Zapatista Army of National Liberation', EZLN) as insurmountable.

8. King 2004.

9. Jamie King extends this insight to free and open-source software communities, "the most open system theoretically imaginable": "limitations to those who can access and alter source code are formally removed. But what then comes to define such access, and the software that is produced, are underlying determinants such as education, social opportunity, social connections and affiliations". King 2004.

10. Ibid. The term 'supernode' is borrowed from this text. Without employing the word, a study by Paul Ormerod and Andrew Roach on the manner in which the Medieval Inquisition was finally capable of eradicating heretical movements points to qualitative evidence of the occurrence of such things as 'supernodes'. See Ormerod and Roach, June 2003a. The authors have recently co-authored a text proposing the application of the strategy of the Inquisition to Jihadist networks. See Ormerod and Roach, June 2003b.
11. Ibid.
12. Freeman, nd [c.May 1970 / 1971].
13. Ibid.
14. Arquilla and Ronfeldt, eds, 2001, p 12.
15. Hurl 2006.
16. Another recurrent source of frustration for activists being, of course, the feeling that these movements can be self-referential and subcultural and that a good deal of 'closedness' is brought about by its being limited to certain social and cultural profiles. Susanne Lang and Florian Schneider also point out how the incapacity to move from swarming to an actual debate may be solved by attracting state repression and, thus, by conjuring a "bad other", create a fictitious unity of "being on the right side of oppression" that substitutes a real, problematic unity that cannot be created in practice. Cf Lang and Schneider, September 2003.
17. Freeman, nd [c.May 1970 / 1971].
18. Dissent! was the loose network that functioned as an umbrella for the mobilisation against the G8 summit in Gleneagles, Scotland, 2005. Among other things, it maintained a long international networking process and organised the convergence spaces in Edinburgh and in Stirling.
19. There was a discussion on the night when the police surrounded the rural convergence space in Stirling on whether the collective should write a statement and submit it to the open assembly in the morning and, there being consensus, issue it as a statement on behalf of the camp. In the end this was decided against, but it opens a debate for the future: At what moments, under what conditions, and through what process can the mandate of the working group be extended?
20. Lang and Schneider, September 2003.
21. Notes From Nowhere, eds, 2003, p 63.
22. Referring to the web of social relations as being 'beneath' activist networks is, of course, entirely metaphorical; there can be no separation between 'us' and 'society', as we are all involved in relations as employers, employees, parents, sons, neighbours, etc. This separation is, however, created by ourselves when we speak in terms of 'us' and 'the others', 'activists' and 'passives'; we ask ourselves how we can communicate with these people, and yet this communication takes place every day. When we speak of our horizontal activist networks as if they were the rightful space of this ideal, transcendent horizontality in society, we are paradoxically placing ourselves in a vertical place above the web of social relations. The term 'beneath' should be then understood as describing this false dichotomy, of questioning it—so it becomes a *real* problem by being posed—rather than accepting its existence. For a development of these themes, see Andrew X, 2001 and Trott 2005.
23. Foucault 2001, pp 1041–62.

24. Arquilla and Ronfeldt, eds, 2001. In fact, distinguishing these from the 'dark side' of the netwar—terrorist networks, hooligans, and organised crime—they welcome their potential "liberalising effects" (p 7). Their appreciation of Seattle lies somewhere between 'hooliganism' and 'extremist single-issue campaign'.

25. A good example of what swarming *can* do is the blockades on the first day of the G8 summit at Gleneagles in 2005. Small groups with little coordination were a lot more effective (as well as more impervious to police infiltration) than a large mass of people gathering in one place. As I have pointed out, however, this is a case where the goal is given from the outside (blockading the roads, stopping traffic, shutting the summit down) rather than constructed through political debate.

26. Wilde 1997 [1890].

27. "The activist role is a self-imposed isolation from all the people we should be connecting to. Taking on the role of an activist separates you from the rest of the human race as someone special and different. People tend to think of their own first person plural (who are you referring to when you say 'we'?) as referring to some community of activists, rather than a class. For example, for some time now in the activist milieu it has been popular to argue for 'no more single issues' and for the importance of 'making links'. However, many people's conception of what this involved was to 'make links' with *other activists* and other campaign groups. June 18th demonstrated this quite well, the whole idea being to get all the representatives of all the various different causes or issues in one place at one time, voluntarily relegating ourselves to the ghetto of good causes" (Andrew X 2001). This is a classic text arguing that social change does not require 'more activists' through a process of linear accumulation.

OpenWord

Worlds in Motion
Movements, Problematics, and the Creation of New Worlds[1]
The Free Association

'People have been saying for some time that what the movement needs are some real victories. But—it's a strange but frequent phenomenon—when movements finally win them, they often go unnoticed.'[2]

'Ding Dong! The Witch is dead. . . . The Wicked Witch is dead!'[3] With the irrecoverable collapse in 2006 of the Doha round of trade talks, the World Trade Organization (WTO) appears to be effectively defunct.[4] The cycle of anti-summit protests of the turn of the century and beyond, and the social movements that formed around them, played a vital role in killing it off. Yet there was no general affect of victory. In fact you could even say the opposite: the 'we are winning' sentiment of the couple of years following Seattle disappeared to be replaced by, at best, head-scratching and soul-searching. More a case of WTF than WTO.[5]

Maybe this paradox makes more sense if we start to think of movements not as concrete blocks of people but as a moving of social relations. Of course, sometimes it's useful to think of the individuals and groups who make up social movements, but such a definition—however broad—will always be limited by the fact that it conceives of the movement as a 'thing'. It is something that can be defined, whose boundaries can be clearly mapped, and which stands *outside* and *against* something else called 'capital'. We may argue over the exact terms of the definition (for example, do we include this campaign or that group?), and we may agree that these definitions will shift, but this movement is still seen as a 'thing'. It is increasingly difficult, though, to reconcile such a static, 'thing-like' view of the anti-capitalist movement with the realities of everyday life—not least our own—where the vast majority of the world's population exists both within and against capital.

Of course social relations are always moving: capital tries to pretend that it is a universal and immutable way of living, when in fact those social relations have to be re-established every day—every time we go to work, exchange money for goods, or act in alienated ways, etc. But every now and then these social relations are fundamentally challenged by our actions as we start to create new worlds. One of the places where that has happened is counter-summit mobilisations: the new worlds we've created there may be temporary or geographically limited (this is the basis of the criticism of 'summit-hopping'), but it's those same limits which have made them such a rich laboratory. They have produced an intensity that enables us to see this moving of social relations on two different levels, one we can call 'demands' and one we can call 'problematics'.

Be Realistic . . .

Demands are by their very nature demands to someone or something. They are demands to an existing state or state of affairs. They might be explicit—when we appeal to governments for a change in policy or we demand that sacked workers be reinstated—or they might be implicit—when we insist on our right to police ourselves. But they are always, to some extent, within the terms and sense of the thing we are trying to escape: in these cases, we are accepting the idea of 'work' or the idea of 'policing'.

Indeed, if demands are ever met it is only done by further reducing a movement's autonomy. The state or capital grants the demand by recasting it in its own terms and within its own logic. This is how mediation works: think, for example, of the way 'green consumerism' is now promoted as a solution to climate change. The incorporation of demands almost always takes the form of a counterattack—the cost of action on climate change, for example, will always be shifted on to us (eg, road pricing, green taxes). As the saying goes, be careful what you wish for.

But it's not as simple as saying that all demands lead to empty recuperation ('bigger cages, longer chains'). Those bigger cages also give us more room for manoeuvre. And it is partly because demands operate on the foreign territory of representation that we fail to recognise the achievement of demands as victories. They appear as the actions of our opponents, the product of their good sense and not of our activity. But we need to dig a little deeper to see what's really going on. In many ways demands involve a freezing of (a) movement, an attempt to capture what we are and raise it to the level of representation. But as a crystallisation, they also contain our logic within them, like a fly trapped in amber. It's similar to the way the product of our work is sold back to us: sometimes it's hard to see the social history buried within the latest government announcement.

There's a second reason why we find it hard to see victories in the realm of representation as winning. There's a time lag to this process: When we stormed through Seattle in 1999 chanting 'Kill the WTO!', we felt like we were winning, but it wasn't until 2006 that the WTO fell to its knees. By the time demands are 'met', movements have moved on. And this isn't just a question of time: it's also to do with speed. During intensive moments, like counter-summit mobilisations, we have moved so incredibly fast that a few days seem like years. Think of the way we have arrived at a convergence centre or campsite: to begin with, it's just a featureless field where we struggle to find our bearings, yet in the space of a few days, we have transformed it into a new world.

. . . Demand the Impossible!

But demands are just one moment that social movements move through. They are necessarily lopsided and partial, because they operate on a terrain that is not ours. We're more interested here in the movement at the level of 'problematics'. Unlike demands that are implicitly vocal or static, problematics are about acting and moving. If demands are an attempt to capture who we are, then problematics are all about who we are becoming.

Social movements form around problems. We don't mean this in a simple functionalist fashion, as if there is a pre-existent problem which then produces a social movement that, in turn, forces the state or capital to respond and solve the problem. Rather, social movements produce their own problematic at the same time as they are formed by them. How does this work in practice?

Firstly, there has to be a moment of rupture that creates a new problem, one that doesn't fit into the 'sense' of contemporary society—this is the grit that the pearl forms around. The Zapatista uprising is one example, but we could just as easily refer to climate change or border struggles. With this rupture come a whole new set of questions, new problems which don't make sense and which don't have a simple solution. As we try to formulate the problematic, we create new worlds. One could call this 'worlding': by envisaging a different world, and by acting in a different world, we actually call forth that world. It is only because we have, at least partially, moved out of what makes 'sense' in the old world that another world can start to make its own sense.

Take the example of Rosa Parks, who simply refused to obey a bus driver's order to give up her seat and move to the back of the bus to make way for a white passenger. She wasn't making a demand, she wasn't even in opposition; she was simply acting in a different world. It's the same with the 'antiglobalisation movement': no sooner had we come into being as a social force than we were redefining ourselves as an *alter*-globalisation movement. In many ways, we were in a novel position of having no one who we could put demands to. How else could we act if not by creating another world (or worlds)? And who would create it if not us? So first we have to create that 'us'.

And here's where we return to the realm of demands, of crystallising, because the process of creating this new agency (this new 'us') also involves acting at the level of 'demands', and this can be an extremely productive moment. The rupture itself can take the form of a demand, maybe a simple 'No!' That can give a movement an identity by providing a static position around which people can orient themselves—a public staking-out of ground upon which an expanded social movement can cohere. This is exactly what happened with summit protests over the last decade. Most of us didn't go to Seattle, yet an identity was forged there which we could loosely relate to. That identity was strengthened and deepened as it moved through Gothenburg, Cancún, etc. In other words, summit protests were not only conscious attempts to delegitimise the meetings of the rich and powerful. They simultaneously legitimised our worlds and widened the space for worlds governed by logics other than that of capital and the state. Summit protests played a vital role in creating a new 'us', an extended 'we'.

On another scale, we were part of exactly the same process at the 2003 G8 summit when there was a mass road blockade at Saint-Cergues: the 'No!' of the front line barricade created space in which a new body could cohere and start to develop consistency. We created new knowledge (tactics for dealing with tear gas and pepper spray); we developed new ways of decision-making (for maintaining food and water supplies and for working out when and how we would withdraw); we extended the problematics (blocking side roads, making connections with local residents). Through these processes we took forward the project of building a 'we'.

This move from opposition to composition, from the level of demands to the problem of practice, is never easy. The UK anti–poll tax movement, for example, never managed to find its own autonomous consistency. When the government finally backed down in 1991, the movement imploded. We had been held together by our *NO!*—it's what allowed us to stand together—but without the emergence of *YES*es we were simply unable to move. But trying to bypass the level of demands altogether is equally fraught. One of the criticisms of the mobilisation against the 2005 G8 summit was that we were too easily outmanoeuvred by a state-orchestrated campaign (Make Poverty History), which was used to make demands 'on our behalf'.[6]

Inevitably this moving has to take into account things that appear to be outside of it, like the actions of the state or the deployment of a police helicopter at Saint-Cergues. So we move in response to new developments, to evade capture. But there is also an internal dynamic caused by the new enriched material that has cohered around the original 'grit'. This new material has its own new properties and might then find itself with new internal problematics.

At a macro-level we can think here of the debates about the Black Bloc or the issue of violence after Genoa, where a whole new set of questions were posed and everything moved on. Or we can look at how the idea of convergence centres at summit protests has been developed to embrace a whole practice around social centres, whether rented, owned, or squatted. These centres, however temporary, are one space within which movements can thicken and start to develop a consistency.

Beneath the Pavement

There is a bigger problem here. There's a relation between our autonomous movements (inventing new forms, throwing up new problematics, etc) and the effects those movements have on capital and state and their mechanisms of capture. But there is a danger that we stay trapped within this relation and never manage to break free. We can never entirely evade capture, but we can try to develop techniques to postpone or minimise it. And this is where counter-summit mobilisations have proved essential.

In everyday life it's quite easy to see the world of demands, of things, but it's more difficult to work out what's going on underneath. We can glimpse traces of the underlying dynamics in spectacular eruptions (Paris 1871, Barcelona 1936, Seattle 1999, Oaxaca 2006 . . .) or by looking at the realm of demands and seeing what's reported in the press or how states act. Summit protests can shatter this everyday equilibrium and make the intensive realm spring to life. At such moments, we can see commodities for what they are—dead. We get a sense that this is real—this is life. And we can see more easily what social movements are made of.

But this also has profound consequences. At these times it becomes obvious that our movement isn't just a movement of 'us' ('activists versus others') but a moving of social relations, an unfreezing of all that is fixed. This moving of social relations is like the breaking of an ice floe: it has no edges or boundaries ('this group is in our movement, this group isn't', etc), or rather the boundaries are always in motion; the moving ripples through everywhere—absolutely everywhere. This is the affect of winning that we experienced in Seattle and elsewhere. We felt we were winning because we weren't 'we' any more; maybe we'd even abolished any idea of a 'we', because there was no outside, no 'us' and 'them' any more. In fact this slippage in 'we' is reflected in this text: the meaning of 'we' goes from 'us the authors' to 'you the readers' to an extended 'we' that defies measurement. Moreover what we do cannot be limited to what is consciously decided: sometimes we 'do' things behind our own backs.

This shattering of the everyday also forms a new point of rupture, a new jumping-off point. And this can be one of the ways we can escape the twin apparatuses of capture that the state deploys. First, at the level of demands, the state attempts to incorporate us into its logic of sense. Here we can think of how the police tried to incorporate into their own logic of legality the squatted Camp for Climate Action next to Heathrow Airport in August 2007. They did this simply by offering to be 'helpful' and just wanting to walk around the camp once. This 'offer' was initially accepted, as there was a need for the camp to feel a certain sense of security. But there was a price to pay: when we moved onto the terrain of legality (whether 'illegal' or 'legal'), we were within their sense, and not ours. Allowing the police on site set a precedent and it became impossible to refuse constant patrols without forcing a new rupture. And if and when we instigate that break and follow the logic of our deepening problematics, we come up against the other pole, the state's machine of outright repression. The danger is that we get trapped in this pincer of incorporation / repression, and our activity in response to either diverts us from our own autonomous movement.

We come full circle: the problem that faces us again and again is the risk of being trapped in the logic of capital and the state, whether as radical reformers, summit protesters, workplace activists, or whatever. Capital always takes its own limits as universal ones, but in truth those limits are 'theirs' not ours. The only way for autonomous social movements to avoid this dance of death is to keep breaking new ground.

In this sense, winning—in the realm of problematics—is just the gaining of extended problematics, as our experimental probing opens up ever-wider horizons. Or more prosaically, all that movements can ever get from 'winning' is more movement. And that's why we kept getting drawn back to counter-summit mobilisations like the anti-G8 mobilisation at Heiligendamm in 2007: they are—or were—one of the places where the movement of movements can break the limits of its formation and ask its own questions.

References

Danny Burns, 1992—*Poll Tax Rebellion*. Edinburgh: AK Press, and London: Attack International

Olivier de Marcellus, 2006—'Biggest victory yet over WTO and "free" trade: Celebrate it!', *InterActivist Info Exchange*, August 18 2006, at http://interactivist.autonomedia.org/node/5349 (Accessed August 12 2017)

'The Doha round . . . and round . . . and round', *The Economist*, July 31 2008, at http://www.economist.com/node/11848592 (Accessed August 12 2017)

'The future of globalisation', *The Economist*, July 27 2006, at http://www.economist.com/node/7223846 (Accessed August 12 2017)

David Harvie, Keir Milburn, Ben Trott, and David Watts, eds, 2005—*Shut Them Down! The G8, Gleneagles 2005, and the Movement of Movements*. Leeds: Dissent! and Brooklyn, NY: Autonomedia

Paul Hewson, 2005—'"It's the politics, stupid": How neoliberal politicians, NGOs, and rock stars hijacked the global justice movement at Gleneagles . . . and how we let them', in David Harvie, Keir Milburn, Ben Trott, and David Watts, eds, 2005—*Shut Them Down! The G8, Gleneagles 2005, and the Movement of Movements*. Leeds: Dissent! and Brooklyn, NY: Autonomedia, pp 135–49

Turbulence Collective, ed, 2010—*What Would It Mean To Win?* Oakland, CA: PM Press

WTO, nd—'Doha Development Agenda', at https://www.wto.org/english/tratop_e/dda_e/dda_e.htm#development (Accessed August 12 2017)

Notes

1. This essay was originally published in the first issue of the journal *Turbulence: Ideas for Movement*, which was distributed at the counter-mobilisation against the G8 summit held in Heiligendamm, Germany, in early June 2007. It was republished in Turbulence Collective, ed, 2010—*What Would It Mean To Win?* (Oakland, CA: PM Press). As always, in writing this piece the authors were helped along the way

by countless others, especially people around The Common Place social centre in Leeds (www.thecommonplace.org.uk); the authors would also like to thank Jai Sen for comments which improved this revised version. Ed: I warmly thank the authors, who are also the editors of *Turbulence*, for their ready agreement to publish a revised, edited, and updated version in this book.

2. de Marcellus 2006.

3. For those not familiar with *The Wizard of Oz*, these lines form a recurring theme in several songs sung by Dorothy (played by Judy Garland) and others in the 1939 film.

4. 'The future of globalisation', July 27 2006. The 'Doha Development Agenda' or 'Doha Development Round' World Trade Organization talks commenced in 2001 with a ministerial-level meeting in Doha, Qatar. Following further ministerials in 2003, 2004, and 2005, negotiations collapsed at the 2006 ministerial meeting in Geneva. Subsequent talks, most recently in 2008, also in Geneva, have also stalled. See 'The Doha round . . . and round . . . and round', July 31 2008; also see WTO, 'Doha Development Agenda', at https://www.wto.org/english/tratop_e/dda_e/dda_e. htm#development (Accessed August 12 2017).

5. WTF is a common abbreviation for the slang expression 'What the fuck?'.

6. A good history of the anti-poll tax movement is Burns 1992. On Make Poverty History and the 2005 G8 summit, see Hewson 2005.

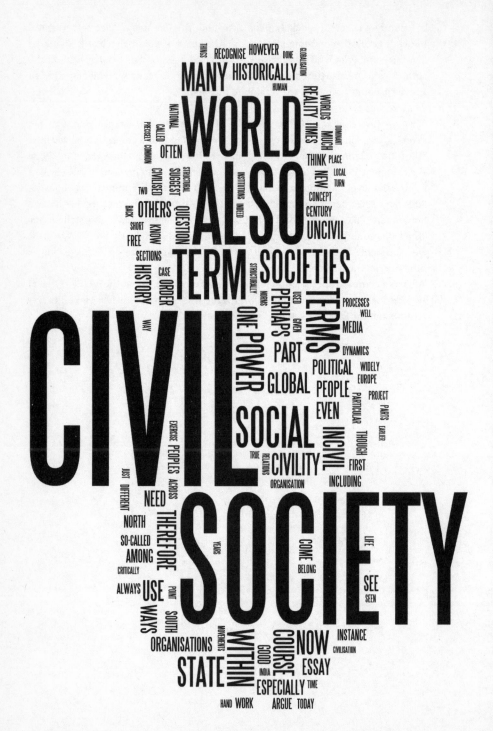

OpenWord

Break Free!
Engaging Critically with the Concept and Reality of Civil Society (Part 1)[1,2]
A Call to People Concerned with Justice, Peace, and Social Transformation
Jai Sen

> *The 'civilized' have created the wretched, quite coldly and deliberately, and do not intend to change the status quo; are responsible for their slaughter and enslavement; rain down bombs on defenseless children whenever and wherever they decide that their "vital interests" are menaced and think nothing of torturing a man to death; these people are not to be taken seriously when they speak of the 'sanctity' of human life or the conscience of [the] civilized world.*
> —James Baldwin[3]

> *'Citizens' have always existed throughout history only in relation to non-citizens, people defined to be of unequal status to those defined as citizens. The concept of citizenship is intimately bound up with the concept of the nation state, and the struggle for alternatives that go beyond the nation state must also point to a conception of the human being that goes beyond citizens and citizenship.*
> —Kolya Abramsky[4]

> *The battle is a spiritual and physical one, fought against the political manipulation of the people's own innate fears and the embedding of complacency, that metastasising weakness, into their psyches.*
> —Taiaiake Alfred and Jeff Corntassel[5]

> *Break all the barriers! Let the captive soul be liberated!*
> —Rabindranath Tagore[6]

In a general sense, this essay hopes to speak to people anywhere who are concerned about justice, peace, and social transformation. But in particular, it hopes to speak to people who see themselves as belonging to what is called 'civil society', and to those who feel they are excluded. Among other things, it is written to urge careful thought about what this now very everyday term, 'civil society' (and the terms behind it—'civility' and 'being civil'), actually means and what it therefore means—in a deeper sense—to identify oneself with it. Suggesting that these are carefully constructed terms that have profoundly contradictory meanings and a deeply problematic history, it discusses other ways to look at things—other lenses, other cracks. In particular, it argues that to achieve our full creative powers, which we need today more than ever before, we need to free ourselves: by breaking free of civility.

I
'Being Civil Is Good': Lifting the Veil, Removing the Mask

In our time, in social and political literature, and in the media, as well as in common exchanges within what is called 'civil society', the term 'civil society' is being increasingly used to refer in particular to the worldwide phenomenon of social and other civil activism—and, in turn, this phenomenon is increasingly being seen and celebrated as a powerful contribution to the democratisation of politics and to bringing common sense and civility to difficult situations. This is perhaps especially the case in the North and among those in international organisations, the media, and academia, but it is also increasingly so among those who belong to 'the North in the South'—and, for me, far more disturbingly, also among too many who would like to otherwise say that they belong to 'the South in both the North and the South'—or the Global South—but who seem to have accepted 'civil society' as a legitimate term and a self-descriptor.

I want to make clear that I recognise and acknowledge the historical contributions to social justice and well-being of both individuals and organisations belonging to 'civil society'. However, I also fundamentally question and contest this term, this idea and how it is used, and argue that the term and the idea mask the reality of what so-called 'civil society' is, does, and has done historically. I put forward the argument that 'civility' and 'civilisation'—which I submit are at the core of the project of civil society—are in fact *structurally suffused* with what in effect are profoundly colonial, patriarchal, oppressive, and anti-democratic undercurrents; and that as a result, and along with its contributions to democratisation, so-called 'civil society' has also, in many periods and in perhaps all parts of the world, been at the cutting edge of barbarism and exploitation. This continues in our time—for instance, in the continued oppression of Dalits in India—and I suspect that this is the case in all societies and has always been so. In this sense, and because of the uniformly positive connotation attributed to the term 'civil', I suggest here that we should see it as a mask or veil that hides reality, moreover as a deliberate mask or veil—and that we therefore need to lift it and look at the face behind.

I argue further that today, at a time when the world is dramatically changing and communities of the historically oppressed and structurally excluded in so many parts of the world are becoming new actors on national and world political stages, the beguiling power of civility' is—even as some sections of 'civil society' continue to make contributions to this resurgence—in many ways also undermining the processes of the much deeper and wider democratisations that are opening up in our time because of the internal structural dynamics of civility.

All this should be reason enough to give pause for thought to those of us who think we belong to 'civil society' and are also concerned about justice and social transformation. Activists, researchers, journalists, and so many others need to step back and question this label and reflect on where we are located with respect to it; to stop using this term as a self-descriptor and an analytical category; and to reflect on and rethink our politics and our lives. I hope that the arguments in this essay may perhaps give those who are excluded from civil society and / or do not see themselves as belonging to 'civil society' a critical lens through which to view it.

In addition, while I acknowledge the importance of what we call 'civil rights', 'civil liberties', and 'civil disobedience', I also question the idea that 'being civil' is uniformly good (and argue that civil disobedience, for instance, is at base incivil) and insist that the use of the word 'civil' in all these terms is part of the same strategic web and the same illusion and deception; and I put forward the social category of the incivil, the concept of 'incivility', and some arguments for critically appreciating and celebrating the power and value of incivility.[7] I go on to argue that for those of us who are, for good or for bad, structurally assigned to being members of 'civil society' being incivil—and learning how and when to be incivil—can help to set us free to achieve our full creative powers.

In short, if we are to address and undo the effects of colonialism, imperialism, capitalism, casteism, racism, sexism, and all the other structural exploitative isms, and if we want to decolonise, de-imperialise, de-capitalise, de-racialise, and de-casteise the world—and build a more free world—then, among many other things, we also need to think about, question, challenge, and free ourselves from the insidious grammar and vocabulary of these processes in all senses. It is no accident that so-called 'civil society' is a powerful vice *where all of these meet and through which all of these act.*[8] If we want to work for justice, peace, and social transformation, then we urgently need to free ourselves of this vice.

Difficult Terrain

All of this is difficult terrain because the term 'civil' and the concept of 'civility' (and their equivalents in perhaps all languages and cultures) are so deeply embedded in our everyday lives and our self-images—whether we belong to the 'civil' world or the incivil, I suspect. In short, and perhaps in all societies, being civil is universally portrayed as being 'good'—unquestionably good. This is a part of our everyday language, norms, and customs; crucially, the idea is embedded in what is called 'law'—this is of course one of the main means by which 'civil(ised)' societies are structured and regulated; it is deeply buried in the fables and stories we tell our children and in storybooks that build and fill our imaginations;[9] it is contained in all the textbooks that shape our professions; it is reflected in mainstream media that fire our imaginations;[10] and it is vividly played out in movies, and now even more universally in what people post and access on YouTube. We, therefore, all use and reproduce this norm, often unwittingly.

To repeat, within 'civil society' these terms and the concepts are seen as normatively positive and beyond question. In many ways, it is like the term 'classical' used in music, dance, or architecture. What does this term actually mean? Does it not also contain centuries—sometimes thousands of years—of exploitation and extraction?

While it is perhaps true of all societies past or present that are or were conscious of themselves as being 'civilised', it is still the case that over the past two to three decades—since the triumph of the North / First World and the collapse of the Soviet Union—the term 'civil' has been vigorously and massively introduced into common usage in governmental policy, academia, and the media—three key circuits of the propagation of ideas—as part of the introduction and use of the term 'civil society'. In turn, the term and the activities of 'civil society' have come in these circles to be seen as a given and a good—a virtually unquestionable good. I see the introduction of this term into everyday vocabulary as a small but important part of the larger project of neoliberal globalisation that took off following the collapse of the Soviet Union.

A key part of the problem of critically looking at and questioning 'civility' and 'civil society' therefore lies in the relations of the production of knowledge: how the norms of civility are defined, how the subject of 'civil society' has historically been defined, and of who does the defining (and the broadcasting). Reflect, for instance, on the list I have just given above of how widely and deeply the concept of 'the civil' penetrates and permeates our lives and of who produces the norms and knowledge. What we call and accept as 'laws', for instance, are norms that are defined by members of civil society (academics, lawyers, jurists, bureaucrats, etc—and, occasionally, activists), and then sanctified by the state. But the state, in turn, has historically been set up by civil society, and the state and civil society both use law to structure and regulate society.

Equally, fable and stories—especially in so-called 'advanced' societies, where oral traditions have fallen into disuse—are authored and composed by members of civil society (and increasingly, it sometimes seems, by the Walt Disney empire alone). The same is true of our textbooks and, at least historically, of the media: newspapers, films, videos, and the radio.

This is of course not 100 per cent true. Oral traditions and history still remain vital for many peoples in most parts of the world; people in struggle throughout the world and throughout history have always appropriated available media and disseminated their own stories, their own messages. There have also been people—rebels—within 'civil society' who have used these media insurgently to open up social and political issues, a balance that is now changing somewhat with the introduction of the internet and more open so-called 'social media'—where, in principle anyway, anyone who has access to these media can post their own messages. This is now happening so widely that the military-industrial complex in the Empire has even come to consider some aspects of this to be geopolitical aggression, has coined the term 'netwar' to describe it and is developing tactics to counter it.[11] These incursions and rebellions not withstanding, these institutions and the media are still hugely dominated by civil society and the state and—going back to my point—civil society plays the overwhelming role in setting social norms.

In terms of power and its exercise, this is of course a very convenient situation. Insofar as it has historically been—and remains—the prominent, rule-making members of 'civil society' who, as its *brahmins*, produce the knowledge that most of us are brought up on (that defines what society is and how it works and establishes the values that it stands for). Because it is also they who establish the rules by which society is ordered, run, governed, and therefore reproduced, this becomes a very convenient self-fulfilling and self-reinforcing circular process that ensures that power—including the power to make rules—always remains with them (us. . .). Equally, it is civil society that owns and / or runs all (or most) educational institutions and the media; and so the meta-exercise of power—the exercise of power beneath the more obvious manifestations—is in a virtual stranglehold.

As I will argue later in this essay, this is true not only in terms of the exercise of power at a macro level but also at the most micro level and in terms of everyday relations in all dimensions of social life, as in how we bring up our children, for example. Going back to my opening point, I believe that we who are concerned about justice, peace, and social transformation, who are struggling for them, but who also accept being part of civil society, cannot disassociate ourselves from these processes of social control, colonisation, and exploitation. We need to critically think about how we should locate ourselves in relation to them. Do we believe that this is how things should be? Are we okay with being complicit in this self-reinforcing, locked-in circle of power? Or are there other ways we can and should be locating ourselves?

Questioning 'civil society' is also difficult because the term 'civil' is so beguiling and reinforcing, perhaps especially for those who feel that they are 'civil' and belong to civil society; it's a very clever term, because it demands a kind of unquestioning loyalty. As I said above, it is an unstated truth that 'being civil' is good; and in the world of civil society, being good in turn requires being civil, and it's almost a given that you cannot be good without being civil.

Arguably, the idea of being 'civil' and of following these norms unquestioningly is also attractive for some or even many among those who have been historically and structurally excluded from 'civil society', precisely because it is equated with being good (who would not like to be good?), and because it seems to be a kind of 'ticket' for entry and 'inclusion'; on the other hand, as I argue further on, one of the ways in which 'civil society' operates—and has historically operated through patriarchy and colonialism—is to create insecurities within those it seeks to dominate. As Indigenous scholar-activists Taiaiake Alfred and Jeff Corntassel say in their essay in this book:

> The battle is a spiritual and physical one, fought against the political manipulation of the people's own innate fears and the embedding of complacency, that metastasising weakness, into their psyches.[12]

Precisely because of these attributes, I argue that we need to see the term 'civil' for what it is—a very skilfully designed veil or mask—and to take care not to get seduced by what it appears to be.

As to why this is difficult terrain, I feel I must also add some more personal notes. At one level, it is difficult for me to interrogate because I myself belong to and come from 'civil society', with a long family lineage on both sides of members who were deeply steeped in 'the civilising of society'.[13] So, to question this, especially at my age, is in many ways to question and to challenge the validity of so much that my family has stood for and lived by. In particular, it is not easy for me to argue, let alone to fully accept, that they—we—too were and are accomplices in the domination and colonisation that I am saying civil society has been and is responsible for. It is also difficult because I was myself a 'civil activist' for decades, and even though I have always questioned things as I went along, I think I have to now admit that I have at times been complicit with some of what I want to fundamentally question in this essay.[14]

This is also difficult ground for me to tread on for other related reasons. I have been working with these ideas for some years now, and from very personal experience I know that while these ideas and this analysis are appreciated by some, they have also been dismissed by others, including by people I respect; beyond this, this discussion has also greatly upset some people, including some very close to me, who feel that what I say here "attacks everything that I do and everything that we as a civil society organisation do". Taken together, this experience has not been easy for me. My decision to continue to work on these ideas has, I think, contributed to some friends and fellow travellers distancing themselves from me and to the loss of some close relationships.

I am not trying to gently back off from my position. While I know what I have to say here is (or aims to be) a *critique* of civility and of what is called 'civil society', it is not meant as an attack on any individuals or their work. Rather, this attempt to explore this subject is at one level only a call for deeply critical reflection—on the terms we use, their history and reality, and what we as concerned people do and how we do it—and for the need to move away from uncritical thought, especially in relation to things that seem self-evidently 'good'.

I am very aware that these are difficult issues to face, because in doing so we are questioning our deepest selves, our very identities—and, to paraphrase Alfred and Corntassel, we have to fight 'a spiritual and physical battle against the political manipulation of our innate fears and against the embedding into our psyches of the complacency of being civil, of being good, of being on the right side'. I am also very aware that I have no monopoly on truth. But this makes these questions no less necessary, even though I know that by raising them we must in many ways face ourselves naked. It goes without saying that I of course welcome comments on and discussion of what I say here.

On the other hand, I confess I have been very encouraged to keep working on the subject by the fact that the earlier version/s of this essay is one of my most widely read, and some people I respect are beginning to use some of the terms I use and to some extent the framework.[15] I'm also encouraged by the further reading and thinking I have done, including of several essays within this book. And so I have pushed ahead.

I try in this essay to be as 'objective' as possible and to critically visit and examine this apparent good by looking at three issues: one, the dynamics of power relations in the building and exercise of 'civil society' in the world as it is unfolding today, especially in relation to emerging movements and alliances among the historically and structurally oppressed and marginalised; two, the structural politics and dynamics of the global civil cooperation that underlie what is called 'global civil society', taking the World Social Forum as an example; and three, and as a counterpoint to my critique of civil society and of civility, I also put forward and explore the idea and practice of what I term 'incivility'.

I should perhaps also explain why I have chosen to focus on the World Social Forum, especially when it is so widely loved and respected. While I have great respect for what the WSF has been and has contributed to society and for many of the individuals who have been involved in its creation and its flowering, I have in part chosen it simply because so many 'civil' activists, students, and researchers, etc have taken part in it and / or know it, and also because it describes itself straightforwardly in terms of civil society (notably, of civil society alone):

> The World Social Forum is an open meeting place for reflective thinking, democratic debate of ideas, formulation of proposals, free exchange of experiences and interlinking for effective action, *by groups and movements of civil society.* . . .
> The World Social Forum brings together and interlinks *only organisations and movements of civil society* from all the countries in the world.[16]

In other words, it is familiar ground for many who might read this essay—ground that I assume they can recognise and identify with—and is therefore a useful example to reflect upon.

But I have also chosen to look at the WSF because I was myself very closely involved with it for many years, at many levels and in numerous ways, and so beyond knowing it quite well I have been in some ways complicit in the 'sins' I accuse it of. I have, I now realise, at times uncritically celebrated it (even as I have attempted to promote a practice of critical reflection on it) and have, therefore, in my own way contributed to veiling and disguising it. Working on this essay has provided me with an invaluable opportunity to reflect on the past decade and more of much of my work, as well as on earlier phases.[17]

In particular, even as I acknowledge the many historical contributions of civil organisations and civil societies, I try to look critically at the question of power relations *within* civil society and *within* organisations and processes that are a part of civil society—doing what some consider to be socially progressive work—and at the internal contradictions of civility. The WSF is again a useful context within which to do this. The question of the power of conventional market corporations and of (market) corporatism has, of course, been well explored, as has the question of the corporate state.[18] But for some reason when we talk of 'power' and institutions, we seem to automatically refer to the state or the market and not, for some reason, to so-called 'civil society'. What I attempt to do here is a parallel exercise of looking not at power between state and market nor at their power over society but at structural power *within* the non-state (and also non-market) world and *among and between* non-state actors; in short, at power not only in the world of 'civil society' but in society at large and at the possibility that classical structural dynamics (gender, race, caste, etc) are also expressed in the form of a meta-structural divide named 'civility'.[19, 20]

I do this at two levels. I first argue that the concept of civility is central to (though not alone in) the exercise of power in the non-state world—and, I feel sure, within the world of the state too. Second, I reflect critically on the democratic options that global civil society is offering us, not normatively but in terms of structural reality, with the hope of getting practitioners and theorists both in the civil world and in what I term the incivil world to engage with this hard question.[21]

I do not, however, try to define—or redefine—the terms. On the one hand, this has been done so richly by others, such as social theorist John Keane;[22] and on the other, fixing their meanings is not my objective. Rather, my purpose is to critically engage with and interrogate them, in order to open them up for debate—and in a way to perhaps unfix them.

Finally, a note on the title, in part because earlier drafts are in circulation. I had initially titled this revised version of this essay 'Lifting The Veil: Engaging Critically with the Concept and Reality of Civil Society', as a simple reflection of the exercise I was then attempting. After struggling with this title for a long time because of the apparently negative way in which it suggests that I see veils—to the contrary, I think the veil is one of the more beautifully designed human creations—I came up with 'Removing the Mask' as an alternative, but then decided to include both phrases in the main title, because I realised that I do different things at different places in this essay: in some places lifting and in others removing, but in both cases addressing the disguising of reality, which is what I wanted this essay to focus on. I also rephrased the subtitle 'Looking at the Concept and Reality of Civil Society in *His* Face', because over these years, I have come to understand civil society as essentially being—aside from its many other attributes—a patriarchal construct.

As I finalised this essay, however, I found that I myself have changed since when I started it, stimulated by the ideas and experiences I explore here and inspired by the growing insurgencies of the incivil that are taking shape around the world, especially in relation to the climate crisis. As a result, i decided that I must grasp this moment to break free, and that the possibility of—and need for—breaking free is, after all is said and done, what this essay is really all about; and so I have retitled it to reflect this. I warmly acknowledge my debt for this breakthrough to the Break Free climate campaign and to all campaigns and struggles for breaking free.[23]

The Terrain

In this perspective, 'others' around the world—including European peasants and workers—were and still are mired in backward religions and cultures, ignorance, irrationality and superstitions, internecine conflicts and wars, and 'poverty'. However, 'progress' was and is argued to be potentially in their future too. For, these scholars insisted, the 'laws' of development are necessarily 'universal'. In its most ambitious expressions, this is thus a social evolutionary worldview, in which, resonating with Darwin's view of biological evolution, all the basic dimensions of human life—consciousness, reason, and society—are evolving in a linear direction from the 'primitive', 'ignorant', 'backward', and 'poverty-ridden' past to the enlightened and rational, modern, peace-loving, and wealthy societies allegedly evident in modern Europe. In addition to claiming to sum up all that could reliably be known about the earth and the human condition, this doctrine of European superiority also legitimised the 'white man's burden' of civilising the 'others' even against their own wills, for the long-term interests of coming generations, if not of the current generation still mired in ignorance and superstition.[24]

In normal discussion within 'civil society' circles—and by implication, not necessarily outside them—the historical and contemporary contributions of civil societies and civil actors are considered to be normatively positive processes. The development and teaching of manners and 'proper' everyday behaviour (in other words, civility), the establishment of welfare institutions in health and education (and in time, the welfare state), and the achievement of human rights, conflict resolution, democracy, and social transformation, these are perhaps uniformly understood and accepted to be the essential and very substantial foundations of a civil(ised) society. All this, I suggest, is a part of the construct of 'civil society'.

The former category, everyday behaviour, refers to everything from eating habits, physical appearance, and personal hygiene to 'proper' ways of speaking, discussing ideas, and resolving disagreements, and so on. While the latter includes contributions ranging from the great democratic breakthroughs and transformations in Europe in the nineteenth century[25] to the role of the bourgeoisie in the same century in the major social reforms in societies of both what are today called the North and the South (such as the abolition of the slave trade in Europe and the Americas—also, although less known, in other parts of the world, including India, for instance, involving millions of people over the centuries; and, for example, the abolition of wife sacrifice and child marriage, again in India / South Asia). It also refers to the beginning of equal political rights by women (even if initially only by some sections among women—essentially, the civil) in some parts of the North in the early part of the twentieth century and to the many contributions of civil actors to national liberation struggles across the world throughout the past two centuries—though this was most often also tied up with the aspirations of coming to power, ie, in terms of their own class, caste, and other interests.

More recently, it is seen to also include the contributions of civil actors to the articulation of the Universal Declaration of Human Rights in the mid-twentieth century; and more broadly, their contributions at local, national, and global levels to deepening the realisation of rights and freedoms won during this period.[26] Amnesty International is only the best known among such initiatives. We now also have any number of awards from within civil society recognising such achievements, ranging from the Nobel Peace Prize through the Right Livelihood Award to the Magsaysay Prize, among many others. The majority of those who receive these awards come from within 'civil society' and are seen as being exemplars of civility.

In many ways, it is now all but taken for granted that it is 'civil society' that is responsible for almost all that is good—all the positive reforms and advances of modernity, anyway. There is also a subtle, implicit message in this belief: that there is something special about 'civil society' and those who belong to it, and that moral fibre is inherent in what is 'civil'. Indeed, and in essence, this is surely what the term 'civil' denotes.

This is perhaps the place where we need to take an initial step back and recognise that most of these great advances have taken place not simply because of the moral fibre and / or vision of the individuals involved (though that too, in some or even many cases). There were other dynamics involved, but the advances have come to be solely associated with individuals and organisations from civil society (and commonly understood to have been authored by them) largely because of civil society's hold over all media of knowledge and propagation and its constant desire to project itself. Most importantly, we need to acknowledge, even as we recognise their contributions, that the steps taken by those of 'civil society' have most often come about as a result of the great pressure 'from below'—in the forms of resistance, rebellion, and revolt—and that very often it was this pressure that forced and / or inspired women and men from within civil society to take the steps they did.[27]

Beyond this, we need to also recognise that it has often been the case that the individuals concerned have taken the steps they have largely because of simple economic advantage to them and their community. One example among many is the fact that at one point having slaves (or bonded labour) became inconvenient or too expensive, making it advantageous for the slave owners to 'set them free'.[28]

As André Drainville graphically put it, the world is not—and has never been—ordered only from above; and to give here just a brief but tantalising quote from his work: "The world economy is [and always has been] wherever social forces meet world ordering".[29]

We need to also recognise and reflect on the contemporary resonance of the term 'civil society' and its deeper meanings. Though the term originated in eighteenth-century Europe,[30] referring to the bourgeoisie, it came to be used by Marx, among others, in the nineteenth century, and then by Gramsci in the 1930s in his groundbreaking analysis.[31] But its present usage comes from somewhere else entirely: it was forcefully brought back into usage in the early 1990s from a very different direction and with a very different purpose. It was reintroduced by the architects of neoliberalism and diffused through the world institutions that they had captured—eg, the UN and the World Bank—becoming and remaining a fundamental building block in the neoliberal campaign for the rethinking of social and economic policies and for the restructuring of societies across the world after the collapse of actually existing socialism in 1989. In particular, paring back the state created space for the emergence of 'civil society' as resistance to the hegemony of the state that had existed till then, simultaneously opening up space and freedom for the market, with all of this done in the name of bringing 'democracy' and 'freedom'. (I come later to why the market must be seen as a part of civil society.) This then is the fundamental genetic message and code of the contemporary encouragement, insertion, and empowerment of 'civil society', and of all the buzz around it: it has been and is the enabler and pacifier for the penetration and restructuring of societies in their 'transition' from socialism to capitalism.

With the neoliberal project—centred in the 'free world's capital, Washington, DC—not only looking outward but also inward and continuing to roll back the gains made by movements in the North during the 1960s and '70s,[32] the term 'civil society' was simultaneously and very deliberately brought into common usage within the 'free world', first with the aim of building a common vocabulary 'worldwide' as a necessary part of neoliberalism as a global project but also and very significantly towards civilising and taming rebellious non-state actors in the 'free world' as a part of the same project.[33]

In short, the promotion and successful propagation of 'civil society' at a world level has been a breathtakingly ambitious project and is an integral part of the vision and strategy of neoliberalism. And those of us who now use the term for ourselves and for others need to very clearly recognise this.

While the rapid and widespread reproduction and usage of the term—in the media, in academia, within governments—is understandable insofar as the term has had powerful legitimisers and promoters such as the World Bank and the UN, it is very interesting (in the sense of very disturbing) to reflect on how easily and quickly this term has also been adopted by a wide range of social and political actors—many who would not like to see themselves as neoliberals or as part of the campaign for neoliberalism—and how widely it has come to be used in just two decades.

Just to take one example, and I am deliberately choosing someone I have the greatest admiration and respect for in terms of his otherwise seminal work in the related field of human rights (including proposing the not unrelated term and concept of a 'globalisation from below' in 1997).[34] Richard Falk, in a 1999 book titled *Predatory Globalisation*, which was a deep critique of and attack on neoliberal globalisation, very easily and without interrogating the concept accepted the term 'global civil society' to describe "social forces that respond to the patterns of behaviour associated with the phenomena of economic globalisation".[35] And interestingly, while he went on to briefly question the appropriateness of the use of the word 'society' in this term, he did not stop to look at the word 'civil'. I am quite sure that this is not because Falk has sympathies for neoliberalism, but simply because being civil is so widely accepted as a good, and so the term just didn't catch his attention.

All those who have been involved in social and political work will recognise that in the North the term 'civil society' has become—in just over two decades—standard vocabulary, and that the term 'civil society organisation' has totally replaced the earlier term 'nongovernmental organisation', or 'NGO', (and the still earlier designation in some parts of the world, 'voluntary organisation', and in others, 'non-profit organisation')—and the term 'global civil society' was quickly coined to accompany it, again as part of this project. This has been one more major achievement for the neoliberal juggernaut.

As André Drainville said in a contribution to the formulation of a project he and I once discussed doing together:[36]

> Unheard of a generation ago, the term 'global civil society' is now used quite matter-of-factly, both by regulatory institutions whose task it is to reproduce neo-liberal world order (the World Bank) as well as by alter-globalization activists of every political persuasion (the World Social Forum et al). With little consideration for the manner of its constitution, for its historical lineage or current boundaries, a thing called 'global civil society' has installed itself at the very centre of thinking about world order and change, with such strength of concord that no politics can be made in the world if not on its behalf.
>
> Such a plastic understanding of 'global civil society' lends itself to all manners of recuperations and distortions. In the end, it disserves the cause of democracy. To move beyond it, we need to look beneath discourses, at the very words by which actually-existing organizations, really acting in the concrete world, recognize one another, define the terms of their relationships, and begin to work

together as a common concern. To do this we need to listen in on conversations held by those who stand between the political agencies and the global market, and begin to recognise the constitutive lexicon of 'global civil society'.[37]

And why has this happened? Because, of course, of the enormous power and reach of the neoliberal juggernaut but also, I suggest, because we who belong to these organisations and initiatives like the resonance of the term 'civil', which—much more than the rather clinical and neutered previous terms such as 'non-governmental', 'non-profit'—has a seemingly positive spin to it. And so we use these terms not only to describe ourselves but implicitly also to locate and position ourselves—but we therefore also become complicit in the globalisation of this term and of this way of seeing the world.

In this process the term 'civil society' has also come to have somewhat different meanings for different people. As was noted above, some use the term 'CSOs', or 'civil society organisations' almost exclusively to refer to what were earlier called 'NGOs' and / or to imply that even if 'civil society' itself is or might be larger and broader (but without defining it), in any case, such organisations 'lead' civil society today. Others use it to refer to all non-state actors involved in social and political issues, including trade unions and social movements but excluding the market (though such users also often seem uneasy about including popular or radical movements or political parties). Yet others, including John Keane, use a much broader interpretation and insist that to be useful the term must include the market.[38]

I belong in the third camp; in simple terms, and as a layperson in the field, because I cannot understand how (or why) anyone could argue that such a key non-state actor as the market not be considered a part of civil society. It completely dominates so much of social, cultural, economic, and political life, and trading and commerce are such a fundamental part of social life at all levels, including in the development and implementation of law. I therefore believe that the market is a fundamental part of civil society and needs to be accepted as such.

Having said this, let me admit that in this essay and elsewhere I use a very similar term, 'civil organisation', to refer to the first camp above, rather than the more common term 'non-governmental organisation' or the new term 'civil society organisation' and have done so for a couple of decades now. I do this, first, since I see no reason to describe a category by a negative nor, moreover, to define what in principle is a non-state actor exclusively in terms of government; second, because I believe my preferred term more explicitly describes and defines such organisations in terms of their values and politics, a point I develop a little further on in this essay; and third, I also see the use of the word 'society' in the increasingly common term 'civil society organisation' as totally redundant—one would not say 'political society organisation' for a political organisation. So I use the word 'civil' merely as a descriptor. And last, simply because it's a shorter and simpler name.

'Global Civil Society'

I now want to briefly explore and address André Drainville's question as to where 'global civil society' has come from and why it has suddenly entered our thinking (even if his question was skilfully rhetorical and polemical). In short, I suggest— consistent with his argument above—that it has come both from below and from above, but that the very specific term 'global civil society' was parachuted in from above sometime during the late 1990s as a part of the juggernaut's larger project. The term is in fact a brilliant concoction: on the one hand, in a world that is for the first time in history being consciously globalised by the capitalist project of neoliberalism, it suggested a glorious, shimmering, world-encompassing unity and solidarity—though leaving the question of who was or could be a part of this world unstated—and therefore creating a desire, an aspiration for membership; and, on the other, again referring back to Taiaiake Alfred and Jeff Corntassel's powerful point, the invention of this term also played on the insecurities of those in more local civil societies who perhaps had larger dreams and larger ambitions.

But there is also a history to this. During the 1970s and subsequently, very much as a consequence of a series of developments in the preceding twenty to twenty-five years,[39] two significant new things took place: a widespread growth of consciousness, resistance, and movement at the local and then national levels in societies across the world, perhaps especially in the postcolonial societies of the South but also in societies of the North, with the emergence of new movements and countercultures; and subsequently, a very substantial thickening of civil organisations and alliances not only at the local and national levels but also at the regional, transnational, and global levels.[40] Most especially, the latter included the emergence of international civil organisations, not only the well known social organisations such as Amnesty, Oxfam, and Greenpeace but also of a wide range and huge number of interconnected business, industry, cultural, media, and religious organisations—a phenomenon that Keane has vividly compared to the formation of a biospheric web of life that envelops the planet:

> Global civil society is a vast, interconnected, and multi-layered social space that comprises many hundreds of thousands of self-directing or nongovernmental institutions and ways of life. It can be likened—to draw for a moment upon ecological similes—to a dynamic biosphere. This complex biosphere looks and feels expansive and polyarchic, full of horizontal push and pull, vertical conflict, and compromise, precisely because it comprises a bewildering variety of interacting habitats and species: organisations, civic and business initiatives, coalitions, social movements, linguistic communities, and cultural identities. All of them have at least one thing in common: across vast geographic distances and despite barriers of time, they deliberately organise themselves and conduct their cross-border social activities, business, and politics outside the boundaries of

governmental structures, with a minimum of violence and a maximum of respect for the principle of civilised power-sharing among different ways of life.[41]

Though this is a subject that needs more careful delineation, to my understanding, the emergence of this web is a function both of the globalisation and financialisation of the economy and of a huge swell of transborder civil activity across the North and, increasingly, the South intersecting with a historically new perception and consciousness of the earth as one and of changing material conditions, including the development of far more 'affordable' international travel and the invention and commercialisation of radically new and globalising information and communication technologies.[42] It has, therefore, come from both below and above.

Within this larger phenomenon, however, one of the strongest manifestations has been the building of activist transnational social organisations, while another has been the emergence of new, more open-ended processes of 'global' activist *association* (rather than organisation) such as the PP21 (People's Plan for the 21st Century),[43] the World Social Forum,[44] and Peoples' Global Action.[45] (As I have already said, it is precisely because these social initiatives are so widely seen to be working towards the common good and to embody civil qualities that I focus in this essay on this part of civil society and in particular on the World Social Forum.)

Even if we now know from the climate crisis that the 'affordability' that made so much of this possible has also had a high price—being subsidised as it was by a false economy of cheap oil and making complicit all those of us who have taken advantage of this—the gradual but progressive articulation of strategic alliances across borders since the 1970s has nevertheless been, in a larger historical perspective, an extraordinary phenomenon. Often struggling against the most brutal and dehumanised circumstances, human beings have found ingenious ways of reaching over the walls that have imprisoned them, and their calls have found resonance in other parts of the world, most often among sections of civil society, especially in the North but also in parts of the South.[46] Sometimes it has also happened the other way round, with individuals such as anthropologists uncovering the most grotesque circumstances, such as in the Amazon from the 1960s to the 1980s, and bringing them to world attention, thus creating linkages.[47] Similarly, the 1980s saw the emergence of local and then national movements around such major international campaigns as the Bhopal gas tragedy and the Narmada dams complex in India,[48] land mines, and countless issues. Think of almost any field, and you can see that this has happened and is continuing.

International campaigns that took shape during the 1980s then matured during the 1990s and moved to a new stage in the 2000s, with the formation of associative spaces such as the World Social Forum and the perception and then portrayal of this as being an 'anti-globalisation movement', or even 'a movement of movements'.[49]

This reached a stage in the 1990s and 2000s where some political scientists suggested that these processes—these organisations and formations taken collectively in civil coalitions, alliances, and other webs of association—were contributing to nothing less than the restructuring of world politics.[50] A related image was the much quoted suggestion in articles in the *New York Times* both in 1999 after the demonstrations in Seattle around the WTO and in 2003 after the global anti-war rally that the emerging global social justice movement now constituted a new "superpower . . . [of] world opinion".[51] In a passionate and forthright interpretation of what was happening, David Korten, an influential writer from within the world of civil organisations, argued that "the globalisation of civil society" is a necessary part of "reclaiming our right to power"—but with no problematisation of which 'we' the 'our' referred to.[52]

Too Simple

Notwithstanding this record and this way of looking at the issue, I submit that this analysis is too simple: that the role of 'civil society' at local and national levels is far more complex; what is happening in the course of the 'globalisation of civil society' is also deeply complex and contradictory. Specifically referring to our discussion here, the terms 'civil society' and 'global civil society' gloss over all manner of striking contradictions and historical sins—contradictions and sins that are only sharpening in our time because of the rise of new actors on the stage, including among those who have been historically excluded from these worlds.

See, for instance, the argument made by Josephine Ho in her essay in this book:

> There is, after all, nothing intrinsically progressive or democratic about international civil society. International NGOs have been known to set up branches in Third World nations not only as channels for needed funding and aid, but more importantly as a field where Western values and interests can exercise their influence and foster checks and balances to resist local state domination and control. Well meaning development projects executed by well-meaning NGOs may intend to promote population management, disease prevention, and maternal and child health, yet they often also end up intentionally or unwittingly shaping ideas about what constitutes 'normal', and thus acceptable, sexual practices and identities.[53]

And by the legendary activist and thinker Muto Ichiyo:

> [C]ivil society is largely a creation of the modern nation state. It is demarcated by national borders and filled with nationalist substance. That is why you call it "inter-national civil society". Shouldn't we envisage broader social relationships

beyond national borders, instead of linking already nationally constituted civil societies? Second, as a concept modeled after European experience, civil society carries with it strong European flavors. I am afraid efforts to deodorate it may turn it into a meaningless abstraction. For instance, is Islamic Ummah a civil society? Civil society is a historical product—a product of modernity which is the creation of the West. Aren't we [today at a stage] where we face the entire consequence of modernity? Third, does civil society include all the residents in a certain territory as its full-fledged members? Weren't the working class in the 18th–19th century considered outcast of civil society? Aren't there their equivalent in civil societies of today? Are "illegal" migrant workers members of civil society? Last but not least, isn't it necessary to transform civil society itself for it is where exploitation of labor takes place and dominance of the poor by the rich, of women by patriarchy, and other social-economic forms of dominance are entrenched. Civil society approach does not give us a guideline as to how civil society should be transformed.[54]

Once again, and cutting to the point, I suggest that we who belong to civil society tend to so unquestioningly use these terms 'civil society' and 'global civil society' largely because we are seduced by their normatively positive value, and perhaps also because of the allure of the power that seems to come from the addition of the term 'global'. The first step that those of us who are disturbed by this possibility need to take is to much more deeply interrogate and understand these terms; it is only by doing so, and through exploring and experiencing the transformative power of critical reflection, that we can rethink and reposition ourselves with respect to this otherwise seemingly inexorable dynamic.

I should perhaps underline the fact that I agree with those who argue that the term 'civil society' should not be summarily discarded[55]—but I do so not because, as they argue, it is "too useful to be discarded" (they seem, in fact, to see it as a positive and useful term), but because focussing on it and unmasking it reveals the face of our world as it really is—and it is, therefore, intensely useful for critically understanding social and political structures and dynamics; I also take this position, of course, because simply discarding or not using the term will do nothing to change the social relations involved.

In short, I suggest that the social and political reality of civil society—and of global civil society—is structurally riddled with power relations that need to be much more clearly read, and that it is only by uncovering and examining them critically that we can begin to seriously understand the roles of civil society in history and in our time, locally, nationally, and globally; and, in turn, that it is only through doing this that we can—and must—radically redefine 'civil society' and also, crucially, build authentic, respectful transcommunal relations with the rapidly emerging 'incivil societies' of the world.[56]

Civil, Incivil, Uncivil: A History, Reality, and Story of Power

My first submission here is something that I have already outlined: that 'civil society' is not what it is said and assumed to be; nor is it what the textbooks say it is, a neutral 'space between the individual (or the family) and the state'. Rather, it is just what common sense tells us it is and what the term itself indicates: *civil* society—a society, or better, a community, that is bounded and governed by the norms of civility that its thought- and rule-givers define for it and a section of any given society that has become—in its own terms and by its own definition—'civilised'. The etymological linkage between these various terms is of course self-evident and unavoidable.

As is perhaps true in all contexts, the rules of civility that prevail are always set by individuals and institutions that consider themselves to be civil and civilised, and the primary aim of the rules is to 'civilise' everything and everyone: to bring order to society by making sure that everything operates within defined limits. These limits and norms of course change over time in all societies, but generally speaking the change is incremental and highly conservative and always remains tightly controlled by the rule-giving institutions and individuals. In particular, there is little or no room for what civil society regards as deviants—for all those sections in society that are different and do not follow the same rules of being 'civilised'—which are, of course, defined by the rule-givers within civil society.[57]

This of course does not mean that 'deviants' do not exist in society or that some so-called 'deviants' do not organise themselves and exercise considerable social force and bring about societal change (think, for instance, of the LGBTQ world, among so many others). Nor is it a refusal to recognize that some whom civil society regards as deviants are people who have consciously dropped out and built alternative ways of living, either outside of society or in its interstices. It is only to argue that the way that 'civil society' attempts to rule excludes deviants and discriminates against them, as an exercise of power-over or an attempt to domesticate and assimilate them, sometimes successfully and sometimes not. In essence, civil society is about the exercise of power.

Just as one instance, allow me to again quote Josephine Ho:

> This essay contends that answers to these important questions are located in our current context of global governance and global civil society. Fortified by UN discourse and worldwide policy directives that have been set in place by aspiring nation-states in collaboration with local civil organisations (the most aggressive ones being fundamentalist Christian), a new 'reign of civility' has been widely popularised in the socially and politically volatile spaces of East Asia, and this is now producing detrimental effects on queer lives through increased media sensationalism, police-baiting, recriminalisation, and recurrent sex panic, not to mention new sex-repressive legislative reform measures.

Ho later asserts:

> It is noteworthy that in East Asia both mainstream women's NGOs and conservative Christian NGOs have chosen to abide by the most basic form of 'sexual fundamentalism': the notion that there is a singular, ideal sexuality (heterosexual, marital, procreative) and two genders (man and woman), and that those conforming to this standard have a right to police and control others, often by creating and enforcing new legislation. With the help of shame and stigmatisation, the legal regulation of sex and the body helps produce other effects of power, including an increasingly conservative social milieu and a chilling effect on sexual dissidence. Since such highly justified regulatory measures not only strengthen state power but also improve state legitimacy, conservative NGOs have enjoyed state support in fortifying the moral regime that now surrounds marginal sexualities in East Asia and elsewhere.[58]

In addition, it is generally the case that those who consider themselves to be 'civilised' also feel threatened—sometimes vaguely, sometimes directly—by those who do not conform to their ideas of how society should be ordered and, indeed, by the very existence of such other worlds. And so their first step is to resort to deliberately using and sometimes coining loaded terms for naming and framing them to depict them as 'others'—terms such as 'antisocial', 'deviant', 'wild', and 'uncivil' and names such as 'nigger' in the US and *achyut* (untouchable) in India,[59] By the using such terms and names, they / we seek relentlessly to stigmatise, intimidate, marginalise, humiliate, subjugate, convert, and tame their / our others; in short, to bind them and so, perhaps, to 'civilise' them. This has been the case historically, and it remains true today—though the boundaries (of who is included and who is not) are constantly changing through processes of negotiation and struggle as social relations evolve. If some such people become sufficiently docile and domesticated, they are left alone and ignored; on the other hand, if they resist or are too assertive, the tactics change and may even include attempts to destroy and exterminate them (but only in the most civilised of ways, of course).

One of the most infamous examples of this in the history of the world has of course been the savage treatment by settler societies—largely immigrants from what is now Europe—of the Aborigines in what came to be called Australia, the 'Indians' in Latin America, the Caribbean, and the USA, and the First Nations in Canada.[60] All of this, including the genocide of so many tribes and nations, was done in the name of "the great cause of civilisation".[61] Indeed, the rise of colonisation and imperialism coincides precisely with the formation of so-called 'civil societies' in colonising countries; the two took place together, and members of European 'civil society' were then among the leading entrepreneurs, let's say, in the 'exploration' and 'civilisation' of the rest of the world.[62]

Equally barbarous has been the enslavement and mistreatment of women, men, and children—again, by the supposedly civilised, in the practice of their supposedly civilised ways—throughout history and across the world, but with the most recent, the largest, and perhaps the most horrifying example being the treatment of Africans from the seventeenth through to the nineteenth century. More recently, the horrors of the atomic bombing of Hiroshima and Nagasaki, and then the war on Vietnam, and more recently the war on Iraq were all committed to protect and promote 'civilisation'. Not to speak of the savagery of the countless other wars and counterinsurgencies that the US and former colonial powers have engaged in or encouraged all over the world over the past half century.

But this behaviour and drive is not only a function of what we commonly understand (or are given to understand) as 'colonisation' and 'war'. This behaviour and this colonisation and war are part of self-styled 'civil societies' as well, and this is as true of what we today call the North as it is of the South. Just as three examples, we have the barbaric treatment of Dalits in South Asia by upper-caste Hindus—where the discrimination, exclusion, and barbarism they have inflicted for over a thousand years have historically been defended and continues today to be defended by the upper castes as a means of protecting their own purity, and through this the purity and order of 'society';[63] the manner in which the Roma—one of the groups referred to as gypsies—have been ostracised, hounded, persecuted, and enslaved in Europe, a practice that continues in our time;[64] and at another level but structurally similar, the manner in which the civilised gentlefolk of, say, the Netherlands 'treated' and 'processed' the Dutch peasantry and working classes in special 'homes' as recently as the early twentieth century, teaching them reading, writing, dressing, table and bathroom manners in their attempt to 'civilise' them into 'proper' citizenship.[65]

(Again, this 'civilisational' project and policing does not stop at civilising our 'others'; the civil also turn in on themselves and their children. For instance, the relentless pressure forces people—especially immigrants, who through daily experience have a self-perception of being 'outsiders'—to monitor and police themselves in terms of their behaviour, colour, dress, appearance, etc, and especially that of their children; because of their insecurity they want their children, and especially their girls, to 'fit in'—all the way down to minute details such as facial and body hair.)[66]

In turn, the third example I have given above, the treatment by parents of their daughters, is of course only a mild version of the brutal treatment by European settler societies of the Aboriginals in Australia or of the First Nations on Turtle Island, especially but not only through the establishment of 'residential schools' and forcibly taking the children for the purpose of civilising them.[67]

In our time, we are seeing the establishment of commissions of enquiry towards processes of 'truth and reconciliation' and apologies issued by heads of state for these historical crimes.[68] These are very important steps, but let us also recognise clearly that these political leaders are in all cases apologising not only for what their respective states have done in history but also, implicitly, for what their respective civil societies have done, and therefore on behalf of civil societies too. These three examples are of course paralleled by, as already mentioned, the horrendous and barbaric experience of Africans over centuries, through slavery by European settlers in the Americas, North and South, and in the Caribbean (and for which there has as yet been no apology forthcoming from the European and Euro-American colonial societies, though the question of reparations is now on the table).

But can this not also be said to be true of the treatment of Jews in relatively recent history? In our time, we tend to not see things this way, I suspect because most sections of the Jewish community have become so deeply assimilated into civil societies since the Second World War—and, indeed, include prominent members of civil society in many countries—and because of the creation of Israel, which has since become a powerful state.

Historically speaking, however, the Jewish experience has been a similar one in Europe and elsewhere. During the nineteenth century, Jews were decisively the 'other' in Europe, and as such, ostracised, hounded, and ghettoised, just as the "gypsies" have been and continue to be (which is why, of course, such huge numbers of Jews fled Europe and migrated to countries across North and South America, and then to the purpose-made, newly created state of Israel). Given this, is it not possible to consider the twentieth-century Holocaust, which occurred not only in Germany but also and significantly in several surrounding countries, as one more ultimate expression of the brutality of those who consider themselves civilised and superior?[69] In this case, Christians.

In short, I want to suggest that the emergence of all so-called 'civil societies' has historically included intensive and often brutal processes of 'civilising' those in societies whom 'the civil' considered as their 'others', not only through war, conquest, slavery, and forced labour but also through the establishment of 'civil' instruments of sustained and permanent enforcement, such as the police and prisons, homes, mental wards, and other institutions where 'unruly and deviant elements' were—and continue to be—incarcerated and 'civilised'; aside from leading to a high rate of suicide among the victim peoples, these 'homes' have also had and continue to have enormous long-term traumatic consequences for the victim societies, including alcoholism, drug abuse, the crippling of minds, and the loss of identity. In some cases the salubrious experience of civilisation has even led to the extermination of those subjected to this treatment.[70]

I submit that all this comes from precisely the same root, and that we need to search for that root, including within ourselves. Conversely, we need to recognise that colonisation and the process and treatment of 'civilisation' are umbilically linked, and that they are not restricted to the conquest and domestication of alien lands and peoples. And that 'civility' and 'civilisation', as much as they are about establishing order for peace and justice are also about the imposition of very particular understandings and worldviews (including of order, peace, and justice) and about creating and instituting structures of religion, race, caste, class, gender, and sexuality. And that for colonisers and civilisers alike, it is their self-appointed historical task to colonise, domesticate, and 'civilise' the world around them and to establish what they define as a 'civil' order, both within what they consider to be 'their' home territories and in territories that they have conquered through war and exploitation. Most centrally, this means establishing and maintaining hegemony over all those who (and all that) they consider to be wild and uncivil.

Who Are the Civil?
In this view then, 'the civil' and the tasks of 'civilisation' and of building civil societies are therefore dialectically tied to the 'uncivil'. As the great African-American writer and philosopher James Baldwin said in his famous interview titled 'Who Is the Nigger?':

Well, I know this. Anyone who has ever tried to live knows this. What you say about somebody else, you know, anybody else, reveals you, what I think of you as being. Thinking about my own—my own necessities, my own psychology, my own fears and desires. I'm not describing you, when I'm talking about you; I'm describing me.

Now here's something: we've got something called 'nigger'. But other than in [indistinct], I beg you to remark that this doesn't exist in any other country in the world. We have invented the nigger. I didn't invent him. White people invented him.

I've always known—I had to know by the time I was seventeen years old— that what you were describing was not me, what you were afraid of was not me. It has to be something else. You've invented it, so it has to be something new, something you were afraid of that you invested me with.

Now if that's so, no matter what you've done to me, I can say to you this, and I mean it, I know you can't do any more, and I've got nothing to lose. And I know, and I've always known—and really always, and that's part of the agony—I've known that I'm not a nigger. But if I am not the nigger, and if it's true that you invented the real Jew, then who is the nigger?

I am not the victim here. I know one thing from another. I know that I was born, and that I'm going to suffer, and that I'm going to die. The way you get through life is one of the worst things about it. I know that . . . a person is more important than anything—anything else. I know this because I've had to learn it. But you still think, I gather, that a nigger is necessary. Well, it's unnecessary to me. So it must be necessary to you. So I give you your problem back. You're the nigger, baby, it isn't me.[71]

In my earlier work on cities and on people's struggles for a place to live, both in my writing and in my organising work, I used the term 'unintended' to try to understand and describe the dynamic tension that I sensed between the different worlds I could see in cities. I argued that within cities there were whole worlds of 'the unintended', and that these unintended build separate, parallel societies and 'cities' of their own through a complex dynamic of relationships with the intended world.[72] Given the contemporary resonance of the term 'civil society', I feel that the term 'uncivil'—and especially and even more so, 'incivil'—is similarly relevant, useful, and necessary.

In this narrative, the 'civil' are those who are otherwise referred to as the middle and upper classes, and earlier as 'the gentlefolk'. In the part of India I come from, Bengal, we have the term *bhadralok*, the 'proper', 'civil', or 'well mannered' (*bhadra*) people (*lok*). Beyond good manners, however, a crucial aspect of civility is power. Members of this civil class see themselves as inherently superior, and by virtue of their superiority, and in order that the world remain civil, it is imperative that they remain permanently in power. Although the proponents of civility would prefer what they do be represented and understood as merely a benign and well intentioned rule by those who have a superior and civil understanding of the world, in reality civility is manifested as power-over—as a force of control not emancipation.[73]

In the Indian state of West Bengal (recently renamed Paschimbanga, the name that Bengalis commonly use, the equivalent of 'West Bengal'), even though there was a government of the left continuously in power for over thirty years (1977–2011), and according to any conventional understanding of 'the left', that government might have been expected to challenge such an order, there was no reduction in the power and hold of the *bhadralok* over the state over these years. To the contrary, the upper and middle castes continuously reigned throughout this period, with little or no change in the caste composition of the government—in many ways, more importantly, there were several instances during this long reign of the massive and brutal repression of Dalits, and on each occasion the Left Front government made strenuous efforts to suppress media coverage.[74] This was accompanied by a sustained history of assaults in the city of Calcutta (now Kolkata) on the labouring poor (many of whom were again, and expectably, Dalits), against which they fought—with some of us alongside them—on the streets, in the courts, and in the media, with some degree of temporary success.[75] In other words, the rule and domination of the civil in India needs to be understood as a direct function of caste and casteism, where casteism works through so-called 'civil society'.

This is unlike, for instance, the neighbouring state of Bihar—which the Bengali *bhadralok* typically still looks down upon as being an 'uncivilised' state—where despite continuing caste warfare and extreme caste atrocities, the OBCs (Other Backward Classes) came to power during this same period; or in the also neighbouring state of Jharkhand where the Adivasis (Indigenous Peoples; literally, 'original dwellers') have come to power. This reading of the dynamics of politics in West Bengal alone speaks volumes about the power, reach, and resilience of civility.[76]

The norms that are established (read: 'imposed') by the civil to define and enforce civility vary of course from context to context and are mediated by other processes ranging from insurrection to globalisation; but I suggest that in all cases the term 'civil society' can be most meaningfully used to refer simply to *those dominant sections of society who define civility in particular ways and consider themselves to be 'civil' or 'civilised' in those particular terms* and to be the guardians of the civility that they have defined. By extension, 'civil society' also struggles to define and impose an order of civility and morality on others, both those immediately around them and those they are attempting to colonise and domesticate.

A crucial aspect of this process is that civil society does not act alone in exercising and retaining this power. In order to do this, it has over time built an instrument—the state—to serve its purposes, and throughout its history has invoked and used the powers that it has invested in the state—with which it is umbilically linked—and which it constantly struggles to control.

This is true and significant in of itself, but the specific relevance of this to our discussion is that the popular impression that is created by other sections of civil society, such as the media, about so-called 'non-governmental organisations' is that they are independent of the state, often critical of it, and sometimes in opposition to it. Contrary to this, the political reality is that while some civil organisations do fight for reforms, civil society as a whole—to which civil organisations belong—*is fundamentally pro-state and in favour of the status quo*. Far from opposing the state or wanting to change the system that is the underlying cause of the injustice around us, civil society needs the state to maintain the social order that it wants and to protect and promote its own existence. In turn, the state draws on 'civil society' to fill its ranks; and, as seen so clearly in our own time, the state also woos civil society in order to do its—often dirty—work, both in the North and the South.[77]

This goes further. Together, over history, civil society and the state have also developed a concept that expresses and embodies this: citizen. As is well known, historically the term 'citizen' was expressly and exclusively reserved for 'the civil' in society. At first equated with the propertied, even with the democratisation of this concept over the centuries (such as men allowing women to vote only in the early twentieth century, and then, gradually, also tenants—lord forbid!), it still remains a boundary, a border of legitimacy. (Till then women and tenants were still seen and portrayed by men as belonging to 'the others'.) More recently, other terms have been brought into play both to portray and victimise 'the others' and as instruments for maintaining both 'order' and 'the other' in our lives: 'aliens', 'illegal immigrants', and so on.[78]

In terms of power and its exercise over the rest of society, locally, nationally, and globally, civil society and the state are deeply interlinked. As so graphically explained by Gramsci, "the institutions of civil society [form] . . . the 'outer earthworks' of the state, through which the ruling classes [maintain] their 'hege-mony' or dominance in society".[79]

A crucial aspect of this is the question of how civil society maintains its con-trol. Here, I would like to again draw on Gramsci, but as outlined by Laurence Cox and Alf Gunvald Nilsen in their work on social movement:

> Gramsci distinguished between two ways in which dominant groups establish and maintain their position in a given social formation. On the one hand, there is the coercive power that is exercised through the state to enforce "discipline on those groups who do not 'consent' either actively or passively" to the prevailing social order. On the other hand, however, there is "[t]he spontaneous consent given by the great masses of the population to the general direction imposed on social life by the dominant fundamental group . . .". This consent, Gramsci argued, ultimately rests on the ability of a dominant group to posit "the development and expansion of the particular group . . . as being the motor force of a universal expansion, of a development of all the national energies".[80]

Having said this, I need however to also problematise the perhaps too easy distinction that I am making between the so-called 'civil' and the others in at least two ways. On the one hand, it is important to recognise that historically, and in relation to colonisation, perhaps the majority of those who have been 'settlers' have not belonged to social sectors that 'the civil' belong to. In most processes of colonisation and the conquest of the others, while the planning, strategisation, financing, and arming has all been done by members of 'civil society'—earlier by themselves and in more recent history through the state—the barons of colo-nialism have also always used the uncivil from within their own worlds to be the actual cutting edge of their conquests, to be the actual settlers, including having to bear the direct costs of the conquests. This continues in our time.

This has applied as much to the colonisation, occupation, and looting by Europeans of what came to be called 'the Americas', 'Australia', and 'South Africa'[81] as, in more recent history, to the forced 'settlement' by postcolonial governments of outlying and border regions of the territories they seek to rule: for instance, the forced settlement and populating of the western Amazon by the Brazilian govern-ment during the 1970s and '80s—till then inhabited only by Indigenous Peoples (and to a limited extent, by communities of rubber tappers brought in by rubber barons from outside the region in the second half of the nineteenth century, who were the first wave of settlers). The Brazilian state induced and transported tens of thousands of peasants from the impoverished northeast of the country to migrate to and settle in the northwest of the country, ostensibly to protect the country's national borders but in reality to open up the region for mining, logging, and industrial development, with massive and tragic human consequences when the

Indigenous Peoples native to the region militantly resisted this invasion.[82] Indonesia and several other governments have done precisely the same in recent decades, through what are politely called 'transmigration projects', financed massively by the World Bank, and with similar results.[83] In other words, it is always important to try and read the hand behind the immediate act of conquest and violence.

On the other hand, it is important also to mention that there are countless current and historical examples of rebels and dropouts from within civil society breaking free sufficiently to withdraw from the civil society that surrounds them and live and act in incivil ways, and who therefore consciously make of themselves another section of 'the others'. I will return to this in the fourth part of this essay, 'On being incivil'.[84]

The Social Character of Civil Society

Let me now try to more specifically sketch out, although still in very broad terms, what I understand to be the social character of civil society and to explain why I propose to use the terms 'incivil' and 'uncivil' as analytical categories alongside but in contradistinction to the term 'civil'. I use these terms, first, in order to focus on and bring out the reality of civility, which I argue is dialectical; where it is not only a question of how 'we' see 'them' as 'the other' but also that this 'other' is, as James Baldwin so powerfully argued, within us. It is important for 'us' to be constantly conscious of this. Second, and to the contrary, I wish to signal the resistance of such peoples to the singular and hegemonic norms of the civil—and, indeed, to implicitly suggest that there are many civilities, many different forms and modes of civilisation and of life, and to incorporate this within a more structural understanding of 'the civil'. And, finally, I use these terms, of course, to politicise the term 'civil' and to draw out its political content and reality.

As I see it, the dynamic of civility plays out in many forms and modes and is multilayered. It is a function not only of class but also of *caste* in those contexts where this applies—right across South Asia, reaching into Southeast Asia, covering over a billion and a half people[85]—of *ethnicity, race, religion, cosmology, sexuality, sexual preference, language*, and *gender*, especially as it intertwines with some or all of the above. This list is only indicative; there may well also be other arenas of social life where this plays out in particular parts of the world.

In this view, those who constitute the core of 'civil society' are in general middle or upper class, middle or upper caste, heterosexual, and male, actively or passively practising the dominant religion in the region, speaking its dominant language (which in most postcolonial countries is usually a foreign language), and, while this of course varies across the world, are white, or at least 'pale' or 'fair' (since in most societies across the world 'fairness' of complexion is something that the upper castes and classes aspire to), and pro-state. This is the broad outline; in reality, such sections often allow peoples of colour and other differentiations and preferences to join them on condition that they use the dominant social sector's language and are loyal adherents to the rules of local and national civil society. In colonised societies, the term 'civil society' historically referred to the colonising settler community but is now no longer limited to this. In more recent decades, this picture is also becoming more complicated, with the widespread migration of settlers of colour that is now taking place.[86]

In contradistinction, and in order to be able to categorise and taxonomise the other, 'the civil' have historically seen their others as 'the uncivil', almost by definition. (As Lee Cormie brilliantly argues in his Afterword to this book, the taxonomisation and compartmentalisation of the world has been a fundamental instrument of European 'civilisation',[87] and this practice of taxonomy has in turn been happily adopted by postcolonial states and endogenous civil societies.) I of course don't mean this in terms of the use of this specific term 'uncivil' as such but as a broad category in relation to which each colonial and postcolonial power developed and develops its own terms as a necessary function of the dynamics of social structure.

The fundamental category of those who constitute 'the uncivil'—as perceived, created, and stigmatised by the 'civil'—has historically included the lower classes, the lower castes and the outcastes, and in general all peoples of colour, especially the black and the Indigenous, and all those of other languages, faiths, genders, and sexual preferences. There are of course some from within this category who have been successfully domesticated and 'civilised', especially through intermarriage and miscegenation, but in a larger sense even such peoples have in many societies been historically stigmatised and left hanging as second-class denizens in a middle world. It is only in our time and only in a few societies that civil society is beginning to recognise and accept such peoples as equal.

Within this overall dynamic of civility and 'uncivility', the *gender* division and discourse is, on the surface at least, perhaps less obvious. But I think it also applies here in much the same way but also in many other ways. Keep in mind the manner in which 'the civil' stigmatise those they label 'uncivil' and the terms they (we) use for the 'uncivil'. Think, for instance, of the (male, civil) association of 'the feminine' with 'the wild' and uncontrollable in so many cultures and religions, of the systems that have historically been put in place to 'husband' and control this nature, in particular, the structure and ideology of patriarchy that is so widely prevalent across the world, where women are seen only as property and as vehicles for reproduction of the (hu)man species, therefore justifying the system of 'husbanding' and domestication and giving men the license to inflict violence on them within the home, on the streets, and in the course of war.[88]

Recalling Josephine Ho's argument that I quoted above—which addressed the control and repression by civil society of sexual freedoms more generally—I would argue that there is every reason to also see the question of the gender division of society through the lens of civility. Very significantly for the arguments of this essay, women have historically gained their freedoms primarily through incivil (and not uncivil) action.

My experience of using these terms and making these distinctions in discussions with Dalit activists in India and with others seems to validate these arguments. As is now widely known, the term 'Dalit' means 'oppressed' or 'crushed', and it is one that the Dalits themselves now use in preference to, say, Gandhi's term *harijan* ('children of god'). Perhaps not surprisingly, I have found that Dalit activists seem to most easily grasp the meaning of the term 'incivil', including its dialectical meaning and usage. My sense is that this is because they see the word—and the world—in terms of relations and not in terms of fixed states.[89] On the other hand, it has been my experience that it has usually been 'civil' activists and researchers who have tended to find these terms and distinctions more difficult to grasp, objecting to the distinctions and dismissing them as merely semantic and superficial. Which is not surprising given the very different location they occupy in these dynamics and the discomfort that arises with recognising these distinctions. I also see this reaction as directly related to the fact that many such activists and researchers are also uncomfortable with Dalits calling themselves 'oppressed' or 'crushed', which they find strange and unnecessary; they would prefer it if they used more 'self-respecting' terms. But as I see it, this is precisely the struggle: to see the world in terms of relations and from the other's point of view, especially from that of the oppressed, and to understand one's own location within this and one's relation to it.

The Incivil and the Uncivil

Having put forward my larger point, I want to try and draw a line between what I am referring to as the 'incivil' and the 'uncivil', or at least a vital distinction.

As is widely known and documented, in our time, a large and growing proportion of ordinary people in societies across the world—and now the majority of people living in most cities of the South—are forced by social, political, and economic forces to live in subhuman extralegal settlements, practise extralegal occupations, and / or migrate extralegally—in short, the peoples who I came in 1973–1974 to refer to as 'the unintended'.[90] They do this not out of choice, but because they are forced by prevailing social and economic conditions over which the state and civil society have command to resort to actions that are termed—by civil society and by the state—as 'informal', 'illegal', and 'unauthorised'. As part of the dynamics I discussed above, they are then criminalised and stigmatised for their actions and widely portrayed as being congenitally uncivil by both state and civil society.[91]

This is not a new phenomenon, however, and although contemporary literature on, say, housing, planning, and urbanisation continues to focus primarily on this (with a sort of orientalist perspective), it has historically not been limited to conditions in 'the South'. To the contrary, this dynamic and the marginalisation, pauperisation, and migration that it causes, with the consequent ghettoisation, has existed from at least the enclosure of the Commons in Europe from the eighteenth century onwards and the so-called 'Poor Laws' of those contexts.[92]

Though I think that it is not yet recognised, I believe that the same structural situation exists today in many parts of the North, for instance in the ghettoisation of the vast majority of the working and labouring peoples who have migrated from Central America to the US ('aliens') searching for a better life or from French colonies in North Africa to France—and similarly elsewhere in Europe. This is also true of the huge number of people who are now migrating as refugees from West Asia (and from farther east, eg, Afghanistan, and farther south, eg, northeast Africa) into Europe, threatening to tear Project Europe apart. Significantly, it is increasingly the case that it is precisely from within these areas and from among these profoundly alienated, stigmatised, and brutalised peoples, the 'others' of contemporary Europe, that jihadis are today being born. As much as the periodic revolts and rebellions that have characterised US society in this past century, and that are now increasingly characterising, say, French society—blacks in the case of the US, Algerians and other North Africans in the case of France—I suggest that this too is a legacy of the dynamics of civility.[93]

But jihad is not the only expression of rebellion and assertion. The new reality is that in many parts of the world we are now seeing precisely these sections of society—peoples who have historically been oppressed, exploited, and marginalised by civil society and the state—organising to peacefully and democratically assert themselves; in contexts such as Bolivia and in parts of large countries like India, where these layers constitute the majority of the population, they are slowly not just accumulating power but also asserting it, often (though not always) in independent and insurgent ways that challenge ruling 'civil society'.[94] At the same time, they are also building their own transnational links and associations and increasingly putting forward their own visions of the world. These historically unintended worlds, which I now also see and term as 'the incivil', are thus new societies in the making—of their own making and on their own terms.[95] These worlds are of course fundamentally different from the uncivil.

It could be argued that what is happening should be described as merely the emergence of 'civil societies' from within the uncivil. I would, however, suggest that this loses sight of and veils the reality that those who are creating these new worlds are simultaneously struggling against both the norms of the uncivil worlds that have created the stigmatisation and exploitation that pervasively surrounds them and their respective dominant civil societies and are forging and asserting a society of their own. We have to find a way of recognising this trivalent struggle and dynamic. I suggest that the categories of civil, incivil, and uncivil may provide a useful approach.

This emergence is of course neither a linear process nor automatically successful in emancipatory terms. There is plenty of evidence already available of inversions and implosions. One reason for this seems to be the tendency of the leadership of such sections, once they are in power, to adopt and reproduce the laws and customs of their former oppressors; another is the tendency to use organisational forms and cultures inherited from dominant civil society and, therefore, the hierarchical social relations embedded in them as a part of the biopolitics of state and society.[96] But these inversions are natural enough. When seen in a longer historical perspective, there is surely no question that we are today at a new threshold of human history, a historic deepening and widening of the democratisation of local and national societies and of global society—a reimagining and rebuilding of the world—that is being undertaken and led not by civil societies but by the incivil of the world.[97]

Asserting this is not to romanticise what is happening. In a very real sense, beyond and in a way 'below' and 'above' the incivil (and always challenging it) lie the other worlds that are the outcomes of centuries of colonisation—internal and external—and structural exploitation by civil society: worlds of gross exploitation, such as those of child prostitution and the trade in women, of bonded labour and other forms of slavery, and of trade in organs, drugs, and arms, worlds of the exploitation of the profound precarity and alienation that such peoples feel by being rendered 'the other' by gang lords, on the one hand, and by religious fundamentalists, on the other. These worlds, which of course overlap with the incivil, are broadly the sections of society where the criminal, the mafia, the fundamentalists, and the criminalised lumpen rule. As films such as *The City of God* and *Dheepan* make so dramatically clear, huge sections of contemporary world society continue to be forced to live these very other lives.[98] Even while recognising that these worlds too are often ultimately controlled and exploited by sections of civil society and also keeping in mind that the very existence of this world is a direct result of the dynamics of civility and 'development'. At the risk of oversimplifying things, in order to distinguish this world from what I am referring to as the incivil, I refer to this world—to the reality rather than to the people—as 'the uncivil'.

Variants in Incivility: The Structurally Incivil and the Consciously Incivil

To this already complex ground, I must add another category that I have signalled but not yet spelled out: those who I term—keeping to the framework I have put forward in this essay and the broad category of the incivil—the 'consciously incivil', as distinct from those I have so far discussed, the 'structurally incivil'. I do this, of course, in order to extend my argument and recognise and include in my analysis the very significant phenomenon of people in all societies who, historically and in our time, have consciously chosen to live alternative lives—'alternative', that is, to the dominant order, which I am characterising as 'civil'.[99]

This phenomenon exists perhaps in all societies and in all fields of life, from religion to art and music to science and philosophy, and of course also in life-style—and very much in social movement and politics. Given that this is such a real and creative force within all societies, often one of the most creative, it is vital for a more complete understanding of social dynamics, and in my present analysis, to embrace this world / these worlds.

At the same time, and even though such sectors and movements are clearly also counterposed to so-called 'civil society', their structural relationship to civil society is fundamentally different from those who are structurally discriminated against. For want of a better term at this point, and keeping within the rubric that I have put forward here, I suggest that only when and as necessary, we could use the term the 'consciously incivil', as distinct from the category I have so far discussed, who by contradistinction and only where necessary, we can refer to as the 'structurally incivil'.

Without elaborating further on this complex point, I suggest that we need to make a distinction between these two broad realities, the incivil and the uncivil, at local, national, and now also transnational and global levels, and that doing this is of vital strategic consequence to the tasks of building other worlds. As a contribution to this rethinking, I propose that we use the term 'incivil' for the victimised and oppressed who are consciously building insurgent societies and challenging existing power structures that are dominated either by the civil or the uncivil and—a point I will return to in Part 2 of this essay[100] to rebels and dropouts from within civil society who act in similar ways, reserving 'uncivil' for all those who, while in some cases resisting and subverting civil society, do so with more limited actions and often material motives and are in general criminal and exploitative. Using the distinction I drew earlier between power-to and power-over, I believe it is significant that while both the civil and the uncivil work through power-over, the incivil of both categories tend to work first through power-to.

In lived reality, I acknowledge that the dividing line between the 'incivil' and the 'uncivil' is often blurred, but I believe that we need to recognise that these are different worlds and, crucially, that they coexist in dynamic tension. I am aware that some civil theorists in the North use the term 'uncivil', but as far as I know only to refer to those limited sections of society that in India are commonly called 'antisocials'.[101] I suggest that this is far too limited a use for a much wider, deeper, and richer social and political phenomenon—now with global dimensions—and urge those who use the term 'uncivil' in this way to think about its wider resonances and to shift to using it in the wider and more structural ways that I propose in this essay.

Many activists and researchers have worked and struggled with aspects of these questions for many years,[102] but as far as I know, without a clear approach and not, in my limited knowledge of the field, within this much larger perspective of global cultural and historical dynamics that I suggest play tectonic roles. I would like to think that this discussion could add some depth to our thinking.

Writing at that point, only with a more limited picture (which is also how I saw the world till not so long ago), when posing the question back in the late 1990s as to what could be an alternative to the kind of assault that the state and civil society had once again unleashed on the 'unintended' in Kolkata, I myself phrased it in terms of how one could achieve a "*civilised* transition" to another future.[103] I have only much later come to realise that I need to fundamentally re-think not just my language but also how I see things, because the achievement of a 'civilised transition' too often signals not emancipation but further domestication and subjugation, sometimes in hidden forms. Even though I had myself intensely questioned and challenged these processes over the previous twenty years, in all my writings and in all my organising and campaigning, I ironically—but I think very tellingly—took the default position that is so embedded in all of us who belong to the civil world.[104]

On Being Incivil

Does the answer perhaps lie not in struggling to be civil or in 'civilised transitions' but in *struggling to be incivil*—or rather, and crucially, in knowing how and when to be civil, and when incivil, as countless peoples have discovered throughout history, and which so many movements in fact are?

[*Continued in Part 2 of this essay, published separately in this book*][105]

References

Taiaiake Alfred, 1995—*Heeding the Voices of Our Ancestors: Kahnawake Mohawk Politics and the Rise of Native Nationalism*. Don Mills, ON: Oxford University Press

Taiaiake Alfred, 1999—*Peace, Power, Righteousness: An Indigenous Manifesto*. Don Mills, ON: Oxford University Press

Taiaiake Alfred, 2005—*Wasáse: Indigenous Pathways of Action and Freedom*. Peterborough: Broadview Press

Taiaiake Alfred and Jeff Corntassel, 2017—'Being Indigenous: Resurgences against Contemporary Colonialism', in Jai Sen, ed, 2017a—*The Movements of Movements, Part 1: What Makes Us Move?*. Volume 4 in the *Challenging Empires* series. New Delhi: OpenWord, and Oakland, CA: PM Press

Dr Bhim Rao Ambedkar, 2014 [1936]—*Annihilation of Caste: The Annotated Critical Edition*. Introduction by Arundhati Roy. New Delhi: Navayana Books

Dr Bhim Rao Ambedkar, nd [c.1936]—'Annihilation of Caste With a Reply to Mahatma Gandhi', at http://www.ambedkar.org/ambcd/02.Annihilation%20of%20Caste.htm (Accessed August 14 2017)

Anon, nd [c.January 2013]—'South Asians in Solidarity with Idle No More', at https://www.facebook.com/nishant.upadhyay.18/posts/10100389033191971?notif_t=like (Accessed August 14 2017)

Jacques Audiard, 2015—*Dheepan* [a French film about the experience of refugees and immigrants in Europe], see http://www.imdb.com/title/tt4082068/ and https://en.wikipedia.org/wiki/Dheepan (Both accessed December 24 2017)

James Baldwin, with KQED, 1963—'Who is the Nigger?', a clip from *Take this Hammer,* 1963, at https://www.youtube.com/watch?v=L0L5fciA6AU (Accessed August 14 2017)

Joe Bandy and Jackie Smith, eds, 2004—*Coalitions across Borders: Transnational Protest and the Neoliberal Order*. Oxford: Rowman & Littlefield

Niyousha Bastani and Melis Çaçan, February 2016—'What's Hair got to do with it? An Ode to unibrows, and other hairy tales', in *McGill Daily*, February 1 2016, at https://www.mcgilldaily.com/2016/02/whatshairgottodowithit/ (Accessed August 14 2017)

Tushar Bhattacharjee, nd [c.2009]—*Marichhanpi 1978–79: Tortured Humanity*, at https://vimeo.com/23944832 (Accessed August 14 2017)

Amit Bhattacharyya, June 2009—*Singur to Lalgarh via Nandigram: Rising Flames of People's Anger Against Displacement, Destitution and State Terror*. Kolkata: Visthapan Virodhi Jan Vikas Andolan ['Movement Against Displacement and For People's Development', in Hindi]

Patrick Bond, August 2007—Post on Debate with Subject '[Debate] Civil Society, not', August 27 2010

Patrick Bond, May 2014—'Civil society positioning on emerging powers' human rights and foreign policy: A view of ideology, social unrest and solidaristic potential from South Africa'. Abstract for talk at the South African Institute of International Affairs, Johannesburg, on May 13 2014, as posted on the Debate list, May 12, 2014

Sandra Braman and Annabelle Sreberny-Mohammadi, eds, 1996—*Globalization, Communication and Transnational Civil Society*. Cresskill, NJ: Hampton Press

Susan Branford and Oriel Glock, 1985—*The Last Frontier: Fighting for Land in the Amazon*. London: Zed Books

Jeremy Brecher, Tim Costello, and Brendan Smith, 2000—*Globalization from Below: The power of solidarity*. Cambridge, MA: South End Press

Urvashi Butalia, January 2005—'A Hierarchy of Violence', Chapter 8 in Jai Sen and Mayuri Saini, eds, January 2005—*Are Other Worlds Possible? Talking NEW Politics*. New Delhi: Zubaan, pp 114–23

Jean Chiappino, 1975—*The Brazilian Indigenous Problems and Policy: The Example of the Aripuana Indigenous Park*. IWGIA Document No 19. Copenhagen: International Working Group on Indigenous Affairs

John Brown Childs, 2003—*Transcommunality: From the Politics of Conversion to the Ethics of Respect*. Philadelphia: Temple University Press

John Brown Childs, 2018—'Boundary as Bridge', in Jai Sen, ed, 2018—*The Movements of Movements, Part 2: Rethinking Our Dance*. Volume 5 in the *Challenging Empires* series. New Delhi: OpenWord, and Oakland, CA: PM Press)

Ward Churchill, 2004—*Kill the Indian, Save the Man: The Genocidal Impact of American Indian Residential Schools*. San Francisco: City Lights Books

Janet Conway, 2012—*Edges of Global Justice: The World Social Forum and its 'Others'*. London and New York: Routledge

Lee Cormie, 2018—'Another World Is Inevitable . . . But Which Other World?'. Afterword for Jai Sen, ed, 2018—*The Movements of Movements, Part 2: Rethinking Our Dance*. Volume 5 in the *Challenging Empires* series. New Delhi: OpenWord, and Oakland, CA: PM Press

Adrian Cowell, 1989—*Banking on Disaster*. Part of the 'Decade of Destruction' series. Central Television of London

Adrian Cowell, 1990—*The Decade of Destruction: The Crusade to Save the Amazon Rainforest*. New York: Henry Holt and Company

Laurence Cox and Alf Gunvald Nilsen, 2014a—*We Make Our Own History: Marxism and Social Movements in the Twilight of Neoliberalism*. London: Pluto

Andrew Crosby, December 2006—'The Principles and Values of Taiaiake Alfred's *Peace, Power, Righteousness* as a Global Model: Bolivia and Other Worlds'. Research paper for PSCI 5501, Carleton University, Ottawa, Ontario, Canada, Fall 2006—'Other Worlds, Other Globalisations', at www.critical-courses.cacim.net (Inactive August 14 2017)

Sanjib Datta Chowdhury, 1993—'A Sociological Study of Institutionalized Aging'. PhD diss, Delhi School of Economics

Shelton H Davis, 1977—*Victims of the Miracle: Development Impact and the Indians of Brazil*. New York: Cambridge University Press

Ali de Regt, 1986—*Arbeidersgezinnen en beschavingsarbeid: Ontwikkelingen in Nederland 1870–1940* ['Workers' families and civilizing work: Developments in the Netherlands, 1870–1940', in Dutch]. Amsterdam: Boom Meppel

Guillermo Delgado-P, 2017—'Refounding Bolivia: Exploring the Possibility and Paradox of a Social Movements State', in Jai Sen, ed, 2017a—*The Movements of Movements, Part 1: What Makes Us Move?*. Volume 4 in the *Challenging Empires* series. New Delhi: OpenWord, and Oakland, CA: PM Press

Paul Divakar Namala, 2011—'Making Caste a Global Issue', in Jai Sen, ed, 2011a—*Interrogating Empires*. New Delhi: OpenWord and Daanish Books)

André Drainville, May 2011—'Draft Proposal for Listening in on Global Civil Society', second draft of proposal for collaboration with Jai Sen. Private correspondence

André C Drainville, 2012—*A History of World Order and Resistance: The making and unmaking of global subjects*. London and New York: Routledge

Roxanne Dunbar-Ortiz, 2014—*An Indigenous Peoples' History of the United States*. Boston, MA: Beacon Press

Richard Falk, 1997—'Resisting "Globalization-from-above" through "Globalization-from-below"', in *New Political Economy* 2, pp 17–24

Richard Falk, 1999—*Predatory Globalization: A Critique*. Cambridge, UK: Polity Press, and Malden, Mass: Blackwell

Philip M Fearnside, 1997—'Transmigration in Indonesia: Lessons from its Environmental and Social Impacts', in *Environmental Management*, vol 21 no 00, pp 1–19

Marc Ferro, 1997—*Colonization: A Global History*. London and New York: Routledge

Paulo Freire, 1970—*Pedagogy of the Oppressed*. New York: Continuum

Elizabeth Furniss, 2000 [1992, 1995]—*Victims of Benevolence: The Dark Legacy of the Williams Lake Residential School*. Vancouver: Arsenal Pulp Press

Lysiane Gagnon, March 2016—'Why Belgium is ground zero for jihadi terrorism', in *Globe and Mail*, March 30 2016, at http://www.theglobeandmail.com/opinion/why-belgium-is-ground-zero-for-jihadi-terrorism/article29425530/ (Accessed August 14 2017)

Marlies Glasius, Mary Kaldor, and Helmut Anheier, eds, 2006—*Global Civil Society 2005 / 6*. London: Thousand Oaks, and New Delhi: Sage, at http://www.lse.ac.uk/Depts/global/yearbook05.htm (Accessed August 14 2017)

Marlies Glasius, Mary Kaldor, and Helmut Anheier, eds, 2007—*Global Civil Society 2006 / 7*. London: Sage, at http://www.lse.ac.uk/Depts/global/yearbook06-7.htm (Accessed August 14 2017)

Adam Gopnik, September 2015—'Blood and Soil: A historian returns to the Holocaust', in *New Yorker*, September 21 2015, pp 100–04

Antonio Gramsci, 1971—*Selections from the Prison Notebooks*. Edited and translated by Quintin Hoare and Geoffrey Nowell-Smith. London: Lawrence and Wishart, and New York: International Publishers

Jorge E Hardoy and David Satterthwaite, 1989—*Squatter Citizen: Life in the Urban Third World*. London: Earthscan Publications

Josephine Ho, 2018—'Is Global Governance Bad for East Asian Queers?', in Jai Sen, ed, 2018—*The Movements of Movements, Part 2: Rethinking Our Dance*. Volume 5 in the *Challenging Empires* series. New Delhi: OpenWord, and Oakland, CA: PM Press

Jude Howell and Jenny Pearce, 1998—*Civil Society & Development: A critical exploration*. Boulder, CO, and London: Lynne Rienner

Carmen Junqueira and Betty Mindlin, July 1987—*The Aripuana Park and the Polonoroeste Programme*. IWGIA Document No 59. Published by IWGIA, Fiolstraede 10, DK-1711 Copenhagen K, Denmark

Fouad Kalouche and Eric Mielants, 2017—'Antisystemic Movements and Transformations of the World-System, 1968–1989', in Jai Sen, ed, 2017a—*The Movements of Movements, Part 1: What Makes Us Move?*. Volume 4 in the *Challenging Empires* series. New Delhi: OpenWord, and Oakland, CA: PM Press

John Keane, 2001—'Global Civil Society?', in Helmut Anheier, Marlies Glasius, and Mary Kaldor, eds, 2001—*Global Civil Society 2001*, pp 28–47

Margaret E Keck and Kathryn Sikkink, 1998—*Activists Beyond Borders: Advocacy Networks in International Politics*. Ithaca, NY: Cornell University Press

Chloé Keraghel and Jai Sen, December 2004—'Explorations in Open Space: The World Social Forum and Cultures of Politics', in *International Social Science Journal*, vol 56 no 182

Sanjeev Khagram, James V Riker, and Kathryn Sikkink, eds, 2002—*Restructuring World Politics: Transnational Social Movements, Networks, and Norms*. Minneapolis: University of Minnesota

Alex Khasnabish, 2017—'Forward Dreaming: Zapatismo and the Radical Imagination', in Jai Sen, ed, 2017a—*The Movements of Movements, Part 1: What Makes Us Move?*. Volume 4 in the *Challenging Empires* series. New Delhi: OpenWord, and Oakland, CA: PM Press

David C Korten, 1998a—*When the Corporations Rule the World*. Mapusa, Goa: The Other India Press

David C Korten, 1998b—*Globalising Civil Society: Reclaiming our Right to Power*. New York: Seven Stories Press

Madhuresh Kumar, nd—*A Toolkit Orientation Programme on Rethinking Rights, Justice, and Development*, Section 4: Programme Resources, subsection 4.1 A Primer on

Rethinking Rights, Justice and Development'. Calcutta Research Group, at http://www.mcrg.ac.in/Toolkit/inside_pgs/keywords.html (Accessed December 25, 2017)

Nilesh Kumar, Ajay Hela, and Anoop Kumar, November 2009—'Marichjhapi and the Revenge of Bengali Bhadralok: The story of a Dalit Genocide that remains untold'. Email from Anoop Keri on Dalits Media Watch on November 30 2009, at http://blog.insightyv.com/ (Inactive August 14 2017)

Mauro Leonel, 1992—*Roads, Indians, and the Environment in the Amazon, from Central America to the Pacific Ocean*. Translated from Portuguese by Edda Frost and Sam Poole. IAMA-2 Studies, IWGIA Document No 72. Published by IWGIA, Copenhagen

Norman Lewis, February 1969—'Genocide: From Fire and Sword to Arsenic and Bullet, Civilisation Has Sent Six Million Indians to Extinction', in *The Sunday Times*, London, February 23 1969

Xochitl Leyva Solano, 2017—'Geopolitics of Knowledge and the Neo-Zapatista Social Movement Networks', in Jai Sen, ed, 2017a—*The Movements of Movements, Part 1: What Makes Us Move?*. Volume 4 in the *Challenging Empires* series. New Delhi: OpenWord, and Oakland, CA: PM Press

Peter Linebaugh and Marcus Rediker, 2000—*The Many-Headed Hydra: Sailors, Slaves, Commoners, and the Hidden History of the Revolutionary Atlantic*. Boston, MA: Beacon Press

Ronnie D Lipschutz, Winter 1992—'Reconstructing World Politics: The Emergence of Global Civil Society', in *Millennium—Journal of International Studies*, vol 21, pp 389–420

Mikael Löfgren and Håkan Thörn, eds, 2007—'Global Civil Society—More Or Less Democracy?', special issue of *Development Dialogue*, at www.dhf.uu.se (Accessed August 14 2017)

Marianne Maeckelbergh, 2009—*The Will of the Many: How the Alterglobalisation Movement is Changing the Face of Democracy*. London: Pluto Press

Eldrid Mageli, June 2005—'Exploring the NGO Environment in Kolkata: The Universe of Unnayan and *Chhinnamul Sramajibi Adhikar Samiti*', in *The European Journal of Development Research*, vol 17, no 2, pp 249–69

Margareta Matache and Jacqueline Bhabha, April 2016—'Roma Slavery: The Case for Reparations', in *Foreign Policy in Focus*, April 22 2016, at http://fpif.org/roma-slavery-case-reparations/ (Accessed August 14 2017)

Fernando Meirelles and Kátia Lund, 2002—*Cidade de Deus* ('City of God', in Portuguese), at http://cidadededeus.globo.com/ (Accessed August 14 2017)

Ritu Menon and Kamla Bhasin, 1998—*Borders and Boundaries: Women in India's Partition*. New Brunswick: Rutgers University Press

Tom Mertes, ed, 2004—*A Movement of Movements: Is another world really possible?* London: Verso

Matt Meyer and Ousseina Alidou, 2018—'The Power of Words: Reclaiming and Reimagining Revolution and Nonviolence', in Jai Sen, ed, 2018—*The Movements of Movements, Part 2: Rethinking Our Dance*. Volume 5 in the *Challenging Empires* series. New Delhi: OpenWord, and Oakland, CA: PM Press

Ministry of Housing and Local Government, Welsh Office (Government of Great Britain), 1967—*Gypsies and other travellers*. London: Her Majesty's Stationery Office

Evo Morales Ayma (President of the Plurinational State of Bolivia), January 2010—'Peoples' World Conference on Climate Change and the Rights of Mother Earth', January 5 2010

Muto Ichiyo, 1993b—'For an Alliance of Hope', in Jeremy Brecher, John Brown Childs, and Jill Cutler, eds, 1993—*Global Visions: Beyond the New World Order*. Boston, MA: South End Press, pp 147–62

Muto Ichiyo, June 2002—'Neo-Liberal Globalization and People's Alliance', Contribution to the People's Plan 21 General Assembly, Rajabhat Institute, Bangkok, June 22–23 2002, at http://www.europe-solidaire.org/spip.php?article2765 (Accessed August 14 2017)

Muto Ichiyo, 2018—'Towards the Autonomy of the People of the World: Need for a New Movement of Movements to Animate People's Alliance Processes', in Jai Sen, ed, 2018—*The Movements of Movements, Part 2: Rethinking Our Dance*. Volume 5 in the *Challenging Empires* series. New Delhi: OpenWord, and Oakland, CA: PM Press

August H Nimtz Jr, 2000—*Marx and Engels: Their Contribution to the Democratic Breakthrough*. Albany, NY: State University of New York Press

'No one is illegal', at https://en.wikipedia.org/wiki/No_one_is_illegal (Accessed August 14 2017)

Rodrigo Nunes, 2018—'Nothing Is What Democracy Looks Like: Openness, Horizontality, and The Movement of Movements', in Jai Sen, ed, 2018—*The Movements of Movements, Part 2: Rethinking Our Dance*. Volume 5 in the *Challenging Empires* series. New Delhi: OpenWord, and Oakland, CA: PM Press

Gail Omvedt, 1994—*Dalits and the Democratic Revolution: Dr Ambedkar and the Dalit Movement in Colonial India*. New Delhi: Sage Publications

Karl Polanyi, 2001 [1944]—*The Great Transformation: The Political and Economic Origins of Our Time*. Boston, MA: Beacon Press

Bruce Rich, 1994—*Mortgaging the Earth: The World Bank, Environmental Impoverishment and the Crisis of Development*. Boston, MA: Beacon Press

Theodore Roszak, 1969—*The Making of a Counter Culture: Reflections on the Technocratic Society and Its Youthful Opposition*. Berkeley: University of California Press

J Sakai, 2014 [1982]—*Settlers: The Mythology of the White Proletariat*. Montreal: Kerplebedeb

Jan Aart Scholte, November 2007—'Global Civil Society: Opportunity or Obstacle for Democracy?', in Mikael Löfgren and Håkan Thörn, eds, 2007—'Global Civil Society—More Or Less Democracy?', special issue of *Development Dialogue*, no 49, pp 15–28, at https://www.researchgate.net/publication/298670331_Global_civil_society_-_Opportunity_or_obstacle_for_democracy (Accessed December 27 2017)

Jared P Scott and Kelly Nyks, 2015—*Requiem for the American Dream: The Noam Chomsky Documentary*, at http://requiemfortheamericandream.com/the-film/ (Accessed August 14, 2017)

Jai Sen, April 1975—*The Unintended City: An Essay on the City of the Poor*. Cathedral Relief Services, Calcutta, at http://www.india-seminar.com/2001/500/500%20jai%20sen.htm (Accessed August 14 2017)

Jai Sen, November 1983—'A Continuing Struggle: Organised and Unorganised Workers', in *Business Standard*, November 2 1983

Jai Sen, August 1984—'Criminalisation of the Poor' and 'Rules with Alternatives', in *Indian Express*, New Delhi, August 10 and 11 1984

Jai Sen, April 1985—'What is the Nature of the Housing Question in India Today?'. Background paper for a 'National Workshop on the Housing Question' organised by Unnayan in Calcutta, April 24–28 1985. Reprinted in revised form in *Lokayan Bulletin* 3 / 3 and 3 / 4–5, June and October 1985

Jai Sen, July 1986—'Anniversaries of another kind', published as 'Ugly life, uglier evictions' and 'Who cares for those who need care the most?', in *Amrita Bazar Patrika*, July 13 and 27 1986

Jai Sen, with Unnayan, December 1987—'Housing Struggles of the Labouring Poor and Urban Planning: Rabindranagar, Calcutta'. Paper presented at the Convention of ISoCARP (International Society of Area and Regional Planners), New Delhi, India, December 1987. Published in the report of the Convention

Jai Sen, September 1989 / May 1990—'Who is the Real Stoneman?', in *Mainstream*, May 19 1990 [First published in Bengali, September 1989—'*Prokrita Stoneman Key?*', NCHR, Calcutta]

Jai Sen, June 1996a—"Participation of the People'—Intentions and Contradictions: A Critical Look at Habitat II', in *Economic and Political Weekly*, June 1 1996, pp 1302–06

Jai Sen, November 1996—'The Left Front and the "Unintended City": Is a Civilised Transition Possible?', in *Economic and Political Weekly*, November 9–16 1996, pp 2977–82

Jai Sen, December 1996—'Deeper Meanings: Explorations into the history and dynamics of movement around the dwelling rights of the *kudikidappukaran* (attached labour) of Kerala, India'. Paper presented at the International Conference on 'Kerala's Development Experience: National and Global Dimensions', New Delhi, December 8–11 1996

Jai Sen, July–September 1998—'*Sha Fu*: The Past, the Present, and the Future of the Hand-rickshaw Pullers of Calcutta: Is a civilised and progressive transition possible?', in *Bulletin of Concerned Asian Scholars* vol 30 no 3, pp 37–49

Jai Sen, June 1999—'On the Dynamics of Strategic Civil Alliance: A Critical Documentation of the Experience of Civil Campaigns around the Narmada Project in India and the Polonoroeste and related projects in Brazil'. Project Proposal to the Ford Foundation

Jai Sen, December 1999—'A World to Win—But whose world is it, anyway?', Chapter 9 in John W Foster and Anita Anand, eds, 1999—*Whose World is it Anyway? Civil Society, the United Nations, and the multilateral future*. Ottawa: United Nations Association in Canada, pp 337–90, at http://cacim.net/twiki/tiki-download_file. php?fileId=17 (Accessed August 14 2017)

Jai Sen, April 2001 [1975]—'The Unintended City'. Reprinted in *Seminar* 500, special issue on 'Seminar through the decades', pp 39–47, at http://www.india-seminar. com/2001/500/500%20jai%20sen.htm (Accessed August 14 2017)

Jai Sen, January 2002a—'The World Social Forum—Some Concerns and Considerations for a WSF Process in India', January 5 2002, at http://www.choike.org/PDFs/concerns. pdf (Inactive August 14 2017). Subsequently published in: Jai Sen with Madhuresh Kumar, compilers, August 2003—*Are Other Worlds Possible? The Open Space Reader on the World Social Forum and its Engagement with Empire*, pp 198–206

Jai Sen, March–April 2002—'On Building Another World (Or: 'Are other globalisations possible?): The World Social Forum as an instrument of global democratisation'. Paper for the Network Institute for Global Democratisation (NIGD) Seminar at the World Social Forum on 'Global Democracy? A North-South Dialogue', February 4 2002, Amarzen, Porto Alegre, Brazil

Jai Sen, November 2002d—'Civilising Globalisation? Or Globalising Civilisation? Some reflections towards civil governance and a conscious, critical globalisation'. Paper for the Opening Session of 'Helsinki Conference 2002: Searching for Global Partnerships' held in Helsinki, Finland, December 2–4 2002. Organised by the Crisis

Management Initiative (Office of President Ahtisaari) on behalf of the Government of Finland

Jai Sen, 2002—'Are other globalizations possible? The World Social Forum as an instrument of global democratization', Chapter 8 in Leena Rikkilä and Katarina Sehm Patomäki, eds, 2002—*From a Global Market Place to Political Spaces*, pp 167–205. NIGD Working Paper 1, 2002. Helsinki: Network Institute for Global Democratization

Jai Sen, May 2003d—'The WSF as logo, the WSF as commons: Take a moment to reflect on what is happening in the World Social Forum'. Discussion note

Jai Sen, July 2005a—'On Incivility and Transnationality: Towards Alliances of Critical Hope. Steps towards critically engaging with Muto Ichiyo's concept of transborder participatory democracy'. Paper presented in Panel One, 'The Long March of 50 Year People's Movement: The Works of Muto Ichiyo', 2005 IACS Conference 'Emerging Inter-Asian Subjectivities in Cultural Movements', at http://www.cacim. net/twiki/tiki-read_article.php?articleId=59 (Available August 14 2017)

Jai Sen, January 2006b—'Some Hard Questions About The WSF', at http://www.choike. org/nuevo_eng/informes/3824.html (Accessed August 14 2017)

Jai Sen, January 2007a—'The World Social Forum as an emergent learning process', in *Futures* vol 39 (2007), pp 505–22

Jai Sen, November 2007b—'Lifting the veil: Marichjhampi then, Nandigram now', on *Sanhati*, at http://sanhati.com/articles/470/ (Accessed August 14 2017)

Jai Sen, November 2007d—'The power of civility', in Mikael Löfgren and Håkan Thörn, eds, 2007—'Global Civil Society—More or Less Democracy?', special issue of *Development Dialogue*, no 49, pp 51–68, at http://www.daghammarskjold.se/wp-content/ uploads/2007/11/development_dialogue_49.pdf (Accessed December 25 2017)

Jai Sen, March 2010b—'Be the Seed: An Introduction to and Commentary on the government of Bolivia's Call for a "Peoples" World Conference On Climate Change and the Rights of Mother Earth', on *CACIM*, at http://cacim.net/twiki/tiki-read_article. php?articleId=64 (Accessed August 14 2017)

Jai Sen, 2010c—'On open space: Explorations towards a vocabulary of a more open politics', in *Antipode*, vol 42 no 4, 2010, pp 994–1018

Jai Sen, 2011d—'Understanding the world: Interrogating empire and power'. Introduction to Jai Sen, ed, 2011a—*Interrogating Empires*. Book 2 in the *Are Other Worlds Possible?* series. New Delhi: OpenWord and Daanish Books

Jai Sen, April 2013a—'The WSF As A Historical Process: Learning by Doing?', on *ALAI*, at http://www.alainet.org/active/63440 (Accessed April 23 2013, inactive August 14 2017)

Jai Sen, 2017a—'The Movements of Movements: An Introduction and an Exploration'. Introduction to Jai Sen, ed, 2017a—*The Movements of Movements, Part 1: What Makes Us Move?*. Volume 4 in the *Challenging Empires* series. New Delhi: OpenWord, and Oakland, CA: PM Press

Jai Sen, 2018—'Break Free! Engaging Critically with the Concept and Reality of Civil Society (Part 2)', in Jai Sen, ed, 2018—*The Movements of Movements, Part 2: Rethinking Our Dance*. Volume 5 in the *Challenging Empires* series. New Delhi: OpenWord, and Oakland, CA: PM Press

Jai Sen, ed, 2011a—*Interrogating Empires*. Book 2 in the *Are Other Worlds Possible?* series. New Delhi: OpenWord and Daanish Books

Jai Sen, ed, 2011b—*Imagining Alternatives*. Book 3 in the *Are Other Worlds Possible?* series. New Delhi: OpenWord and Daanish Books

Jai Sen, ed, 2017—*The Movements of Movements, Part 1: What Makes Us Move?*. Volume 4 in the *Challenging Empires* series. New Delhi: OpenWord, and Oakland, CA: PM Press

Jai Sen, Anita Anand, Arturo Escobar, and Peter Waterman, eds, 2004—*World Social Forum: Challenging Empires*. New Delhi: Viveka. Slightly edited version at http://www.choike.org/nuevo_eng/informes/1557.html (Accessed August 14 2017)

Jai Sen with Madhuresh Kumar, compilers, 2003—*Are Other Worlds Possible? The Open Space Reader on the World Social Forum and its Engagement with Empire, Volume One: On the Forum*. New Delhi: CACIM

Jai Sen and Madhuresh Kumar, compilers, with Patrick Bond and Peter Waterman, 2007—*A Political Programme for the World Social Forum? Democracy, Substance, and Debate in the Bamako Appeal and the Global Justice Movements—A Reader*. New Delhi: CACIM, at http://www.cacim.net/bareader/ (Accessed December 25 2017)

Jai Sen and Peter Waterman, with Madhuresh Kumar, December 2003—'The World Social Bibliography: A Bibliography on the World Social Forum and the Global Solidarity and Justice Movement', at http://www.cacim.net/twiki/tiki-index.php?page= Publications (Accessed December 25 2017)

Jai Sen and Peter Waterman, eds, 2009—*World Social Forum: Challenging Empires*, second edition. Montreal: Black Rose Books

Martin Shaw, 2008—'Civil society', in Lester Kurtz, ed, 2008—*Encyclopaedia of Violence, Peace and Conflict*, second edition. San Diego: Academic Press, pp 269–78, at http://www.sussex.ac.uk/Users/hafa3/cs.htm (Accessed October 8 2017)

Jackie Smith, Charles Chatfield, and Ron Pagnucco, eds, 1997—*Transnational Social Movements and Global Politics: Solidarity Beyond the State*. Syracuse, NY: Syracuse University Press

Jackie Smith, Marina Karides, Marc Becker, Dorval Brunelle, Christopher Chase-Dunn, Donatella della Porta, Rosalba Icaza Garza, Jeffrey S Juris, Lorenzo Mosca, Ellen Reese, Peter (Jay) Smith, and Rolando Vazquez, 2008—*Global Democracy and the World Social Forums*. Boulder, CO: Paradigm Press

Truth and Reconciliation Commission of Canada, 2015a—*Honouring the Truth, Reconciling for the Future: Summary of the Final Report of the Truth and Reconciliation Commission of Canada*, at http://nctr.ca/reports.php (Accessed August 14 2017)

Truth and Reconciliation Commission of Canada, 2015c—*The Survivors Speak*. A Report of the Truth and Reconciliation Commission of Canada, at http://nctr.ca/reports. php (Accessed August 14 2017)

Truth and Reconciliation Commission of Canada, 2015d—*Canada's Residential Schools: The History, Part 1: Origins to 1939*. The Final Report of the Truth and Reconciliation Commission of Canada, Volume 1, at http://nctr.ca/reports.php (Accessed August 14 2017)

P E Tyler, February 2003—'A new power in the streets', in *New York Times*, February 17 2003, at http://www.nytimes.com/2003/02/17/world/threats-and-responses-news-analysis-a-new-power-in-the-streets.html (Accessed August 14 2017)

UNI-Norte (União das Nações Indígenas do Acre e Sul do Amazonas) ['Union of Indigenous Nations', in Portuguese], 1989—'Open Letter from UNI-North to PMACI and IDB', in *Cultural Survival Quarterly* vol 13 no 1

Unnayan, July 1982—'Hand-rickshaws in Calcutta: Who decides?', in *Mainstream*, July 10 1982, pp 26–27

Unnayan, February 1983—'Towards Planning for the Real Calcutta'. Paper for seminar on 'Economy & Employment, Calcutta Metropolitan District 1983–2001', in *Business Standard*, July 28, 29, and August 1 1983

Harsha Walia, 2013—*Undoing Border Imperialism*. Oakland, CA: AK Press and IAS (Institute for Anarchist Studies)

Peter Waterman, 2001b—'Conclusion: Globalization, Civil Society, Solidarity', in Peter Waterman, *Globalization, Social Movements and the New Internationalisms*. London and New York: Continuum, pp 198–245

Franke Wilmer, 1993—*The Indigenous Voice in World Politics, Since Time Immemorial*. Newbury Park, London, and New Delhi: Sage Publications

Notes

1. This is the first part of a totally revised essay titled 'The power of civility' that first appeared as a contribution to a special issue of the journal *Development Dialogue* under the title 'Global Civil Society—More Or Less Democracy?' (Löfgren and Thörn 2007; Sen, November 2007)—which in turn was the text of a presentation I made to a seminar organised by the Committee on Civil Society Research (Sweden) at the World Social Forum in Nairobi, Kenya, on January 22 2007. Even though this version is very different, and my arguments substantially developed, I nevertheless thank the publishers of my 2007 essay, the Dag Hammarskjöld Foundation, and the editors Mikael Löfgren and Håkan Thörn, for their ready respective agreements to my request in 2008 to republish that essay in revised form. This essay as it stands has been a long time in the making. Vipul Rikhi was the Content Editor for the first finalised version, some years ago. With delays in the publication of the book/s in which it was to appear, I ended up developing and reworking several of my arguments. Vipul bears no responsibility for the essay as it now stands. My thanks to him for doing a wonderful job that first time around. Last: I have taken the enormous liberty of having access—as editor—to all the great essays in this book and the companion volume (Sen, ed, 2017) to quote from several of them.

2. Because this essay is long, it is being published in two parts. Part 2 appears at the end of the third section of this book. This essay takes more space than the other essays in this book for two reasons. One, this is perhaps the last time I will write on this subject, which I have been working and writing on for a decade now. And, two, the theme of this essay is in fact a chord that many contributors to this book also strike in their own ways and for their own reasons; aside from other contemporary writers also addressing some of the same questions. I believe that this is significant, and I decided to allow this synergy to shape my essay and to express itself here as a celebration of contributors walking together and dancing together, as a contribution to the theme of this book, and in a small way—along with the Afterwords to this book and to Part 1 (Cormie 2018, Cox 2017)—towards this essay also being something of an additional exercise of reading across essays in these books.

3. Baldwin 1998 [1976].

4. Abramsky 2018.

5. Alfred and Corntassel 2017.

6. Tagore 1933—'*Bandh Bhengey Dao*' ['Break all the Barriers', in Bengali].

7. On reflection and in some self-criticism, I should clarify that although I have used the term 'civil' as an adjective in this area since at least 1996 (Sen, November 1996; Sen, June 1999), it was because at that time I saw 'civil' as being a better descriptor for what then in India were still described as 'voluntary organisations' (or soon after, 'non-governmental organisations'). I still understood 'civil' in an uncritical way, and in my own writings appealed—as is 'normal' in civil society—to its normatively positive ('civilised') qualities. It was only in 2002 that I started interrogating the idea of 'the civil' and exploring the contradictions of civility (Sen, November 2002d) and only in 2005 that I started more specifically exploring the dialectical relationship between civility and incivility (Sen, July 2005a). And this, even though in my first essay in this broad area, back in 1973, I had explored what I now realise is the related concept of 'unintendedness' (published in 1975 and subsequently as 'The Unintended City: An Essay on the City of the Poor' [Sen, April 1975]; most easily accessible in edited form as Sen, April 2001). I then worked as an organiser and strategist from 1977 until 1991 within the 'Unintended City Project'. I now see that the idea I had then was in some ways not unrelated. There was and is a thread running through all this. The section of society I refer to in this essay as 'the civil', or as 'civil society', are of course also 'the intended'. This is therefore an appropriate place for me to again acknowledge my profound debt in this stream of thought, reflection, and action to US Professor Glean Chase, who in a lecture in Oxford, UK, in 1974, talked about the 'unintended' in society. Focussing on 'social deviants', he said something along the lines of: "There are two classes of citizens—the intended and the unintended. The intended are the class depended on for progress by the experts—the Galbraiths and the Wards; the unintended are the rest". This resonated closely with questions I was then struggling with in relation to the literature I was reading about 'Third World urbanisation' and led me first to think about and develop the concept of unintendedness, and then over time to thinking more dialectically about social dynamics. Though I acknowledged Professor Chase in my 1975 essay as the source of the term 'unintended', I had no idea then of what effect this would have on me. In short, hearing him speak in 1974 changed my way of thinking and, over time, my life.

8. And with the word 'vice' used here, of course, in the sense of "any of various devices, usually having two jaws that may be brought together or separated by means of a screw, lever, or the like, used to hold an object firmly while work is being done on it" (http://www.dictionary.com/browse/vice?s=t).

9. In the English-speaking world, think for instance of the story 'Three Little Pigs'. A little reflection will quickly reveal that the house built with bricks is the one worth having—and, implicitly, that the pig living there is the brighter one, the more accomplished one; and the home built with straw is. . . . I leave the rest to your imagination.

10. Though given the rabidly partisan way that some sections of the (read: 'dominant') media are behaving these days, in India, in the US, and perhaps all over the world—losing all pretence of civility—maybe the generalisation I have made here is becoming less true.

11. For a discussion of 'netwars', see the essay in the accompanying volume by Xochitl Leyva Solano on 'Geopolitics of Knowledge and the Neo-Zapatista Social Movement Networks' (Leyva Solano 2017).

12. Alfred and Corntassel 2017.

13. Aside from my father being a very well known and successful doctor, my maternal uncles rising to the most senior positions in the Indian civil and military service (my mother died when I was still very young), and a maternal aunt being a well known social worker and politician, my grandfather on my father's side, for instance, was— as well as being a prominent practicing barrister—a minister in the Brahmo Samaj, at one time a very prominent, progressive reformist movement in India that played an important role in the nineteenth and early twentieth centuries in a whole host of areas (such as banning the practices of child marriage and widow sacrifice that were once so prevalent in Hindu society). He also wrote what is perhaps the authoritative history of this movement. Equally, my great-grandmother on my mother's side was a great educationalist—establishing several important institutions, and through them influencing generations of people in civil society. And there have been other such figures in my family, going way back. Even though I learned about all this only quite recently in my life (because of the particular circumstances under which I grew up and my life took shape, I was not exposed to much of this earlier on), and I was therefore not brought up to specifically 'do' any of these things, I think I was nevertheless brought up with many of the values that imbued their lives, and therefore come from civil society, whether I like it or not.

14. See note 6 above for an account of my own relation to the term 'civil'.

15. When I first presented my core arguments in this area in their still raw form at the seminar in Nairobi in 2007, specifically differentiating between the civil, the incivil, and the uncivil, one of the other panellists, Patrick Bond, dismissed my arguments as being merely a semantic distinction. Imagine my surprise—and pleasure—to see a post by him on the Debate listserv some years later, in August 2010, where he said (to someone else): "Comradely suggestion: when you see something in 'civil society' you don't like, try calling it 'civilised society'. As for the rest, we like 'uncivil society'. How would that work for you, com Dom? Works well for us in Durban". (Bond, August 2007); Bond then further developed this in 2014 by saying, in the abstract for a talk: "An overly vague term, 'civil society' usually experiences divides between *civilised* society (NGOs and trade unions) and *uncivil* society (radical social movements and a new labour / community left)" (Bond, May 2014; emphases in original). As will become clear in this essay, I find this categorisation too restricted, but I've been glad to see that Patrick and I are at least now—perhaps—in the same field.

16. Extracts from Articles 1 and 5 of the WSF's Charter of Principles (World Social Forum Organising Committee and World Social Forum International Council, June 2001). Emphases added.

17. I have been intensively involved with promoting critical reflection on the WSF since 2002, first raising hard questions about the World Social Forum being parachuted into India in relation to social politics in the country at that juncture and through a number of interrelated activities: being closely involved with the initial preparations for WSF process in India; writing on it and editing books on it; organising seminars and workshops on it (both during WSF meetings and outside); conceiving and moderating a listserv on it, WSFDiscuss; conceiving and being partially responsible for a website complementary to the WSF and to the idea of the WSF, OpenSpaceForum; and co-organising and mentoring fellowships on it. For an overview of the work that fellow members and associates and I have done on the WSF through CACIM, the

organisation some of us set up in 2005, see http://www.cacim.net/twiki/tiki-index.php?page=WSF (Accessed August 14 2017); Sen, January 2002a; Sen, March–April 2002; Sen, May 2003d; Sen with Kumar, compilers, August 2003; Sen and Waterman, with the help of Kumar, December 2003; Sen, Anand, Escobar, and Waterman, eds, 2004; Keraghel and Sen, editorial advisers, December 2004; Sen and Saini, eds, January 2005; Sen, January 2006b; Sen and Saini, eds, March 2006; Sen, January 2007a; Sen and Kumar, compilers, with Bond and Waterman, January 2007; Sen and Waterman, eds, 2009; Sen 2010; Sen, ed, 2011a and Sen, ed, 2011b; Sen, April 2013a; and Sen, ed, 2017d.

18. See, for instance, Korten 1998.

19. As mentioned above, this essay is a substantially developed version of my earlier attempts to explore this question. In the course of doing this, I have had the privilege of discussing these ideas with various people and / or getting comments from them and of reading other people's work. One of the most interesting aspects of this ongoing exchange has been to see how others have explored similar ground. And among the most stimulating has been the major—even magisterial—work by Janet Conway titled *Edges of Global Justice: The World Social Forum and its 'Others'* (2012). By focussing on the subject in great depth, she has opened up some of the issues I have been trying to explore but in far greater depth and with far greater nuance; I am deeply indebted to her. I have also discussed the subject with many others, a list too long to give here. In short, I want to express here my debt to all those I have discussed these ideas with over the past decade or so, and with whom I have worked on these issues; in particular, to the contributors to this book (and to its companion volume *The Movements of Movements, Part 1: What Makes Us Move?*; Sen, ed, 2017), many of whom also interrogate these questions in their own way. It feels good to be walking together!

20. I am going to leave this as a footnote, but I am well aware that there is a crucial realm of "structural power *within* the non-state (and also non-market) world and *among and between* non-state actors" that I have not discussed at all in this essay: the world of religion. I can only hope that someone else may try to do this as a parallel and perhaps converging exercise.

21. I again refer readers to Janet Conway's book (Conway 2012), and I also especially welcome the hard questioning that Josephine Ho does of this subject in her essay in this book, 'Is Global Governance Bad for East Asian Queers?' (2018).

22. Keane 2001.

23. For details on the Break Free climate campaign, see, for example, http://breakfreepnw.org/ (Accessed August 14 2017).

24. Cormie 2018.

25. Nimtz Jr 2000; Polanyi 2001 [1944].

26. For a sometimes critical anthology of the role of civil organisations at a global level, see the *Global Civil Society Yearbook*, produced annually since 2001 by Mary Kaldor and her colleagues at the Centre for Global Governance, at the London School of Economics. See, among others, Glasius, Kaldor, and Anheier 2006, and Glasius, Kaldor, and Anheier 2007.

27. See, for instance, Linebaugh and Rediker 2000, Drainville 2012, and Cox and Nilsen 2014.

28. Most famously perhaps, this was the case at the time of the Emancipation Proclamation—the freeing of slaves—in the US in the nineteenth century. But my own studies into movements for a place to live have shown this in the Indian context; see Sen, December 1996.

29. Drainville 2012. See also Cox and Nilsen 2014 for a great discussion of this subject.

30. I am here focussing only on this (European) lineage and on the forward and outward projection of this in the form of colonial power relations, because it has been and remains the dominant discourse during our stage of history. As I mention elsewhere in this essay, we have a very similar term—and section of society and norms—in the part of the world I come from, *bhadralok*, meaning 'the civil (or proper) folk', and I would guess that this is likely to be the case for many other societies in the world. We each need to reflect on and do similar work on our own societies and political cosmologies.

31. Gramsci 1971; see also Shaw 2008. See also the entry for 'Civil Society' in Madhuresh Kumar, nd.

32. For a discussion of these movements and the gains they made (along with a lot else), see the Afterword in this book by Lee Cormie (2018).

33. For a gripping presentation and discussion of both the movements and the project of rolling back, watch Noam Chomsky on Scott and Nyks 2015. Characteristically, Chomsky wonderfully problematises the term 'civil' (and this essay!) by passingly saying that the movements in the United States in the 1970s that were so brutally suppressed played the useful role of "civilising society". Thus turning the table on its head.

34. Falk 1997.

35. Falk 1999, p 137. Similarly, Falk also goes on to say on the same page, "A similar issue arises with respect to the terminology useful in aggregating the actors. *It seems convenient* to retain the term 'non-governmental organizations' (NGOs) to designate those actors associated with global civil society, *because it is accurate and convenient, being so widely used and thus easily recognizable*". Emphases added.

36. André Drainville, a contributor to this book, is professor of Transnational Sociology at Université Laval in Québec City, Canada. He has been writing for more than twenty years on forms of resistance to capitalist world ordering. His most recent book is titled *A History of World Order and Resistance: The Making and Unmaking of Global Subjects* (London and New York: Routledge, 2012).

37. Drainville 2011.

38. Keane 2001.

39. A good deal of this background is discussed in essays in this book and in its accompanying volume, *The Movements of Movements, Part 1: What Makes Us Move?* (Sen, ed, 2017a). See, in particular, the essay in this book by Muto Ichiyo (2018) and in the accompanying book by Fouad Kalouche and Eric Mielants (2017).

40. Lipschutz, Winter 1992; Braman and Sreberny-Mohammadi 1996; Smith, Chatfield, and Pagnucco 1997; Keck and Sikkink 1998; Brecher, Costello, and Smith 2000; and Keane 2001.

41. Keane 2001. Note, of course, his emphasis on "*civilised* power-sharing". Emphasis added.

42. For a discussion of the role and influence of new conditions on the emergence of transnational activities till the mid- to late 1990s, see Keck and Sikkink 1998; and for a discussion of the role and influence of subsequent developments, see the essay by Rodrigo Nunes in this book (2018).

43. For an overview of the PP21, see the essay in this book by Muto Ichiyo (2018) and Muto 1993.

44. For an overview of the history and emergence of the World Social Forum, see: Sen, Anand, Escobar, and Waterman, eds, 2004; Sen and Waterman, eds, 2009; Sen and Waterman, eds, 2012; and most accessibly, Sen April 2013a.

45. There is surprisingly little solid published work on the PGA, but for a lucid introduction, see the essay by Alex Khasnabish in the companion volume to this book (2017).

46. For one of the first and best accounts, see Keck and Sikkink 1998.

47. For the campaign that unfolded around 'Indians' in the Brazilian Amazon over decades, see Lewis, February 1969; Chiappino 1975; Davis 1977; and Junqueira and Mindlin, July 1987; and for a comprehensive sketch, Cowell 1990.

48. For the Bhopal campaign, see the website for Students for Bhopal / the International Campaign for Justice in Bhopal, at http://www.studentsforbhopal.org/ (Accessed August 14 2017); and for the Narmada campaigns, see the website of Friends of Narmada, at http://www.narmada.org/ (Accessed August 14 2017). I should acknowledge here that I did a decade of in-depth research during the 1990s on the Narmada movements and their globalisation, but for various reasons—most especially that I hijacked myself into working with and on the World Social Forum from 2002 on—I have not yet completed writing up that work. For an essay that discusses a part of the wider dynamics of the globalisation of movement, see Sen, December 1999.

49. Many people have written on this (for instance, see Bandy and Smith, eds, 2004; Mertes, ed, 2004; Smith, Karides, Becker, et al 2008). While I have great respect for the movements themselves—and for the authors—in my Introduction to the companion volume to this book, *The Movements of Movements, Part 1: What Makes Us Move?*, I contest the idea of a singular 'movement of movements' and it portrayal by the authors (Sen 2017a).

50. Lipschutz, Winter 1992; Khagram, Riker, and Sikkink, March 2002; and Maeckelbergh 2009.

51. Tyler, February 2003.

52. Korten 1998b.

53. Ho 2018.

54. Muto, June 2002. Since I am citing this, I should clarify that I do not agree with Muto-san's argument in the opening sentence in this quote that "[C]ivil society is largely a creation of the modern nation state". Other than in the very particular and recent sense of its promotion by the architects of neoliberalism, I think that in a longer history it has been the other way around.

55. For instance, Peter Waterman and Jan Aart Scholte; Waterman 2001b, and Scholte, January 2007.

56. For a discussion of the crucial concept of transcommunality, see the classic work of the Afro-Indigenous scholar John Brown Childs (2003) and his beautiful essay in this book (Childs 2018).

57. I again acknowledge my debt here to Professor Glean Chase; see note 5 above.

58. Ho 2018.

59. And even more specific and precise terms such as *kudikidappukaran*, in the state of Kerala in southern India, referring to a subsection of Dalits and a particular form

of land tenure in that part of the country. The most common colloquial translation of the term *kudikidappukaran* into English is 'hutment dwellers', but the underlying meaning of the hutment itself, *kudikidappu*—because of the deeper meanings of the term *kudi*—is 'the place where drunkards lie'. By extension, the deeper cultural meaning (and use) of the term *kudikidappukaran* is 'congenital drunkards'. For a detailed discussion of the etymology of this term—where the struggle around the rights and freedoms of the *kudikidappukaran* (who finally gained their freedom from servitude only in the 1970s) played a major role in the formation of Kerala as a state and society—see Sen, December 1996.

60. For an informative and challenging discussion on the use in the US context of the term 'Indian' to refer to the Indigenous Peoples—including militantly by some among them—see the essay in this book by Matt Meyer and Ousseina Alidou (2018).

61. Wilmer 1993, especially Chapter 4, 'The Great Cause of Civilization', pp 95–126. See also Churchill 2004; Furniss 2000 [1992, 1995].

62. Ferro 1997.

63. For those interested in knowing more about this subject, see Ambedkar nd [1936]; for a more recent and annotated version, see Ambedkar, 2014 [1936]. For the role of Dalits in the democratisation of Indian society, see Omvedt 1994.

64. See Matache and Bhabha, April 2016. For a governmental report from the 1960s on the Roma in Europe, see Ministry of Housing and Local Government, Welsh Office (Government of Great Britain), 1967.

65. Datta Chowdhury 1993, citing de Regt 1986. See also the graphic discussion of this issue and a comparison to what was happening in the empire's colonies by Lee Cormie in his Afterword to this book (2018).

66. For an interesting and revealing discussion about how this force manifests itself in relation to everyday things, such as facial and body hair, see: Bastani and Çaçan, February 2016.

67. Churchill 2004; Dunbar-Ortiz 2014; Furniss 2000 [1992, 1995]; Truth and Reconciliation Commission of Canada, 2015a; Truth and Reconciliation Commission of Canada, 2015c; and Truth and Reconciliation Commission of Canada, 2015d.

68. For instance, the Truth and Reconciliation process in Canada, on Turtle Island (Truth and Reconciliation Commission of Canada, 2015a), but this has equally been true of New Zealand, or Aotearoa in Maori—where Maori has been recognised as an official language, as a part of the process of reconciliation.

69. On the question of widespread anti-Semitism in Europe, see, for instance, Gopnik, September 2015: "The great and sympathetic historian of Christianity Diarmaid MacCulloch writes that it is still 'necessary to remind Christians of the centuries-old heritage of anti-Semitism festering in the memories of countless ordinary twentieth-century Christians on the eve of the Nazi takeover. In the 1940s, this poison led not just to Christian Germans, but [also] Christian Lithuanians, Poles, and many others gleefully to perpetuate bestial cruelties on helpless Jews who done them no harm'".

70. As in note 61 above.

71. Baldwin, with KQED, 1963.

72. Sen, April 2001 [1975]. As already explained in note 5, I learned of the term 'unintended' in a lecture by Professor Glean Chase, who used it in a more focused way to refer to the 'deviant' in society.

73. For a discussion of power-over and power-to, drawing on the work of John Holloway, see Sen 2010d.

74. Kumar, Hela, and Kumar, November 2009; Bhattacharjee nd [c.2009]; Sen, November 2007b; and in general, http://sanhati.com/ (Accessed August 14 2017).

75. Through Unnayan, the organisation I had helped form in 1977 and was with until 1991, and through the several incivil formations we at Unnayan and others in Calcutta (now Kolkata) helped form during the 1980s, including the Chhinnamul Sramajibi Adhikar Samiti (Organisation for the Rights of Uprooted Labouring People). See, for instance: Unnayan, July 1982; Unnayan, February 1983; Sen, November 1983; Sen, August 1984b; Sen, April 1985; Sen, July 1986; Sen, with Unnayan, December 1987; Sen, September 1989 / May 1990; Sen, November 1996; and the independent researcher Eldrid Mageli (June 2005).

76. In 2008–2009, potentially major changes seemed to be taking place in West Bengal, where peasants and agriculturalists, backed by significant sections of the independent progressive intelligentsia—civil society—as well as by some political parties, rose to challenge the seemingly unbreakable hold of the left parties over developments in the state. See Bhattacharyya, June 2009, and http://sanhati.com/ (Accessed August 14 2014). With respect to the arguments of this essay, however, this is not to suggest that this rebellion was necessarily going to challenge civil society's essential control of the state and society in West Bengal (or was even interested in doing so); it is only to put on record that change was in the air. On the other hand, while in what was otherwise a historic moment, the Left Front was defeated in 2011, after thirty-four years in continuous power and a new populist government led by present Chief Minister Mamata Banerjee came to power and has remained in power, there has been no change in terms of the arguments of this essay.

77. See also the quote from Josephine Ho's essay, as in note 51 above; another example—among many—is the generous funding that was provided by the US government and its allies to civil organisations that were willing to do 'constructive social work' in Afghanistan in the period after 9/11 in a blatant attempt to improve the image of the Western powers that had created the Taliban, and had then invaded and occupied that country once their creation turned on them.

78. For critical discussions of these crucial contemporary instruments of state and civil power, see Walia 2013 and the work of 'No One Is Illegal', at http://www.noii.org.uk/ (Accessed August 14 2017).

79. Quoted in Shaw, 2008, pp 1, 3.

80. Cox and Nilsen 2014.

81. See, for instance, Sakai 2014 [1982].

82. See, for instance, Branford and Glock 1985; Cowell 1989; Cowell 1990; Leonel 1992; Rich, February 1994; and UNI-Norte 1989.

83. Fearnside 1997.

84. The fourth section of this essay appears in Part 2 (Sen 2018).

85. This discrimination involves an even larger number of people in many parts of the world from Fiji to the Caribbean to South Africa, because a large proportion of the huge South Asian diaspora that is scattered across the world are the descendants of people, many of them Dalits by caste, who were exported around the world by the British empire in the second half of the nineteenth century as 'indentured labour', after the banning of slavery.

86. For a discussion of the contours of this issue, see Anon, nd [*c.*January 2013].

87. Cormie 2018.

88. Butalia, January 2005; Menon and Bhasin 1998.

89. See, for example, Divakar Namala 2011.

90. Sen 2001 [1975]. See also note 4 above.

91. For an early discussion of this criminalisation and stigmatisation, see Sen, August 1984b. For a less pointed but far more comprehensive discussion, see Hardoy and Satterthwaite 1989.

92. For a discussion of this landscape as a part of a much wider canvas, see Polanyi 2001 [1944].

93. See, for instance, Gagnon, March 2016—not as an authoritative statement but as a sign of increased understanding of this growing phenomenon.

94. For a rich discussion of the extraordinary historic, social, and political experiment taking place in Bolivia, with the Indigenous Peoples coming to power, and on—among many other things—the struggle between the Indigenous Peoples and the non-indigenous settlers in eastern Bolivia, see the essay in the accompanying volume to this book by Guillermo Delgado-P (2017).

95. See, for instance, Alfred 1995; Alfred 1999; Alfred 2005. See also Crosby, December 2006.

96. For the classic discussion of these dynamics, see the great work by Paulo Freire, *Pedagogy of the Oppressed* (1970). See also Alfred 1999 for a trenchant critique of and reflection on this tendency and how to overcome it. See also the essay in the accompanying volume by Taiaiake Alfred and Jeff Corntassel (2017).

97. A powerful contemporary example has been the world leadership in relation to the climate crisis that was shown in 2010 by the Indigenous-led government of Bolivia in convening the 'World Peoples' Conference on Climate Change and the Rights of Mother Earth', in Cochabamba, in April 2010, not as a follow-up to the disastrous UN Conference on Climate at Copenhagen but as a counterpoint—as an insurgent action from the South and from and by Indigenous Peoples. For details of the Conference, see Morales Ayma (President of the Plurinational State of Bolivia), January 2010; and for an introduction to the Conference and a commentary, see Sen, March 2010b.

98. Meirelles and Lund 2002; Audiard 2015.

99. See, for instance, Roszak 1969.

100. Sen 2018c.

101. See, for instance, Howell and Pearce 1998.

102. See, for instance, Hardoy and Satterthwaite 1989. For a discussion of this issue in a symbolically important situation at a very local level, the struggles for survival of hand rickshaw pullers in Calcutta (now Kolkata), see Unnayan, July 1982.

103. See my articles Sen, November 1996; Sen, July–September 1998. Emphasis added.

104. For those interested, I develop these arguments to some extent in another paper, Sen, November 2002d. See also note 6 above.

105. Sen 2018c.

OpenWord

Believing in Exclusion
The Problem of Secularism
in Progressive Politics
Anila Daulatzai[1]

This essay seeks to interrogate the privileged place implicitly assigned to secularism in contemporary radical / progressive political spaces. I will argue that the relation and adherence of progressive politics to secularism constitutes an existential crisis for radical / progressive political movements that further mirrors a crisis within Europe and the US with regard to the relation between religion and politics.

The critical conundrum begins with the fact that secularism seems to pursue a politics of diversity and non-exclusion even while negating or denying the possibility that pluralism can be pursued in non-secular ways. As I will argue, many who are explicitly committed to a politics of diversity and self-determination embrace an inherently exclusionary stance vis-à-vis political movements or individuals with religious convictions.

My earlier attempt to bring out the critical debates circulating around secularism in relation to the World Social Forum (WSF) was somewhat anaemic.[2] Since then I have been inspired by elegant elaborations which support the suspicions I have had about the privileged place assigned (unconsciously and consciously) to liberal secular ideas in the crafting of a 'new' more plural public sphere, such as the WSF. I thus reiterate my plea to those who see themselves as stakeholders in progressive political spaces to break down global power into its constitutive elements, which include discursive power and the more elusive practices and manifestations, including sentiments and affects,[3] that secularism is enmeshed in.

For the purposes of this essay, I am limiting my definition of 'progressive political spaces' to the generic. I thus include anti-war movement/s as well as the alter-globalisation and anti-neoliberalism movement/s, as exemplified by the concerns of the participants and supporters of the space created by the World Social Forum. These movements seem to share (at the minimum) a compulsion to critique existing power constellations in the world, an allegiance to a philosophy that favours self-determination and social justice, as well as a strong commitment to the advancement of diversity and pluralism.

Secularism

Secularism has come to be known as the separation of church and state; yet in this essay the meaning of secularism extends beyond this distinction to a more differentiated understanding as elaborated by Elizabeth Shakman Hurd, who explains the authoritative nature of the discourse of Euro-American forms of secularism and how they are implicated in the production of knowledges, behaviours, habits, sentiments, and practices by states, institutions, and individuals. Hurd writes that secularism "refers to a public settlement of the relationship between politics and religion", and that secularisation is "the historical process through which these settlements become authoritative, legitimated and embedded in and through individuals, the law, state constitutions, and other social relationships".[4]

Drawing on Asad, Connolly, Hirschkind, Mahmood, Scott, and others, Hurd demonstrates that secularism should not be viewed merely as the separation of church and state, but that the practices and processes that have been enabled by the demand for such a separation must be considered as central to understanding secularism. She makes the following critical points: 1) secularism is a central organisational principle of political modernity and as such is infused with power; 2) secularism is a discursive tradition and a form of political authority, an authoritative discourse; 3) the secularist imperative produces a division between religion and politics—a division not fixed but socially and historically constructed; and 4) secularism is an important locus of authority—moral, political, and cultural— that extends well beyond the reach of the state, thus sustaining enduring relations with forms of global capitalism and other overt sites of power.[5]

Secularism exists in different forms across the world depending on social and historical contingencies particular to places, as well as to the shifting and manipulative workings of the state. In India, for example, secularism is largely based on what is known as Nehruvian secularism[6]—a "demand for symmetric political treatment of different religious communities",[7] meaning that the state should protect all religions equally. Rajeev Bhargava identifies a problem with this definition of secularism: "India has yet to resolve whether non-sectarianism or non-religiosity is the true meaning of secularism appropriate in its context".[8]

The situation in Europe diverges in important ways from the Indian case, since secularism in Europe signifies primarily the separation of religion from politics and a privatisation of religion. European secularism was called into existence at a very particular historical moment (1648, with the Peace of Westphalia) to transcend certain difficulties within Christendom and the churches' involvement with politics. Although secularism was a specific theological and political move to avoid the spread of religious sectarianism throughout Europe, the limitations of secularistic practices must now be recognised. It is the Euro-American varieties of secularism—mainly laicism and Judeo-Christian secularism[9]—that I will take issue with, not only due to their sheer force but also because of the resemblances I have witnessed between these forms of secularism and the practices and sentiments with regard to religion, ethics, and politics expressed in progressive political spaces, including the WSF.

In the spaces of the WSF, which was founded in Brazil, for instance, Euro-American forms of secularism appear to be treated as normative and thus as authoritative. This is equally true of the WSF in India, underlining the normativity of the Euro-American understanding within progressive political spaces across the world. My purpose here is to critique secularistic practices, both in the North and in the South, that sanitise the public realm and public reason of religious sentiments and leave the guttural registers of being mediated by religious sentiments and affects out of public life.

My earlier rendition of this argument[10] was understood largely as critiquing progressive political spaces for not providing religion or people with religious convictions a comfortable position in the proclaimed 'open' space of progressive politics; and furthermore as claiming that progressive spaces not only excluded religion per se but one faith in particular, Islam.[11] I did make these points, yet they did not encompass the entire scope of my argument. The actions expressed by followers of the WSF (and similarly other progressive political spaces) reflect a deep critique of the global architecture of power, particularly with regard to notions of social and economic justice. Yet it seems this critique of and vigilance towards authoritative power structures is somehow suspended with regard to secularism. A replication of existing power structures takes place as a secularist ethic of political participation is promoted unquestionably in progressive political spaces such as the WSF. It is an affront to the ideals promoted by the WSF to endorse secularism when the forms of secularism expressed at the WSF replicate the authoritative forms of secularism found in Europe as well as the United States of America, which have failed miserably in attending to the dynamic relationship between religion and politics.

In this essay, Islam is the religion I discuss most, but this is not only because of the particularly suspicious and difficult position it, as well as its followers, have been mercilessly propelled into at this historical moment. As Hurd says in relation to how Islam is currently viewed in the West: "More than any other single religious or political tradition, Islam represents the 'non-secular' in European and American political discourses. . . . [A] laicist and Judeo-Christian secular West has been consolidated in part through opposition to representations of an anti-modern, anti-Christian and theocratic Islamic Middle East".[12] Beyond this, Hurd goes on to elaborate at length on how negative connotations of Islam have in fact come to constitute Euro-American secular traditions as practiced today.

I also focus on Islam, however, in order to highlight the relative ease with which sentiments hinged to Islam are instantly excluded from consideration from political action or debate by progressive movements due to forms of Islamophobia prevalent today. In this critique of the privileging of a secularistic[13] culture of politics in contemporary progressive political movements, it is not my intention to dislodge secularistic practices and replace them with a privileging of Islamic principles. My approach is rather to consider such secularistic practices as potentially problematic and full of rigidity, contradictions, and anxieties. Presenting them as problematic will hopefully push open the doors of debate enough to enable productive discussions to ensue within the space of radical / progressive politics. The aim is not to eliminate secularism or secularistic practices but to decentre their position as the only authoritative sources of public reason and to translate the normative position currently occupied by secularism into a political ethics of a plurality of norms.

In the shadows of this essay, however, there is also a preliminary interrogation of the criteria that define 'progressive' and 'radical' politics and their often taken for granted composition. These criteria are often predetermined and thus marginalise or exclude what falls outside them. I begin this interrogation by pausing at two nodal points on the plane of contemporary progressive politics—one looks at the proximity of practices of secularism to Islamophobia, and another looks at the slippages between forms of feminism and secularism. I have deliberately chosen these examples as paradigmatic of the embodiment and enactment of a particular posture of progressive politics that I seek to question. The first example is from an experience in anti-war organising and activism in the United States, and the following ones are from my experience at the WSF in India in 2004.

Practising Secularism

Professor Joe and the Muslims
An anti-war movement was developing in a politically conservative and rather elite university on the East Coast of the United States, in 2005. A young professor, whom I will call Joe, was helping the movement by trying to find ways of cultivating a greater appeal in the eyes of the students and the larger community. Joe and others asked a certain student to make efforts to encourage student groups to join the movement, as for some time the same eight to ten people had been attending the meetings. The student at the university met with and invited the representatives of eight student groups on campus, who all agreed to play a supporting role in the anti-war evening. The student came to the next organisational meeting and informed Joe and the others of what she thought of as good news.

The conversation went something like this:

Joe: "That is wonderful, which groups will be co-sponsoring the event?".

The student replies excitedly: "I managed to get the support of the Muslim, the Middle Eastern, the Iranian, and the Pakistani Student Groups, as well as the Amnesty International Chapter on Campus, the Black Student Union, the Campus Justice group concerned with diverse social justice issues, the Feminist Group on Campus, as well as full support from the Campus Inter-faith Council".

"Oh", says Joe, appearing surprised: "There seems to be an over-concentra-tion of people from over there . . . Pakistanis . . . Iranians . . . Middle Easterners . . . and then the Muslim Student Union. The groups you assembled don't seem very objective, and frankly that makes me a bit nervous. I mean we can align maybe with only some of them. It certainly makes me nervous to align with the Muslim Student Group, particularly because, you know, they come in all shapes and sizes".

Joe's 'nervousness' seemed to be shared by the other eight committed mem-bers of the anti-war group at some level or another. Did Joe (and the others) ex-pect students of Pakistani, Middle Eastern, or Iranian origin to be less concerned about the current wars with Afghanistan and Iraq? Or did their connections to these places disqualify them as legitimate anti-war activists? The sentiments Joe expressed about his discomfort with the idea that many Middle Easterners or South Asians would be joining alongside him in protest, and also his discomfort with the possibility of Muslims sharing the same protest space with him, ran dan-gerously close to a form of Islamophobia[14] on two different but related registers: firstly, Joe was nervous that the presence of Muslims and / or students from 'over there' would compromise the legitimacy of the anti-war movement; and secondly, the idea of aligning himself with a Muslim organisation triggered an instinctive discomfort in Joe and other members of the organisational committee. However, the tension, nervousness, and unease were in relation not only to Islam and Muslims but also to religious sentiments more generally. Joe was totally baffled that the student would even approach the inter-faith council to get their support: "They hardly seem radical to me".

In judging the potential political radicalism and legitimacy of certain groups, Joe appropriated and normalised notions of 'radical' and 'progressive' politics. As I argue in the next section, he thus ended up committing as well as fostering exclusionary practices, whether intended or not, based on visceral and affective registers of reflexivity. Similarly exclusionary instincts are at work in the implicit assumptions I encountered at the WSF, where I found Muslims being considered incapable of pursuing progressive political positions and Islam in itself being un-derstood as organically unable to cultivate such positions. The following example may serve to illustrate this.

The Professor at the WSF

"Why don't we admit it and say it plainly and simply?" demanded a twenty-some-thing Indian male of a small group of delegates gathered in a tent-like structure in Mumbai at the January 2004 meeting of the WSF. "Why aren't we straightforward and say that the reason Afghanistan is a failed state is its religion, the religion of Islam. Why don't people see that the real fault is in the religion?" The young man was addressing his questions to a panel of self-proclaimed 'experts' in a session titled 'Afghanistan: The First Target in the War on Terror'.

Initially, there was a gasp, as many in the room could not imagine how such words might be uttered in the sacredly tolerant space that the WSF supposedly offers. One panellist, an academic from Pakistan whom I will call 'the Professor', was the main respondent. Surprisingly, he began to give examples to support the position of the young man. His main point was that nothing positive ever came out of a place where Islam was predominant. The young man continued with disparaging comments about Islam in India and later openly declared his allegiance to the Hindu right.

This unusually explicit example about the place of religion in the WSF is not to accuse it of being anti-Islamic or of supporting the militant Hindu right, but rather to question a particular secularistic vocabulary, grammar, and culture of politics exhibited at the Forum in Mumbai, as well as at prior and subsequent Forums. Must the political arena of the WSF, which is defined as an 'open space', necessarily be a 'secular' one? Does 'open' necessarily—and only—mean 'secular'? Is it only the 'secular' who can be open? Or is this a limitation that closes potentialities by narrowing the possibilities for anti-imperial critiques and by excluding valid forms of dissent?

With this essay, I hope to show how secularistic politics can be an impediment for an emerging and growing revolutionary phenomenon because of their exclusionary and limiting tendencies. The question of *how* such practices have come to be seen as the normative expression of oppositional politics (and everything else as a deviation or an irrational misapprehension) lingers throughout the essay.

In the following sections, I draw attention, with the help of William Connolly's work, to registers of subjectivity that I suggest are being excluded from public discourse today. I also discuss particular expressions of feminism at the WSF that have an underlying 'family resemblance'[15] to secularistic practices, in terms of the way some forms of feminism privilege a particular historically and ideologically specific point of view as normative, as well as neutral and / or objective.

Lastly, in the light of this critique, I raise the possibility of a culture of politics that does not alienate believers and instead opens up the potential for new models of political pluralism. This possibility is presented against the background of the 'ethos of engagement' of William Connolly's political philosophy.[16] Throughout, I will expand and illustrate the critique by discussing specific cases, primarily from the WSF 2004 in Mumbai but also historically specific examples, to illustrate as precisely as possible my objection to the centrality of the position accorded to secularistic modes of political participation.

Affects, Experience, and Subjectivity

Connolly refers to what he calls the "visceral registers of subjectivity and intersubjectivity" as he describes the sentiments, or emotions, that secularism disallows from entering into public life.[17] I understand these visceral registers to be the historical and cultural inheritances that inform gut reactions. He uses the works of Friedrich Nietzsche, Gilles Deleuze, Michel Foucault, Talal Asad, and others, who may have differences—at times substantial and at other times more subtle—in their notions of ethics, democracy, justice, the role of religion in public life, etc, but all of whom share and maintain what Connolly refers to as "the ethical importance of engaging the visceral registers of subjectivity and intersubjectivity".[18]

Connolly outlines how instincts, the changing position of symbol and ritual in religion, and affects operate at different registers of being. He also mentions how, in expanding the possibilities for a more generous ethos of public life, these scholars emphasise a metaphysical viewpoint that is marginalised in relation to the more dominant and central (but nevertheless metaphysical) perspectives of the West. In this task of accentuating more marginal metaphysical understandings, these scholars reveal the strategies often used by secularists, in which the latter encourage others to transcend personal, culturally rooted affects, while surreptitiously allowing their own (ie, secularistic) rooted affects in through the back door—ultimately resulting in secularists assuming the authoritative position and secularistic practices being privileged as the only acceptable modes of reason in public life.

In order to illustrate my discomforts with the ethical (and other) dilemmas that lie within the problematic of secularistic practices, I offer a few specific examples from WSF 2004, held in Mumbai, India.

One of the organisations present at the Mumbai Forum was the Revolutionary Association of the Women of Afghanistan (RAWA), which in the previous years had been presented to the Western public as a paradigmatic example of progressive and transformative politics. RAWA spokesperson Sahar Saba spoke at two events in Mumbai: one was a large WSF-organised panel with Arundhati Roy, Nawal El Saadawi, and others titled 'Wars Against Women, Women Against Wars', and the other a much smaller panel organised by the Afghan Women's Mission. In both events, Saba repeatedly referred to the *burqa* as "a disgusting piece of clothing". In one event, she spoke of how the *burqa* disgusts her and how the mere sight of it sickens her.

I believe that it is critical—especially for those who consider themselves to be liberal-secular—to attend carefully to this feeling of disgust and to avoid the secular tendency that ignores altogether the visceral levels of human reaction, almost as if they do not exist. Attending to these registers would be a first step in appreciating their importance and in cultivating a culture of politics that values a plurality of sensibilities. I wish to state quite clearly that it is not that Saba had this feeling of disgust that I find problematic but the way this affect is privileged and propagated as normative over other equally valid affects.

But where do such feelings of disgust as expressed by Saba come from? Reactions like hers are an example of what Connolly refers to as the "visceral registers of subjectivity and intersubjectivity". They are formed when human beings tap into the sedimented reservoir—or "cultural repertoire" of sorts, as Asad calls it[19]—that we all have, which is a series of historical and cultural inheritances that makes a person who he or she is. Such inheritances can be contingent on and formed by multiple religious, cultural, class, gender, fashion / stylistic, and other sensibilities. The reservoir or repertoire is instinctual and often takes shape unsolicited. Connolly refers to these as "thought-imbued feelings" and emphasises Nietzsche's understanding of the "thoughts behind your thoughts and thoughts behind those thoughts"; although these are instincts, they are much more than muscular reactions or predetermined biology-based forces—rather, they are thoughts located in culturally shaped affects.[20] Connolly points to the importance of attending to these visceral registers not only because doing so will require one to work very specifically on one's own thinking, but also because it will advance a politics of becoming that is more ethical and generous, and hence more appropriate for the sort of pluralistic political ethics that this historical moment demands.

The WSF 2004 meeting in Mumbai was not the first time that RAWA and the Afghan Women's Mission had expressed feelings of repulsion and disgust not only for the Afghan *burqa* but for any headscarf for Muslim women. In numerous public fundraising events of RAWA over the prior decade, the representatives of RAWA (almost always Sahar Saba) had frequently shown videos with commentary and given lectures that communicated their disgust with the *burqa* and the veil. RAWA appeared and continues to appear as if it represents 'Afghan women', yet its political position invalidated the subjectivities of a significant majority of women in Afghanistan—local or regional, class differences notwithstanding—for whom wearing a *burqa* or a headscarf is a matter of personal choice and / or piety that is deeply rooted in their cultural and / or religious sensibilities. In many ways then, RAWA is paradigmatic of the much larger sentiment within the culture of politics that I critique here.

A RAWA spokesperson was asked in March 2004 for the magazine *Counterpunch* if she considered secularism to be a prerequisite of a successful democracy. The representative replied: "In our opinion, secularism and democracy are two sides of the same coin. Democracy without secularism is incomplete".[21] In an article written by RAWA for *Radical History Review*, it described itself as follows: "RAWA, in short, supports all movements in favor of democracy, freedom of expression, and the fulfillment of human rights and social justice".[22] The

RAWA website opens with the following statement: "If you are freedom-loving and anti-fundamentalist, you are with RAWA". Finally, the mission statement of their website offers this: "RAWA is the oldest political / social organisation of Afghan women struggling for peace, freedom, democracy and women's rights in fundamentalism-blighted Afghanistan".

These self-descriptions by RAWA, coupled with their position on the role of religious sentiment in public life, attempt to represent the organisation as embodying a normatively *superior* mode of political participation. They equate their secularistic politics with promoting human rights, democracy, peace, freedom—in essence, all that is good and rational. Crucially, implied in this is the converse of such a thought, ie, that non-secularistic politics, or political participation inflected by religious sentiments, are irrational and less capable of promoting democracy—and perhaps even incapable of doing so. What RAWA representatives and supporters may or may not have realised is that by attempting to unfetter the political sphere from the authority of the religious, they are merely replacing religion with another authority—that of secularism or secularists.

These exclusionary practices and modes of political participation / normativity were also present in the much larger session at the Mumbai WSF on women and war, with Nawal El Saadawi as one of the speakers. In my understanding, the forms of feminism maintained and promoted by both RAWA and El Saadawi are dismissive of the possibilities of religious feminisms, most specifically of Islamic feminism. Secularistic politics and Western feminism as upheld paradigmatically by RAWA entirely foreclose the possibility that a woman might autonomously choose to be veiled or covered, and that progressive politics and religion can also be two sides of one coin.

Similar to the secularistic culture of politics, notions of feminism present at the WSF operated along comparable exclusionary lines, suppressing alternative modes of female sovereignty. In the larger panel 'Wars Against Women, Women Against Wars', Egyptian scholar Nawal El Saadawi referred to Muslim women who veil themselves as "oppressed", and compared them to women who wear earrings and / or make-up, calling the latter ornaments "the postmodern veil". Similarly, in her article 'Another world is necessary', El Saadawi mocks a young veiled Pakistani woman who confronted her after her speech at the 2003 Social Forum in Porto Alegre. The young Pakistani informed El Saadawi that it was, in fact, her own decision to wear the veil, as an expression of her personal freedom. El Saadawi also mentions in the article a US woman who reprimanded her along similar lines, saying that it was her choice to wear make-up: "Why are you against make-up? How can you call it a postmodern veil?! It is a free choice!"[23]

In both instances, El Saadawi summarily dismisses the possibility that the veiled woman and / or the make-up wearing US female could exercise their freedoms and produce outcomes that were devoid of influences from what El

Saadawi calls religious and market "fundamentalisms".[24] In her speech at WSF 2004, El Saadawi further clarified her position as she spoke of Muslim women in France who were protesting against the French government's *laïcité* (secularism) law banning the veil from schools:

> In these demonstrations the young women and girls who marched in them wearing the veil were often clothed in tight fitting jeans, their faces covered with layers of make-up, their lips painted bright red, the lashes around their eyes thickened black or blue with heavy mascara. . . . Their demonstration was a proof of the link between Western capitalist consumerism and Islamic fundamentalism—how in both, money and trade ride supreme, and bend to the rule of corporate globalisation.[25]

I object to these links made by El Saadawi, as well as to her reductionist tendencies with regard to the potential roles that religion can play in a woman's life. She repeatedly refers to women who chose to wear the veil as suffering from "false consciousness", which ultimately makes such women "enemies of their freedom, enemies of themselves".[26] She even goes as far as to collapse veiling with horrific acts of rape and violence against women: "Women are increasingly exposed to patriarchal oppression; to violence; to rape; to loss of their rights in the family; to segregation, discrimination, veiling, and female genital mutilation".[27] In a similar vein, in the Afghanistan panel session with Saba, the professor I mentioned earlier followed RAWA's denouncements of the veil by adding a comparison with slaves who were liberated, but when given the choice, chose to remain slaves. He repeatedly attributed the decision to veil oneself to "false consciousness".

The core issue here is not whether wearing a veil is false consciousness or not; the question is: What kind of radical politics is promoted by such imperatives of marginalisation and exclusion? Veiling is a controversial and highly complex issue. It has received much attention, and has become an emblematic symbol of the discourse on gender and Islam—sometimes with the consequence of obscuring historical, regional, and individual particularities. Islamic feminist scholar Homa Hoodfar deepens and complicates a discussion of veiling by documenting how, for the West, the veil has symbolised, since as early as the nineteenth century, the inferiority of Muslim societies.[28] She discusses how the veil continues to be a powerful symbol both in the West and in Muslim societies. In the West, its meaning has remained largely unchanged, while in Muslim societies its function and significance have developed greatly in response to political and social movements. Hoodfar focuses on veiling as a lived experience full of contradictions and manifold meanings. She recognises how the veil has served and continues to serve as a tool in the service of patriarchal mechanisms that control women's lives, but she gives much attention to the ways Muslim women have reinscribed the significances of the veil, and in the process challenged and reformed social institutions. At the WSF, however, the veil as an expression of piety, resistance, or both was explained away as mere false consciousness by El Saadawi and the Professor. The question arises whether the enforcing of a normative, unveiled woman would be less paternalistic than the better recognised patriarchal interpretations of Islam.

The particular feminism El Saadawi is promoting is clearly a secularistic one that not only marginalises but also ridicules forms of feminism or femininity inspired by Islam, as well as other contemporary interpretations of female self-determination. I believe it is important to pay attention to the assumptions that underlie judgements about women who veil themselves; about what 'others' do and how they live their lives. Connolly warns us that the development of sensibilities is critical. When one allows one's personal gut feelings to be left unanalysed and unattended, as is the case in secularistic notions of public life such as discussed above, ethical thoughtlessness results.[29] It is precisely these sorts of exclusionary positions that I think are compromising the spirit of the open space of the WSF. El Saadawi herself nicely describes its process: "The WSF is not merely an annual event in Porto Alegre. It has become a global movement, a continuous process to create an open space *for free and equal exchange of thoughts and action*".[30] I am concerned here with the contradictions El Saadawi poses for herself, and perhaps for others. I wonder how any 'equality of exchange' can be possible when those motivated by expressions of religiosity are dismissed as 'brainwashed', suffering from false consciousness, or victims of multiple fundamentalisms. I wonder what this disquiet and these admonitions do, not only to those they are addressed to but also to those who express them.

The very simple point I am trying to make here is not so much that Saba, El Saadawi, the Professor from Pakistan, or Joe the campus anti-war organiser react to expressions of religiosity with discomfort, but that they present these reactions as *the only valid position*, and therefore as having normative status. If we are trying to create an idealised open space for 'progressive' politics, we must allow a plurality of justice-oriented sensibilities without privileging some and disallowing others. Presently, a hierarchy of affects seems to be established. One is given more value than others, and is seen as more rational and reasonable, and therefore more valid. Secularistic ideologies have come to be assumed neutral, value-free, and uncharged with historical contingency, whereas everything else is considered loaded, biased, and non-objective. As a consequence of this hierarchy, which normalises certain affects and dismisses others, people of faith are expected to contain their religious sentiments. This is an impossible task to perform. One cannot distil one's politics so that a sensibility informed by gender, culture, history, and class is completely isolated from one informed by religious sentiments. And in the case of the WSF, it is surely an unethical demand if participants whose culturally sedimented reservoir is in complete consonance with its Charter are expected to suppress just one particular aspect of what they bring into the open space of the Forum—here, the religious.

Ecologies and Emergences

A useful practice, or concept, for burgeoning political and social movements is Boaventura de Sousa Santos's idea of 'translation', with which he calls upon movements and NGOs to create contact zones open for other movements, discourses, practices, knowledges, and strategies.[31] The celebration of diversity through solidarity and the identification of shared sentiments are foundational for any counter-hegemonic movement, says Santos.

In speaking of what he calls "the sociology of absences", he identifies processes of hegemonic reason and rationality that create "non-existence", which "is produced whenever a certain entity is disqualified and rendered invisible, unintelligible, or irreversibly discarded".[32] Thus, a successful counter-hegemonic movement would include turning these absences into equally critical components of the "ecologies of knowledge".[33] Religion and religious sentiments come to my mind as such absences. Santos seems to think along similar lines: "The future of counter-hegemonic globalisation depends on a process that allows for mutual clarity among the experiences of the world, both available and possible. For example, between the concept of human rights and the Hindu and Islamic concepts of human dignity; between Western strategies of development and Gandhi's *swadeshi*".[34] A rich corpus of understanding and debates on ethics, democracy, metaphysics, and human rights is lost by the privileging of secularistic configurations—thus creating unintended forms of exclusion and marginalisation.

Connolly maintains that secularism, as it exists today in the West, is no longer an appropriate model for restricting religious dogmatism or potential sectarian conflict from entering into public life. He thoughtfully remarks that agreeing to a separation of church and state does not necessarily mean acquiescing to formations of public life laid out by secularism. Throughout his text, Connolly refers to these formations of public life constructed by secularism as "immodest" and "tone-deaf to multiple modes of suffering and subordination".[35] How can we afford to favour a conception of public life and public space that not only is 'tone-deaf' to the sufferings of many but also ignores entire registers of instincts and sensibilities? While avoiding formulaic prescriptions, it is useful to be attentive to the suggestions that Connolly offers us to begin renegotiating the terms of secularism in order for it to be more vigilant to the sensibilities that abound in contemporary political life.

Connolly repeatedly refers to several strategies that I understand as important in his concept of a public ethos of engagement—a politics of becoming that would allow for a more imaginative and deeply democratic space to emerge. He provides lucid discussions of the conservative pluralism that abounds in progressive spaces and leaves it wide open for activists and others to enact the project of radical pluralism. These strategies include but are not limited to critical responsiveness, critical reflexivity, the cultivation of ethical sensibilities, and the ethical arts of the self. Part of the artistry of the self, which Connolly views as essential, means confronting with generosity and forbearance those identities of difference each of us constructed, maintained, and participated in marginalising in order to validate our own identities. He uses Deleuze and Guattari's image of rhizomatic pluralism to outline the overlapping connections and multiple entryways for collaboration that would allow us to organise without the need for a centre.[36] He further speaks of a "plurivocity of being" that allows for similar sentiments to arise from different moral sources. In thoughtfully and thoroughly negotiating these tensions, a politics of becoming infused at every moment with a deep commitment to justice could potentially emerge.

What are the kinds of moments of agreement or potentialities that are possible but diminished by the secularistic politics of today? As an instance, at a nodal point of the so-called antiglobalisation movement in Europe, certain alliances between the movement and Islamic intellectuals have occurred and have been strongly criticised. Controversies arose, for example, about the participation of the philosopher and Islamic scholar Tariq Ramadan in the European Social Forum.[37] He was accused of anti-semitism, an accusation that thwarted more thoughtful discussions on the role of Muslims in a progressive political space. In this case, the fact that an alliance had occurred across very different domains of resistance became the issue instead of the possibilities of the alliance itself.

Ramadan's writings extensively detail the Islamic principles of justice, social welfare, community, struggles against oppressions, solidarity, education, etc and conclusively show the deep commensurability of Islam with the anti-neoliberal globalisation resistance movements.[38] He has criticised the antiglobalisation movement for a "lack of openness" to "the world of Islam".[39] In essence, he criticises the 'open space' for not allowing an alliance between the progressive movement and followers of Islamic principles. In his scholarly work, Ramadan asserts the universality, inclusivity, and openness of Islam, as a consequence of which he encourages Muslims to join resistance movements. He pleads with Muslims to understand Islamic principles such that they fight against all injustices and all forms of oppression, not only those that affect their ethnic or religious communities. Ramadan's approach is a theological one; the argument I make is rooted in the ethics of political participation. Nonetheless, we arrive at similar conclusions about the place of religion in progressive politics.

Religious Ethics and Political Action

The political sentiment represented by the WSF, according to its Charter, is supposed to celebrate diversity, to cultivate a substrate where movements can be incubated and prosper. Could it also contain the capacity to support a movement based on or inspired by Islam, or religion in general, as Ramadan advocates? Expressions of religion that do not resort to violence in any way to achieve political goals would be in consonance with the values expressed by the Charter of the WSF. I am thinking here, to give a historical example, of the anti-imperialist, non-violent *Khudai Khidmatgar* (Servants of God) movement in the North-West Frontier Province of present-day Pakistan.[40] It was inspired by Islam and led by Abdul Ghaffar Khan (1890–1988), a companion of Mahatma Gandhi (who, for his part, was inspired by Hinduism) in the independence struggle against the British Empire.

Ghaffar Khan's Islam was inclusive. It did not marginalise or alienate but presented a line of reasoning and a sentiment of sovereignty that could be reciprocated by those adopting a secularistic line (or informed by other religious traditions). Abdul Ghaffar Khan is rarely mentioned in Pakistani history books because of the particularities of the postcolonial history of Pakistan.[41] Yet his life project had many significant consequences for the subcontinent, and well beyond. Abdul Ghaffar Khan waged a relentless non-violent freedom struggle against the British Empire at great personal sacrifice. In 1929, he organised an 'army' of 100,000 Pashtuns from the North-West Frontier Province (NWFP) who vowed to fight non-violently against colonial rule, exploitation, poverty, ignorance, and injustice.

Ghaffar Khan's undertaking was a difficult one. He spent half of his life behind bars, in chains, and in exile. Yet for more than eighty years, he struggled incessantly, not only for independence from the British but also for social reform. Ghaffar Khan opened schools throughout the North-West Frontier Province, brought women into the mainstream of society, fought for more equitable land distribution, and encouraged his non-violent soldiers to commit to at least two hours of social work a day. His activism was unfalteringly rooted in his understanding of Islam, which he summarised as *amal, yakeen,* and *mohabbat* (selfless service, faith, and love).[42] Ghaffar Khan continuously challenged those who commented on the unique nature of his movement, as many erroneously believed that Muslims and Pashtuns were an inherently violent people.[43] To Ghaffar Khan and the *Khudai Khidmatgars,* there was nothing incommensurate about Islam and their anti-imperialist struggle. He would repeatedly assert:

> There is nothing surprising in a Muslim or a Pathan like me subscribing to the creed of nonviolence. It is not a new creed. It was followed fourteen hundred years ago by the Prophet all the time he was in Mecca, and it has since been followed by all those who wanted to throw off an oppressor's yoke.[44]

Ghaffar Khan and the *Khudai Khidmatgars* located the foundations for social reform, self-determination, justice, and non-violence in Islam, which enabled them to be patient and forbearing, even against the staggering violence of the British. Throughout the 1930s and '40s, the British tortured the *Khudai Khidmatgars*, imprisoned them, set their homes and agriculture fields ablaze, and massacred them, yet the *Khidmatgars* refused to abandon their non-violent resistance. Although motivated by Islam, the movement was non-sectarian. It transcended ethnic, religious, class, and national limitations.[45] When Sikhs and Hindus were attacked in Peshawar (now in Pakistan), during the partition of India by the British in 1947 into India and Pakistan, 10,000 *Khidmatgars* protected their lives and property. Similarly, as riots enveloped the central Indian state of Bihar in 1946 and 1947, Ghaffar Khan journeyed there with Gandhi to quell the violence. He worked closely with Gandhi throughout the independence movement, becoming a valued Muslim ally of Gandhi. This alliance helped to free India from the British in one of the most memorable and effective anti-imperialist struggles in history.

For Ghaffar Khan, Ramadan, and many others, religion is not an optional attachment to the resistance movements they were or are engaged in; it is elemental to it, as it is to the integrity of their personae, and their subjectivity. Religion cannot be dismissed if it has the scope to allow a person to make connections between who they are and the world they inhabit, and when it contributes to struggles against injustice and oppression without exclusion. To the contrary, the imperative of a politics of resistance free from religious sentiments will fail to address the needs of vast majorities of the planet's inhabitants as well as continue to provide opportunities for more fundamental and violent alternatives to flourish.

Conclusions

Scholars, activists, and journalists have meticulously detailed the failures of religious dogmatism. Should we not be equally thorough about addressing the limits, incongruities, and dogmatisms of secularistic politics in our world? Many philosophers and political theorists worldwide have engaged with the problematic of secularism and offered a vision of post-secularistic reason. I strongly advocate that these discussions take a more central role in emerging counter-hegemonic movements. Such movements would undermine their critical potential for a politics of diversification by being complicit in aligning uncritically with secularistic modes of political participation that speak of tolerance, democracy, non-violence, and universality but systematically impose on believers a secularistic political ethos. This complicity often aggravates and obscures the modes of suffering of those who are most marginalised. Consequently, many people are left alienated and refrain from participation in counter-hegemonic movements altogether, while believers who have chosen to participate are welcomed only as fragments.

I believe that by attending to the "visceral registers of subjectivity and intersubjectivity" it will become evident that the affective politics of secularists have been privileged and reified as normative at the expense of the affective politics of believers. The metaphysical realm constantly enters into politics, but it is not always at a level of perception that is visible to us. Thus, we must be more vigilant about addressing the relevance of bringing this metaphysical register into public discourse and debate, particularly in progressive political spheres. Neglecting this can have horrendous consequences, especially because right-wing and neoconservative political movements are successfully exploiting these affects. Attention to these affective realms would allow us to identify and dismantle the hierarchy of affects that has been unwittingly maintained in the open space of progressive politics. Focusing on the "visceral registers of subjectivity and intersubjectivity" will enable the possibility of building a movement infused with deep pluralism. Connolly lucidly argues that this would be a critical part of building a public ethos of engagement which would allow alliances between secularists as well as believers who enter into politics and advance towards the same goals but from differing starting points. As Connolly affirms, "nothing is more unrealistic today than to insist upon the incontrovertibility of a particular metaphysical faith or to pretend to bypass this dimension of politics altogether".[46]

Although general suggestions have been made here about the possibilities of reassembling progressive political spaces, I refrain from offering these suggestions as prescriptive. However, beginning discussions within and between progressive spaces directed towards addressing the affective levels of politics could be one place to start.

Finally, at the risk of appearing anachronistic, I borrow—at length—from Frantz Fanon, who, in the final chapter of *The Wretched of the Earth*, gives advice that is remarkably relevant to the problematic I have outlined in this paper. Fanon lays out the design for a new way forward. I direct his words towards those who consider themselves part of progressive movements such as the WSF, and who envision the possibility of building a new, more just, less violent world:

How is it that we do not understand that we have better things to do than to follow that same Europe?

That same Europe where they were never done talking of Man, and where they never stopped proclaiming that they were only anxious for the welfare of Man: today we know with what sufferings humanity has paid for every one of their triumphs of the mind.

Come, then, comrades, the European game has finally ended; we must find something different. We today can do everything, so long as we do not imitate Europe, so long as we are not obsessed by the desire to catch up with Europe.

Europe now lives at such a mad, reckless pace that she has shaken off all guidance and all reason, and she is running headlong into the abyss; we would do well to avoid it with all possible speed.

Yet it is very true that we need a model, and that we want blueprints and examples. For many among us the European model is the most inspiring. . . . European achievements, European techniques and the European style ought no longer to tempt us and to throw us off our balance. . . .

Let us decide not to imitate Europe; let us combine our muscles and our brains in a new direction. Let us try to create the whole man, whom Europe has been incapable of bringing to triumphant birth.

Two centuries ago, a former European colony decided to catch up with Europe. It succeeded so well that the United States of America became a monster, in which the taints, the sickness and the inhumanity of Europe have grown to appalling dimensions.

Comrades, have we not other work to do than to create a third Europe? The West saw itself as a spiritual adventure. It is in the name of the spirit, in the name of the spirit of Europe, that Europe has made her encroachments, that she has justified her crimes and legitimized the slavery in which she holds four-fifths of humanity. . . .

Today, we are present at the stasis of Europe. Comrades, let us flee from this motionless movement where gradually dialectic is changing into the logic of equilibrium. Let us reconsider the question of mankind. Let us reconsider the question of cerebral reality and of the cerebral mass of all humanity, whose connexions must be increased, whose channels must be diversified and whose messages must be re-humanized. . . .

So, comrades, let us not pay tribute to Europe by creating states, institutions and societies which draw their inspiration from her.

Humanity is waiting for something other from us than such an imitation, which would be almost an obscene caricature.

If we want to turn Africa into a new Europe, and America into a new Europe, then let us leave the destiny of our countries to Europeans. They will know how to do it better than the most gifted among us.

But if we want humanity to advance a step farther, if we want to bring it up to a different level than that which Europe has shown it, then we must invent and we must make discoveries.

If we wish to live up to our peoples' expectations, we must seek the response elsewhere than in Europe. [47]

My use of Fanon's words here is not intended as a critique of Europe per se but as a cautionary note. If the credo of the WSF—'Another World Is Possible'—is to be taken seriously, this new world should not be built on exclusionary grounds by adhering to a political ethic which caters only to those whose life choices resonate with Euro-American forms of secularism, unless the intention is to limit the possibilities for another world as to rely exclusively on Euro-American versions of the other world.

Throughout this essay I have called secularistic politics exclusionary; it might, however, be more accurate to refer to them as *unethical*. Let me use a quote by Deleuze and Guattari that I feel points out, although somewhat too harshly, the reactionary potential of the secularistic imperative: "Leftist organisations will not be the last to secrete microfascisms. It's too easy to be antifascist on the molar level, and not even see the fascist inside you, the fascist you yourself sustain and nourish and cherish with molecules both personal and collective".[48]

The way I understand it, the WSF, and progressive politics in general, need to be particularly vigilant about the creation of a space that might nurture the becoming of subjected peoples. The space must allow, on equal footing, for various possibilities of life and ways of inhabiting the world. Only through work on ourselves and on relations and understandings with others, imbued with forbearance and generosity, can we remake ourselves, remake our political community, and actively participate in the remaking of our world.

References

Talal Asad, 2003—*Formations of the Secular: Christianity, Islam, Modernity*. Stanford: Stanford University Press

Mukulika Banerjee, 2000—*Pathan Unarmed: Opposition and Memory in the North West Frontier*. Oxford: Oxford University Press

Rajeev Bhargava, 1998—'Introduction', in Rajeev Bhargava, ed, 1998—*Secularism and its Critics*. Oxford: Oxford University Press

William E Connolly, 1995—*The Ethos of Pluralisation*. Minneapolis, MN: University of Minnesota Press

William E Connolly, 1999—*Why I am Not a Secularist*. Minneapolis, MN: University of Minnesota Press

Anila Daulatzai, 2004—'A Leap of Faith: Notes on Secularistic Practices and Progressive Politics', in *The International Social Science Journal*, issue 182, December 2004

Gilles Deleuze and Félix Guattari, 1980—*Mille plateaux*. Paris: Minuit. [Published in English as *A Thousand Plateaus: Capitalism and Schizophrenia*, translated by Brian Massumi. Minneapolis, MN: University of Minnesota Press, 1987]

Eknath Easwaran, 1984—*Nonviolent Soldier of Islam: Badshah Khan, A Man to Match His Mountains*. New Delhi: Penguin

Nawal El Saadawi, 2003—'Keynote address', at the 'European Union Forum on Gender, Peace and Foreign Policy', Athens, June 12 2003, at http://www.nawalsaadawi.net/articles/2003/athenskeynote.htm (Accessed September 7 1999, inactive August 16 2017)

Nawal El Saadawi, 2004a—'Another World Is Necessary', in Jai Sen, Anita Anand, Arturo Escobar, and Peter Waterman, 2004—*World Social Forum: Challenging Empires*. New Delhi: The Viveka Foundation, pp 136–39

Nawal El Saadawi, 2004b—'War against Women and Women against War: Waging War on the Mind'. Paper presented at the World Social Forum, Mumbai, at www. nawalsaadawi.net/oldsite/articlesnawal/MumbaiNawalPaper.DOC (Accessed September 7 1999, inactive August 16 2017)

Arturo Escobar, 2004—'Other Worlds Are (Already) Possible: Self-Organisation, Complexity, and Post-Capitalist Cultures', in Jai Sen, Anita Anand, Arturo Escobar, and Peter Waterman, eds, 2004—*World Social Forum: Challenging Empires*. New Delhi: The Viveka Foundation, pp 349–358, at http://www.choike.org/documentos/ wsf_s506_escobar.pdf (Accessed August 16 2017)

Frantz Fanon, 1963—*The Wretched of the Earth*. New York: Grove Press

Homa Hoodfar, 1997—'The Veil in Their Minds and on Our Heads: Veiling Practices and Muslim Women', in Lisa Lowe and David Lloyd, eds, 1997—*The Politics of Culture in the Shadow of Capital*. Durham, NC: Duke University Press

Elizabeth Shakman Hurd, 2007—*The Politics of Secularism in International Relations*. Princeton: Princeton University Press

Jeffrey S Juris, 2008—*Networking Futures: The Movements Against Corporate Globalization*. Durham, NC: Duke University Press

Muhammad Soaleh Korejo, 1993—*The Frontier Gandhi: His Place in History*. New York: Oxford University Press

Brian Massumi, 2002—*Movement, Affect, Sensation: Parables for the Virtual*. Durham, NC: Duke University Press

Caroline Mannot and Xavier Ternisien, 2003—'Tariq Ramadan accused of anti-Semitism', in *Watch*, October 14 2003

Tariq Ramadan, 2004—*Western Muslims and the Future of Islam*. New York: Oxford University Press

Ra Ravishankar, 2004—'Afghanistan: The Liberation That Isn't: An Interview with "Mariam" from RAWA', in *Counterpunch*, March 2 2004, at http://www. counterpunch.org/rawa03022004.html (Accessed October 21 2009, inactive August 16 2017)

RAWA (Revolutionary Association of the Women of Afghanistan), 2002—'Shoulder to Shoulder, Hand in Hand: Resistance under the Iron Fist in Afghanistan', in *Radical History Review*, 82

Boaventura de Sousa Santos, 2004a—'The World Social Forum: Towards a Counter-Hegemonic Globalisation (Part I)', in Jai Sen, Anita Anand, Arturo Escobar, and Peter Waterman, eds, 2004—*World Social Forum: Challenging Empires*. New Delhi: The Viveka Foundation, pp 235–45, at http://www.boaventuradesousasantos.pt/media/ wsf_JaiSenPart1.pdf (Accessed August 16 2017)

Boaventura de Sousa Santos, 2004b—'The WSF: Towards a Counter-Hegemonic Globalisation (Part II)', in Jai Sen, Anita Anand, Arturo Escobar, and Peter Waterman, eds, 2004—*World Social Forum: Challenging Empires*. New Delhi: The Viveka Foundation, pp 336–43, at https://pdfs.semanticscholar. org/0931/749f4fb530d9e82f2ed58d8ef652c387d9a3.pdf (Accessed August 16 2017)

Joan Wallach Scott, 2007—*The Politics of the Veil*. Princeton: Princeton University Press

Amartya Sen, 1998—'Secularism and its Discontents', in Rajeev Bhargava, ed, 1998—*Secularism and its Critics*. Oxford: Oxford University Press

Ludwig Wittgenstein, 2001—*Philosophical Investigations: The German Text, with a Revised English Translation*, third edition. Oxford: Blackwell

Notes

1. I am grateful for the friendship and intellectual support given to me by Roger Begrich and Hussein Agrama, especially during the writing of this essay. I also thank Jai Sen and Vipul Rikhi for their patience and skilful editorial comments. I would like to extend my gratitude for the support given to me by Professor George Fisher, the Institute for Global Studies and the Center for a Livable Future at Johns Hopkins University for making possible my presence at the WSF 2004 in Mumbai, India, and UNESCO and Jai Sen for my presence and participation at the WSF 2005 in Porto Alegre, Brazil. My acknowledgments for my work here (and in general) end where I began—my parents and my siblings, for their endless commitment to my development as a scholar and human being.

2. Daulatzai 2004.

3. The term 'affect' will often be used in this essay. Although a much more nuanced conception of affect has been carefully worked out by Brian Massumi in his book *Movement, Affect, Sensation: Parables for the Virtual* (Massumi 2002), 'affect' can more simply be understood as emotion, intensity, or feeling.

4. Hurd 2007.

5. Hurd 2007.

6. For details on the specifics surrounding debates on secularism in India, I recommend *Secularism and its Critics* (Bhargava, ed, 1998).

7. Sen 1998, p 484.

8. Bhargava 1998, p 19.

9. The two most significant forms of secularism in contemporary politics have been laicism and Judeo-Christian secularism. Both of them try to maintain the separation of church and state in different arrangements and with different claims. Laicism is the French version of secularism (unique to French history and linked with French republicanism and universalism): it is the separation of church and state through the state's protection of individuals from the claims of religion. It rests heavily on the assumption that a neutral space is created where religious belief and practice are distinct from politics or the political. Judeo-Christian secularism does not seek to banish religion entirely from public life—or at least not the Judeo-Christian faiths—because the instincts and affects of Judeo-Christianity are already inscribed in the political order, thus not requiring the complete banishment of religion from politics. For more detail on laicism, please refer to Scott 2007; for more elaboration of both laicism and Judeo-Christian secularism see Hurd 2007.

10. Daulatzai 2004.

11. Juris 2008.

12. Hurd 2007, p 7.

13. Throughout this essay I use the adjective 'secularistic' in order to describe practices or forms of political ethics that are informed by imaginations of secularism. It is therefore related to, but not synonymous with, the term 'secular'.

14. The Oxford English Dictionary defines Islamophobia as "a hatred or fear of Islam or Muslims, especially feared when it is a political force". Islamic scholar Tariq Ramadan makes a critical distinction in defining Islamophobia: "We have to distinguish between two things. To criticise the religion and Muslims is not Islamophobia; a critical attitude towards religion must be accepted. But to criticise someone or discriminate against them only because they are Muslim—this is what we can call Islamophobia, this is a kind of racism" (Ramadan 2004).

15. The idea of "family resemblances" to describe the ways in which certain aspects are common to a category, ie, through their similarities and the relationships between them, goes back to Ludwig Wittgenstein's philosophy of language (Wittgenstein 2001).

16. Connolly 1995, 1999.

17. Connolly 1999.

18. Connolly 1999, p 15.

19. Asad 2003.

20. Connolly 1999, p 28.

21. Ravishankar 2004.

22. RAWA 2002.

23. El Saadawi 2004a. El Saadawi mocks these two women with these words: "I smiled, 'Yes, you are free like the free market, like George W Bush, like Ariel Sharon, like Adolf Hitler; you are free!'"

24. El Saadawi 2003, 2004a.

25. El Saadawi 2004b.

26. El Saadawi 2003, 2004a, 2004b.

27. El Saadawi 2003.

28. Hoodfar 1997.

29. Connolly 1999.

30. El Saadawi 2004a, p 138. Emphasis added.

31. Santos 2004a, 2004b.

32. Santos 2004a, p 238.

33. Santos 2004a, p 239.

34. Santos 2004b, p 342.

35. Connolly 1999.

36. Gilles Deleuze and Félix Guattari introduce the concept of the *rhizome* as an emblem for new forms of politics, thought, and ways of life that are not trapped within the rigid confines of totalising Western thought and hierarchical structures, such as those within and between nation-states, languages, and so on. Rhizomes are horizontal, root-like stems that extend underground and send out shoots to the surface, connecting plants in a living network. They are particularly appealing as a metaphor because, in contrast to trees, which are stationary, of a single origin and firmly rooted, rhizomes constantly negotiate and create new roots and lines of connections in the processes of their development. A rhizome rejects authoritarian logics and is nomadic and acentric, which enables it to capture multiplicities of meaning in the processes of becoming. Deleuze and Guattari advocate revolutionary practices that nurture metaphysical relations and propagate assemblages of affect that affirm differences. The "assemblages" they describe are created by linkages

between differing systems of knowledge formation, which can connect and produce potential new forms of thought and politics in nomadic and non-hierarchical ways within and across domains. With their concepts of *rhizome* and *assemblage*, Deleuze and Guattari deliver analytical tools that can help in sketching out the possibilities of pluralistic, transformative progressive politics. Manuel de Landa's notion of "meshworks" is very similar, described by Arturo Escobar as a metaphoric network topology that should be considered for a politics of emergence (Escobar 2004).

37. I commend the organisers of the European Social Forum (ESF), and particularly Jose Bové, for allowing Ramadan to contribute actively to the ESF despite the intense pressure on them to ban his participation.

38. Ramadan 2004.

39. Mannot and Ternisien 2003.

40. Books on the life and work of Abdul Ghaffar Khan are limited. In fact, it is difficult to find a single book on him in Pakistan due to his anti-Partition stance. The books by Banerjee (2000), Easwaran (1984), and Korejo (1993) have been quite useful to me in understanding various aspects of Ghaffar Khan and his movement. I have done much research, including oral histories, over fifteen years of visiting the majority Pashtun areas of Pakistan, as well as speaking to non-Muslims who now live in India, but who lived in Pashtun areas of what is now Pakistan during the *Khudai Khidmatgar* movement. I have done this to augment, and sometimes question, the information presented in these books. This has been an ongoing and endless process of inquiry for me. I owe my knowledge of Abdul Ghaffar Khan to my father Mohammad Ashiq Daulatzai. I am grateful for being truly enriched by his expansive knowledge of the region and enchanted by his compassionate yet critical comments on Abdul Ghaffar Khan. I also thank B P Singh for his generous spirit and infectious love for and knowledge of Abdul Ghaffar Khan.

41. To say that Abdul Ghaffar Khan's omission from Pakistani national history is due to the 'particularities of the postcolonial history of Pakistan' could be considered euphemistic. State-engineered amnesia resulted in Abdul Ghaffar Khan and the *Khudai Khidmatgars* being written out of the national history of Pakistan or, if present, being represented as traitors. Furthermore, the newly found freedom for the subcontinent meant nothing but continued subjugation for Abdul Ghaffar Khan and the Pashtuns. While people from NWFP built the core of the masses who fought against British imperialism, the state of Pakistan made sure that there would be no rightful place in the country's memory for those who opposed bifurcating the subcontinent along religious lines. As a result, Abdul Ghaffar Khan alone spent fifteen years behind bars *after* independence, while scores of his followers spent countless years in Pakistani jails as well. Cricket players, musicians, and politicians line the avenue in Rawalpindi as recognised heroes of Pakistan, but there is no place there for Abdul Ghaffar Khan and the *Khudai Khidmatgars*.

42. Easwaran 1984, p 63.

43. Pashtuns are also referred to as Pathans, Pukhtoons, Pakhtuns, and Pushtuns. Pashtuns are separated by the Durand Line, a somewhat arbitrary border between Afghanistan and Pakistan that was engineered by the British in 1893. Timothy Flinders notes that the word Pakhtun became Pathan in British India, and it is the word that is used in the English language to describe Pashtuns. However, the word

Pathan contains vestiges of colonial manipulation and thus Pashtun / Pakhtun / Pukhtoons / Afghans are the dialect variations and preferred terminology not only for Ghaffar Khan, but for most Pashtuns, in order to reflect the unity of Pashtuns on both sides of the Afghanistan-Pakistan border.

44. Easwaran 1984, p 103.

45. Although India gained independence in 1947, it was a time of great sorrow for Abdul Ghaffar Khan and his movement. They had vehemently opposed the partitioning of India, and once Pakistan was created Abdul Ghaffar Khan refused to accept its existence. He was therefore imprisoned for more than fifteen years by the Government of Pakistan, and later lived in self-imposed exile. He unfortunately resorted to ethnic nationalism after the partition of India in attempts to disallow the marginal treatment of Pashtuns.

46. Connolly 1999, p 187.

47. Fanon 1963.

48. Deleuze and Guattari 1980 [1987], p 215.

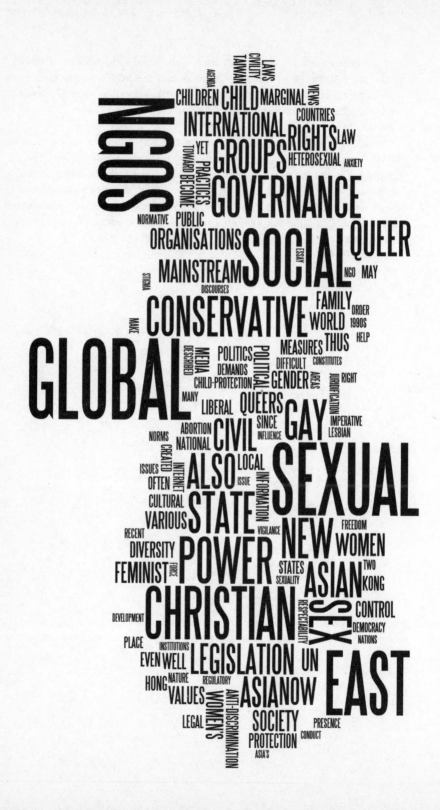

Is Global Governance Bad for East Asian Queers?[1]
Josephine Ho

Introduction

The rise of transnational systems and networks of governance and norms since the 1990s has fostered the hope that a new global order, described by the UN as "global governance", operating through shared goals, purposes, and values, as well as consensus, would be created in place of state authority and brute force.[2] The emergence of a so-called 'global civil society' holds out further hope for democratic potentials that promise to promote the spirit of responsible humanitarianism as well as respect for diversity, while weakening state power and domination in certain national contexts. In the developing liberal democracies of East Asia, optimistic LGBT advocates and marginal groups look to changing, and seemingly liberalising, political regimes and expanding civil society as sites for possible leverage or gains, while pride marches, lesbian and gay cultural events, and booming queer Internet communities corroborate the impression that queer Asia may be much more than a concept.[3]

Yet as the new global order evolved in recent years, such euphoric feelings have been punctured by growing retrenchment in the same region as various states take up measures quite inhospitable to queer existence. Police raids on Taiwan's only gay bookstore in 2003 and on gay home parties since 2004 fuelled public impression of gay decadence and a resultant spread of HIV; subsequent litigation further intensified fear and intimidation.[4] Gatherings such as gay parties, exhibitions, performances, and forums, even picnics were banned in Singapore in 2004 and 2007.[5] On the grounds that lesbian and gay rights have not achieved social consensus, gay-sponsored anti-discrimination legislation met with repeated defeat in Hong Kong, and broad-based anti-discrimination legislation ended up excluding sexual orientation in both Singapore and South Korea in 2007.[6] Gay- and lesbian-oriented radio programme content was chastised by broadcasting authorities as outright obscene in Taiwan in 2004 or characterised by Christian civil organisations as "biased towards homosexual marriage and thus inappropriate for children" in Hong Kong in 2007.[7] Thanks to the efforts of Christian child-protection organisations, helped in no small way by East Asia's sensationalising media, a heightened sense of vigilance is now pervasive with the result that, depending on the national context, legislation is either in place or underway to circumscribe all sexual communication and contact on the Internet.[8]

While such events are often described as either the natural outcome of democratic processes or well-meaning universal measures of obscenity and crime prevention, two significant observations demonstrate otherwise. First, Christian-based civil organisations were not only actively involved in many of these processes but quite aggressive in promoting social discontent and mobilising opposition against the growing visibility of gay lifestyles and the equity demands launched by queer activism.[9] Beyond this, East Asia's new liberal states, interpreting democracy as majority rule, have made it conveniently workable to claim respect for diversity while staunchly upholding and reaffirming mainstream values. Curiously, these two developments mostly work together to boost the public image and political power of both the Christian organisations and the liberal states. One cannot help but wonder: How do Christian civil organisations achieve such influential positions within East Asian societies despite the Christian community's minority status?[10] And what do these recent developments in East Asia reveal about liberal democracy's own limits in promoting marginal issues of social justice?

This essay contends that answers to these important questions are located in our current context of global governance and global civil society. Fortified by UN discourse and worldwide policy directives that have been set in place by aspiring nation-states in collaboration with local civil organisations (the most aggressive ones being fundamentalist Christian), a new 'reign of civility' has been widely popularised in the socially and politically volatile spaces of East Asia, and this is now producing detrimental effects on queer lives through increased media sensationalism, police-baiting, recriminalisation, and recurrent sex panic, not to mention new sex-repressive legislative reform measures.

The analysis that follows centres on two major aspects of this development. First, the emerging global hegemony of morality that is stepping up its assault on queer representations and queer interaction through new local legislation and litigation against queer social presence, as well as through mobilising and transforming conservative vigilance into an active surveillance network that thrives on fanning sex panic. Second, the construction of 'child protection' as a universal imperative that in actuality both reinforces heterosexual monogamy and attacks cultural diversity as inherently confusing and thus harmful for children.[11] This hegemony of morality and its child protection campaign constitutes an important and growing offensive by conservative forces as they navigate the new world order of global governance.

Global Governance and the Reign of Civility and Respectability

Since the 1990s, 'governance' has been used by international organisations such as the World Bank and the International Monetary Fund (IMF) to evaluate the political status of countries in need of aid as well as their suitability for a free market economy, so as to remove all obstacles to free trade while ensuring the countries' ability to repay debt. Viewed in this light, the release in 1995 of the United Nations report *Our Neighbourhood: Report of the Commission on Global Governance* and the urgency and speed with which 'global governance' has been popularised and aggressively promoted in various regions reflects efforts to forge new social realities in preparation for economic globalisation.[12] In place of state-oriented approaches to global politics, this UN report proposed a new conception (and the emerging operations) of the institutions, practices, and processes for organising global politics in the post-Cold-War era.

This new global order is being conducted mainly through multiple and flexible interactions among intergovernmental organisations (IGOs), such as the UN, the World Trade Organization (WTO), the World Bank, and the IMF, and their various treaties; NGOs (non-governmental organisations) and their activism; multinational corporations (MNCs) and their operations; and existing but allegedly weakened nation-state governments. In addition to the usual powerful players in international politics, the UN Secretary General envisions 'NGOs' as "indispensable partners" of the UN "in the process of deliberation and policy formation", as well as in "the execution of policies".[13] The UN has since enlisted an army of NGOs to raise public awareness of the need for international cooperation and to advance the report's agenda, outlined as the 'Charter for Global Democracy'.[14] Participation in such UN projects in turn adds to the political weight of local NGOs, which now find themselves involved in global negotiations and international politics, even capable of formulating rules of conduct for nation-states.[15] The resulting complex, explicit, implicit, and evolving system of interlocking unilateral, bilateral, and multilateral bodies of rules and documents gradually assumes the role of global principles and values, while new circuits and networks of power continue to emerge.

While the complex nature of and vast differences among transnational NGOs are said to mitigate the possibility of a benign and integrated 'global civil society' working towards the common dual goals of human rights and democracy, the actual politics of NGOs working across national borders is much more volatile and often variously implicated in different circles of political involvement.[16] There is, after all, nothing intrinsically progressive or democratic about international civil society. International NGOs have been known to set up branches in Third World nations not only as channels for needed funding and aid but more importantly as a field where Western values and interests can exercise their influence and foster checks and balances to resist local state domination and control.[17] Well meaning development projects executed by well-meaning NGOs may intend to promote population management, disease prevention, and maternal and child health, yet they often also end up intentionally or unwittingly shaping ideas about what constitutes 'normal', and thus acceptable, sexual practices and identities.[18]

Conversely, East Asia's liberal states are increasingly aware of the political expedience of choosing the right NGO delegates to attend international gatherings so as to guarantee presence but also safeguard national image; the choice of delegates naturally favours the mainstream and normative over the marginal and difficult. Tensions and contradictions among civil organisations of different origins and ideologies are also complex. Within this new global public, emergent indigenous social movements could even find themselves suffering more from policy directives enforced by world powers at the urging of such NGOs than from the usual culprit of the authoritarian state.[19] In these and other cases, the intermingling of NGOs of different calibres, with governments of different democratic formations, further complicates regional differences, resulting in complex webs of conflicting and collaborating forces that range far beyond the circuits of power described by the so-called boomerang pattern of transnational advocacy.[20]

Despite the structural complexity of this expanding global civil society, the consensus-building negotiations of global governance are predisposed to favour visions and values that congeal towards mainstream normative values, now expressed as global commonalities. The UN report calls for establishing a "global civic ethic" based on "a set of core values that can unite people of all cultural, political, religious, or philosophical backgrounds".[21] As appealing as this imaginary brotherhood or sisterhood may sound, such core values have had only partial success, and mostly only on broad topics such as universal human rights or global environmental concerns, but even there disputes and cultural differences run deep. The problems of universalism aside, the envisioned 'global' and 'civic' ethic—with its inherent assumptions about shared cultural commonality and cherished nationalistic civility—has tended to find its baseline of agreement in those areas most deeply entrenched in benign but unreflexive humanism, areas where longstanding differences are glossed over and long-held prejudices and fears remain buried and unchallenged, areas where the demands of modernisation and the civilising process find ready and unproblematic targets for scorn; and there is perhaps no better choice for targeting than the long stigmatised subject of sex.[22] And as technology enabled global access to sexual information and sexual contact, further heightening social anxieties, media-produced sex panics have helped facilitate the compelling success of global ratification of international agreements on stringent but often indiscriminating measures directed at Internet content monitoring in the name of the prevention of (sex) trafficking, child pornography, and paedophilia.[23]

This success in global negotiations over the restriction of sexual information and contact has a lot to do with the specific nature of power under global governance. As Raimo Väyrynen points out:

In the multicentric world, power not only is dispersed, but it also assumes more forms than the traditional power analysis suggests. For instance, power can also be *symbolic and reputational*, as well as material, and it may reflect conventions and narratives. The fluidity of "soft" power means that it is difficult to capture and use for specific purposes. One implication of this state of affairs is that, in the multicentric world, traditional power resources alone cannot assure stability and progress; the management of power must be based also on *norms and institutions*.[24] Emphasis added.

"Norms and institutions" refer to structural constraints embodied in various international conventions and agencies and more significantly in local legislations; in other words, they tend to presume normative lifestyles and values that are to be regulated by legal frameworks. "Symbolic and reputational", on the other hand, signals a form of power that rides mostly on gestures and tokens and consequently is extremely sensitive and apprehensive about possible scandal, which finds its most potent embodiment in things sexual. In other words, the nature and structure of the world of diffused power also render it vulnerable to populist demands, demands that are usually inclined to sidestep the difficult, the unpopular, and, in particular, the stigmatised. The norms underlying global propositions thus tend to gravitate towards 'respectability', and towards: "norms that repress sexuality, bodily functions, and emotional expression. . . . [T]he respectable person is chaste, modest, does not express lustful desires, passion, spontaneity, or exuberance, is frugal, clean, gently spoken, and well mannered. The orderliness of respectability means things are under control, everything in its place, not crossing the borders".[25]

Such norms of civility and respectability, with their inherent proclivity for order and control, are most relevant for our understanding of East Asia's new liberal democracies and their increasing collaboration with Christian NGOs in the construction of what looks more and more like what Jock Young has described as "exclusive societies". What interests me most about Young's theory is his attention to the ever-expanding exclusionary system of crime prevention (detailed in the next section) and its correlation with the increase of "difference and difficulty", the pluralisation and fragmentation of identities and lifestyles, and the fears and responses they engender.[26] While Young's analysis centres mainly on changes in technologies of social control that constitute the changing nature of state, civil society, and public realm in post-war United States, his observation is illuminating for our understanding of recent developments in East Asian democracies as the latter scramble to rein in increases in incivilities and active challenges to rules that accompany profound transformations in political and economic restructuring. As contemporary conflicts around sexual relations tend to acquire "immense symbolic weight" in the process,[27] such exclusive measures also tend to concentrate on the sexual realm and its emergent diversity.

What is unique about East Asian exclusive societies is that an exclusive civil society made up of Christian NGOs and morally like-minded conservative NGOs has now emerged in the newly invigorated public sphere. This is a civil society that embraces mutual interpenetration with the state so as to help better manage what is perceived as the unruliness of contemporary sexual libertarianism. As compliance with standards of civic respectability has become a token of legitimacy and political correctness in international relations, this new deployment of normative power also tends to favour a global social milieu in which non-normative sexualities are deemed possible threats or undesirable practices. Significantly, it is in the *legal* domain that this suturing of global governance, nation-state aspirations, and pastoral impulses of Christian NGOs into a reign of civility and respectability is most concretely effected, as fragile nation-states, with the help of Christian NGOs weaving anxiety and uncertainty into popular support, fortify themselves into new regulatory states by increasingly regulating sexual acts, identities, information, and exchanges through codified laws aligned with so-called global standards. The fiercest battles have been fought in the legal domain as marginal NGOs working towards sexual justice and freedom of expression struggle against the 'soft power turned iron rule' of governance.[28]

The Juridification of Global Governance

The UN Commission on Global Governance decrees that governance be underpinned by democracy on all levels and ultimately 'by the rule of enforceable law'. Nations are thus strongly encouraged to bring their laws into alignment with UN decrees. With the blessing of the UN, conservative NGOs in various East Asian countries have been rallying legislators to amend old laws and institute new laws concentrated in sex-related areas in accordance with a conservative agenda now described as concretising UN standards. This significant redeployment of power, which Jürgen Habermas has aptly described as "juridification" in our late modern era, asserts itself by having more and more formal laws created in the sociocultural sphere, the private sphere, and the body-related sphere, the density of which leaves little social space outside the reach and definition of the law.[29] In fact, with the active involvement, if not total initiative, of mainstream women's NGOs in collaboration with conservative Christian NGOs, legislation that aggressively regulates sexual conduct, contact, and information—in the name of modern civility and gender equity—has already come into place all over East Asia despite resistance by sex emancipationist feminists.[30] Along with the regulation of sexual harassment and sexual assault, these now include artificial insemination, HIV-status, new sex-related drugs such as RU486, and, most importantly, sexual information and interaction on the Internet. The increasing codification of conduct previously located in the private realm is interpreted by such mainstream

NGOs as enhancing protection for women and children and by the state as proof of responsible government, ready to be presented to the international community as evidence of democratic progress towards a rational 'rule of law'. Yet for those who now fall victim to such jurisdiction, the laws have practically redefined their daily life practices as nothing short of criminal.

In many East Asian countries, NGO-sponsored conservative legislation and surveillance of sex-related activities and information on the Internet have made it quite difficult for queers to conduct their most common forms of flirtation and sexual negotiation. In Taiwan, where nation-statehood is fragile and juridifica-tion fiercely underway as a top priority for Christian NGOs, any sexually explicit message on the Internet (such as describing the size of one's penis or inviting a bottom or a master to collaborate in sexual play), even in clearly marked adult chat rooms or adult BBSs, is now considered harmful for the young and thus subject to indictment.[31] Local gay and lesbian groups have joined human rights groups in 2006 in demanding that the Constitutional Court examine such legal clauses to ascertain whether they violate basic freedoms of speech and expression as decreed by the Constitution.

Unfortunately, the Justices of the Constitutional Court came up with only an equivocal response that again affirms the importance of child protection over freedom of speech.[32] It is now obvious that comprehensive and universal child protection legislation, which is in effect also anti-sex legislation, has greatly exac-erbated the already existing social and sexual stigma of marginal sexualities and their practices, not to mention bringing actual litigation against many individ-uals. Increasingly, social differences are no longer dealt with through the com-municative reason of public debate; instead, the force of law is directly applied. Non-negotiable disciplinary management has now replaced rational debates and communication in dealing with gender and sexual diversity.

Incidentally, as NGOs find more and more room for involvement in na-tional and transnational politics in the age of global governance, NGO status has also become desirable and even profitable currency. Significantly, aggressive Christian groups in East Asia have learned to refrain from presenting themselves as 'Christian' groups or churches to the public; instead, they have created par-allel civil organisations to soften their religious image. Describing themselves as conducting the business of 'social movements', a string of such parallel civil organisations has come into being since the 1990s in various East Asian coun-tries and areas.[33] As only officially registered NGOs are eligible for government funding and franchise application, the transformation does bring important and practical benefits, but it also crowds out marginal and difficult NGOs that do not necessarily tow the mainstream line.[34] Such parallel civil organisations also make it more convenient to rally other social movement groups around topical though conservative causes such as media monitoring.[35] The NGO-isation of Christian groups has been so successful that one of them has even won quite a few NGO-related international awards, thus greatly enhancing its social status and power of influence in national politics.[36] The flexibility with which Christian groups in East Asia adapted to this age of secularism and NGO operation often obscures their origin to such an extent that it is increasingly difficult to recognise their true nature, which also complicates the struggle of social movements in general when opposing views stand starkly against each other on the same issue within civil society.

With its pernicious effect clearly in sight, juridification also holds out the prospect of protection by the law. East Asian queers, like queers everywhere, had hoped that new anti-discrimination legislation could help mitigate the social ills of homophobia and sex phobia. Yet as we have witnessed so far, such proposed legislation, if it comes up at all, has already been rejected in Singapore, South Korea, and Hong Kong. The obstacles that such legislation has faced have a lot to do with two NGO conglomerates whose recent aggressiveness has received increasing encouragement from the general system of global governance.

The first NGO conglomerate that poses a problem is, surprisingly, mainstream women's (not necessarily feminist) NGOs in East Asian countries. While pushing for general anti-discrimination legislation, most women's NGOs are reluctant to incorporate sexual orientation in their claims, fearing that sexual stigma would hinder women's own hard-fought equal rights claims.[37] UN-sponsored 'gender mainstreaming' may have propagated the gender analytic with its implicit biological framework, but that analytic has often elided discussions about sexual orientation and gender variance. After all, gender mainstreaming aims to mainstream gender, not gender marginalities, much less sexual marginalities and diversity. On the issue of sexuality, the core feminist project of sexual self-determination has continuously restricted itself to heteronormalcy and the right to refuse unwanted sexual advances, which in turn converges nicely with Christian NGOs' advocacy of abstinence-oriented sex education. In that sense, such a feminist agenda may not cohere with queer sex rights at all.

Aside from the mainstreamers, feminist sex radicals do exist in East Asia, but their presence and power of influence are continually circumscribed by mainstream feminists who denounce sex-positive views as un-feminist.[38] In Taiwan, where feminist sex radicals, including the present author, spearheaded liberal and radical views on female sexuality, our sex-positive views met with a string of purges in the feminist community. Sex emancipationist feminists were excommunicated in 1995 from the Taiwanese Feminist Scholars Association that they had helped create,[39] and feminist staff members who supported sex work rights were fired from a leading feminist organisation in 1997.[40] And, as this happened, so-called 'state feminists' were invited to join the government cabinet in 2000, which gave them a chance to turn their own family-oriented heteronormal agenda into state policies and laws in regard to childcare and prevention of domestic violence.[41]

Simply put, most women's NGOs in East Asia are not ready to tackle the force of sexual stigma that surrounds issues of sexual diversity or sexual pleasure. Some even capitalise on such social inhibition by demanding, to the dismay of queers, more protective surveillance or correction institutions, as well as sex-phobic legal codes, all in the name of protecting women or, ominously, children.

In addition to the cold shoulder of mainstream women's groups, queer causes face real and formidable foes in East Asia's Christian-based conservative NGOs. Spurred on by a sense of imminent crisis in the profound social change resulting from globalisation but feeling 'liberated' by the ideas of pluralism and multiculturalism to propagate their discriminatory discourses and their vendetta against anything non-normative, conservative religious (Christian) groups have become dramatically outspoken in their concerted opposition to gay rights in recent years. In Hong Kong, Alliance for Family, an anti-gay Christian front, bought a four-page advertisement in a major local newspaper on April 29 2005 detailing the dangers of homosexuality and calling on Hong Kong residents to rise up against the proposed anti-discrimination legislation that, according to the Christian group, would unleash the danger of gay sex for public health in addition to eroding the monogamous heterosexual family. This was the first massive and open demonstration of conservative forces against queers in Hong Kong.[42] In Taiwan, city legislators associated with Exodus International, an international Christian organisation that advocates "freedom from homosexuality through the power of Jesus Christ", demanded in 2006 that Taipei city government withdraw its annual funding for gay civic causes, which had been the city's pledge to diversity.[43] In South Korea, a powerful conservative Christian lobby triumphed by persuading the legislative body that if the non-discrimination bill were passed, "homosexuals will try to seduce everyone, including adolescents; victims will be forced to become homosexuals; and sexual harassment by homosexuals will increase".[44]

It is obvious that the religious right in East Asia has stepped up its efforts to stop anti-discrimination legislation. With a longstanding global missionary network, loaded with historical ties to the colonial past and its hierarchies, the Christian-based opposition has, in a perverted way, usurped the strategies and energies created by marginal social movements and now works aggressively to characterise queer existence as an alarming global trend that will damage the young and fragile.[45] For the traditional family-oriented Chinese, the 'queer scare' has not only displaced social and parental anxiety and fear induced by globalisation onto local queers and the latter's proposed anti-discrimination legislation but also encouraged litigation against previously acceptable queer practices. The prosecution and eventual conviction of Taiwan's only gay bookstore, GinGin's, in 2005 for "dissemination of obscene materials" serves as a sobering reminder that the law is now being employed to make a statement about queer cultural visibility.

It is noteworthy that in East Asia both mainstream women's NGOs and conservative Christian NGOs have chosen to abide by the most basic form of 'sexual fundamentalism': the notion that there is a singular, ideal sexuality (heterosexual, marital, procreative) and two genders (man and woman), and that those conforming to this standard have a right to police and control others, often by creating and enforcing new legislation. With the help of shame and stigmatisation, the legal regulation of sex and the body helps produce other effects of power, including an increasingly conservative social milieu and a chilling effect on sexual dissidence. Since such highly justified regulatory measures not only strengthen state power but also improve state legitimacy, conservative NGOs have enjoyed state support in fortifying the moral regime that now surrounds marginal sexualities in East Asia and elsewhere.

Conversely, in a context where such sexual fundamentalism pervades major conservative NGOs, women's NGOs, and the tabloid media in Asia, the inevitable result is that emergent sexual practices, values, and activism easily become occasions for moral and sexual panics. The media consistently scrutinise the daily lives of marginal sexual subjects, probing and exposing intimacies, demonising alternative lifestyles, confirming stereotypes and prejudices, and sometimes even fabricating sex scares. While gay activism rarely receives media coverage, gay saunas, lesbian bars, and arrests at gay home parties regularly come under media scrutiny, and the stories are always narrated from a conservative and normative point of view. Media reports characterise safe sex measures (such as the presence of used condoms) as evidence of promiscuity and lifestyle stimulants as narcotics. As sexual hysteria has become a mainstay in East Asian media, they are unfailingly and flexibly used by the conservative NGOs as well as the state to encourage social vigilance against the non-normative.

Such sexual regulation has met with fierce resistance from radical sex groups in East Asian countries where the forces of modernisation have only begun to take root. Yet as social mobility and keen competition in the newly prospering East Asian states continue to make the reproduction of class unpredictable, there is plenty of (middle-)class anxiety to be galvanised and transformed into fear for the safety of children and aggressive efforts to keep them safe (from anything characterised as harmful or distracting to their 'normal' development into designated class, gender, and sex positions). Middle-class parents thus make up the staunchest supporters of conservative NGOs in the latter's crusade to purify the world. And as East Asian nations race towards liberal democracy on this wave of middle-class self-affirmation, the Christian NGOs' active promotion of the imperative to protect children greatly contributes to the codification and juridification that helps bolster state power and state legitimacy.

The Child Protection Imperative

Do you understand that children are the stem cells for the culture? The environment that you put them in is what they grow up to be. And if you can control what they hear, if you could control what they're told, if you have access to their minds . . . you can make them into just about whatever you want them to be.
—James Dobson, Focus on the Family, USA

The immense power of the cultural imaginary of the child can be partially glimpsed in the extraordinary success of the ratification of the UN Convention on the Rights of the Child. The convention is the most universally accepted human rights document in history, ratified by every country in the world except two (at last count, 192 total). By ratifying this document, national governments commit themselves to protecting and ensuring children's rights, and they agree to hold themselves accountable for this commitment before the international community.[46] As the convention protects children's rights by setting standards in health care, education, and legal, civil, and social services, many Asian countries are urged by their NGOs to bring national laws and practices in line with the UN's definition of children's rights.

While the Convention beckons forth its own global vision for child protection, the adoption of the child protection imperative proves effective in managing local issues and struggles too. Three areas of intense NGO vigilance in Taiwan are instructive for my discussion here.[47] To begin with, the perennial oppression of pornography and sex work had glimpsed some hope for relief in the 1990s, as an indigenous feminist discourse of sexual freedom spread throughout East Asia, opening up social space for more liberal views on sexual representation and transaction. The advent of cable television and the Internet also provided channels for communication and transaction beyond existing state measures of control. Fierce debates thus erupted between feminist sex radicals and various conservative voices (from the medical profession to the Christian groups to the women's groups) as they fought for popular support. Yet with the advent of the child-protection imperative through amendments and new legislation enacted by 2000, adults seeking their right to freedom of (sexual) speech and information suddenly found themselves interpellated as parents or would-be parents with solemn duties to perform in order to safeguard the well-being of all children. And as age and generation stratification still constitutes a core belief and institution in Asian societies, constitutional rights to freedom of expression and information proved fragile when faced with the higher calling of the protection of offspring.

Deeply ingrained sex negativity eventually triumphed over newly affirmed entitlement to autonomy and pleasure.

The second area has to do with the institutionalisation of homosexual relationships. Lesbian and gay couples of a previous generation were unable to gather enough force to challenge the heteronormative system. All they could hope for was to be able to pass and lead a secluded life. Yet since the 1990s, with the aggressive activism of an indigenous gay liberation movement, a new generation of lesbians and gays has emerged who may still suffer from prejudice and discrimination individually but who have acquired enough collective presence to make demands on society. Anti-discrimination bills are drafted in various nations, and the right to marry constitutes an additional demand. It almost looks as if growing social tolerance might allow for stable gay relationships. At this critical moment, Christian NGOs have come forth in various alliances to ensure that the institution of family stays heterosexual. Unable to issue any argument against lesbian and gay love, the issue of children is raised as Christian NGOs caution against the radical changes that will take place in the home and in schools if homosexual marriages are legally recognised.[48] Once again, duties to the young prove to be formidable obstacles to social change.

The last and most recent development directly bears on the child as foetus. Abortion in East Asia is a complicated issue connected to sociohistorical conditions as well as life politics. In difficult times of limited means and resources and before the use of oral contraceptives became common practice, abortion, in keeping with state policies of population control, had been a popular and acceptable solution for unwanted pregnancies in marriage.[49] The social meaning of abortion was transformed after the 1980s as a rapid increase in premarital sex shifted the demography of abortions, and in response to the social condemnation of abortion, indigenous myths about how 'the foetus's spirit will haunt the mother' began to spread as various temples devised special rites to ease the mother's guilt and dread by helping put the foetus's spirit to rest. Guilt and shame gradually replaced pragmatism as the dominant emotion associated with abortion, which articulated nicely with emerging Christian right-to-life discourses. Equally, the introduction of abortifacients (emergency contraceptives) such as Mifepristone (better known as RU486) since the late 1990s brought hope that the social stigma and danger associated with abortion would no longer plague women. On the other hand, however, reading this development as encouraging irresponsible sexual conduct in the midst of a blatant sex revolution, Christian NGOs in Taiwan quickly responded by urging the state to institute regulatory measures that included parental consent for minors, waiting periods, and mandatory consultation.

In the meantime, as much as the Chinese value fertility for the sake of family lineage, the availability of artificial insemination procedures nevertheless met with resistance from Christian NGOs—who believe that only the natural family should give birth to children—and from mainstream women's NGOs— who fear the procedure would revive the age-old belief that women are nothing but childbearing vessels for patriarchy.[50] Following this, and through deliberative democracy, it was decided that artificial insemination procedure should be accessible only to married couples, which effectively excludes lesbians and gays. The insistent involvement of the conservative NGOs in debates surrounding abortion and artificial insemination boils down to requiring that the foetus be produced only through normal heterosexual sex conducted in state-sanctioned marriage.[51]

Underneath the emotional investment in the child and foetus is thus a deeply rooted fixation on the heterosexual monogamous family, which alone—it is argued—can guarantee the child's proper birth, upbringing, acculturation, gender socialisation, and emotional maturity. 'The child', understood as the future of humankind, carries a pre-emptive authority that decrees heterosexuality to be elemental to the survival of the family, the clan, and the nation, a noble obligation that queers have been shown to deliberately evade. The popular complaint that 'gayness will cause the family (and the nation) to perish' aptly expresses the deep-rooted anxiety of reproduction-oriented East Asian cultures.[52] Here, Christian (anti-gay) doctrines and Asian heterosexual family traditions converge on the issues of the family and child protection. And the result is none other than a rejuvenation and legitimation of parental power, which had been greatly diminished and challenged in the sweeping influence of modern individualism but is now amplified to fortify the state into an all-powerful overseeing parent.[53]

The child, now understood as supremely innocent, must therefore be kept safe from harmful influences that could distract it from the heteronormative track of 'developing to its fullest'—and influences that clearly encompass anything queer. To ensure the intactness of that innocence, new forms of discipline and regulation are created that end up affecting all adults, queer or straight. All things sexual, whether gay or straight or other kinds, must be kept out of sight; all sexual knowledge and representation, gay or straight or other kinds, must be considered taboo; all non-normative sexualities are presented as pathological; all interactions must be desexualised. In collaboration with this protectionist mode of thinking, *child protection* discourses quickly become aligned with like-minded anti-sex *women protection* discourses. Without a critical perspective, it is only a matter of time before these become *foetus protection* discourses, as is already the case in East Asia, where an inflated concern for the extremely young and vulnerable has been constructed to justify the rigorous regulation of society and the promotion and enforcement of 'civility'.

Finally, this continuously broadening circle of protection works also to strengthen the conservative NGOs' power of influence, which in the final analysis contributes significantly to the grand project of the legitimacy both of state and of 'global governance'. The child protection imperative thereby constitutes the ultimate trump card in enforcing the most rigid forms of social control today, and thus has become a key point of struggle for East Asian queers.

Conclusion: Lessons for Movement

That figural Child alone embodies the citizen as an ideal, entitled to claim full rights to its future share in the nation's good, though always at the cost of limiting the rights 'real' citizens are allowed.
—Lee Edelman, *No Future*

The title of the present essay is a spin-off from the feminist political philosopher Susan Moller Okin's 1997 essay, 'Is Multiculturalism Bad for Women?' Okin's argument is that multiculturalism, a justice- and equality-oriented worldview, may help to preserve some minority cultural values and practices that are oppressive to women and violate the demands of modern gender equality.[54] While I do not share Okin's views entirely, the structure of her logic is illuminating for the issues discussed in the present essay.[55] For what appears to be justice- and equality-oriented global governance is shown to help propagate juridical tendencies and policy strategies that violate the basic demands of equality and diversity and are oppressive to queers, freaks, and other disenfranchised, disinherited, criminalised, and pathologised populations created by increasing modernisation, civilisation, juridification, and, not least of all, global governance.

Saskia Sassen has proposed that the relocation of various components of sovereignty onto supranational or non-governmental institutions could create "institutional voids resulting from the shrinking regulatory umbrella of the state" that strengthen "the ascendance of women . . . as subjects of law and the formation of crossborder feminist solidarities".[56] It is true that in many parts of East Asia and elsewhere, women have risen in status and have built cross-border solidarities, but as I have tried to demonstrate in this essay, the ones who have soared on the wings of global governance are specific groups of women, including women with class privilege, women of heterosexual persuasion, women of Christian vigilance, and women with conservative views of sexuality. They have transformed themselves into subjects of law by creating legislation that subsumes many more (queer and sexually non-conforming) subjects. By doing so, they have helped broaden, rather than shrink, the regulatory umbrella of the state. The conjunction of social change and social anxiety, of nationalistic uncertainty and global aspiration, has created fertile ground for conservative manoeuvres that often ride on the sweeping force of moral hysteria and social stigma against sexual dissidence.

If the Christian NGOs readily insert their conservative agenda into the normative nature of global governance, and if mainstream women's NGOs easily align themselves with the state and its schemes of governance, are queer NGOs immune from such opportunism or co-optation? If global governance or global civil society is proving to be not so good for East Asian queers, how should they respond to its continued spread?

The lesson of the Independent Gay Forum in the US is still fresh, and we have already been cautioned by activist scholars such as Lisa Duggan about the co-optation of mainstream gay groups by the discourse of neoliberalism and the fluidity of NGO affiliation.[57] In East Asia, the same tension and possibility exists. Internal struggle has never been absent from the gay community as mainstreaming gays and militant queers diverge on strategies and issues. Yet one is also encouraged by the fact that at the December 2005 WTO ministerial meeting in Hong Kong, queer groups from quite a few East Asian states lined up with other social movement groups (labour, farmer, women, sex worker) in fierce protest against WTO policies. Such collaboration has proven to be both educational and solidarity-building. Queer groups from across Asia have also banded together to protest local legislation and litigation in, for example, Hong Kong and Taiwan that threaten to jeopardise queer existence. When marginal groups confront the state machine and its legal arms, valuable lessons about governance are learned. East Asian queer groups have also been a common presence at rallies for workers, including sex workers, in Taiwan, Hong Kong, and South Korea for the past ten years. The alliance provides a sobering experience for groups that have lingering hopes that the state will live up to the ideals of diversity and equality. Such coalition politics encourages us to imagine a power that continues to contest any firm grasp of identity formation, a power that continues to constitute new and unexpected modes of intimate alliance, a power that is always quick in forging and consolidating new coalitions, and, of course, a power that continues to resist the temptation of the new state-NGO power bloc. It is towards this alternative kind of global solidarity that East Asian queers are struggling.

References

Kenneth Anderson and David Rieff, 2005—'Global Civil Society': A Sceptical View', in *Global Civil Society 2004/5*, edited by Helmut Anheier, Marlies Glasius, and Mary Kaldor. London: Sage, pp 26–39, at https://papers.ssrn.com/sol3/papers.cfm?abstract_id=899771 (Accessed August 16 2017)

Steven Angelides, 2004—'Feminism, Child Sexual Abuse, and the Erasure of Child Sexuality', in *GLQ* vol 10, pp 141–77

Associated Press, December 2004—'Singapore Bans Christmas Because It Might Be Gay', December 9 2004, at http://www.yawningbread.org/apdx_2004/imp-168.htm (Accessed April 18 2011, inactive August 16 2017)

Alex Au, August 2007—'A Ban(ner) Week in Singapore', August 15 2007, at fridae.com/newsfeatures/article.php?articleid=2014&viewarticle=1 (Inactive August 16 2017)

Kate Bedford, 2005—'Loving to Straighten Out Development: Sexuality and "Ethnode-velopment" in the World Bank's Ecuadorian Lending', *Feminist Legal Studies*, 2005, no 13, pp 295–322

Doris Buss and Didi Herman, 2003—*Globalising Family Values: The Christian Right in International Politics*. Minneapolis, MN, and London: University of Minnesota Press

Charter for Global Democracy (Charter 99), 1999—'A Charter for Global Democracy', September 17 1999, at www.i-p-o.org/global-democracy.htm (Accessed August 16 2017)

Commission on Global Governance, 1995—*Our Global Neighbourhood: The Report of the Commission on Global Governance*. Oxford: Oxford University Press

Anila Daulatzai, 2018—'Believing in Exclusion: The Problem of Secularism in Progressive Politics', in Jai Sen, ed, 2018—*The Movements of Movements, Part 2: Rethinking Our Dance*. Volume 5 in the *Challenging Empires* series. New Delhi: OpenWord, and Oakland, CA: PM Press

Lisa Duggan, 2003—*The Twilight of Equality? Neoliberalism, Cultural Politics, and the Attack on Democracy*. Boston, MA: Beacon

Lee Edelman, 2004—*No Future: Queer Theory and the Death Drive*. Durham, NC: Duke University Press

Jürgen Habermas, 1987—*Life World and System: A Critique of Functionalist Reason*, vol 2 of *The Theory of Communicative Action*. Boston, MA: Beacon

Josephine Ho, 2005—'From Anti-Trafficking to Social Discipline: The Case of Taiwan', in Kamala Kempadoo, Jyoti Sanghera, and Bandana Pattanaik, eds, 2005—*Trafficking and Prostitution Reconsidered: New Perspectives on Migration, Sex Work, and Human Rights*. Boulder, CO: Paradigm, pp 83–105

Josephine Ho, 2008—'Is Global Governance Bad for Asian Queers?', in *GLQ: A Journal of Gay, Lesbian, and Queer Studies*, volume 14 no 4, pp 457–79

Caroline Hong, 2004—'Sister Radio in Sex Sounds Row', *Taipei Times*, May 16 2004, at www.taipeitimes.com/News/taiwan/archives/2004/05/16/2003155678 (Accessed August 16 2017)

Wei-Po Ka, July 2001—'Women-centered Feminism and Sex Rights Feminism in Taiwan', in *Cultural Studies Monthly: An Online Journal*, vol 5, July 2001, at http://www.ncu.edu.tw/~eng/csa/journal/journal_forum_52.htm (Accessed November 25 2010, inactive August 16 2017)

Margaret E Keck and Kathryn Sikkink, 1998—*Activists Beyond Borders: Advocacy Networks in International Politics*. Ithaca, NY: Cornell University Press

'NGOs and the United Nations', *Global Policy Forum*, June 1999, at www.globalpolicy.org/ngos/docs99/gpfrep.htm (Accessed August 16 2017)

Susan Moller Okin, 1999—'Is Multiculturalism Bad for Women?', in Joshua Cohen and Matthew Howard, eds, 1999—*Is Multiculturalism Bad for Women?* New Haven: Princeton University Press, pp 7–24

Jan Nederveen Pieterse, 1992—'Emancipations, Modern and Postmodern', in Jan Nederveen Pieterse, ed, 1992—*Emancipations, Modern and Postmodern*. London: Sage

James N Rosenau, 1992—'Governance, Order and Change in World Politics', in James N Rosenau and Ernst-Otto Czempiel, eds, 1992—*Governance without Government: Order and Change in World Politics*. Cambridge: Cambridge University Press

Gayle Rubin, 1999—'Thinking Sex: Notes for a Radical Theory of the Politics of Sexuality', in Richard Parker and Peter Aggleton, eds, 1999—*Culture, Society and Sexuality: A Reader* London: University College London

Saskia Sassen, 1996–1997—'Towards a Feminist Analytics of Today's Global Economy', in *Indiana Journal of Global Legal Studies* vol 4, p 7

Jai Sen, 2018b—'Break Free! Engaging Critically with the Concept and Reality of Civil Society (Part 1)', in Jai Sen, ed, 2018—*The Movements of Movements, Part 2: Rethinking Our Dance*. Volume 5 in the *Challenging Empires* series. New Delhi: OpenWord, and Oakland, CA: PM Press

Jai Sen, 2018c—'Break Free! Engaging Critically with the Concept and Reality of Civil Society (Part 2)', in Jai Sen, ed, 2018—*The Movements of Movements, Part 2: Rethinking Our Dance*. Volume 5 in the *Challenging Empires* series. New Delhi: OpenWord, and Oakland, CA: PM Press

Evelyn Shih, June 2004—'No Guilt and Not Guilty, Say Homosexual Protesters', June 16 2004, at www.taipeitimes.com/News/taiwan/archives/2004/06/16/2003175251 (Accessed August 16 2017)

'Treatment of Homosexual Men Caught at Party Outrages Gay Rights Activists', *Taipei Times*, January 23 2004, at www.taipeitimes.com/News/taiwan/archives/2004/01/23/2003092323 (Accessed August 16 2017)

Raimo Vayrynen, 1990—'Norms, Compliance, and Enforcement in Global Governance', in Raimo Vayrynen, ed, 1990—*Globalization and Global Governance*. Lanham, MD: Rowman and Littlefield Publishers

Iris Marion Young, 1990—*Justice and the Politics of Difference*. Princeton, NJ: Princeton University Press

Jock Young, 1999—*The Exclusive Society: Social Exclusion, Crime and Difference in Late Modernity*. London: Sage

Notes

1. An earlier version of this essay was published as Josephine Ho, 2008—'Is Global Governance Bad for Asian Queers?', in *GLQ: A Journal of Gay, Lesbian, and Queer Studies*, volume 14 no 4, pp 457–79 (which in turn was a revised version of the author's keynote address to 'Sexualities, Gender, and Rights in Asia', the First International Conference of Asian Queer Studies, Bangkok, Thailand, July 7–9, 2005). Ed: I warmly thank Josephine Ho for agreeing to publish this revised version of her essay, for all her work in revising it, and for requesting permission from the publisher of the earlier version to publish this revised version. We made every effort to get reprint permission from the publishers, but since we have not heard back from them despite several reminders, we are going ahead with this open acknowledgement in good faith.

2. Rosenau 1992, pp 4–5.

3. The spread of global governance is quite uneven across Asia. The discussion here will be limited to those nations in East Asia that share certain common features of (Confucian) cultural heritage, but even more important the common experience of having been active players in Asia's economic boom in the 1990s. The former produces a context in which the state strives to manage developing democratic impulses

while maintaining a lingering authoritarianism that stabilises the ruling power; the latter produces a context in which traditional class reproduction is disturbed by globalisation. Both factors contribute to states of confusion, uncertainty, and anxiety that help make the Christian NGOs' conservative agenda increasingly palatable.

4. All adult publications sold in the bookstore had been wrapped in plastic and clearly marked for those eighteen and older only. Still, police ripped open the wrapping and charged the owner with disseminating obscenity. Gay groups repeatedly protested against the litigation; unfortunately, the gay owner still suffered a final conviction in 2005. (Evelyn Shih, 'No Guilt and Not Guilty, Say Homosexual Protesters', *Taipei Times*, June 16 2004, at www.taipeitimes.com/News/taiwan/archives/2004/06/16/2003175251) (Accessed August 16 2017). In front of media cameras, partygoers in their shorts or briefs were marched out of the building and required to take urine and blood tests at the police station (*Taipei Times*, January 2004). Still, thanks to token gestures of tolerance from the Taiwan government, Wikipedia describes Taiwan as "one of Asia's most progressive countries as far as LGBT rights are concerned". ('LGBT Rights in Taiwan', en.wikipedia.org/wiki/LGBT_rights_in_Taiwan) (Accessed August 16 2017).

5. Associated Press, December 2004; August 2007.

6. 'Sexual Orientation Discrimination Legislation for Hong Kong', at www.ipetitions.com/petition/sodbhk/ (Accessed August 16 2017). Despite a massive petition drive by gay and lesbian groups to demand equal treatment under the law, Singapore's lawmakers voted in October 2007 to retain section 377A of the penal code, which decrees that any male person found guilty of engaging in "gross indecency" with another male, whether in private or in public, faces a jail term of up to two years (Sylvia Tan, 'Allow Space for Gays but Gay Sex Ban to Stay: Singapore PM', *fridae*, October 24 2007, at http://www.fridae.asia/gay-news/2007/10/24/1970.allow-space-for-gays-but-gay-sex-ban-to-stay-singapore-pm [Accessed August 16 2017]). The South Korean Ministry of Justice announced a bill in October 2007 to criminalise discrimination on twenty grounds, including race, sex, educational status, and sexual orientation. In the end, sexual orientation was removed from the list of inclusions (Matt Kelly, 'Exclusion from Non-Discrimination Bill Mobilises Korea's LGBT Community', *fridae*, November 23 2007, at http://www.fridae.asia/gay-news/2007/11/23/1947.exclusion-from-non-discrimination-bill-mobilises-koreas-lgbt-community [Accessed August 16, 2017]).

7. Caroline Hong, *Taipei Times*, May 2004. The case was repealed one year later after much protest. In the case of Hong Kong, one militant fundamental Christian NGO, Alliance for the Protection of Family, filed the complaint and demanded that all gay programming henceforth must include opposed (Christian) views in order to meet parity standards for broadcasting, while religious programmes are automatically exempt from this requirement under the principle of religious freedom. The case is now under review, and the final ruling will have far-reaching impact on advocacy for any unpopular views ('Gay Marriage Show Sparks TV Row in Hong Kong', *fridae*, January 24 2007, at http://www.fridae.com/newsfeatures/article.php?articleid=1844&viewarticle=1 [Inactive August 16, 2017]).

8. Ed: This essay was finalised in 2010. Given recent developments in relation to the rights of the LGBT community in different parts of the world (India, Russia, and

Uganda during 2013–2014, to cite just a few), and given the powerful description and analysis in this essay of the situation and the balance of forces in Taiwan and in other parts of East Asia during the mid-2000s, there is every reason to assume that there have also been similar things happening there during this subsequent period.

9.   Such aggressiveness may remind the reader of the Christian right in the United States. Researchers maintain that the Christian right's political activism focuses on different targets domestically and internationally, with the former concentrated on "issues such as gay rights and school vouchers" and the latter on "United Nations population policy, women's rights, and children's rights". See Buss and Herman, 2003, p xviii. Christian-based NGOs in East Asia, however, merged the issues and turned gay rights into an issue that threatens women's rights and children's rights, with its obvious challenge to the institution of the family as well as its insistent demand on sexual openness and diversity.

10.   Christians may have been a minority in these nations, yet their colonial lineage and financial advantage afforded them the opportunity to occupy morally mainstream positions through establishing schools and relief agencies, and individual Christians also occupy positions of political and social influence. Their role as independent social service providers also facilitates their later transformation into government franchises.

11.   Ed: It surely only speaks to the power of this essay that Russia, for instance, deployed precisely this logic for its 2013 anti-gay legislation ahead of the Winter Olympic Games at Sochi.

12.   Commission on Global Governance, 1995.

13.   NGOs and the United Nations', June 1999 (Accessed August 16 2017).

14.   Charter for Global Democracy (Charter 99), 1999, at http://www.i-p-o.org/global-democracy.htm (Accessed September 5 2017).

15.   The states, of course, have made arrangements to ensure that no such dramatic turn takes place. After all, indigenous NGOs in East Asia are mostly financially ill-equipped to attend such international functions and must rely on the state governments to supply funding and bestow legitimacy to the delegation. It is little wonder that the chosen delegates almost always come from those mainstream NGOs friendly with the government. (Where nation-state status is questionable, such as Taiwan, the funding blatantly comes from the Ministry of Foreign Affairs, where NGO participation in international conventions is considered a matter of national diplomacy.)

16.   Anderson and Rieff 2005, pp 27–29.

17.   The concentrated presence of international NGOs along with their provision of abundant grants in the economically booming but ideologically restrained People's Republic of China serves as a prime example of such political motivation.

18.   Kate Bedford's seminal study of the World Bank's lending policies highlights one set of such manoeuvres geared towards fine-tuning local heteronormative arrangements to collaborate with global economic transformation. See Bedford 2005.

19.   New 'moral' strings added to U.S. funding policies by President Bush since 2004 aim to exclude those NGOs, domestic or international, that support sex workers' rights or needle exchange programmes, as well as other harm-reduction strategies and HIV / AIDS prevention advocacy. This moral decree is already having a serious

impact on Asia's nascent sex workers' rights movements, which are hard-pressed not only by the continued illegal status of sex work but more profoundly by the insistence of First World anti-trafficking NGOs that women's migration towards economic betterment and their choice of sex work are nothing but acts of trafficking and exploitation.

20. Keck and Sikkink 1998, p 13.

21. Commission on Global Governance, 1995—Ingvar Carlsson and Shridath Ramphal, chairs. *Our Global Neighbourhood: The Report of the Commission on Global Governance*, chapter 2. Oxford, UK: Oxford University Press, at http://www.gdrc. org/u-gov/global-neighbourhood/chap2.htm (Accessed October 6 2017).

22. In many Asian countries where nation-statehood is still a relatively recent achievement, 'civic' is often understood as something closely aligned with nationalistic sovereignty. In the 1910s, the early years of the Republic of China, opponents of masturbation exclaimed: "Masturbation is the draining of national energy?" Civic duties to the nation thus denote things serious and solemn, to the absolute exclusion of things sexual.

23. Significantly, such international agreements rarely promote sex-positive measures. Lesbian and gay rights, sex work rights, freedom to access sexual information, rights to sexual pleasure, and so forth encounter either defeat and frustration or total neglect and disdain.

24. Vayrynen 1990, p 27.

25. I M Young 1990, p 136.

26. J Young 1999, p 65.

27. Rubin 1999, p 143.

28. Ed: For something of a companion essay in terms of the discussion of the dynamics of civil society, see the essay in this book by Jai Sen, 'Break Free! Engaging Critically with the Concept and Reality of Civil Society' (Parts 1 and 2) (Sen 2018b and 2018c).

29. Habermas 1987, pp 357–73.

30. Western readers may be more familiar with the liberal concept of sex liberation or sexual freedom. In Taiwan, feminist sex radicals chose the term 'sex emancipation' in 1994 to describe their project so as to highlight its linkage to the Enlightenment tradition and its vision of self-liberation of the oppressed. See Nederveen Pieterse 1992, pp 5–41.

31. At the urging of Christian child protection NGOs, article 235 of the criminal code, which originally indicted the commercial production and sale of pornography for dissemination of obscenity, is now generously applied to individual Internet sex messages. Article 29 of the Child and Juvenile Sexual Transaction Prevention Act (1995, with a number of amendments in the following years) further criminalises any Internet message or content that hints at or discusses sexual transaction in whatever indirect fashion. For a detailed analysis of this gradual process of juridification in Taiwan, see Ho 2005.

32. For the English version of Constitutional Court Interpretation no 617 pertaining to article 235 of the criminal code (dissemination of obscenities), see www.judicial.gov. tw/CONSTITUTIONALCOURT/EN/p03_01.asp?expno=617 (Accessed August 16 2017). For the English version of Constitutional Court Interpretation no. 623 pertaining to article 29 of the Child and Juvenile Sexual Transaction Prevention Act

(inducing people to engage in unlawful sexual transaction), see www.judicial.gov.tw/CONSTITUTIONALCOURT/EN/p03_01.asp?expno=623 (Accessed August 16 2017).

33. Taiwan's Garden of Hope Foundation hired the veteran journalist Hui-jung Chi as its new CEO in 1992. Since then, the foundation has benefited greatly from her experience and expertise in public relations and has come to describe its various campaigns as 'social movements', adopting strategies of emergent social movements in organising marches, rallies, petitions, fundraising drives, and so forth for conservative causes. Chi herself admitted to such a manoeuvre in a 1997 interview (in Chinese). See www.ccea.org.tw/soc/17.htm (Accessed February 14 2008, inactive August 16 2017). The most aggressive of civil society organisations that tackle sex- and gay-related issues in East Asia include Hong Kong's Society for Truth and Light, Hong Kong Sex Culture Society, and Hong Kong Alliance for Family; Taiwan's Garden of Hope Foundation, End Child Prostitution Association Taiwan, Exodus International, and Center for the Study of Bio-Ethics; Singapore's Liberty League; and South Korea's Assembly of Scientists against Embryonic Cloning.

34. NGO-isation proves to be highly profitable. The annual budget of two of the largest Taiwanese Christian NGOs, Garden of Hope Foundation and Catholic Good Shepherd Sisters Foundation, has grown tenfold since the transformation, with hundreds of full-time staff members and many more volunteers. Delegates from these conservative NGOs also enjoy privileged membership on most of the important policy-setting committees in the government, setting policy priorities that empower and benefit their cause while creating formidable obstacles for queers and other groups.

35. Christian-based NGOs have been most keen in organising a media monitoring alliance with other NGOs. As public discontent with the tabloid media runs high, the conservative agenda has successfully diverted social energy away from questions of ownership and control to questions of content and morality.

36. Probably the most aggressive of such Christian NGOs, Taiwan's Garden of Hope Foundation, has won international NGO awards repeatedly, including Kellogg's Child Development Award, World of Children Awards (2005); Changemakers Innovation Award, Ashoka Foundation (2005); and Citigroup's NGO of the Year, Asia-Pacific Region, Resource Alliance (2004). The awarding agencies may be merely corporate subsidiaries, and the awards more significant in image than in actuality, but the international status of such awards carries a weight that makes them irresistible to the aspiring Taiwan (non-)state.

37. The hesitation and reluctance remain undocumented except through reports from frustrated LGBTQ representatives who attended such negotiation meetings. Years of experience in political correctness have taught many NGO groups never to put their criticism of marginal views into writing for fear of being cited and rebuked. It is the underdog NGOs that tend to be explicit about their own nonconforming views in trying to open up social space.

38. Mainstream feminist writings on sexuality centre mostly on the dangers of sex, pornography, and pleasure.

39. Ka, July 2001.

40. 'Family Feud within the Awakening Foundation: Employees Received "Adjustment of Duties" over Support for Prostitutes and Lesbians', in *United Daily*, December 5 1997, page 6.

41. The Chinese term state-feminism describes the vision that encouraging housewives to become political agents and enter the public realm of the state apparatus en masse can help realise feminist ideals. The sheer presence and number of women would then swallow up the public realm, feminising the state and forcing it to take up the job of caring, which has been women's domain and responsibility. It is with this vision in mind that mainstream feminists developed an unusually high interest and investment in the project of state-building.

42. To the dismay of gay rights organisations and activists, even after the newspaper campaign, this anti-gay NGO still won the 'human rights education project' in 2005 from Hong Kong's Education and Manpower Bureau, with exclusive rights to train teachers and to produce educational materials—on the subject of *human rights*—for middle schools all over Hong Kong. And in the extracts from the teaching course outline, the Society for Truth and Light is already saying that one of the themes it will discuss is "excessive use of human rights".

43. 'Taipei Hosts Gay Civic Event; Religious Group Contests', in *United Evening News*, August 25 2006, Metropolitan Section, at gsrat.net/news/newsclipDetail.php?ncdata_id=3013 (Inactive August 16 2017).

44. Kelley, November 23 2007, at http://www.fridae.asia/gay-news/2007/11/23/1947.exclusion-from-non-discrimination-bill-mobilises-koreas-lgbt-community (Accessed August 16 2017).

45. See www.hkchurch.org/family/sub/1.htm (Accessed February 10 2008, inactive August 16 2017).

46. The convention is the first legally binding international instrument that incorporates the full range of human rights—civil and political rights as well as economic, social, and cultural rights. Yet while it decrees that children be protected from abuse, violence, deprivation, and economic exploitation, the most active and fruitful NGO efforts in East Asia have been those that aim at protecting children from *sexual* abuse and exploitation. This focus on the negative aspects of sex reflects significant historical shifts in feminist movements and discourse. Just as the iconoclastic sex liberation discourse in the United States in the early 1970s was eventually eclipsed by women's painful narration of rape and abuse experiences that culminated in the 'Take Back the Night' rally in 1978, the celebratory pro–child sexuality milieu of late 1970s was also eclipsed by protection-oriented discourse on child innocence and vulnerability that culminated in moral panics such as the McMartin Preschool sex scare case in the 1980s. Steven Angelides has documented the feminist evasion of the issue of child sexuality in his important essay, 'Feminism, Child Sexual Abuse, and the Erasure of Child Sexuality' (Angelides 2004). A similar shift has also taken place in Taiwanese feminism, where talk of subject-centred female sexuality and sexual emancipation in 1994–1995 was silenced as mainstream women's groups chose to focus on victim-centred sexual harassment and sexual violence from 1996 on.

47. The case of Taiwan supplies the most emblematic example for my observation here because, given its unique and tumultuous process of ongoing democratisation and uncertain nation-state status, it has afforded social movements the most fertile ground for active yet limited intervention. Moreover, Taiwanese gender / sexuality

activists have produced the most sophisticated discourses on women's issues and lesbian and gay issues, which are now being disseminated throughout Asia.

48. Such views are most clearly stated on the web page of the Hong Kong Alliance for Family, while opposition to the homosexual marriage bill in Taiwan took more veiled forms. See www.hkchurch.org/family/sub/2.htm. (Accessed February 10 2008, inactive August 16 2017).

49. Only when conception was out of wedlock did it entail family shame, and even then the shame mostly had to do with the fact that the woman was not married but had already consented to sex with men.

50. Buss and Herman write about a shift in the Christian Right's UN rhetoric on defending the "rights of poor women" in its opposition to abortion (*Globalizing Family Values*, p 58). The argument about "rights of poor women" is also invoked by conservative Christian NGOs in Taiwan but only in relation to their opposition to surrogate motherhood, which they see as serving the needs of the rich exclusively.

51. To safeguard the welfare of children from the earliest moment possible, article 32 of the Child Welfare Act of Taiwan (2003) even prohibits pregnant women from ingesting any substance (cigarettes, alcohol, betel nuts, LSD, or other intoxicating drugs) that might be considered harmful for the foetus. Nor are they allowed to engage in activities deemed dangerous for the foetus.

52. Uttered by Taiwan's ruling party legislator Hou Shui-Sheng in 2004, this quotation coincides with Lee Edelman's delineation of the politics of "reproductive futurism", in which the figure of the child represents the possibility of the future against which the queer serves as a negating drive. See Edelman 2004.

53. I thank my colleague Naifei Ding for reminding me that the convergence of the 'colonial-modern' (Christian) and the 'feudal-cultural' (in various Chinese contexts, transfer of ancestor-worship to children-fetish) is a historical phenomenon quite typical of many East Asian societies.

54. Okin 1999.

55. Ed: For a related discussion on the limitations and contradictions of progressive secularism and feminism, see the essay in this book by Anila Daulatzai (Daulatzai 2018).

56. Sassen, 1996–1997.

57. Duggan 2003, chapter 3.

OpenWord

Incorporating Youth or Transforming Politics?
Alter-Activism as an Emerging Mode of Praxis among Young Global Justice Activists
Jeffrey S Juris and Geoffrey Pleyers

On January 26 2005, then Brazilian president Luiz Inácio Lula da Silva (Lula) addressed a packed crowd at the Gigantinho Stadium in Porto Alegre during the World Social Forum (WSF). Two years earlier, Lula had drawn widespread adulation within the forum as the first elected president from the leftist *Partido dos Trabalhadores* (PT, 'Workers' Party'), but this year he was roundly criticised in many circles for allying himself with local and transnational financial elites against the interests of his grassroots base. And when a group of hecklers began taunting Lula during his speech, the president retorted:

> Those of you who aren't from here, don't be afraid. These people that don't want
> to listen are sons and daughters of the PT who rebelled. That's typical of youth,
> and one day they are going to mature, and we'll be here with open arms to wel-
> come them back.[1]

According to Lula, youth is thus a stage of development characterised by disobedience and rebelliousness along the inevitable path towards adulthood. The young are given to unruliness and excess but will evolve into 'mature' political beings. The category of youth is pathologised, and thus de-politicised. Many older activists and politicians conceive of young people as raw material to be shaped through careful cultivation within formal political organisations. A related version of this life-cycle model views the young as political actors in training. Here, although cast in a more positive light, young people are still treated as less than full political subjects.

An alternative view floating around the Forum sees young people as political agents but still projects their agency towards a distant future. For example, Kamal Mitra Chenoy, then a member of the WSF Ad hoc India Organising Committee (IOC), pointed out in *Terra Viva*, an independent newspaper covering the 2005 Forum, that "The real constituency of the WSF is the youth. They are the future. And if an alternative world is possible it is for them and they are the ones who are going to build it".[2] On January 30, during an open discussion on the future of the forum at the Youth Camp, another IOC member pointed out that "When you are old the dreams grow faint, but when you are young the dreams are stronger".[3] Here, young people are romanticised, transformed into symbols of future hope and potential, rather than regarded as coeval participants.

In this article we conceptualise young political actors in a different light, as active political and cultural agents, thus contesting the view of the young as political actors in training. Specifically, we explore an innovative mode of activism practiced by many (though certainly not all) young global justice activists, which we call *alter-activism*.[4] Alter-activists are developing alternative forms of grassroots participation based on informal network structures that many view as an alternative to representative democracy. At the same time, many young people continue to participate in traditional leftist organisations, including youth wings of various communist and other leftist parties.[5] However, despite this diversity, we argue that alter-activism is a particularly influential mode of activism among young global justice activists. Rather than 'maturing' into traditional political actors, as we shall see, alter-activists are transforming the very nature of political action itself. In what follows we outline several key aspects of alter-activist practice, including an emphasis on lived experience, horizontal networking, creative direct action, and the innovative use of new information and communication technologies (ICTs). We then conclude by considering how such practices have influenced the global justice movement, and the WSF in particular.

Social Change and Lived Experience

Young alter-activists view social transformation as an ongoing collective process. Rather than messianic visions or an already established project, alter-activists focus on day-to-day practices. As a leaflet introducing a youth autonomous space at the European Social Forum (ESF) held in Paris in 2003 explained, "We are feeling our way, seeking out concrete and emancipatory paths towards the transformation of social relations". In this sense, collaborative, interactive practices are reflected in the emergence of new political visions and forms of interaction. These combine elements of traditional ideologies, such as anarchism, an emphasis on internal democracy and autonomy—feminism and grassroots movements such as the Zapatistas have been particularly influential in this respect—as well as a commitment to openness, collaboration, and connectedness, which is also evident in recent technology-oriented activism, including the free software movement.

Alter-activists emphasise the importance of directly democratic processes, often contrasting their own practices with those of more institutionalised parties, trade unions, and non-governmental organisations (NGOs). For example, as an activist from the Barcelona-based *Movimiento de Resistencia Global* ('Movement for Global Resistance', MRG) pointed out, "We are promoting decentralised participation, making each group responsible for their part so decisions are taken among many people as opposed to the old politics where a small group has all the information and decides everything".[6] Moreover, alter-activists have a distinctly global vision, although they emphasise the importance of autonomy and local self-management. For example, another MRG-based activist described his ideal world as follows, "Regions would be self-sufficient and would have food sovereignty, but they wouldn't close themselves off. Instead, they would articulate and work together through a kind of anarcho-eco-regionalist global government".[7]

At the same time, unlike traditional actors, alter-activists stress grassroots participation and personal interaction in the context of daily social life. Meetings, neighbourhood relations, and protest camps become spaces to experience and experiment with alternative forms of life, as a document from the Parisian alter-activist network Vamos explains, "We do not separate our practices and aims. We opt for a horizontal, anti-sexist, self- and eco-managed way of operating". This distinguishes alter-activists from NGO participants and other global justice activists who are criticised for "not being aware of process, which means there is no difference between means and ends. Our manner of working has to reflect the values we are defending as part of our resistance".[8] Moreover, alter-activists combine virtual networking with the creation of interstitial physical spaces, including action camps and interactive workshops such as the *Caracol* at the 2005 WSF.[9]

Horizontal Networking

Alter-activists have developed decentralised network-based organisational forms, including highly flexible, diffuse, and often ephemeral formations, such as the Direct Action Network (DAN) in the United States, MRG in Catalonia, Vamos in Paris, GAS9 in Mexico City, and People's Global Action (PGA) on a global scale. Given the rise of new information and communications technologies (ICTs), activists can now connect directly without the need for organisational hierarchy.[10] Whereas in the past movements needed centralised structures to facilitate communication and coordination over vast distances, new ICTs allow activists to maintain such interactions through horizontal, peer-to-peer communication. Moreover, such informal grassroots forms of political participation are increasingly viewed as concrete political alternatives to traditional political parties and unions.

Decentralised networks tend to involve more informal modes of political commitment and participation, including temporary, ad hoc coalitions. At the same time, many alter-activist networks that began as temporary coordinating vehicles continued to operate long after specific mobilisations had ended. Seattle DAN, for example, was founded as a loose coalition among direct action groups, radical environmentalists, and grassroots NGOs to plan and coordinate the anti-WTO actions in Seattle in November 1999. Activists then went on to build a continental DAN structure. Although the national network quickly faltered, local DAN chapters remained active in several US cities. MRG was similarly created to mobilise Catalan activists to the protests against the World Bank and IMF in

Prague in September 2000. After nearly three years of organising actions, gatherings, and workshops, the network finally 'self-dissolved' in January 2003.

Similarly, Paris-based Vamos, formed during the 2001 anti-G8 protests in Genoa, began by carrying out public education regarding the neoliberal agenda of multilateral summits and organising busloads of students to attend international counter-summit mobilisations. In 2002, Vamos started organising symbolic direct action focusing on issues such as migration, the war in Iraq, multinational corporations, and neoliberal reforms. The network created alternative spaces and activist camps during both the anti-G8 protests in Geneva and the ESF in Paris in 2003. Likewise, GAS9 was founded to mobilise young Mexicans against the 2003 WTO summit in Cancún. Together with similar groups, they went on to organise youth assemblies that involved more than 200 young people from distinct backgrounds—students, libertarians, communist militants, NGO workers, and educators. The group has changed its name several times, but remains active despite heavy turnover among participants. After the summit protest against the Inter-American Development Bank in Guadalajara, activists decided to focus on local activities, alternative media, and support for Zapatistas campaigns.

Alter-activist networks also challenge representative logics. Rather than identifying with a specific organisation, activists are committed to the wider movement and its guiding values. Participation is thus individualised but still concerned with collective goals and collaborative practice. As MRG's manifesto declares, "We understand MRG as a tool for collective mobilisation, education, and exchange, which, at the same time, respects and preserves the autonomy of participating people and groups, reinforcing all the voices taking part in the action". Alter-activist networks thus provide open spaces for communication and coordination around concrete projects, favouring open participation over rigid membership. As another early MRG document explained, the network "has a diffuse structure, and involves a diffuse sense of individual identification with the movement. MRG should therefore be understood as a movement 'without members'; membership leads to static, non-dynamic structures".[11]

Finally, despite internal conflicts and contradictions, alter-activist networks have no formal hierarchies, elected positions, or paid staff, and decisions are taken by consensus. For example, the organisational structure of Vamos remains dynamic and participatory, involving nearly 200 activists during preparatory meetings. US-based activists in particular, including those formerly associated with DAN, have specialised in the practice of elaborate forms of collaborative decision-making designed to build compromise agreements rather than majority voting. Although not always the most time-efficient ways to operate, alter-activist networks emphasise horizontal structure and democratic process as political ends. This leads to an egalitarian, dynamic, and flexible form of activism. At the same time, however, alter-activist networks have clear limitations. For example, they can be highly unstable over time, given the lack of formal structure and clear chains of responsibility. Moreover, despite a commitment to non-hierarchical relations, in practice, informal hierarchies, which are often less democratic and more difficult to control, can contradict the expressed egalitarian values of alter-activist networks.[12]

New Information and Communication Technologies (ICTs)

Alter-activism is in fact characterised by the innovative use of new ICTs. Given that younger generations have grown up with computers, it should come as no surprise that they have been at the forefront of incorporating new technologies within their ongoing organising. Alter-activists have specifically employed new ICTs to organise direct actions, share information and resources, and plan and coordinate activities. Although alter-activists primarily use e-mail and electronic listservs, they also create temporary web pages during mobilisations to provide information, resources, and contact lists; post documents and calls to action; and sometimes house discussion forums and IRC chat rooms. Moreover, particular networks have their own web pages, where activists post reflections, analyses, updates, calls to action, and links, together with more logistical information. Meanwhile, interactive websites offering multiple tools for coordination are becoming increasingly popular, including open publishing projects like the Independent Media Centre (IMC) or Indymedia, which allow users to post news and information without editorial selection and control.

Independent media activism also forms part of an emerging radical media culture among young alter-activists. Indymedia, established during the anti-WTO protests in Seattle, has become a global network of local web-based media projects, allowing alter-activists to circulate alternative news and information. There are now more than 160 local IMC sites around the world, while the global network receives up to 2,000,000 page views per day[13] Moreover, alter-activists also practice 'tactical media', including the playful parodying of corporate advertisements, such as 'culture jamming', or new kinds of electronic civil disobedience, including the 'virtual sit-in'.[14]

Beyond their instrumental goals, alter-activists have used new ICTs during temporary media labs featuring digital audio, video, and streaming as a way to experiment with horizontal collaboration and express their directly democratic ideals. For example, the Euraction Hub Project at the November 2002 ESF in Florence was an open space for sharing ideas and experiences, experimenting with new ICTs, carrying out autonomous actions, and, above all, organising in a horizontal and participatory fashion. Inside the Hub, young media activists organised workshops on themes such as Hacking the Borders and Corporate Europe, Digital Media Activism, and Culture Jamming. The project was also meant "as an implicit critique of vertical, non-inclusive, and non-participatory structures", in order "to reflect on activist communication and new forms of expression of antagonism and conflict".[15] In this sense, the Hub was conceived as an alternative to the hierarchical practices associated with the official forum. At the same time, its egalitarian, playful, and exploratory spirit reflected a broader emphasis on process, experimentation, and lived experience within alter-activist culture.[16]

Creative Direct Action

Alter-activism is also associated with nonconventional, creative, and expressive forms of direct action protest. Despite emerging in different cultural contexts, the tactics employed by young alter-activists all produce theatrical images for mass mediated consumption. In addition, the blockade strategy, in which diverse formations 'swarm' their target,[17] produces high-powered social drama. Beyond their utilitarian purpose—shutting down major summit meetings—mass actions are complex cultural performances that allow participants to communicate symbolic messages to an audience while experiencing symbolic meanings through embodied ritual practice.

During mass actions, alter-activists appropriate, recombine, and assemble diverse commodity signs, including white overalls, industrial tubes and tires, wigs, and pink dresses, to express the values and identities associated with alternative activist youth subcultures. This uncanny, festive element of alter-activist protest is particularly evident in the case of the Pink and Silver Bloc, which first appeared at the September 2000 anti–World Bank and IMF protests in Prague; as well as the Italian *Tute Bianche* ('White Overalls'), a tactic developed by the Milan-based Ya Basta! collective in which large, orderly groups of activists advance behind plastic shields towards police lines, where they initiate 'non-violent' physical contact. In Prague, for example, hundreds of *Tute Bianche* marched together wearing white overalls, protective shields, and spectacularly coloured padding, while another several dozen young revellers from the Pink and Silver Bloc, decked out in pink and silver lingerie, bright glitter, and feathers, danced their way behind a Samba band. Meanwhile, Radical Cheerleaders and Pink Fairies entertained the crowd, taunting police lines and performing ironic cheers inspired by the mobile street parties and aesthetics of UK-based Reclaim the Streets. In this sense, alter-activism is not only festive; it also reflects the emphasis on creativity, diversity, innovation, and symbolic protest among young activists.

Similar scenes have occurred repeatedly across the world. For example, after the final march against the WTO in Cancún in 2003, thousands of activists approached the fence dividing the city centre from the resort area where the WTO meetings were being held. Suddenly, young Mexican women and Korean trade unionists began attacking the fence, while others shouted slogans and sang. After an hour a hole finally appeared in the fence, leaving protesters directly facing the police who were guarding the "no-protest zone". Although police and journalists expected violent confrontation, protesters immediately sat down and observed a moment of silence commemorating Lee Kiung, the Korean peasant leader who had committed suicide three days earlier to denounce the impact of WTO commercial agreements on small farmers. Following speeches by Latin American and Asian activists, protesters burned an effigy representing the WTO and laid flowers before the police. As the riot cops looked on, confused and impotent, hundreds of alter-activists began dancing to the beat of Korean, Latin, and North American music to celebrate their symbolic victory.

Alter-Activist Camps

Over the past few years, alter-activist camps, including 'No Border' camps, protest camps during mass mobilisations, and youth camps during world and regional social forums, have emerged as a key political strategy among young global justice activists. In Mexico, for example, national and international autonomous youth camps have been organised in the Mexican state of Oaxaca and along the US-Mexico border. These spaces constitute laboratories where alter-activists experiment with new ideas, practices, and forms of social action. Beyond opposing neoliberalism, such camps provide spaces for socialising, sharing ideas and experiences, celebrating, mixing private and public activities, making friends, and developing new commitments. Physically assembling in large numbers also generates strong emotions that deepen participants' commitment to the struggle for a better world.[18] Moreover, they provide opportunities for experimenting with alternative forms of participation and social interaction. Indeed, despite internal conflicts and contradictions, youth camps are organised along directly democratic lines: there are no formal leaders, decisions are made collectively, and all residents are encouraged to take part in the construction, organisation, and daily administration of the camps.

The International Youth Camp (IYC) that took shape alongside the WSF in Porto Alegre provides a particularly good example of these alter-activist dynamics. While counter-summit actions had given visibility to a new kind of movement, forum organisers felt it was time to build a concrete, less diffuse vision of how to build an alternative world. However, the younger direct action–oriented sectors most active within earlier mass protests have been underrepresented within the WSF. Some of these alter-activists view the forum as an attempt by the traditional left to establish hegemony over an emerging form of movement that had escaped their control. Meanwhile, direct action–oriented activists who have taken part in the WSF have tended to focus their energy on the IYC and its autonomous spaces.

Many observers have characterised the IYC as a political Woodstock, involving thousands of shabbily dressed young people living collectively, taking communal meals, selling their wares, dancing, drinking, and listening to live and recorded music throughout the night. Moreover, the long lines for bathrooms and showers give the appearance of a mass refugee camp. At the same time, however, there is also significant political discussion and debate, particularly within more organised spaces, such as the Intergalactic Laboratory of Disobedience, or *Intergaláctika* (2002 and 2003) and the more recent *Caracol* project (2005).[19] Moreover, after the first edition of the IYC in 2001, organisers began to view the Camp as a laboratory for experimenting with new forms of horizontal collaboration. It was during this time that the Free Metropolitan Council of Architecture Students, together with the autonomous and more loosely organised Architecture Students' Movement, developed the concept of the Youth Camp as a city, involving self-managed, directly democratic forms of organisation and the increased use of alternative media and ecologically friendly construction techniques.[20]

The concept of the IYC as a city was taken even further during the 2005 WSF. The idea was to fully transform the camp from an alternative sleeping area into an innovative space for generating new forms of social, political, and cultural interaction. The IYC was organised into zones around seven Action Centres intended to promote the convergence of activities around similar themes. Moreover, all residents were encouraged to participate in construction, administration, and decision-making. Indeed, the Camp was conceived of as a laboratory for generating new network-based social and political practices. As the manual pointed out, the IYC was designed to "short-circuit . . . old forms of political representation. It's a laboratory of the new political militancy seeking to make resistance an act of creation, to promote counter-power". Thus, instead of organising around youth-based identities and traditional notions of inclusion, alter-activists primarily wanted to practice new models of horizontal organisation. As we shall see, the organisation of the official forum underwent a similar transformation in 2005.[21]

Alter-activist camps provide a time out of time, a communal space where hierarchical relations are suspended. Indeed, such intense 'liminal spaces'[22] are particularly productive moments for experimenting with alternative ways of life, new social identities, and novel forms of interaction. At the same time, despite their utopian thrust, alter-activist camps also present complex, often intractable challenges, including the rise of informal hierarchies, the need to delegate despite an emphasis on participation, differential levels of involvement among residents, and the emergence of political divisions. These camps are ephemeral: once they end, groups tend to dissolve and networks dilute. Nevertheless, such camps provide important occasions, however brief, where alter-activists are able to physically assemble in large numbers and actually live the utopian worlds they are attempting to create. These experiences produce intense emotions and powerful feelings of collective solidarity, which are often perceived as personally, socially, and historically transformative. In this sense, as several studies have shown, intense experiences of political activism during one's younger years can transform social identity and political beliefs in lasting ways.[23]

Young Alter-Activists and the WSF

Many younger global justice activists reject the category of youth owing to its paternalist overtones. Rather than 'young' versus 'old', a more important cleavage involves a conflict between 'networking' and 'command logics'.[24] The latter, characteristic of traditional formations such as political parties, trade unions, and NGOs, is based on the recruitment of new members, the forging of unified strategies, political representation, and the struggle for hegemony. The former involves the creation of umbrella spaces, where diverse movements converge around common hallmarks, while preserving their autonomy and specificity. Thus, rather than identifying in generational terms, many younger activists see themselves as part of a new way of doing politics involving people of all ages. In theory, the WSF is an example of this new politics. Indeed, the Charter of Principles defines the forum as an open meeting space for reflection and debate. Consequently, no one person or group is authorised to represent the forum or speak in its name. In practice, however, the forum involves an ongoing conflict between newer and traditional actors. In this sense, the hecklers mentioned at the beginning of this article not only criticised Lula for abandoning his political base, they also chastised him for attempting to 'represent' the WSF at the World Economic Forum in Davos.

Many of the innovative practices and ideas emerging among young alter-activists have already had a significant impact on the political and organisational dynamics associated with contemporary global justice movements, particularly the social forums. For example, the grassroots participation and decentralised forms of organisation within the IYC have had a major influence on the 'official' forum, which was evident during the 2005 WSF. For one, previous editions of the forum had been based at the Pontifícia Universidade Católica do Rio Grande do Sul (PUC, a Catholic University) located on the outskirts of Porto Alegre, far from the IYC. The forum was not only spatially centralised, it also revolved around large plenary sessions involving high-profile intellectuals. Influenced by the critiques of the institutional, hierarchical WSF in 2003, the more grassroots, popular feel of the 2004 WSF in Mumbai and the alternative model provided by the IYC, the decision was taken in 2005 to hold forum activities in a series of makeshift tents, shifting from the PUC to a large open-air ground surrounding the Youth Camp along the banks of Guaiba Lake. The 2005 IYC thus found itself at the centre of the forum, while its decentralised, network-based model of organisation was incorporated into the wider event. Specifically, the 2005 WSF was conceived of as a 'World Social Territory', involving eleven horizontally linked thematic areas, each with auditoriums, stages for cultural events, food courts, markets, and information centres. Although some participants complained of fragmentation and long distances, it was relatively easy to move fluidly between the different spaces, including the activities organised within the IYC. The idea of a singular open space thus moved towards a decentralised network of horizontally connected spaces, while the entire forum had a more popular grassroots feel.

Second, whereas prior editions of the WSF had relied on the Organising Committee (OC) to plan and choose the speakers for the plenary sessions, the 2005 forum was entirely self-managed. Workshops and sessions were organised through an electronic consultation process in which delegates proposed themes and submitted proposals for their activities within the resulting terrains. Through its decentralised territorial organisation, non-institutional infrastructure, and predominantly self-organised programme and methodology, the official forum in 2005 thus moved closer to the grassroots, network-based model of the Youth Camp. In this sense, there has been a process of migration through which practices and values related to horizontal coordination and grassroots participation once associated with 'youth' have diffused more widely, ultimately transforming the larger forum itself.

Conclusion

In this essay, we have outlined an emerging mode of political praxis among young global justice activists we call alter-activism. As an innovative set of cultural ideas and practices, alter-activism will not necessarily disappear when young people 'grow up' and begin to participate in formal political institutions in relatively traditional ways. Of course, this may happen, but once we start to view young people as active political and cultural producers other possibilities emerge. Perhaps some alter-activists will continue to engage in alternative modes of political engagement throughout their lives. Alternately, others might bring their novel ideas, values, and practices to bear on more traditional settings. Indeed, rather than asking how democratic institutions can better reach out to and integrate youth, we should ask how young political actors might influence emerging forms of political practice. Nowhere is this process more evident than within and around the social forum process.

In this sense, the growing influence on the official forum of many of the ideas, practices, and organisational models developed by alter-activists within the IYC and other global justice spaces and networks over the past decade clearly demonstrates the capacity of young people to act as political subjects in their own right. Rather than moving towards 'mature' forms of political participation, young alter-activists have significantly influenced the way 'adult' leaders conceive and organise the forum. Although surely utopian, at its best alter-activism can help generate new ways of thinking and acting that respond to emerging possibilities and challenges at local, national, and global scales.

References

Michael Albert, 2004—'WSF: Where to now?', in Jai Sen, Anita Anand, Arturo Escobar, and Peter Waterman, eds, 2004—*World Social Forum: Challenging Empires*. New Delhi: Viveka Foundation

Anon—'Call to Eur@action Hub Project', at http://www.nadir.org/nadir/initiativ/agp (Accessed November 13 2005, inactive August 17 2017)

John Arquilla and David Ronfeldt, 2001—*Networks and Netwars*. Santa Monica, CA: Rand

Todd Benson, January 2005—'Brazilian Leader Hears Boos From Unusual Direction, the Left', in *The New York Times*, January 28, 2005, p A9, at http://query.nytimes.com/gst/fullpage.html?res=9C05E1D7173BF93BA15752C0A9639C8B63 (Accessed October 7 2017)

Randall Collins, 2001—'Social Movements and the Focus of Emotional Attention', in Jeff Goodwin, James M Jasper, and Francesca Polletta, eds, 2001—*Passionate Politics*. Chicago: University of Chicago Press, pp 27–44

Jeffrey S Juris, 2004—'Networked Social Movements: Global Movements for Global Justice', in Manuel Castells, ed, 2004—*The Network Society: A Cross-Cultural Perspective*. Cheltenham: Edward Elgar

Jeffrey S Juris, 2005a—'Social Forums and Their Margins: Networking Logics and the Cultural Politics of Autonomous Space', in *ephemera*, special edition on the World Social Forum, Vol 5 no 2, pp 253–72, at https://www.researchgate.net/publication/228618673_Social_Forums_and_their_margins_Networking_logics_and_the_cultural_politics_of_autonomous_space (Accessed August 17 2017)

Jeffrey S Juris, 2005b—'The New Digital Media and Activist Networking within Anti-Corporate Globalization Movements', in *The Annals of the American Academy of Political and Social Science*, vol 597, special edition on 'Cultural Production in a Digital Age', pp 189–208

Ron Kassimir, 2005—'Youth Activism: International and Transnational', in Lonnie R Sherrod, ed, 2005—*Youth Activism: An International Encyclopedia*. Westport, Connecticut: Greenwood Press

Doug McAdam, 1989—'The biographical consequences of activism', in *American Sociological Review*, Vol 54, No 5, October 1989, pp 744–60

Kamal Mitra Chenoy (interview), January 2005—*Terra Viva*, January 31 2005, p 11

Rodrigo Nunes, 2005—'The International Youth Camp as the Unthought of the World Social Forum', in *ephemera*, vol 5 no 2, pp 277–96, at http://www.ephemerajournal.org/sites/default/files/5-2nunes1.pdf (Accessed August 17 2017)

Rodrigo Nunes, 2012—'The Intercontinental Youth Camp as the Unthought of World Social Forum, Revisited', in Jai Sen and Peter Waterman, eds, 2012—*World Social Forum: Critical Explorations*. Volume 3 in the *Challenging Empires* series. New Delhi: OpenWord

Michal Osterweil, 2004—'De-centering the forum', in Jai Sen, Anita Anand, Arturo Escobar, and Peter Waterman, eds, 2004—*World Social Forum: Challenging Empires*. New Delhi: Viveka Foundation

Geoffrey Pleyers, 2004—'Social Forums as an ideal model of convergence', in *International Social Science Journal*, Vol 56, Issue 182, pp 507–17

Geoffrey Pleyers, 2005—'From disillusionment to a new culture of participation: Young alter-globalisation activists' commitment', in Joerg Forbrig, ed, 2005—*Revisiting youth political participation*. Strasbourg: Press of the Council of Europe

Jai Sen and Peter Waterman, eds, 2012—*World Social Forum: Critical Explorations*. Volume 3 in the *Challenging Empires* series. New Delhi: OpenWord, at http://www. into-ebooks.com/book/world_social_forum/ (Accessed August 17 2017)

Gregor Stangherlin, 2005—*L'Engagement pour l'Autre Lointain. Une Etude des Acteurs des ONG* ['A Commitment to a Distant Other: A Study of NGO Actors', in French], Paris: L'Harmattan

Kamal Mitra Chenoy (interview), January 2005—*Terra Viva*, January 2005, January 31 2005, p 11

Victor Turner, 1969—*The Ritual Process*. Chicago: Aldine Publishers

Notes

1. Benson, January 2005 (Accessed October 7 2017).
2. Mitra Chenoy, January 2005, p 11.
3. Field notes.
4. This study is based on field research conducted between 1999 and 2005 at five World Social Forums, international protests, and activist gatherings in the Americas and Europe, as well as long-term ethnographic observations of activist networks in Spain, the United States, France, Belgium, and Mexico. We have also carried out textual analyses and seventy semi-structured interviews.
5. Indeed, the young people with whom we work are often critical of traditional political and civil society associations, including political parties, unions, and large non-governmental organisations (NGOs) (Pleyers 2005; Juris 2004, pp 341–62). These institutions are generally viewed as hierarchical, bureaucratic, and overly removed from their grassroots base (Kassimir 2005, pp 20–28).
6. Personal interview.
7. Ibid.
8. Ibid.
9. The *Caracol* was an autonomous space organised by young European, US, and Latin American alter-activists at the 2005 Youth Camp. Inspired by the Zapatistas, the *Caracol* was a place to share ideas, information, and experiences with the goal of constructing another world. Discussions also focused on strategies for building a more open and horizontally-organised WSF.
10. Juris 2004, pp 341–62.
11. Cited in a document produced by MRG activists regarding network identity, structure, and functioning that circulated on the global@ldist.ct.upc.es listserv, October 18 2000.
12. Albert 2004, pp 323–28; Juris 2005a, pp 253–72; Pleyers 2004, pp 507–17.

13. Juris 2005a, pp 253–72.
14. Juris 2005b, pp 189–208.
15. 'Call to Eur@action Hub Project'.
16. Ed: This essay was finalised in 2008. Given the (increasingly) relentless developments that have taken place since then in the world of ICT—including in social media—the vocabulary of actions that those who the authors call alter-globalists now use, in 2018, will surely be even wider than the already impressive outline given here, but this only strongly underlines the points made by them.
17. Arquilla and Ronfeldt 2001.
18. Collins 2001, pp 27–44.
19. A precursor to the *Caracol, Intergaláctika* similarly provided a space for more radical, direct action–oriented activists to share their ideas, practices, and experiences in a horizontal and participatory fashion (Juris 2005a, pp 253–72; Osterweil 2004, pp 183–90).
20. Nunes 2005, pp 277–96. Ed: See also the substantively revised and expanded version of this essay in a companion volume, *World Social Forum: Critical Explorations* (Nunes 2012, in Sen and Waterman, eds, 2012).
21. Ed: See also Nunes 2012.
22. Turner 1969.
23. McAdam 1989, pp 744–60; Stangherlin 2005.
24. Juris 2004, pp 341–62.

The Antiglobalisation Movement
Coalition and Division[1]
Tomás Mac Sheoin and Nicola Yeates

Rather than the prophesied end of history, the last two decades—from the 1990s through to the 2000s—have seen a huge growth in international and transnational political mobilisation by non-state actors. The growth of this activism has prompted the appearance of a large social sciences literature, much of it enthusiastically celebrating the arrival of this 'new' actor on the global stage,[2] analysing the arrival of 'transnational advocacy networks', 'transnational social movement organisations', 'global social movements', and 'global civil society'.[3] These analyses attempt to explain what are considered to be 'new' politics, involving non-traditional political actors, organising methods, and tactics, and taking place 'above' and 'beyond' the national. Beyond this, various academic (and other) analysts have acclaimed the arrival of a new phase of contestation where social movement organisation has moved from the national to the transnational level, with new targets (transnational governmental institutions) and a concomitant reduction in the importance and occurrence of national contention.

The antiglobalisation movement (AGM)[4] has been widely used to illustrate this 'new' politics, combining as it does the varying scalar and spatial dimensions held to be key to these developments. To begin with, the AGM opposes nothing less than a world system: its target is truly transnational. In addition, the AGM is a global social movement par excellence, uniting as it does all the other major global social movements. Furthermore, it is organisationally new in its use of social and technological networks, such as the Internet, and its use of consensus methods of decision-making and lack of hierarchy in—often temporary—organisational structures. This research has included claims that antiglobalisation campaigns and networks are forging new modes of collective political action and constructing a new 'global' political community, a 'global citizenship'.[5]

However, research on the AGM has major failings. As Tarrow argued, too many observers have made hasty analytical leaps from protests against globalisation to transnational social movements to global civil society.[6] Just as in the policy area global influences have not succeeded in rolling over national ones, as theories of strong globalisation suggest,[7] so transnational activism has not broken free of the state. It is still shaped by the history and characteristics of national social movements and contention. We find ourselves agreeing with Worth and Abbott that "[m]uch of what has been written still tends to 'over-romanticise' the aims and objectives of the variety of diverse groups that favour an 'antiglobalisation' and 'anti-capitalist' agenda".[8]

In this essay, we attempt to correct this unbalanced emphasis on the novelty of the AGM by first drawing attention to the national bases / aspects of summit mobilisations, social forums, and transnationally coordinated days of action, and secondly by stressing the continuities between the AGM and the previous generation's means of political contestation. We accomplish this second aim by demonstrating the survival of decidedly 'old' politics in this 'new' movement, by tracing the cleavage between reformists and radicals, and through a short exposition of the continuities in the characteristics of the AGM's cadre and that of previous movements.

The AGM: Diversity and Division

The most striking characteristic of the AGM is its diversity.[9] In terms of composition, it involves the convergence of many global social movements, both 'old' social movements—labour, peace—and 'new' social movements—environment, women, human rights, and development. In terms of participants, della Porta reports on "the generational, gender, social, religious, ideological diversity of the global justice movement".[10]

The diversity is evident in terms of the methods deployed as well. It ranges from "[a] rich and growing panoply of organisational forms and instruments—affinity groups, spokescouncils, facilitation tools, break-outs, fishbowls, blocking concerns, vibes-watchers and so on",[11] to innovative tactics including the development of tactical frivolity—from street theatre to teddy bear catapults (in Canada), and from radical cheerleading in the US to the Clown Army at the anti-G8 protest at Gleneagles in the UK, in 2005. Street protests, however, are only part of a much wider range of tactics, which include lobbying and letter-writing campaigns; action through the courts; pickets, strikes, and riots; and consumer boycotts and physical attacks on products, centres of consumption, and infrastructure. These campaigns are the base from which the AGM mobilises. Finally, the AGM operates on a variety of geographical scales: at the global level in opposition to institutions of global governance, be they the IFIs (international financial institutions), such as the IMF and the World Bank, or other multilateral economic coordination groupings, such as the G8 or OECD; at the regional level in opposition to regional and trans-regional trade agreements and economic coordination (NAFTA, FTAA, APEC, ASEM); at the national level in opposition to SAPs (structural adjustment programmes) and other neoliberal economic policies; at the local level in opposition to privatisation of local government services and local branches of TNCs (transnational corporations); as well as at the virtual level through its use of the Internet.

While the AGM's shared ideology is opposition to neoliberalism, there is no agreement on either strategy or tactics. The primary tension exists between those who want to reform the international financial and economic system and those who want to abolish it. On the one side are mainly NGOs and leftist political parties and their fronts, which believe that the IFIs can be reformed, and on the other is the direct action contingent, with strong anarchist representation and influence. The latter uses direct democracy and confrontational tactics up to and including violence and holds the political position that the IFIs are unreformable. Each side is further divided. For example, there are radical reformists, left reformists, and centrist reformists, all with a different version of 'globalisation with a human face'.

As Juris notes, these tensions between grassroots network-based movements and their more traditional organisational counterpoints have been integral to the AGM from the beginning.[12] There are two main parallel processes of organisation in the AGM. The first is radical, anarchic, confrontational, prefigurative in its politics, decentralised, non-hierarchical, anti-capitalist, and anti-statist. Its place is in the streets and its exemplar is the Black Bloc. The second is reformist, hierarchical, and more centralised, and involves civil society / NGO and more traditional political groups. Its place is in the Social Forum and its exemplar is the self-appointed Organising Committee (OC) of the World Social Forum. The following table summarises the division between the reformist 'verticals' (hierarchical national and international NGOs and political parties) and the radical or revolutionary 'horizontals' (looser affinity groups, anarchists, and direct actionists):

Table 1: Reformist and Revolutionary wings of the AGM

	Reformist / Vertical	Revolutionary / Horizontal
Exemplar AGM group	ATTAC (Association for the Taxation of Financial Transactions for the Aid to Citizens)	PGA (People's Global Action)
Exemplar AGM institution	World Social Forum	Indymedia
Position on globalisation	Globalisation with a 'human face'	Antiglobalisation
Organisational format	Centralised hierarchy Permanent administrative apparatus Directed organisation	Decentralised network Temporary administrative apparatus Self-organisation
Democracy	Representative Non-transparent Closed participation	Direct Transparent Open participation
Tactics	Lobbying, alternative policy formation	Confrontational
Strategy	Reform system Statist	Overthrow system Anti-statist

(from Mac Sheoin and Yeates 2006)

These tensions have surfaced in the demonstrations themselves. While many have praised the alliance between labour and new social movements in some demonstrations, labour has consistently maintained its separate space in such situations and at times forcefully maintained separation between its members and AGM militants. For instance, in many cases trade union marches in Europe have been kept separate from social movement / general marches.

The issue of the tactical use of violence at mass demonstrations is another major dividing line, as well as providing a handy marker as to whether fractions of the movement are reformist or revolutionary (and thereby recipients of mass media attention and condemnation). It is also the axis on which the state has tried to split the AGM, calling for the 'respectable' NGOs to denounce the 'hooligan violence' of some protesters.

To many detached observers, the emphasis on violence in some of the actions of the revolutionary / horizontal tendency often seems excessive. Much of the 'violence' has, however, been symbolic in nature rather than actual, as evidenced by the low level of casualties. Indeed what is startling about the AGM is how non-violent it has actually been. To quote a Marxist observer:

> [W]hat precisely characterises this generation and this movement in contrast with earlier ones on the European and North American left is the explicit eschewal, even among its most militant elements, of either armed revolutionary struggle or terrorism . . . as a means of effecting change in the advanced capitalist countries.[13]

Despite these tensions, the AGM has been able to maintain its unity through inclusiveness. The response of the AGM to the debate over violence has created "an evolving framework of 'diversity of tactics' . . . while also maintaining a united front of solidarity among activists and organisations with divergent beliefs about tactics".[14]

As one example of this, at the anti-World Bank / IMF demonstrations in Prague in the Czech Republic in September 2000, there were three separate axes of action exemplified in the Yellow march (Tute Bianche and Ya Basta!—symbolic opposition oriented to communication and mediation), the Blue march (anarchists and autonomen—direct and confrontational), and the Silver / Pink march (Earth First and Reclaim the Streets—playful and carnivalesque protest).[15] Along with this has been the development of what della Porta calls 'tolerant identities': "The self-definition as a 'movement of movements' . . . emphasises the positive aspects of heterogen[eity]".[16]

Gleneagles G8

Despite this toleration, on many occasions the splits within the AGM have been manifested on the ground. One example was provided by the mobilisation spurred by the G8 meeting in Gleneagles, Scotland, in July 2005. The reformist campaign Make Poverty History (MPH) involved the sale of white wristbands and a march in Edinburgh, combined with the speedily arranged Live8 concerts.

MPH's attitude towards their demonstration was summed up by its official, Bruce Whitehead:

> It's not a march in the sense of a demonstration, but more of a walk. It is going to be very much a family affair. The emphasis is on fun in the sun. The intention is to welcome the G8 leaders to Scotland and to ask them to deliver trade justice, debt cancellation and increased aid to developing countries.[17]

Around 225,000 people marched with MPH. Radicals accused MPH of co-opting concern over global poverty into spectacular and consumerist activities, noting how "the major civil society mobilisation for the G8—the MPH—comprising the major trade unions, development NGOs, and faith groups with 'political celebrities', shamelessly organised *in favour* of the summit", and how, by organising its march in Edinburgh (whereas the G8 summit was in Gleneagles), "MPH succeeded in simultaneously mobilising hundreds of thousands of people to Scotland but away from the G8".[18] On the other hand, the radicals organised marches towards the actual location of the G8 summit, which they considered more effectively protested the summit despite a huge security apparatus assembled to prevent protest.

MPH's campaign not only involved a diversionary spectacular and consumerist politics—'buy a white wristband / ticket to a concert and take part in a major march' which was nowhere near the G8 meeting. The campaign's activities were also tightly controlled, with no possibility of spontaneity, and they were effectively an attempt to depoliticise the summit. In contrast, the radicals' campaign involved a DIY approach—do something rather than buy something—whose decentralised organisation welcomed autonomous actions and was characterised by innovative tactics such as the Clown Army. The radical campaign was also aimed at the summit itself. Finally, its organisation was seen by those taking part in it as prefigurative of a new society.[19]

The National and the Regional in the Transnational

The celebration of the transnationality of the AGM has encompassed a variety of meanings, including "national mobilisations in a globalised world" and "mobilisations beyond the nation state".[20] This section looks first at available surveys of protesters and participants at major AGM summit demonstrations and social forums, before turning to look at the international solidarity demonstrations that accompany major AGM summit demonstrations.

While the existence of transnationally mobile demonstrators is undeniable, surveys of participants in social forums and demonstrations repeatedly make obvious the markedly 'national' composition of AGM manifestations. At Seattle the vast majority of demonstrators were North American: of the 50,000 protesters, at most 3,000 came from outside Canada and the US. Data assembled from four AGM protests confirms the paucity of transnational participation in protest mobilisations at summits in North America, finding just 3.2 per cent of their sample at the February 2002 WEF protests in New York to be international (and 0 per cent at the A20 WB demo in Washington, DC, in April 2000); 2.3 per cent at the anti-G8 action in Calgary in Canada in June 2002; and 2.2 per cent at the WB in Washington in September 2002.[21] Regarding the September 2001 protests in Washington, DC, Tarrow reports: "Only one group in the Washington protest even took it upon itself to maintain ties with foreign allies, and there were almost no foreigners present at the demonstration".[22]

Similarly, an analysis of EU summit demonstrators at Brussels, Belgium, on December 14 2001 found that 62 per cent of the demonstrators were Belgian and 31 per cent were from the four nearest EU countries, with the remaining 7 per cent from "elsewhere".[23] While the demonstrations at Prague have been described as the most international of the European summit protests, of the 400 people arrested, "about 100 [were] foreigners, and the rest Czechs".[24] Similarly, for the MPH march in Edinburgh, a survey found that "over a third of our respondents (37 per cent) lived in Edinburgh itself, with another fifth (20 per cent) living elsewhere in lowland Scotland. Overall, the majority of our respondents (65 per cent) lived in Scotland. Most of the rest lived in England, notably northern England and London".[25]

There are also differences in the composition of the AGM in different countries. Surveys at the European Social Forum held in Florence in Italy in 2002, and at the anti-G8 protest that took place in Genoa, also in Italy, in 2001, found that "[n]ew social movement (NSM) and environmental activists were much more present among British or German participants than among French ones. French participants were characterised by a strong union component to a much greater extent than German or Spanish ones".[26] Further surveys of the French and Swiss participants in the protests in Evian, France, in June 2003 found that "Swiss and French participants in that event were embedded in different organizational networks", with more NSM organisations (environmental, human rights, peace) on the Swiss side and more AGM organisations present on the French side.[27]

The overwhelmingly 'national' composition of the AGM is shown again in the social forums. Ninety per cent of the delegates at the first ESF in Florence, Italy, were Italian.[28] The Profile of Participants at the WSF in Porto Alegre, Brazil, found nearly 86 per cent of the total 170,000 officially registered participants at the first three WSFs were Brazilian; the largest foreign delegations were from nearby Latin American countries. Similarly, "the ASF [Asian Social Forum, held in Hyderabad, India, in January 2003] was a pan-Asian meeting only to a very limited degree, with only a few hundred out of the total 20,000 participants coming from other parts of Asia".[29] With respect to two Australian social forums in 2004, Bramble has noted that "[v]ery few were attending from overseas".[30]

If the demographic composition of the main summit protests is not where the transnational content of the AGM is located, it is reflected in the geographic spread of solidarity protests. Wood reports that demonstrations took place in forty-one countries throughout the world in May 1998, fifty-three in June 1999, ninety-seven in November 1999, eighty-eight in September 2000, and 152 in November 2001,[31] while the anti-FTAA protest in Québec in April 2001 was accompanied by solidarity protests in at least fifty cities outside Canada.[32]

There is thus no doubt that in these demonstrations the AGM is manifesting itself in transnationally coordinated protests on a global scale. However these protests also show a variety of regional characteristics. Wood goes on to suggest that "protests target neoliberalism differently on each continent", adding that "in order to understand the variation between continents in terms of target choice, one must consider pre-existing political repertoires, social movement networks, and the diffusion processes that spread innovations to new sites".[33]

Regional differences, as well as divisions between reformists and revolutionaries, are also expressed in the choice of targets for demonstrations. Demonstrations linked to ATTAC, ICFTU, and Jubilee 2000 tend to target WTO, G8, IMF, and / or WB, while those associated with PGA and RTS (Reclaim the Streets) were more likely to select a local target. Of local targets, 27 per cent of actions aimed at local branches or headquarters of MNCs, especially prevalent targets in Canada, Australia, New Zealand, Europe, and the US—countries without an already existing anti-neoliberal repertoire. Nineteen per cent of the protests targeted national governments, mainly in Africa and Asia. The third most popular target (15 per cent of the sample) were banks and / or stock exchanges, with Latin America specialising in this target.[34]

Overall, then, there is no one unitary AGM to be described, and diversity is the essence of the AGM. It is highly diverse in composition, organisational features, targets, and tactics; it expresses itself at local, national, regional, and global levels in very different ways. To explore this feature further—after a brief discussion of social composition—in the second section we contrast modes of organisation by looking at two transnational organisations, one from each wing of the AGM: PGA and ATTAC. And in the third section we focus on the tensions between the movement's wings as expressed in social forums.

The Return of the 'New Middle Class'

Surveys on the AGM also show a social composition similar to that of NSMs: "[T]he Forum is an initiative that still belongs mostly to the middle class, middle and upper castes, and male leadership of the 'civil', 'present' world".[35] According to the WSF participants' profile, around 73 per cent of those attending both WSF

2001 and WSF 2003 had begun, attended, and / or finished university; a survey of WSF India in 2004 found 63 per cent of attendees had university degrees; a survey at WSF 2005 found "an overrepresentation of Latin American and European activists, affluent people with high levels of education and whites"; among Florence ESF activists, "[a] very high number (14.6%) of activists are teachers or university professors, with higher representation for the French (19%) and British (25.5%)".[36]

In surveys carried out at the Paris ESF and the anti-G8 demonstrations in Evian in France, both in 2003, only 3 per cent of respondents at the ESF and 6 per cent at Evian had no school diplomas, while 17 per cent of ESF and 19 per cent of Evian participants had attended college, and 50 per cent of those at the ESF and 34 per cent of those at Evian had attended university. Regarding professional status, 31 per cent at ESF and 19 per cent at Evian were managers or members of intellectual professions, while 31 per cent of ESF and 16 per cent of Evian participants belonged to intermediate professions. The commentators note that those at both Evian and the ESF who work "often own favoured positions: professionals, executives, managers and employees, rather than work [wo]men", of whom there were 2 per cent at ESF and 4 per cent at Evian. As they note, these sociological characteristics correspond to "middle class radicalism".[37]

University educated, working in the knowledge industries, predominantly in the public sector . . . the list is beginning to sound familiar. The explicit connection is made by a study of activists at Australian social forums, which found two-thirds had undergraduate or postgraduate degrees, with a disproportionate number working in the public sector (34 per cent) or non-profit sector (26 per cent):

> [T]he backgrounds of participants at Australian social forums clearly match those of the NSMs of the 1980s and, indeed, the radical movements of the late 1960s and early 1970s. They are highly educated, come from professional families and are either students, full-time activists or work in the public sector and or social / community professions. To the extent that the concept of a 'new middle class' is meaningful, it would appear to fit the current or likely future occupations of the large majority of participants.[38]

This study also notes that the "[p]articipants in the Australian social forums exhibit the classic split between radicals and moderates evident in the social movements of the 1970s and 1980s".[39]

Transnational Organisations

PGA—People's Global Action

Founded in Geneva in 1998, the original impetus for the PGA (People's Global Action) stemmed from the International Encounters called by the Zapatistas in

1995 and 1997. A new kind of International, the PGA describes itself as having neither membership nor a juridical character. No organisation or person represents the PGA, nor does the PGA represent any organisation or person. The PGA is a transnational network comprised of a loose coalition of ninety-four 'core' organisations from forty-three countries. This coalition-network facilitates communication, information sharing, solidarity, coordination, and resource mobilisation, mainly through its websites, email lists, and conferences. The PGA has been key to issuing AGM calls to action,[40] and a total of more than 1,500 organisations attended its regional fora, three international conferences, and / or participated in five 'global days of action' between 1998 and 2001.[41]

PGA involves a remarkable coalition between mass-based (primarily peasant and Indigenous) organisations in peripheral countries and activists in core countries who are unaffiliated to any mass-based organisation and who are committed to direct democracy and new forms of organisation. As Petras notes, "[t]oday, the most promising and dynamic movements—the unemployed workers' movement in Argentina, the MST in Brazil, the Cocaleros of Bolivia, the Zapatistas in Mexico—are based on popular assemblies and consultation, direct democracy".[42] Its ideological commitment to new forms of organisation has allowed the PGA to coordinate highly diverse organisations transnationally.

This success is not, however, unqualified. Problems include lack of transparency regarding roles, lack of accountability mechanisms, uncertainty over responsibility for various network functions, and the predominant importance of specific activists and support groups.[43] There is also the issue of 'core' country dominance due to differential access to resources, with activists from core countries in Europe and North America better able to bear the costs of international travel and having better Internet access. The importance of Europe-based support group activists in propelling PGA activities has reinforced this 'core / periphery' division.

The PGA has tried to address this issue by stressing the diversity of policy responses to neoliberalism articulated by its members, including the local development of alternatives, and limiting participation by European and North American groups in its conferences. However, much remains to be done: the contradictions between mass peasant and Indigenous organisations and their core country allies, manifested in the PGA network relying on communication by computer (to which most members of mass organisations have no access) and in dominant Western languages,[44] remain unresolved.

ATTAC—Association for the Taxation of Financial Transactions for the Aid to Citizens

Whereas the PGA is comprised of local groups co-operating as a transnational network, ATTAC's mode of organisation is essentially national and hierarchical. Founded in 1998, ATTAC is a radical reformist group characterised by its supporters as a 'triple movement'—a popular education movement with a goal of action, a protest movement, and one that "wishes to be present where real decisions are made, not after the fact or 50 kilometres away".[45] From the beginning, ATTAC France has enjoyed strong trade union and other institutional support. It launched its international presence in Paris in December 1998, attended by representatives from Africa, Asia, Europe, and Latin America. By summer 1999, its first major international conference had taken place in Paris.[46] It has no global organisational structure, being essentially an international network of national organisations. By 2003, it had local branches in forty-eight countries, which were however concentrated in Western Europe and Latin America, with only a few adherents in North America and five branches in Africa, all in former French colonies. It is absent from Asia-Pacific and the Middle East.[47]

National formations vary. While ATTAC France is a group with extensive membership and support, ATTAC Germany is "a product for and of the media",[48] though it later became a "breeding ground for the new left party".[49] ATTAC Denmark has been described as a marketing and political project by a newspaper.[50] Some national organisations are less hierarchical, such as ATTAC Sweden, which has neither a chairperson nor an official spokesperson. Others have been successful in opposition to neoliberal policies locally: Norway, in conjunction with unions and NGOs, "successfully used an election campaign to stop all privatisations, cancel odious debt and move the government to the left".[51]

ATTAC France has a markedly hierarchical structure, with a central secretariat, chairperson, and spokespeople. Decision-making takes place at its General Assembly where decisions are made by a majority vote. Members and local groups have little influence compared with that of the non-elected members of the *collège des fondateurs* (or in English, 'foundation board').[52] This political model was explained by ATTAC founder and first president Bernard Cassen as follows:

> I proposed national statutes that on first sight might appear undemocratic, but in my view are by no means so. There are 30 members of the national executive, of whom 18 are elected by the 70 founders of ATTAC, and 12 by the 30,000 membership at large.[53]

The reason for this was to defeat possible entryism. Thus, to prevent undemocratic manipulation of the national structure, the national structure was made undemocratic. George notes that this organisational structure is so locked in that the ATTAC dissidents were unable to change it.[54]

This tight hierarchical control became a cause of division and split within ATTAC France. The internal strife and lack of democracy also led to a decrease in membership from 28,000 in 2002 to less than 10,000 in 2007.[55]

Despite its internationalist rhetoric, ATTAC France has concentrated on national politics and national demands. And if the demands are national, so are the institutions on whom the demands are made. In France (and Sweden), "national institutions (parliament, government) absolutely dominate as primary targets for the groups' actions, and amount to around half of those. In contrast, global institutions are only rarely targeted".[56] ATTAC's demands are oriented towards the state: "ATTAC calls for a re-affirmation of State power—the State alone is seen as capable of resisting and containing rampant market forces and of protecting democratic values and the general interest".[57]

ATTAC's membership is dominated by intellectuals, with an independent survey in 2002 reporting that over 45 per cent of its membership discovered ATTAC through its readership of the monthly *Le Monde diplomatique*. For the rest of its membership, 38 per cent worked in the public sector, 23 per cent were teachers, 3 per cent workers, 1 per cent farmers, with the remainder working in the private sector, mainly in professional and managerial grades.[58] As Cassen himself noted:

[W]e are an association recruited from the lower-middle classes upwards, above all in the public services, with a significant proportion of students and teachers, but employees and executives of the private sector are also present. We also have a sprinkling of farmers and unemployed. What we do not possess—any more than anyone else—are roots in the working class, or popular sectors more broadly.[59]

Its tactics mirrored its cadre: "[E]mphasis is placed on intellectual production as a tool of social change and it is through argument rather than direct action that it confronts its enemies".[60] Waters sees this intellectual credibility as central to ATTAC's success, which was considerable:

[I]t achieved unparalleled success in the very political establishment it set out to criticise. In the space of a few years, it acquired representation in the French and European parliaments, developed alliances with the ruling government coalition and was courted by political leaders on the Left and Right.[61]

This section has focused on two organisational models that co-exist within the AGM. The PGA is an exemplar of the new global politics, a non- or virtual organisation, which operates through its website, its conferences, and its global coordination of days of action. Despite this global organisational form, the constituents of the PGA are locally- and nationally-based groups whose main activity is local or national mobilisation, as shown by their target selection. In comparison, ATTAC appears decidedly French in its nature, stemming from the unique position that interventions by the intellectual elite are accorded within the French political position, while also being an exemplar of the 'old' politics, with strong trade union support and more than a whiff of 'democratic centralism' to its mode of organisation. Despite the formation of ATTACs in several parts of the world, the national organisations do not give high priority to transnational matters. The major transnational contribution ATTAC made was its involvement in the World Social Forum (WSF), of which Cassen was one of the main architects, and it is to the WSF that we now turn.

Transnational Spaces

Social Fora

Social forums and counter-summits are a major manifestation of the AGM's existence. Dating to the Zapatista Encounters and to the alternative summits of the 1980s, these events have proliferated over the last twenty years.[62] Half of the sixty-one parallel summits have been located in Europe, one-quarter in the US, and one-quarter in the rest of the world.[63]

The first major social Forum—the World Social Forum—took place in Porto Alegre, Brazil, in January 2001, organised by Brazilian NGOs with assistance from ATTAC France. Its Charter of Principles declared it to be "an open meeting place" to oppose neoliberalism and for "building a planetary society centred on the human person".[64]

Social forums have been characterised as prefigurative of future forms of political organisation, a new way of doing politics, a process rather than an institution. On closer inspection, however, they suffer from exceedingly old forms of political organisation and are not as democratic, open, and accountable as sometimes represented. The following are the main areas in which tension has arisen.

First, the organisation of and range of discussion in social forums have been strongly controlled by political parties (which are supposedly excluded from participating). The first three WSF meetings—all held in Porto Alegre in Brazil—benefitted (like all the European Social Forums) from the political parties who were in power in the cities where the fora were held. The most obvious problem raised by this return of the social democrats is that of democracy. In Porto Alegre, and then the WSF held in Mumbai, and in the case of the ESF in London control by political party cadres led to allegations of lack of accountability, democracy, and transparency, along with problems of exclusion of groups and movements, as well as tight control over the fora sessions. Sen notes that "the actually existing Forum is not the 'open space' that it is said to be, but is instead highly structured and, in several dimensions, exclusive", and observes "the tendency of the organisers, both in Brazil and India, to *control* things".[65]

Secondly, the WSF excluded groups "that seek to take people's lives as a method of political action", such as those sympathetic to the Maoist People's War Group (PWG) in India, Basque organisations, and the Zapatistas.[66] However, this critical attitude to violence was not applied to mainstream politicians: various European politicians who are leaders of states with large armies visited the WSF without a problem. The best example is provided by French politicians who lead a state that bombed the Greenpeace ship *Rainbow Warrior*, maintains weapons of mass destruction in the form of a nuclear arsenal, undertook armed interventions in former African colonies, and supported the war in Afghanistan. Both the BBC and the *Wall Street Journal* reported in 2002 that six ministers from the Jospin government attended the WSF.[67]

Third, the WSF is dominated by a particular section of civil society. As one member of the Brazilian Organising Committee has noted: "[W]e are an elite of citizen activism. The larger, more excluded sectors, although organised in social movements and networks, do not participate in a meaningful way in the Forum".[68] Petras echoed the complaint:

> Many of the European and US NGOs present are paper organisations and the majority of Third World NGOers are members of small groups of professionals with few, if any, organised supporters and possess little power of convocation. On the other hand, there were a small number of representatives from mass movements in Africa, particularly South Africa, and Asia who represent hundreds of thousands of grassroots activists. Yet it was the well-known intellectual notables from the NGOs which crowded the platforms and informed the public about the movements in their regions.[69]

Related to the charge of elitism is that the WSF reduced most of its attendees to passive 'consumers' of sessions and workshops at which noted speakers took up most of the time with speeches, allowing little time for discussion or contributions from the audience.

Fourth, despite the ready availability and power of feminist critiques of neoliberalism, the WSF, like the AGM, has failed to adequately take on board issues such as reproductive rights, male violence, and patriarchy, and has also failed to provide a safe space for women, a charge also laid against the autonomous spaces at the WSF, ie, those most associated with the radical wing of the AGM.

Fifth, there has been strong criticism of the sources of funding, including Ford, Rockefeller, and other foundations, while many NGO sponsors of the fora are themselves funded by corporations.[70] The failure of the WSF organisers to provide detailed information on the size and conditionalities of funding contradicts the transparency that many of its proponents would demand from MNCs. In September 2006, an internal report on the WSF's finances commissioned by its International Council (IC) provided only a very basic summary of income and expenditure for the WSF from 2001 to 2005. However, it also noted that "many interviewees felt they lacked essential information about income, expenditures and decisions that were taken in that regard. The problem is that there is no system of reporting back on financial matters in the IC".[71] No financial malfeasance is implied here, rather a failure to attribute a high enough priority to transparency (a problem that dogs much of the WSF).

Finally, major tensions resulted from attempts to turn the Forum from an open space to an arena for "deliberation, decision, organisation and action".[72] Related to this is the concern over the growth of 'platformism'. Critics attacked the Appeal of the 19 produced at WSF 2005 (as a suggested programme for the AGM) and the Bamako Appeal of 2006 as programmes for global transformation, going against the spirit of the Forum. There is tension also over those attracted by the possibility of turning the WSF into the next International or the base for a global political party.[73]

These contradictions affect all social forums. Sen expresses a problem basic to the WSF process: "[O]rganisation with *old* vocabularies of politics, and old ways of organising and relating to others, are leading the process of forging what are said by some to be *new* politics".[74]

With the ESF in London in October 2004, this contradiction reached a breaking point. By all accounts, except, understandably, those of the organisers, the London 'bid' to hold the ESF was secretly produced and implemented by a small coalition of Greater London Authority (GLA) officials and the Socialist Workers Party.[75] Much of the organising work was contracted out to commercial companies. Instead of prefiguring their desired society, as the autonomous spaces did by using activist kitchens, at the ESF "the food was all provided by catering companies employing low-wage work, plastic packages and corporate brands everywhere".[76] This commercialisation was reflected in the high cost of attendance, ranging from £20 to £40.

Overall, the WSF and ESF in their organisation seem to deny the democracy that is claimed to be characteristic of the AGM. Indeed, it is feared that they are being used by a minority of individuals to parachute themselves as leaders onto a movement that developed without their participation in the first place. In some ways it seems hard not to interpret the social forums as attempts by the traditional left—social democratic, radical reformist, and ex-communist—to obtain hegemony over the AGM.

Counter-Summits

Because of their exclusionary organisation and capture by political parties, the social forums have generated their own organised opposition—inside, outside, and close to the official fora themselves—through the establishment of parallel summits by groups excluded from the official fora. In most of these, the opposition was anarchist, but in Mumbai it was Maoist, with Marxist-Leninist elements and mass-based organisations organising their own counter-summit, Mumbai Resistance 2004 (MR).

Certainly there were class differences between MR and WSF Mumbai, with Bavadam noting that "[t]he majority of MR participants were peasant farmers and field-based activists. The disproportionately high number of police personnel at the MR venue bore testimony to this".[77] In the London ESF, the direct action fraction of the English AGM, acting in cooperation with sympathetic transnationals, organised their own parallel fora. The Athens ESF in 2006 also saw four alternative fora.

This founding of alternative fora seems to be the most satisfactory response to the criticisms of actually existing fora:

> Our movements are too diverse, even contradictory, to be contained within a single space, however open it may be. This does not mean abandoning the process, but rather building on the London experience to recast the forum as a network of interconnected, yet autonomous spaces converging across a single urban terrain at a particular point in time. . . . Moreover there will necessarily be contradiction and struggle, even within and between our networks. Such conflict should not be feared, but rather recognised as an integral part of the forum itself.[78]

Our examination of social forums has shown a similar division between 'old' and 'new' politics as the previous section on PGA and ATTAC did. Despite the rhetoric of 'open space' and 'new politics', the organisation of WSF (and ESF) has shown the continued existence in the AGM of 'old' forms of politics masquerading as the 'new', leading to conflict between both wings of the movement.

Conclusions

Much emphasis has been placed on the novelty of AGM politics both in its transnational / global scope and its constituent actors, but this essay has tried to show that this emphasis needs to be tempered with caution. Not all the actors involved are new. Indeed, the example of the 'new public space' we examined most closely in this chapter, the WSF and ESF, contains some political groups and practices that are decidedly 'old'. While the AGM is a 'new' global movement, it is also locally or nationally based. AGM demonstrations have been markedly national in composition, and the accompanying solidarity demonstrations, while obviously manifesting the international spread of the AGM and the transnational coordination of demonstrations also show regional characteristics. Furthermore, in general the AGM is not only exemplary of new politics but shows evidence of decidedly old politics. The AGM has continued to contain these two contrasting and often contradictory modes of organising in a coalition, the basis for which is respect for the movement's diversity, whether in accepting diversity of tactics in street demonstrations or in including in social forums spaces for both wings of the movement.

References

Paul D Almeida and Mark I Lichbach, 2003—'To the internet, from the internet: Comparative media coverage of transnational protests', in *Mobilization*, vol 8 no 3, pp 249–72

Helmut Anheier, Marlies Glasius, and Mary Kaldor, 2001—*Global Civil Society 2001*. Oxford: Oxford University Press

Anon, 2002—'Alternative forum tries to define agenda', on *BBC*, at http://news.bbc. co.uk/2/hi/americas/1797557.stm (Accessed August 17 2017)

Lyla Bavadam, January 2004—'A militant platform', in *Frontline*, vol 21 no 3, January 31 2004, at http://www.frontline.in/static/html/fl2103/stories/20040213004702200.htm (Accessed August 17 2017)

Isabelle Bédoyan, Peter Van Aelst, and Stefaan Walgrave, December 2003—'Limitations and possibilities of transnational mobilization: The case of the EU summit protesters in Brussels, 2001'. Paper to the symposium '*Les mobilisations altermondialistes*' ['Alterglobalist Mobilisations', in French], Association francaise de science politique, Paris, December 3–5 2003

Vicki L Birchfield, 2004—'Institutionalised power and anti-establishment politics in France: The case of ATTAC'. Paper to the conference 'Interest Groups in 21st Century France and Europe'. IEP / CEVIPOF, Paris, France, September 24–25 2004, at http://www.cevipof.msh-paris.fr (Inactive August 17 2017)

Philippe Blanchard and Olivier Fillieule, 2006—'Individual surveys in rallies (INSURA): A new Eldorado for comparative social movement research?', on *ResearchGate* at https://www.researchgate.net/publication/237227953_Individual_Surveys_in_ Rallies_INSURA_A_new_Eldorado_for_Comparative_Social_Movement_Research (Accessed August 17 2017)

Patrick Bond, Dennis Brutus, and Virginia Setshedi, July 2005—'Average white band' in *Red Pepper*, July 2005, at www.redpepper.org.uk/global/x-jul05-whiteband.htm (Accessed April 14 2009, inactive August 17 2017)

Tom Bramble, 2006—'Another world is possible: A study of participants at Australian *alter-globalization* social forums', in *Journal of Sociology*, vol 42 no 3, pp 287–309

Bart Cammaerts and Leo Van Audenhove, 2003—'ICT-usage among Transnational Social Movements in the Networked Society: to organize, to mediate, and to influence'. Amsterdam: ASCoR (Amsterdam School of Communications Research), Amsterdam Free University, at http://www.lse.ac.uk/media@lse/research/EMTEL/ reports/cammaerts_2003_emtel.pdf (Accessed August 17 2017)

Bernard Cassen, January–February 2003—'On the attack', in *New Left Review*, no 19, January–February 2003, pp 41–63

Graeme Chesters and Ian Welsh, November 2001—'Rebel colours: "framing" in global social movements', on *ResearchGate*, at https://www.researchgate.net/publication/ 27312969_Rebel_colours_'Framing'_in_global_social_movements (Accessed August 17 2017)

B M Christensen, 2002—'Constructing a social movement: The case of ATTAC—a case of constructive journalism'. Paper to the Making Social Movements conference, Edgehill College, Ormskirk, England, June 26–28 2002, at http://www.modinet.dk/ pdf/WorkingPapers/No1_Constructing_a_Social_Movement.pdf (Accessed April 14 2009, inactive August 17 2017)

Robin Cohen and Shirin Rai, 2000—'Global social movements: Towards a cosmopolitan politics', in Robin Cohen and Shirin Rai, eds, 2000—*Global Social Movements*. London: Athlone, pp 1–17

Massimo De Angelis, 2018—'PR Like PRocess! Strategy from the Bottom Up', in Jai Sen, ed, 2018—*The Movements of Movements, Part 2: Rethinking Our Dance*. Volume 5 in the *Challenging Empires* series. New Delhi: OpenWord, and Oakland, CA: PM Press

Olivier de Marcellus, 2000—'People's Global Action: a brief history', in *Race and Class*, vol 1 no 4, pp 92–99

Donna della Porta, 2005a—'The Social Bases of the Global Justice Movement: Some Theoretical Reflections and Empirical Evidence from the first European Social Forum'. Geneva: UNRISD, at http://www.unrisd.org/unrisd/website/document. nsf/(httpPublications)/C779023A61701329C125710F00300361?OpenDocument (Accessed August 17 2017)

Donna della Porta, 2005b—'Multiple belongings, tolerant identities and the construction of another politics', in Donna della Porta and Sidney Tarrow, eds, 2005—*Transnational Protest and Global Activism*. Lanham, MD: Rowman and Littlefield, pp 175–202

Linden Farrer, 2004—'World Forum Movement: Abandon or Contaminate', in Jai Sen, Anita Anand, Arturo Escobar, and Peter Waterman, eds, 2004—*World Social Forum: Challenging Empires*. New Delhi: The Viveka Foundation, pp 168–77

D Ferre, 2002—'A look at some of the French delegates to Porto Alegre 2', in *Informations Ouvrieres*, February 12 2002, at www.owcinfo.org/ILC/WSF/Report_WF2_Brazil_ html (Accessed November 10 2008, inactive August 17 2017)

Dana R Fisher, Kevin Stanley, David Berman, and Gina Neff, 2003—'How do organizations matter? Mobilization and support for participants at five globalization protests', in *Social Problems*, vol 52 no 1, pp 102–21

C Fleming, January 2002—'Anti-globalization movement gains support from both sides in France', in *Wall Street Journal*, January 29 2002, at http://news.infoshop.org/article/php?story+02/01/30/2105549 (Accessed November 11, 2008, inactive August 17 2017)

Eddy Fougier, 2003—'The French Anti-Globalisation Movement: A New French Exception?', IFRI Policy Paper 2, at https://www.ifri.org/en/publications/enotes/notes-de-lifri/french-antiglobalization-movement-new-french-exception#sthash. qNRDSr72.dpbs (Accessed August 17 2017)

Susan George, 2006—'A New Beginning for ATTAC', on *tni*, December 28 2006, at https://www.tni.org/en/archives/act/16059 (Accessed August 17 2017)

Sven Giegold, 2008—'Do we need a post-altermondialisation? Report from the WSF 2008 in Paris', at www.forumsocialmundial.org.br/noticias_textos.php?ed_news=453 (Accessed November 4 2008, inactive August 17 2017)

Marco Giugni, Marko Bandler, and Nina Eggert, 2005—'The Global Justice Movement: How Far Does the Classic Social Movement Agenda Go in Explaining Transnational Contention?'. Geneva: UNRISD, at http://www.unrisd.org/unrisd/website/document .nsf/(httpPublications)/8647C951DCB7E800C12571D1002D7BE4?OpenDocument (Accessed August 17 2017)

Hugo Gorringe and Michael Rosie, January 2006—'Pants to poverty?', at Making Poverty History, Edinburgh 2005, on *Sociological Research Online*, vol 11 no 1, 2006, at http://www.socresonline.org.uk/11/1/gorringe.html (Accessed August 17 2017)

David Graeber, 2001—'The Globalisation Movement: Some Points of Clarification', in *Items*, vol 2, nos 3–4, pp 12–14, at http://mailman.lbo-talk.org/2001/2001-November/025048.html (Accessed August 17 2017)

Devashree Gupta, Sidney Tarrow, and Melanie Acostaville, 2001—'Transnational politics: A bibliographic guide to recent research on transnational movements and advocacy groups', at http://falcon.arts.cornell.edu/sgtz/contention/Transnational-Bibliography.htm. (Inactive August 17 2017)

Paul Hewson, 2005—'It's the politics, stupid! How liberal politicians, NGOs and rock stars hijacked the global justice movement at Gleneagles. And how we let them', in David Harvie, Keir Milburn, Ben Trott, and David Watts, eds, 2005—*Shut Them Down! The G8, Gleneagles 2005, and the Movement of Movements*. Leeds: Dissent! / New York: Autonomedia, pp 135–50

John H Henning Center for International Labour Relations, nd—'The Bibliography', at http://henningcenter.berkeley.edu/projects/abstracts.html (Accessed April 14 2009, inactive August 17 2017)

IPS Correspondents, 2004—'Challenges, Limits and Possibilities of the Word Social Forum', on *IPS*, at http://ipsnews.net/news.asp?idnews=21938 (Accessed August 17 2017)

Jeffrey S Juris, 2004a—'The London ESF and the Politics of Autonomous Space', at https://static1.squarespace.com/static/53fde28ee4b0f7be79e00d95/t/54121603e-4b0a1dd950d55d2/1410471427903/the-london-esf-and-the-politics-of-autonomous-space.pdf (Accessed August 17 2017)

Boris Kagarlitsky, 2003—'Prague 2000: The People's Battle', in Eddie Yuen, Daniel Burton-Rose, and George Katsiaficas, eds, 2003—*The Battle of Seattle*. New York: Soft Skull Press, pp 253–67

Anastasia Kavada, 2005—'Exploring the role of the internet in the movement for alternative globalization: The case of the Paris 2003 European Social Forum', in *Westminster Papers in Communication and Culture*, vol 2 no 1, pp 72–95, at https://www.westminsterpapers.org/articles/abstract/10.16997/wpcc.9/ (Accessed August 17 2017)

Margaret Keck and Kathryn Sikkink, 1998—*Activists Beyond Borders: Transnational Advocacy Networks in International Politics*. Ithaca: Cornell University Press

Felix Kolb, 2003—'The impact of transnational protest on social movement organizations: Mass media and the making of ATTAC Germany'. Paper to the conference 'Transnational Processes and Social Movements', Bellagio, Italy, July 22–26 2003, on *ResearchGate*, at https://www.researchgate.net/publication/229002881_The_impact_of_transnational_protest_on_social_movement_organizations_mass_media_and_the_making_of_ATTAC_Germany (Accessed August 17 2017)

Gordon Laxer and Sandra Halperin, 2003—*Global Civil Society and its Limits*. Basingstoke: Palgrave Macmillan

Rolando Lopez, Theo van Koolwijk, and Nandita Shah, 2006—'World Social Forum Financial Strategy: Report and Recommendations', at www.massglobalaction.org/projects/WSF_finstrategy_FinalReport_EN.pdf (Accessed August 17 2017)

Tomás Mac Sheoin and Nicola Yeates, 2006—'Division and Dissent in the Anti-Globalisation Movement', in Samir Dasgupta and Ray Kiely, eds, 2006—*Globalization and After*. New Delhi: Sage, pp 360–91

Hermann Maiba, nd—'"We are everywhere": Transnational grassroots against capitalism', at http://www.hermann-*maiba*.de/Final%20report.doc.pdf (Accessed April 8 2014, inactive August 17 2017)

Carlos R S Milani, 2007—'Review of *L'altermondialisme en France: La longue histoire d'une nouvelle cause* ['Alternative globalisation in France: The long history of a new cause', in French], in *International Social Science Journal*, vol 58 no 189, pp 527–30, at http://onlinelibrary.wiley.com/doi/10.1111/j.1468-2451.2007.00650.x/abstract (Accessed August 17 2017)

Rodrigo Nunes, 2004—'Territory and Deterritory: Inside and outside the ESF, new movement subjectivities', on *Interactivist Information Exchange*, at http://www.openspaceforum.net/twiki/tiki-print_article.php?articleId=30 (Accessed August 17 2017)

Leo Panitch, 2002—'Violence as a Tool of Order and Change', in *Monthly Review*, June, vol 54 no 2, pp 12–32, at http://www.monthlyreview.org/0602panitch.htm (Accessed August 17 2017)

Tasos Papadimitriou, April 2008—'A Social Experiment in the Midst of G8 Power: Creating "Another World" or the Politics of Self-Indulgence?', in *Transformative Studies* vol 1 no 2, April 2008, at http://transformativestudies.org/wp-content/uploads/2008/04/a-social-experiment-in-the-mhe-politics-of-self-indulgence2.pdf (Accessed August 17 2017)

Florence Passy, 1999—'Supranational Political Opportunities as a Channel of Globalisation of Political Conflicts: The Case of the Rights of Indigenous Peoples', in Donna della Porta, Hanspeter Kriesi, and Dieter Rucht, eds, 1999—*Social Movements in a Globalising World*. London: Macmillan

James Petras, December 2001—'Non-Governmental Organisations in a Conjuncture of Conflict and War Psychosis', at http://www.rebelion.org/hemeroteca/petras/english/ngo170102.htm (Accessed August 17 2017)

James Petras, 2002—'Porto Alegre 2002: A tale of two forums', at http://www.rebelion.org/hemeroteca/petras/english/twoforums170202.htm (Accessed August 17 2017)

Mario Pianta, 2001—'Parallel Summits of Global Civil Society', in Helmut Anheier, Marlies Glasius, and Mary Kaldor, eds, 2001—*Global Civil Society 2001*. Oxford: Oxford University Press, pp 169–94

Rebecca Álvarez, Erika Gutierrez, Linda Kim, Christine Petit, and Ellen Reese, c.2005—'The Contours of Color at the World Social Forum: Reflections on Racialized Politics, Representation, and the Global Justice Movement'. IROWS Working Paper #36. UCR Institute for Research on World-Systems, University of California-Riverside, at http://www.irows.ucr.edu/papers/irows36/irows36.htm (Accessed October 7 2017)

Research Unit for Political Economy, 2007—'Foundations and Mass Movements: The Case of the World Social Forum', in *Critical Sociology*, 33, pp 505–36, at http://journals.sagepub.com/doi/abs/10.1163/156916307X189004?journalCode=crsb (Accessed August 18 2017)

Gustavo Lins Ribeiro, 2006—'Other globalisations: Alter-native Transnational Processes and Agents'. Brasilia: Universidade de Brasilia. Série Antropologia 389, at www.centro-edelstein.org.br/PDF/WorkingPapers/WP_4_English.pdf (Accessed August 18 2017)

Paul Routledge, 2004—'Convergence of Commons: Process Geographies of People's Global Action', at www.commoner.org.uk/08routledge.pdf (Accessed August 18 2017)

Günther Schonleitner, 2003—'World Social Forum: Making another world possible?', in John Clark, ed, 2003—*Globalizing Civic Engagement: Civil Society and Transnational Activism*. London: Earthscan

Jai Sen, 2004c—'The Long March to Another World: Reflections of a Member of the WSF India Committee in 2002 on the First Year of the World Social Forum Process in India', in Jai Sen, Anita Anand, Arturo Escobar, and Peter Waterman, eds, 2004— *World Social Forum: Challenging Empires*. New Delhi: Viveka, pp 293–311, at http://www.choike.org/nuevo_eng/informes/1557.html (Accessed August 18 2017)

Jackie Smith, Charles Chatfield, and Ron Pagnucco, 1997—'Social Movements and World Politics: A Theoretical Framework', in Jackie Smith, Charles Chatfield, and Ron Pagnucco, eds, 1997—*Transnational Social Movements and Global Politics: Solidarity Beyond the State*. Syracuse, NY: Syracuse University Press, pp 59–80

Amory Starr, 2003—'". . . (Excepting Barricades Erected to Prevent Us from Peacefully Assembling"): So-called "Violence" in the First World Anti-globalization Movement', in *Social Movement Studies*, vol 5 no 1, May 2006, pp 61–81, at https://www.researchgate.net/publication/242165889_'_Excepting_Barricades_Erected_to_Prevent_Us_from_Peacefully_Assembling'_So-called_'Violence'_in_the_Global_North_Alterglobalization_Movement (Accessed August 18 2017)

Laura Sullivan, 2012—'Activism, Affect, and Abuse: The Emotional Contexts and Consequences of the ESF Organising Process 2004', in Jai Sen and Peter Waterman, eds, 2012—*World Social Forum: Critical Explorations*. Volume 3 in the *Challenging Empires* series. New Delhi: OpenWord, at http://www.ephemerajournal.org/sites/default/files/5-2lsullivan.pdf (August 18 2017)

Sidney Tarrow, 2001—'Transnational Politics: Contention and Institutions in International Politics', in *Annual Review of Political Science*, 1, pp 1–20

Sidney Tarrow, 2005—*The New Transnational Activism*. Cambridge: Cambridge University Press

E Toscano, 2008—'Tensions and boundaries of alterglobalisation: Is it still alive?'. Presented at First ISA Forum of Sociology: Sociological Research and Public Debate, September 7 2008, Barcelona, Spain, at www.isarc47.org/Files/Toscano.pdf (Accessed November 9 2008, inactive August 18, 2017)

Fredrik Uggla, April 2004—'A Movement of Popular Education Oriented towards Action? ATTAC in France and Sweden'. Paper to the European Consortium of Political Research Workshop 'Emerging Repertoires of Political Action', Uppsala, Sweden, April 14–18 2004, at https://ecpr.eu/Filestore/PaperProposal/df936790-fbd7-4d3b-a170-67e9cda0198c.pdf (Accessed August 18 2017)

Peter Waterman, 2003e—'The WSF and a Global Justice and Solidarity Movement: A Rough Guide to Print and Web Publications', at http://www.labournet.info/wsfbook2004/guide.doc/view (Accessed April 14 2009, inactive August 18 2017)

Peter Waterman, 2006—*The Bamako Appeal of Samir Amin: A Post-Modern Janus?*. Warwick: CSGR. Working Paper 212/06, at http://www2.warwick.ac.uk/fac/soc/pais/research/researchcentres/csgr/research/abstracts/212/ (Accessed August 18 2017)

Sarah Waters, 2004—'Mobilising against Globalisation: ATTAC and the French Intellectuals', in *West European Politics*, vol 27 no 5, pp 854–74, at http://www.tandfonline.com/doi/abs/10.1080/0140238042000283292 (Accessed August 18 2017)

Sarah Waters, 2006—'A l'attac: Globalisation and Ideological Renewal on the French Left', in *Modern and Contemporary France*, vol 14 no 2, pp 141–56, at http://www.tandfonline.com/doi/abs/10.1080/09639480600667665 (Accessed August 18 2017)

Lesley J Wood, 2002—'Bridging the divide: The case of People's Global Action', at https://www.nadir.org/nadir/initiativ/agp/new/en/bridging_the_divide.htm (Accessed August 18 2017)

Lesley J Wood, 2004—'Breaking the bank and taking to the street: How protesters target neoliberalism', in *Journal of World-Systems Research*, vol X no 1, pp 69–89, at https://www.academia.edu/1282558/Breaking_the_bank_and_taking_to_the_streets_how_protesters_target_neoliberalism (Accessed August 18 2017)

Owen Worth and Jason P Abbott, 2006—'Land of false hope? The contradictions of British opposition to globalisation', in *Globalizations*, vol 3 no 1, pp 49–63, at http://www.tandfonline.com/doi/abs/10.1080/14747730500502902 (Accessed August 18 2018)

Nicola Yeates, 2001—*Globalisation and Social Policy*. London: Sage

Notes

1. Ed: This essay was originally written for the first 2006–2007 version of this book, based on work that the authors were doing then. I would like to warmly thank the authors for preparing this essay for me, and since they were among the first contributors, for their enormous patience in the subsequent course of its publication.
2. See, for instance, bibliographies by Gupta, Tarrow, and Acostavalle 2001, John H Henning Centre nd, and Waterman 2003.
3. Keck and Sikkink 1998, Smith Chatfield, and Pagnucco 1997, Cohen and Rai 2000, Anheier, Glasius, and Kaldor 2001, respectively.
4. Labels attached to this movement by academics and movement members and intellectuals have proliferated over time and often represent ideological orientation or repositioning (for instance in the labels 'anti-capitalist movement' or 'movement against neoliberal globalisation'). Given the plethora of competing labels and lack of agreement over the correct label we retain the use of 'antiglobalisation movement' for purposes of continuity and convenience.
5. Anheier, Glasius, and Kaldor 2001; Keck and Sikkink 1998; Laxer and Halperin 2003.
6. Tarrow 2001.
7. Yeates 2001.
8. Worth and Abbott 2006.
9. Diversity and diverse are used in this essay purely in their dictionary definition of variety and varied.
10. della Porta 2005.
11. Graeber 2001.
12. Juris 2004.
13. Panitch 2002.
14. Starr 2003.
15. Chesters and Welsh 2001.
16. della Porta 2005b.
17. Bond, Brutus, and Setshedi 2005.

18. Hewson 2005.
19. For a critical reading of this, see Papadimitriou 2008.
20. Milani 2007, p 529.
21. Fisher, Stanley, Berman, and Neff 2003.
22. Tarrow 2005.
23. Bédoyan, Van Aelst, and Walgrave 2003.
24. Kagarlitsky 2003.
25. Gorringe and Rosie 2006.
26. Giugni, Bandler, and Eggert 2006.
27. Ibid.
28. Farrer 2004.
29. Sen 2004c.
30. Bramble 2003.
31. Wood 2004.
32. Almeida and Lichbach 2003.
33. Wood 2004.
34. Ibid.
35. Sen 2004c.
36. Schonleitner 2003; Gryzbowski 2004; Ribeiro 2006; Álvarez et al, c.2005; and della Porta 2005a, respectively.
37. Blanchard and Filliele 2006.
38. Bramble 2003.
39. Ibid.
40. Wood's (2002) data set shows that 53 per cent of the demonstrations were organised by groups identified as parts of the PGA (through inclusion on the PGA webpage).
41. Routledge 2004; de Marcellus 2000; Wood 2002. Ed: This essay, which refers to the PGA in the present tense, was originally written in late 2006. By 2008 however, PGA activities seemed to have subsided.
42. Petras 2001.
43. Maiba 2005.
44. PGA conferences are conducted in English and Spanish. (Routledge 2004, p 12).
45. Susan George cited in Birchfield 2004. Ed: The authors finalised this essay in 2009. As is to some extent normal in any active social formation, several developments have taken place in ATTAC since then, and especially within its founding unit, ATTAC France. The outline given here may not completely apply today, but is certainly sufficient for the arguments developed here.
46. Birchfield 2004, p 14.
47. Cammaerts and Van Audenhove 2003.
48. Kolb 2003.
49. Giegold 2008.
50. Christensen 2002.
51. Giegold 2008.
52. Uggla 2004.
53. Cassen 2003.
54. George 2006.
55. Toscano 2008.

56. Uggla 2004.
57. Waters 2006.
58. Ibid.
59. Cassen 2003.
60. Waters 2004.
61. Ibid.
62. A chronology of regional, thematic, and national social forums from December 2001 to July 2004 listed seventy-three events: twenty-six in Latin America, twenty-one in Europe, fifteen in Africa, seven in North America, three in Asia, and one in Oceania; see http://www.transform.it/newsletter/892004530007.php (Inactive August 18 2017).
63. Pianta 2001.
64. The WSF Charter of Principles.
65. Sen 2004c. Emphasis in original.
66. Sen 2004c.
67. Anon 2002; Fleming 2002.
68. Gryzbowski 2004.
69. Petras 2002.
70. For a critical view of foundation funding of the WSF, see Research Unit in Political Economy 2007. Ed: By the time of publication, most of the foundations that funded the World Social Forum in its early years have dropped away.
71. Lopez, Koolwijk, and Shah 2006.
72. Waterman 2006.
73. See for instance, http://www.nigd.org/globalparties/ (Inactive August 18 2017).
74. Sen 2004c.
75. Nunes 2004. Ed: For detailed discussions of the political dynamics of the organisation of the London ESF, see the essay by Laura Sullivan in a companion volume in the *Challenging Empires* series (Sullivan 2012) and the essay by Massimo De Angelis in this book (De Angelis 2018).
76. Nunes 2004.
77. Bavadam 2004.
78. Juris 2004.

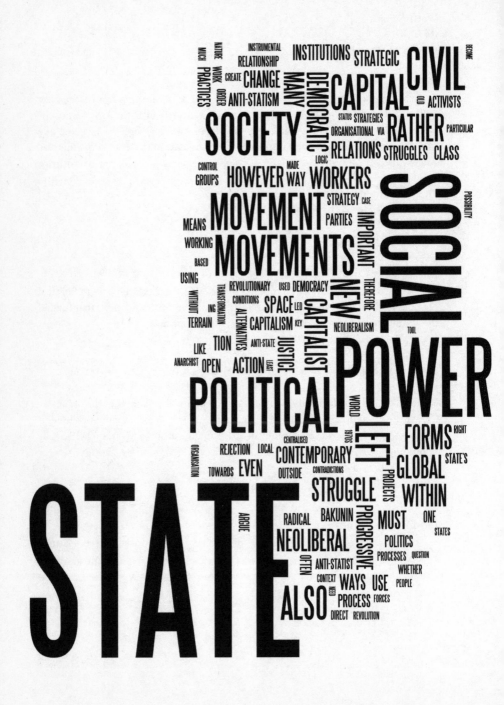

The Strategic Implications of Anti-Statism in the Global Justice Movement[1]

Stephanie Ross

A key feature of influential sections of the global justice movement continues to be experimentation with 'new' and recovered democratic forms. In the diffuse and multifarious 'movement of movements', some argue that a common approach to democratic organisation forms the main basis of unity. According to anarchist anthropologist David Graeber, the movement is about "reinventing democracy" and "creating new forms of organisation".[2] Given the dramatically reduced scope for meaningful democratic deliberation in state legislatures claiming to be hemmed in by the prerogatives of global capital, it is no wonder that the (re)invention of democratic forms and experiences is a key motivation for many of today's activists.

Given democracy's long historical entanglement with the state, attempts to rethink democratic practice are always, if only implicitly, based on a theory of both the state and its power. When the state is deemed an inappropriate space for deliberating over, deciding upon, and implementing the democratic will of the community, a particular understanding of its nature, capacities, and limits is invoked. The anti-hierarchical organisational commitments of a substantial segment of the global justice movement guide not only their internal practices but also their philosophical and strategic attitude towards the state.

It is right to reject the atrophied version of democracy offered up by the contemporary neoliberal state and to insist upon a deeper and more thorough democratisation of both institutions and social relations. However, does the global justice movement provide the intellectual, political, and strategic resources to counter power in its neoliberal, capitalist, or imperialist guises?

In this paper I will argue that pervasive anarchist and postmodern assumptions have led not only to a critique of the contemporary state but also to a tendency towards 'anti-statism' within the movement: a rejection of the possibility that state power can be used by progressive forces to create alternatives to capitalism. Using insights from Gramscian and neo-Marxist theory, I argue that such anti-statism is rooted in an impoverished and monolithic understanding of the state, is accompanied by a romanticised view of civil society as a realm of freedom and autonomy, and results in the adoption of easily marginalised forms of resistance. Even where activists are more ambivalent in their attitude towards the use of the state by the left and prefer to focus on building 'non-state' forms of power, the practical outcome can be a failure to think through ways of articulating those struggles along with ones aimed at using state power, especially where anti-state voices are particularly strong. To illustrate, I will examine two of the most influential contemporary sources of such ideas: the Social Forum Movement and the autonomist movements of Argentina.

Finally, I will argue that an abandonment of the state as a terrain of struggle permits its continued and unhindered use by capital reinforces the neoliberal mantra that the state should not be used to subject the market to social values and abandons the possibility of creating a unified, sustained, and effective counter-hegemonic political project.

Theories of the State, Power, and Democracy in the Global Justice Movement

As Graeber notes, there is a pole of unity in the global justice movement around organisational questions.[3] Although by no means universal, my reading of the global justice movement is that major sections of the movement are committed to the following political and organisational practices, which they see as fundamental to progressive social change: decentralised decision-making structures in which small groups are autonomous from the decisions of superordinate bodies; participatory (rather than representative) forms of democratic deliberation, in which consensus rather than majority rule is preferred; rejection of internal hierarchies and, in particular, of leaders; and a commitment to a diversity of tactics rather than a single, common strategy.[4] While most visible in the dynamics of public protest since the late 1990s, these commitments also guide the less dramatic activities of many groups, such as day-to-day decision-making and strategic analysis.

Each of these principles is grounded in a suspicion, if not complete rejection, of centralised forms of power in general and of the state as a particular type of centralised institution. Three major reasons are generally forwarded to reject the state as a terrain of struggle. First, the state is inherently a concentration of coercive 'power-over'[5] used to dominate others, and power itself is a corrupting force that inevitably produces hierarchy. To use the state as an instrument is to become infected with the very thing that should be resisted, namely power relations themselves. Second, as an institution, the state is inherently capitalist, thoroughly penetrated by and biased towards the capitalist class, and therefore cannot be turned towards non- or anti-capitalist ends. Third, even if it has fostered greater equality and democracy in the past, the state is now strategically impotent in the face of contemporary global capitalism and the hegemony of neoliberal practices and ideas. Anyone attempting to use the state today gets entangled in the reproduction of global capitalist dynamics, at best mitigating their negative effects but never mounting a radical challenge to its power. All these variants lead to the same conclusion: the state is useless in the struggle for progressive social change. This anti-statist orientation can be traced to at least one of three political-ideological roots: historical and contemporary forms of anarchism, the New Left social movements of the 1960s and 1970s, and postmodern / post-Marxist theorising of the 1980s and 1990s.

Anarchism

In the anarchist tradition, authority outside of the individual is rejected as an unacceptable limit on individual freedom and creativity. As a major source of such external control, the state is deemed illegitimate in both form and content. Major historical proponents of this view include Pierre Proudhon, Mikhail Bakunin, and Emma Goldman. Bakunin is the most useful here: in a vigorous debate with Karl Marx within the First International, he expressed most clearly the classical anarchist position on the political action of the working class and its relationship to the question of state power.

Both Bakunin and Marx shared an understanding of the state as capitalist and as implicated in the reproduction of inequality, and therefore believed it must ultimately be overthrown. However, where Marx held that the proletariat would need to use the state to dismantle capitalist social and economic conditions and create socialist ones, Bakunin insisted that while the proletariat "must overthrow the existing state apparatus in order to liberate itself, it must not set up in its place its own political power, as by doing so it necessarily substitutes a new authoritarian apparatus which will perpetuate its oppression".[6] For Bakunin, "Every state power, every government, by its very nature places itself outside and over the people and inevitably subordinates them to an organisation and to aims which are foreign to and opposed to the real needs and aspirations of the people".[7] As such, governmental power would "deprave . . . those who wear its mantle" and transform the class position of its holders: "[W]orkers . . . as soon as they become the rulers of the representatives of the people, will cease to be workers and will look down at the plain working masses from the governing heights of the State".[8]

In concrete strategic terms, rather than organising a working-class political party in order to win state power (political revolution, whether through electoral or insurrectionary means), Bakunin advocated the "build(ing) of the new society within the old", namely through self-organisation "from the bottom up, created by the people themselves, without governments and parliaments", to be achieved by "the free participation of associations, of the agricultural and industrial workers, of the communes and the provinces", which would form the basis of post-revolutionary societies.[9] As Richard Day points out, Bakunin distinguished this as social revolution, whose aim is "*breaking* rather than *taking* state power".[10]

A contemporary version of anarchist-inspired anti-statism is found in the work of John Holloway, whose *Change the World Without Taking Power* generated a political-strategic debate on the left which mirrored that between Marx and

Bakunin. Holloway characterises himself as an 'open' Marxist, but embraces the central anarchist theme of rejecting the state as an emancipatory tool. Holloway's thinking is inspired by the Zapatistas' dramatic rejection of the state, in both its neoliberal guise and as a potential source of liberation. Holloway argues that the Zapatistas' revolutionary contribution is precisely in their insistence on "changing the world without taking power" and detaching the revolutionary process from the project of seeking to control the state.[11] For him, the "state paradigm" of social transformation is the "assassin" of hope.[12] Struggles premised on winning state power involve a false sense of what it can accomplish as a tool in the 'right' hands and pervert progressive movements themselves. Like Bakunin, Holloway asserts that once the state becomes central to social change,

> [t]he struggle is lost from the beginning, long before the victorious party or army conquers state power and 'betrays' its promises. It is lost once power itself seeps into the struggle, once the logic of power itself becomes the logic of the revolutionary process, once the negative of refusal is converted into the positive of power-building. . . . You cannot build a society of non-power relations by conquering power.[13]

For Holloway, then, statism is the left's "original sin",[14] and human emancipation requires the emancipation of revolutionary theory from the mirage of state power.

New Left Social Movements of the 1960s and 1970s

New Left social movements, and in particular the feminist, student, environmental, and peace movements of the 1960s and 1970s, also took up antiauthoritarian themes and practices which continue to inform the anti-statism of contemporary activism. These movements' orientation against centralised institutions is often discussed in terms of their revival of anarchist- and libertarian-inspired internal organisational practices, such as: the valuation of tacit and experiential (rather than expert) knowledge; an emphasis on the prefigurative over instrumental aspects of activism (or at least an insistence that means and ends are organically connected); and the use of consensus-based, dialogical, direct, and participatory decision-making processes, rotation of leadership, and horizontal networks of autonomous groups.[15] However, equally important were the strategic conclusions many of these so-called 'new' social movements came to about how and whether to engage with the state.

An important explanation for New Left anti-institutional politics is rooted in Jürgen Habermas's observation that "large, anonymous social institutions have become especially intrusive and invasive in the late twentieth century",[16] penetrating the "lifeworld" with the values of instrumental rationality. Fordist regulation of capital accumulation and class conflict, in which unionised workers traded greater ambitions to control the labour process for capital's participation in bureaucratic collective bargaining processes, both deepened Taylorist[17] production methods with ongoing centralisation, rationalisation, and reorganisation of the production process, as well as encouraged workers to trade quality of work life for expanded consumption via higher wages.[18] Young workers and activists chafed against the constraints of centralised unions and social democratic parties, which in many places used corporatist institutions to regulate national industrial sectors via the restraint of wage militancy, with corrosive effects on left political institutions and legitimacy.[19]

While capital and the trade unions drew much fire in this period, so too did the increasingly centralised and interventionist state. The post-war state's expansion into more areas of economic and social life, whether to "smooth out the accumulation process and contain the system's disruptive tendencies",[20] to redistribute wealth and opportunity and to regulate the more negative effects of capitalism via the welfare state,[21] or to engage in corporatist industrial and economic planning, also meant bureaucratisation, rationalisation, greater social and ideological control, and the dominance of technocrats and instrumental reason.[22]

The greater visibility and "transparence of the state's impact on daily life", which politicised "matters that previously were perceived as outside the reach of political solutions", combined with the contradictory results of those interventions to foster "antiparty and anti-state values" in "virtually all new political movements of both the Right and the Left in Europe" in the 1970s.[23] As it became clear that the state was no panacea for the problems of social inequality, and that both social democratic and Leninist party organisations continued to be attached to this notion, many—if not all—New Left movements turned to other strategic terrains.

Reviving Bakunin's notion of social revolution, many New Left movements focused on strategies of personal or cultural transformation in the realm of civil society and outside established political institutions. While not always eschewing power as such, these movements engaged in struggles that were more local, challenged the habits and meanings of everyday life, built new institutions and ways of living, and destabilised and subverted accepted meanings and norms.[24] If not entirely anti-state in the way that Bakunin was, many elements of the New Left were deeply sceptical of the state and preferred to engage in non-state-oriented struggles. These practices were subsequently theorised and valorised by the post-Marxists and postmodernists of the 1980s and 1990s.[25]

The Influence of Post-Marxism and Postmodernism

Post-Marxism and postmodernism have reiterated and extended the rejection of the state as a potentially democratic and progressive space. In attempts to explain the significance of the new social movements of the 1960s and 1970s, many post-Marxists argued that radical transformations in the structure of advanced capitalism (discussed above) had destabilised old class-based political identities, brought forth new ones based on diversified, complex, and contradictory experiences, and necessitated multiple forms of resistance and emancipatory strategy.[26] Others emphasised the way in which power, rather than concentrated in the hands of the state or capital, was diffuse and present in social relations of all types,[27] which rendered the focus on the state as a vehicle of emancipation both incorrect and futile.[28]

These perspectives tended to produce either a dilution of the Gramscian notion of *counter-hegemony*—the strategy by which the working class exercises moral and intellectual leadership to construct a progressive alternative to capitalism via alliances with other social groups—or its rejection in favour of *anti-hegemony*. For some, counter-hegemony remains a goal but is primarily a discursive rather than organisational accomplishment in which various democratic—and not necessarily class-based—struggles are brought together through a "chain of equivalence" linking their (contingent and indeterminate) meanings.[29]

Postmodernists, however, tend to reject counter-hegemonic projects altogether. For them, attempts to construct unity and to generalise progressive alternatives are forms of power-over, reproducing a "totalising logic" that destroys diversity and autonomy.[30] Counter-hegemony thus reflects "the assumption that effective social change can only be achieved simultaneously and en masse, across an entire national or supranational space", and hence remains within the logic of neoliberalism.[31] Postmodernists thus tend to advocate *anti-hegemonic* oppositional practices, which are at most micro-disruptions of dominant discourses challenging normativity and disorganising consent.

Contemporary Anti-Statism and the Neoliberal Conjuncture

Contemporary anti-statism is informed both by the political and theoretical commitments of these movement traditions, and by the specific conjunctural effects of neoliberal globalisation on the role of the state and its relationship to citizens. As Alfredo Saad Filho has argued, "[t]he most basic feature of neoliberalism is the systematic use of state power to protect capital and disarticulate the working class through the imposition of financial market imperatives and under the ideological veil of nonintervention", which has led to a "hollowing out" of even the most limited forms of representative democracy.[32] As the state's relationship with global and local capital has deepened and become more evident, growing numbers of leftists have abandoned it as a tool of social transformation.

The *non-statist* response to neoliberalism is prominent, for instance, in the World Social Forum movement, having been written into several foundational documents and celebrated by some as one of its most innovative aspects. The

WSF's Charter of Principles explicitly places itself on the terrain outside of states, a "non-governmental and non-party context" bringing together "only organisations and movements of civil society from all the countries in the world". The Charter does not permit official representation by states or political parties and allows participation from government officials only "in a personal capacity".[33]

These criteria reflect the desire of many for social forums to be something other than representative or decision-making bodies. These roles are explicitly rejected in the WSF Charter of Principles: no binding decisions are to be made, no meetings are to be treated as a "locus of power to be disputed by the participants", and no one is to "be authorised, on behalf of any of the editions of the Forum, to express positions claiming to be those of all its participants".[34]

Instead, many commentators emphasise the Social Forum's status as a *space* of encounter and learning "outside the immediate spheres of capital and state",[35] not an *agent* or *movement* as such.[36] Its non-deliberative character is seen to be central to building a new, open, and heterogeneous political culture on the left that emphasises "open debate" and "horizontal social relations and politics",[37] rather than a "single, deliberative and, by definition, unitary political process",[38] and that prefigures future relations. This open-endedness is "alchemical" and creative, producing outcomes that cannot—and could not—be planned, pre-determined, or assessed in the short-term.[39]

For some, these characteristics constitute the social forums's radical departure from state-oriented forms of political organisation and must be defended as debates emerge over its future. The major tensions emerging over the question of "forum-as-space" versus "forum-as-movement"[40] have led proponents like Waterman to caution against the experiences of past movements, which were "dominated by the institutions they spawned, by political parties that instrumentalised them", and were "state-oriented and / or state-identified".[41] The desire for strategies or unifying projects is symptomatic of the "old kind of power politics . . . that seeks to control, that distrusts plurality, and that effectively shuts down space for diversity and for debate".[42] Those who insist that the state power is an important tool in fighting capital or making progressive social change are "haunted by the political imaginary of an old left", in which "the state and the national scale remains at the centre of political vision and strategy".[43] Even if the proponents of and participants in the World Social Forums are not united on the question of the state as a terrain of struggle, there is at least a pervasive scepticism about what can be achieved in that domain and a desire to focus energies elsewhere.

More explicitly, *anti*-statist currents are visible in anti-neoliberal movements at the national level. Like the Zapatistas in 1994, Argentina's most recent round of social mobilisation emerged in response to the contradictions of the neoliberal economic model. The pressures of '*el modelo*' (literally, 'the model', which is how neoliberalism is often referred to in Argentina) introduced by Carlos Menem had long been felt in various social sectors, and multiple forms of resistance had been building through the 1990s. As these policies predictably resulted in higher rates of unemployment (due to a contraction of the public sector and the closure of many domestic small- and medium-sized enterprises unable to compete with transnational corporations), workers, their families, and their communities initially sought relief from the state within the boundaries and conventions of the formal democratic process. However, unemployed workers soon turned to more radical forms of extra-parliamentary action, such as occupations of government offices, mass pickets, and, most notably, blockades of strategic roadways, as their petitions and peaceful protests were ignored.[44] The *piqueteros'* evolution from engagement *with* the state to direct action *against* it was mirrored by other movements whose claims were also repeatedly ignored. By late 2001, an explosion of protest emerged in the wake of a political crisis within the governing coalition led by Fernando de la Rua, who was elected in 1999 on an anti-neoliberal platform, but then continued Menem's policies.[45]

The slogan under which this broad social mobilisation took place—"*¡Que se vayan todos, que no quede ni uno solo!*" ('They All Must Go; Not a Single One Can Remain')—contains within it multiple meanings. For some, as James Petras contends, this rejection was conjunctural, an indictment of the entrenched political class whose clientelist, paternalistic, and corrupt practices required a thorough housecleaning.[46] For others, however, the saying indicated a more profound disenchantment with politicians, political parties, and electoral representative processes as such, as well as a deep scepticism about the state as a tool for progressive social transformation. For Ana Dinerstein, it represented a "reinvention of politics as negative politics", even a "collective action against power" in which the form, substance, and representativeness of democratic institutions, the law, and their relationship to capital are questioned and rejected.[47] In place of the traditional left of trade unions and political parties, organised hierarchically and with a statist (and, in this case, collaborationist) orientation, there has been a flowering of "non-identity, horizontal, democratic, and anti-institution politics", focused on local and direct forms of democracy and self-determination.[48]

For instance, the weekly meetings of the *asambleas barriales*—'neighbourhood assemblies' that emerged as a means to discuss the political-economic crisis and to organise mutual aid at the neighbourhood level—discussed the question of the state and power in a way that "question[s] the whole *system* of political representation" and aimed "not to contest constituted power but rather to constitute power against it".[49] Dinerstein interpreted their choice to address each other as *vecino*—neighbour—rather than 'citizen' as a discursive means of establishing direct, solidaristic relations between people without the mediation of the state.[50] The anti-institutional politics of a new generation of Argentinian social movement activists is vividly depicted in Avi Lewis and Naomi Klein's

2004 film, *The Take*, which chronicles the progress of the recovered factories movement and its relationship to other 'anti-political' movements in the country. Matty, an activist with the unemployed workers' movement and worker at the Zanon Ceramics factory, explains why she will not vote in the 2003 presidential election, even though the architect of neoliberalism, Carlos Menem, was in the running and abstention from voting is illegal: "This graffiti says 'Our dreams don't fit on your ballots'. That's how I feel. What I want, what I need, I'm not going to get by voting".[51]

In sum, anti-statist and non-statist themes in the contemporary global justice movement are in part a product of several important strands of twentieth-century political thought and practice. Underlying these positions is a deep suspicion of power as such, given its equation with power-over. In this view, institutions like the state that centralise power are seen as antithetical to emancipatory projects. Anti-statist groups often seek to create a society in which power relations are no longer present; they argue that the state is not to be used towards this end, but rather to be sidelined and, for some, perhaps, destroyed. Instead of reengineering society from the top down, these groups emphasise prefigurative struggle, or what Gramsci called the 'war of position': struggles which create new ways of living, thinking, feeling, and relating that challenge the 'common sense' of the age.[52] Though alternatives to dominant social arrangements are sought, these projects tend to be local, autonomous, and anti-hegemonic, in that there is a reluctance to create generalised strategies that unite particular struggles. At best, horizontal networked relationships of mutual support are to be created rather than relations of collective discipline and obligation. Left political projects that continue to prioritise contesting state power and the strategies that accompany such a goal are not just 'old hat' and 'passé' but also obstacles to genuinely radical social transformation.

There is much to be valued in such an approach. The emphasis on the subjective moment of struggle, of transforming both individual and collective consciousness and capacity, and of creating strong and independent forms of political and social organisation is crucial. This is a necessary response to errors in past left strategies that pursued political revolution without also attending sufficiently to social revolution, and which therefore had to impose forms of discipline in order to maintain revolutionary processes.

However, these insights also raise several important strategic questions. First, is the state really so pervaded with coercive power that it is hopeless to try to use it? Second, if we must abandon the terrain of the state, what kind of space is 'civil society' and is it necessarily freer than the state from power?[53] Finally, is work within civil society rather than the state sufficient to the task of developing effective strategic responses to the contemporary neoliberal state, not to mention building sustainable alternatives to capitalism?

Recuperating the State

For many global justice activists today, the state is understood as a coercive and repressive force with little independence from the imperatives of global capital. While there is a prima facie truth to these observations, the anarchist-inspired idea that the state is seamless in its unity and therefore unrecuperable for left projects is based on a simplistic, monolithic view. Although debates over the capitalist state are complex and extensive, most Marxists agree its capitalist nature does not prevent it from being internally contradictory. Indeed, as a terrain on which class struggles are played out, the state expresses at different points in time the particular balance of power that exists within and between various classes and other social forces. As such, it is not always the case that capital can 'get its way' or that 'getting its way' is unproblematically clear or exactly the same in concrete time and place.

Contradiction is also a product of the multiple roles that states play within capitalist societies. The state's involvement in establishing and maintaining the conditions for capital accumulation often conflict with other important goals, like securing legitimation and stability through active consent. One of Gramsci's important insights into the dynamics of hegemony was to point to the material concessions that ruling groups make to subordinate classes in order to win the latter's consent to be governed.[54] However, that need to secure consent is always in tension with the pressures that competition imposes to continually intensify exploitation and extend the reach of capitalist social relations. It is in the fissures of these contradictory pressures that working classes, for instance, have been able to extract gains like the welfare state, the conversion of many essential services (state-provided healthcare or education, for instance) from private commodities to public entitlements, and legal recognition for workers' independent organisations. While not without their own internal contradictions and unforeseen consequences, these victories represent the possibility of using the state, albeit in conjunctural ways, to open up space for progressive alternatives.

The struggle of Argentinian social movements illustrates well the fallacy of the monolithic conception of the state, as well as the possibility of using the state strategically. While many in the movements rejected the state on principle, their projects were dependent upon a sympathetic legal-institutional framework that only the state could create and protect. As depicted in *The Take*, workers' initial expropriations "bubbled up from below", having been achieved through direct action rather than imposition "from on high by a socialist state or bureaucrats".[55] Workers physically occupied their workplaces and organised around-the-clock defence brigades armed with slingshots. While some asserted that such direct action was sufficient and in fact superior to legal sanction or electoral struggle, other activists recognised the state's centrality in determining their fate and took advantage of other avenues. With the judiciary and police often uncritically protecting employers' private property rights, the municipal, provincial, and national legislatures were seen as more open to popular pressure, and therefore became key sites for winning (at least temporary) legal backing for workers' expropriations. Even some judges were willing to interpret the law in ways that legitimated worker ownership. Although divisions within the judiciary were strategically important, this was also recognised by some as insufficient: one of the Zanon activists made an impassioned plea for the need to "go to the legislature", and the workers from Forja San Martin concentrated much energy on getting legislative backing for their cooperative.[56] This example indicates a tacit knowledge among some elements of the movement of not only the state's importance in creating space for alternative economic relationships but also of its fragmented and internally contradictory nature, making it possible for workers' cooperatives to fight on numerous fronts for a national expropriation law.

Taking advantage of internal divisions within the state of course raises the issue of electoral engagement as a strategy, for if legal sanction for worker-owned enterprises is to be won, there must be at least some sympathetic elected representatives open to these arguments and pressures. Although the recovered factories movement remained insecure and even under siege under Néstor Kirchner's presidency, one must ask what would have happened had Menem, with his close ties to internationalised Argentine capital and his 'order and security' platform, won the 2003 presidential elections. Despite horizontal networks of mutual support between cooperatives, the struggle of the recovered factories movement revealed the impossibility of completely rejecting formal political processes and institutions, even for anarcho-syndicalist strategies based on direct action and workers' control.

Anti-statism can, therefore, have on the whole a debilitating effect if and where it prevents the identification of divisions or contradictions within the state that may offer important avenues to use institutional power, not to substitute for movements but rather to further empower them by sustaining and extending their achievements.

De-romanticising Civil Society

This example also raises the question of civil society, and whether social change can be made wholly within this realm. In important ways, the rejection of the state by anti-statists is based upon an implicit dichotomisation of 'inside' versus 'outside' the system of power, which has historically specific contours. As Ellen Wood points out, the delineation of "some notion of 'society', distinct from the body politic and with moral claims independent of, and sometimes opposed to, the state's authority" has long been part of the Western intellectual tradition; however, with the rise of capitalism and the *formal* (if not real) separation of capitalist accumulation from the mechanisms of political rule, the state-civil society opposition took its modern form, the latter often synonymous with "the community of private-property holders" who seek to maintain their autonomy from the absolutist state.[57] More contemporary conceptions of civil society have expanded it to include the full range of voluntary human association and activity, "distinct from both the state and capitalist production", where both interests and identities are formed, organised around, and contested.[58]

However, the 'distinctive' status of civil society is often conceptualised quite rigidly by anti-statists, such that an unproblematically capitalist and coercive state is contrasted with civil society as a realm of freedom and autonomous action.[59] Not only does this ignore the contradictions within the state's multiple institutions (as argued above), it also hides the way that civil society is *also* capitalist and rife with hegemonic practices. Gramsci's notion of the "integral state" highlights the way that civil society is not independent of the power of capital; instead, the state is that terrain on which capital organises its material, ideological, and cultural hegemony, mediated as much through civil society institutions like the church, schools, the family, and non-governmental organisations, as through coercion.[60] Emir Sader argues that to invoke civil society as a pure space of action unhindered by power differentials and in opposition to the state is "to mask . . . the class nature of its components—multinational corporations, banks, and mafia, set next to social movements, trade unions, civil bodies",[61] as though these are all equally powerful. Instead, both the state and civil society are profoundly (if not exclusively) shaped by capitalist social relations, and it is neither accurate nor strategically useful to privilege one site of struggle over the other in some transhistorical way.

Some may—and do—argue that such an analysis inevitably leads to pessimistic conclusions: if both the state and civil society are thoroughly penetrated with capitalist logic, there are no possibilities for collective resistance and thus all that remains is critique or perhaps individual hedonism. However, like the state, civil society is not an unproblematically unified whole either. For Carroll and Ratner, "[p]eople's everyday lives are permeated not only by hegemonic practices that legitimate . . . inequities, but also by acts of subversion and adaptation" that provide the materials out of which alternatives can be fashioned.[62] Moreover, the balance of social forces, and therefore of relations inside and between state and civil society, is historically contingent and therefore variable. In certain periods or contexts, the avenues for state-based action may be closed or so risky that civil society organising is to be preferred. However, just as Leninists were mistaken to generalise a form of party organisation and revolutionary change based on the specific circumstances of Tsarist Russia, so too is it wrong to claim that only non- or anti-state means can produce progressive social change.

Indeed, many 'civil society struggles' are strengthened precisely by the actions of state-based agents who use their strategic location to further open up and protect spaces for the exploration and development of alternatives. In Argentina, even temporary legalisation of cooperative status released workers in the re-covered factories from the constant threat of police violence and requirement of armed defence and allowed attention to be put towards strengthening both internal organisation and external relationships of support. For instance, having won three years of legal status in October 2005, the FASINPAT cooperative that runs the Zanon Ceramics factory could "concentrate on production planning" and "improve working conditions and community projects".[63] Similarly, the Social Forum movement, though explicitly identified with 'civil society', emerged in the particular context of Brazil for a reason: the "success of specific political measures, implemented by a left party through a process of democratic state re-forms" not only attracted global justice activists to Porto Alegre but also made the initial organisation of the World Social Forum possible.[64] In other words, where anti-statist elements in the movement are not allowed to dominate strategic de-cisions, it becomes possible for hard-won gains to be consolidated.

The fact that state action can open up space in civil society for radical organ-ising is not new. In her discussion of the New Left social movements of the 1960s, Hilary Wainwright reveals that self-organisation and the creation of autono-mous, participatory institutions relied upon a permissive institutional-political context. The "sustainability" of local institutions "has depended, ironically, on social democracy—the very political strategy they were often initiated against".[65] Wainwright's insight into the conditions of possibility for autonomist movements implies that the choice facing activists is not between civil society and formal political institutions of the state, but rather how to engage the state in ways that both preserve and protect independent spaces for self-organisation and partici-patory democracy as well as challenge the state itself to become more thoroughly democratised.

Of course, as Gramsci pointed out, the state can also act on civil society in ways that close down the possibilities for radical and democratising alternatives and promote those which reinforce the status quo. Hence, as Emir Sader has put it, the consequences of accepting the civil society / state dichotomy are

> serious, not only because it means rejecting a potential weapon in a radically
> unequal contest but also, and more importantly, because the movement distanc-
> es itself from the themes of power, the state, public sphere, political leadership,
> and even, in a sense, from ideological struggle. . . . The result of this exclusion of
> parties and the state . . . severely limit[s] the formulation of any alternatives to
> neoliberalism, confining such aspirations to a local or sectoral context.[66]

As such, a negative case for contesting state power can also be made: not only does some control over the state imply the power to do but also the power *to prevent others*, namely capital, from using the state unhindered.

Perils of Abandoning the State to Neoliberal Capitalism

A rigidly anti-statist position, rooted in misconceptions about the state, civil society, and their relationship, impedes the global justice movement's capacity to confront the contemporary state, whether in its neoliberal or imperialist guise. The wholesale rejection of political projects that involve capturing state power—particularly via elections—accounts in part for the left's current inability to roll back or contain neoliberal state policy both domestically and internationally. However, it is insufficient to merely say that the left needs a strategy to win state power. A case must be made for why such power is *necessary* both to block capital and to create more space for social movement organising and *usable* in a way that does not fundamentally pervert the democratic commitments and practices of the left, but rather strengthens and empowers them.

When we accept the argument that the state as a representation of the democratic will of the community, however constituted, is powerless in the face of global capitalist interests, we accept the core of the neoliberal message. The powerless state is the ideology of neoliberal capital, which disarms and disempowers popular forces. Interestingly, Suzanne Berger noted a convergence of right-wing and left-wing anti-statism in the late 1970s, both of which involved a profound loss of confidence about the possibility of using the state to "good ends".[67] However, despite its claims, the right has since regained its 'faith' in the state and has been using it effectively to remake the world in its own image. Rather than being 'decentred' or less important, as many postmoderns have claimed, the state has become even *more* central to the process of capitalist restructuring. As Leo Panitch points out, "the process of globalisation, far from dwarfing states, has been constituted through and even by them".[68] The state remains a fundamental weapon for capital to organise and reinforce its own power and to disorganise and fragment the power of its opponents. Why else would capital be willing to spend so much of its resources on financing electoral campaigns and lobbying efforts to secure favourable legislation? As Boron argues, we must learn to distinguish between the right's "anti-state rhetoric" and the reality of "the ever-increasing strategic nature that the state has assumed in order to guarantee the continuity of capitalist domination".[69]

In some ways, then, the commitment to 'anti-hegemony' and the abandonment of counter-hegemonic struggle signals a victory for capital. Convincing the working class (or popular forces more generally) to abandon a broader and large-scale transformative vision is central to the capitalist strategy of passive revolution, in which the bourgeoisie decapitates and tames its opponents by keeping them focused on the defensive protection of corporate or particularistic interests.[70] In some ways, localism is a symptom of how the left, demoralised by past mistakes and the difficulties of anti-capitalist struggle, now thinks small rather than big and does not present a real systemic challenge to capitalism, neoliberal or otherwise.

Indeed, anti-hegemony favours not only the local scale as the terrain of action but also the present over the future. In that sense, anti-hegemony is also increasingly anti-utopian: some argue that the future no longer figures prominently in the practice of anarchist-inspired groups and has been replaced by a focus on carving out space in the present to live in radical or revolutionary ways.[71]

As elements of the left retreat from contesting state power, whether out of anti-state or non-state political commitments, capital retains unchallenged access to a crucial and potent weapon and, via its own parties and politicians, continues to act on civil society relatively unhindered. The case of Argentina is again illustrative: in the 2003 presidential election, "[t]he anti-political slogan 'que se vayan todos' ('They All Must Go') intimidated any promising left candidates and ultimately led to the total domination of electoral politics by the traditional right parties".[72] Emilia Castorina argues that the "political fragmentation" between "reformists, revolutionaries, and autonomists" resulted in the movements' incapacity in that election "to build a unified, plausible alternative from 'below'", which opened the way for the clientelistic co-optation of the *piqueteros* movement by a reinvigorated Peronist state.[73] Similarly, North and Huber document how, while the spontaneously created 'convergence spaces' of the *Argentinazo* (the period of civil uprising, unrest, and revolt in Argentina in December 2001) were "bubbling away without a coherent attitude to the state, the politicians were reorganising".[74] In the context of struggles by cooperatives to extract both resources and legitimacy from the state, the lack of progressive voices within legislatures was a weakness. In that sense, anti-statism can strengthen the power of those it seeks to resist, entrenching the power of capital and fortifying the bureaucratic state.[75]

Anti-statist presumptions are thus clearly underwritten by a deeply spontaneist understanding of social transformation. In the absence of any specified ideas about the processes and practices involved in effecting large-scale social change, it is assumed that building alternative ways of thinking and living in the cracks of the system would eventually destabilise and overwhelm that system in some way. This both underestimates the power and solidity of systemic processes and overestimates the impact that civil society struggles can have on their own. On the first, while neoliberal capitalism produces deeply destructive contradictions, this does not guarantee that the system will collapse in on itself. Indeed, as Saad Filho sagely points out, neoliberalism is a fairly stable system of accumulation, not only because it "fosters modes of behaviour that contribute to its reproduction over time", but also because it does so *through the very crises it produces*, imposing further discipline and austerity on both capital and workers.[76] On the second, as Boron argues, the key difference between change enacted at the levels of the state and civil society is that the latter, while "extremely important, lacks imperative effects", as the state is the site where interests are transformed into laws and normative and institutional frameworks are created.[77]

In his reflections on the rise of new social movements and their strategic challenge to the old left, Carl Boggs argued that the "ongoing conflict between prefigurative (value-oriented) and instrumental (power-oriented) dimensions of popular movements has all too often been resolved in favour of the prefigurative, with typically fatal results".[78] Overemphasis of the instrumental element no doubt led to the problems of Leninist and social democratic forms of political struggle. However, solutions to these problems are not to be found in abandonment of the state in favour of exclusively 'subjective transformations'. While convincing people that 'another world is possible' is key, how much more demoralising is it to see that belief unsupported by material changes in relations of power and wealth? Rather than favouring the prefigurative over the instrumental, political and theoretical work must focus on the dialectic relationship between the subjective and objective or structural bases for change. In other words, social transformation is the product of interactions between changes in people's beliefs, relationships, and organisational practices, *and* the arrangement of other social forces and structures, which can be used to open up and reinforce certain kinds of subjective capacities and diminish others.

Reclaiming the State for Social Justice

To argue that the state must figure importantly in left political strategy is not to be uncritical or naive about the dangers of using the state to make radical change. Indeed, the potential for internalisation of the neoliberal logic into the policies and practices of governments that swept to power on the wave of social movement activity is serious and real. Moreover, such defeats dangerously reinforce the conclusion that, despite what we do, the state will always assimilate and transform those who occupy it. Despite this, the call to develop different relationships between parties and strong social movements should be heeded. The state continues to be an important terrain of struggle because it holds out important resources for progressive movements, resources that the right will use to our detriment if permitted to do so.

In order to move forward, the global justice movement must chart a strategic direction between the positions of 'state as panacea' and 'state as useless'. The difficult work lies, as Boggs says, in constructing "a new politics", one which "integrates both state and civil society in a manner that allows for a dynamic relationship between the two, between the 'political' and 'social' realms, parties and movements, institutional activity and grassroots mobilisation".[79] This also means developing an analysis of the political-economic and organisational conditions under which social movements can use states to open up more space while also transforming states themselves.[80] The means for developing such conditions cannot be determined through theoretical-intellectual work alone: the proper marriage of strategies within and outside the state must be worked out in the context of struggle. However, practical insights can be drawn from revisiting theoretical debates over the state and civil society as well as a careful reading of past political experiences. At a minimum, we urgently need a critical examination of contemporary anti-statist political projects and whether they are condemning the left to guerrilla warfare at the margins of an ever more powerful capitalism.

References

Amy Allen, 2005—'Feminist Perspectives on Power', in Edward N Zalta, ed, 2005—*The Stanford Encyclopedia of Philosophy*, Winter, at http://plato.stanford.edu/archives/win2005/entries/feminist-power/ (Accessed August 18 2017)

Mikhail Bakunin, 1873—*Statism and Anarchy*, on *Marxist Internet Archive*, at http://www.marxists.org/reference/archive/bakunin/works/1873/statism-anarchy.htm (Accessed August 18 2017)

Marc Becker, 2007—'The Future of the Forum', on *Midwest Social Forum*, at www.mwsocialforum.org/node/1244 (Accessed July 30 2007, inactive August 18 2017)

Daniel Bensaïd, 2005—'On a Recent Book by John Holloway', in *Historical Materialism*, vol 13 no 4, pp 169–92

Suzanne Berger, 1979—'Politics and Antipolitics in Western Europe in the Seventies', in *Daedalus*, vol 128, Winter 1979, pp 27–50

Carl Boggs, 1986—*Social Movements and Political Power: Emerging Forms of Radicalism in the West*. Philadelphia: Temple University Press

Atilio Boron, 2005—'Holloway on Power and the "State Illusion"', in *Capital & Class*, vol 85, Spring 2005, pp 35–38

Steven M Buechler, 2000—*Social Movements in Advanced Capitalism: The Political Economy and Cultural Construction of Social Activism*. Oxford: Oxford University Press

William K Carroll and Robert S Ratner, 1994—'Between Leninism and Radical Pluralism: Gramscian Reflections on Counter-Hegemony and the New Social Movements', in *Critical Sociology*, vol 20 no 2, pp 3–26

Emilia Castorina, 2007—'The Contradictions of "Democratic" Neoliberalism in Argentina: A New Politics from "Below"?', in Leo Panitch and Colin Leys, eds, 2007—*Socialist Register 2008: Global Flashpoints: Reactions to Imperialism and Neoliberalism*. London: Merlin Press, pp 265–83

Janet Conway, June 2005—'Social Forums, Social Movements and Social Change: A Response to Peter Marcuse on the Subject of the World Social Forum', in *International Journal of Urban and Regional Research*, vol 29 no 2, June 2005, pp 425–28

Richard Day, 2005—*Gramsci Is Dead: Anarchist Currents in the Newest Social Movements*. London: Pluto Press

Ana Dinerstein, 2003—'¡Que se Vayan Todos! Popular Insurrection and the *Asambleas Barriales* in Argentina', in *Bulletin of Latin American Research*, 22 (2), pp 187–200

Ana Dinerstein, 2002—'The Battle of Buenos Aires: Crisis, Insurrection and the Reinvention of Politics in Argentina', in *Historical Materialism*, vol 10 no 4, pp 5–38

Terry Eagleton, 2003—*After Theory*. London: Penguin

David Fernbach, 1974—'Introduction', in Karl Marx, 1974. *The First International and After: Political Writings*, Vol 3., edited by David Fernbach. London: Pelican, pp 9–72

Michel Foucault, 1980—'Two Lectures', in *Power / Knowledge: Selected Interviews and Other Writings, 1972–1977*. New York: Pantheon, pp 78–108

Uri Gordon, 2005—'Liberation Now: Present-Tense Dimensions of Contemporary Anarchism'. Graduate Student Conference, 'Thinking the Present: The Beginnings and Ends of Political Theory', University of California Berkeley (unpublished manuscript)

David Graeber, 2003—'The New Anarchists', in *New Left Review II*, no 13, January–February 2003, pp 61–73

John Holloway, 2005—*Change the World Without Taking Power: The Meaning of Revolution Today*. London: Pluto Press

Ernesto Laclau and Chantal Mouffe, 1985—*Hegemony and Socialist Strategy: Towards a Radical Democratic Politics*. London: Verso

Avi Lewis, dir, 2004—*The Take*. Montreal: National Film Board of Canada

Warren Magnussen and Ron Walker, 1988—'De-Centring the State: Political Theory and Canadian Political Economy', in *Studies in Political Economy*, no 26, Summer 1988, pp 37–71

Karl Marx, 1874—'Conspectus of Bakunin's *Statism and Anarchy*', on *Marxist Internet Archive*, at http://www.marxists.org/archive/marx/works/1874/04/bakunin-notes. htm (Accessed August 18 2017)

Alberto Melucci, 1989—*Nomads of the Present: Social Movements and Individual Needs in Contemporary Society*. Philadelphia: Temple University Press

David Miller, 1985—*Anarchism*. London: J M Dent & Sons

Peter North and Ulli Huber, 2004—'Alternative Spaces of the "*Argentinazo*"', in *Antipode*, vol 36 no 5, pp 963–84

Claus Offe, 1987—'Challenging the Boundaries of Institutional Politics: Social Movements since the 1960s', in Charles S Maier, ed, 1987—*Changing Boundaries of the Political: Essays on the Evolving Balance between State and Society, Public and Private in Europe*. Cambridge: Cambridge University Press, pp 63–105

Leo Panitch, 1986—*Working Class Politics in Crisis*. London: Verso

Leo Panitch, 2000—'The New Imperial State', in *New Left Review II*, no 2, March–April 2000, pp 5–20

James Petras, January 2002—'The Unemployed Workers Movement in Argentina', in *Monthly Review*, vol 53 no 8, January 2002, at http://www.monthlyreview.org/ 0102petras.htm (Accessed August 18 2017)

James Petras, 2003—'Argentina: 18 Months of Popular Struggle—A Balance', at http:// petras.lahaine.org/b2-img/030604petras.pdf (Accessed August 18 2017)

Francesca Polletta, 2002—*Freedom is an Endless Meeting: Democracy in American Social Movements*. Chicago: University of Chicago Press

James Rinehart, 2006—*The Tyranny of Work: Alienation and the Labour Process*, fifth edition. Toronto: Thompson Nelson

George Ross and Jane Jenson, 1986—'Post-war Class Struggle and the Crisis of Left Politics', in Ralph Miliband, John Saville, Marcel Liebman, and Leo Panitch, eds, 1986—*Socialist Register 1985/86*. London: Merlin

Stephanie Ross, 2003—'Is this What Democracy Looks Like? The Politics of the Anti-Globalization Movement in North America', in Leo Panitch and Colin Leys, eds, 2003—*Socialist Register 2003: Fighting Identities*. London: Merlin, pp 281–301

Alfredo Saad Filho, 2006—'Contesting the State in the Era of Globalization'. Canadian Political Science Association annual conference, York University, Toronto (unpublished manuscript)

Emir Sader, 2002—'Beyond Civil Society: The Left after Porto Alegre', in *New Left Review*, no 17, September–October 2002, pp 87–99

Anne Showstack Sassoon, 1987—*Gramsci's Politics*. Minneapolis: University of Minnesota Press

Jai Sen, 2006—'Understanding the World Social Forum: The WSF as an Emergent Learning Process—Notes on the Dynamics of Change', in *Mainstream* (New Delhi), March 25 2006

Jai Sen, 2018b—'Break Free! Engaging Critically with the Concept and Reality of Civil Society (Part 1)', in Jai Sen, ed, 2018—*The Movements of Movements, Part 2: Rethinking Our Dance*. Volume 5 in the *Challenging Empires* series. New Delhi: OpenWord, and Oakland, CA: PM Press

Steve Sherman, 2007—'Achievements and Limits of the First United States Social Forum', in *Monthly* Review, July 4 2007, at http://www.monthlyreview.org/mrzine/sherman040707.html (Accessed September 5 2017)

Maria Trigona, November 2006—'Workers without bosses at a turning point', on *ResearchGate*, November 9 2006, at https://www.researchgate.net/publication/265104404_Workers_without_bosses_at_a_turning_point (Accessed August 18 2017)

Hilary Wainwright, 1994—*Arguments for a New Left: Answering the Free Market Right*. London: Blackwell

Peter Waterman, 2003—*Place, Space and the Reinvention of Social Emancipation: Second Thoughts on the Third World Social Forum*. The Hague: Institute of Social Studies Working Paper, no 378, at https://www.researchgate.net/publication/5130659_Place_space_and_the_reinvention_of_social_emancipation_on_a_global_scale_second_thoughts_on_the_Third_World_Social_Forum (Accessed August 18 2017)

Chico Whitaker, 2004—'The WSF as Open Space', in Jai Sen, Anita Anand, Arturo Escobar, and Peter Waterman, eds, 2004—*The World Social Forum: Challenging Empires*. New Delhi: The Viveka Foundation, pp 111–21

Ellen Meiksins Wood, 1990—'The Uses and Abuses of "Civil Society"', in Ralph Miliband and Leo Panitch, eds, 1990—*Socialist Register 1990: The Retreat of the Intellectuals*. London: Merlin Press, pp 60–84

World Social Forum Organising Committee, 2001—'World Social Forum Charter of Principles', at http://www.colorado.edu/AmStudies/lewis/ecology/wsfcharter.pdf (Accessed August 18 2017)

Notes

1. Ed: This essay was originally published in *Labour, Capital and Society*, vol 41 issue 1, in April 2008, at http://www.lcs-tcs.com/ (Accessed August 18 2017). I thank both the author and the editor for their permission to publish this essay here in edited form.
2. Graeber 2002, p 70.
3. Graeber 2002, pp 70–72.
4. Ross 2003, pp 283–89.

5.   'Power-over' is a term used primarily by feminists to distinguish between power understood as domination and 'power-to', which refers to the capacity to act, whether individually or collectively. See Allen 2005.
6.   Fernbach 1975, p 45.
7.   Bakunin 1873.
8.   Ibid.
9.   Ibid.
10. Day 2005, p 113. Emphasis in original.
11. Holloway 2005, pp 20–21.
12. Holloway 2005, pp 12, 19.
13. Holloway 2005, p 17.
14. Bensaïd 2005, p 172.
15. Polletta 2002; Wainwright 1994, pp 76–84; Buechler 2000, p 48; Offe 1987, pp 63–65; Berger 1979, p 37.
16. Buechler 2000, p 46.
17. Taylorism refers to the practice of 'scientific management' of the production process in order to centralise knowledge in the managerial strata and dramatically reduce workers' discretion and capacity to interfere with managerial decisions. Developed in the early twentieth-century US by Frederick Taylor, 'scientific management' involved observing workers to capture their 'trade secrets', fragmenting and reorganising these tasks in order to minimize wasteful movements, using time-motion studies to set benchmarks for the pace of production at the "physiological maximum", and instituting forms of discipline to ensure conformity with such a reorganised labour process. See Rinehart 2006, pp 37–41.
18. Ross and Jenson 1986, p 24.
19. Panitch 1986.
20. Boggs 1986, p 24.
21. Berger 1979, p 29.
22. Wainwright 1994, pp 68–69.
23. Berger 1979, pp 30–31.
24. Buechler 2000, p 47; Boggs 1986, pp 47–52.
25. Foucault 1980, Laclau and Mouffe 1985, Magnussen and Walker 1988.
26. Laclau and Mouffe 1985, pp 81–85.
27. Foucault 1980.
28. Magnussen and Walker 1988.
29. Laclau and Mouffe 1985, pp 113, 153.
30. Carroll and Ratner 1994, p 13.
31. Day 2005, p 8.
32. Saad Filho 2006, pp 1, 2.
33. World Social Forum Organising Committee 2001.
34. Ibid.
35. Waterman 2003, p 2.
36. Becker 2007; Sen 2006, p 7.
37. Sen 2006, p 5.
38. Conway 2005, p 427.
39. Sherman 2007.

40. Whitaker 2004, p 111.
41. Waterman 2003, p 7.
42. Whitaker, in Conway 2005, p 425; also Sen 2006, p 9.
43. Conway 2005, p 426.
44. Petras, January 2002.
45. Dinerstein 2002, p 19.
46. Petras 2003.
47. Dinerstein 2002, pp 8, 23, 25–26.
48. Dinerstein 2002, pp 25–26.
49. Dinerstein 2003, pp 196–97.
50. Dinerstein 2003, p 196.
51. Lewis 2004.
52. Sassoon 1987, pp 193–204.
53. Ed: For a related discussion of the relationship between civil society and the state and the question of power, see the essay by Jai Sen in this book (Sen 2018b).
54. Sassoon 1987, p 116.
55. Lewis 2004.
56. Ibid.
57. Wood 1990, p 61.
58. Carroll and Ratner 1994, p 6. See also Melucci 1989.
59. Wood 1990, p 64.
60. Carroll and Ratner 1994, p 11.
61. Sader 2002, p 93.
62. Carroll and Ratner 1994, p 6.
63. Trigona 2006.
64. Sader 2002, p 91.
65. Wainwright 1994, p 76.
66. Sader 2002, p 92.
67. Berger 1979, p 33.
68. Panitch 2000, p 14.
69. Boron 2005, p 36.
70. Carroll and Ratner 1994, p 23 fn 8; Sassoon 1982, p 136.
71. Gordon 2005.
72. Petras 2003, p 18.
73. Castorina 2007, pp 271, 279–80.
74. North and Huber 2004, p 981.
75. Boggs 1986, p 19.
76. Saad Filho 2006, p 3.
77. Boron 2005, p 37.
78. Boggs 1986, p 19.
79. Ibid.
80. Carroll and Ratner 1994, p 21.

Negativity and Utopia in the Global Justice Movement[1]
Michael Löwy

The global justice movement—or the global justice and solidarity movement, or the global resistance movement, or, in the Latin languages, *el movimiento altermundialista* ('the alterglobalist movement')—is, without doubt, the most important phenomena of antisystemic resistance at the beginning of the twenty-first century. This vast galaxy, a sort of 'movement of movements' whose most visible manifestations are the social forums—local, continental, or international—and the great demonstrations of protest against the World Trade Organization (WTO), the G8 (the annual meeting of the eight great powers), and the imperial war in Iraq—does not correspond to the usual forms of social or political action. Being a large, decentralised network, it is multiple, diverse, and heterogeneous, bringing together workers' unions and peasant movements, NGOs and Indigenous associations, women's movements and ecological initiatives, senior intellectuals and young activists (and vice versa). Far from being a weakness, this plurality is one of the sources of the movement's growing and expansive power.

The international solidarities that grow inside this vast network are of a new sort, somewhat different from those of the internationalist mobilisations of the '60s and '70s. In those years, solidarity networks would support liberation movements, either in the Global South—the Algerian, Cuban, or Vietnamese revolutions—or in Eastern Europe—the Polish dissidents, the Prague Spring. A few years latter, in the 1980s, important movements of solidarity emerged, this time to support the Sandinistas in Nicaragua or Solidarność in Poland.

This fraternal and generous tradition of solidarity with the oppressed has not disappeared from the new global justice movement that started in the '90s—far from it. An obvious example is the sympathy and the support on an international scale for the Zapatistas after the Indigenous uprising of January 1994 in Chiapas, Mexico. But, one sees here already something new emerging, a change of perspective. In 1996, the Zapatista Army of National Liberation called for an 'Intercontinental—poetically described by Subcomandante Marcos as "Intergalactic"—Encounter against Neoliberalism and for Humanity'.[2] The thousands of participants, originating from forty countries, who came to this encounter—which can be considered the first event of what would later be called the *movimiento altermundialista*—were doubtless motivated *in addition* by feelings of solidarity with the Zapatistas. But the aim of the meeting, as defined by its organisers, was much larger: the search was for convergences in the common struggle against a common enemy—neoliberalism—and the discussion of possible alternatives for humanity.

Here, therefore, is the new characteristic of the solidarities woven inside or around the Global Resistance Movement against capitalist globalisation: the struggle to achieve immediate aims common to all—for instance, the defeat of the WTO—and the common search for new paradigms of civilisation. In other words, instead of a solidarity *with*, it is a new solidarity *between* various organisations, social movements, or political forces from different countries or continents that help each other and cooperate in the same battle against the same planetary enemies. This new tendency is, to some extent, the result of the process of capitalist globalisation itself, which, by imposing the dictatorship of financial capital on the whole planet, produces the need for a common resistance.

To give a concrete example: the international peasant network Via Campesina connects movements as diverse as the French Conféderation Paysanne ('Peasant Confederation'), the Brazilian Landless Movement (MST), and some great peasant movements in India. These organisations support each other, exchange experiences, and act in common against neoliberal policies and their common opponents: agribusiness multinationals, seed monopolists, producers of genetically modified organisms (GMOs), big landowners. Their solidarity is *mutual* and they make up one of the most powerful, active, and vocal components of the world movement against capitalist globalisation. One could cite other examples among trade unionists, feminists (the World Women's March), ecologists, and others. For sure, this process of revitalisation of ancient solidarities and invention of new ones is still nascent. It is fragile, limited, uncertain, and quite unable, for the moment, to threaten the overwhelming domination of global capital and the planetary hegemony of neoliberalism. It is nevertheless the strategic place where tomorrow's internationalism is being elaborated.

The Three Moments of Global Justice

The dynamics of the global justice movement includes three distinct but complementary moments: a *negativity of resistance*, *concrete propositions*, and a *utopian vision of another world*.

The first moment, the starting point of the movement, is the *great refusal*, the protest, the imperative need to *resist* the existing order of things. This is why the global justice movement constitutes, in fact, the "International of Resistance" that Jacques Derrida hoped for in his book *Spectres of Marx*.[3] The initial motivation for the multitudes that mobilised against the WTO in Seattle in 1999 was the wish to actively oppose not 'globalisation' as such but its capitalist and liberal form, that is corporate globalisation with its consequence of injustices and catastrophes:

growing inequality between North and South, unemployment, social exclusion, destruction of the environment, imperial wars, and crimes against humanity. It was not by accident that the *altermundialista* movement was born with this cry issued by the Zapatistas in 1994: "*Ya basta*! Enough of that!" The strength of the movement comes first of all from this radical negativity, inspired by a deep and irreducible indignation. Celebrating the dignity of indignation and the unconditional rejection of injustice, Daniel Bensaïd wrote, "The burning current of indignation cannot be dissolved into the lukewarm waters of consensual resignation. . . . Indignation is a beginning. A way to stand up and to start on the road. People are indignant, they rise up, and then see what happens".[4] The radicality of the movement comes to a large extent from this capacity for rebellion and non-submission, from this uncompromising disposition to say: *No!*

Hostile critics of the movement and the conformist media insist on its excessively 'negative' character, its nature of 'pure protest', the absence of 'realist' alternative propositions. One must resolutely reject this blackmail; even if the movement did not have one single proposition to make, its rebellion would be entirely justified. The street protests against the WTO, the G8, or the imperial war are visible, concentrated, and vocal expression of this defiance against the powers that be and their rules of the game. The movement is proud of its active negativity, its rebellious complexion. Without this radical feeling of refusal, the global justice movement simply would not exist.

Against which enemy is this rejection directed? The international financial institutions (the WTO, the World Bank, and the International Monetary Fund)? Or neoliberal policies? Or, beyond this, the great multinational monopolies? All these forces responsible for the commodification of the world are favourite targets. But the movement is more 'radical'. This word means, as we know, to go to the roots of a problem. Now, what is the root of the banks and monopolies' total domination, of the financial markets' dictatorship, of the imperialist wars, if not the *capitalist system* itself? For sure, not all components of the global justice movement are ready to draw this conclusion; some still dream of a return to the neo-Keynesianism of the so-called 'thirty glorious' years of growth or of regulated capitalism with a human face. These 'moderates' have their place in the movement, but usually the radical tendency predominates. Most of the documents issued by the movement challenge not only neoliberal and bellicose policies but also the power of capital itself.

Let us take, for instance, the World Social Forum's (WSF) Charter of Principles, issued by the Brazilian Organising Committee—composed not only of delegates from unions and peasant movements but also of NGOs and the Peace and Justice Commission of the Catholic Church—and approved, with small changes, by the WSF's International Council. This document, among the most representative and 'consensual' of the *altermundialista* movement, states:

The World Social Forum is an open space of encounter whose aim is to deepen reflection, debate democratic ideas, formulate propositions, freely exchange experiences, and articulate in view of efficient actions, organisations and movements of civil society that are opposed to neoliberalism and to the domination of the world by capital and all form of imperialism, and which wish to build a planetary society grounded on the human being. . . . The alternatives proposed by the WSF are opposed to a process of capitalist globalisation commanded by the great multinational enterprises.[5]

The main *parole* of the movement, "the world is not a commodity", is not so far from the ideas of a certain Karl Marx, who denounced in his *Manuscripts of 1844* a system—capitalism—in which "the worker becomes a commodity, whose worthlessness increases with the quantity of commodities it produces. The depreciation of the human world increases in direct relation with the rise in value of the world of things".[6] In other words, the radicality of the movement's *great refusal* aims at the capitalist nature of domination.

However, in contrast to the assertions of establishment scribes, the global justice movement does not lack concrete, urgent, practical, and immediately feasible alternative propositions. For sure, none of its bodies has approved a 'common programme', and no project belonging to a political force has become dominant. But during Forums and mobilisations several demands appear that are, if not unanimous, at least largely shared and carried by the movement. For instance, cancellation of Third-World debt, taxation of financial transactions, abolition of fiscal paradises, a moratorium on GMOs, the right of peoples to nourish themselves, effective equality between men and women, the defence and extension of public services, a priority for health, education, and culture, and the protection of the environment. These demands have been elaborated by the movement's international networks—World March of Women, the *Association pour la Taxation des Transactions Financières et pour l'Aide aux Citoyens* ('Association for the Taxation of Financial Transactions for the Aid to Citizens', ATTAC), Focus on the Global South, Via Campesina, Committee for the Abolition of the Third World's Debt—and various other social movements, and discussed in the Forums.

One of the great qualities of these Forums is to permit encounters and sharing of mutual knowledge between feminists and trade unionists, ecologists and Marxists, believers and non-believers, activists from the North and the South. In this process of confrontation and mutual enrichment, disagreements do not disappear but, little by little, emerges a body of common propositions.

Are these propositions 'realistic'? The question is poorly formulated. In the existing relationship of forces, power elites and ruling classes refuse en bloc to consider them; they are literally unimaginable to the neoliberal *pensée unique*, intolerable to the representatives of capital; or, in the hypocritical variant of social-liberals, they are 'unfortunately unfeasible'. But it is enough that the relationship of forces changes and public opinion mobilises for the powerful to be forced to retreat and make concessions, even while trying to empty them of all substance. The important thing in these propositions is that they are extensible: every partial victory, every concession obtained, every step forward permits advancement to the next, higher stage, to a more radical demand. We have here, in a different form than the traditional labour movement, a 'transitory' dynamic that leads, sooner or later, to challenging the system itself.

We reach now the third moment, as important as the others: the *utopian dimension* of the 'movement of movements'. It too is radical: for it proclaims that 'Another World Is Possible'. The aim is not simply to correct the excesses of the capitalist / industrial world and its monstrous neoliberal policies but to dream and to struggle for another civilisation, another economic and social paradigm, another way of living together on earth. Beyond its multiple concrete and specific propositions, the movement harbours a more ambitious, more 'global', more universal transformative perspective. Here too one would search in vain for a common project, a consensual reformist or revolutionary programme. The *altermundialista* utopia shows itself only in the sharing of certain common values that sketch the outline of this other 'possible world'.

The first of these values is the human being. The utopia of the movement is *resolutely humanist*; it requires that the needs and aspirations of human beings become the vital centre of a reorganisation of economy and society. Its rebellion against the commodification of human relations, against the transformation of love, culture, life, and health into commodities, supposes another form of social life beyond reification and fetishism. Not by accident does the movement address all humans, even if it privileges the oppressed and the exploited as actors of social change. The defence of the environment is also of humanist inspiration: to save the ecological equilibrium and to protect nature against the predatory attacks of capitalist productivism is necessary to ensure the continuity of human life.

Another essential value of the *altermundialista* utopia is *democracy*. The idea of participatory democracy as a superior form of citizenship—beyond the limits of traditional representative systems because it permits the population to exercise its power of decision and control directly—has a central place in the discussions of the movement. It has a 'utopic' value in so far as it questions existing forms of power and, at the same time, it is already being put into practice under limited and experimental forms in several towns, beginning, of course, with Porto Alegre, Brazil, where the WSF began. The great challenge from the viewpoint of an alternative society project is to extend democracy to the economic and social sphere. Why permit, in these areas, exclusive power to an elite, which is denied them in the political sphere?

Capital has replaced three great revolutionary values of the past—liberty, equality, fraternity—with more 'modern' concepts: liberalism, equity, charity. The utopia of the global justice movement takes up the values of 1789 but gives them new scope. For instance, liberty is not only the freedom of expression, organisation, thought, criticism—won at a high price through fierce struggles over centuries against absolutism and dictatorship. It is also, today more than ever, the freedom from another form of absolutism: the dictatorship of financial markets and the oligarchy of bankers and heads of multinational enterprises imposing their interests on the whole planet. As for equality, it concerns not only the 'social fracture' between the richest elite and the dispossessed masses but also the inequality between nations and continents—the North and the South—as well as between men and women. Finally, fraternity—which seems to limit itself to brothers (*frates* in Latin)—is replaced by *solidarity*, by relations of cooperation, sharing, and mutual help. The expression 'civilisation of solidarity' is perhaps the best summary of the movement's alternative project. This requires not only a radically different economical and political structure but also an alternative society that cherishes the ideas of common good, general interest, universal rights, and gratuity.

Another important value of the Global Justice culture is *diversity*. The new world of which the movement dreams is anything but homogeneous, where all are supposed to imitate a unique model. We want, said the Zapatistas, *a world where different worlds can find their place*. The plurality of languages, cultures, music, food, and life forms is an immense wealth which one must learn to cultivate.

All these values do not define a model of society for the future. They provide paths, openings, windows towards the possible. The road to utopia is not yet traced: it is the marchers themselves who shall trace it.

For many of the participants in Forums and demonstrations, *socialism* is the name of this utopia. It is a hope shared by Marxists and anarchists, radical Christians and left ecologists, as well as by a significant number of activists in the labour, peasant, feminist, and Indigenous movements. A socialist democracy would mean that the great socioeconomic and ecological choices, priorities in terms of investment, the basic orientations of production and distribution would be democratically discussed and decided by the population itself, not by a handful of exploiters in the name of the so-called 'laws of the market' (nor, in a variant which failed, by an all-powerful Politburo). It wouldn't make sense to impose socialism as the programme of the global justice movement, but the debate on socialism—very much at the centre of political life in several Latin American countries, in the form of debates on 'socialism in the twenty-first century'—is a legitimate part of the discussion of alternative projects and ideas.

In any case, the global justice movement is not waiting for this utopian future to arrive, but acting and struggling, here and now. Each Social Forum, each local experience of participatory democracy, each collective land occupation by peasants, each internationally coordinated action against war is a prefiguration of the *altermundialista* utopia and is inspired by its values, which are those of a civilisation of solidarity.

References

Daniel Bensaïd, 2001—*Les irréductibles. Théorèmes de la résistance à l'air du temps* ['The Unsubmissive Ones: Theses on the Resistance to Conformism', in French], Paris: Textuel

Bernard Cassen, 2003—*Tout a commencé à Porto Alegre . . .* ['Everything started in Porto Alegre . . ', in French], Paris: Mille et une nuits

Jacques Derrida, 1993—*Spectres de Marx* ['Spectres of Marx', in French], Paris: Galilée

Karl Marx, 1962—*Manuscrits de 1844* ['Manuscripts of 1844', in French], Paris: Ed Sociales

Zapatista Army of National Liberation (EZLN), May 1996—'Invitation-summons to the Intercontinental Encounter for Humanity and Against Neoliberalism, Mexico, May of 1996', at http://www.nadir.org/nadir/initiativ/agp/chiapas1996/en/invite.html (Accessed August 19 2017)

Notes

1. Ed: The author Michael Löwy sent me the original of this essay back in 2007 ('*Negativité et utopie du mouvement altermondialiste*'), which was then not available in English, and then very kindly translated it for us. I believe it is being published here for the first time. I want to most sincerely and warmly thank him for his embrace of our book project and for his generosity of spirit.

2. Zapatista Army of National Liberation (EZLN), May 1996.

3. Derrida 1993, pp 141–42.

4. Bensaïd 2001, p 106.

5. Cassen 2003, p 166.

6. Marx 1962, p 57.

The Global Moment
Seattle, Ten Years On[1]
Rodrigo Nunes

A Spent Force?

What are we to make of a tenth anniversary of a key event that no one celebrates? The year 2009 may be remembered for many things: the greatest capitalist crisis in over a century, the first year of the Obama presidency in the US, the transformation of the G8 into a G20 (the first massive geopolitical rearrangement since the fall of the Soviet bloc), the ecological crisis definitively establishing itself as a widespread concern (even if it means very different things to different groups). One thing, however, was conspicuously absent from the year's calendar: the tenth anniversary of the protests in Seattle against the World Trade Organization (WTO), which made 1999 the year when the 'anti' or 'alter-globalisation' movement, or the 'movement of movements' or 'global movement', became a visible phenomenon across the world.

In 2009, of course, 'celebration' was not very high on the agenda, even—or especially—if looked at from the point of view of those protests. If anything, the problems highlighted then seem even more pressing now, the threats they pose more acute. More importantly, while the danger grows, the redeeming power seems to recede. It is tempting to say that time has proved those protesters ten years ago right, but the capacity for immediate action in the present seems ever more remote. Today, the liveliness of debate, the wealth of different experiences, and—more importantly—the intensity of mobilisation, the determination and the hope of those years, seem far away.[2] Surely this is sufficient reason to revisit the period as a source of inspiration and a way of stoking whatever embers are left? In which case, should the silence be interpreted as yet another symptom of the present lethargy? Or could it also be a sign of a something else: an unspoken avoidance or implicit recognition of that period as a source of impasse, a dead end?

The failure of the 2003 anti-war mobilisations to stop the Iraq war opened the season of public questioning regarding the effectiveness of 'the movement'. Thus, for instance, Paolo Virno, writing in 2004:

> The global movement, from Seattle forward, appears as a battery that only half works: It accumulates energy without pause, but it does not know how or where to discharge it. It is faced with an amazing accumulation, which has no correlate,

at the moment, in adequate investments. It is like being in front of a new tech-nological apparatus, potent and refined, but ignoring the instructions for its use.[3]

By 2007, a major player in the World Social Forum process wondered whether the time had not come for it, "having fulfilled its historic function of aggregating and linking the diverse counter-movements spawned by global capitalism . . . to give way to new modes of global organisation of resistance and transformation".[4] It became common to hear that 'the movement' had failed to produce 'proposals' or 'alternatives', and hence squandered its accumulated energy and opportunities to deliver on the promise that the blue-sky lightning of Seattle had suggested. There were many alleged culprits: the incapacity to deal with diversity or an ab-solute emphasis on diversity making political definitions impossible, depoliticised 'movementism' and 'life-stylism', and the atavistic reformism of parties and unions (and of course NGOs).

Yet if one asks the seemingly straightforward question of what has been achieved since Seattle, it is just as true to say 'a lot' as 'not nearly enough'. The various blows to the WTO project, successful anti-privatisation campaigns such as the ones around water and gas in Bolivia, the election of progressive govern-ments across Latin America, the opposition to the neoliberal constitution in Europe, the defeat of the CPE in France . . . plus a huge number of local victories, small victories, partial victories, even defeats that resulted in the creation of new possibilities that might one day result in victories. One could certainly ask: What does any of this have to do with the 'global movement' as such? But this, precisely, takes us to the crucial difficulty in talking about a 'global movement': How are we to tell it apart from its constituent parts? How are we to isolate whatever these parts do as parts from what they do in conjunction with others, or the aggregate effect of what all of them do?

Take the struggles against the WTO—the one example from those above that can be least problematically attributed to the 'global movement'. Until the Seattle protests, negotiations soldiered on with the time's distinctive sense of in-evitability, and governments would hardly bother to inform let alone consult their citizens. That sudden crystallisation managed to foreground a dissent that could have remained marginal and powerless if not for that instant when certain forces recognised themselves in a common struggle, and it certainly began to tilt the agenda. A sequence was opened that made it possible for opposition to neoliberal policies to grow, for different movements to communicate with and reinforce each other, and for other moments of convergence to occur, in a chain of positive feed-backs that undoubtedly contributed to, for example, the election of progressive governments in Latin America. It may be that the effective cause of the WTO's 'derailing' was, in the end, the stronger stance taken by the governments of some developing states around the negotiating table; this, however, would probably not have happened had it not been for the presence of movements outside the gates or for the broader sequence at the turn of the century through which this series unfolded. But despite this, at the time when these ultimate effects were produced, the 'global movement' was already regarded by many of its participants as a spent force.

How are we to think through this paradox: that its greatest victory arrived after its wane? What if the reluctance to celebrate today comes from a difficulty in thinking of a 'global movement' in any meaningful way? What if this, rather than dichotomies such as 'openness' versus 'decision-making', is the impasse that is sensed? And what if—to advance a hypothesis in the bluntest possible way—the global movement never existed? What if it was a moment, rather than a movement?[5]

One World Is Possible

The most literal way of speaking of a 'global movement' would be as a reference to those groups posing only explicitly global goals, or whose space of action was essentially transnational. In the face of the plethora of social forces mobilised around the world at the time, however, such a definition seems scandalously narrow. (The greater currency enjoyed among many by the phrase 'global movement of movements' was no doubt due precisely to its indefinite, near-infinite inclusivity.) To limit the frame of reference in such a way would turn 'global movement' into a very reductive synecdoche. Yet this is exactly the *pars pro toto* logic that was (and is) often used by media commentators, whereby the expression comes to refer to what, in the Global North, was the period's most visible manifestation: the cycle of summit protests (Seattle, Prague, Québec City, Genoa, and so on) and of counter-summits (the social forums and the like).

Avoiding this synecdoche is crucial, not only to stay close to the self-understanding of the actors concerned but also to undo the confusion at the source of the present impasse. Thinking in terms of moment allows us to do so. This was a moment, first, because there was an intensification of activity on various fronts, including mobilisations against structural adjustment and privatisation (Bolivia, South Korea, various African countries, Canada), against multinational corporations (oil companies, as in the Niger Delta; sweatshop-based brands, as in the USA), against migration policies (the *sans papiers*—'without papers'—in France, various border camps in Europe, North America, Australia), against GMOs (several Via Campesina campaigns around the world), and many more. In most cases, these were not pitched as 'global' campaigns as such; they took place in the space of local or national politics, had national legislation and policies as their referents, and unfolded within a complex, multilayered field of relations and causal series where their 'global' dimension was always filtered by local, national, and regional struggles, correlations of forces, institutional arrangements, conjunctures, and contingent events. In this case, speaking of a 'global movement' appropriately would refer to nothing more than the sum total of these various forces' activities, the outcome of their political interventions and the transformation of social relations they managed to produce. Except that 'movement' would still have a metaphorical sense, calling a whole what is really only a collection: something whose only criteria for membership would be existence on the same globe, something that could never be totalised or given any kind of unitary shape or direction—a 'wild' in-itself, never to be fully appropriated for-itself.

However, there is one characteristic of the moment that began in the mid-1990s that sets it apart from previous cycles of struggle that took place simultaneously in various parts of the globe, such as those of the 1840s, 1920s–30s and 1960s–70s. In the sense disclosed by it, the 'global movement' would in fact exist only for-itself, and this for-itselfness would be the very quality making its emergence unique: a for-itself whose in-itself is not given. What is the unique characteristic of that emergence? This was the first cycle of struggles that defined itself in terms of its global dimension. The material element determining this difference was, of course, capitalist globalisation itself, which created and strengthened structures and flows of communication, movements of people and goods to such a scale that the potential for connections between different local realities became widely accessible not only to the actors instrumental in the advance of capital, but potentially also to those who wished to resist it. This expanded potential for exchange and the production of commonalities resulted in enhanced awareness of the different impacts of neoliberal globalisation, their interconnectedness, the forms taken by resistance to them, and the ways in which these resistances could be placed in relation with each other. This, in turn, enabled concrete exchanges and mutual support between different local experiences, which, finally, conjured a potential: that of momentarily focusing this localised political activity into moments of shared relevance, whether at a global level (such as the mobilisations against the WTO or the Iraq war) or more locally.

These three factors—awareness, concrete exchanges, and potential for convergence—constitute that moment's global dimension. There is no contradiction between affirming this dimension as its defining feature and the fact that most of the movements and campaigns then active had local or national politics as their space of action and main referents. As a matter of fact, these three factors are precisely what created the mirage of a movement, when in fact what one had was a moment of rapidly increased capacity for communication and coordination, and wide-eyed astonishment at a just discovered potential for channelling much of that activity into determinate spatio-temporal coordinates, creating moments of convergence whose collective power was much greater than the sum of its parts.

Thus, while most of the activity effectively occupied the national or local political space, the key characteristic of that period was the widened perception of global processes. The 'global movement', in this sense, was something that existed in people's heads and in the communication between them.

This is distinct from previous generations' 'internationalism': rather than an aggregate of nation-states to be revolutionised or reformed one by one, it refers to a shared belonging to an interconnected, interdependent world.[6] This means not only a heightened awareness of the commonality of natural commons but a clearer grasp of the effects at a distance produced by a global market and of the possibility of intervening in relation to these effects in ways that are necessarily restricted neither to national borders nor to the nation-state as the sole agency to be addressed. It is the increase in types of connection today—supranational (multilateral organisms, information networks), transnational (migrant networks), and infranational (among different regions affected by the same problem, for example, dams)—that opens up the possibility of interventions that need neither depart from the nation-state nor retain it as their sole or immediate referent.

It has been argued that the famous 'Earthrise' photograph had an effect on the development of environmentalism; and indeed there is enormous power in the idea that 'there is only one world': once a physical limit is placed on the capacity to universalise, the rational operation of seeing one's lot as necessarily tangled with that of others is given a concrete outline. That this 'concrete universalism' is coupled with the increase in the capacity to exchange and cooperate with 'concrete others' from all over the globe is one of the novelties of 'globalism'. Under its light, every struggle appears as neither exclusively local nor exclusively global: all struggles communicate on different levels, while no struggle can in practice subsume all others. There are no partial 'local' solutions that can stand in isolation, and there is no 'global' solution unless this is understood as a certain possible configuration of local ones. What ended up being labelled as a 'movement' (the cycle of summit protests and counter-summits) was, therefore, nothing but the tip of the iceberg: the convergences produced by a much wider and deeper weft of connections, both direct (as when groups engaged in communication and coordination with each other) and indirect (when struggles resonated and reinforced each other without any coordination), among initiatives that were sometimes very local, sometimes very different, sometimes even contradictory.

That there was no 'movement' as such does not mean that it did not produce concrete effects; every moment of convergence fed back into these initiatives, creating and reinforcing connections and strengthening the globalism that defined the moment, nourishing the (subjectively effective) notion that all of this belonged in the same movement. This strength, however, would reveal itself as also being a weakness. The 'we' of that period became progressively stabilised as the 'we' of the summit protests and counter-summits—certainly a multitudinous, diverse 'we', but one which managed to sustain itself largely because of the short-lived nature of those convergences, their externally, negatively given object (where the 'one no' always had precedence over the 'many yeses'), and the positive feedback produced by their own spectacular mediatic strength. The more entrenched the synecdoche became, the more these convergences came to be treated as an end in themselves, rather than strategic tools and tactical moments in what should be the constitution of 'another world'.[7]

Yes and No

That moment's passing can be partially explained by the impossibility of inhabiting the global level as such. The technological and tactical innovations ('swarming', the 'diversity of tactics' principle) that enabled large-scale convergences can only function at such a scale when their objects are externally given and negatively defined: anti-WTO, anti-war, and so on. The much lamented lack of 'proposals' was never actually that; there was a dizzying collection of proposals, and what was perceived as a lack was in fact the impossibility of having 'the movement' sub-scribe to any of them as global movement—that is, as a whole. Moreover, there is a serious difficulty in thinking of global 'proposals' by analogy with those that can be placed in national political space, given that at the global level there is no one to address directly. One cannot lobby or influence transnational structures in the same way as national governments, as the unaccountability and imperviousness of the latter to political process is structural rather than contingent; whatever accountability they may have is ultimately mediated by national structures.

This became evident in 2005 in the attempt by a group of intellectuals asso-ciated with the World Social Forum to elaborate what they saw as a distillation of that profusion of ideas into a minimal consensual programme.[8] Ultimately, the main problem with this document was not the way in which it was drafted, the lack of gender balance, or any of the other criticisms raised at the time, but that it is entirely unclear what its presumed target audience (the WSF, 'the movement') could actually do about proposals pitched at such a global level—apart from organising demonstrations incorporating them as rallying points. They do not even function as demands, as there is no one to demand them from. At this level, antagonism remains purely representative: expressing a dissent that has no means of enforcement. This kind of dissent has some effectiveness in a parliamentary de-mocracy, of course, provided it corresponds to a large enough constituency rep-resenting a relevant electoral variable. The problem is that at the global level this is impossible. However crucial it is to keep open the potential to focus political activity on singular global moments, such potential exists only as a consequence of capacity built at the local level, not as its substitute; it is only to the extent that local struggles enhance their capacity to act in their immediate environment that they can act globally in meaningful ways. In fact, privileging convergences can sap resources from local capacity-building, when the point should be precisely that the former reinforce the latter. If they do not, antagonism, rather than being the other half of building autonomy, comes to replace it; and, in doing so, it loses the grounds on which it can find support. It becomes the expression of political contents from which it is impossible to draw political consequences.

There was another reason why the global became uninhabitable. The context in which the 'global moment' unfolded changed drastically with the onset of the 'War on Terror'. Not only was the main focus of conflict moved elsewhere ('good' versus 'rogue' states, 'fundamentalism' versus 'democracy', 'Islam' versus 'the West'), it was displaced to a level of confrontation no movements were willing or able to occupy (state apparatus versus 'terror'). Moreover, the combination of an atmosphere of constantly reiterated alarm and the creep into spheres of legislative and policing measures that served to criminalise social movements had the subjective impact of reinforcing feelings of isolation, fear, and impotence. Many individuals abandoned political involvement altogether; individuals and groups disengaged from the global level, refocusing on the local. In other cases, investment in the global at the expense of the local led to a disconnection between politics and life, representation (or antagonism) and capacity-building, burn-out, or a replacement of slowly built consistency for the quicker, wider, but also less sustainable effects of the media.

Is the 'global moment' over? Yes and no. The material conditions that enabled it to become manifest remain, as do the elements of awareness of global processes and (the potential for) concrete exchanges. There is no going back on this, as there is no going back on 'globalism', or the political consciousness of belonging to a single world. Whatever movements appear in the future will in all likelihood share these features, and they will do well to look back to those years and draw some lessons from what went right and wrong. To say that the expectations then built around the use of information technology (as almost a substitute for other forms of political action) were exaggerated does not mean that their possibilities have been exhausted, the recent Iranian protests being a good example. If anything, one would expect to see much more made of their potential for diffuse initiative and rapid dissemination; yet the question will always be, once the 'great nights' they can produce have passed, how to give consistency to the excess they throw up.

On the other hand, these movements would do well to disarm some false dichotomies that were strong then, such as the supposedly definitive choices between autonomy-building and antagonism (the latter requires the former to exist, the former at various junctures requires the latter to expand), between absolute openness and capacity to act (any movement, any decision always strikes a balance between the two), or even between 'taking' or 'not taking' power (recognising the limits of what the state can deliver does not diminish the need to always push beyond them). It is far more important to develop the collective capacity to choose what mediators to have, what mediation to accept, and when. Building on these, managing to move beyond them; now that would be cause for celebration.

References

Walden Bello, 2007b—'The Forum at the Crossroads', at http://www.cadtm.org/The-Forum-at-the-Crossroads (Accessed August 20 2017)

Walden Bello, 2012—'World Social Forum at the Crossroads', in Jai Sen and Peter Waterman, eds, 2012—*World Social Forum: Critical Explorations.* Volume 3 in the *Challenging Empires* series. New Delhi: OpenWord, at https://www.tni.org/en/archives/act/16771 (Accessed August 20 2017)

Susan George, 2008—'Contribution to the Debate on the Future of the Social Forums and the Alter-globalization Movement', at www.tni.org/detail_page.phtml?&act_id=18081 (Inactive August 20 2017)

Group of Nineteen, February 2005—'Porto Alegre Manifesto', February 20 2005, at http://www.openspaceforum.net/twiki/tiki-read_article.php?articleId=276 (Accessed August 20 2017)

Renato Poggioli, 1968—*The Theory of the Avant-Garde*. Cambridge, MA: Harvard University Press

Paolo Virno, 2004—'Facing a New 17th Century', at www.generation-online.org/p/fpvirno4.htm (Accessed August 20 2017)

Notes

1. This essay was first published in *Radical Philosophy*, January–February 2010. I thank Emma Dowling for bringing it to my notice; we are reprinting it here with the agreement of the author and with the prompt and generous permission of the publisher.

2. Ed: This essay was written and first published in 2010, just a year or so ahead of the irruptions at a world scale that broke out in 2011.

3. Virno 2004.

4. Bello 2007b. Ed: See also Bello 2012.

5. Poggioli 1968.

6. Even before the thesis of 'socialism in only one country' and the tactical retreat into nationalism, proletarian universalism necessarily required the (national) communist party and trade union movement as the initial supports and local agents of 'world revolution'; solidarity and collaboration among revolutionary movements mirrored the bourgeois internationalism of solidarity among nation-states.

7. One example of this entrenchment is the current [2008] proposal for a permanent International Day of Action every two years. Tellingly, one proponent says of this

idea—where "one central subject, which touches everyone in the world, can be commonly put forward once every two years" as the theme for simultaneous worldwide demonstrations—that the theme "could be global warming, trade, out-of-control finance, debt. . . . I don't even care what the theme is; it's the principle of choosing it and of the unity that creates visibility that I think is important". See: Susan George 2008.

8.   Group of Nineteen, February 2005.

OpenWord

Autonomous Politics and Its Problems
Thinking the Passage from the Social to the Political[1,2]
Ezequiel Adamovsky

My aim in this essay is to present some hypotheses on issues of strategy for anti-capitalist emancipatory movements. The idea is to rethink the conditions for an effective politics with the capacity to radically change the society we live in. Though I don't have the space here to analyse concrete cases, these reflections are not a purely 'theoretical' endeavour but spring from the observation of a series of movements I have had the chance to be part of—the movement of neighbourhood assemblies in Argentina, some processes of the World Social Forum, and other global networks—or that I have followed closely in the past years, the *piquetero* (unemployed) movement also in Argentina and the Zapatistas in Mexico.

From the viewpoint of strategy, the current emancipatory movements can, somewhat schematically, be said to be in two opposite positions.[3] The first is where they manage to mobilise a great deal of social energy in favour of a political project but in a way that makes them fall in the trap of 'heteronomous politics'. By 'heteronomous' (as opposed to 'autonomous') I refer to the political mechanisms by means of which all that social energy ends up being channelled in a way that benefits the interests of the ruling class or, at least, minimises the radical potential of that popular mobilisation. This is, for example, the fate of Brazil's PT under Lula (Partido dos Trabalhadores, the 'Workers' Party') and of some social movements (for example, certain sections of the feminist movement) that turned into single-issue lobby organisations with no connection to any broader radical movement.

The second position is of those movements and collectives that reject any contact with the state and with heteronomous politics in general (parties, lobbies, elections, etc), only to find themselves reduced to small identity groups with little chance of having a real impact in terms of radical change. This is the case, for example, of some of the unemployed movements in Argentina but also of many small anti-capitalist collectives throughout the world. The cost of their political 'purity' is the inability to connect with larger sections of society.

To be sure, this is just a schematic picture: there are many experiments here and there of new strategic paths that may escape these two dead-end situations (the most visible example being that of the Zapatistas and their 'Sixth Declaration').[4] The reflections I present here are aimed at contributing to these explorations.

Two Hypotheses on a New Strategy for an Autonomous Politics

Hypothesis One: The left has a difficulty when it comes to thinking of power (or, what truth can be discerned in people's support for the right).

Let us face this awkward question: Why is it that the left, in spite of being a better option for humankind, almost never succeeds in getting the support of the people? Moreover, why is it that people often vote for obviously pro-capitalist options—sometimes even very right-wing candidates—instead? Let us avoid simplistic and patronising answers such as 'the people don't understand', or 'the pervasive power of the media', and so on. These sorts of explanations give us an implicit sense of superiority that we do not deserve and do not help us, politically speaking. Of course, the system has a formidable power to control culture and so to counter radical appeals. But we cannot only look for an answer there.

Leaving aside circumstantial factors, the perennial appeal of the right lies in that it presents itself as (and to some extent really is) a force of order. But why would order be so appealing for those who do not belong to the ruling class? We live in a type of society that rests upon (and strengthens) a constitutive, paradoxical tension. Each day we become more 'de-collectivised', that is, more atomised, increasingly isolated individuals without strong bonds with each other. But, at the same time, never in the history of humankind has there been such an interdependence when it comes to producing social life. Today, the division of labour is so deep that each minute, even without realising it, each of us is relying on the labour of millions of people from all over the world. In the capitalist system, paradoxically enough, the institutions that enable and organise such a high level of social cooperation are the very same that separate us from the other and make us isolated individuals without responsibility to other people. Yes, I am talking about the market and the (its) state. Buying and consuming products and voting for candidates in elections involves no answerability. These are actions performed by isolated individuals in solitude.

But such is our current interdependence that (global) society requires, like never before, that each person behave as they are supposed to behave. Yes, we have the freedom to dress like a clown if we want to, but we can't do anything that may affect the 'normal' course of society—because today, a small group of people or even one person has a bigger chance than ever to affect that normal course if they want to. Like never before, a single person has the chance to affect the lives of millions and to cause chaos. Why is this the case today more than in the past? Let us consider an example: if a peasant in seventeenth-century France decided not to farm his land he would not be putting his neighbours' lives in jeopardy but only his own. Imagine that he was angry or mad and set out to impede his neighbours from harvesting. In that case, the community would deal with him very soon; in the worst scenario, he might be able to affect one or two of his neighbours. Fast forward to any country in the twenty-first century. If three operators of a subway security system decide not to work (or to mess with the system just for fun), or if this important guy from the stock exchange lies about the prospects of AOL (America Online), they would be affecting the lives and labours of thousands of people, without those people even knowing the reason for the accident they had or the loss of their jobs. The paradox is that the ever-increasing individualism and lack of answerability makes it more likely that, in fact, there will be people who will be ready to cause trouble or harm other people's lives and interests, even without good reasons. Ask the students of Columbine about that.[5] In some respects our mutual dependence paradoxically contrasts with our subjectivity as isolated, non-answerable individuals.

As people who live in this constitutive tension, we all to some extent feel the anxiety for the continuity of social order and of our own lives, in view of the vulnerability of both. We unconsciously know that we depend on other individuals doing the right thing, but we don't know who they are or how to communicate with them. They are close but alien at the same time. This is the anxiety that popular movies enact time and again in hundreds of films whose narrative structure and themes are almost the same. A person or a small group of people puts society or other people's lives in jeopardy—be it because of evilness, criminal orientation, madness, strange political reasons, you name it—until some powerful intervention restores order—a caring father, Superman, the police, the president, Charles Bronson, etc. As moviegoers we come out with our anxiety sedated, but that comfort only lasts for some minutes. . .

Just like in such films, the political appeal of the right-wing calls to order comes from society's anxiety about the ever-increasing possibility of catastrophic disorder. From the viewpoint of an isolated individual, it makes no difference whether disorder is produced by another individual for random reasons or by a progressive collective that does it as part of a political action. It does not matter if it is a criminal, a madman, a union striking, or an anti-capitalist group doing direct action: whenever there is fear of catastrophic disorder and of the dissolution of social bonds, right-wing calls to order find a fertile soil.

There is no point in complaining about the situation: this fear is part of the society we live in. And it is not a matter of attitude. Popular support for right-wing options is not due to 'lack of political education'—something that could be remedied by simply telling the people what to think in a more persuasive way. There is no 'error' in popular support for the right: if there are reasons to believe that social life is in danger (and there usually are), the choice for more (right-wing) 'order' is a perfectly rational option *in the absence of other feasible and more desirable options*.

What I am trying to argue is that there is a valuable truth to be learnt in the perennial appeal of the calls for more 'order'. It is time we considered that, perhaps, what we (the radical left) are offering is not perceived as a feasible or a better option simply because, well, it isn't. The left has indeed the best diagnosis

244 | The Movements of Movements, Part 2

of what's wrong with society. We now also have a fairly decent offer of visions of what a better society would look like. But what about the question of how to get there? When it comes to that, we either have the option of traditional Leninist parties taking power (sorry, neither desirable nor better for me) or vague and sometimes utterly non-realistic generalisations.

In any case, we invite people to destroy the current social order (which is obviously necessary) so that we can then build something better. However, our political culture so far has more been about destroying, criticising, attacking the present for the sake of the future than about building and creating new and effective forms of cooperation and solidarity here and now. As we live in the future and despise the present, and as we do not bother to explain how we will protect people's lives from catastrophic social disorder while we try to build a new society, it is normal that the people perceive (rightly) that ours are nothing but vague, unreliable promises.

For reasons I will not have the space to explain here, the tradition of the left has inherited serious impediments when it comes to thinking about social order and, therefore, to relating to society as a whole.[6] In general, the left is not able to think of power as *immanent* with respect to social life. We tend instead to think of it as an *external* thing, a sort of parasite that colonises society 'from without'. In turn, we tend to think of society as a cooperative whole that exists before and independently from that *external* entity. Hence the Marxist idea that the state, the laws, etc are nothing but the 'superstructure' of a society that is defined primarily in the economic realm. Hence also the attitude of some anarchists who tend to consider all rules (with the exception of those freely and individually accepted) as something purely external and oppressive, while believing that the state could simply be destroyed with no cost to a society that—they think—is already 'complete' and exists 'beneath' the state and beyond its domination. Hence also the distinction that some autonomists propose between power as 'power-over' (the capacity to command) and as 'power-to-do' (the capacity to do), as if it were a struggle between two independent and clearly distinguishable 'sides'—the one evil, the other good.

What matters for our purposes is to understand that from all three cases mentioned above, there follows a strategic viewpoint (and also a certain 'militant culture') that is based in an attitude of pure hostility and rejection of social order, the laws, and all institutions. While some Marxists reject that order for the sake of the new order to be created after the Revolution, some anarchists and autonomists do so in the belief that society already possesses an 'order' of its own ready to flourish as soon as we get rid of all the political-legal-institutional burden.

Maybe it made sense in the past to think of social change as, first and foremost, a work of *destruction* of the social order. The situation today makes that strategic choice completely non-viable. Because nowadays there isn't any society 'beneath' the state and the market. Of course, there are many social connections and forms of cooperation that happen beyond them, but the main social bonds that organise and produce social life today are *structured by means of the market and the (its) state.* The market-state has already transformed social life in such a way that there is no 'society' outside of it. What would be left if we could make the state and the market cease to function right now by some magical twist? Certainly not a liberated humankind but catastrophic chaos: more or less weak groupings of decollectivised individuals here and there and the end of social life as we know it.

It follows that if we adopt a political strategy for radical change that is completely 'external' with regards to the market and the state, we would be choosing a strategy that is also, and by the same token, 'external' with regards to society. In other words, any emancipatory politics that explicitly (in its programme) or implicitly (in its 'militant culture' or 'attitude') presents itself as a purely *destructive* endeavour (or that only offers vague promises of reconstruction of social order *after* the destruction of the current one) will never manage to attract a large number of adherents. This is due to the fact that the others perceive (correctly) that this sort of politics puts current social life in jeopardy, with little to offer in its place. We are asking the people to trust us and jump into the abyss, but the people know (and they are right) that the complexity of our society is such that they cannot take that risk. In conclusion, the people do not trust the left, and they have very good reasons not to.

I would argue that we need to rethink our strategy taking into account this fundamental truth: the rules and institutions that enable and organise oppression are, at the same time, the rules and institutions that enable and organise social life as such. They are immanent and constitutive of society. Of course we can have other non-oppressive rules and institutions, but for the time being the market-state has become the spinal column of the one and only social life we have. In view of this, we cannot continue to offer a political option aimed at simply destroying the current social order. On the contrary, we need to present a strategy (and a 'militant culture' or 'attitude' based on it) that *makes explicit the path* by which we plan to replace the market and the state with *other forms of management of social life.* While struggling against the current order, we need, at the same time, to *create* and develop *institutions of a new type* that are able to deal with the complexity of society's common tasks on the appropriate scale.

In conclusion, no emancipatory politics has a chance to succeed if it has a strategy that, implicitly or explicitly, remains external to the issue of the alternative (but actual and concrete) management of social life. There is no autonomous politics or autonomy without taking responsibility for the overall management of the actually existing society. In other words, there is no future for any strategy that refuses to think of the creation of alternative forms of management here and now, or that resolves that problem either by means of an authoritarian device (such as the traditional Leninist left) or by utopian daydreaming and magical thinking (such as 'primitivism', the reliance on angelic and altruistic 'New Men', abstract schemes of direct democracy, and so forth). To avoid any misunderstanding: I am not suggesting that we anti-capitalists should find and get involved in a nicer way of managing capitalism (that would be the traditionally 'reformist' or social-democratic option). What I am trying to argue is that we need to create and develop *our own* political devices—devices that are able to manage the current society (thus avoiding the danger of catastrophic dissolution of all social order) while we walk towards a new world free of capitalism.

Hypothesis Two: There is a need for an 'interface' that enables the passage from the social to the political.

If we are to present a new political strategy that is both destructive and creative at the same time, we need to collectively explore and design an autonomous 'interface' that enables us to link our *social* movements to the *political* plane of the global management of society. I do not mean by this to endorse the standard prejudice of the traditional left, according to which social self-organising is just fine but where the 'real' politics starts only in the realm of party and state politics. When I refer to the 'passage from the social to the political' I do not impute any higher value to the latter. On the contrary, I believe that autonomous politics needs to be firmly anchored in processes of social self-organisation, but it also needs to expand in order to 'colonise' the political-institutional plane. Let me explain what such an 'interface' would be.

In capitalist society, power structures itself on two fundamental planes, the general social plane (biopolitical), and the political plane properly speaking (the state). I call the social plane 'biopolitical' because, as Foucault has shown, power has so deeply penetrated our own lives and daily relationships that it has transformed the social plane according to its image and likeness. Market and class relations have shaped us in such a way that *we ourselves reproduce the capitalist power relations*. Each and every one of us is an agent who produces capitalism. In other words, power not only dominates us from without but also from within social life. Yet in capitalist society the biopolitical plane of power is not enough to ensure the reproduction of the system. It also needs a plane that I call simply 'political'—the state, laws, institutions. That political plane makes sure that biopolitical power relations continue to function properly: it corrects deviations, punishes infractions, decides where to channel social cooperation, deals with larger scale tasks that the system needs, and monitors everything. In other words, the political plane deals with the global management of society; in a capitalist kind of society, it does so under the form of the state.

In current capitalist societies, the social (biopolitical) plane and the state (political plane) are not disconnected. On the contrary, there is an 'interface' that links them—the representative institutions, political parties, elections, etc. Through these mechanisms (usually called 'democracy') the system gets a certain basic legitimacy such that the global management of society can take place. In other words, it is this 'elective' interface that ensures that society as a whole accepts that a particular body of authorities makes all the important decisions that then everybody else must accept. Needless to say, this is a *heteronomous* interface, for it builds legitimacy not for the cooperative whole that we call society but only for the benefit of the ruling class. The heteronomous interface channels the political energy of society in a way that impedes society from making its own decisions and being autonomous (that is, self-managed).

I would like to argue that the new generation of emancipatory movements that is emerging has already carried out some amazing experiments in the *biopolitical* realm but is facing great difficulties when it comes to the *political* plane. There are numerous movements and collectives throughout the world that are practising forms of struggle and organisation that challenge oppression and capitalist domination. Their biopolitics creates—even if in small-scale, local territories—human relations of a new type, relations that are horizontal and collective and bring about solidarity and autonomy instead of competition and oppression.

However, we—emancipatory movements—have still not found the way to transport these values so that they also become the core of a new strategy for the political plane. As I have argued before, this is indispensable for changing the world. In other words, we still need to develop an interface of a new type, an autonomous interface that allows us to articulate forms of political cooperation on a higher scale, thus connecting our movements, collectives, and struggles with the political plane where the global management of society takes place. We have rejected the other interface models that the traditional left offered, namely, the parties—be they electoral or vanguardist—and the 'enlightened' leaders, for we understood that they were nothing but a (slightly) different form of a heteronomous interface. Indeed, this is an interface that instead of colonising the political plane with our values and ways of life has operated the other way round, bringing the hierarchical, competitive values of the elite into contact with our movements. So the rejection was healthy and necessary. But we still have to explore and design our own autonomous interface. Without resolving this question, I am afraid that our movements will never establish stronger ties with society as a whole and will remain in a state of constant vulnerability. (The current experience of the Zapatistas' 'Other Campaign' will perhaps bring important developments in this respect.)[7]

The Autonomous Interface as an Institution of a New Type

What would an autonomous interface look like? What kind of new political organisation, different from parties, would allow us to articulate vast sections of the emancipatory movement on a large scale? What should it be like, if it also has to be able to deal with the global management of society, thereby becoming a strategic instrument for the abolition of the state and the market? These are questions that social movements are beginning to ask themselves and that only they can resolve. The following ideas are aimed at contributing to this debate.

Thesis One: The need of an ethics of equality

Since there is no point in thinking of rules and institutions for abstract human beings without taking into account their customs and values (that is, their specific culture), let us begin by a thesis on a new emancipatory culture.

One of the most serious tragedies of the left tradition has been (and still is) its refusal to consider the *ethical* dimension of political struggle. In general, in both practice and theory, the typical attitude of the left regarding ethics—that is, the principles that must orient us towards good actions by distinguishing these from the bad actions—is to consider this merely an 'epistemological' issue. In other words, political actions are considered 'good' if they correspond with a 'truth' that we know beforehand. The issue of the ethically good / bad is thus shrunk down to the problem of the correct / incorrect political 'line' to be followed. In this way, the left often ends up implicitly rejecting any ethics of care for the other (and I mean here the *concrete* other, our fellow beings); instead, the left replaces it with a commitment to a certain ideology-truth that alleges it represents an 'abstract' other ('humankind'). The concrete effect of this absence of ethics can be seen in our concrete practice, in countless cases in which otherwise good-hearted activists manipulate and inflict violence upon others in the name of 'the truth'. (No wonder, then, that common people tend to keep as far away as possible from those activists.)

Additionally, this non-ethical attitude is often an unconsciously elitist behaviour that impedes true cooperation among equals. If you think you own the truth, then you will not 'waste' your time listening to the others, nor will you be ready to negotiate consensus. That is why a real emancipatory politics needs to be based on a firm and radical ethics of equality and of responsibility before (and care for) the *concrete* other. We still have a long way to go in this sense if we are to create, divulge, and embody a new ethics. Luckily, many movements are already walking along this path. The Zapatista slogan, "we walk at the pace of the slowest", is nothing but the inversion of the relation between truth and ethics that we are proposing here.

Thesis Two: Horizontality needs institutions (badly)

Our institutions of a new type need to be 'anticipatory', that is, they must embody in their own shape and forms the values of the society we are striving to build.

One of our main problems when it comes to building new institutions lies in two wrong (but deeply rooted) beliefs: first, that organisational structures and rules conspire per se against horizontality and against the openness of our movements; and second, that any kind of division of labour, specialisation, and delegation of functions brings about a new hierarchy. Luckily, social movements in many corners have started to question these beliefs.

Any person who has participated in a non-hierarchical organisation, even a small one, knows that in the absence of mechanisms that protect plurality and foster participation, 'horizontality' soon becomes a fertile soil for the survival of the fittest. This person also knows how frustrating and limited it is to have organisations in which everyone is always forced to gather in assemblies to make decisions on every single issue of a movement—from general political strategy to fixing a leaking roof. The 'tyranny of structurelessness', as Jo Freeman used to say, exhausts our movements, subverts their principles, and makes them absurdly inefficient.[8]

Contrary to usual belief, autonomous and horizontal organisations are *more* in need of institutions than hierarchical ones; for the latter can always rely on the will of the leader to resolve conflicts, assign tasks, etc. I would like to argue that we need to develop *institutions of a new type*. By institutions I do not mean a bureaucratic hierarchy but simply a set of democratic agreements on ways of functioning that are formally established and that are endowed with the necessary organisational infrastructure to enforce them if needed. This includes:

a) *A reasonable division of labour*, which is indispensable if we are to have a higher scale of cooperation. If everybody is responsible for everything, then no one is accountable for anything. We need clear rules as to which decisions are to be taken by the collective as a whole and which are to be decided by individuals or smaller groups. This division of labour, needless to say, has to be in agreement with our values: tasks and responsibilities have to be distributed in a way that each person has a relatively equal share of empowering and of repetitive, tedious duties.

b) *'Weak' forms of delegation and representation.* We are right in being sceptical about representation, in that representatives often end up 'replacing' the rank and file and accumulating power at the expense of the rest. But it does not follow from this that we can have large-scale cooperation without any form of delegation. The belief that we can do with simply calling an assembly and practising (abstract) direct democracy whenever something needs to be decided or done is nothing but magical thinking. We need to develop forms of representation and delegation that make sure that no group of people becomes a special body of decision makers detached from the rest. We need to move from strong leaders to soft 'facilitators' who put all their capacity and knowledge at the service of organising collective deliberation and decision-making processes, and from strong forms of delegation and representation to 'weak' ones. For this, again, we need clear rules and procedures.

c) *A clear delimitation* between the rights of the collective and its majorities and those to be kept by individuals and minorities. The idea that a collective organisation needs to 'transcend' the diverging needs or interests of its members is authoritarian and harmful. Individuals and minorities cannot and should not 'dissolve' within a collective. We need to accept the fact that in any human collective there always remains an irresolvable tension between the will and needs of the individual person and those of the collective. Instead of denying or trying to suppress that tension, an organisation of a new type needs to acknowledge it as a legitimate fact and behave accordingly. In other words, we need to reach collective agreements on the limits between individual (or minority) rights and collective imperatives. And we need institutions to protect the former from the latter and to defend the decision of the collective from unduly individual behaviour.

d) *A fair and transparent conflict-management code of procedure*, so as to resolve the inevitable internal conflicts in ways that do not lead to divisionism and to the end of cooperation.

Thesis Three: A political organisation that 'mimics' our biopolitical forms

Forms of political organisation tend to establish a 'mimetic' relation with regards to biopolitical forms. They crystallise normative and institutional mechanisms that 'copy' or 'imitate' certain forms that are immanent to society's self-organisation. This does not mean that they are 'neutral'; on the contrary, the shape that political organisations acquire may direct social cooperation in a sense that either strengthens heteronomy (power-over) or, inversely, favours autonomy (power-to-do). The political-institutional-legal organisation of capitalism is a good example of the first situation: its pyramidal form both mimics and strengthens the basic vertical and centralised relationships of domination.

Our organisations of a new type can be better thought of as an 'imitation' of the way cooperative biopolitical networks function. Let me explain by using the example of the Internet. The Internet's technical frame and its network-like structure have provided unexpected opportunities for the expansion of social cooperation to a scale that we had never imagined before. The existence of vast 'intelligent communities' on the Internet created spontaneously by the users themselves has been well documented. These communities are non-hierarchical and decentralised, and yet they manage to learn and act collectively without the need of someone shouting orders. These communities have achieved impressive levels of cooperation.

However, the Internet also displays opposite tendencies towards the concentration of information and exchanges. I am not referring to the fact that certain governments and corporations still control important technical aspects of the web but to phenomena of emergence of 'centres of power' as part of the very life of cyberspace. In theory, in an open network any given point can connect with any other in a free, unmediated way. And yet we all use websites and search engines such as Google, which both facilitate connectivity—therefore expanding our possibilities for cooperation and our power-to-do—and centralise the traffic. Sites like Google thus play an ambivalent role: on the one hand, they 'parasite' the web, on the other, they are part of the very architecture of it.

For the time being, the negative effects of the centralisation of traffic are not very noticeable. But that centralisation can potentially be easily transformed—and is already being transformed—in a form of power-over and a hierarchisation of the contacts within the web. Take for example the recent agreements between the Chinese government and Google and Yahoo to censor and control the Chinese cybernauts. Take also the possibility of paying Google in order to appear prominently in searches. These examples show how easily the most important sites can restrict and / or channel connectivity.

What to do then with Google-like sites? They help us find each other, but the very use we give them puts in corporate hands a great power that can easily be used against us. What is to be done? Let me answer with a joke. The strategy of the traditional left would be that the party has to 'take over Google', eliminate their owners, destroy any rival (such as Yahoo), and then 'put Google at the service of the working class'. We all know the authoritarian and ineffective consequences of such politics. But equally, what would be the strategy of a naive libertarian? He or she would probably argue that we need to destroy Google, Yahoo, etc and make sure that no other big sites emerge, so no one can centralise the traffic. But the result of this would be the virtual destruction of the potential of the Internet and of the experiences of cooperation that the web enables. We would still in theory be able to communicate with each other. But in practice it would be extremely difficult to find each other. In the absence of better options, and in view of the virtual collapse of the possibilities of cooperation, we would all end up surrendering to the first would-be businessman that offers us a new Google.

What would be the strategy of an autonomous politics of the kind we are trying to describe in this text when it comes to resolving the (rather silly) example that we are discussing? It would probably start by identifying the main crossroads of the web of cooperation that the Internet articulates and the loci of power and centralisation (such as Google) that the very life of the web produces. Having identified the immanent tendencies that might give birth to forms of power-over, the strategy of an autonomous politics would be to create an organisational alternative that would help us perform the tasks that Google performs in favour of our power-to-do. It would do so by surrounding any necessary concentration of traffic with an institutional framework that makes sure that that concentration will not subvert the emancipatory values present in the 'daily (biopolitical) life' of the web. This strategy is about creating a political-institutional device (one that transcends the possibilities of the web's own biopolitical plane) that protects the network from its own centralising, hierarchical tendencies. An autonomous strategy would not protect the web by denying those tendencies but by acknowledging them and giving them a subordinate place within an 'intelligent' institutional framework that keeps them under control.

This kind of 'intelligent' institutional operation is an illustration of my thesis on the 'mimetic' nature of the institutions of a new type with regard to biopolitical forms.

Imagining an Organisational Model of a New Type

Mutatis mutandis, the example of the problems of the Internet may be applied to emancipatory movements as a whole. We have today a loose network of social movements connected at the global level. As part of the very life of that network there are also loci of centralisation and (some) power comparable to Google. The World Social Forum, the 'intergalactic' initiatives of the Zapatistas, some NGOs, and even some national governments have helped to expand the connectivity of that network and, therefore, the possibilities of strengthening its cooperative capacities. But that concentration is also potentially dangerous for the movements, for they may easily become a door for the return of heteronomous politics.

How to think of an autonomous strategy in this context? Who would do it, and how? The hypothesis of an 'autonomous interface' is about answering these questions. It goes without saying that any strategy has to be developed in and for concrete situations. The following thoughts do not intend to be a model or a recipe but only an imaginative exercise aimed at expanding our horizons.

We have already argued that an organisation of a new type that may perform the task of an autonomous interface has to have an anticipatory design (that is, it has to agree with our fundamental values) as well as the capacity to 'colonise' the current state structures in order to neutralise or replace them, or to put them within a different institutional framework so that we can walk along the path of emancipation. In practical terms, this means that the fundamental virtue of a new type of organisation lies in its capacity to articulate non-oppressive, solid forms of social cooperation on a large scale.

While all this may sound new, the tradition of emancipatory struggles has already experimented with forms similar to the 'autonomous interface' we are talking about. The most famous example would be that of the soviet during the 1905 and 1917 revolutions in Russia. As an autonomous creation of the workers, the soviets emerged primarily as bodies for the coordination of the strike movement. But during the course of the revolution, and without 'planning' it in advance, they started to perform tasks of 'dual power' or, to use the terminology we have been using here, of a 'global management of society'. The soviets were the meetings of the 'deputies' that each factory or collective appointed in a number relative to their size. In 1917, they offered an open and multiple space for the encounter and horizontal deliberation of a variety of social groupings—workers, but also soldiers, peasants, ethnic minorities, etc—with diverse political inclinations. Unlike political parties that demanded exclusive membership and competed with one another, the soviet was a space of political cooperation open to everybody. Besides, during the revolution they dealt with issues such as the provision of food for cities, public transport, defence against the Germans, etc. Their prestige before the masses came from both aspects we have been discussing: they 'represented' the whole of the revolutionary movement in an anticipatory way, and they also offered a real alternative of political management.

The soviet 'interface' had different strategies towards power during 1917: they initially 'collaborated' with the provisional government but without being part of it; then there was the time of 'coalition', when the soviets decided to appoint some ministers to the government; and then, in October, they decided to get rid of the state altogether and replace it by a wholly new government of their own 'people's commissars'. During that process the dynamics of soviet self-organising had multiplied itself; hundreds of new soviets emerged throughout the country, which came together in the All-Russian Congress of the Soviets.

True, the experience of the soviets was soon to collapse under the Bolshevik leadership, for reasons I don't have the space to discuss here. What matters for our present purposes is the historical example of an autonomous interface that was able to articulate the cooperation between groups and sectors that were in favour of the revolution, and at the same time to take care of the global management of society.

How to imagine a comparable interface adapted to our times? Let us imagine an organisation designed to be, like the soviets, an *open space*, that is, an arena of deliberation for all groups committed to social change (within certain limits, of course). In other words, it would be an organisation that does not establish 'what to do' beforehand but offers its members the space to decide it collectively. Let us imagine that this organisation emerges by defining itself as a plural space for the coordination of anti-capitalist, anti-racist, and anti-sexist movements; let us call it the 'Assembly of Social Movement' (ASM).

The ASM would be formed by one spokesperson from each of the collectives accepted as members (individuals who want to participate first need to group in collectives). Like the soviets, it would be the Assembly itself that decides whether or not to accept new collectives as members. One of the criteria for the inclusion of new members would be to have the highest possible multiplicity by having collectives representative of different social groups (workers, women, students, Indigenous People, lesbians and gays, etc) and also of different types of organisations (small collectives, large unions, NGOs, movements, campaigns, parties, etc).

Unlike the soviets, the larger member organisations would not have the right to more spokespersons, but would have the right to more 'votes' in proportion to its relative importance for the ASM as a whole. For example, the spokesperson of a small collective of political art would have the right to cast two votes, while the spokesperson of a big metal workers union would have the right to cast 200 votes. The 'voting capacity' would be assigned by the Assembly to each member according to a series of criteria defined beforehand (of course, democratically decided). Thus, the ASM would be able to acknowledge differences in size, previous trajectory, strategic value, etc according to an equation that also makes sure that no single group gets the capacity to unilaterally condition the decision-making process. The ASM would try to decide by consensus or at least by qualified majority on important matters. If voting became necessary, each member organisation would have the chance to use its 'voting capacity' the way it prefers. Thus, for example, the metal workers union may decide to cast all of its 200 votes in favour of, say, the direct action against the government that is being discussed. However, if the union was internally divided on this matter, they might decide to 'represent' their minority opinion in the ASM as well, by casting 120 votes for the direct action and 80 against it, for instance. In this way, the ASM's functioning would not 'force' the homogenisation of the opinions of its members (which usually brings about divisionism).

Important decisions would always remain in the hands of each member organisation, which would decide freely the style of their spokespersons. Some may prefer to delegate in them the capacity to make all decisions, while others would prefer them to be representatives only in a weaker sense. In any case, the ASM would implement decision-making mechanisms that allow each organisation to have the time to discuss the issues beforehand, and then give their spokesperson an explicit mandate on how to vote. Member organisations would also have the chance to use electronic means to express their views and cast votes from afar if they couldn't be present for any reason or if they want to follow the debates and make a decision in 'real time'.

The ASM's decisions would not compromise the autonomy of each member; the ASM would not claim to be the exclusive representative of all struggles, nor would it demand exclusive membership. There may exist several organisations like the ASM operating at the same time, with some overlapping members, without that being a problem. It would be in the interest of all to cooperate with any organisation that represents a valid struggle.

The ASM would not have 'authorities' in the strong sense of the word (that is, leaders). Instead, it would appoint task groups of facilitators to deal with different functions, such as the admission of new members, their 'voting capacities', funds and finances, internal conflict management, urgent tactical decisions, specific campaigns, and the like. The post of facilitators would have a limited duration, and they would rotate between different member organisations to avoid accumulation of power for some at the expense of others and the typical struggles for power between leaders.

What would such an organisation be good for? Depending on the political context, it could serve different goals. Let us imagine a context in which the ASM is only starting to organise. It has a small number of member organisations, and therefore has little social impact. In such a context, the ASM would be a sort of 'political cooperative'. Each member would contribute with some of its resources—contacts, experience, funds, etc—for common goals (for example, to organise a demonstration). This cooperative work would, in turn, help strengthen links between social movements in the network in general.

Let us now imagine a more favourable context. In view of the evidence that the ASM has been working for some time, and that it has helped to articulate forms of cooperation useful for all and in accordance with the emancipatory values it claims to represent, several new organisations have decided to join. The ASM has grown, and it now gathers a good number of organisations of all types; its voice is already audible in society as a whole, and many people listen to its messages with interest. In this context, the 'political cooperative' may mobilise its resources to have a direct impact on state policies. The ASM may, for example, threaten the government with strikes and direct actions if it decides to sign a new free trade treaty. If convenient, the ASM may call for an electoral boycott for the next elections. Alternately, the ASM may decide that it would be more useful to have its own candidates run for the legislative elections. According to its main tenets, those candidates would only be spokespersons for the ASM, without the right to decide anything by themselves and without the right to be re-elected for a second term. As the candidates would run not as individuals or as representatives of particular organisations but as spokespersons of the ASM, political 'accumulation' would be in favour of the ASM as a whole. Moreover, in view of the great capacity for cooperation thus displayed by the ASM, and given that the ASM would make sure that its candidates do not become a caste of professional politicians, its prestige would surely grow in the eyes of society as a whole.

Let us now imagine an even more favourable context. The ASM already has a long experience of work in common. It has grown and has several thousand member organisations. It has perfected its decision-making procedures and its internal division of tasks. It has contributed in spreading a new militant culture and ethics. It has a proficient method of dealing with internal conflicts and making sure that no person or organisation accumulates power at the expense of the rest. Its debates and political positions are followed with great attention by the whole of society. The strategy of electoral boycott has been effective and the government and all parties are losing all credibility. Or, alternately, the strategy to 'colonise' parts of the state with their own people has been successful, and the ASM now controls vast sections of legislative power and some executive power. In either case, the state has lost credibility and a vast social movement is demanding some radical changes. There are strikes, civil disobedience, and direct action everywhere. In this case, the 'political cooperative' may be used to prepare the next strategic step by proposing itself as an alternative means (at least transitionally) for the global management of society. The strategy here may vary: the ASM may decide to continue to 'colonise' the electoral positions that state politics offer, thus taking over more and more sections of the state until it controls most of it. Or, alternately, the ASM may promote an insurrectional strategy. Or a combination of both.

Needless to say, this was just an imaginary exercise aimed at providing an example of an 'autonomous interface' at work. In this hypothetical case the ASM has worked both as a tool for the cooperation of emancipatory movements and as an institution able to take care of the management of society *here and now*. Its strategy consisted in, first, developing an institutional model that 'mimics' the multiple shapes that structure our cooperating networks (that is, an open and plural space endowed with clear rules), with an 'anticipatory' character (it is horizontal and autonomous; it expands our power-to-do without concentrating power-over). Secondly, the ASM developed an intelligent strategy by 'reading' the configuration of the main links of cooperation of the current society. Thus, the ASM identified the crossroads at which the power-over has an ambivalent role (that is, those tasks performed by the state that are to some extent useful or necessary) and offered a better autonomous alternative. In this way, the ASM's strategy was not purely destructive. Unlike political parties—including the Leninist ones—which 'colonise' social movements with the forms and values of heteronomous politics, the ASM provided an interface between our movements and the state that ended up 'colonising' the state with the forms and values of the movements. It did so either by occupying state positions, by draining their power, or by destroying them when necessary.

Once again, this does not intend to be the model of a perfect political machine. The ASM does not require 'angelic' beings. Of course, there would be internal struggles for power and conflicts of all kinds. And, of course, such an institution would not resolve and eliminate for good the intrinsic distance between the social and the political. Emancipatory politics would continue to be, as it is today, a difficult task with no guarantees aimed at expanding our autonomy day by day. The benefit of such an institution of a new type is that all those struggles, conflicts, and tensions would be at the same time acknowledged and regulated, so that they do not inevitably destroy the possibilities of cooperation.

Even if this was a purely imaginary exercise with many limitations, I hope it may contribute to expanding our horizon of possibilities when it comes to answering the crucial question of an emancipatory strategy: *What is to be done?*

References

Ezequiel Adamovsky, 2003—*Anticapitalismo para principiantes* ['Anti-capitalism for Beginners', in Spanish]. Buenos Aires: Era Naciente

Ezequiel Adamovsky, 2007—*Más allá de la vieja izquierda: Seis ensayos para un nuevo anticapitalismo* ['Beyond the Old Left: Six essays for a new anticapitalism', in Spanish]. Novedad Editorial. Buenos Aires: Promoteo

EZLN (Zapatista Army of National Liberation), 2006—'Sixth Declaration of the Selva Lacandona', at www.zaptranslations.blogspot.com (Accessed August 23 2017)

Jo Freeman (aka Joreen), nd [c.May 1970 / 1971]—'The Tyranny of Structurelessness', at http://www.jofreeman.com/joreen/tyranny.htm (Accessed August 23 2017)

Notes

1. Ed: A more 'idiomatic' (and slightly longer) version of this text was first published in Spanish in 2006 as '*Problemas de la política autónoma: pensando el pasaje de lo social a lo político*', on *Indymedia Argentina*, at http://argentina.indymedia. org/news/2006/03/382729.php (Accessed August 23 2017). An earlier version of the essay in English can be found at http://transdada3.blogspot.ca/2006/05/ autonomous-politics-and-its-problems.html (Accessed August 23 2017), but to my knowledge, this is the first time it is being published in a book. I warmly thank the author, Ezequiel Adamovsky, for revising the essay and for giving us permission to publish it.

2. Ed: Originally published in 2006, this essay remains as radically relevant today as then—and perhaps even more so, given the experience and dynamics of the 'take the square' movements since 2011. This essay in many ways anticipates and 'looks ahead' to these movements.

3. Ed: given that this essay was written and published in 2006, by 'current emancipatory movements' the author is referring to movements at that time, in Argentina, in Latin America / Abya Yala, and globally—the so-called 'global justice movement' that had exploded onto the scene around 1999.

4. EZLN 2006.

5. Ed: 'Columbine' refers to a shooting massacre in a high school in the US that occurred on April 20 1999 and became a standard reference for a culture of violence at that time. See http://en.wikipedia.org/wiki/Columbine_High_School_massacre (Accessed August 23 2017).

6. For a detailed treatment of this issue, see my essay '*Sensatez y Sentimientos en la cultura de izquierda*' ['Sense and sentiment in the culture of the left', in Spanish] in Adamovsky 2007, pp 31–59.

7. Ed: This essay was written in 2006 and is referring to the Zapatistas' 'Other Campaign'—*La otra campaña*—which began in January 2006. See http://en. wikipedia.org/wiki/The_Other_Campaign (Accessed August 23 2017).

8. Freeman nd [c.May 1970 / 1971].

OpenWord

Boundary as Bridge
John Brown Childs

Ntunnanquomen, mattapsh yoteg awaissh, cuttaunchemokous.
(I have had a good dream, come sit by the fire, warm yourself, I will tell a story.)
—from the Algonkian language of my Indigenous Massachusaug ancestors in
what is now called 'New England', USA

Space
    needs Boundaries
otherwise we step into the void.

    My Indigenous ancestors of North America
    the Massachusaug people and the Brothertown-Oneida people

    believed in boundaries
    and negotiation
    and dialogue.

Boundaries were to be respected.

They were places of respect and
places in which to enact respect.

Jai Sen remarks that "the concept of open space and the contemporary rise
of the concept and practice must . . . be located in [a] much wider context".[1]
That context has many historical antecedents. So with this focus on the 'vocabulary' and 'grammar' of open space in mind, I begin with the words of
the Haudenosaunee, or People of the Confederacy known as the Longhouse
('Iroquois'). Starting in the fifteenth century, this confederacy, or Great League
of Peace, originally included the five Indigenous nations of the Seneca, Cayuga,
Onondaga, Oneida, and Mohawk people in what is now the northeast US and
southeastern Canada. The Great League of Peace, created under the inspiration
and guidance of a man known generally as the 'Peacemaker', or Deganawidah,
came about in the midst of a violent war of reprisal among these nations. Its creation and longevity are an important example of making not just peace a reality
but also highlight the significance of respect for social, cultural, and political

heterogeneity as a potential basis for, rather than a barrier to, cooperation and mutual understandings.

The Haudenosaunee, 'People of the Longhouse', had and have a special ceremony for visitors and visits in which boundary plays a major role as bridge not barrier. Called 'At the Woods' Edge', this ceremony highlights respect for visitors and respect by the visitors who live in the clear fields beyond the edge of the woods.

In part it goes:

> Today
> we have arrived at the appointed time
> where we are supposed to be
> here, in this place,
> where our ancestors made solemn agreements.

> And now,
> as to our custom in the olden times, and as we do today also,
> whenever we receive visitors that enter into our country,
> then we say these words to them:

> Perhaps maybe,
> when you came here
> on your way here
> you travelled through many dangerous areas and places.

> Those things that you went through,
> maybe could have hurt you,
> but we are thankful,
> we, the People of the Haudenosaunee,
> for you have arrived here safely to be with us today.

> In your travels maybe you have accumulated much dirt
> from the roads that maybe were dusty.

> And now we use a nice feather, a nice soft feather
> and from the top of your head to where your feet are resting,
> we wipe away all the dust.

> And sometimes when you went into
> some bushes that contained thorns and briars
> then what we do now

is we take them away from your clothes
so you can be comfortable while you are with us.

Now sometimes what happens to people,
when they arrive from different directions as we have today.
Perhaps recently we have experienced a great loss in our family.
But because of the importance of our having clarity in our mind,
we now say these words to you.

If you have tears in your eyes today, because of a recent loss,
today we have brought a white cloth,
and we use this to wipe away your tears,
so that your future will become clearer
from this moment forward.

Perhaps some dust has accumulated in your ears
because of your recent losses.
Then what we will do
is we will take a soft feather and wipe away the dust
so that your hearing will be restored.

And now we will give you a pure medicine water for you to drink
to wash away anything that might be obstructing your throat,
and so that your voice will be restored
and so may your words be good
when you start to speak to our peoples.

And so now we welcome you
into our territory of the Haudenosaunee.
We hope that you have had a safe journey to be with us today.
And we give thanks to all the people
that have come forward to observe today's event.
—From: 'The Edge of the Woods', delivered by Chief Jake Swamp, Mohawk
Nation, November 11 1794.[2]

My Algonkian-speaking Massachusaug ancestors spoke of *chaconabomgam-aug*, which at one level means simply the 'boundary' between peoples; but at a deeper level it means a boundary not as separation but as the place of negotiations, the place of meetings, the place of respect—in other words, the woods' edge.

And how often do we do this in our meetings, be they big or small, global or local?

Do we pay heed to the pain and fear with which humans wrestle—do we endeavour to recognise such feelings and to offer solace—to use a nice soft feather to wipe away some of the dust of life?

Do we recognise the challenges that all of us have faced and continue to face just to come together as we talk about how to come together?

The soft feather wiping away the dust, the medicine water to clear the throat, are necessary (say the Haudenosaunee and Massachusaug, and others) in order for people to have their voices restored, so that their "words may be good" when they "start to speak".

Boundaries are absolutely vital here.

An open space that obliterates individual and group realities in the name of some all-encompassing unity will miss the distinctions, both positive and negative, that we bring with us. The woods' edge requires respect. It is a place of welcome, but those coming there must ask permission to enter, not just break down the doors. And those inside must provide the welcome, not just superficially but as a form of restoration and hope.

In African-American classical music, or 'jazz', there is often a form of what can be called 'collective improvisation' that is a variation of the above. In a jazz group there are several individuals. They work in concert with one another. But each has her or his own distinctive instrument, insights, and creative explorations that cannot be subsumed under one person's direction. There is collective action that flows from a highly diverse autonomy. *The autonomy exists only because of the respect for the boundaries that mark each person.* Each person stands at the boundary—the woods' edge—ready to ask permission to enter and ready to give such permission.

How often do we do this in our meetings about cooperation?

The Five Nations of the Haudenosaunee had originally been at war with one another. It was a terrible time of revenge and murder—sometime in the 1300s in what is now the New York State area in the northeast of the United States and the southeast of Canada. According to Haudenosaunee history, sometime before the arrival of the Europeans, probably in the late 1300s or early 1400s, a man appeared during this time of conflict—The Peacemaker, with a Message of Peace that after much struggle was accepted by all of the Five Nations, thus ending their wars and creating what came to be known as the Great League of Peace. The Great League is also known as the Longhouse.

The Peacemaker's story is attributed with what is widely recognised by non-Indigenous historians as historical authenticity; yet it also carries the enveloping aura that we see with many great spiritual figures who are historically real but who come bearing messages about change in the world. His well-detailed recommendations for the protocols and social structures—in which peace plus heterogeneity and common action could coexist—were of significance to a wide range of writers, from one of the founders of anthropology in Lewis Henry Morgan through Marx and Engels to a continued parade of scholars past and present (see the many writings about the categories 'Iroquois', 'Great League of Peace', or 'the Iroquois Confederacy' as examples). In his practical yet 'out of the box' visionary suggestions for peace in times of conflict, the Peacemaker has something in common with peacemakers and alliance builders today, from those involved with Northern Ireland to gang impacted city streets.

The Peacemaker used the pragmatic and—for the Haudenosaunee—immediately recognisable image of a common structure among the Five Nations, a communal longhouse in which lived many families, each with its own hearth but all together in that one structure. Each family was autonomous and went about its own affairs in the way it wanted. Yet all the families could and did come together for discussions about events and circumstances that impacted all of them. So with this image in mind the Peacemaker said both to those who eagerly accepted his Message of Peace and to the sceptics and followers of the warpath: we can be as a longhouse, with each nation having its own central fire, its own identity, its own way of being; yet we can also at the same time be one people with one mind as the many compartments of the longhouse are part of one common structure. This was a coordinated autonomy, a cooperative diversity that one sees among many Indigenous North American alliances—and which one sees in the collective improvisations of such great African-American musicians as Thelonious Monk and John Coltrane.

This 'longhouse' of peoples—that has many distinctive compartments that are autonomous yet cooperative (which elsewhere I call "coordinated autonomy")[3]—is an intellectual and spiritual cousin of what Martin Luther King, Jr called the 'World House', in which there are many rooms, some cold, some hot, some well provided, others in disrepair—but all of them part of one architectural reality.[4] In that image of reality, the travel along corridors from room to room requires respectful request for interaction but also, as a common structure, necessitates that interaction. As Patricia Hill Collins says, "everyone has a voice, but everyone must listen and respond to other voices".[5]

The great poet from Argentina Jorge Luis Borges (1899–1986) captured the contradictory yet conciliatory sense of many places within one place, which in turn is one place filled with many places, in the following lines from his poem 'Elegy':

Oh destiny of Borges
    to have sailed across the diverse seas of the world
    or across that single solitary sea of diverse
    names . . .

So both occur—the many diverse names and the one sea, perhaps un-named. Each named sea is real, distinct, and important for those who sail it. The Mediterranean is not the Caribbean, the Pacific is not the Atlantic, and so on. Yet we can sail from one to the other. We are all connected in one giant ocean (both literally and metaphorically). Many places, one location, many compartments, one structure; no matter what we call this manyness and oneness, it is a reality from which we cannot escape. Moreover, it should be a reality that tells us that respect for high ranges of heterogeneity and equal recognition of and respect for that of which we are all part is absolutely necessary.

Manyness and Oneness

A while ago I saw a progressive student poster at the university where I work. The poster was for a commendable conference on global progressivism. It read:

One People
One Struggle
One Love

I appreciate the positive intention of the poster. But given my transcommunal impulse, as described elsewhere,[6] in which many come out of one and one out of many, and in which we must recognise that egalitarian oneness interlaced with and drawing from human heterogeneity *rather* than a top-down unification struc-ture—no matter how progressive—I would write it differently (but with much of the same positive intentionality):

Many Peoples
Many Struggles
One Love

Are we ready for mutual respect in the midst of many different ideological and philosophical rooms and starting points? Can we respect the fact that there are doors of importance to those within and that sometimes for some reasons at some moments those doors may be locked while at other moments they may be open? Can we wipe the dust from others who come to visit and have it wiped from us when we go to visit, no matter whether they or we are from the east or west or north or south in the great global longhouse?

If we can address these questions to ourselves (rather than me forcing my own answers) then we will have made a great step. We must ask not only what is to be done but also, with respect, what is being done. And there we will have to show great flexibility for the wide varieties that the spirit of freedom and justice takes among the many diverse peoples of the world.

Allow space for bounded differences:
Differences that allow space for bridging contacts.

As the great African-American jazz composer Sun Ra said (thinking, I believe, both of the cosmos and of the distance among us that can be simultaneously great and small):

Space is the Place![7]

References

John Brown Childs, 2003—*Transcommunality: From the Politics of Conversion to the Ethics of Respect*. Philadelphia: Temple University Press

Patricia Hill Collins, 1990—*Black Feminist Thought: Knowledge, Consciousness, and the Politics of Empowerment*. New York: Routledge

G Peter Jemison and Anna M Schein, eds, 2000—*Treaty of Canadaigua, 1794*. Santa Fe, New Mexico: Clear Light Publishers

Martin Luther King, Jr, 1967—*Where Do We Go from Here: Chaos or Community*. New York: Harper and Row

Jai Sen, May 2007b—'Opening open space: Notes on the grammar and vocabulary of the concept of open space', on *OpenSpaceForum*, May 7, 2007, at http://www.open spaceforum.net/twiki/tiki-read_article.php?articleId=429 (Accessed August 23 2017)

Notes

1. Sen, May 2007b.
2. See Jemison and Schein 2000, pp. 13–14.
3. Childs 2003, pp 49–56.
4. King, Jr 1967.
5. Collins 1990, p 23.
6. See Childs 2003.
7. Sun Ra used this phrase in numerous performances, many unrecorded. I heard it several times personally at concerts in New York and California. It is also the title of an offbeat film that came out in 1974. The film was directed by John Coney and co-written by Sun Ra.

OpenWord

Effective Politics or Feeling Effective?[1]
Chris Carlsson

We fought the police with words, dances, clown-armies, yoga, laughs, music . . .
they tried to stop us with gas, batons, water cannons, bulldozers, helicopters, stop
and search actions, blockades, riot gear and intimidation. . . . We are happy. Any
action is better than none. We're having fun.[2]

Despite all the dozens of beautifully designed posters all around Germany calling people to come and blockade the G8 meeting at Rostock in June 2007 and to 'smash capitalism', capitalism was not smashed. But the week-long protests still felt like a success to most participants, as the quote above indicates. Thousands of people converged in Rostock to partake in marches, discussions, meetings, and symposia, and some 6,000–10,000 marched to the security fence (erected by the German State at great expense) to 'blockade' the G8 summit. Real courage and creativity buoyed the blockaders and kept the security forces in an exhausting round-the-clock state of alert while politicians wined and dined in monarchical splendour behind the formidable barriers. Their vapid pronouncements were dutifully reported by the world's media but always, a few paragraphs down, the presence of thousands of blockading protesters had to be mentioned too. Little coverage was offered of the multiple critical views and myriad alternatives to 'business as usual' presented by the assembled protesters, but the 'global war' hysteria whipped up in the past few years has clearly failed to silence the growing global chorus of people who insist that 'Another World Is Possible'.[3]

The anti-G8 protests have to be seen against the background of a steadily increasing delegitimisation of representative democracy. Politics has become an empty ritual in most Western democracies. Moreover, political formations based on class and community have also dissipated in the past two generations to the point that most formal politics is more a habit than a living, breathing engagement.

This demise of formal politics coincides with increased polarisation of wealth both inside and between nations. Leaders of the wealthiest countries who meet at the G8 summit every year are managers of an ever more brutal world system that keeps billions in catastrophic, intolerable misery, and many millions more just a step or two away from immiseration themselves. Political systems drained of meaningful choices, combined with a fragmented and largely numb polity, have pushed those seeking change towards developing new forms of doing politics.

Crucial to these forms is a need to *feel* effective in ways that regular politics has prevented.

June Camping in Germany

At the beginning of June 2007, anti-G8 summit protesters from around the world descended on northern Germany, united in their determination to 'shut down' the summit through direct action. Prior to the June 1–8 gathering in the former East German countryside, an Asian-European Market summit in Hamburg on May 28 was confronted by protesters led by several thousand Black Bloc anarchists and squatters and joined by hundreds of others. This was the warm-up for the coming days of protest and for those inclined towards brawling with the police it was a tantalising taste of what was to come—or so they hoped—because they certainly 'got their riot on' in Hamburg that day, as the streets filled with tear gas, high-powered water cannons, burning cars, and smashed windows.

As it turned out, the only time the anti-G8 protests resembled that day in Hamburg was at the end of the first day's legal march, on June 2, a Saturday, when Black Bloc marchers attacked the police and a riot erupted, injuring 250 protesters and 250 police, some seriously. A sea of words was rapidly splashed across the Internet and the world's newspapers, a remarkably large proportion of them dedicated to reporting on and discussing the infamous Black Bloc. Though commentary in the first few days of June focused on the question of anarchist violence (both in the press and among the protesters themselves), by the end of the week the analysis of anti-G8 protest in Germany had gone well beyond that narrow framework.

There was a range of preferences regarding tactics among demonstrators aiming to shut down the G8, as there have been since the 1999 WTO protests in Seattle. German organisers accommodated this difference of tactics by setting up three different camps to house protesters. Closest to the 'red zone' was Camp Reiddelich, where anarchists and 'hardcore' protesters concentrated. Furthest away, but closest to the largest nearby city, Rostock, was Camp Rostock, located on the northern outskirts of the urban area, and among its over 5,000 inhabitants were many of the more organised NGO groups and political parties, as well as a large number of independent demonstrators. The last, Camp Wichmannstorff, was far away to the northeast, more than an hour from the other camps, and was supposed to be home to experienced anti-nuclear blockaders but never had nearly as much attendance as Camps Rostock and Reiddelich.

Relations among the various tendencies remained largely cordial. The exception to this was the French NGO Association for the Taxation of Financial Transactions for the Aid to Citizens (ATTAC), which after the June 2 riot in Rostock publicly denounced the Black Bloc. This was at odds with German

NGOs organised under the umbrella Block G8 who saw themselves as occupying the ground between the more cautious ATTAC on the one side and the more provocative Black Bloc anarchists on the other extreme. Another non-profit NGO, Via Campesina, present at previous summits, once again brought their message on behalf of the Global South's millions of impoverished peasants and farmers. When they were hectored to denounce the Black Bloc's violence during a press conference, they firmly refused to accept the framing of the discussion. Similarly, a spokesperson for Block G8, Christophe Kleine, also turned the tables on the press, urging the discussion to focus on the structural and day-to-day violence imposed on most of the world by the policies of G8 countries. In this way a solidarity was maintained that avoided splitting the movement over tactical disagreements, even as the press and police sought to expand that division. Instead, a mutual respect and acceptance was based on the shared knowledge that everyone there needed everyone else for the concept—anti-G8 protests—to be effective. Riots alone would not achieve political results, just as political demonstrating without any militancy could be easily absorbed and trivialised.

Beyond the attempt to blockade the meetings in Heiligendamm, there were also four separate legal marches in Rostock on different but related themes between June 1 and June 4, as well as an alternative summit, nightly music concerts, and an unknown number of decentralised actions around the vicinity. Thousands of protesters set up tents in camps and held meetings, ate meals together, staged concerts, showed films, and carried on debates and discussions in many languages. Remarkable global villages took root in the German countryside, but these were no ordinary villages: the anti-G8 gathering sprawled over three camps, two convergence centres, and two Indymedia centres. At the level of infrastructure it was impressive. Big, expensive tents, 200 portable toilets, daily food for thousands, communications facilities, even a tent dedicated to recharging mobile phones, and another with ten open-access Internet computers.

As at the summit battles of past years in Seattle, Washington, Genoa, Québec, Gleneagles, etc, protesters were inventing a new culture in the camps, workshops, and protest marches, or at least many were trying to. Camp Rostock, where I stayed from Friday night to Monday night, was jumping nearly twenty-four hours a day. Impromptu stages featured hip-hoppers, beatboxers, speeches, bands, DJs, and movies, while bars in many group camps poured out an endless sea of beer. Camp Rostock became quite intimate and resembled the Nevada desert's annual Burning Man Festival—wall-to-wall tents made it quite cozy, even too cozy! A hundred porta-potties dotted the perimeter, and within the space was crowded with a big communal kitchen, meeting tents, 'streets' (mud paths) called Durruti Blvd, Via Guiliani, Rue de Arundhati Roy, Kurt Eisner Platz, Rosa Luxembourg Allée, and Leiselotte Meyer Weg. We had speed tweakers next to us the first night, but they thankfully slept through the next day and night.[4] On Sunday night, there was an absolute roar surrounding us until at least 3:00 in the morning. The nearest stage had beatbox and rap performances in German, English, French, and Spanish, but terrible-quality speakers make it pretty loud and bad at our distance.

Amidst all this noisy cultural invention, I had a strange thought about the camp experience—one dark view would see it as practice for involuntary life in camps in the future . . . with fewer resources and pleasures one might assume, but who knows? And, beyond this, that this might be as much an experiment for the state as for the 'multitude', which seems more true in light of the official cooperation that was given to open and maintain camps large enough to accommodate thousands of people. It was a remarkable blend of political camp, a dash of Boy Scouts, and an ample splash of Burning Man—though unlike the last, everyone here was intentionally political. I saw a lot of affinity groups meeting, characteristically held in the open, and undoubtedly self-consciously transparent and oblivious to who stopped to listen. I overheard Greek, Spanish, and Francophone African groups (Senegalese and Malian, I believe), but mostly the groups were German, French, a few Danish, a smattering of Russians and Poles, and some US Americans. The few Latin Americans and Asians present were probably already living in Germany.

Protesting Success

The structure of the week of protests was complex, with hundreds of affinity groups intersecting with a large number of NGOs and somewhat fewer political parties. Issues that usually get Balkanised and kept apart are continually brought together at summits like this; one of the better aspects of the whole thing. So after the big opening anti-G8 demo, again using the slogan 'Another World Is Possible', the second day had a big demo against GMO agriculture and in support of food sovereignty and local farmers with the slogan 'Resistance Is Fruitful'. It was a spirited march of several thousand, very well decorated and quite mellow in terms of police response, who only put a few dozen '*antikonflikt*' cops in windbreakers around the march.

The demo on the next day, June 4, was called The Right to Movement. It was aimed at addressing the plight of immigrants in Germany and Fortress Europe, which is generally as bad or worse than in the United States. In Germany an immigrant is placed in a certain district, usually rural and poor, and while they await processing it is illegal for them to leave that district. Later, if they get legal residency status, and if they are still on welfare, it is illegal for them to leave that district unless they have a job outside of it. Of course, it might be tricky to arrange a job somewhere that you are banned from visiting! This Kafkaesque nightmare of harsh restrictions on migration stands in sharp contrast to the ever-easier movement of capital, whipping to and fro in a frenzy of speculation across the planet.

The police, however, turned the march into an exercise in patience and attrition. Its route was to be the same as that of the agriculture march, but at the gathering point there were a lot more of us than the day before; and it began with several thousand participants, seemingly more determined and 'militant'. Before too long hundreds of heavily armoured riot police had spread out in the forests, surrounding us completely. As soon as the march started it was stopped. From the sound truck came the news that the police had detected 500 protesters who had evaded their control and infiltrated the march, and who they were sure were going to be violent. After an hour and a half of negotiations, the march organisers and police agreed that we could proceed only if no one wore a mask, a hoody, sunglasses, or any kind of face-obscuring clothing. It's officially illegal to hide your face in Germany during demonstrations, though that rule had been flouted by 2,000 Black Blocers on Saturday.

So finally we moved a bit, only to be stopped again after a few hundred yards. Now the police insisted on lining the route of the march with riot cops, three deep on either side. The organisers refused to proceed under those conditions, so another hour went by as they negotiated. Finally, we got to move without that level of police accompaniment, though there were thousands of riot cops all around, along with giant water cannons and fleets of police vans constantly moving around Rostock. These form the backbone of the police infantry, their twenty-first-century horses, which at times they park three to four rows deep, crisscrossing the road to serve as barricades.

Capitalism was never threatened directly by these protests, to no one's surprise. At this point in history, we are creating the foundations for a challenge to capitalism rather than taking it on directly. Still, it's important for many participants to claim that the anti-G8 protests were successful on many levels. Of course, measuring 'success' in this kind of week-long event is a pointless exercise, akin to reducing a complex moment in social and political history to a football match with a final score, a winner, and a loser. It's an inappropriate framework for understanding the meaning of this, and insofar as we accept it we succumb to the logic of Spectacle, flattening complexity into bite-sized nuggets of unnourishing mystification.

The individuals who animated the camps, marches, and blockades contributed to a process of political reinvention and re-engagement. No one protesting the G8 would have been satisfied by merely writing a letter to a politician or a newspaper (though some of them undoubtedly did that too), let alone accepting that the proper way to respond to this self-designated global elite was to await the next election in their home country. It is precisely against the impotent rituals of modern democracy that these folks are in motion. For those 10,000 plus who hiked miles across open fields to sit on roads and rails to blockade the summit, direct action was a far more potent act than any of the activities that preceded it, even if politicians and supplies were flown over the blockades by helicopter.

Among the people who took time out of their normal lives to camp and march and argue and blockade, there were more differences than commonalities, but they represented a continuum of subjective choices, refusals of the limits of politics, and embrace of 'action', defined in various ways. There are sharp differences on appropriate tactics and behaviours. For some, showing up in Rostock and walking in legal marches and attending workshops was already a break from the atomised lives most of their compatriots accept as normal. For many others, participating in a legally approved political demonstration was to affirm one's own passivity in the face of a system that demands acquiescence. Some of them wanted to make music, to dance and sing together, to make wild and marvellous artistic floats and puppets with subversive messages. For them, drumming and dancing was to throw their bodies into another level of engagement, to feel their own participation in a visceral and sometimes powerful way. By introducing this Dionysian element of pleasure and even celebration, they were refusing the sombre, obedient, sheep-like behaviour acceptable to both the state and leftist organisers. At their most extreme, they were creating the beginnings of a new post-capitalist culture, filling the streets with art and music in the here and now. For those who wanted to connect through pleasure and joy, the passivity and quietude of many demonstrators was what they were trying to break through.

Seen from outside, the Black Bloc seems like a Calvinist nightmare, all colour and individuality expunged from their ranks, while their hostility to the limitations of legal marches or to the 'hippy' fun of drummers and dancers is palpable. In a real way Black Blocers are 'throwing down'—throwing their bodies on the gears of the machine as best they can (to echo Mario Savio's epochal call during Berkeley's 1964 Free Speech Movement). It's a romantic and ultimately doomed approach—fighting military with military will fail even if the insurgents 'win'. Though the 'machine' may use the police as its first line of defence, the cops are replaceable parts too, and underneath the ninja turtle suits, much to the dismay of those who have demonised them in their symbolic roles, they are people whom we need to have join us not fight us.

This became even clearer to me as I enjoyed a walking tour of Berlin after returning from Rostock. It ended with a stirring account of the revolt that finally brought down the Berlin Wall. In October / November 1989, in Leipzig, hundreds, and then thousands, of demonstrators had turned out until a crucial evening when the mobilised armed forces of the East German state were sent to crush them—but the soldiers refused to fire on the crowds. Weeks later the iron curtain was kaput! Mass demonstrations were crucial, but the subversion of the police and army, not their military defeat per se, was equally important.

Black Bloc 'anarchists' got most of the press here between Saturday and Tuesday, at the expense of the other 75,000 protesters and their respective messages, because of the riot at the end of Saturday's big anti-G8 march. This obsessive press angle led eleven US protesters to write an open letter in which they argued:

> Summit after summit, we have seen the same pattern in the media. The images of black-clad protesters hurling rocks at police, the stories of senseless hooligans—those whom the government says should be punished and locked away. These stories and images of street fighting do nothing but spread fear, criminalise protests, divide social movements, and distract the public from the story of the G8 and their unaccountable polices that are spreading militarism, poverty, violence, environmental destruction and climate change.[5]

Only US Americans can be surprised that the media does not communicate their message properly! However, it is true that few commented on the strange psychological operations undertaken by the police as they continuously made bizarre claims about nonexistent weapons (potatoes spiked with nails?) and nonexistent combatants, filling the air with disturbingly unverifiable claims that went unchallenged by the media.

There was actually a striking parallel in the behaviour of the mainstream press and many protesters in their mutual obsession with and focus on the Black Bloc and violence. At a breakfast table on Monday morning, everyone was reading about Saturday's demonstration. At the Indymedia Centre (IMC), most of the international writers and bloggers uploading pictures and stories were using images of the riot. My friend browsed English-language Indymedia sites, and in the first few days there wasn't much mention of any other aspect of the protests at Rostock. In this sad way, the anti-G8 protesters perfectly mirrored the mainstream: if it bleeds, it leads. Conflict and violence are much easier to capture and communicate and resonate much louder than any of the dozens of other messages, groups, and creative expressions.

Anti-G8 Protests, Rostock

There wasn't anything particularly new or different about this anti-G8 protest compared to the protest at Gleneagles in Scotland in 2005 or to the longer history of protests against other summits (and before that, the anti-nuclear and anti-military protests in the 1970s and 1980s). It might have been more effective to have the blockades at the gates of Heiligendamm matched by mass strikes and urban demonstrations in Berlin and Hamburg, but the protests were not embraced by a sufficiently broad swathe of the population to bring that about.

Waiting for politicians or legal protest to bring about radical change is hopeless. But as people 'take action', curious questions emerge about how feeling effective is not necessarily the same as effective politics. Obviously the people in motion are an evolving social and political movement, and Rostock is another important chapter in that evolution. Just as obviously though, capitalism is not directly threatened by dancing in the streets or brawling with the police, though it may someday be challenged by the culture that these activities help nurture. If anything, we might note that security bureaucracies are responsive and evolving too, learning lessons and making adjustments in response to the endless creativity of their opponents. And as protests grow larger, so too do the resources dedicated to repressing them.

Is the summit-hopping culture too insular and self-referential? Is it too disconnected from the daily lives of everyday workers and citizens? Aren't protesters themselves everyday workers and citizens? Why the separation then? These are among the questions that summit protesters will have to face in the coming years.

Can the movement escape the cycle of predictability and a politics of ineffective self-gratification? Can more of the same, bigger and better, produce more subversive results? Or might there be a lesson in the disobedience of the Eastern Bloc soldiers back in 1989? A new world beyond borders and capitalism is in formation. Will it burst forth one day, inspiring even those who are employed to suppress it to join in? Our protests and creative alternatives have to inspire even our enemies to join us. That's a big challenge, to be sure. Revolution is not something to be imposed but, rather, should be an irresistibly compelling invitation. That other world we keep claiming? It beckons some of us already, because in it we'll feel and taste and know things we've only dreamed about. Are our protests communicating that dream, those implausible hopes, those urgent necessities? Would your mother want to come along?

References

Dissent Netzwerk, at http://dissentnetzwerk.org/node/3116 (Accessed August 23 2017)
Jai Sen, 2012b—'Another World Is Possible!': Critical Explorations of the World
    Social Forum and the Dreams It Has Inspired', Introduction to Jai Sen and Peter
    Waterman, eds, 2012—*World Social Forum: Critical Explorations.* Volume 3 in the
    Challenging Empires series. New Delhi: OpenWord
Voluntari@s IMC-PT, 2007—'Protests in Rostock, Now', on *Indymedia*, at http://de.
    indymedia.org/2007/06/183147.shtml (Accessed August 23 2017)

Notes

1. Ed: This is a somewhat revised version of an essay first published on *Mute magazine—Culture and politics after the net*, June 26 2007, at http://www.metamute.org/en/Effective-Politics-or-Feeling-Effective (Inactive August 23 2017). My thanks to

Mute for publishing this article on an open basis—we too are publishing it similarly, as is our preferred policy—and my thanks to the author for working with our content editor to revise the essay.

2. From Germany and Portugal and the rest of the world, Voluntari@s IMC-PT, June 8 2007, Rostock, Germany, at http://de.indymedia.org/2007/06/183147.shtml (Accessed August 23 2017).

3. Ed: For those not familiar with the contours of the social movement world of the early 2000s, 'Another World Is Possible?' is / was the slogan coined for the World Social Forum in about 2001. (For a quick history, see Sen 2012b.) To the extent that the anti-G8 protests—held in Germany in June 2007, but which also took place in several other parts of the North during those years—were far more front-line direct action than the WSF, it is in some way even a little surprising that the Rostock protests should have adopted this very vague, open call as its slogan. It is also an indication of how strongly the WSF had 'arrived' in that decade and perhaps also of how attractive the idea of 'another world' seemed. Also important was the strong presence in European protests of ATTAC France, which was one of the founders of the WSF and whose president, Susan George, is credited for this concept and slogan.

4. Speed tweakers are abusers of methamphetamines. They stay awake for days at a time and tend to play loud music and behave very antisocially, so when they sleep it off it is a relief to anyone who has had to be near them during their binge.

5. At http://dissentnetzwerk.org/node/3116 (Accessed August 23 2017).

PR Like PRocess!
Strategy From The Bottom Up[1]
Massimo De Angelis

Evaluating the London ESF after the Horizontal Posse Came to Town

From the perspective of those who seek a politics of alternatives, one firmly rooted in a critique of the beasts we are confronting, capitalism and war, the story of the internal contrasts in the process that led to the European Social Forum (ESF) in London, UK, in 2004 might seem trivial, far removed from the high theoretical plateaux that characterise debates on strategy in our movements. However, often these plateaux turn into platitudes, banal assertions of the 'right' way forward that select out the motivations and aspirations of real struggles and lived practices emerging from the ground up, and instead follow templates rooted in timeless ideological models. In this piece I want to contribute to the broad debate on strategy for overcoming capitalism by drawing a connection between the struggles for democracy, inclusiveness, and participation within the ESF process, and the struggles for overcoming capitalism as a mode of production, a mode of doing, and consequent social relations.

The story of the battle inside the ESF process in 2004 is the story of the contrast between those coming from many networks and organisations to make the ESF a temporary space-time commons that would prefigure alternative practices and multiple nonexploitative doings in a 'global city' like London, with the efforts of those following variations of bureaucratic socialist lines to monopolise and centralise the event.[2] This came to be known as the struggle between 'horizontals' and 'verticals'.[3] I must make clear to the reader that I have actively participated in this struggle and sided with the 'horizontals'.

Perhaps this distinction caused some confusion, since the definition of 'horizontality' or 'verticality' did not identify a specific group, organisation, or network but a *mode of doing* predicated on opposite *organising* principles and modes of doing and relating that were common to many belonging to a variety of networks and organisations. One based on participatory, open, and inclusive democracy, in which participants through their iterative relational practises sought to reach consensus on both the means to be employed and the ends to be achieved and were willing to engage in the continuous learning process necessary for these practices. The other in which democracy was identified with a rigid vertical structure within which ends are defined by the few and means seen purely as

278 | The Movements of Movements, Part 2

instrumental to those ends. For 'horizontals' the means embody values as much as the ends (whether we use free or patented software, whether information is posted freely or under a coordinating committee's control, whether working groups emerge from the ground up or are 'allowed' by a coordinating committee) and indeed, because of this, the shape of ends *emerge* from negotiations of means. For the 'verticals' it was just about 'getting the job done'—their concept, that is, of 'job' and final outcome.[4]

A brief history here is perhaps useful. The first reference to 'horizontals' in the context of the ESF process was in an email that Stuart Hodkinson sent to the democratise_the_esf list on January 30 2004.[5] This was already a few months after activists from loose networks and movements had begun growing frustrated with what they saw to be traditional devious and manipulative tactics to monopolise and push through pre-established agendas by the usual suspects from UK left-wing politics. In this e-mail, Stuart tells a little anecdote:

> Last year, I went to the Argentina Puppetista show as it toured around the UK. It was a beautiful event for many reasons, but I remember one thing more than any other. The *piquetera* sister from Argentina was explaining the political divisions within the *piquetera* movement (roadblockers' movement). She was an autonomist and explained how in her part of the movement, they worked in a non-hierarchical way: with assemblies meeting, deciding by consensus and then selecting delegates to go meet with delegates from other assemblies, relaying information and finding a common agreement. However, they were constantly undermined by Trotskyist parties who tried to hijack protests, reneged on agreements and would not work by consensus. She said they had all tried to work together, to find a common way of working, but in the end, she had found it impossible. Her explanation was simple but perfect: "Horizontal people cannot work with vertical people".

He continues with a comparison between the way that this and the ESF meetings were conducted:

> That meeting was organised in a circle, there was a facilitator who simply facilitated the discussion, ensuring that everyone who wanted to speak could speak, was respectful of everyone's views and created an atmosphere of common humanity. Because we all agreed with the process of the discussion, what the discussion would be on, what time we would finish, who would provide translation etc, etc, and because we all wanted to work together to be able to hear about what was happening in Argentina, the meeting worked beautifully. The ESF process in the UK, from the moment it began in the minds of the [Socialist Workers Party] SWP central committee last year, right through to now has never, ever been conducted

in such a way, nor have those people pushing the process forward ever wanted us to work in such a way. They are not interested in the process of consensus-based decision-making. They do not respect it, do not agree with it, and will never, ever work in that way. Neither will trade union officials, nor most representatives from NGOs and mainstream campaign groups. They are vertical people!

In this original intervention, verticality and horizontality do not define states of being but *modes of doing*, that is, modes of *relating* within *processes* of social production. Also, as it became clear in the months that followed, these modes of doing are not a static set of procedural rules to be agreed upon once and for all and then applied in various contexts. Instead, they are modes that develop and emerge from among the interacting agents themselves. The anecdote captured very well the feeling and experience of the people involved. Soon after this email was sent around, people whose attempts to democratise the ESF process in the previous months were frustrated immediately recognised themselves in the experience of the *piquetera* sister and started to refer to themselves as 'horizontals' and to their opponents as 'verticals'. A few days later, beginning on February 7, a 'log of evidence' was circulated through lists and posted on the ESF.net website, providing a case against the organisations which had begun to monopolise the process of the ESF. Concerns ranged from the opaque ways followed in order to make London a candidate for the next ESF without proper consultations with social movements to the abolition of working groups that were emerging spontaneously to deal with a variety of organisational aspects, from the 'blackmail' of the type 'either this way or without trade unions' money' to what was seen as the opportunistic management of general assemblies, little respectful of the democratic principles of inclusion and participation, principles that many sought to be at the very basis of the World Social Forum (WSF).[6]

On the basis of this document, a Call for Democracy was then circulated,[7] signed by 128 people belonging to a wide range of groups, loose networks, and organisations, from the European Parliament, trade unions, and NGOs to a Northern Anarchist Network, Indymedia, and local social forums.[8] The signature methodology was revealing: it listed all individuals and affiliations in two different places, making clear that individuals were not representing organisations and, at the same time, that "horizontals are everywhere, even in the organisations of the verticals".[9] Hence, from the beginning, the political identity and positionality of horizontality was not defined in terms of a label or as belonging to a particular group but as a mode of doing that was *transversal* to a variety of groups and networks, to a variety of identities and positionalities.[10]

The conflict among what were clearly appearing as two divergent political cultures[11] would explode publicly and openly during the European assembly for the preparation of the ESF held in London on March 6–7 2004. The European delegates could bear witness to the accusations made by 'horizontals' about the way the meeting was chaired and the blatant tactics used to force through a pre-established and controversial agenda.

The 'verticals' were forced to the negotiating table in the middle of the assembly in order to renegotiate the terms within which the ESF process should proceed. The outcome of what several horizontals saw as a major victory would, however, in the following months be frustrated by the continuation of the same practices in an endless war of attrition between the two political cultures. By June, only a few months from the event, most people involved in horizontal networks opted to put their organisational energies and skills in the organisation and logistics of seminars, workshops, and accommodations in autonomous spaces (www.altspaces.net), which, as I will briefly discuss below, became the most diverse, vibrant, and well attended in the brief history of the ESF.[12]

Indeed, the latter spaces showed that the two camps held quite different meanings of democracy; they *valued* different aspects of it. On the one hand, a hierarchal concept of democracy, rooted in apparatus, in which the powers of the social body (in this case the people involved in the production of the Forum) were articulated through a vertical scale of representations and mediations that constructed and rigidified roles, bureaucratically defined the boundaries of the subjects' inputs, of *what* they could or could not contribute to, of *how* they could and could not contribute, and confined the free expression of their *powers* within a wall well guarded by bureaucratic socialist principles. In this country, this vertical line is the mainstream of politics. On the other hand, there was a horizontal plateau of encounters, relations, and doing, through which the exercise of the subjects' powers and their reciprocal feedbacks constructed norms, rules, spaces, and temporarily defined roles.

Keeping in mind this contrast, what can we say post facto about the 'event' ESF held in London in October 2004? Ambiguous result. On the one hand, it represented a clear step forward for our movement not only because 25,000 people attended, and because all large events like this encourage encounters across networks, but also and especially because a section of the movement overcame its insularity at events like this and, working with organising principles based on horizontality, inclusiveness, and participation, broadened substantially the programme of and participation in self-managed and autonomous zones. About 5,000 people, many of whom were wearing the bracelet of the 'official' event, are estimated to have participated in the broad range of activities in the autonomous zones and defined future action programmes on crucial themes such as precarity, refugees, and communication rights.

On the other hand, there is also a sense in which the process of the 'official' ESF in London was not a way forward for our movement but a serious step back. The degree of subcontracting of various processes at 'official' events, culminating

with the hiring of an 'event management' company; the environmental unaware-
ness of its practices; the vertical control freakery that dominated all moments of
its production, suspicion of all productive networks within the movement that
did not match the habitual practices of union bureaucracies and socialist parties;
the contractual 'terms and conditions' email sent to anyone purchasing tickets;
the petty self-promotional splashing of UK union names on the walls of meeting
rooms instead of symbols that belong to all movements across the globe; not to
mention the bullying, the trade unions' and Greater London Authority's financial
blackmail, and the monopolisation of platforms such as the final rally—these
were just an indication that in terms of these practices, another world was still
far away. In the effort to 'build' the movement, to 'outreach' to people who have
not yet heard about the horrors of the world, the organisers forgot that a process
of radical social transformation takes much more than an increasing number of
people laid down as 'building blocks'. This relational incompetence is a heavy
political liability in our movement and cannot be justified by the ends argued, for
example, by Callinicos,[13] of 'educating' more people or outreaching into mainstream union organisations.

From the London ESF to the World

We need to zoom out at this stage because the 'verticals' strategy of excluding
subjectivities, themes, and organisational processes not compatible with their
ideological templates was not particular to the production of one specific ESF
event. The struggle that emerged in London also happened during the preparatory process in India for the World Social Forum held in Mumbai, earlier in
2004[14] and, more generally, has been reproduced within the movement at many
occasions: within the anti-war movement in London, on the streets and in the assemblies in Argentina,[15] and so on. There are always 'template strategists' ready to
fly in circles over concrete problems encountered by the movement and processes
such as social forums, who read the problems in their own terms and offer solutions that go in the direction of the goals hidden and predefined in their particular
political cookbook. 'Verticality' in this sense is not simply the 'management' of
an event such as the ESF but *a culture of politics that is managerial*. Let us zoom
out then and reach those plateaux of generalisations that characterise debates on
strategy in our movements, without, however, losing our sanity.

A recent contribution by Susan George[16] offers a good and intelligent entry
point to tackle this managerial conception of politics, a culture that by and large
informs many of the 'reformists' and 'revolutionary' tendencies in our movement,
to use an old classification not very meaningful today.[17] In 'Taking the Movement
Forward', she raises some serious strategic reflections and confronts us with the
problem of how our movement can win its battles, and push "'our adversaries

backward' until they fall over the edge of the cliff". She raises four main points that are "vital for the continuing success of the movement". For mnemonic reasons, they all begin with PR: "PRogrammes, PRiorities and PRagmatism, ending with a warning about PRecautions". PRogramme has to do with the activities at our social forums, which she sees quite correctly as dispersive and repetitive, lacking focus on strategic reflections, a clear understanding of the powers of our enemy, etc. PRiorities is where the problems start. They indicate the need for "defining a minimum, common programme every activist in the world (or, when relevant, in Europe or another region) can agree on and in whose service political campaigning can be undertaken and pressure applied, right now". This is a common programme that not only identifies the most urgent and strategically important battles but also states the kind of globalisation we want, "otherwise, why should anyone bother listening to us, much less joining us?"

PRagmatism is a sober reminder that our priorities cannot be a laundry list, that they have to be selected with intelligence, and that intelligence is to step out of one's partial worldview and preferred 'pet issues' and embrace the perspective of the whole, of what is doable here and now, what issue would bring us more allies, what type of victory would most weaken our opponents, etc. Finally, PRecaution is a reminder that "in order to take the movement forward, let's not get side-tracked or bogged down with huge, unwieldy abstractions like 'defeating the market' or 'overthrowing capitalism'". Since there is no Winter Palace to seize, any victory we achieve will always be a partial victory.

What Kinds of Victory Do We Need?

Let me engage with the type of argument that Susan George puts forward, starting, however, with a different concept of precaution, one that recognises the fact that there is no centre of power, no Winter Palace to storm, and hence that any victory is a partial victory, but one that, at the same time, does not want to root its strategic horizon and thinking in anything other than overcoming capitalism, that is 'overthrowing of capitalism' through a process of social radical transformation and constitution.

Now the recognition that any victory is a partial victory implies that we need to be able to judge the value of such a victory. In traditional socialist mythology, there are two ways to judge a victory. One is to consider a victory as an achievement that goes in the direction of a new social deal with capital. The other considers a victory as an achievement that goes in the direction of the seizure of state power. We have here the classic dichotomy between 'reform' and 'revolution'. A third option, closer to a horizontal approach than the socialist mythology, is that a victory is something that goes towards the abolition of exploitation and oppressions, as well as promoting empowerment, self-determination, and autonomy over our lives and contexts of interaction. Some may say that these three are complementary, and others would disagree. I say, maybe so, and it depends on contexts—but I am not interested to debate the issue here. What interests me is to reclaim a unit of measurement, a yardstick by which we can formulate and frame our broad strategic judgments. To do this, we must ask: Which of these three is our ultimate end, our goal? What are we really fighting for? My stand is that if any generalisation is possible regarding the goals of the people engaged in struggles, it is closer to the last of these three options, which, given the multiplicity of positionalities, desires, and needs, means a multiplicity of goals and new relational fields to articulate them in.

Obviously, one can make the argument that institutional 'victories', whether through 'reforms' or 'revolutions', are means to realise empowerment, autonomy, and an end to exploitation. Fine, make this argument. In any case, they are means, not goals. The question then becomes whether these 'victories' also become means for our opponents; that is, if they are also means to goals that go against our own goals, then it is strategically shortsighted to embrace them as our means. For example, the goal of the ESF event as defined through the means of its verticalisation made it uniquely an event to be 'consumed'. The goal of 'environmental sustainability' through the means of sustaining business and capitalism metabolises the original meaning of sustainability and turns it into a means for 'competitive advantage'. The goal of 'poverty reduction' through extending the realm of markets and competition turns the discourse on poverty into an instrument to promote a social mechanism through which somebody else's livelihood is threatened (this is what market competition is all about).

It is very dangerous these days to make people think that we are going to have 'victories', or that we even should hope to get them. I mean those types of victories that imply or even hint at a 'progressive' institutional shift of paradigms: something like the Tobin Tax (ATTAC), a world parliament (Monbiot), a Keynesian-inspired International Trade Organisation (George), or, broadly, a system of governance of global markets predicated on a deal between capital and selected organisations of civil society. This is not a judgment on the merits of such regulatory reforms in the abstract. It is a judgment on the processes that such victories would imply and a rejection of an approach that aspires to the institutionalisation of social movements. Within the boundaries of capitalist systems, institutional shifts in paradigms never come without some forms of exclusion and militarisation in our lives, because they have to be contained within the limits acceptable to start a new round of accumulation.

The last big 'progressive' shift of paradigm was the welfare state and Keynesianism, and this would not have been accepted by capital without the Second World War, which turned trade unions into bureaucracies,[18] coupled with the priorities of growth and global (under)development that is capital accumulation.[19] No welfare state would have been possible without the Cold War, the constant fear of nuclear obliteration, and the networks of spies infiltrated in our movements, which attempted to confine struggles within geopolitically compatible limits.[20]

Linear Thinking and the Marginalisation of Struggles

The emphasis on empowerment and autonomy is not simply an 'ideological preference'. It is also a question of the constituent social powers we are capable of mobilising when we ground our politics in this. Thus, for example, we have to realise that not one of us, including the most trained and up-to-date political campaigner on any particular issue, has sufficient knowledge of what is at stake for any particular community in struggle, let alone the innumerable priorities of our global movement. Nobody knows what priorities might emerge from the ground up on the day after some steering committee has decided a list of priorities as they see fit. Nobody has full knowledge of context, desires, needs, and aspirations except the subjects themselves.

The 'swarm' nature of our movements allows the best use of knowledge of priorities that is available because it relies on peoples and communities to ground them in their own contexts, to share that knowledge and articulate their priorities with those of others as they see fit in their own processes of empowerment, struggle, and production of relational fabrics. Knowledge, including the knowledge of priorities, can only be conceived in a networked form, as an ongoing relational field among the many worlds and aspirations we comprise. Hence, while it is tactically important, sensible, and conceivable that in given times and circumstances, and for short periods of time, we reach consensus and focus our efforts on specific objectives, it would be a disaster for our broad movement to strategically prioritise campaigns and define a common programme for which, in the article quoted, Susan George hopes "every activist in the world (or, when relevant, in Europe or another region) can agree on and in whose service political campaigning can be undertaken and pressure applied". This way of putting it risks reproducing the worst of political parties, the hierarchy between a central committee (read 'secretariat') entitled to shape broad political ends and all the rest who 'service political campaigning' and serve as means to externally defined ends. We would lose our flexibility and replace the dynamic swarm nature of our movement with a new bureaucracy.

These types of arguments are predicated on a linear, cumulative understanding of social transformation, with no connection to the dynamics of existing social struggles. In this George is not alone, she shares much with the many classical 'revolutionary socialist' tendencies she seems to oppose. The metaphor she uses, for example, the idea that by pushing and pushing we can send our opponents off a cliff, and the representation of this pushing in term of a series of 'victories', evokes a football competition more than the 'game' of social transformation. In the latter, there is no independent recording of the score, the rules of the game are not accepted by all, and, most importantly, our 'scoring' a victory today may well result (as it has often resulted) in changing some aspects of the 'game' in such a way that the fundamental aspects we are opposed to remain untouched! The storming of the Winter Palace implied some real material gains for the Russian people, but its institutionalisation deep froze hierarchical social relations (and consequent gulags) for seventy years in a process of 'socialist accumulation'. The working of the Keynesian state implied the institutionalisation of wage rounds and the entrance of trade unions into the 'deal' room with governments and bosses. Yet women remained confined as unwaged workers in patriarchal homes, US American black communities were confined to their poverty stricken ghettoes, South East Asian peasants were bombed and napalmed in their villages and rice paddies, while the CO_2 emissions of the 'golden age of capitalism' are choking us all and are the basis of today's changing weather patterns.

There is a long and variegated tradition of autonomist thinking rooted in the 1960s and 1970s Italian movements and *operaismo* ('workerism'), but then branching out into a broad range of contributions worldwide, according to which one does not just come up with strategies. Instead, strategies must be 'read from the struggles', and their evaluation should begin with the present complexity and urgency. Thus, for example, what is the status of the cancellation of debt versus the Tobin Tax strategies now? Which of the two has been more effective in recomposing movements in Africa, South America, and Asia? How would popular movements be (dis)empowered by a tax negotiated and administered from above? By a generalised refusal to pay the debt imposed on states by the movements themselves? What would cause capitalist institutions like the World Bank and IMF to retreat? How does the debate around the Iraqi debt cancellation create a contradiction in the capitalist structural adjustment strategy? It is only with a discussion of questions in such detail that debates between the different strategies can be evaluated.

It is obvious that from the perspective of a concept of social transformation that wants to promote empowerment, we must abandon linear thinking, since social transformation emerges out of our actions, subjectivities, desires, organisational capability, ingenuity, and struggles in unpredictable ways. Indeed, we must be very wary of thinking that the achievement of a victory, of any victory, is a move towards the promised land. This is because what we call victories (or defeats for that matter) represent turning points for both us and our opponents. And by our opponents I do not mean a particular set of elites, specifically and contingently defined. From the broad *strategic perspective* of social transformation, our enemies are not Bush and Blair, not this or that corporate shark. These only serve the machine in particular contexts, and they are our enemies within those contexts. Strategically speaking, what we are confronting are not personalities but social roles, and roles emerge out of social relations and the processes of particular forms. When a pope dies, goes an Italian saying, another takes his place, and the death of a pope does not question the role of the pope, his position within a hierarchical scale, or the ongoing processes that reproduce that hierarchy. Our movement, like each and every one of us, has the potential to transform those roles or to fall back into the old ones.

Tactically speaking, we simply do not know who will take the place of our particular adversaries in the here and now after a 'victory' on this or that issue has been achieved; we do not know what strategic direction capital will take to perpetrate the social system most congenial to it. We can identify some general lines on current debates within the elite, we can learn from history; however, we do not know how, whether, and to what extent our victory will bring about a realignment of social forces that will help to redefine a new era of capital accumulation, with its inevitable injustices, exclusions, stupidity, and madness.

Just to make a simple illustration: the Bolkestein Directive, to which Susan George draws our attention, which "would introduce a new legal principle and allow firms to apply the social and labour laws of the 'country of origin' to workers in all the European countries where the firms might happen to do business", is not particularly incompatible with the strategic aspirations of some tendencies in international trade unions. I am thinking, for instance, about global business unionism, for which international unions must engage in alliances with global capital to compete against other global capitalist alliances.[21] Who are our adversaries here, the proponents of the EU directive who set the legal framework within which corporate-union alliances on a global scale would also become possible or those trade unionists who work for making such an alliance the policy of trade unions? They sound complementary to me, in that they are both ways to understand human social production as competitive and profit-oriented, that is, they envisage a process of doing that is incompatible with our transformative goals. Such complementarities are discernable only if we measure the proposal strategically in the sense discussed before, asking whether it will help further capitalist disciplinary markets or set a limit to them and open spaces for empowerment and new modes of doing and social relations.

From the perspective of radical transformation and moving beyond capitalism, our true enemy, the beast we are confronting, is how we articulate our social doing and (re)produce our livelihoods, our needs and desires, in a social process predicated on a certain distribution of property rights and access to resources. This is what we call capitalism. This is what our historical memory and diverse body of knowledge in the form of theoretical and empirical work, as well as lived experience and biographical narrative, tells us: however regulated and however fine-tuned, capitalism reproduces the same patterns of injustices and delirium.

This form of human doing and mode of articulation of difference through disciplinary markets has always proved dynamic and flexible enough to absorb, contrast, and co-opt any fixed 'institutional progressive' programme that we come up with. Instead, we need to beat it by spreading alternative modes of doing, *alternative processes of social cooperation*, and the articulation of diversity a billion times more creative, flexible, innovative, as well as communal and cohesive, than capitalist disciplinary markets. But in order to be emancipatory and empowering, these processes can only be defined by the interacting agents themselves, not by a grand design or by a 'general programme'.

A programme and the prioritisation of action can only be helpful in concentrating our forces in specific contexts and situations, in order to build a critical mass *to set a limit to capital*. But even this limited understanding of programme must *emerge* from a process that is alternative to the mode of doing of capital. Even this programme must be *produced* by an alternative mode of production and social relations. It is for this reason that struggles for the problematisation of process within our movement, like the one that emerged at the London ESF, are so strategically important.

PRocess!

How can we reconcile our broad strategic goal of the radical transformation of global society beyond capitalism with the tasks of activism, the nitty-gritty of political campaigning, of defining priorities, mobilising, agitating, educating, and setting contexts and goals that are workable? To me, the answer is centred around the 'PR' left out from the list provided by Susan George: PRocess. This in a twofold sense.

First, we have to see the whole of our diverse movements as setting a limit, an insurmountable barrier to the process of the social doing of capital. This is a process of social reproduction based on pitting one against the other, one's livelihood against those of others'. The barrier is a multitude of 'No!' to this type of process. We do this in the diverse struggles that emerge: against debt, against further trade liberalisations, against privatisations, for land, for food sovereignty, and for different relations to nature. And we do this by pushing back the market agenda from pervading all dimensions of our lives.

Second, from the perspective of a radical transformation of society, these capital-limiting struggles also enable us to do two other things. They enable not only to quantitatively 'build' the movement but, more importantly, to thicken the networks and extend the relational fields of action of social cooperation *predicated on values other than market values*. Also, and consequently, since thickening the web implies the extension of relational fields of action, of social cooperation, we have opened new spaces within which we consolidate our relational practices. Our many powers have grown, and they have grown not arithmetically but exponentially.

We can understand these two dimensions of our struggles in terms of "One No, Many Yeses" vis-à-vis capital, a slogan that emerged from the second *Encuentro* promoted by the Zapatistas, in 1997. The "One No" that keeps throwing spanners at its wheels, seeking to push it back and keep it at bay. The "Many Yeses" that thicken the web of social cooperation grounded on different values. The "One No" that dents, challenges, and destroys its drive to colonise life with monetary values. The "Many Yeses" that push desires and aspirations away from being coupled with disciplinary market loops. The "One No" that cuts back enclosures and the "Many Yeses" that create new commons predicated on new communities and relational practices. In this framework, we can hail as 'victories' all the moments, opportunities, events, and spaces of empowerment, whether these achieve the establishment of a new connection among communities in struggle or the winning of a major concessions from the state that effectively reduces the dependency of people on markets.

The dictatorship of capitalist markets is predicated on a social consensus that makes us act in ways compatible with them, makes us follow our desires and meet our needs within social forms that pit our livelihoods against each other's. To the extent that consensus is manufactured, we have then to challenge how that manufacturing takes place and practice a different type of production process through which a new consensus emerges. Again, it is a question of process as, for example, our independent media people teach us again and again. To the extent that manufacturing is the result of our daily engagements within markets, an iteration that creates and normalises rules of engagement with the other, we must find ways to disengage, construct a politics of alternatives that focuses on a reduction of the degree of our dependence on markets, and therefore struggles for different types of commons. In other words, to the extent that we do not consent—'we must interact in these ways because this is what our livelihoods depend on'—our struggle must seek to push back our degree of dependence on capitalist markets, reclaim resources at whatever scale of social action, and on this basis invent and practice new forms of exchanges across the social body, creating new types of local and translocal communities. In all these cases, what is required is an emphasis on relational and communicational processes, as well as on the conditions within which we access resources. Competition is replaced by communication and enclosures by commons.

References

Ezequiel Adamovsky, 2018—'Autonomous Politics and its Problems: Thinking the Passage from the Social to Political', in Jai Sen, ed, 2018—*The Movements of Movements, Part 2: Rethinking Our Dance*. Volume 5 in the *Challenging Empires* series. New Delhi: OpenWord, and Oakland, CA: PM Press

Alex Callinicos, 2004—'Building on the Success of the London ESF', at http://www.euromovements.info/newsletter/callinics.htm (Inactive August 24 2017)

Massimo De Angelis, 2000—*Keynesianism, Social Conflict and Political Economy*. London: Macmillan

Susan George, October 2004—'Taking the Movement Forward', at http://www.tni.org/archives/archives_george_forward (Inactve August 24 2017)

Marty Glaberman, 1980—*Wartime Strikes: The Struggle Against the No-Strike Pledge in the UAW During World War II*. Detroit, MI: Bewick

Stuart Hodkinson, 2004—'Is There a New Trade Union Internationalism? The ICFTU and the Campaign for Core Labour Standards in the WTO', in *School of Politics and International Studies*, Leeds, University of Leeds

Horizontals, 2004a—'European Social Forum (ESF) in UK in 2004; What's Happening? Log of Evidence', at http://esf2004.net/en/tiki-index.php?page=LogOfProcess (Inactive August 24 2017)

Horizontals, 2004b—'Call for Democracy in the ESF Process', at http://esf2004.net/en/tiki-index.php?page=CallForDemocracy (Inactive August 24 2017)

Horizontals, 2004c—'Call for Democracy Signatures', at http://esf2004.net/en/tiki-index.php?page=CallForDemSigs (Inactive August 24 2017)

Horizontals, 2004d—'Horizontals Statement: The Horizontals Come to Town', at http://esf2004.net/en/tiki-index.php?page=HorizontalsStatement (Inactive August 24 2017)

Horizontals, 2004e—'ESF in London: A Celebration For All and An Invitation From Few Horizontals', at http://esf2004.net/en/tiki-read_article.php?articleld=6 (Inactive August 24 2017)

Les Levidow, 2004—'European Social Forum: Making Another World Possible?', in *Radical Philosophy*, 128, pp 6–11, at https://www.radicalphilosophy.com/commentary/making-another-world-possible (Accessed August 24 2017)

Vincenzo Ruggiero, April 2004—'*Orizzontali e Vertical*' ['Horizontals and Verticals', in Italian], in *Carta*, vol 15, pp 46–49

Jai Sen, 2004—'The Long March to Another World: Reflections of a Member of the WSF India Committee in 2002 on the First Year of the WSF Process in India', in Jai Sen, Anita Anand, Arturo Escobar, and Peter Waterman, eds, *2004—World Social Forum: Challenging Empires*. New Delhi: The Viveka Foundation

Notes

1. Ed: This essay was first published in *ephemera, theory & politics in organization*, vol 5 no 2, pp 193–204. I warmly thank the editors for their prompt and generous permission to publish this slightly edited version and the author for working with our Content Editor to prepare his essay for publication.

2. In this context, these included the Social Workers Party and Socialist Action lines, union bureaucracies mentalities, and the directives of Ken Livingston's office.

3. For a broad account of this story, see Levidow 2004.

4. Horizontals define themselves as those "who believe that the most important thing in the politics for a New World is how we relate to each other in making it happen" (Horizontals 2004d). This means to "recognise and respect our differences and always strive to find common ways to articulate them in order to meet the challenges of the day". Furthermore, horizontals believe that "our organising and getting things done must be founded on the non-hierarchical contribution of all, including decision making powers".

5. The democratize_the_esf list was one of two lists in Britain where participants discussed, coordinated, and often ranted on themes surrounding the ESF in London. The other was the ESF_UK list, which attracted a core of more conventional 'vertical' political activists. There was, of course, a lot of overlap between the two, as debates occurring in one list spilled over to the other. There were two other lists that were European based: the 'official' FSE_ESF list that pulled together activists from a broad range of social movements, trade unions, and NGOs across Europe and the esfdemocracy_eurodebate list, which was set up to inform and coordinate actions among European activists and social movements who were sympathetic to the 'horizontal' case.

6. See Horizontals 2004a.

7. Horizontals 2004b.

8. Horizontals 2004c.

9. Horizontals 2004e.

10. Indeed, this is also demonstrated by the resistance I have witnessed by several practicing 'horizontals' against defining themselves as such, perhaps fearing that labels could rigidify identities in such a way as to contradict the necessary fluidity of 'horizontal' practices.

11. Ruggiero 2004.

12. Ed: Unlike the 'world' WSF process, which started with a great flourish with a first event in Florence, Italy, in 2002, and then Paris, France, in 2003, continuing in Tunis in 2015 and then in Montréal, Canada, in 2016, the ESF process seems to have ended, with its last meeting in Istanbul, Turkey, in 2010.

13. Callinicos 2004.

14. Sen 2004.

15. Ed: For a discussion of the dynamics and politics of the assemblies in Argentina, see the essay in this book by Ezequiel Adamovsky (Adamovsky 2018).

16. George 2004.

17. I want to make clear that in what follows I will only engage with one of George's many short contributions to the debate in our movement, because it is a straightforward piece that poses some very relevant questions and that enabled me to clarify my own thinking while critically confronting them. My engagement does not pretend to pass judgment on her overall valuable work as intellectual and activist, which extends far beyond the short contribution cited.

18. Glaberman 1980.

19. De Angelis 2000.

20. Indeed, a reading of the end of this era would involve a more grounded analysis of struggles and capital reactions than those provided by George (2004). She blames it on "self-gratifying hippies" who have abandoned the movement to get jobs in advertising, thus opening up a space for Maggie and Ronnie? Ed: For those from other parts of the world, this is British shorthand for Margaret Thatcher and Ronald Reagan—respectively the prime minister of Britain and president of the United States in the early and mid-1980s.

21. Hodkinson 2004.

The Power of Words
Reclaiming and Reimagining Revolution and Non-Violence
Matt Meyer and Ousseina Alidou

It is not our differences which separate [us], but our reluctance to recognize those differences and to deal effectively with the distortions which have resulted from the ignoring and misnaming of those differences.
—Audre Lorde[1]

Our words have failed to adequately describe the world we wish to see.

From Kiswahili to Gujarati to Mandarin and Spanish—to French and, most especially, the imperial polyglot known as English—we have not always succeeded in communicating our messages in consistently coherent and inspiring ways. The workers of the world have not united; too many still live in mental and physical chains. At least some of the responsibility for this fact must be faced as an internal weakness: the international left has not been able to consistently 'speak' to 'the people'.

It is more than not reaching people. It is also a fact that radical ideas have been widely co-opted, commoditised, and betrayed before reaching fruition. Our most creative struggles have yielded so many vital lessons that a language of movement building must describe. But too many movements, in moving from one demonstration to the next, and from one campaign to another, have trouble finding not only the strategic next step but also, and crucially, the words to help imagine and build the new societies we envision; in this situation, too many of us use words and ideas that have already been co-opted, sometimes with tragic consequences.

Most of the people we are trying to reach already understand that another world is possible, and many believe that there are things we can do, individually and collectively, to help bring that new world about. But—as representatives of movements and participants in them, moving within and between broad sectors of civil society—we have not figured out how to imagine liberation in a way that deeply and collectively challenges the purveyors of oppression and crisis. There are many people out there who are willing to do a small part to bring about social change, but as movements struggling to move forward more effectively, we have not yet found common ground or a communal voice.

As we look carefully at words, including the use of the term 'movement' to describe grassroots civil society efforts for peace and justice, it is hard—at least in the US—not to come across the famous civil rights spiritual 'We Shall Not Be Moved' and the many ways in which resisting being moved and standing steadfast in civil disobedience shut-down actions became powerfully symbolic of a burgeoning mass consciousness which brought reform to much of North America.[2] For too many who remember (and perhaps tend to romanticise) the heady days of revolutionary moments long past, we have not been moved.[3] But on the other hand, we have allowed the basic calls for Black Power and Black Liberation, for instance—which included African, Asian, and Latin American components (and which also specified a role for those of European descent to lead the work against empire in their own communities)—to be mystified and misquoted, and generally ignored, for almost half a century now. Following the successes of the late 1950s and early 1960s, there has been little movement indeed and few examples of the effective building of ongoing movements—either in regards to racial justice within the US or to the context of social and economic justice throughout the world. Ironically, and in contrast to the intent of the oft-referenced song, the racial, cultural, class, and patriarchal divisions (among others) have proven more intractable than most activists and academics ever expected: even as radicals, we have not been moved beyond our comfort zones and familiar points of reference. In the course of this, the nexus between what is meant by 'revolution' itself and the ideals of non-violent 'beloved communities'—yet another term developed during the Civil Rights Movement in the US in the 1950s–60s—has similarly been misunderstood.

Beyond the need for better rhetoric about our "beautiful trouble-making",[4] if we are to reach wider numbers and unite more diverse groups of people we must be able to conceptualise what 'revolution' means in the twenty-first-century context. Our movements must reach beyond what was conceived of as 'national liberation' (state power and independence for those on the 'periphery' of empire) and beyond what has been conceptualised as personal power (via feminist notions and / or identity politics). Giving voice to all the new revolutionary concepts that could make up modern-day movements is beyond the focus of this essay. But we will at least try to raise some key questions, to challenge certain key assumptions and their underpinning phrases that we believe hold us back from forging the dynamic, unified movements of movements that our twenty-first-century moment requires.

Ocupado: The Meanings of Occupy and the Importance of Meanings—What's in a Word?

It may be easiest to illustrate the problems and possibilities we see by starting with the meanings of Occupy and of Occupation.

The first essential lesson of the Occupy Wall Street (OWS) 'movement' that irrupted in New York in September 2011,[5] and perhaps especially so when viewed from the perspective of many long-time, direct action–oriented native New York City–based activists and analysts, is simply this: we didn't see it coming.

When the takeover of a small park near Wall Street in downtown Manhattan went from a several-hour civil disobedience to an overnight affair, we were amused.

When that occupation lasted more than a couple of days and began receiving some positive press and attention, we were pleased. When it quickly and clearly evolved into the go-to spot for all progressive New Yorkers, a place to check out and be checked out, to bring one's support and ideas and books and food and blankets and friends, it was almost like a dream. This space in our unconscious or distant memories, in our hopes and dreams of mass movements and community-building and of social-political space and economic alternatives, now had an address, an actual place one could go to, which, like the city that birthed it, never slept, was open '24/7' and had become a glorious piece of liberated territory in the literal shadow of the corporate world. When Occupy Wall Street at Zucotti Park continued to get positive local press, as well as national and international attention, it was an outright shock; and by the time the movement began spreading to other cities around the USA and the world, we were almost too busy to once again be surprised.

Why, then, were the hearts and minds of so many 'First World' leftists, hardened and experienced progressive thinkers, organisers from every sect and sector, spanning people who came of age in the 1950s, '60s, '70s, '80s, and '90s so preoccupied with 'other' work, thinking about other issues, campaigns, and approaches, that we didn't see a movement of this type, magnitude, scope, or scale coming? We ask this question not to berate nor to say that we should've known the exact time and space that the first wave of protesters would take over Zucotti Park on September 17 2011, or that *this* was going to be the next big thing. We raise it to frankly assess why so many radicals over such diverse ideological terrain hadn't even imagined an upsurge of OWS proportions as a possibility at *that* historic time and in *that* historic space.

So much of the answer to this, and this is the first major lesson of OWS, has to do with the effectiveness of the rhetoric and revisionism of the 'post-1960s' establishment: that movements are an anomaly, a thing of blessed and saintly moments and peoples, or else a thing of intricate planning and financing. We need to ask ourselves: How much have our movements—not only of reformists but also of revolutionaries—integrated this false logic of right-wing revisionism into our subconscious daily practice? Though this may not be readily admitted, or is perhaps even consciously understood, in reality how many 'strategic plans' that we have formulated have been based on the connected ideas and catchphrases which have been well-honed and often-repeated by those who seek to maintain the status quo?

The terrain that this revisionism covers is vast and insidious. In its understanding, large-scale war is a thing of the past; low intensity conflicts fought out of the range of mainstream media (and fought, more than ever, by proxy forces) have taken the place of global conflicts ever since the 'Vietnam syndrome' saw to the rise of massive anti-war movements throughout the US and Europe—not to mention the multifaceted resistance of the people of Vietnam and South East Asia themselves. Equally, racism and sexism are things of the past; Obama is king, more women are in leadership positions of power on every continent, and there are more rich elites in Africa, Latin America, and Asia than ever before. When race, ethnicity, gender, or caste appears to be at the centre of oppression and inequality, it must be just a glitch in the system; no radical remediation need be applied. Perhaps most significantly, with labour and work itself now decentralised, internationalised, and fragmented, with membership in trade unions at an all-time low, and with the disintegration of nation-states based on anti-capitalist economic, the possibility of class struggle must surely be over. One of their key publicists, Francis Fukuyama, famously suggested in the '90s that 'the end of history' was already in sight.[6]

We were therefore surprised by OWS because, in part, we had allowed ourselves to believe this hype; and we had lost faith in the ability and interest of 'the people' to be moved to militant action. That more people, previously unorganised or at least not in well-defined leftist cadre organisations, were willing to come out to support a call against Wall Street was our first surprise. That they / we were willing to take part in an action which required some amount of risk, some flexibility and discomfort, was our second great surprise. Here folks were willing to face the discomfort of—hell, be spurred on by—rain and snow and police harassment and a lack of centralised support from movement heavies; they were willing to do all this in order to take part in something challenging to the powers that be. This is what felt meaningful about Zucotti: it was a real action, not stage-managed or orchestrated using tactics which seemed tired and uncreative to many. But we had been convinced by three decades of the words and worries of naysayers, who had assured us that rebellions and uprisings were things of the past, at least in the North.

The second main lesson of OWS, therefore—beyond the fact that we must be cautious about the ways in which we have accepted false rhetoric into our movements—is that neoliberal rhetoric has also largely been completely incorrect: large numbers of people are not only willing to come out and protest against structural and systemic forms of oppression but are in fact *more willing* to do so if the protests are inspiring, constructive, filled with do-it-yourself energy, and even militant, or at least mildly risk-taking.

Many pages have been written about the reasons for the successes and failures of 'the Occupy movement', but few have arrived at these simple truths. We suggest that some of this is because our basic definitions and verbiage have not correctly assessed what, at its root, Occupy was and was not. Using the term 'movement' to describe Occupy has been one of the problems, referencing far more long-term and better coordinated efforts (the 'civil rights' or Black Power movements, the anti-war and anti-dictatorship movements, etc) and setting OWS up for inevitable disappointment and failure to live up to lofty past examples. In short, Occupy was not a movement; it was not even a strategic action that was a key part of an already-existing movement. It was, to be clear, a semi-spontaneous action in search of and with the hope of a movement.

One of those closest to the centre of the action at Zucotti from the very beginning of the occupation, journalist and Waging Nonviolence co-founder Nathan Schneider, came closest to hitting the definitionally correct mark when he wrote that Occupy was at that time "a viral phenomenon replicated worldwide at will and whim".[7] Occupy must therefore be understood within the context of a time period that had—in the North—been relatively devoid of strict coordination and organisational unification; and also as part of the resonance of the early 'Arab Spring' takeovers in Western Sahara, Tunisia, and Egypt that in many ways inspired it. In the US, even coalition structures had been less prevalent than the more decentralised use of affinity groups or on the spot small group action initiatives. Post-Occupy analysis hasn't been helped by the fact that, as Schneider put it, those in Occupy "resisted boundaries between what it was and what it wasn't"—but this, in fact, was part of the reason for its success. Building people's power across the boundaries of individual versus organisation, across the boundaries of this nation-state versus the one next door, and across boundaries which many have directly or intuitively deemed inherently false is part of the beauty of twenty-first-century social change. That beauty was also evident, as noted, in the North African events which inspired OWS: from the Gdeim Izik protest camp outside of the Moroccan controlled Saharawi capital of El Aaiun to Tahrir Square in Cairo, Egypt, and beyond. All of this was 'Occupy'.

Of course, within the wonder of Occupy spaces—and perhaps especially in the so-called North—there were also plenty of prejudicial and problematic behaviours, as has been well documented.[8] Racist, paternalist, and imperialist attitudes mingled side by side within the Occupy actions with the sexist, homophobic, transphobic, and patriarchal rape culture that has come to pervade most post-industrial societies.

In New York and elsewhere, Indigenous groups also challenged the words used at the very heart of OWS, thus also challenging basic assumptions about space, land, and people's relationship to it. They argued that the 'occupation' of the land had in fact been accomplished by European settlers centuries before, so what was needed now was something radically different. The slogans they proposed, cleverly appropriating the words used by OWS, included:

TAKE BACK WALL STREET: OCCUPIED SINCE 1625! DECOLONIZE WALL STREET: ON ALGONQUIN LAND, DEFEND MOTHER EARTH![9]

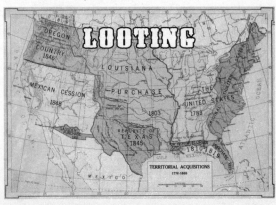

Resistance in Brooklyn, a New York–based anti-imperialist collective that helped organise a Halloween 'anonymous' action around Occupy Wall Street 2011 noted that words mattered greatly in the original OWS General Assembly discussions about the Declaration, when many in the 'people of colour' caucus within OWS worked hard to strike from the OWS materials the offensive phrase "being one race, the human race, formerly divided by race [and] class". Pretending that divisions don't exist or that we live in a colour-blind post-oppression world is most certainly not the way towards collective liberation.[10]

Fast forward four years to the 2015 mass, spontaneous anti–police violence protests in the US, instigated and informed by the Twitter handle #BlackLivesMatter, and we find many commentators suggesting that this was the next phase of twenty-first-century North American uprisings that had begun with OWS. Like OWS, Black Lives Matter was multigenerational and rose quickly in many different cities with only tangential organisational connections between them. But unlike OWS, the protests were significantly Black-led in most instances and included some attempts at broad unity, or at least communication, that many saw as a more significant step to genuine movement building. Organisations like Occu-evolve, which was among the only OWS-related subgroups still functioning four years after the start of the action, stayed intact in part because of their consistent commitment to direct work with the disenfranchised—and perhaps not surprisingly, they were led by 'people of colour'.[11]

Unsurprisingly, however, many of these unresolved problems of wording, clarity, and the ways in which they negatively affect movement building continue to emerge. What revolution itself (and / or revolutionary strategies and tactics) mean in these circumstances comes to the fore: Do we need to abandon reformist ideas such as 'No police misconduct' in order to be truly radical? Is calling for the death of racist cops an important revolutionary demand? Is there a need to choose between the ideological or methodological examples of Martin Luther King, Jr and Malcolm X?

These surely are deeply political questions, but they are further complicated by linguistic issues when organisers use words poorly—for instance, by not understanding that all revolutionary movements have also had tactically reformist aspects to them or that non-violence and reformism are not the same thing (and by the same token, that violence and revolution are not identical). As student activist Ashoka Jegroo, writing on just these issues, puts it: "Language has become one of the main sources of conflict among [the] #Black Lives Matter movement".[12]

What's in a Name?

The same is as true of names. In the early days of the push for 'multicultural education'—a post-ethnic studies moment in the US particular to industrial urban public education districts trying to increase diversity—an organisation called the R.E.A.C.H. Center published a series of popular booklets on African-American, Latino, Native, and Asian communities, focused on the history of naming and the politics of self-determination.[13] In short, the booklets showed that the names that oppressed groups chose to define themselves were and are not only important in terms of rights and principles; they are significant also in terms of emphasising social consciousness and political-economic direction. While many on the individual level can understand the power of choices regarding naming (Should a life partner take on their significant other's last name? What significance should we give to the naming of children?), movement builders too often overlook the power of clearly naming ourselves and the institutions we fight to change.

Some debates, like those involving the 'correctness' of saying 'Latino' (or even more correctly, 'Latin@', with the '@' used to combine the male Latino and female Latina in a gender-neutral term) to refer to Spanish-speaking peoples versus 'Hispanic', spoke to the connectedness of a given group's relationship to a colonising power (in this case, the state of Spain). 'American Indians' are well aware that they were never from the Asian subcontinent of India, but many Indigenous radicals still use the phrase after hundreds of years of misuse, and some even forged the militant 'American Indian Movement' (AIM) in the US in the late 1960s, deliberately using the Settlers' term. One of the most vocal, active, and analytical of united fronts among such peoples—including peoples from North, South, and Central Americas—is the 'International Indian Treaty Council', which serves as one of the leading voices regarding Indigenous rights at the United Nations level.[14] On the other hand, the fact that some other equally proud 'Indians' choose to instead call themselves 'Native Nations' or 'Indigenous Peoples' only underlines the difficulty in some aspects of 'naming' as it relates to cross-ethnic unity.

The question of naming, revolution, and reform among oppressed peoples of the Americas is arguably most central in the case of so-called 'African Americans'. Upon first contact between Africans and the people of the 'New World' under the harsh conditions following the Middle Passage, the most popular name for those captured and sold was not 'slave' but simply 'African'. For centuries, 'Africans' were understood as a distinctive group, even with mixed-race generations growing due to the widespread rape of African women and some intermarriage between Africans and Indigenous Peoples and Latinos in the South of the US. Of course the term 'African', while historically more respectful than the generic and confusing 'Black', still masked the many different ethnic, religious, sociocultural, economic, political, and linguistic variations that existed among people kidnapped from assorted parts of West and Central Africa. Extensive intermarriage and relationships between these various peoples undoubtedly produced a particular new 'people'—but how they should self-define has been a matter of intense political conflict for at least the last hundred years.

The Spanish- and Portuguese-related term 'Negro' (translating to Black) was considered an appropriate term by people of European descent; this term was also adopted by many Africans who saw it as preferable to 'black'—which had for most of the eighteenth and nineteenth centuries been portrayed by the dominant Eurocentric society (and had been internalised by them) as being equivalent to dirty, evil, and bad. The term 'coloured' also came to be used by whites—even though Native peoples have long suggested that *all* ethnicities and people have 'colour' of some kind.

A broad spectrum of early twentieth-century leaders of African descent in the US—from Harvard-educated W.E.B. DuBois to Tuskegee Institute founder Booker T Washington to militant Africanist Marcus Garvey—also began using the term 'Negro'. Despite widespread differences between these groups and their leaders, they almost defiantly appropriated the word (which is at least preferable to the overly derogatory 'nigger', which some twenty-first-century hip hop groups have tried to re-invent). Thus, the early twentieth-century organisation that was founded by DuBois and the Niagara Movement—which came to be regarded as highly respectable—was called the 'National Association for the Advancement of Colored People' (NAACP); alongside this, the 'United Negro College Fund' led self-help efforts within the community and the Garvey-founded back to Africa organisation (the largest in the history of the African Diaspora) was the 'Universal Negro Improvement Association'.

By the mid-1960s, however, much had changed. This was the time in the US when Malcolm X famously critiqued Martin Luther King, Jr and the Civil Rights Movement he led as being too tame, and when Malcolm X struggled to internationalise the movement by looking to the United Nations and the protection of *human* rights beyond specialised US-only *civil* rights.[15] Earlier, he also decried the notion of being 'American' in any way, stating that he was certainly not an American, but rather one of the 22 million Black people who are the "victims of Americanism . . . victims of democracy, nothing but disguised hypocrisy".[16] His criticisms in fact challenged the whole notion of naming, arguing that the terms 'Negro' and 'Coloured' were antiquated—but even as he was arguing this, he and Martin Luther King, Jr were also drawing closer to one another in their last years, and Malcolm X himself was working to develop united fronts under the banner of his 'Organization of Afro-American Unity'—and he had therefore accepted and incorporated the term 'American' within his own strategy.

After the assassination of Malcolm X in 1965, the question of moving from reform to revolution was echoed in militant slogans and rhetoric. Somewhere in between it all was student leader Stokely Carmichael—a colleague of Martin Luther King, Jr but also deeply respectful towards Malcolm X; a student of them both. His was the loudest, sharpest voice to articulately raise the call for 'Black Power', shouting the phrase at demonstrations and laying out the basis for the phraseology in a classic book cowritten by Charles V Hamilton.[17]

Giving birth to the prideful assertion that 'Black is beautiful!' and to the internationally appealing concept of 'Black Consciousness' (as reflected, for instance, in the South African / Azanian movement's parallel phrase and embodied in the work of Steve Biko), the concept of Black Power completed the task of reclaiming the word, including a *very* capitalised 'B!' Though Black Power itself was never a template for revolutionary programmes (Black-owned businesses, for example, could just as easily work within a capitalist model), the Black Panther Party and the related Black Liberation Army, which came to the forefront of the US movement following King's assassination in 1968, had an overtly revolutionary nationalist and internationalist programme.[18] The embracing and naming of 'Black' as the forefront of revolutionary organisation among people of African descent in the US, South Africa, and elsewhere underscored a political sophistication which rejected old notions of European wording and asserted an anti-colonial internationalism that was neither strictly African nor unconnected to African roots.

It is no coincidence that by the mid-1970s, however, and following the assassinations of both Malcolm X and of Martin Luther King, Jr in the 1960s, the label 'African American' became a favourite within the mainstream US media. It was a term that was easy to line up next to 'Irish American' or 'German American' or 'Chinese American'—on the road to an apparently 'level playing field' and to a period of colour-blindness. Followers of Stokely Carmichael (who, like many of his generation renamed himself based on traditional African names—in his case, adopting the name Kwame Ture after two freedom fighter mentors, Ghana's Kwame Nkrumah and Guinea's Sekou Toure) insisted on just using 'African' as their identifiers, without the 'American' modifier. Members of the Malcolm X Society (made up of friends and radical associates of Malcolm X) developed a new term altogether: 'New Afrikan'. This self-description was based on an understanding that a new sociocultural identity had been formed in the years of enslavement and post-slavery terror, a merged identity born of the struggle and of the mixing of diverse West and Central African ethnic groups with Indigenous and European customs. This 'New Afrikan' nation also developed its programmes based on the political-economic centrality of a land base; it argued that the five southern states in the US where slavery was most central (South Carolina, Georgia, Mississippi, Alabama, and Louisiana) should make up a new, independent nation—separate from the USA and led by conscious New Afrikans.[19] Several organisations and individuals (including hip hop icon Tupac Shakur and recently mayor-elect of Jackson, Mississippi, Chokwe Lumumba) argue that this naming—of their identity and the movement of which they are a part—is the most historically powerful remedy to centuries of forced labour, citizenship, and injustice.

As unlikely as it may seem in contemporary realpolitik that a New Afrikan liberation movement will win military, political, or economic victories against the US, in many ways the New Afrikan movement is at the pinnacle of ideological self-determination and self-definition. Their outlook, while far from obvious in a traditional sense, is based on an analysis of the US that draws on a historical perspective that doesn't view it as a humanitarian democracy with some failings but as an imperial power based on premeditated capitalist designs and colonial military acquisitions. Given the revolutionary need to sharply and correctly name one's oppressor in order to overcome them, it would be foolish to ignore developments in the New Afrikan sector.

Empire, Power, and Solidarity

Understanding empire and understanding the unique ways in which the twentieth-century USA developed its empire is key to developing effective twenty-first-century anti-imperialist struggle. The US has long transcended early twentieth-century versions of colonial design. Only Puerto Rico still fits the traditional definition of what a colony was meant to be and is, thus, one of the last territories still under consideration by the United Nations Decolonisation Committee of 24.[20] The preferred practice within the US now is an 'internal colonisation' process. The reality of the country is that fifty states of the United States subsume hundreds of Native nations, almost one-third of the Mexican subcontinent, the schizophrenic Puerto Rican subnation of 'immigrants' living on the *main*land (who have 'full but second class' citizenship rights by virtue of their street address, losing and gaining nationality based entirely on residence),[21] and—most disputed—the Black / New Afrikan / African-American Nation. That these entities are, in fact, 'nations' is definitionally obvious as far as common language, culture, ethnicity, descent, and history are concerned, but the reality is that they lack the political and economic sovereignty to hold power over the 'mother country'—which makes them colonies, albeit in a non-traditional, internal sense. Leading US critics have shared an understanding of this, such as when Malcolm X focused upon 'human' rather than 'civil' rights as a case for UN consideration, and when Martin Luther King, Jr's confidant and speech writer Vincent Harding noted that the Civil Rights Movement should more correctly be called the pro-democracy, "southern-based, Black-led Freedom movement".[22]

Leading peace researchers and political economists have also begun to consistently write of the oncoming dissolution of the US Empire. Johan Galtung, for instance, speaks of an inevitable ten-year decline in US hegemony, followed by the possibilities of an increasingly divided and closed fascist society or, very much on the other hand, the flourishing of beloved communities of decentralised justice.[23] While the word 'fascism' itself is fraught with poor and uncertain usage,[24] it is clear that 'false consciousness' among US progressives has led to general confusion regarding how to build revolutionary united fronts with principled anti-imperialist programs.[25]

Equally, Samir Amin's work begins to outline, for anti-imperialists the world over, the urgent tasks ahead in countering the diminishing US imperial project. He asserts that a strategic audacity must exist within movements located both inside the imperialist centre and outside of it, each with a response particular to the challenge of their place in the global order.[26]

It should be clear that national liberation movements, which provided leadership for revolutionary change in the past century, no longer play such a central role. It is not simply that the victorious among such movements ended up winning little more than 'flag independence', as Mwalimu Julius Nyerere of Tanzania put it.[27] Over recent decades, the prominence of the nation-state itself has also receded on a world scale, as multinational corporations and regional entities have replaced nations in terms of influence and power.[28] Some socialist-oriented national projects continue—such as Venezuela, which has not only pulled itself out of impoverishment over the last decade, but whose oil-rich Bolivarian radicals were at one point even able to offer discounts and subsidies to impoverished inner city neighbourhoods in the USA.[29] But in Occupied Palestine and elsewhere, despite the abomination of settler colonialism and neocolonialism, statehood, as the leading solution to oppression at all levels, no longer holds out the promise it did only a quarter-century ago. And the spectre of failed states across the world and the failure to produce socialism in an isolated country (Cuba notwithstanding) has cast too long a shadow.

The word 'solidarity', in a revolutionary twenty-first-century non-state-based context, is thus also in urgent need of review and resuscitation. Mozambique's Samora Machel noted that true solidarity must mean two fists coming together to strike a single blow against a common enemy. This vision, which goes well beyond the top-down, paternalistic notions common to North-South solidarity that resemble 'aid' rather than mutual cooperation, relates well to the notion of solidarity as a "transformative political relation" which de-emphasises actions of left elites and prefigures a new anti-neoliberal internationalism.[30]

Ironically, the contemporary understanding and exercise of internationalism and solidarity in many ways harks back to the days of Bandung in 1955, when the leaders of African and Asian descent who shared common ground in their resistance to direct European colonialism gave birth to the Non-Aligned Movement (NAM). Gathering in Sukarno's socialist Indonesia under the leadership of Pan-Africanist Kwame Nkrumah of Ghana, Pan-Arab Gamal Nasser of Egypt, as well as India's Nehru and Yugoslavia's Tito, Bandung represented a South-South interstate solidarity which viewed as similarly problematic the neocolonial interests of both the US and the Soviet Union. While initially an economic forum, it established ongoing state-to-state dialogue for strategising about how best to counter the foreign quest for control of land and other natural resources that was present even before the postcolonial period began.[31]

The notion of a 'Third World'—emphasising the possibility of alternative paths of development that are neither capitalist ('First World') nor state communist ('Second World')—arose out of this movement and came to define wider geographic and demographic spaces that are today referred to as 'the South', reaching well beyond Afro-Asian literal or cultural borders. The spirit of Bandung continues to inform many movement actors, especially given the assault of borderless multinational corporations which immiserate communities around the world—from land dispossession and displacement to mass killings of those who dare to resist. Solidarity and resistance within and between peoples of the South now mark new possibilities for power over imperial and sub-imperial gatekeepers.

Fundamental Struggles over Meanings

As explosive conflicts over land, gender, and power emerge sharply throughout the world in our times, the issues of anti-colonial national liberation struggles and of identity politics that were so central to the previous era are today intersecting starkly and fundamentally with theocratic, orthodox, fundamentalist groups of the current era, with some leading examples to be found in, for instance, Palestine / Israel and northern Nigeria. To take our discussion forward, we want here to look at the latter.

The abduction in April 2014 of 276 female students from the Government Secondary School in Chibok, in Borno State in northern Nigeria, showed starkly how land, gender, and geopolitical competitions are intimately intertwined. A close look at what happened—and seen from *within* Nigeria and the region, and not from outside with Northern eyes—reveals the many ways in which control of raw materials and natural resources is increasingly subject to the interconnected forces of patriarchy, religious fundamentalism, and globalised militarisation, which can then in turn become the basis of cultural and political resistance to Empire—even if a resistance that may be very different and alien for many of us.

The entire Sahel-Sahara region has become one of the planet's most intensely contested terrains, as the scramble for uranium, petroleum, diamonds, and coltan has given rise to international arms deals, drug trafficking, mercenaries, and corruption. And here too, the deliberate misuse of words and the classic colonialist tactic of the appropriation of control over meanings through renaming, has been and remains a major impediment to dealing with the crisis of the abduction. Specifically, and as a direct result of the use—and widespread broadcast—of this term by Northern governments and media, the group that did the abduction is now known across the world as Boko Haram, and—equally important—as an Islamist jihadist group linked to al-Qaeda. It is vitally important, however, if we want to effectively understand and combat the reactionary policies of both decentralised political Islam and centralised neoliberal capitalism that we both name things correctly and also contextualise them, with cultural respect and without sloppiness or caricature.

The real name of the group that is responsible for the abductions is not 'Boko Haram' but Ahi al-Sunna Li'l-D'awa wa'l-Jihad 'ala Minhaj as-Salaf (the 'Association of the People of the Sunna for the Missionary Call and the Armed Struggle, according to the Method of the Salaf', in Arabic). This name may not fit into a neat Western sound bite, but as the name employed by the founders and members of the Nigerian group, it conveys a precise and authentic message about the politics of power in the region.

The reality is that the term *boko* is one that was originally used during the British colonial rule of Nigeria, especially by the peoples of the Hausa-dominated north—which is where the 2014 abduction took place—refers not to a resistance to Western education alone, but rather to the imposition of any educational system which undermines and erases local traditions and Islamic culture or fails to deliver promised socioeconomic advantages. The common translation in English of the words Boko Haram—'western education is forbidden'—is therefore a misnomer and an oversimplification that comes directly out of colonial prejudices[32] that is now part of a Western / Northern media fixation on the idea that 'western education is forbidden'.

Furthermore, if we use the actual and full title of the fundamentalist organisation popularly called Boko Haram, the abduction of the female students can be easily and immediately linked—both linguistically and politically—to the armed Salafist movements so prevalent in and funded by certain Saudi Arabian Muslim groups. Thus, the change of name maintained outside of the Muslim and African worlds needs to be understood not merely as being a condensed title; it also conveniently directs attention away from the group's connections to the leading loyal ally of the West and of international capital. and at the same time equates legitimate anti-colonial struggle (and, by extension, anti-neocolonial and neoliberal efforts) with religious fanaticism and terror methods.[33]

These correctives are vitally important because they reveal both the organisation's root connections and sponsors and expose the Islamophobia of Western / Northern mass media. The Western media has in fact worked hard to sensationalise the issue by transforming the meaning of Boko Haram from its intended rejection of the governing institutions in the region by a select few Islamic orders in northern Nigeria—in other words, a local (or at most, a local-regional) struggle over meanings—to a wholesale representation of Islam throughout Africa. Although the majority of Sunni Muslims of the region, and also the Muslim elite in the north, are against the destructive ideology of this movement, and while there is also no doubt that the movement developed from a Sunni Islamic tradition in Nigeria, the portrayal of them as 'simple Muslim fanatics' covers up both the more complicated truth and also the ways in which the organisation's actions are based not only on religious precepts but on the larger regional questions of land, resource control, and power.

Feminist autonomist Silvia Federici has described how, while the 'land question' may be a dim memory for many leftists in the North (where most land has already been ultra-developed and is now corporate controlled), "in most of Africa, communal land relations still survive . . . a factor bemoaned by leftist and rightist developers alike as the main reason for Africa's economic 'backwardness'".[34] In short, and although the Ahi al-Sunna Li'l-D'awa wa'l-Jihad 'ala Minhaj as-Salaf can in no circumstance be seen as a progressive or positive force, it is nevertheless important for us in the rest of the world to understand it outside of a simplistic 'black and white' defined world, just as a previous generation's 'East-West' obsessions failed to fully understand the Non-Aligned Movement and the significance of independent action and ideology from the South.[35]

A parallel and vital aspect of these politics is the equally sustained misrepresentation of the position and role of women—of women in society and of women in movement. The reality is that it is still true in the second decade of the twenty-first century that women make up a significant part of the world's unregulated and non-formal workforce. This makes them not only a target for super-exploitation but also a potential motor force for revolutionary change. Success stories centring on women taking on multinational corporate, dictatorial, and oppressive power structures abound—from throughout Nigeria,[36] to specific campaigns of the Ijaw women's movement against transnational oil corporations in the Niger Delta region,[37] to the Liberian women's peace actions for a just end to the civil war,[38] and in the work against autocracy, corruption, and underdevelopment in Kenya by Wangari Maathai and the Green Belt Movement.[39] These are but a few examples of success on the African continent alone. Similarly, women and men who fall outside of the traditional, highly structured credit system, such as those in Zapatista-controlled Mexico, are free to discover new directions of revolutionary engagement.[40] Our ability to support, develop, and unite with these movements is at least in part dependent on our ability to understand the fundamental origins, goals, and meanings of the conflicting struggles around us.

On Revolution and Non-Violence: A Half-Century of Divisive False Dichotomies

As Patrick Bond has recently noted, an urgent task for contemporary movements is to "treat the non-governmental organization disease of silo-isation: being stuck in our little specializations with historic privileges intact, unable to lift up our heads and use the full range of human capacities to find unity".[41]

Perhaps the most vexing false dichotomy still perpetuated throughout much of the left is the concept—alluded to earlier—that revolution and non-violence are opposites. At best, the idea that revolution always requires some armed component and that non-violence always connotes reformism are regarded as almost incontestable truisms despite a growing body of evidence to the contrary. Some may well argue that most modern revolutions which have included armed components do, in fact, fully comply with international guidelines regarding self-defence, self-determination, and the acceptance of the right of armed combatants in anti-colonial struggle. It can also be argued that too many campaigns using the monikers of 'non-violence' and 'pacifism' have been misused to support the status quo of state violence and oppression (which should be viewed as far worse than reformist, and rather as counter-revolutionary and violent in their essence). Nevertheless, the potential conclusions that armed struggle is revolutionary and that non-violence is, by definition, not revolutionary presents a problematic which too many movements of the North and South appear still to be stuck in.

To negotiate this ground, we must always be more careful with our words. If we wish to break free from tired old debates that are no longer relevant to the conditions faced in many communities, we must learn some linguistic and political lessons based on the past half-century of movement building.

Examining Mohandas Gandhi's advocacy of militant civil disobedience, it can be made clear that his confrontational tactics were a new way of looking at non-violence, one which at first had as many detractors as it did supporters. Like King, Mandela, and so many others iconised in less grand and global ways, the movement lessons of these tactics have been surgically removed, leaving us with a saintly hero whose work is impossible to replicate. Post-Gandhian leaders in India—most notably socialist activist Jayaprakash Narayan (JP)—attempted to deepen and broaden Gandhi's methodology, calling for a 'Total Revolution' that would merge militant non-violence with a desire to dislodge all oppression and transform society from the roots.[42] But these examples, pushing non-violent techniques to as revolutionary objectives as possible, have been left largely unstudied, unknown, and therefore underutilised in the current context—in India and throughout the world.

'Revolutionary non-violence'—a powerful and meaningful term that grew out of these experiments for use of militant, non-violent direct action in revolutionary situations—has begun to generate some interest, despite it being largely underdeveloped in philosophical and practical terms. This only occasionally used phrase—primarily cited by small, radical sectors of the peace movement alone[43]— nonetheless keep coming up in debate and dialogue all over the world. Frantz Fanon's insightful texts on the psychological significance of armed struggle, for instance, were met with feminist Barbara Deming's eloquent urgings for an experimental "revolution with equilibrium".[44] But deeper interrogation of the nexus between Fanon, Deming, or other such thinkers has barely begun. Fanon's own key essay on 'Why we choose violence'—which was based on his reflections on the Algerian war for independence and delivered to a Pan-African conference as far back as in the early 1960s—was only translated into English from the original

French forty years later, in 2015, and the publication has yet to receive widespread circulation.[45]

Similarly, many treatises on the failures of non-violence, perhaps most famously in the post-Sharpeville anti-apartheid struggle, have been shown to be at best severely limited in scope.[46] And the warnings of the greatest guerrilla commanders, such as Guinea-Bissau's Amílcar Cabral, have been edited to half-truths with their messages missed or lost. The phrase that Cabral famously used when directing his troops, "Tell no lies, claim no easy victories", has been widely broadcast, but the rest of his message is always omitted. What he also said, very meaningfully, was meant to warn his vanguard armed forces to guard against an "attitude of militarism" and to never forget the fact that there is a significant distinction to be made between militants and militarists.[47]

In the wake of contemporary movement against police brutality in the USA and the #BlackLivesMatter upsurge, which at its core is a manifestation of anti–white supremacy, the revolution versus reform, violence versus non-violence debate has resurfaced with a fury. Some young commentators have understood that there is no such dichotomy, rather, that there is a dialectical relationship between the strategies, tactics, and ideologies employed, and furthermore that "both these wings of the movement . . . ultimately need each other". Then as now, "each wing of the movement essentially helped create space for the other to operate. . . . The differences . . . will only allow their common enemy to divide and conquer them as the powerful have done to past movements. If they're smart, the moderates and militants won't allow themselves to be hoodwinked by this old trick. Instead, their unity lets them pull some tricks of their own".[48]

One new call might well be to 'refuse to choose between Malcolm X and Martin Luther King, Jr'. This was a choice that may possibly have been necessary in 1962, at the height of the time when the two men were critiquing one another, but it is surely not needed today. Both men and the parts of the movements they led contributed deep and different insights into the nature of modern oppression and the most effective ways to combat it. Each also grew and learned in their final years, eventually coming to similar conclusions about the importance of class issues in addition to the racial justice issues they championed, about the need for an internationalist perspective, and even regarding an openness about coalition building across diverse tactics, strategies, and ideologies.[49]

An understanding of the dialectical thinking and lessons which undercut unnecessary divisions and divisiveness has proven important in every historical situation where one might apply it—from North America to Asia, Africa, and beyond.[50] Most late-twentieth-century revolutions (and perhaps many earlier ones as well) have combined violent and non-violent aspects, with many armed activists—including the proud combatants of Mozambique—suggesting that a high price has been paid in post-revolutionary society for an unchecked use of an overly militarised perspective in bringing about radical change.[51] A growing body of research suggests that non-violent means have been far more effective than was previously considered,[52] and that non-violent rather than traditional military approaches can be more effective in isolating and defeating indigenous grassroots paramilitaries, such as in the Nigerian context of Ahi al-Sunna Li'l-D'awa wa'l-Jihad 'ala Minhaj as-Salaf (aka 'Boko Haram'). These tactical and strategic means and the ends which result from different actions are in need of much greater and deeper academic exploration and activist reflection—including how one may best define 'violent acts' that are carefully designed to not harm civilians or are essentially carried out against property.[53]

Speaking Truth to Power: Turning Speech Freedoms into Strong Voices

No matter where and when this takes place, one can always feel the divides which still exist between us when a word as innocuous as 'peace' is used in a movement context—divides that make some feel weak and impotent; and similarly, when fist-pumping calls for 'people's power' or for 'Black Power' make others feel threatened. Some pacifists change the words of popular phrases to muted cries of 'Power to the Peaceful', while militants implore their fallen comrades to 'Rest in Power'. Whether peaceful or not, revolutionary thinking must address the root issues of power and powerlessness. We can no longer afford divides that imply that only minor reforms are open for discussion.

In our travels across borders and our dialogues within movements, both co-authors of this piece found ourselves debating words at a book launch at Columbia University in New York. Because the book was on African affairs and Matt was one of the editors, another speaker—in an act of kindness and connectedness—said of this Brooklyn-born man of European descent: "Oh, but truly Matt is an African!" Ousseina, the next speaker, was compelled to disagree: "In his heart and ours he may be a great *ally* of Africa, but he doesn't have to be African for that".

Our examination in this essay of the need for a more careful use of words brings us back to that evening and the ongoing need to not only be more precise in our language and our naming but also in how we understand the contours of movement building. We are not all the same and should not need or want to be. Pretending otherwise—like pretending that we live in colour-blind societies or that we can 'be' at peace just because no one happens to be hitting us at the moment—doesn't sharpen our vision. It blurs it.

A precise and concise use of words can very significantly help us further our objectives. This becomes most significant when the words we are using bear special meaning for the movements we are struggling to build—be they 'non-violent' or 'violent', 'Black', 'white', 'African', 'Indigenous', and / or other, fighting against 'empires' internal and / or external, working in 'solidarity' in whatever manner seems most effective, and whether using English or the chorus of other languages for which this essay has only provided two limited examples: the legacy of Mahatma (meaning 'Great Soul') Gandhi and the strategic meanings and use of the term 'Boko Haram'. If our movements of movements aim to ultimately centre on fundamental global transformation—around 'revolution' in all its forms and multiple interconnected meanings—then the need for clarity, unity, and power becomes nothing short of essential. Like 'revolution' and 'non-violence', we must build our movements in ways that celebrate continuums rather than overemphasise competitive constructs.

As Viet Nam's Ho Chi Minh taught us all, our job is to make the world we leave behind "ten times more beautiful" than the one we inherit.[54] With this in mind, we must make our very words more beautiful, filled with the power to build bridges across borders, ideologies, and peoples. We must refuse to choose between non-violence and revolution, looking instead to fit our actions and strategic thinking to the specific places and spaces around us, rather than adopt foreign and imperial names or outmoded concepts. We must revitalise our voices, reclaim words that describe our power, and discard those terms that serve only to confuse, distort, or divide. From an urban world trade centre city to a rural village of unenclosed common land, our own personal movements inform us about our political-economic movements. It is a time, once more, to teach one another how best to speak.

References

Ousseina Alidou, 2005—'Through the Eyes of Agaisha: Womanhood, Gender Politics, and Tuareg Armed Rebellion', in Ousseina Alidou, 2005—*Engaging Modernity: Muslim Women and the Politics of Agency in Postcolonial Niger*. Madison: University of Wisconsin Press, pp 171–84

Ousseina Alidou, 2010—'Rethinking the Nation in Post-War Reconstruction in Niger Republic', in Elavie Ndura-Ouedraogo, Matt Meyer, and Judith Atiri, eds, 2010—*Seeds Bearing Fruit: Pan African Peace Action for the Twenty-First Century*. Trenton, NJ: Africa World Press, pp 359–78

Ousseina Alidou, Summer 2014—'The Militarization of the Sahel Region and the Abduction of the Chibok School Girls', in *African Studies Association Women's Caucus Newsletter*, pp 13–19

Samir Amin, 2014—'Popular Movement towards Socialism: Their Unity and Diversity', in *Monthly Review*, vol 66 no 2, at https://monthlyreview.org/2014/06/01/popular-movements-toward-socialism/ (Accessed October 1 2017)

Margiej Bartkowski, 2013—*Recovering Nonviolent History: Civil Resistance in Liberation Struggles*. New York: Lynne Reinner

Scott H Bennett, 2003—*Radical Pacifism: The War Resisters League and Gandhian Non-violence in America, 1915–1963*. Syracuse, NY: Syracuse University Press

Joshua Bloom and Waldo E Martin, 2014—*Blacks against Empire: The History and Politics of the Black Panther Party*. San Francisco: University of California Press

Patrick Bond, March 2015—'Disconnecting the minerals-energy-climate dots: Intersectionality missing-in-action at Cape Town's Alternative Energy Indaba', in *Pambakuza News*, March 4 2015, at http://allafrica.com/stories/201503131682.html

Andrew Boyd, with Dave Oswald Mitchell, compilers, 2012—*Beautiful Trouble: A Toolbox for Revolution—From the People Who Brought You the YES Men, Billionaires for Bush, Etc*. New York: O/R Books

Erica Chenoweth and Maria J Stephan, 2011—*Why Civil Resistance Works: The Strategic Logic of Nonviolent Conflict*. New York: Columbia University Press

James H Cone, 1991—*Malcolm and Martin and America: A Dream or a Nightmare?*. New York: Orbis Books

Chris Crass and the Catalyst Project, 2012—'Occupy Resource Center', on *Catalyst Project: Anti Racism for Collective Liberation*, at http://collectiveliberation.org/resources/occupy-resource-center/ (Accessed August 26 2017)

Franz Fanon, 2015 [April 1960]—'Why We Use Violence'. Translation by Timur Ucan. Accra, Ghana: Conference on Peace and Security in Africa

David Featherstone, 2012—*Solidarity: Hidden Histories and Geographies of Internationalism*. London: Zed Books

Silvia Federici, September 2001—'The Debt Crisis, Africa, and the New Enclosures', in *Midnight Notes*, September 10 2015, at http://www.midnightnotes.org/pdfneweng2.pdf (Accessed August 26 2017)

Francis Fukuyama, Summer 1989—'The End of History?', in *The National Interest*, at http://www.wesjones.com/eoh.htm#source (Accessed August 26 2017)

Johan Galtung, 2009—*The Fall of the US Empire: And Then What?*. Grenzach-Whyen, Germany: TRANSCEND University Press

Leymah Gbowee, 2011—*Mighty Be Our Powers: How Sisterhood, Prayer, and Sex Changed a Nation at War*. New York: Beast Books

Eddie James Girdner, 2013—*Socialism, Sarvodaya, and Democracy: The Theoretical Contributions of M N Roy, J P Narayan, and J B Kripalani*. New Delhi: Gyan Publishing House

Global Information Network, 2015—*Burundi-Watchers See Erosion of Human Rights and Civic Freedoms*. New York: Global Information Network

Kathleen Gough, 1978—*Ten Times More Beautiful: The Rebuilding of Vietnam*. New York: Monthly Review Press

Vincent Harding, 2010 [1990]—*Hope and History: Why We Must Share the Story of the Movement*. Maryknoll, NY: Orbis Books

François Houtart, 2018—'We Still Exist', in Jai Sen, ed, 2018—*The Movements of Movements, Part 2: Rethinking Our Dance*. Volume 5 in the *Challenging Empires* series. New Delhi: OpenWord, and Oakland, CA: PM Press

G Howard, 2015—'Welcome to the New Reach Center', at http://www.reachctr.org/index.html (Accessed August 26 2017)

International Indian Treaty Council, 2015—'IITC Submits Urgent Communication to the United Nations', February 17 2015, on *Last Real Indians*, at http://lastrealindians.com/for-immediate-release-iitc-submits-urgent-communication-to-the-united-nations-citing-human-rights-violations-and-death-threats-against-indigenous-human-rights-defenders-in-mexico/ (Accessed August 26 2017)

Ashoka Jegroo, Spring 2015—'Revolution and Reform: Martin's and Malcolm's Tactics, Strategies and Ideology in the BlackLivesMatter Movement', in *The CUNY Graduate Center Advocate*, Spring 2015, vol 26 no 1, pp 22–27

Jeffrey S Juris, 2005c—'Violence Performed and Imagined: Militant Action, the Black Bloc and the Mass Media in Genoa', in *Critique of Anthropology*, volume 25 no 4, pp 413–32

Xochitl Leyva Solano and Christopher Gunderson, 2017—'The Tapestry of Neo-Zapatismo: Origins and Development', in Jai Sen, ed, 2017—*The Movements of Movements, Part 1: What Makes Us Move?*. Volume 4 in the Challenging Empires series. New Delhi: OpenWord, and Oakland, CA: PM Press

Audre Lorde, 1984—'Age, Race, Class, and Sex', in Audre Lorde, 1984—*Sister Outsider*. New York: Crossing Press

Matthew N Lyons, March 2011—'Two Ways of Looking at Fascism', in *Socialism and Democracy*, March 8 2011, at http://sdonline.org/47/two-ways-of-looking-at-fascism/ (Accessed August 26 2017)

Wangari Maathai, 2009—*The Challenge for Africa*. New York: Pantheon

Ifeamo N Malo, 2011—'Positive Peacemaking and the Women of Nigeria', in Elavie Ndura-Ouedraogo, Matt Meyer, and Judith Atiri, eds, 2010—*Seeds Bearing Fruit: Pan African Peace Action for the Twenty-First Century*. Trenton, NJ: Africa World Press, pp 257–84

Roel Meijer, 2017—'Fighting for Another World: Yusuf al-'Uyairi's Conceptualisation of Praxis and Permanent Revolution', in Jai Sen, ed, 2017—*The Movements of Movements, Part 1: What Makes Us Move?*. Volume 4 in the *Challenging Empires* series. New Delhi: OpenWord, and Oakland, CA: PM Press

Matt Meyer, 2011—'Occupation: Liberation—Building Sustainable Resistance Movement', on *The War Resisters League Blog*, at https://warresisters.wordpress.com/2011/11/29/occupation-liberation-building-sustainable-resistance-movements/ (Accessed August 26 2017)

Matt Meyer, 2012—'The Marriage of Gandhi and Che', in Andrew Boyd, with Dave Oswald Mitchell, compilers, 2012—*Beautiful Trouble: A Toolbox for Revolution— From the People Who Brought You the YES Men, Billionaires for Bush, Etc*. New York: O/R Books

Matt Meyer, 2014—'Rebuilding Revolutionary Nonviolence in an Anti-Imperialist Era', in *Peace Review: A Journal of Social Justice* 03/2014; vol 26 no 1, pp 69–77, at http://www.tandfonline.com/doi/abs/10.1080/10402659.2014.876319 (Accessed August 26 2017)

Matt Meyer, ed, 1992—*Puerto Rico: The Cost of Colonialism*. Nyack, NJ: Fellowship of Reconciliation

Matt Meyer, Mandy Carter, and Elizabeth Martínez, 2012—*We Have Not Been Moved: Resisting Racism and Militarism in 21st Century America*. Oakland, CA: PM Press

Ruth Milkman, Stephanie Luce, and Penny Lewis, 2015—'Occupy Wall Street', in Jeff Goodwin and James M Jasper, eds, 2015—*The Social Movements Reader: Cases and Concepts*. Chichester, West Sussex: John Wiley and Sons Ltd, pp 30–44

Thomas Mosch, 2005—'*Nigeria: Une Société Civile Très Eveillée, mais fragmentée*' ['Nigeria: A Civil Society Very Awakened but Fragmented', in French], in *L'Autre Afrique* ['The Other Africa', in French], pp 22–24

Imari Abubakari Obadele, 1984—*Free the Land: The True Story of the Trials of the RNA-11 in Mississippi and the Continuing Struggle to Establish an Independent Black Nation in Five States of the Deep South*. Jackson: House of Songhay

Occu-evolve, 2012—'A New Day in Occupy: Our 10 Point Declaration of Interdependence with the 99%', at http://occuevolve.com/what-is-occu-evolve/about/a-new-day-in-occupy-our-10-pt-declaration-of-interdependence-wthe-99/ (Accessed August 26 2017)

J Reardon, 2011—'US Poor to Benefit from 6th Year of Subsidized Venezuelan Heating Oil', on *Venezuelanalysis.com*, January 28 2011, at https://venezuelanalysis.com/news/5965 (Accessed August 26 2017)

J Sakai, 2014 [1983]—*Settlers: The Mythology of the White Proletariat*. Montreal: Kersplebedeb Publishing, 2014 [Chicago: Morningstar Press, 1983]

William W Sales, 1999—*From Civil Rights to Black Liberation: Malcolm X and the Organization of Afro-American Unity*. Boston, MA: South End Press

Nathan Schneider, 2013a—*Thank You, Anarchy: Notes from the Occupy Apocalypse*. San Francisco: University of California Press

Nathan Schneider, 2013b—'Occupy Studies Itself', December 14 2013, on *Waging Nonviolence*, at http://wagingnonviolence.org/2013/12/occupy-studies/ (Accessed August 26 2017)

Bill Sutherland and Matt Meyer, 2000—*Guns and Gandhi in Africa: Pan African Insights on Nonviolence, Armed Struggle and Liberation*. Trenton, NJ: Africa World Press

Michael Thelwell and Stokely Carmichael, 2005—*Ready for Revolution: The Life and Struggles of Stokely Carmichael (Kwame Ture)*. New York: Scribner

Kwame Ture and Charles V Hamilton, 1967—*Black Power: The Politics of Liberation*. New York: Random House

Malcolm X, 1964—'The Ballot or the Bullet', talk at Cleveland, Ohio, USA, at https://www.youtube.com/watch?v=7oVW3HfzXkg (Accessed August 26 2017)

R J Young, 2005—'Postcolonialism: From Bandung to the Tricontinental', in *Historein* pp 1–16, at http://www.nnet.gr/historein/historeinfiles/histvolumes/hist05/historein5-young.pdf (Accessed August 26 2017)

Notes

1. Lorde 1984.
2. Ed: https://en.wikipedia.org/wiki/I_Shall_Not_Be_Moved (Accessed August 26 2017).
3. Meyer, Carter, and Martínez 2012.
4. The phrase 'Beautiful Trouble' in part refers to a recent book with the work of a collective of global radicals, titled *Beautiful Trouble: A Toolbox for Revolution—From the People Who Brought You the YES Men, Billionaires for Bush, Etc* (Boyd, with Mitchell, compilers, 2012). The volume brings out a wide variety of tactics, principles, theories, and case studies, 'assembled' (as opposed to authored or edited) by Andrew Boyd and a cast of thousands. It also has gone well beyond a simple book or even web-based resource guide; the Beautiful Trouble got 'more beautiful than ever' in 2015, as they launched Beautiful Solutions, an online gallery for sharing ongoing stories of struggle, as well as Beautiful Rising, a showcase of innovative

social movement from the southern hemisphere with connections in Myanmar / Burma, Uganda, Jordan, Zimbabwe, and El Salvador. With an emphasis on creative thinking, writing, messaging, and action, they have spotlighted new ideas that build creatively on classic progressive notions with the purpose of building newer, stronger movements. They can be reached at http://beautifultrouble.org/ (Accessed August 26 2017).

5.   Milkman, Luce, and Lewis 2015.

6.   Fukuyama, Summer 1989.

7.   Schneider 2013b; see also Schneider 2013a.

8.   For instance, in Crass and Catalyst Project 2012.

9.   See 'Unsettling America: Decolonizing in Theory and Practice', a blog site which has included a number of poignant critiques from Native Nations within North America, at https://unsettlingamerica.wordpress.com/2011/10/ (Accessed August 26 2017).

10.   Meyer 2011.

11.   Occu-evolve 2012.

12.   Jegroo 2015.

13.   Howard 2015.

14.   International Indian Treaty Council 2015.

15.   Sales 1999.

16.   Malcolm X 1964.

17.   Carmichael and Hamilton 1967.

18.   Ture and Martin 2014.

19.   Obadele 1984.

20.   Though Hawaii in many ways is even more overtly colonized than the US, its full incorporation as a state formally suggests that its status in international terms is resolved. Native Hawaiian peoples struggle within the United Nations and other international bodies as Indigenous Peoples, and a growing number present their struggles as anti-colonial in nature, but they are not under formal UN review. The situation of Guam, Samoa, and other US-related territories outside of the US continental land mass are noteworthy in the cultural sense but have seen little movement for social or status change, in part due to their extremely small populations and their almost complete economic reliance on tourism. For more in formation, see http://everything-everywhere.com/2013/06/27/everything-you-need-to-know-about-the-territories-of-the-united-states/ (Accessed August 26 2017).

21.   There is a wealth of information written about the unique colonization of the people of Puerto Rico, where an eighteen-year-old male based in San Juan can be drafted into the US Armed Forces but cannot vote in US Presidential or Congressional elections. A simple plane ticket and an address in one of the fifty states will automatically get this same person voting privileges. For more information, see Matt Meyer, ed, 1992—*Puerto Rico: The Cost of Colonialism* (Nyack: Fellowship of Reconciliation).

22.   Harding 2010.

23.   Galtung 2009.

24.   Lyons 2011.

25.   Sakai 2014 [1983]. Though the work of J Sakai and his book *Settlers* has been kept in print by various collectives, it is the anarchist movement in Canada which now

houses most of that work. In addition, the related text *False Nationalism, False Internationalism* sheds light on the global implications of this settler-colonial analysis. See Kersplebedeb for more information, at http://kersplebedeb.com/posts/settlers-the-mythology-of-the-white-proletariat-from-mayflower-to-modern/ (Accessed August 26 2017).
26. Amin 2014.
27. Sutherland 2000.
28. Alidou 2011.
29. Reardon 2011.
30. Featherstone 2012.
31. Young 2005.
32. Alidou 2014.
33. Ibid.
34. Federici 2001.
35. Ed: For a comparable analysis and discussion of this complex and difficult terrain, see the essay by Roel Meijer in the companion volume to this book on the life and struggle of Yusuf Al-'Uyairi, "the founder and first leader of al-Qaeda on the Arabian Peninsula . . . is regarded as among the foremost ideologues of Jihadi Salafism by both Jihadis themselves and terrorism experts" (Meijer 2017).
36. Malo 2011.
37. Mosch 2005.
38. Gbowee 2011.
39. Maathai 2009.
40. Ed: For a discussion of the emergence, cosmology, and politics of the Zapatista movement, see the essay by Xochitl Leyva Solano and Christopher Gunderson in the companion volume to this book (Leyva Solano and Gunderson 2017) and in this book by François Houtart (Houtart 2018).
41. Bond 2015.
42. Girdner 2013.
43. Bennett 2003.
44. Meyer 2012.
45. Fanon 2015 [1960].
46. Sutherland and Meyer 2000.
47. Meyer 2014. Ed: Again, for a discussion of this crucial ground in terms of the experience and practice of the Zapatista movement in Mexico, see the essay by Xochitl Leyva Solano and Christopher Gunderson in the companion volume to this book (Leyva Solano and Gunderson 2017).
48. Jegroo 2015.
49. Cone 1991.
50. Alidou 2005.
51. Bartkowski 2013.
52. Chenoweth and Stephan 2012.
53. Ed: For a rare discussion of this important ground, see Juris 2005a.
54. Gough 1978.

OpenWord

Break Free!
Engaging Critically with the Concept and Reality of Civil Society (Part 2)[1]
A Call to People Concerned with Justice, Peace, and Social Transformation
Jai Sen

[*This is Part 2 of a longer essay; for Part 1, see pp 65–113 above.*]

On Being Incivil

Does the answer perhaps lie not in struggling to be civil at all or in 'civilised transitions', but in *struggling to be incivil*—or rather, and crucially, in knowing how and when to be civil and when incivil, both from within civil societies and from within incivil societies? Something countless peoples have discovered throughout history, and which so many movements, in fact, understand.

As a counterpoint to my discussion and critique of civility up to this point, I think it makes sense for me to now talk, walk, and dance incivility a bit. But since 'being incivil' has such a vast and varied lineage—and since 'it' has not even been called this, so far—I feel I have to make clear that this section contains only some broad strokes to stake out some of the ground, and that I do not pretend to be thoroughly discussing the subject. That would require a different time, a different space, and, perhaps, first 'breaking down the barriers'. . .[2] In any case, I am perhaps only exploring here what many already know, pulling some of it together and putting it on the table. So, as somebody said before me: let's just do it!

Being incivil is not just about 'being the other' (let alone posturing or pretending to be incivil). Being incivil has a life of its own; a meaning, vocabulary, and discipline of its own; and a philosophy and cosmology of its own. It is a conscious position, an act of critical self-awareness. Incivility is not merely a label but a counterposition, another address (or '*thikana*', in Hindi), a counter-location, another way of thinking in movement, another way of dancing, and another level of dance.

(Yes, one can perhaps choose to be uncivil, and that too would be a conscious act—but even phrasing it like this brings out the stark difference between 'uncivility' and incivility.)[3]

Given that I have critiqued the fact that the term 'NGO' is the 'non' of government, I should perhaps clarify from the outset that although the term I am proposing, 'incivil', and therefore also the practice of incivility, perhaps sounds like the opposite of 'civil', there is a big difference. Most importantly, incivil is not in any way the 'non' of civil. (If anything, 'uncivil' might be.) To the contrary, incivil has a space of its own at the same 'level' as civil; in a way, its sibling, but not really.

As I see it, 'being incivil' (and / or choosing to be incivil) is—unlike 'NGO'—a positive (and strategically useful) address for people in movement, whether they belong the incivil or civil world. This is especially so given that the term and practice of civility is so fundamental to language and culture in perhaps all societies (and to the exercise of power-over); so even the most immediate connotation of the term 'incivil'—rebellious, mischievous, and even fun—is surely worth considering as a way to be. But there are many deeper meanings and practices of incivility, where being incivil disempowers the civil.

Focussing for a moment on those of us who feel we belong to 'civil society', a fundamental part of being incivil is—at the most basic level—just a matter of letting go; but we need to accompany 'letting go' with a realisation that we are who we are and behave as we do, *because* we have been civil-ised: that we have been tamed, domesticated, and taught to behave as we do. And to let go of all that.

Beyond this, being incivil is a moment—a chance in life—when one comes into command of one's full creative powers and breaks out into new level of existence. Given this, it is worth thinking of incivility and 'the incivil' not merely as a counter to civility and the civil, not even solely as 'resistance', but as *another way of being*, as *a different imaginary*—with a wide spectrum of possibilities—and as a voyage of discovery and a positive state in and of itself. Fundamentally, being incivil is an act of recovering oneself / ourselves, of being ourselves, and of asserting our selves; by virtue of all of this, it is simultaneously also a fundamental decentring and displacing of the centrality of the civil in the political discourse of dominant societies.

It's partly also a function of how you use the term and own it. Like some other terms, it is—or can be—contagious and insurrectionary. Think of the terms *Sufi*, *dance*, and *warrior*. Or *crack*. Or *rap*. Each of these words has a conventional meaning in dominant cultures—but these meanings have, as is the rule, all been attributed to them by those who are dominant in those societies. Now, however, by virtue of the incivil taking them over and repurposing them, along with other distinctly incivil uses, each one of these terms has other meanings and has become a term or a space that individuals and communities enter, occupy, and transform insurgently into a state of being.

On Being a Warrior
Consider the following as a fundamentally different exploration of and meditation on the meaning of the term 'warrior'—breaking out of the confines of the meanings that dominant society gives it and belonging to an entirely different cosmology:

> A Warrior is the one who can use words so that everyone knows they are part of the same family. A Warrior says what is in the people's hearts, talks about what the land means to them, brings them together to fight for it.
> —Bighorse, Diné

If there is an Onkwehonwe warrior creed, it is that he or she is motivated in action by an instinctual sense of responsibility to alleviate suffering and to recreate the condition of peace and happiness. The warrior's first battle is with himself or herself; having fought that battle his or her responsibilities are extended to immediate family and other human beings. The warrior takes action to change the conditions that cause suffering for the people in both the immediate (self-defence) and long-term (self-determination) sense. The warrior does not focus on abstract or historical injustice and believes wholeheartedly that the ability to generate change is within the power of the people.

What kind of people do we need to become in our personal transformations into warriors? There are myriad examples of cultures bringing to reality the universal concept of devotion to service, self-discipline, and the ethic of courage. The ideal was expressed most elegantly, perhaps, in the fourteenth century Japanese Samurai prayer that has come to be widely known among practitioners of the martial arts as the Warrior's Creed:

I have no divine power.
I make honesty my divine power.
I have no magic secrets.
I make character my magic secret.
I have no sword.
I make absence of self my sword.

The way of the new warrior is as much a tactical battle against the patterns of our modern existence as a philosophical and political struggle. The warrior will be reborn inside and among us if we simply do the things that make and have always made a warrior. . . .[5]

Similarly, consider the following:

Break. We are here to break. To break a continuity, to break policies, to break governments, to break the self-satisfied smile on the face of the mass murderers, to break capitalism. To break our own traditions, to break ourselves, to break their expectations, to break our own expectations. The future of the movement depends on our ability to break, to surprise them and to surprise ourselves.

Let us be careful, then, when we talk about the future of the movement. The danger of talking of the future is that we project the present, that we give things a definition and exclude the possibility of surprising ourselves. The movement is a series of breaks. The Zapatista uprising on the 1st of January 1994, Seattle in 1999, Heiligendamm [in 2007] perhaps. Any attempt to predict the future of the anti-capitalist movement just before those events would have been looking in the wrong direction.

The Free Association, in their article in *Turbulence*,[6] speak very beautifully of this process. Social movements articulate demands, but there often comes a moment of rupture, when a new problematic emerges and new perspectives open up, theoretically and practically. A new world is created: "[B]y envisaging a different world, by acting in a different world, we actually call forth that world. . . . Take the example of Rosa Parks who simply refused to move to the back of the bus. She wasn't making a demand, she wasn't even in opposition, she was simply acting in a different world". That, they suggest, is the importance of the big counter-summits: in the best of cases, they open up a new world, carry us into a whole new array of hopes and worries and ways of organising and acting that we had not foreseen and could not have foreseen.

Break, then, is the key to thinking of the future of the movement. . . .[7]

"You're the nigger, baby, it isn't me"

Let me now try and illustrate the idea I am putting forward with some examples from movement and struggle by both categories of the incivil, the structurally incivil and the consciously incivil.[8] I have already cited one example in the first part of this essay, the manner in which the African-American writer James Baldwin, when asked the question 'Who is the nigger?', answered, "You're the nigger, baby, it isn't me". Though I know I am repeating, let me again quote the key paragraph here:

> *I am not the victim here.* I know one thing from another. I know that I was born, and that I'm going to suffer, and that I'm going to die. The way you get through life is one of the worst things about it. I know that . . . a person is more important than anything—anything else. I know this because I've had to learn it. But you still think, I gather, that a nigger is necessary. Well, it's unnecessary to me. So it must be necessary to you. So I give you your problem back. *You're the nigger, baby, it isn't me.*[9]

By doing this, he completely turned the epistemological table on white racist society—and did so knowingly; and, I would say, in an act of profound and brilliant incivility.

A second example is not just the work but also the life of Taiaiake Alfred, who I have also already quoted. Though still quite young when he wrote his magisterial work *Wasasé*,[10] he had already developed with formidable discipline and rigour a whole body of thought. For instance, even when he discusses a seemingly well established subject such as globalisation or revolution, he challenges and implicitly rejects the dominant discourse around the subject and develops and puts forward his own; he flips the game.

In addition, to read him constantly reminds you of who you are and how and where you are located with respect to what he is discussing; it is a demanding and bracing exercise. Far from carrying you along, he demands that you be as rigorous as he is, that you move with him, and perhaps join him in the dance. For me, reading him always reminds me of the passage from his book quoted above: that he is constantly struggling to be a warrior and to dance the dance of a warrior, *Wasáse*. To read him infects you, contaminates you . . . and makes you aware of your self.

At quite another level, not the least of Alfred's intellectual and political accomplishments is something apparently very small that signifies—in relation to the demands of the intellectual academy that he now inhabits—militant and incivil resistance: the simple, seemingly innocuous fact that the majority of his references and citations are to works by other Indigenous authors—almost by definition lesser known—and not to members of Settler societies / civil societies (not even to the progressives and radicals in such societies, unless he is specifically discussing their work).[11] At one level, by ignoring established convention, he is both challenging academia and implicitly taking away the privileged central position that such scholars and / or activists otherwise occupy in terms of knowledge and wisdom, almost by assumed right (but in reality, of course, because of their / our location in the knowledge industry or the movement world). Indeed, I am constantly reminded when I read Alfred that after all is said and done it is the rest of us who, by constantly (usually, almost exclusively) relying on such sources and their insights, give them their power and constantly communicate their centrality to others, only further propagating their power.

At another level, I am sure that Alfred is acutely conscious of the historical context in which he does this—a time of the resurgence of Indigenous Peoples on Turtle Island (the term Indigenous Peoples use for what Settlers call 'North America').[12] It would be politically incorrect and very difficult for Settlers to question his decision to largely or even exclusively cite Indigenous authors in the current context. What he has done here, like James Baldwin, is an act of cultural-political *ju jitsu*.

Each one of these steps—small and big—challenges the system and turns things around, making Taiaiake Alfred's dance beautiful to behold.[13] It is almost like watching *capoeira*, the Brazilian martial dance, in exquisite and reverential slow motion. As in *capoeira*, the observer is inexorably drawn in to this cosmic dance of life. It is definitely *Wasáse*.

My third example is the work of Dr B R Ambedkar—Babasaheb, as he was popularly known—the great Indian scholar-activist and lawyer, a Dalit who founded the modern Dalit movement, and whom I cited in the first part of this essay.[14]

Through his writings but also through his actions throughout his life, Ambedkar challenged orthodoxies and built on the work of earlier reformers to forge a new consciousness of social relationships in Indian society, especially among Dalits, thereby laying the foundations of social revolution: a revolution that continues to unfold in our own time.[15] We are talking of someone who did everything from leading marches in the 1930s to opening temples and water tanks to Dalits—who, as 'untouchables' were and still are prohibited from entering and using them in some parts of India—to playing a leading role in drafting the constitution of the independent state of India during the late 1940s, then resigning from the first Parliament after India gained political independence in 1947 out of disgust with the decisions that his fellow parliamentarians were taking. He would later convert to Buddhism and leave the world of Hinduism, taking thousands of fellow Dalits with him.

Through his life and his work,[16] Ambedkar mastered the task of living and acting militantly in these two radically different and opposed worlds. He did this while waging—in the most civil yet also most profoundly incivil ways—one of the most difficult struggles of all against someone within what from outside looked like the same movement for independence and the democratisation of a colonised society and country, one that also suffered the profound internal colonisation of caste. His formidable opponent was no less a warrior than Mahatma Gandhi.[17]

I've never seen the use of the term 'dance' in relation to Ambedkar's extraordinary life or the extraordinary politics that he to all intents and purposes invented and practised, but he was most certainly a warrior in the Alfredian sense, and I think it could be very interesting for someone to attempt this task.

My next example is the breathtaking thesis put forward by John Murray Cuddihy in his book *The Ordeal of Civility: Freud, Marx, Lévi-Strauss, and the Jewish Struggle with Modernity*.[18] Cuddihy argues that because of major changes taking place in Eastern Europe, Jews migrated in large numbers into Central and Western Europe. Their very different customs made them the great domestic 'other' in nineteenth- and early twentieth-century Europe. Freud, Marx, and Lévi-Strauss (and other diasporic Jewish intellectuals), in the course of their own individual struggles with how to relate as Jews with civil society in Europe, consciously manoeuvred to not assimilate into the prevailing discourses as defined by the dominant Gentiles, which was what was expected of them. Instead, Cuddihy argues, they did nothing less than completely redefine their respective fields and—among other things—forge new discourses in their areas that completely redefined the 'other' that they belonged to, as well as developing new ways to see and to understand this 'other'. They not only succeeded in doing this, they also "drew upon their genius to construct theories calculated to tear away at what each felt was the superficial mask of Western—Christian—superiority".[19] And, therefore, in terms of the arguments of this essay, of 'civility'.

This is, of course, a very major and provocative thesis, and it arguably requires a mastery over the lives and work of the three individuals and of the period they lived in to be fully understood, let alone to be critically engaged with and interrogated—which I certainly don't have. But my reading of his book within the limits of my understanding suggests that Cuddihy's argument is certainly worthy of consideration—understanding what these individuals did in relation to, say, what Ambedkar and Gandhi have contributed in more recent times (I come to Gandhi below). Quite aside from the extraordinary intellectual contributions of each of these giants, what they did was also a truly astonishing cultural-political achievement; I would argue that what each did was not only 'intellectual' in nature but also a great act of incivility.

Let me jump forward in time, though plenty happened in the first half of the twentieth century that could be mentioned here, including in art and music. A completely different mode of incivility characterised Europe and North America, the 'advanced' and 'free' world, during the 1960s. I'd like to look here at the work of Jerry Rubin, a US American activist, anti-war leader, and counterculture icon of the 1960s and '70s, who along with social and political activist Abbie Hoffman and satirist Paul Krassner was one of the founding members of the Youth International Party (YIP), or Yippies,[20] and later the author of *Do It! Scenarios of the Revolution*[21]—and my inspiration for 'doing it' here!

I want to do so not because Rubin was himself especially extraordinary or unique, but because what he did, along with other activists at that time, played an important role in hugely widening—blowing open—what had till then been considered 'politics'. By being radically and creatively incivil and of using political theatre in movement to challenge and to change meanings, Rubin and others greatly influenced subsequent generations of activists, including in terms of the direct action that we see in our own time.[22] In his book, Rubin describes the inspiration drawn from the Dadaist movement, "an anti-rational, anti-art cultural movement" that took shape in Europe in the 1910s and then spread, through Marcel Duchamp and others, to the US. (One of the best-known works of the Dadaist movement is Duchamp's 'Fountain'—an everyday ceramic urinal turned upside down and presented as a work of art.)[23]

Rather than quoting from Rubin's book, which is difficult to do succinctly, given the way he writes, I could do worse than to quote Wikipedia:

> Rubin began to demonstrate on behalf of various left-wing causes after dropping out of Berkeley. Rubin also ran for mayor of Berkeley, on a platform opposing the Vietnam War, and supporting black power and the legalization of marijuana, receiving over twenty per cent of the vote. Having been unsuccessful, Rubin turned all his attentions to political protest.
>
> . . .
>
> . . . The Yippies were not a formal organization with a membership list or a direct relationship with constituency, but played upon the media's appetite for anything new and different. They were influenced by Marshall McLuhan's ideas on the importance of electronic communication, and believed that if radical events were made more entertaining the media, especially television would give them greater coverage.

As Rubin recollected:

> . . .[T]he more visual and surreal the stunts we could cook up, the easier it would be to get on the news, and the more weird and whimsical and provocative the theater, the better it would play.
>
> Rubin's appearance before the House Un-American Activities Committee (HUAC) hearings is a good example of the Yippies emphasis on conducting political protest as theater and creating as much attention as possible to their dissent by turning it into a spectacle. Rubin was subpoenaed by HUAC in Washington but instead of pleading the Fifth Amendment as was common, he entered the room dressed in a rented 18th-century American Revolutionary War uniform, proudly claiming to be a descendant of Jefferson and Paine. "Nothing is more American than revolution", he told the committee. Rubin showing total lack of concern or worries, lightheartedly blew soap bubbles as members of Congress questioned his Communist affiliations. He subsequently appeared before the HUAC as a bare-chested guerrilla in Viet Cong pajamas, with war paint and carrying a toy M-16 rifle, and later as Santa Claus.[24]

Rubin's actions and those of the Yippies were not unique; the 1960s was a time of a reinvention of politics in the United States and much more widely across the world.[25] The 1960s and '70s was also a time when many different streams of movement met and influenced each other, which, as I argued in the first part of this essay, only dramatically blossomed from the 1980s onwards with a kind of 'globalisation' that started taking place in movement and of movement. One of the most interesting outcomes of this globalisation has been the degree to which non-violent civil disobedience has become universal and the degree to which so-called 'ordinary' people have become involved in movement and in what I call incivil resistance: a breaking out of conventional bounds and a resistance—and overturning—of tradition and of so-called 'authority'.

One of the most interesting and inspiring examples of this breakout emerged from conflict-ridden Israel in the late 1980s—the Israeli anti-war Women in Black movement following the first Intifada, which then spread to many other countries and contexts. The women's simple and solitary action was to dress in black—a symbol of mourning for all victims of the conflict—and to conduct silent vigils in public spaces. I encountered their practice during different editions of the World Social Forum in the early and mid-2000s. It was simultaneously an act of deep civility and of profound incivility.[26]

Another example that emerged during the same period was the life and work of Chandralekha, the contemporary Indian dancer, choreographer, designer, and feminist, who died in 2006. Originally a dancer in the Bharatnatyam tradition—one of the highest and most orthodox of all Indian classical dance forms—and one of the most celebrated soloists in her field, she consciously moved away from performing in the late 1950s into an intense twenty-five-year period of reflection. She continued to be creative throughout this period in several other fields (writing, design, and feminist and human rights activism), but went deep into her self and into the traditions she had been schooled in during this time.[27] She emerged in the 1980s with an extraordinarily sensuous form of dance-theatre that fused everything that she was, that she had learned, and that she knew, believed in, and sensed. The dance she forged deeply challenged the orthodoxies of classical dance by positing a radically new interpretation of tradition and a vocabulary and syntax of dance and of body movement and expression that was stunningly new and 'radical' in the other and more generic sense. The form was widely understood as being 'erotic', but as Sadanand Menon explains, she was never afraid of the term or the idea; to the contrary, she celebrated this quality as a part of her reverence for the human body and for the deeper meanings of sensuality. She always explained that her dance was rooted in the fundamentals of tradition—she seemed to implicitly suggest that dance over time had been tamed and 'civilised' and needed, along with human beings, to be liberated.[28]

In terms of the viewer's experience (but perhaps also the performer's experience), her productions were an intensely sensual, deeply moving, and profound fusion of the personal and the political. In doing all this, by no means was she merely 'cocking a snook' at tradition and authority, and thereby 'being incivil' in the very superficial sense; to the contrary, she was—like Taiaiake Alfred is today—a warrior who meditated on life, and through her dance and choreography hugely contributed to new understandings of the life of dance and movement; and by doing this, also to the dance of movement, the dance of life.

Looking back on it, Chandra's work—her body of work and her work on and of the body—was a profound expression of the dialectics of incivility and an extraordinary and beautiful exploration of one of her favourite themes, the dialectical unity of life itself: of the feminine and the masculine, of (as she termed it) "inner and outer spaces", and of freedom and discipline.

There are many other examples, but I will give just one more to indicate this ground: music. Think of reggae, think of rap; and listen, for instance, to the group Indigenous Resistance.[29]

Finally, as an example of contemporary incivility and contemporary movement and action, I would like to cite Jeremy Brecher's discussion of what he argues is a "climate insurgency" taking shape, with ordinary people all over the world coming to realise that nation-states are not respecting their constitutional duty to protect the environment—to the contrary, are grossly violating it—and taking it upon themselves to non-violently enforce laws and to perform their fundamental legal duties to enforce the state's responsibility on it:

> The climate protection movement, by adopting civil disobedience, has moved beyond conventional political and lobbying 'pressure group' activity to become

a protest movement prepared to violate the law. Civil disobedience, while generally recognizing the legitimacy of the law, refuses to obey it. Civil disobedience represents moral protest, but it does not in itself challenge the legal validity of the government or other institutions against which it is directed. Rather, it claims that the obligations to oppose their immoral actions—whether discriminating against a class of people or conducting an immoral war or destroying the climate—*is more binding on individuals than the normal duty to obey the law.*

A constitutional insurgency goes a step further. It declares a set of laws and policies themselves illegal and sets out to establish law through nonviolent self-help. It is not formally a revolutionary insurgency because it does not challenge the legitimacy of the fundamental law; rather, it claims that current officials *are in violation of the very laws that they themselves claim provide the justification for their authority.* Such insurgents view those whom they are obeying as merely persons claiming to represent legitimate authority, but who are themselves violating the law under color of law—on the false pretense of legal authority. Their 'civil disobedience' is actually obedience to law, even a form of law enforcement.[30]

Once again, the movement is overturning the table at a very fundamental level.

Being Incivil

By citing these examples—each of which has to be seen in relation to the respective contexts and times in which they occurred—I am not trying to suggest a simple formula or vocabulary of being incivil but to indicate ground for us to dwell on and think about, perhaps even to consider occupying and inhabiting as our own.

I also do not mean to suggest that this 'overturning of the world' can only be done by the structurally incivil. Let me give one more example. One of the best known—and arguably, greatest—exponents of this militant art has, of course, been Gandhi. (Just for clarity, Gandhi was—aside from being male—a Hindu, by far the dominant religion in India (and not just Hindu but an ardent Hindu) of the *Kshatriya* caste by ancestry, an upper-middle caste. He was, therefore, from well within so-called 'civil society' in India, and he always insisted on respecting those norms.

As is well known, among Gandhiji's most powerful contributions were the concepts and practice of *non-violence* (or, in the original, *ahimsa*, which is a little different from the immediate and apparent meaning of 'non-violence') and of *civil disobedience.* Consider the practice of civil disobedience, which is now widely accepted as one of the most fundamental of all tactics and strategies in the repertoire of movement. This was not literally Gandhiji's own idea,[31] but even if his own life and practice were full of profound contradictions,[32] he explored and honed this tactic as political practice to extraordinary depths, including coining wholly new terms to express what he meant, such as *satyagraha* ('being tied to the truth' or 'the struggle for truth'—within oneself as much as in the outside world). Through his practice—both in 'action' and in the way he lived his life (a lifestyle he insisted that others in the communes he built adopt as well)—he developed and forged these concepts into powerful instruments of emancipation of self, community, and society—but also, brilliantly, of the other, his opponent. In turn, his tactics have subsequently been very widely adopted, adapted, and further developed as instruments of action and thought, including by Martin Luther King in the context of the Civil Rights Movement in the US in the 1950s and '60s. They have also been subsequently codified and widely adopted by many movements as part of their own vocabularies of social and political action.[33]

The discourse and praxis of 'civil disobedience' is in a sense especially interesting and important for our discussion here, for two reasons: one, insofar as the discourse and the practice specifically posits the imperative to *always be civil* during acts of civil disobedience no matter what the provocation or assault or how grave; and two, the accompanying, intertwined, and dialectically related imperative of *always being disobedient* when faced by a moral choice—in particular, to be disobedient towards one's opponent, and by implication, when one's opponent is the state, towards civil society, which is the state's earthwork. In Gandhi's case, the power against which he used this instrument most famously was the British Empire, which considered itself to be the fount of civility. He used the moral code of his 'other'—British civilisation—as the devastating means by which to delegitimise, disable, and over time disempower it; and he did this to such an extent that with the simultaneous crushing impact of the Second World War the entire edifice of the British Empire disintegrated and crumbled in the subsequent years. I therefore see Gandhi's thought and action—while labelled 'civil'—as fundamentally incivil.

Moreover, while I have deep reservations about some of Ghandi's practices, which I see as profoundly contradictory to what he professed, in his own way Gandhiji also struggled to be a warrior in the sense put forward by Taiaiake Alfred.

To a degree, it could even be argued that the World Social Forum—which as I said in the first part of this essay is absolutely 'civil' by self-definition—also started out as something of an experiment in conscious incivility. In its first incarnation, it was conceived as something of a 'incivil counter' (my words) to the World Economic Forum in several dimensions: in the name chosen—deliberately positing the centrality of the social rather than the economic; and insofar as it was over the first five years very consciously organised during the same days as the WEF (and, symbolically, in the South, while the WEF was held in a remote, heavily guarded, elite ski-resort in the mountains of the North). In short, the World Social Forum was consciously designed to create a counterposition in world space for that week, and the organisers paid a great deal of attention to getting international media coverage so that this act of incivility was enacted in public. To a considerable degree, they succeeded.

In addition, and very importantly, the WSF organising concept of 'open space' was also fundamentally opposed and counterposed to the conceptual closedness of the WEF and neoliberalism's mantra of 'There Is No Alternative'. Finally, the fundamental organisational idea of the World Social Forum—being an open space (even though its implementation was riddled with problems)[34]—in principle encouraged diversity and plurality of participants, which was also very different from the WEF.

That said, this was perhaps true of 'the young WSF'. As it moved into middle age, it lost its incivil, insouciant, and strategic outlook at life and politics and all too quickly became far more concerned about rules, about itself, and about territory, and as a result became far more careful and 'civil' (and all of the subconscious rules of 'civil society' and 'being civil' came into play).[35]

Equally, it could be argued that the conceptualisation and articulation of a regime of human rights—as enshrined in the Universal Declaration of Human Rights and in the constitutions of some nation-states—has a similar quality: the capacity of being used creatively and insurgently for confronting the state (and, I would argue, civil society) with its own professed ideas and standards, insisting that they be equally applied—that all human beings are equal.

Finally, there is the question of how we live our lives and the possibility of living organically other lives—lives that practice alternative values that challenge the limits of conventional discourse and exercise of power, through which we can all, in John Holloway's beautiful term, create 'cracks' in the system.[36]

Creating cracks—and, more importantly, being conscious of creating cracks—is not something 'new'; it is already practised quite widely in different dimensions. I have already indicated some practices that I believe are important—such as a primary reliance in our studies and our writing on material generated by people in struggle rather than by those who are outside, however well connected or well-meaning they might be. There are of course also many examples of people consciously living alternative lives in resistance and in celebration, with some of them having liberated whole areas and regions.[37] And in the time and space in-between, there is the possibility and necessity of expressing ourselves in 'other' ways, in our resistance to domination and the permanent colonialism that we all face, through the use of theatre, music, magic, puppetry, and dance in all its forms.[38]

The question still arises: Is this enough? Is civil disobedience, for instance, however remarkable a strategy it has been and is (see, for instance, Erica Chenoweth's powerful argument that non-violent civil resistance has historically been more effective in bringing about social transformation than strategies of violence),[39] enough to bring about the fundamental revolutionary changes that are required to address what we today face in the world?

The answer, as Bob Dylan once sang, may well be blowing in the wind. But what then, as the winds blow around us, are our next steps? What, in the dance of life, are our next moves? How do we do what the great Indian poet Rabindranath Tagore once sang of?

"Break all the barriers! Let the captive soul be liberated!"[40]

The World Social Forum as an Arena of Global Civility: Is This What Democracy Looks Like?

The dynamics of civility that I outlined in the third section of Part 1 of this essay[41] are of course not abstractions but play themselves out in our daily social and political lives at home, at work, and at local and global levels. To both illustrate this reality and to develop it, I look now at the World Social Forum, precisely because it is so widely regarded as an important contribution to social inclusion and global democratisation[42]—but also as an act of critical reflection, since I was intensely involved with the WSF process for a decade or more.[43]

At the risk of taking several liberties at once, I suggest—on the basis of my research on the history and dynamics of transnational civil alliances and my involvement in and reflection on the World Social Forum process—that while there is much reason to believe that 'the young WSF' was in many ways somewhat incivil in nature, the broad sketch of a process of 'civil' domination that I have attempted in this essay applies to the World Social Forum as it matured, and more generally to other alliances among civil organisations and movements: not uniformly, not absolutely, but all too widely.[44] An examination of the WSF in these terms also yields some insights into other, related tendencies of civil corporatisation and the exercise of civil power.

To speak of the civil domination of transnational alliances is not to say that the incivil of the world are not establishing transnational or global alliances—they are[45]—but it is to suggest that the *centres* of power in global civil alliance are still very strongly located in the North, and in the 'North within the South'; that these centres of power still very much lie with the middle and upper castes and classes and among white and fair males; and that many if not all transnational *incivil* alliances are still somewhat dependent on these power centres and have an uneasy relationship with them. This remains the case even if some incivil alliances are acutely aware of this centrality and reality of power and strategically work with it. One example is the *Minga* process that was launched by the Indigenous Peoples of Latin and Central America in 2009, with one foot in the WSF,[46] and another is the struggle of third-generation Dalits in India, who have equally consciously used the WSF as a convenient platform over the past decade or more, including organising a 'World Dignity Forum' at the World Social Forum in Mumbai, India, in 2004. Here, for instance, are the reflections of Paul Divakar, General Secretary of the National Campaign on Dalit Human Rights and a leading Dalit activist and organiser in India and in global space:

> The World Social Forum is an important platform to raise these issues. For us, it is easier to get through to civil society at the level of social organisations, so that we can ride on their shoulders for a while and ask them to also fight for our cause. The WSF also identified casteism as one of the main aspects of not just globalisation, not just of war and militarism, but also of patriarchy and communalism, and so we feel that if we have comrades who will join with us in this fight against casteism as part of their struggles, why not?[47]

Civilising Caste, Colour, Race, and Faith?

Notwithstanding this aspiration, the hard reality is that wherever mixed alliances have appeared, or even in most of the big actions in multicultural contexts like the US (such as at the protests against the WTO in Seattle in November 1999 or against the World Bank and the IMF in Washington, DC, in April 2000), Canada (the FTAA [Free Trade Agreement of the Americas] in Québec City, in 2001), the UK (the G8 at Gleneagles, in 2005), or Germany (Heiligendamm, in 2007), the consciously incivil have been prominently present, while peoples of colour, Indigenous Peoples, and the structurally incivil were hardly to be seen.[48] While, by and large, the consciously incivil strongly challenge this domination through their actions, perhaps all their initiatives were and still are dominated by members and organisations of civil society.

As Elizabeth Betita Martínez once so graphically put it in the title of her great essay on the issue: "*Where was the colour in Seattle?* Looking for reasons why the Great Battle was so white".[49] One of the activists Martínez interviewed in Seattle remarked:

> I was at the jail where a lot of protesters were being held and a big crowd of people was chanting 'This Is What Democracy Looks Like!'. At first it sounded kind of nice. But then I thought: Is this really what democracy looks like? Nobody here looks like me.
> —Jinee Kim, Bay Area youth organiser[50]

Even if this is not always the case—for instance the Occupy actions in the US from 2011 on and the protests against the G20 Summit in Toronto in 2010 were more mixed—this tendency is still a hard reminder of this lingering social and political reality of transnational civil alliance and action in our time. How and why does democracy often look so white (or pale)? And how and why is it all too often so male? And civil?

Despite some promise of change early on in the WSF process as a result of the decision to hold the third meeting in India, this question of colour and race has also been an issue for a long time at the World Social Forum. It was the case at the first and second WSFs in Brazil, and it was true also of the third in India, in a different way. Aside from my personal experience at several WSF meetings over the first decade, many studies have shown that it has been all too widely a white male process,[51] though the colour and race composition has naturally changed over time with the world meetings being held in Africa (Nairobi in 2007, Dakar in 2011, Tunis in 2013 and 2015). This was the case despite the fact that Brazil (where the Forum was born) is such a mixed society. From experience, I know that the same was the case at the European Social Forum (ESF) held in London in October 2004, despite the extremely rich multicultural character of that city.

The question of colour and race is not just about whiteness; it gets played out in other ways. This was also true of the Mumbai Forum, though this is much less talked about. There, it was not so much in terms of colour or race but of *caste*—keeping in mind that the caste spectrum in many ways mirrors the colour spectrum and that some, even many, Dalits see caste and race as closely interrelated—and of *religion*.

While the Mumbai Forum has been widely celebrated, especially by people from outside India, as a place where 'the masses came out' and 'where the Dalits of the country asserted themselves', beneath the surface, the general social reality that I sketched out above was largely also the case there. First and most crucially, the Dalits who came to the Mumbai Forum belonged to what can be called the third generation of Dalits, who are part of 'NGO' Dalit organisations not the main first- and second-generation mass Dalit formations.[52] The latter—which are fundamental to the Dalit movement in India—stayed away from the Mumbai WSF, as they have from all such constructs of Indian and world civil society, in large part because they see them as 'brahminical' (read: civil) constructs, and in particular because the WSF in India was led by representatives of the communist parties and their mass fronts, which Dalits have historically also been alienated from and do not trust, as Dalit activist and strategist Anand Teltumbde argues in his essay in the companion volume to this book.[53] Although he does not use the term, I understand Teltumbde in part to be saying that Dalits perceive the left as being captured by what I call 'the civil'.

This dynamic also played itself out at the Mumbai Forum in terms of faith. Despite Mumbai being a huge metropolitan city with a very substantial Muslim population, there were very few local Muslims present at the 2004 Forum. In addition, in a country where Muslims constitute the largest 'minority' and one of the largest such populations in the world, there were *none at all* on the WSF India Organising Committee, and the organisers were understandably accused—by a Muslim activist—of discrimination and domination.[54] Finally, no less striking than this absence and exclusion was the massive attempt apparently made by the WSF leadership in India—most of whom belonged to the majority faith (Hindu)—to tame, suppress, and downplay this sensitive question when it was raised, instead of addressing the huge contradiction in front of them.[55]

In a perceptive and courageous essay Anila Daulatzai has discussed the highly orthodox and regulatory roles that secularism and feminism, which so many in civil societies today consider to be articles of faith, played in the Mumbai Forum.[56]

I do not know how the issues of colour and race played out at the polycentric Forum that was held in Bamako, Mali, in January 2006, or at the two meetings of the World Social Forum organised in Tunis, in 2013 and 2015. I was not there and to my knowledge no one has written on this aspect of those meetings as yet. But the events that unfolded at the World Social Forum organised in Nairobi, Kenya, in January 2007—the exclusion of the members of local labouring class communities and the popular movements, the gross commercialisation of the Forum, and the very prominent presence of fundamentalist religious groups— clearly indicate that similar exclusionary dynamics regularly play themselves out in such contexts.[57]

This was equally true, though again in a different way, of the WSF that was held in January 2009 at Belém, in Brazil—every context has its particularities. Many observers saw the Belém Forum as a sign of change in these terms and accepted and celebrated the official WSF position that the world meeting was organised that year in that city (on the mouth of the Amazon and of Amazonia) to highlight both the global ecological crisis and the struggles of the Indigenous Peoples who live in such regions, as well as celebrating the fact that the Belém Forum saw the presence of a thousand Indigenous warriors—just as they did about Dalits at the Mumbai Forum.

The on the ground reality of the Belém Forum was far more complex, and there is much reason to think that the official reasoning was also instrumental and disingenuous. The Forum aimed at making the WSF a locus of world ecological activity at this crucial juncture of world history—and of climate crisis—and showcased Indigenous Peoples, seemingly to show the WSF's concern for such peoples. But the enormous irony of the Belém Forum was that it was organised on colonised and occupied land that once belonged to the peoples being showcased, and instead of the Indigenous Peoples being at least the co-hosts (which would almost certainly have led to the meeting being organised very differently), the warriors were instead 'invited' (and mobilised) to come into the heavily guarded and fortified university campus where the Forum was held with entry badges hanging around their necks. Literally. Not as hosts, not as co-hosts, not even as guests of honour.

This most fundamental issue, irony, and tragedy either seems to have completely eluded the organisers of the Belém Forum and of the WSF (its International Council, etc) or they simply wanted to deny this reality. What happened (and didn't happen) in Belém though needs to be understood as being not an isolated instance but part of a general structural pattern. As Janet Conway has written:

In neither the documents nor the discourses nor the organizing practices of the WSF in Belém, where indigenous peoples had greater prominence than ever before, was there any recognition of Brazil or other nation-states of the Americas as settler-colonial societies, founded on the theft of indigenous land and destruction of indigenous societies. A similar point could be made about the absence of reference to the trans-Atlantic slave trade and the labour of millions of Africans and Afro-descendants in establishing Euro-colonial societies in the Americas.

These observations raise the question of history, memory, and forgetting in the constitution of global justice. In Chapter 1, I noted that various lineages of global justice function like prisms, bringing into view specific histories, places, actors, and aspects while occluding others. *The naturally subordinate position of Indigenous and Black histories that prevails in the settler-colonial societies of the Americas can also be seen at work in the WSF.* Indigenous and Afro-descendent discourses of global justice confront the WSF, particularly in the Americas with its prominent European and Euro-descendent demographic, with histories of the present that are rather left forgotten. Throughout the Americas, there is widespread official and popular denial, which functions through silence, forgetting, and cultivated memory loss, of the acts of violence, dispossession, and enslavement that founded modern nation-states in which Euro-descendants overwhelmingly continue to rule. The vast majority of global justice movements in the Americas are struggling to expand representation and distribution within these racial formations rather than to fundamentally contest their legitimacy.[58]

It is also not as if at least some of the Indigenous Peoples who were present at the Belém Forum—from Amazonia and from other parts of Abya Yala (the continent of South America)—did not see what was going on and had no opinion on it. Even if it is true that the Indigenous Peoples of South and Central America successfully—and skilfully—used the Belém Forum as a platform to advance the struggle they launched that year on a world scale,[59] some of their representatives were very critical of the way the event was organised and the way they were treated by the organisers and spoke openly about this, including at a meeting that some of us from outside Brazil had organised to look at precisely these questions.[60]

Echoing what Janet Conway has said—even if the Indigenous Peoples of the Americas were able to successfully use the Belém Forum to advance their own struggles, for its part, so-called 'global civil society' lost a historic opportunity to own up to complicity in the genocide of the aboriginals on Abya Yala and to attempt a process of reconciliation—in itself and in terms of the planetary crisis we are facing today.[61] This is of course a generous interpretation of what happened; another way to look at it, as Conway argues so clearly, is that the organisers were actually in denial and avoided and suppressed this truth.

An even more critical way to look at what took place at Belém was that while the organisers—all belonging to civil society—were happy enough to be impresarios and stage managers for the event and to get the credit, they made sure that *their* event remained theirs, did not go out of hand, and that they did not have to go as far as becoming political partners with the warriors in their struggles.

As I said in the introduction in Part 1 of this essay,[62] these are not easy things to say, especially as I know and respect some of the people who were involved in the organisation of these events and processes. But these are patterns that need to be written about and—I hope it will be agreed—spelled out in public. This is the only way we can learn and move forward.

Event Planning as an Instrument of Imposing Civility

As I have discussed elsewhere, this characteristic of the WSF—the denial of class, caste, race, faith, and other structural features of social reality is largely a function of the dominant class, caste, race, and *civil* character of the organisers—has also, perhaps expectably, manifested itself in the physical planning and conceptualisation of most WSF meetings, including the choice of location. This too is how 'civility' plays out in reality—planning and design are fundamental tools and expressions of civility.

The first (and strongest) indication of this has been the choice of the location of most WSF events: within the walls of university campuses, with all that this choice of location signals in terms of divisions within society, even if this balance and division is gradually changing. While undoubtedly 'convenient'—insofar as such campuses provide distinct spaces where the dozens and even hundreds of simultaneous meetings that are typical of large WSF forums can take place—the fact that the event as a whole is being held within a secluded walled campus (where, normally speaking, labouring and working-class people do not enter, and are generally welcome only to do the work that such service classes are meant to do) and that individual events are held in classrooms and lecture halls, with all the disciplining restrictions that come along with such spaces, inevitably results in the exchanges that take place also to a considerable extent being 'civilised' and disciplined—incivility is discouraged.

This WSF culture started with the first two meetings in Porto Alegre, in southern Brazil—again, notwithstanding my argument that the young WSF could be seen as having started out as an initiative in incivility. Both were held in the campus of the PUC (Pontifícia Universidade Católica—'Pontifical Catholic University', in Portuguese), a private, fairly wealthy university run by a religious denomination. (I still remember vividly, as a participant at the second WSF, being first annoyed and disturbed by the music and drumming that periodically broke out outside those walls and windows, and then, as I began to read about what was happening, being delighted by a huge, noisy, colourful, and rambunctious gathering of people who were quite obviously troublemakers that snaked its way through the campus. . . .)[63]

This pattern was temporarily broken when the 2004 Mumbai Forum was held in a disused industrial complex (with the larger events taking place in huge sheds and the smaller in temporary purpose-built stalls). The relative informality of this experience powerfully influenced the design of the next WSF, which was again held in Porto Alegre but this time in a public park on the river front, with the events largely held in tents (albeit much 'nicer' and more civil, sturdy, and expensive ones than those in Mumbai).[64] But the initial physical planning culture quickly reasserted itself, with the following world meeting—in Nairobi, Kenya, in 2007—being organised in a heavily fenced and guarded stadium and the subsequent one, in Belém in 2009, again in a campus.

In Belém, as mentioned, not only were the Amazonian warriors only allowed in with badges hanging around their necks, but the campus was also heavily guarded and patrolled—in part against the dwellers living in the *favelas* ('slums') opposite. There seems little doubt that one factor that led to this armed defence was that similar dwellers had successfully broken into and swarmed through the previous Forum in Nairobi, in 2007. 'Never again!' must have been the WSF's call. . . .

Just try and imagine, therefore, the cruel double irony of what happened in Belém in terms of how the World Social Forum—a process that claims to be about democracy and rights—treated and related to 'the others' of Brazilian society. From then on, university campuses—one of the great historical achievements of civil society, after all—have continued to be the default location of choice for WSF events, in Africa, in Canada, almost everywhere.[65]

The mark of civility seems indelible in the WSF, in more senses than one. This is the case, of course, because the civil always control the organisation of such events and the World Social Forum process.

The mark is there in a different dimension as well, as a kind of invisible disciplining, to keep things civil. From 2002 to 2014, I attended seven WSF world meetings, the only Asian Social Forum that has so far been held, two sessions of the European Social Forum, one US Social Forum, and the (Canada-Quebec-Indigenous) People's Social Forum. Although I cannot deny there has always been a certain magic about taking part, and there has also—on many occasions and in many spaces—been a kind of craziness (along with a lot of networking and deep social, political, and cultural engagement), and although I also accept that each event is enormously demanding logistically, and therefore a huge achievement, I have also almost always felt that there was a kind of invisible 'hyper-organisation' and resulting disciplining in the air that tended to discourage the unpredictable.

Perhaps the only example in my experience of the WSF where this pattern was somewhat turned on its head and where peoples of colour, women, the queer, and others of the incivil have been dominant was at the US Forum in Detroit, in

2010. I understand from what has been written about it that this was also the case the first USSF held in Atlanta, in 2007, and to a more limited degree at the WSF in Mumbai in 2004. However, as the organisers of the Atlanta Forum and analysts of the experience make clear, this was the case because the incivil literally took over the organising process in the US right from the beginning, consciously turning the tables and excluding and marginalising the traditional civil formations who otherwise dominate such processes (including the big progressive civil rights, labour, and environmental organisations). By doing so, they radically reinterpreted—and intentionally inverted—the concept of open space on which the WSF is supposedly founded.[66] In other words, it takes this kind—and scale—of insurrection and ambition to break through the walls of civility that surround the WSF.

I will end this survey of the WSF as a civil construct by again quoting Janet Conway's extraordinary book, this time at some length—underlining, as she does, that her discussion is not only about the WSF but also about 'global civil society' more generally:

> The grammar of modern politics deeply pervades the practices and discourses of the WSF, indeed, its very constitution. The preeminence of the following modalities and discourses in the WSF all testify to its modern character: national states as the sites and containers of politics; the national scale in modes of organization and representation; national identities and attachments; discourses of citizenship and rights; and discourses of civil society, whether national or global. This modern character is barely noted, rarely problematized, and so is naturalized. Relatedly, as noted, the colonial character of nation-states is almost completely unrecognized in the WSF and by the majority of movements present therein whose politics take the state form and its mechanisms of representation, rights, and entitlements for granted.
>
> . . . [T]he WSF is constituted unproblematically as a civil society space in that it is autonomous of states, parties, and armed groups. However, as Sen argues, civil societies are the settler societies whose dominance is established through the colonization of subaltern populations, their lands, and their labour. Many of the entities present in the WSF, as organizations of civil society, have been implicated in colonial projects, past and present: including churches and NGOs, along with states and TNCs. While the positionality of churches and NGOs in the WSF is highly variable in terms of critical awareness of coloniality, the ambiguous history of relations between these kinds of organizations and indigenous peoples is rarely spoken of. Further to this point about its civil society character is the WSF's *de facto* privileging of the urbanized, lettered, professionalized, fluent in the colonial languages, internationally-networked, internet-connected, funded, and formally-organized cultures and modalities of non-governmental organizations.

Indigenous peoples, Afro-descendants, *dalits*, and other racialized groups appear constantly in the lists of movements in the WSF and as an attribute of its 'diversity'. Their bodies often serve as icons for the forum. Yet racialized and subalternized movements attest to multiple barriers to their full participation, their generalized under-representation in both the space and the organizing processes, and the lack of serious engagement with their knowledges.

. . . [A]ny capacity to confront these contradictions is hampered by an enduring refusal to recognize race in the WSF. This extends to many spaces of the anti-globalization movement worldwide which are dominated by white people. The silence about race, coupled with the *de facto* denial of contemporary nation-states as racially-stratified formations grounded in colonial histories, combined with liberal discourses of equality, pluralism, and diversity in an open space make it exceedingly difficult to talk about racism, racial exclusion, subalternity, or coloniality within the global justice movement.

The presence of subaltern movements in the WSF confronts the global justice movement with its class, caste, and race privilege, as well as its civilizational specificity. As Peter Waterman astutely observed early on, the WSF, and with it 'global civil society', represents not a globalization from below, as has often been heralded, but a 'globalization from the middle'. It is a phenomenon of the world's middle classes, still disproportionately European or Euro-descendants, professionals and students, the urban, and the literate, organized primarily through NGOs, and increasingly globally networked through their access to the internet, international travel, and fluency in colonial languages. The lived subalternity of the movements under discussion issues a silent rebuke to this cosmopolitan politics and to the modern modes of life and consumption on which it is grafted. It also poses deep challenges to the modern subjectivities at its heart—those autonomous, empowered, and highly individualized citizen-activists of global network society.[67]

In conclusion, even this overview of the WSF suggests clear patterns that reinforce my more general argument: in the WSF—in its events and in its organisation—civility rules, and incivility struggles insurgently. I do not mean to suggest that this is an absolute, predetermined, and inevitable path; only that this has been the general tendency so far. It is true that some individual organisations and actors within civil societies, and perhaps especially those associated with the emerging 'global social justice movement', are struggling to break out of these confines and redefine the rules, and the boundaries are therefore not always so clear. Nevertheless, the continuing experience of the WSF makes clear that the deep dialectic of civility is an issue that all those who are in transcultural and transnational alliance building—civil or incivil—need to engage with and reflect upon.

Civility, Corporatism, and Power[68]

I turn now to the related question of corporatisation within civil processes and of the power relations that are contained in such processes. I argue that the power relations inevitably and necessarily build and consolidate on the structural relations, realities, and dialectics of civility and civil society. I will again take the WSF as an example, not to target the WSF as such but as one example of what is happening much more widely in 'global civil society'.

The WSF was ten years old in 2010. Even though I have argued that it is an extraordinary example of a process in organic emergence in terms of learning from its own experience,[69] I believe that by as early as 2004 it had reached a stage where it was beginning to corporatise, and thereby was losing its soul, its essence. By 2009, this was abundantly clear. Since I have already presented these arguments in detail elsewhere,[70] I will only summarise them here.

The WSF calls itself an 'open space'—open to pluralism and diversity[71]—but its history shows a strong tendency towards structural exclusion and co-option and the periodic articulation of strict and exclusionary rules for membership and / or participation; as Janet Conway has so powerfully shown, being—despite all its other strengths—blind to or in denial about the implications of these rules as a consequence of the structural prejudices that are embedded in and coursing through what it does and is (or, as I have argued above, simply because it quickly became middle aged). Keeping in mind that the WSF calls itself an open space, examples of such rules include the requirement on one occasion of a written declaration of adherence to the Charter of Principles of the Forum for membership on its committees and the coercive questioning of people registering for the Mumbai Forum in 2004 as to whether or not they agreed with the Charter of Principles.

This in addition to the fact that in the otherwise resonant Charter of Principles drafted in 2001, the founders of the World Social Forum specifically excluded all movements that had any history of armed struggle.[72] It is of course understandable that the initiators of the WSF would not want armed militants to be present within Forum meetings, but how could a world process with the kind of social and political ambition that the WSF had look at armed struggle in such a simplistic way and decide that it would not even talk with such people? For instance, why could it not have followed the simple rule successfully followed for decades by the legendary café in Manila (Café 57)—a place created specifically for differing, highly militant (and armed) political factions in the Philippines to meet in a social environment—of recognising that all those who enter are warriors and asking them to surrender their arms at the door? Literally but in reality also metaphorically. As a result, other than individual activists from such movements who entered without declaring their identities, the WSF closed itself off from whole worlds of contemporary movement, including the Basque movement, the

Palestinian movements, and even the Zapatista movement—although early in the WSF process many felt that the World Social Forum itself was in many ways inspired by the *encuentros* (encounters) that the Zapatistas organised in the mid- and late 1990s.[73]

As the late Peter Waterman observed, this proscription raised the very serious question of whether the "the conditionalities of the Charter have not been exercised [by the WSF] more against the ultra-left than the parliamentary left and centre ([which are] often complicit with [the] neo-liberalism [that the WSF says it opposes])".[74]

In other words, there has been a current running through the WSF process that shows that the organisers—of different meetings and at different times—have tended to be so conservative and concerned about the possibility of having people present either on its committees or in its events who hold dissenting opinions that they attempted to screen them out. Given what the WSF has proclaimed as its fundamental philosophy—open space—this has been both deeply troubling and revealing.

Beyond this, and as is true of many corporate structures, this gatekeeping takes place not only through articulated rules but also through a 'tyranny of structurelessness' where a barely visible leadership makes (and breaks) the rules and decides who is eligible to join without making the procedures public.[75] The social and political dynamics that lie behind such control are always disguised by a veil of civility, and it takes determined investigation and exploration to remove the mask and show the real face.[76]

These tendencies also include an increasingly intense—and tense—discourse over the years about the representativeness of the International Council (IC), even though the Charter of Principles specifically declares that the WSF "is not a representative organisation" and "does not seek to represent world civil society".[77,78] Although the IC took some steps in the late 2000s towards systematising the processes of application and approval, the rules and criteria by which decisions were (and, even today, are) made remained unclear. The longstanding non-democratic and non-transparent organisational culture of the IC contrasts sharply with the notionally democratic ideal and debate about representativeness that the authors of the WSF declared.

There was some possibility that this might change after the IC adopted a resolution in Nairobi in January 2007 calling for an assessment of the internal functioning of the WSF. As it turned out, despite public reminders,[79] the Commission established to undertake this review chose to focus only on the much simpler question of the logistical organisation of events and ducked the far more difficult issues that are involved in regulating relations between different bodies, including power relations. Moreover, the final report of the committee remains unavailable and the rules apparently framed back in 2007[80] still remain invisible. This issue reached a crisis stage in 2012–2013, when one of the founders and father figures of the WSF, Chico Whitaker, put forward a proposal for the IC to be dissolved.[81]

This behaviour is also manifested in the degree to which the WSF has, despite protest to the contrary in its Charter of Principles, often become a piece of territory to be struggled over, gained, and retained at almost any cost, especially by those with political ambitions. The experience of the WSF in Mumbai in January 2004, the ESF in London in 2004, and the WSF India process as a whole are classic examples of this.[82] In most cases the leadership of the Forum, once installed, never changes, simply because it has established no procedures for doing so, and no one ever seems to be willing to initiate processes for doing so. This is another classic manifestation of the tyranny of structurelessness, and it is always the already powerful who take advantage of such a situation.

Furthermore, we need to recognise that those who are in the leadership of the WSF—as manifested in the membership of its International Council—are also in the leadership of many other significant civil alliances and coalitions at national, regional, and global levels: not only among civil organisations but also among social movements.[83] In social and structural terms, this is uncomfortably similar to the case of the conventional corporate world, which Sklair has described as the emergence of a 'transnational capitalist class'.[84] On the one hand, this prominence in national and global society has been the driving force behind the formation and expansion of the IC; on the other, it makes the IC a hugely powerful body—in effect, a supra-board of the activist civil world—despite the WSF Charter and spokespersons' very civil insistence that it does not see itself as a locus of power. It is again precisely the formal denial of this power that is a manifestation of civility's power.

Over the years, and through all these actions, the leadership of the Forum has also at times behaved like the Forum was the temple of an orthodox sect or party,[85] with its priests, its faithful constituency, and its rituals. Its priests have often expressed alarm at the suggestion that the provisions of the WSF's Charter should be reviewed and debated, or that non-believers—such as people who were not staunch declared opponents of neoliberalism or those who hold that armed resistance is justified under certain circumstances—be allowed into the Forum; even while they have been willing to compromise the rules of the Charter on other grounds of their choosing.[86]

There are two aspects to all of this. On the one hand, a tendency to plan and conduct the WSF events and processes such that they can be and are carefully controlled, starting from the location and going from there; and on the other, there is a tendency among many organisers of WSF events to perceive and portray the WSF not as one site within a much, much larger burgeoning of movements worldwide (even if its own Charter of Principles resonantly declares this) but as *the* movement of movements itself. Even notionally independent commentators have unfortunately come around to describing and celebrating the WSF in this way.[87]

But there are, of course, also other perceptions of what it is and represents:

> The suppression by WSF elites of diversity, complexity, and contestation as con-stitutive features of globalisation *movements* (plural) operates by virtue of an idealised and singular globalisation *movement*, whose assumptions of unity and coherence are required by the institutional realm the elites themselves aspire to inhabit.
>
> . . .The transformation of the WSF into a machine for the repressive dis-ciplining of the politics of the poor is not just a matter of ideology, but has to do with knowledge as well. The established left discourse projects a mode of knowledge onto the social subjectivities of the subaltern, which aims to 'format' them into desirable, prescribed political behaviours. The imposition of old left modes of analysis on the knowledge that social movement struggles produce of themselves, coupled with the temptation in the official discourse of forums like the WSF to argue for social movements that want to become institutions of state and global governance, raises troubling questions. Everywhere in the Global South, for example, states and ruling parties have often attempted to square their enduring adherence to neoliberal policymaking with rhetorical openings in the direction of state-driven developmentalism. In South Africa, a 'developmental state' has indeed become the rallying cry of a government that, while trying to regain support from organised labour constituencies, continues to privatise housing, water, and electricity, evicting those who cannot pay, repressing those who protest, and generally condemning to invisibility the vast numbers of those deemed unproductive in the country's formal 'first economy'. What have WSF representations, and documents like the Bamako Appeal, to say in this regard? Are they conducive to building, as we advocate, life forms and strategies that con-flictually *autonomise* themselves from the state, capital, and wage labour, or are they in fact meant to endorse struggles to shape the heart and soul of the state?[88]

Within this larger dynamic, there have constantly been calls over the years for the Forum to be 'constructed from the grassroots'. In principle, this sounds good, but in practice, this idea has usually come from the top and has been con-ceived not as direct democracy but as a process of delegation from the bottom up to a 'top' in the classic conceptualisation of a world political party. In the ESF in London in 2004, at the session on the future of the ESF and the WSF, the two strongest calls were for strengthening the anti-war struggle and for the formation of a world party. Eminent political scientist Samir Amin, an influential member of the IC, has held for several years that the WSF is—or can be—an important step towards the formation of a Fifth International.[89] Thus, just as there have been calls for reconstructing the WSF from the grassroots, there have also been much stronger calls for the articulation of a clear political programme for the WSF—so that it can behave 'as one body'.[90]

Finally, notwithstanding the declared progressive political intentions of these calls, the social reality of the leadership of the WSF is that until 2011 it was largely led by aging males, mostly white or honorary white, from middle- and upper-class and caste sections of settler societies around the world—and this despite the broadening at that time of the membership of the IC to include more movements.

On the whole, the spirit of openness and consensus that characterised the Forum in its early days has largely been lost and progressively replaced by what seems to be a far more categorical, hierarchical, and corporate civil structure. I say this even though I have argued that the WSF has been an extraordinary example of institutional emergence (where the process of horizontal spread and proliferation is far more important than any single event) and recognise that the leadership of the Forum has often been unusually creative in terms of responding to challenges and introducing change.[91] This is not, however, mutually contradictory; this ability to learn and adapt is also an intrinsic attribute of civility—and, more broadly, the struggle of civil society to retain control and power.

I make these observations not to comment on the Forum alone but on trends that I have perceived taking place in global civil cooperation more generally over the past two to three decades.[92] It is not my intention to malign the Forum, an experiment that I respect a great deal. 'Representative democracy'—where processes such as the Forum might attempt to embrace incivil societies by ensuring their representation on its committees—is not, however, the answer to my concerns. It may be a necessary step, but the principle has to be political and, as Massimo De Angelis says elsewhere in this volume, *processual*:[93] a shift in the agenda of the Forum (and of other such civil processes) towards *a process built and predicated on and centred in the lives and struggles of those it seeks to embrace*, and *towards an open-ended process of connectivity*, which, as Marianne Maeckelbergh has so richly shown, is a hallmark of the alter-globalisation movement and of the new politics that it is building.[94] And as John Brown Childs has so powerfully described—not in specific relation to the WSF but in social and political life more generally—what is needed is a shift in the active organising principle underlying what we do from a politics of conversion to an ethic of respect.[95] The WSF remains some way from that.

The Civilising Role of NGOs: Globalisation from Below?

Finally, I wish to take this line of argument a few steps further—and to move away from the WSF and broaden my argument, looking at civil organisations more generally. First, we need to take a deeper, more critical look at the roles of 'NGOs', or civil organisations. To do this, we need to re-examine the significance that is so widely attributed to them not only by, say, the World Bank, the UN, and private foundations, which is predictable, but by so many social analysts.

To take as an example the work of someone I greatly respect, Japanese activist-scholar Muto Ichiyo,[96] we need to seriously think about and engage with his proposition—which is shared widely, especially within civil organisations—that 'NGOs' can and do play the role of 'helping "the people" come forward' towards a "steady but systematic replacement of NGOs with people's organisations as the representation in the global arena".[97] It is clear from the writings of this visionary thinker and legendary political strategist that he is by no means unqualifiedly celebrating NGOs, as some authors do, but rather challenging them to review their role in society.[98]

While I would very much like to share Muto-san's hope, my experience of and research into transnational civil politics suggest that in practice the reverse has been happening and will necessarily continue to happen.[99] While one result of NGO mobilisation of 'people's organisations' is certainly greater exposure for those who have been historically marginalised and excluded, and through this, undeniably, some degree of self-awareness and self-confidence, there are many other results as well. One very common experience is that those in the leadership of popular organisations often get 'lifted off' the ground and uprooted. They either get increasingly deeply drawn into international work by their sponsors, to whom they provide legitimacy, or they are attracted by the perks and power of international work. There are legion instances of this happening.

As important as this tendency is, the fact that the leadership of the NGOs that sponsor such individuals tend to move into constantly more powerful positions, often behind the scenes, in part by gaining credibility for having successfully sponsored these individuals. Notwithstanding my respect for him, I therefore question Muto-san's unqualified proposition that NGOs play the role of helping 'the people' come forward and believe that the counter-tendencies I describe are not accidental; to the contrary, they are structurally contained within the situation. We need to be far more critical of the structural dynamics involved in such situations.

Secondly, civil organisations need to far more explicitly recognise that we live in a time when more than ever before the incivil are independently and insurgently building their own organisations and their own transnational coalitions and alliances within and beyond 'national' societies—and they also need to far more explicitly decide how they are going to position themselves in relation to this emerging process. Not as sponsors but as equals.

Relatedly, civil organisations need to recognise the reality that whereas they almost unquestioningly accept the reality of the nation-state within which they work—it is the air they breathe, the water they swim in—in many instances the incivil reject the concept and project of the dominant 'nation' within which they find themselves and which they seek to transcend.

They need moreover to recognise and accept that in some cases incivil initiatives are emancipatory and progressive and in others, regressive, and relate to them accordingly—but this is also true of the initiatives of civil organisations.

Thirdly, and in relation to the much celebrated thesis of 'globalisation from below', in which civil organisations ('NGOs') are so often projected as playing a key role, I believe that such organisations would do well to recognise that, as Peter Waterman has argued in the case of the WSF,[100] what they are involved in is not 'globalisation from below' (GfB) but 'globalisation from the middle'.[101] And, far more importantly, that the real globalisation from below is taking place in very different ways and largely independently of the celebrated version.

I am speaking here not of a single parallel world of globalisation from below nor of a simple or single parallel process of building other worlds. We need to shift our gaze and bring into focus the reality that the world is changing in myriad, intertwined ways, not only as a result of or in reaction to neoliberal globalisation (which the celebrated GfB is largely focused on).[102] Myriad globalisations from below have taken place in history and are today taking place; and, crucially, both incivil and uncivil societies all over the world are taking part in this drama, both independently of and interdependently with yet other actors, such as faith-based institutions. The world-changing role of former African slaves over the past two centuries in so many arenas of life—including music, literature, dance, sports, movement, and politics—is just one example among many.[103]

I like the idea and thesis of a 'globalisation from below', which—as I have already said—was first put forward by Richard Falk,[104] and then substantially developed and elaborated by Jeremy Brecher and his colleagues in their landmark book on the subject in 2000.[105] But several years later, after reflecting on the concept and practice of civility and thinking back to the argument made by another influential thinker, David Korten (that the 'globalisation of civil society' is a necessary part of "reclaiming our right to power"),[106] I now feel that the way the term developed in fact makes it a cousin of the term 'civil society', further legitimising its role and power. I therefore believe that this usage needs to be challenged if we are aiming for deeper democratisation.

When I made a very similar point in discussion with Brecher and his colleagues while commenting on the manuscript for their book back in 2000,[107] they acknowledged my concerns but said it would take another book to address them.

Even though some great work has been published on world movement, this particular and very major issue has not yet been addressed. This urgently needs to be done: first, as a matter of respect for the struggle of ordinary people and to build relations of solidarity rather than dominance; second, because if we don't have this picture, we will continue to grope in the dark, to guess our way through, and to tend to work on the basis of default positions (which largely come from civil sources). It is only by accepting that what they (we . . .) are doing is 'globalisation from the middle', and by engaging with and relating to the issues I have tried to raise in this essay, essentially that civil organisations and individuals who think that they are globalising from below should begin to authentically take part in the much larger, wider, and deeper processes of democratisation from below that are opening up in our time. Unless they / we do this, I suggest that they / we are in reality competing with and contradicting these deeper processes, and thereby—precisely because of the power of civility—undermining them, however valid their / our concerns and articulations might otherwise seem to be.

One simple example is the well established practice of civil organisations co-opting (and thereby 'civilising') incivil movements and tendencies. To cite an instance, there is a world of difference in the manner in which many Dalit organisations perceive neoliberal globalisation as potentially being one more tool to blow open the caste structure that has imprisoned them for over a thousand years, which they regard as their primary issue,[108] and the formal ideology of the WSF and the alter-globalisation movement of opposing neoliberal globalisation. Despite this major, even fundamental, contradiction with its declared objectives, the WSF never objects to the presence in its events of Dalits with such beliefs (to the contrary, the WSF wants and celebrates this presence). We need to question and reflect upon this selective openness. If we accept that the WSF's opposition to neoliberalism is based on principle, then we need to recognise that there are deeper reasons than mere opportunism behind the leadership's willingness to accept this contradiction but not, for instance, to allow the participation of armed organisations. The answer, I suggest, lies in the historical task of civil organisations to civilise the incivil: in this case, by co-opting them.

As Cox and Nilsen explain in their book on social movement:

> Thus social movements from above shape the common sense which gives meaning to everyday routines in a way that enables dominant groups to manage the task of providing effective directions and orientations to the life-activity of subaltern groups. On a wider scale it is also about meeting some of their diverse needs selectively, in ways which reinforce existing power relations, and about providing a political language in which they can express their thoughts about the world they inhabit. In this complex process, the existing social order is variously represented and experienced as natural (unchangeable), as purposive (and beneficial to subaltern interests), and as legitimate (and offering a language through which subaltern grievances can be expressed).[109]

Fourth, especially in this context of competing alter-globalisms, we need to far more seriously read and recognise the degree to which the leadership of international civil organisations, private foundations, and social movements promoted by such organisations is coagulating into something that has many of the characteristics of a powerful 'transnational social class'. As I have argued above in terms of the WSF, these characteristics include key individuals (mostly males) across the world being on the boards of each other's organisations, thereby building ever-larger webs of interlinked control.[110] This is not only true of the WSF.

Finally, it is vitally important to remember that the recent and current phenomenal growth and expansion of civil society and of transnational civil organisations is not merely a result of spontaneous association and action, though this has played an important role. As I have already argued in this essay and elsewhere, it is also a function of Northern governments being far more flexible in terms of selectively funding international NGOs from the 1990s onwards, as a part of the neoliberal project and as a part of attempting to secure global hegemony through the dominance of the Washington Consensus.[111] Both governments and corporations see civil organisations at local, national, and transnational levels as playing a useful role in their larger geopolitical ambitions.

See, for instance, the following discussion by Julian Assange, the founder of Wikileaks, on Google, governments, and global civil society:

> [Jared] Cohen's world seems to be one event like this after another: endless soirees for the cross-fertilization of influence between elites and their vassals, under the pious rubric of "civil society". The received wisdom in advanced capitalist societies is that there still exists an organic "civil society sector" in which institutions form autonomously and come together to manifest the interests and will of citizens. The fable has it that the boundaries of this sector are respected by actors from government and the "private sector", leaving a safe space for NGOs and nonprofits to advocate for things like human rights, free speech and accountable government.
>
> This sounds like a great idea. But if it was ever true, it has not been for decades. Since at least the 1970s, authentic actors like unions and churches have folded under a sustained assault by free-market statism, transforming "civil society" into a buyer's market for political factions and corporate interests looking to exert influence at arm's length. The last forty years have seen a huge proliferation of think tanks and political NGOs whose purpose, beneath all the verbiage, is to execute political agendas by proxy.
>
> It is not just obvious neocon front groups like Foreign Policy Initiative. It also includes fatuous Western NGOs like Freedom House, where naïve but well-meaning career nonprofit workers are twisted in knots by political funding streams, denouncing non-Western human rights violations while keeping local abuses firmly in their blind spots.
>
> The civil society conference circuit—which flies developing-world activists across the globe hundreds of times a year to bless the unholy union

between "government and private stakeholders" at geopoliticized events like the "Stockholm Internet Forum"—simply could not exist if it were not blasted with millions of dollars in political funding annually. . . .[112]

To conclude, I suggest that the emerging global alliance and cooperation between civil, social, and political actors—collectively referred to as 'global civil society'—is first and foremost a crucial vehicle for transnational *civil* solidarity, which translates into the consolidation of the hold of civil societies transnationally, and through them, the hold of corporations. In a very and superficial and limited sense, it is true that non-state actors coming on to the world stage, a stage that has so far been monopolised by nation-states, is contributing to the democratisation of institutionalised world politics—but as Assange reminds us, we need to look at the larger picture and be realistic about what is really happening.

In this bigger picture, and seen through the lens of the larger and wider democratisation that is beginning to unfold in our time, this cooperation and consolidation is, far more importantly—due to the dynamics of civility and its internal tendencies to co-option and corporatisation—merely an instrument for the consolidation, strengthening, and imposition of historically unequal social and political relations and entrenched interests at local, national, regional, and global levels. In fundamental terms, what is called 'global civil society' is today contributing to less democracy—not more.

There Is No Conclusion . . . !

Almost by definition, there is no final conclusion to be drawn about the dynamics I have tried to explore in this essay—simply because they are an integral part of the existing social structures, which continue to unfold. This essay is by definition a work in progress. I have tried here to lift the veil called 'civility' and discuss it for what it really is and has historically been, to remove the mask and to look at the face behind it. While I acknowledge that the idea of civility and its practice have made a major contribution to the establishment of order and balance in societies everywhere, with many—perhaps countless—positive manifestations, we need to recognise that civil society necessarily aims for a very particular 'order and balance', and that there has also been a hidden iron fist of power within this order and balance and the way it was established, a fist that has exercised and continues to exercise huge power and that has played—and continues to play—a profoundly negative role in human affairs, simply by virtue of being a fist—and then there is the purpose of that fist.

Those of us who like to consider ourselves 'civil' need to think deeply about this: about being 'civil', about what this means not just on the surface but deeper down, and about how well we are perceiving and comprehending the implications of 'being civil'. In short, we need to shed our innocence about 'civilisation', about being civil, and about what is so innocuously called 'civil society'—and consider breaking free of this.

I have tried to pull together evidence for my arguments from a wide range of contexts, cultures, and experiences, and I can only hope that by doing so this essay can contribute to stimulating critical reflection and encourage others to deepen and expand this argument.

I have also tried to explore what being incivil is and can be and what an important and creative force it is.

Much about 'being civil' is good. But as someone who was born, bred, and brought up within civil society, I believe that we need to accept, in all humility, that 'being civil' is not all good. It is of the greatest importance that all of us—wherever we fall on the civil-incivil spectrum—recognise that each one of us, both individually and collectively, is necessarily complicit in what is taking place and in what has historically taken place—the good and the bad, including the barbarism. It is only by examining our consciousness and our conscience and deeply reflecting on who we are—in our deepest selves—and what our roles in what is happening are and can potentially be that we can influence the unfolding of this drama.

In short, I believe that we need to break free—and doing so is perhaps more important and urgent today than ever before in history.

References

Elizabeth Abraham, August 2010—*Pluralities of Open Space: A Reading of Dalit Participation in WSF 2004*. Final paper as CACIM Forum Fellow 2008–09. Volume 7 in *Critical Engagement*—CACIM's Occasional Publications Programme. New Delhi: CACIM, at http://www.cacim.net/twiki/tiki-index.php?page=Publications/ Elizabeth%20Abraham (Accessed August 29 2017)

Taiaiake Alfred, 2005—*Wasáse: Indigenous Pathways of Action and Freedom*. Peterborough: Broadview Press

Taiaiake Alfred and Jeff Corntassel, 2017—'Being Indigenous Resurgences against Contemporary Colonialism', in Jai Sen, ed, 2017a—*The Movements of Movements, Part 1: What Makes Us Move?*. Volume 4 in the *Challenging Empires* series. New Delhi: OpenWord, and Oakland, CA: PM Press

Tariq Ali, 2017—'Storming Heaven: Where Has The Rage Gone?', in Jai Sen, ed, 2017a—*The Movements of Movements, Part 1: What Makes Us Move?*. Volume 4 in the *Challenging Empires* series. New Delhi: OpenWord, and Oakland, CA: PM Press

Rebecca Álvarez, Erika Gutierrez, Linda Kim, Christine Petit, and Ellen Reese, 2008—'The Contours of Color at the World Social Forum: Reflections on Racialized Politics, Representation, and the Global Justice Movement', in *Critical Sociology*, vol 34

Sonia E. Alvarez, 2012—'Globalised Localisms: The Travels and Translations of the World Social Forum Process', in Jai Sen and Peter Waterman, eds, 2012—*World*

Social Forum: Critical Explorations. Volume 3 in the *Challenging Empires* series. New Delhi: OpenWord

Bhim Rao Ambedkar, 2014 [1936]—*Annihilation of Caste: The Annotated Critical Edition.* with an Introduction by Arundhati Roy. New Delhi: Navayana Books

Bhim Rao Ambedkar, nd [1936]—'Annihilation of Caste With a Reply to Mahatma Gandhi', at http://www.ambedkar.org/ambcd/02.Annihilation%20of%20Caste.htm (Accessed August 29 2017)

Samir Amin, 2006b—'Towards a Fifth International?', in Katarina Sehm Patomäki and Marko Ulvila, August 2006—'Democratic Politics Globally: Elements for a Dialogue on Global Political Party Formations'. NIGD Working Paper 1 / 2006, Network Institute for Global Democratisation, pp 121–44

Samir Amin, 2018—'Towards a Fifth International?', in Jai Sen, ed, 2018—*The Movements of Movements, Part 2: Rethinking Our Dance.* Volume 5 in the *Challenging Empires* series. New Delhi: OpenWord, and Oakland, CA: PM Press)

Arab American National Museum, 2013—'Creative Dissent: Art of the Arab World Uprisings', at http://artsofthearabworlduprisings.com/ (Accessed August 29 2017)

Julian Assange, October 2014—'Google Is Not What It Seems', in *Newsweek*, October 23 2014, at http://www.newsweek.com/assange-google-not-what-it-seems-279447 (Accessed August 29 2017)

James Baldwin, with KQED, 1963—'Who is the Nigger?', a clip from *Take this Hammer*, at https://www.youtube.com/watch?v=L0L5fciA6AU (Accessed August 29 2017)

Franco Barchiesi, Heinrich Bohmke, Prishani Naidoo, and Ahmed Veriava, 2012—'Does Bamako Appeal? The World Social Forum Versus the Life Strategies of the Subaltern', in Jai Sen and Peter Waterman, eds, 2012—*World Social Forum: Critical Explorations.* Volume 3 in the *Challenging Empires* series. New Delhi: OpenWord

Rustom Bharucha, 1995—*Chandralekha: Woman, Dance, Resistance.* New Delhi: Indus South Asia Books (HarperCollins India)

Tiana Bighorse, 1990—*Bighorse the Warrior.* Edited by Noel Bennett. Tucson, AZ: University of Arizona Press

Jeremy Brecher, 2015—*Climate Insurgency: A Strategy for Survival.* Boulder, CO, and London: Paradigm Publishers

Jeremy Brecher, Tim Costello, and Brendan Smith, 2000—*Globalization from Below: The power of solidarity.* Cambridge, MA: South End Press

CACIM and NFFPFW, May 2009—'Indigenous Peoples: "Another World Is Possible" Only If . . .'. Report on the seminar 'The Politics, Potentials, and Meanings of the WSF in Belém: The Significance for the World Social Forum of the Participation of the Indigenous Peoples of the World', Belém, Brazil, January 29 2009, organised by CACIM and NFFPFW (National Forum of Forest People and Forest Workers—India), at http://openspaceforum.net/twiki/tiki-read_article.php?articleId=798 (Accessed August 29 2017)

CAOI (Coordinadora Andina de Organizaciones Indígenas), ECUARUNARI (Confederación de Pueblos de la Nacionalidad Kichwa del Ecuador), ONIC (Organización Nacional Indígena de Colombia) et al, February 2009a—'Declaración de los pueblos indígenas, Foro Social Mundial 2009, Belem, Amazonia, Brasil' ('Declaration of the indigenous peoples, World Social Forum 2009, Belém, Amazonia, Brazil', in Spanish), at http://www.cadtm.org/spip.php?article4133 (Accessed August 29 2017)

Chris Carlsson, 2017—'Effective Politics or Feeling Effective?', in Jai Sen, ed, 2018—*The Movements of Movements, Part 2: Rethinking Our Dance*. Volume 5 in the *Challenging Empires* series. New Delhi: OpenWord, and Oakland, CA: PM Press

William K Carroll, December 2013—'Alternative Policy Groups and Global Civil Society: A report from the field', at https://www.academia.edu/5567548/Alternative_policy_groups_and_global_civil_society_a_report_from_the_field (Accessed August 29 2017)

Giuseppe Caruso, December 2004—'Conflict management and hegemonic practices in the World Social Forum 2004', in *International Social Science Journal*, Issue no 182, pp 577–90, at http://www.openspaceforum.net/twiki/tiki-read_article.php?articleId=20&highlight=giuseppe (Accessed August 29 2017)

Nayan Chanda, 2007—*Bound Together: How Traders, Preachers, Adventurers, and Warriors Shaped Globalization*. New Haven: Yale University Press

Chandralekha, 1997—'Choreographer Chandralekha in interview—Part II'. Recorded by Richard Tremblay, at https://www.youtube.com/watch?v=5d7Br9Yvq10 (Accessed December 30 2017)

Erica Chenoweth and Maria J Stephan, 2011—*Why Civil Resistance Works: The Strategic Logic of Nonviolent Conflict*. New York: Columbia University Press

Mayur Chetia, August 2008—'World Social Forum and the Reaction from the Indian Left'. *Critical Engagement* Document no 5. Paper prepared as CACIM Forum Fellow 2007–08. New Delhi: CACIM, at http://www.cacim.net/twiki/tiki-searchresults.php?highlight=Critical+Engagement+Document+no+5&where=pages&search=Go (Accessed August 29 2017)

John Brown Childs, 2003—*Transcommunality: From the Politics of Conversion to the Ethics of Respect*. Philadelphia: Temple University Press

John Brown Childs, 2018—'Boundary as Bridge', in Jai Sen, ed, 2018—*The Movements of Movements, Part 2: Rethinking Our Dance*. Volume 5 in the *Challenging Empires* series. New Delhi: OpenWord, and Oakland, CA: PM Press

Janet Conway, 2012—*Edges of Global Justice: The World Social Forum and its 'Others'*. London and New York: Routledge

Jeff Corntassel, 2006—'To be ungovernable', in *The New Socialist*, issue 58, special issue on 'Indigenous Resurgence', September–October 2006, at http://www.corntassel.net/ToBeUngovernable.pdf (Accessed August 29 2017)

Jeff Corntassel, 2017—'Rethinking Self-Determination: Lessons from the Indigenous-Rights Discourse', in Jai Sen, ed, 2017a—*The Movements of Movements, Part 1: What Makes Us Move?*. Volume 4 in the *Challenging Empires* series. New Delhi: OpenWord, and Oakland, CA: PM Press

Glen Coulthard, 2006—'Indigenous peoples and the "politics of recognition"', in *The New Socialist*, issue 58, special issue on 'Indigenous Resurgence', September–October 2006, at https://www.cpsa-acsp.ca/papers-2006/Coulthard.pdf (Accessed August 29 2017)

Laurence Cox and Alf Gunvald Nilsen, 2014—*We Make Our Own History: Marxism and Social Movements in the Twilight of Neoliberalism*. London: Pluto

John Murray Cuddihy, 1974—*The Ordeal of Civility: Freud, Marx, Lévi-Strauss, and the Jewish Struggle with Modernity*. New York: Dell

Dennis Dalton, 1998 [1993]—*Gandhi's Power: Nonviolence in Action*. New Delhi: Oxford University Press

Anila Daulatzai, December 2004—'A leap of faith: Thoughts on secularistic practices and progressive politics', in *International Social Science Journal*, Issue no 182, pp 565–76, at http://onlinelibrary.wiley.com/doi/10.1111/j.0020-8701.2004.00517.x/abstract (Accessed August 29 2017)

Anila Daulatzai, 2018—'Believing in Exclusion: The Problem of Secularism in Progressive Politics', in Jai Sen, ed, 2018—*The Movements of Movements, Part 2: Rethinking Our Dance.* Volume 5 in the *Challenging Empires* series. New Delhi: OpenWord, and Oakland, CA: PM Press

Massimo De Angelis, 2018—'PR like PRocess! Strategy from the Bottom Up', in Jai Sen, ed, 2018—*The Movements of Movements, Part 2: Rethinking Our Dance.* Volume 5 in the *Challenging Empires* series. New Delhi: OpenWord, and Oakland, CA: PM Press

Paul Divakar Namala, 2011—'Making Caste a Global Issue', in Jai Sen, ed, 2011a—*Interrogating Empires.* New Delhi: OpenWord and Daanish Books

Emma Dowling, 2005—'The Ethics of Engagement Revisited: Remembering the ESF 2004', in *ephemera*, Vol 5, No 2, pp 205–15, at http://www.ephemerajournal.org/contribution/ethics-engagement-revisited-remembering-esf-2004 (Accessed August 29 2017)

Jennifer Dunning, January 2007—'Chandralekha, 79, Dancer Who Blended Indian Forms, Dies', in *New York Times*, January 7 2007, at http://www.nytimes.com/2007/01/07/arts/07chandralekha.html?_r=0 (Accessed August 29 2017)

Richard Falk, 1993a—'The Making of Global Citizenship', in Jeremy Brecher, John Brown Childs, and Jill Cutler, eds, 1993—*Global Visions*, pp 39–50. Boston, MA: South End Press

Richard Falk, 1997—'Resisting "Globalization-from-above" through "Globalization-from-below"', in *New Political Economy* 2, pp 17–24

Forum pour un Autre Mali, Forum Mondial des Alternatives (France), Forum du Tiers Monde (Sénégal), ENDA (Sénégal) et al, February 2006—'The Bamako Appeal', January 18 2006. Text circulated by Samir Amin, President of the World Forum for Alternatives, at http://www.openspaceforum.net/twiki/tiki-read_article.php?articleId=66 (Accessed August 29 2017)

The Free Association, June 2007—'Worlds in motion', in *Turbulence*, Issue 1, June 2007, at http://turbulence.org.uk/turbulence-1/worlds-in-motion/ (Accessed August 29 2017)

The Free Association, 2018—'Worlds in Motion: Movements, Problematics, and the Creation of New Worlds', in Jai Sen, ed, 2018—*The Movements of Movements, Part 2: Rethinking Our Dance.* Volume 5 in the *Challenging Empires* series. New Delhi: OpenWord, and Oakland, CA: PM Press

Jo Freeman (aka Joreen), nd [May 1970 / 1971]—'The tyranny of structurelessness' at http://www.jofreeman.com/joreen/tyranny.htm (Accessed August 29 2017)

Rajmohan Gandhi, January 2015—*Independence And Social Justice: Understanding the Ambedkar–Gandhi Debate.* New Delhi: Gandhi Foundation, at https://gandhifoundation.files.wordpress.com/2015/01/independence-and-social-justice-jan-2015.pdf (Accessed August 29 2017)

Marlies Glasius, Mary Kaldor, and Helmut Anheier, eds, 2006—*Global Civil Society 2005 / 6.* London, Thousand Oaks, and New Delhi: Sage, at http://www.lse.ac.uk/Depts/global/yearbook05.htm (Accessed August 14 2017)

Marlies Glasius, Mary Kaldor, and Helmut Anheier, eds, 2007—*Global Civil Society 2006 / 7*. London: Sage, at http://www.lse.ac.uk/Depts/global/yearbook06-7.htm (Accessed August 14 2017)

John Holloway, 2010—*Crack Capitalism*. London: Pluto

John Holloway, nd [c.June 2007]—'Break, Breakdown, Breakthrough'. Note for presentation at Panel Discussion at Alternative Summit at Rostock, Germany, June 5 2007

Jude Howell and Jenny Pearce, 1998—*Civil Society and Development: A critical exploration*. Boulder, Co, and London: Lynne Rienner

Chris Hurl, November 2006—'Challenging Empires: Retrocolonialism, Neocolonialism, and Dissent within Dissent'. Note for presentation to graduate course at the University of Carleton, Open Space and Dissent in Movement, Sociology 5805, on November 2 2006

Indigenous Resistance, 2007—*IR10 Indigenous Dublands*, at https://www.beatport.com/release/indigenous-dublands/110890 (Accessed December 30 2017)

Jamaa Al-Yad, at http://www.jamaalyad.org/ (Accessed August 29 2017)

Jeffrey S Juris, 2012b—'Opening Spaces at the US Social Forum', in Jai Sen and Peter Waterman, eds, 2012—*World Social Forum: Critical Explorations*. Volume 3 in the *Challenging Empires* series. New Delhi: OpenWord

Alex Khasnabish, 2017—'Forward Dreaming: Zapatismo and the Radical Imagination', in Jai Sen, ed, 2017a—*The Movements of Movements, Part 1 What Makes Us Move?*. Volume 4 in the *Challenging Empires* series. New Delhi: OpenWord, and Oakland, CA: PM Press

David C Korten, 1998b—*Globalising Civil Society: Reclaiming our Right to Power*. New York: Seven Stories Press

Corinne Kumar, ed, 2007—*Asking, We Walk: South as New Political Imaginary*. Bangalore: Streelekha Publications

Sashi Kumar, 2004—'Chandralekha—Choreography', in *'Kāya Taran' (Chrysalis)*, at http://www.kayataran.com/behindscenes/chandralekha.htm (Accessed August 29 2017)

Labofii—Laboratory of Insurrectionary Imagination, at https://labofii.wordpress.com/ (Accessed August 29 2017)

Michael Leon Guerrero, Tammy Bang Luu, and Cindy Wiesner, 2009—'The Road to Atlanta', in Jai Sen and Peter Waterman, eds, 2009—*World Social Forum: Challenging Empires*, second edition. Montreal: Black Rose Books, pp 315–31

Xochitl Leyva Solano, 2017—'Geopolitics of Knowledge and the Neo-Zapatista Social Movement Networks', in Jai Sen, ed, 2017a—*The Movements of Movements, Part 1: What Makes Us Move?*. Volume 4 in the *Challenging Empires* series. New Delhi: OpenWord, and Oakland, CA: PM Press

Marianne Maeckelbergh, 2009—*The Will of the Many: How the Alterglobalisation Movement is Changing the Face of Democracy*. London: Pluto Press

Elizabeth Betita Martínez, January 2000—'Where Was The Color in Seattle? Looking for reasons why the Great Battle was so white'. Extended version of article in *ColorLines*, February 2000, at http://www.nadir.org/nadir/initiativ/agp/free/seattle/color.htm (Accessed August 29 2017)

Mauvaise Troupe Collective, February 2016—'Defending the Zad: A new little book about the struggle against an airport and its world', on *Laboratory of Insurrectionary*

Imagination, February 9 2016, at https://labofii.wordpress.com/2016/02/09/defending-the-zad-a-new-little-book-about-the-struggle-against-the-airport-and-its-world/ (Accessed August 29 2017)

S R Mehrotra, 2014—*The Mahatma & The Doctor: The Untold Story of Dr Pranjivan Mehta, Gandhi's Greatest Friend and Benefactor*. Mumbai: Vakils, Feffer, and Simons

Sadanand Menon, interviewed by Shobha Warrier, January 2007—'For Chandralekha, the body was erotic, sensuous', on *Rediff.com*, January 3 2007, at http://www.rediff.com/news/2007/jan/03inter.htm (Accessed August 29 2017)

Matt Meyer and Ousseina Alidou, 2018—'The Power of Words: Reclaiming and Reimagining Revolution and Nonviolence', in Jai Sen, ed, 2018—*The Movements of Movements, Part 2: Rethinking Our Dance*. Volume 5 in the *Challenging Empires* series. New Delhi: OpenWord, and Oakland, CA: PM Press

Muto Ichiyo, June 2004—'Alliance of Hope and Challenges of Global Democracy'. Keynote address at 'Alliance of Hope: Encounter of 1993 Regional Networks', June 18–22 2004, Geneva, at http://onlinelibrary.wiley.com/doi/10.1111/j.1758-6623.1994.tb02906.x/full (Accessed August 29 2017)

Muto Ichiyo, 2018—'Towards the Autonomy of the People of the World: Need for a New Movement of Movements to Animate People's Alliance Processes', in Jai Sen, ed, 2018—*The Movements of Movements, Part 2: Rethinking Our Dance*. Volume 5 in the *Challenging Empires* series. New Delhi: OpenWord, and Oakland, CA: PM Press

NCDHR (National Campaign on Dalit Human Rights), 2003—*Dalits on Globalisation : Making Another World Possible*. Secunderabad: National Campaign on Dalit Human Rights

Notes from Nowhere, eds, 2003—*We are Everywhere: The Irresistible Rise of Global Anti-Capitalism*. London and New York: Verso, at http://artactivism.members.gn.apc.org/stories.htm (Accessed August 29 2017)

Rodrigo Nunes, 2012—'The Intercontinental Youth Camp as the Unthought of World Social Forum, Revisited', in Jai Sen and Peter Waterman, eds, 2012—*World Social Forum: Critical Explorations*. Volume 3 in the *Challenging Empires* series. New Delhi: OpenWord

Onyango Oloo, National Coordinator, Kenya Social Forum, March 2007—'Critical Reflections on WSF Nairobi 2007', at http://www.cadtm.org/Critical-Reflections-on-WSF (Accessed December 30 2017)

Gail Omvedt, 1994—*Dalits and the Democratic Revolution: Dr Ambedkar and the Dalit Movement in Colonial India*. New Delhi: Sage Publications

Gail Omvedt, 2001—'Ambedkar and After: The Dalit Movement in India', in Ghanshyam Shah, ed, 2001—*Dalit Identity and Politics*. New Delhi: Sage Publications

Marie-Emmanuelle Pommerolle and Nicolas Haeringer, 2012—'The WSF at Test: Extraversion and Controversies during the World Social Forum in Nairobi', in Jai Sen and Peter Waterman, eds, 2012—*World Social Forum: Critical Explorations*. Volume 3 in the *Challenging Empires* series. New Delhi: OpenWord

Vinod Raina, October 2007—'Guiding Principles for Holding WSF Events', at http://openspaceforum.net/twiki/tiki-read_article.php?articleId=501 (Accessed August 29 2017)

Leena Rikkilä and Katarina Sehm Patomäki, eds, 2002—*From a Global Market Place to Political Spaces—the North South Dialogue continues*. NIGD Working Paper 1 / 2002, at http://www.nigd.org/publications (Inactive August 29 2017)

Arundhati Roy, 2014—'Introduction' to Dr Bhim Rao Ambedkar, 2014 [1936]—*Annihilation of Caste: The Annotated Critical Edition*. New Delhi: Navayana Books

Jerry Rubin, 1970—*Do It! Scenarios of the Revolution*. New York: Simon and Schuster

Jerry Rubin, 1971—*We Are Everywhere*. New York: Harper & Row

Boaventura de Sousa Santos, 2006—*The Rise of the Global Left: The World Social Forum and Beyond*. London: Zed Books

Ronald Segal, 1995—*The Black Diaspora*. London: Faber and Faber [in North America, *The Black Diaspora: Five Centuries of the Black Experience Outside Africa*. New York: Farrar, Straus and Giroux]

Jai Sen, June 1996a—'"Participation of the People"—Intentions and Contradictions: A Critical Look at Habitat II', in *Economic and Political Weekly*, June 1 1996, pp 1302–06

Jai Sen, December 1999—'A World to Win—But whose world is it, anyway?', Chapter 9 in John W Foster and Anita Anand, eds, 1999—*Whose World is it Anyway? Civil Society, the United Nations, and the multilateral future*. Ottawa: United Nations Association in Canada, pp 337–90

Jai Sen, May 2000d—'Some comments [to Jeremy Brecher] on the March 31 2000 draft of 'Globalisation from below'. Personal correspondence, May 2000

Jai Sen, 2002—'Are other globalizations possible? The World Social Forum as an instrument of global democratization'. Chapter 8 in Leena Rikkilä and Katarina Sehm Patomäki, eds, 2002—*From a Global Market Place to Political Spaces*, pp 167–205

Jai Sen, December 2004 [October 2004c]—'*Supermakt!* Superpower! But through Global Cooperation or Global Corporation? Some critical reflections on democratic options'. Notes for a presentation at the public meeting on 'Global cooperation: What democratic possibilities are there?', Norwegian Social Forum, Oslo, Norway, October 22 2004

Jai Sen, 2004b—'How Open? The Forum as Logo, the Forum as Religion—Scepticism of the Intellect, Optimism of the Will', in Jai Sen, Anita Anand, Arturo Escobar, and Peter Waterman, eds, 2004—*World Social Forum: Challenging Empires*. New Delhi: Viveka, pp 210–27, at http://www.choike.org/nuevo_eng/informes/1557.html (Accessed August 29 2017)

Jai Sen, 2004c—'The Long March to Another World: Reflections of a member of the WSF India Committee in 2002 on the first year of the World Social Forum process in India', in Jai Sen, Anita Anand, Arturo Escobar, and Peter Waterman, eds, 2004—*World Social Forum: Challenging Empires*. New Delhi: Viveka, pp 293–311, at http://www.choike.org/nuevo_eng/informes/1557.html (Accessed August 29 2017)

Jai Sen, 2004d—'A Tale of Two Charters', in Jai Sen, Anita Anand, Arturo Escobar, and Peter Waterman, eds, 2004—*World Social Forum: Challenging Empires*. New Delhi: Viveka, pp 72–75, at http://www.choike.org/nuevo_eng/informes/1557.html (Accessed August 29 2017)

Jai Sen, July 2005a—'On Incivility and Transnationality: Towards Alliances of Critical Hope. Steps towards critically engaging with Muto Ichiyo's concept of transborder participatory democracy'. Paper presented at 'The Long March of 50 Year People's Movement: The Works of Muto Ichiyo', IACS Conference 'Emerging Inter-Asian Subjectivities in Cultural Movements', Korean National University of the Arts at the

Ilmin Museum of Art, Seoul, South Korea, July 22–24 2005, at http://www.cacim. net/twiki/tiki-read_article.php?articleId=59 (Accessed August 29 2017)

Jai Sen, March 2006—'Understanding the World Social Forum: The WSF as an Emergent Learning Process—Notes on the Dynamics of Change', in *Mainstream* (New Delhi), March 25 2006, pp 9–24

Jai Sen, January 2007a—'The World Social Forum as an emergent learning process', in *Futures* vol 39 (2007), pp 505–22

Jai Sen, February 2007—Course Outline for 'Other Worlds, Other Globalisations', Institute of Political Economy, Carleton University, Ottawa, Canada, at http:// critical-courses.cacim.net/twiki/tiki-index.php?page=OWOGHome (Inactive August 29 2017)

Jai Sen, November 2007a—'Some Hard Questions, 2: A Source Of Considerable Worry; Some Suggestions for the Forum', on *WSFDiscuss*, November 1 2007, at http:// openspaceforum.net/twiki/tiki-read_article.php?articleId=502 (Accessed August 29 2017)

Jai Sen, May 2009b—'Towards Walking the Earth Together: An Open Letter to the Puno Cumbre / *Caminar Hacia la Tierra Juntos: Una Carta Abierta a la Cumbre de Puno*', May 22 2009, at http://www.openspaceforum.net/twiki/tiki-index. php?page=MingaInDefence&highlight=towards%20walking (Accessed August 29 2017)

Jai Sen, 2010—'On open space: Explorations towards a vocabulary of a more open poli- tics', in *Antipode*, Vol 42 No 4, 2010, pp 994–1018, at http://onlinelibrary.wiley.com/ doi/10.1111/j.1467-8330.2010.00785.x/full (Accessed August 29 2017)

Jai Sen, 2017a—'The Movements of Movements: An Introduction and an Exploration'. Introduction to Jai Sen, ed, 2017a—*The Movements of Movements, Part 1: What Makes Us Move?*. Volume 4 in the *Challenging Empires* series. New Delhi: Open- Word, and Oakland, CA: PM Press

Jai Sen, 2018b—'Break Free! Engaging Critically with the Concept and Reality of Civil Society (Part 1)', in Jai Sen, ed, 2018—*The Movements of Movements, Part 2: Rethink- ing Our Dance*. Volume 5 in the *Challenging Empires* series. New Delhi: OpenWord, and Oakland, CA: PM Press

Jai Sen and Madhuresh Kumar, compilers, with Patrick Bond and Peter Waterman, January 2007—*A Political Programme for the World Social Forum? Democracy, Substance, and Debate in the Bamako Appeal and the Global Justice Movements—A Reader*. New Delhi: CACIM, and Durban: University of KwaZulu-Natal Centre for Civil Society (CCS)

Jai Sen and Mayuri Saini, eds, January 2005—*Are Other Worlds Possible? Talking NEW Politics*. Book One of *Are Other Worlds Possible?* series. New Delhi: Zubaan Books

Jai Sen and Peter Waterman, eds, 2012—*World Social Forum: Critical Explorations*. Volume 3 in the *Challenging Empires* series. New Delhi: OpenWord

Shuddhabrata Sengupta, February 2016—'Break Down the Barriers: Reading Robin T, Bhimrao, and the Nation State at JNU', on *Kafila*, February 16 2016 , at https:// kafila.online/2016/02/16/break-down-the-barriers-reading-robin-t-bhimrao-and- the-nation-state-in-jnu/ (Accessed January 12 2018)

Gene Sharp, 1973—'Gene Sharp's 198 methods of nonviolent action', on *War Resisters' International*, at http://www.wri-irg.org/node/4558 (Accessed August 29 2017)

Gene Sharp, 1973—*The Methods of Nonviolent Action*. Boston MA: Porter Sargent Publishers

Leanne Simpson, 2011—*Dancing on Our Turtle's Back: Stories of Nishnaabeg Re-creation, Resurgence, and a New Emergence*. Winnipeg: Arbeiter Ring Publishing

Oishik Sircar, May 2010—'Sexing Spaces of Emancipation: The Politics and Poetics of Sexuality Within The World Social Forum Process', in *Critical Engagement Occasional Publication* 9. New Delhi: CACIM, at https://www.academia.edu/5547204/Sexing_Spaces_of_Emancipation_The_Politics_and_Poetics_of_Sexuality_in_the_World_Social_Forum_Process_2010_ (Accessed August 29 2017)

Marina Sitrin, ed, 2006—*Horizontalism: Voices of Popular Power in Argentina*. Oakland, CA, and Edinburgh: AK Press

Leslie Sklair, 1991—*Sociology of the Global System*. London: Harvester Wheatsheaf

Leslie Sklair, March 2005—'The silent qualifiers of globalization'. Public Lecture, London School of Economics and Political Science, March 1 2005, at https://digital.library.lse.ac.uk/objects/lse:ner413qow (Accessed August 29 2017)

Jackie Smith, Marina Karides, Marc Becker, Dorval Brunelle, Christopher Chase-Dunn, Donatella della Porta, Rosalba Icaza Garza, Jeffrey S. Juris, Lorenzo Mosca, Ellen Reese, Peter (Jay) Smith, and Rolando Vazquez, 2008—*Global Democracy and the World Social Forums*. Boulder CO: Paradigm Press

Peter J Smith, 2008—'Going Global: The Transnational Politics of the Dalit Movement', in *Globalizations*, volume 5 no 1, pp 13–33

Laura Sullivan, 2012—'Activism, Affect, and Abuse: The Emotional Contexts and Consequences of the ESF Organising Process 2004', in Jai Sen and Peter Waterman, eds, 2012—*World Social Forum: Critical Explorations*. Volume 3 in the *Challenging Empires* series. New Delhi: OpenWord

Rabindranath Tagore, 1933—*'Bandh Bhengey Dao'* ['Break all the Barriers, Let the captive soul be liberated', in Bengali], performed in Q, 2013—*Tasher Desh* ['Card Country'], based on lyrics and music by Rabindranath Tagore, on *YouTube*, at https://youtu.be/Pd45sWu_8Dg (Accessed August 29 2017)

Teivo Teivainen, 2016—'Occupy representation and democratize prefiguration: Speaking for others in global justice movements', in *Capital & Class*, vol 40 no 1, pp 19–36

Anand Teltumbde, 2017—'Dalits, Anti-Imperialism, and the Annihilation of Caste', in Jai Sen, ed, 2017a—*The Movements of Movements, Part 1: What Makes Us Move?*. Volume 4 in the *Challenging Empires* series. New Delhi: OpenWord, and Oakland, CA: PM Press

James Toth, 2017—'Local Islam Gone Global: The Roots of Religious Militancy in Egypt and its Transnational Transformation', in Jai Sen, ed, 2017a—*The Movements of Movements, Part 1: What Makes Us Move?*. Volume 4 in the *Challenging Empires* series. New Delhi: OpenWord, and Oakland, CA: PM Press

Paul Treanor, November 2002—'Who controls the European Social Forum?', at https://www.indymedia.org.uk/en/2002/11/45734.html (Accessed August 29 2017)

Virginia Vargas, 2017—'International Feminisms: New Syntheses, New Directions', in Jai Sen, ed, 2017a—*The Movements of Movements, Part 1: What Makes Us Move?*. Volume 4 in the *Challenging Empires* series. New Delhi: OpenWord, and Oakland, CA: PM Press

Immanuel Wallerstein, August 2006—'The Curve of American Power', in *New Left Review*, vol 40, August 2006

Peter Waterman, November 2003—Personal communication with Jai Sen, November 20 2003

Peter Waterman, 2004a—'Globalisation from the Middle? Reflections from a Margin', in Jai Sen, Anita Anand, Arturo Escobar, and Peter Waterman, eds, 2004—*World Social Forum: Challenging Empires*. New Delhi: Viveka, pp 87–94, at https://www.tni.org/es/node/14407 (Accessed August 29 2017)

Chico Whitaker, December 2012—'World Social Forum: Space or movement? Thinking about the WSF International Council future in new perspectives', on *WSFDiscuss*, December 16 2012 (Inactive August 29 2017)

World Social Forum Organising Committee and World Social Forum International Council, June 2001—'World Social Forum Charter of Principles', June 10 2001, at https://www.colorado.edu/AmStudies/lewis/ecology/wsfcharter.pdf (Accessed December 31 2017)

Zapatista Army of National Liberation (EZLN), May 1996—'Invitation-summons to the Intercontinental Encounter for Humanity and Against Neoliberalism, Mexico, May of 1996', at http://www.cacim.net/bareader/pages/Beyond%20Bamako5.html (Accessed August 29 2017)

Zapatista Army of National Liberation (EZLN), 1997—'Summons to the Second International Encounter For Humanity and against Neoliberalism (26th July to 3rd Aug. 1997)', at http://216.239.39.104/custom?q=cache:QWpaVO0UpRkJ:www.pangea.org/encuentro/convocatoria_in.htm+zapatistas+world+include+other+worlds&hl=en&ie=UTF-8 (Inactive December 31 2017)

Notes

1. This is Part 2 of a revised version of an essay titled 'The power of civility' that first appeared in a special issue of the journal *Development Dialogue* titled 'Global Civil Society—More or Less Democracy?' (Löfgren and Thörn 2007; Sen, November 2007)—and prior to that was the text of a presentation to a Committee on Civil Society Research (Sweden) seminar at the World Social Forum in Nairobi, Kenya, January 22 2007. This version is very different and my arguments substantially developed, but I nevertheless thank the publishers of my 2007 essay, the Dag Hammarskjöld Foundation, and the editors Mikael Löfgren and Håkan Thörn for their ready respective agreements to my request republish the essay in revised form. This essay as it stands has been a long time in the making. Vipul Rikhi was the Content Editor for the first version some years ago. Given the delays in the publication of the book/s in which it was to appear, I further developed and reworked several of my arguments. Therefore Vipul bears no responsibility for the essay as it now stands. But my thanks to him for doing a wonderful job the first time around. Finally, I want to acknowledge that I have taken the enormous liberty of having access—as editor—to all the great essays in this book and its companion volume (Sen, ed, 2017a) to quote from several of them. This essay is published here in two parts. Part 1 appears as the third essay in the third section of this book (Sen 2018).

2. Sengupta, February 2016, which I urge everyone to read. Thanks for the inspiration, Shuddha! I want to take this opportunity to acknowledge that in 2008 Corinne

Kumar of CIEDS in Bangalore (now also Bengaluru), India, and El Taller in Tunisia, on reading the original 2007 version of this essay invited me to write a contribution on incivility for a book she was working on, book 3 of a trilogy, *Asking, We Walk: South as New Political Imaginary* (Bangalore: Streelekha Publications, 2007). In doing so, she put her finger on a key missing part in my argument and text, which I address here. So, thanks to you too, Corinne!

3.   For a discussion of my distinction between uncivil and incivil, see the third section in the first part of this essay (Sen 2018).

4.   Alfred 2005, p 39, citing Bighorse 1990.

5.   Alfred 2005, pp 86–87, pp 77–97. *Onkwehonwe* means 'original people'.

6.   The Free Association, June 2007. See also their essay in this book (2018), a revised version of this 2007 essay.

7.   Holloway, nd [*c*.June 2007]. For a related and much developed discussion of the word 'crack', see Holloway 2010.

8.   In Part 1 of this essay.

9.   Baldwin, with KQED, 1963. Emphases added.

10. Alfred 2005.

11. The written and unwritten requirement to advance in academia is to publish in specific established journals that cite well respected authors; in other words, academics are guided towards living and working within civil society.

12. Simpson 2011.

13. I am always delighted and deeply moved to also see this quality in the work of Alfred's colleagues and students, such as Jeff Corntassel and Glen Coulthard, and to come across the work of people inspired by Taiaiake Alfred, such as Leanne Simpson. Jeff Corntassel is a co-author with Alfred of an essay in the companion volume to this book (Alfred and Corntassel 2017) and of an independent essay there (Corntassel 2017); see also Corntassel 2006. Glen Coulthard has gone on to work—and dance—independently. For an early piece, while with Alfred, see Coulthard 2006. For the work and dance of someone inspired by Alfred's dance, see Simpson 2011. It is empowering to see this resurgence taking place.

14. Ambedkar 2014 [1936].

15. See Omvedt 1994 and 2001.

16. See, especially, Ambedkar 2014 [1936].

17. See Ambedkar, nd [1936].

18. Cuddihy 1974.

19. Extract from the back cover text of Cuddihy 1974. In the book, following some discussion of the life and work of other Jewish intellectuals in Europe at that time, Cuddihy says: "Our analysis of Freud, Marx, and Lévi-Strauss, then, would seem to be applicable—*mutatis mutandis*—to other intellectual giants of the [Jewish] Diaspora" (p 234). In a footnote, he adds: "This volume, in fact, is but a fragment of work completed and work in progress that deals with Kafka, Wittgenstein, Hannah Arendt, and many others".

20. See https://en.wikipedia.org/wiki/Jerry_Rubin (Accessed August 29 2017).

21. Rubin 1970.

22. It is not unimportant that one of the most significant books about recent / contemporary world movement is titled *We Are Everywhere: The Irresistible Rise of Global*

Anti-Capitalism (Notes From Nowhere, eds, 2003)—Jerry Rubin authored a book with the same main title in 1971.

23. https://en.wikipedia.org/wiki/Fountain_%28Duchamp%29 (Accessed August 29 2017).

24. https://en.wikipedia.org/wiki/Jerry_Rubin (Accessed August 29 2017).

25. For an exploration of some of this ground, see the essay by Tariq Ali in the companion volume (2017).

26. https://en.wikipedia.org/wiki/Women_in_Black (Accessed August 29 2017).

27. Personal conversation, early 1980s.

28. See S Menon, January 2007, Bharucha 1995, Kumar 2004, and Dunning, January 2007; watch and listen to Chandralekha herself at Chandralekha 1997. Watching this, and looking back at the photos in these articles, has reminded me of how much Chandralekha's students have, like Taiaiake Alfred's, gone on to contribute to dance and movement in their own very creative and powerful ways.

29. For instance, Indigenous Resistance 2007. For information on the group, see https://www.sonicbids.com/band/indigenousresistance/ (Accessed August 29 2017).

30. Brecher 2015, pp 73–74. Emphases added.

31. Gandhi was deeply moved by and drew on the writings of Rousseau and Tolstoy, among others, and his own thinking was forged through extensive discussion. For a fascinating history of another influence on his thinking—little known till now—see Mehrotra 2014.

32. See, for instance, Roy 2014; for a rejoinder, see R Gandhi, January 2015.

33. For the codification, see Sharp 1973 and Dalton 1998 [1993]; for the adoption, application, and dissemination of these ideas, see, for instance, Sharp 1973.

34. A great deal of interesting work has discussed the concept of open space; at the risk of being self-referential, I here again primarily cite my own work. See Sen 2004b; Sen 2010; and Juris 2012b.

35. I tried opening up these questions at a fairly early stage of the WSF's life—when I still thought of it as young—but to little avail. See Sen 2004b. I am very aware that this is not how other commentators on the WSF, whom I respect a great deal, see and assess the WSF. For instance, Sonia Alvarez, in her wonderful essay on the World Social Forum in an earlier book in this series, 'Globalised Localisms: The Travels and Translations of the World Social Forum Process' (2012) says: "By contrast, the WSF has focused on challenging and undermining the workings of hegemonic global institutions". Interestingly, she cites the work of the editorial-activist collective Notes from Nowhere, which I too cite—but I see their work very differently: through the lens of civility.

36. For instance, Holloway 2010.

37. Such as in Argentina in the early 2000s; see Sitrin, ed, 2006. For a contemporary example, see Mauvaise Troupe Collective, February 2016.

38. See, for instance, the work of Labofii—Laboratory of Insurrectionary Imagination, at https://labofii.wordpress.com/ (Accessed August 29 2017); see also Creative Dissent: Art of the Arab World Uprisings, at http://artsofthearabworlduprisings.com/ (Accessed August 29 2017) and Jamaa Al-Yad at http://www.jamaalyad.org/ (Accessed August 29 2017).

39. Chenoweth and Stephan 2011.

40. Tagore 1933.

41. Sen 2018b.

42. Rikkilä and Sehm Patomäki, eds, 2002; my contribution to their book, Sen 2002; Santos 2006; Smith, Karides, Becker, Brunelle, Chase-Dunn, della Porta, Garza, Juris et al 2008.

43. For details of my involvement with the World Social Forum, see note 14 in Part 1 of this essay.

44. For an initial discussion of these dynamics, see Sen, December 2004 [October 2004]; for a detailed ethnographic discussion of a major transnational civil campaign at the World Bank around the Narmada dams in India, see Sen, December 1999; for a masterful, comprehensive discussion of the dynamics of 'othering' in the WSF and in global social movement, see Conway 2012.

45. On the global networks created by and around the Zapatista movement, see, for instance, Zapatista Army of National Liberation (EZLN), May 1996, and the essays by Alex Khasnabish and Xochitl Leyva Solano in the companion volume to this book (Khasnabish 2017; Leyva Solano 2017). On global networks by and among Dalits, see P Smith 2008 and Divakar Namala 2011; by and among women, see the essay by Gina Vargas in the companion volume to this book (2017); on the Muslim Brotherhood, see the essay by James Toth in the companion volume to this book (2017); by African Americans and the Indigenous Peoples / Indians of the US, see the essay by Matt Meyer and Ousseina Alidou in this book (2018).

46. CAOI (Coordinadora Andina de Organizaciones Indígenas), ECUARUNARI (Confederación de Pueblos de la Nacionalidad Kichwa del Ecuador), ONIC (Organización Nacional Indígena de Colombia) et al, February 2009a.

47. Divakar Namala 2011. At the time that he said this, Paul Divakar Namala was National Convenor of the NCDHR (National Campaign for Dalit Human Rights) in India. He is now its General Secretary.

48. For a close discussion of the dynamics of the actions in Heiligendamm in 2007, see the essay by Chris Carlsson in this book (2017).

49. Martínez, January 2000.

50. Ibid.

51. For a full discussion of colour in the WSF, see Álvarez, Gutierrez, Kim, Petit, and Reese 2008.

52. For a more comprehensive discussion of Dalits at the Mumbai WSF, see Abraham, May 2010.

53. Teltumbde 2017.

54. For a detailed discussion of these dynamics, see Caruso, December 2004.

55. Caruso 2004.

56. Daulatzai, December 2004. See also her essay in this volume. See also Sircar 2010 for similar dynamics in the WSF in terms of sexuality.

57. For a terse but comprehensive critical reflection on the issues of exclusion and commercialisation at the Nairobi Forum by one of its organisers, see Oloo (National Coordinator, Kenya Social Forum), March 2007. For a discussion of the presence of fundamentalist religious groups, see the essay by Virginia Vargas in the companion volume to this book (2017). For an archive of reflections on the Nairobi Forum and on the WSF as a whole, see http://openspaceforum.net/pipermail/

worldsocialforum-discuss_openspaceforum.net/ (Accessed August 29 2017). For a more nuanced analysis of the dynamics at play, see Pommerolle and Haeringer, 2011.

58. Conway 2012. Emphases added.

59. CAOI (Coordinadora Andina de Organizaciones Indígenas), ECUARUNARI (Confederación de Pueblos de la Nacionalidad Kichwa del Ecuador), ONIC (Organización Nacional Indígena de Colombia) et al, February 2009a.

60. For a discussion of this complex terrain, see CACIM and NFFPFW, May 2009.

61. Sen, May 2009b.

62. Sen 2018b.

63. See the cover of one of the books I published at that time for a picture from those moments; Sen and Saini, eds, January 2005, at http://books.google.co.in/books?id=yeh6sswTy8MC&pg=PA1986&dq#v=onepage&q=&f=false (Accessed August 29 2017).

64. For a very interesting discussion of "the Mumbai effect" in the planning of the WSF, see Nunes 2012.

65. The World Social Forum in Montréal, Canada, in August 2016, took place largely, though not exclusively, on college campuses. See https://fsm2016.org/en/sinformer/ (Accessed December 31 2017).

66. Leon Guerrero, Luu, and Wiesner 2009; for an analysis of the concept and practice of 'intentionality', see Juris 2012a, in the same series as this book, see Sen and Waterman, eds, 2012.

67. All quotes from Conway 2012, Chapter 6.

68. This section of this essay was finalised in 2014–15. The World Social Forum process has continued to unfold thereafter, including two world gatherings (in Tunis in 2015 and in Montréal in 2016) and some regional and / or thematic events (such as a Pan-Amazonian Social Forum in 2017). This section does not reflect any of the changes that might have taken place in the WSF since 2014 in relation to the concerns raised here.

69. Sen, January 2007; for a more easily accessible but earlier version, Sen, March 2006.

70. Sen, December 2004 [October 2004].

71. World Social Forum Organising Committee and World Social Forum International Council, June 2001.

72. See the WSF Charter of Principles; World Social Forum Organising Committee and World Social Forum International Council, June 2001. For a discussion of this, see Sen 2004d.

73. Zapatista Army of National Liberation (EZLN), May 1996 and May 1997.

74. Waterman, November 20 2003.

75. For the concept of the tyranny of structurelessness, see Freeman (aka Joreen), nd [May 1970 / 1971].

76. For a study of the dynamics of control in the case of the WSF in India, see Chetia, August 2008.

77. World Social Forum Organising Committee and World Social Forum International Council, June 2001.

78. For a recent intervention on this longstanding and tortured debate, see Teivainen 2016.

79. Sen, November 2007a.
80. Raina, October 2007.
81. Whitaker, December 2012.
82. For a discussion of the WSF in India, see Sen 2004c and Chetia, August 2008; for a discussion of the ESF in London, see Treanor, November 2002. See Dowling 2005 and Sullivan 2012 for careful reflections on and analyses of the power dynamics that were involved in establishing and maintaining control at the London ESF and the brutalisation involved.
83. I assert this about the WSF, even though I am aware of William (Bill) Carroll's conclusion in his otherwise very interesting and useful study of "alternative policy groups"—that their leadership does not sit on each other's boards (Carroll, December 2013). He has drawn his conclusion on the basis of a very specialised sample: almost by definition, the organisations that he chose to study were likely to be somewhat different in how they and their members behaved from the much broader mass of entities that make up 'global civil society'.
84. For a discussion of the emergence of a transnational capitalist class, see Sklair 1991. For a first exploration of its parallels in so-called 'alternative globalisation', see Sklair, March 2005.
85. Sen 2004b.
86. The most prominent and well-known examples are inviting political leaders to speak at the WSF, including Lula, the former president of Brazil, and the late Hugo Chávez, the former president of Venezuela, despite the WSF Charter of Principles specifically proscribing this (and worse, then saying that 'the WSF' didn't invite them, that 'some organisation taking part in the WSF' had!), and accepting corporate sponsorship, even from corruption-ridden corporations such as Petrobras (the same Petrobras that is today at the centre of the huge political storm in Brazil over bribery and corruption).
87. See my introduction to the companion volume to this book, *The Movements of Movements, Part 1: What Makes Us Move?* (Sen 2017a).
88. Barchiesi, Heinrich Bohmke, Prishani Naidoo, and Ahmed Veriava 2012.
89. For Amin's call, see his essay in this volume. Amin first made his call for a Fifth International back in mid-2006 (2006b) but preceded this by taking the initiative to organise a meeting just before the Polycentric World Social Forum in Bamako, Mali, in January 2006, which issued what came to be called the 'Bamako Appeal'. This Appeal strongly leaned in this direction; see Forum pour un Autre Mali, Forum Mondial des Alternatives (France), Forum du Tiers Monde (Sénégal), ENDA (Sénégal) et al, February 2006.
90. Sen and Kumar, compilers, with Bond and Waterman, January 2007.
91. Sen, January 2007a and Sen 2010.
92. I found very similar trends in emerging global civil alliances during the 1980s and '90s—in other words, well before the WSF took shape; see Sen, December 1999.
93. De Angelis 2018.
94. Maeckelbergh 2009.
95. Childs 2003.
96. Muto, June 2004. For a discussion of this paper and its proposals, see Sen, July 2005.
97. Muto, June 2004, pp 11, 12.

98. See also the essay by Muto Ichiyo in this volume. As I have explained in this essay, I do not find the term 'NGO' useful; to the contrary I find it to be negative, so I do not use it. But I do so in this section because the author whose work I am referring to uses it.

99. For a detailed discussion of the dynamics and politics of the representation of CBOs (community-based organisations, a UN term) on 'national civil committees' established to democratise the preparations for and agenda of Habitat II, the second UN Conference on Human Settlements in 1996, see Sen, June 1996a; for the dynamics in a major transnational civil campaign, see Sen, December 1999.

100. Waterman 2004a.

101. Brecher, Costello, and Smith 2000; Glasius, Kaldor, and Anheier, eds, 2006 and 2007 also tend to celebrate 'global civil society' as GfB, but in a carefully muted way. See, for instance, the covering letter to the 2006–2007 Yearbook. For another discussion of the issue with respect to the WSF, see Waterman 2004a. Since I have included a quote from Janet Conway in this essay where she specifically attributes this insight and phrase—'globalisation from the middle'—to Peter Waterman and his 2004 essay, I should perhaps add that I happened to come up with the same term and argument in a somewhat earlier exchange with Jeremy Brecher, the lead author of the book I cite here (Sen, May 2000d). Great minds evidently think alike!

102. A small contribution to this task of examining how change is taking place and of rethinking 'globalisation' took place during a course I ran at Carleton University, Ottawa, Canada, during the Fall semester 2006, titled 'Other Worlds, Other Globalisations'; for details, see Sen, February 2007.

103. For a discussion of the role of the African diaspora in world history, see Segal 1995; for a broader discussion of how the world has 'globalised' in myriad ways, see Chanda 2007.

104. Falk 1993a and Falk 1997.

105. Brecher, Costello, and Smith 2000.

106. Korten 1998b.

107. Sen, May 2000d.

108. See, for instance, NCDHR (National Campaign on Dalit Human Rights) 2003.

109. Cox and Nilsen 2014.

110. See Sklair 1991 and Sklair, March 2005.

111. Point made in Hurl, November 2006, referring to Wallerstein 2006.

112. Assange, October 2014.

4
REFLECTIONS ON POSSIBLE FUTURES

'Becoming-Woman'?
Between Theory, Practice, and Potentiality
Michal Osterweil

Although all becomings are already molecular, including becoming-woman, it must be said that all becomings begin with and pass through becoming-woman. It is the key to all other becomings.
—Gilles Deleuze and Felix Guattari [1]

There are no shortcuts and if there are they are only 'table tricks'. There is only experimentation as method and substance of the 'becoming-movement'.
—Global Project, Invisibili, Ya Basta [2]

Io credo que questo movimento sia una donna!
('I believe that this movement is a woman!')
—(Male) Italian activist [3]

To the extent that the figure of woman signals unfixed or incomplete identity, she is the subject to be constructed through politics. She is the subject of becoming, whose failed identity stands for the possibility of politics itself.
—J K Gibson-Graham [4]

Introduction

This essay takes its title (in part) from a concept coined by the philosophers Deleuze and Guattari. The reasons for this naming, though, don't only have to do with the meaning these authors gave to the term, but also to the term's productivity as a source of debate and critique in various spaces attempting to engage and rethink a critical leftist or progressive project. Introduced by Deleuze and Guattari, 'becoming' (as opposed to being) is key to the ontology of minoritarian, and potentially revolutionary, subjects / projects. Moreover, while for Deleuze and Guattari there are many becomings (becoming-animal, becoming-minoritarian, etc), 'becoming-woman' is special among them. As the quote above illustrates, for them the concept 'becoming-woman' has a certain primacy, privilege, or universality among all minoritarian / revolutionary projects. For feminists, however, this privileging is problematic for many reasons, not least of which is the fact that the use of the term 'woman' has little to do with an actual commitment to feminism, to any privileging of the feminine perspective, or to feminist forms of

367

theorising. As Rosi Braidotti, simultaneously inspired by and critical of the work of Deleuze and Guattari puts it:

> Whereas Deleuze situates his project of becoming within philosophy—albeit against the grain of the dominant canon—feminists think about their becoming outside the beaten tracks of academic life, as a project that reunites life and thought into a far-reaching project of transformation. Feminism is a philosophy of change and of becoming: it functions through creative mimesis, that is to say by activating counter-memories.[5]

In this essay, departing from a recognition of the growing prominence of both Deleuzian and feminist theoretical terms within networks affiliated with the 'alter-globalisation movement' (AGM), or the 'movement of movements',[6] I puzzle through this productive yet problematic use of theory, focusing especially on the difference between a philosophical project and a feminist one that reunites "life and thought". Ultimately I argue that if the 'movement of movements' is to reach the potentials implied in terms such as 'becoming' it must better understand this difference—one I call experiential versus abstract—which itself requires a more micropolitical notion of politics and political effects.

I think a big part of why so many people have been so excited about the politics ushered in by the Zapatistas, by 'Seattle', and by the World Social Forum/s (WSF)—to name just a small part of what has come to be known as the 'movement of movements'[7]—is that, in addition to making opposition and alternatives to the ills of modern capitalism seem possible after some had declared "the end of history", the politics of these movements have embodied and posited deliberate and explicit responses to both the practical and theoretical failures of previous political approaches by the left. Despite much good work done by various movements, unions, and others fighting for social change throughout history, hardly anyone would dispute that leftist movements, unions, and parties of the past failed to achieve or effect change according to their own ambitions: they did not defeat capitalism or achieve equality. But these failures were not only due to a thwarted strategy, a forced compromise, or a political loss to another side. Rather, I believe there were fundamental problems with the theories, political visions, and modes these leftist movements were using; moreover, there were insufficient means for engaging problems—such as the reproduction of oppression within progressive organisations or the inability to deal with different cultures—as they arose.[8]

One of the most inspiring things about this 'movement of movements' is the visibility and centrality of critical and reflective practices that seek to both avoid the repetition of old mistakes and to find new modalities for achieving social change. This reflexive ethos is embodied perhaps most famously by the phrase coined by the Zapatistas, *caminar preguntando* ('to walk while questioning')—but resonates with a great deal of contemporary movement language and concepts, including those of 'open space', 'horizontality', 'encounter', 'affect', etc. While movements have always produced concepts and theories to help guide their actions, what is particularly notable among many of today's movements are what appear as some common tendencies with respect to both the content of the theories and how they are produced. They seem based in an ethic of partiality, specificity, and open-endedness; a willingness to revise and rework depending on their lived effectiveness; and a sensitivity to the fact that unexpected consequences can arise when different subjects or circumstances come into contact with these theories. This also means they are wary of positing new truths or formulas for social change that everyone must adhere to. Finally, they are more attuned to the inextricably political nature of many things previously relegated to superstructure or 'fluff'. This includes the nitty-gritty, day-to-day aspects of life, social relationships, forms of organisation, meeting structure, pleasure, etc.[9]

Notably, all of these qualities are similar to forms of political practice and theorising associated with feminism. In recent years, in fact, academics and activists alike have begun to refer, both directly and indirectly, to the feminist, even feminine, nature of these 'new' politics.[10] This evocation of feminist theory and politics in the language, concepts, and aspirations of our movements is, however, consistently and often quite strikingly, undermined in practice. On the one hand, such appeals to feminism are not matched by greater inclusion of women or feminist concerns in positions of visibility or authority in many movement spaces, and, on the other, they are not matched by any *actual* change in political practice. So, despite embracing visions and imaginaries of partiality, difference, micropolitics, and critical reflexivity, often our supposedly 'new' politics look and feel an awful lot like the traditional, ends-oriented, party-, state- and male-centred politics we claim to have surpassed.

As a female academic-activist who has been inspired by, participated in, and worked to make sense of this movement, I have been struck by the gap between our theories and practices, our imaginaries and actualities, time and again. After several years of both experiencing and puzzling over this gap, I have come to believe that this ironic and disappointing relationship between feminism and the supposedly 'new politics' of the 'movement of movements' points to a key and complex problem for movements, and for politics more broadly. Far from only being a matter of achieving equality for women, this problem—what I will refer to as the 'gender problem'—forces us to look at and rethink the place and significance of *difference* in contemporary politics, while at the same time raising critical questions about the relationship between political potentialities (theories, discourses, imaginaries) and actualities. In so doing, this 'gender problem' poses a fundamental challenge to the very ways our analytical and political language and categories are used and created—modalities that themselves have yet to bridge the messy and difficult gap between theory and experience. As such, just finding the appropriate terms and means to adequately delineate the problem is itself not a simple task. It is, however, what I hope to achieve with this essay.

Mind the Gap!

I first heard a reference to feminism and the 'movement of movements' in 2003.[11] I was visiting Italy to learn about the phenomenal movement that had brought over 300,000 people to the streets of Genoa; had made Italians among the most active participants in myriad alter-globalisation meetings and protests outside Italy; and had seen the emergence of local social forums—where non-representative forms of government were experimented with on a regular basis—in many Italian cities.[12] The Bologna Social Forum (BSF) was one of most active of these local forums. I am told that at its height it was not unusual for 500 people to attend, many of whom were individuals not affiliated to any party, union, or militant organisation. At the first BSF meeting that I attended, one of the leaders of the then *Disobbedienti* ('Disobedients') opened his remarks with a bold and strange statement. He declared, "*Io credo che questo movimento sía una donna*"—"I believe that this movement is a woman". He then went on to explain that what he meant was that this movement was female because it functioned according to logics that differed from those of previous movements, logics of difference, dispersion, and affect. No central group or singular ideology could control it, and it was propelled by an energy from subjects and places that far exceeded those of traditional forms of leftist organisation and practice. To him, this was intimately tied to feminine / feminist notions of politics—and therefore to women.

After his remarks the space was filled with silence, smirks, smiles, and some hesitant nods of agreement. I shared the ambivalence. On the one hand, I was intellectually intrigued and somewhat in agreement with his claim about the 'feminine' or minoritarian logic of this movement; on the other, I was a bit disturbed by the comment. Besides a visceral reaction to the essentialism lurking behind the very use of the term 'woman' (by a man) to describe something as dynamic and heterogeneous as the (Italian) alter-globalisation movement, it made me uncomfortable because throughout a meeting lasting well over two hours, only two or three women had actually spoken. Moreover, when they did speak, they took less time and spoke with less authority than the many male activists. In spite of, or perhaps because of, this rather blatant tension—that the movement was a woman, but the women hardly spoke—the phrase and analogy struck me quite profoundly.

Two years later, I had a conversation with another male activist, again part of the *Disobbedienti* network. Once again I was referred to feminism as a theoretical perspective I really ought to get familiar with if I wanted to make sense of the 'movement of movements' and its potentials. I smiled and raised my eyebrows so this activist, excited by my apparent interest in his own interest in feminism, jotted down a few books and essays that he believed were critical reads. I smiled again and nodded, starting to make more sense of the cause of the uncomfortable ambivalence provoked by such moments.

In each of these moments I was simultaneously compelled and disturbed by references to women and, more explicitly, to feminism. I was excited because I agreed that there was something to this linking of feminism with the emergent and 'new' politics of contemporary movements. But I was disturbed because the theoretical potentials were not being matched in reality, and the feminist theory that paralleled the emergent politics of the AGM was cited *despite* the continued marginalisation and exclusion of women (and feminist concerns) in many movement spaces. Moreover, and despite the rhetorical commitment to moving beyond traditional politics, characterised by dogmatic or formulaic approaches, to embracing partiality and fluidity, in practice, our movements also often seemed to revert back to old-school, unreflexive, and masculinist approaches, unable to deal with discrepancies between theory and practice.

For example, during one of the last days of the 2005 WSF—arguably one of the events and political ideas most influenced (co-authored even) by feminism[13]—a group of nineteen prominent personalities associated with the alter-globalisation and WSF movements published a document referred to as the Porto Alegre Consensus. The document, basically a manifesto, was published in the Forum's daily paper *Terra Viva*.[14] It implored all those present at the Forum to get serious about action and to sign on to a clear programme for social change in order to move beyond the Forum as just a wishy-washy site of encounter and engagement to a subject with 'real', 'political' power. In other words, the Porto Alegre Consensus was, in both content and style, a clear reassertion of a classical political approach.

At the same time, it is also notable that only one out of this 'Group of 19' was a woman. So, while, on the one hand, it is infuriating to think that this group of de facto leaders and spokespeople had no qualms about coming out publicly with only one woman in their ranks (a good example of how little things had changed in terms of gender parity), on the other, it is quite provocative to consider that only one woman was involved in an action that treated the WSF as important only insofar as it constituted itself into a more classical political subject, like a political party or International. While it would be a lie to state that women never participate in old-school politics, the fact that so few did in this case is nonetheless noteworthy and might have something to do with the subtleties and complexities of the 'gender problem'.

More recently, on a more personal scale, I experienced another case of the 'gender problem', while working on the editorial collective of an experimental journal called *Turbulence: ideas for movement*.[15] The journal-cum-newspaper was quite specifically meant to serve as a space for engaging and interrogating the diverse perspectives and positions within the 'movement of movements' on their versions of social change. As such, it was particularly disheartening when, despite the stated desire by the collective to have more pieces by women and other marginalised voices, ultimately very few women ended up contributing to the publication.[16] (There was only one woman on the editorial board—me—and there were very few pieces actually written by women.) While we can identify a lot of specific reasons for such an obvious and outrageous imbalance—and even point out the fact that several women were invited and even intended to contribute articles (but either didn't or weren't ultimately selected)—it was clear (to me at least) that the absence of many voices, especially those of women, was far from coincidental or accidental.

This then was—for me—a particularly poignant and difficult encounter with and re-articulation of the gender problem. On the one hand, it was a very concrete experience in which the absence of women's voices was far from a simple matter of obvious sexist exclusion. On the other, it was also clearly far from coincidental or unrelated to the imbalance of our own collective (made up of seven men and one woman) and its priorities. In fact, to me, it was undeniable that it was a direct result of dynamics that themselves have everything to do with the mostly white male editorial board, as well as cultural-structural factors harder to articulate. However, every time we tried to address the absence of women's and other peoples' voices, we came up against the accusation, or fear, that we were falling into a tokenistic logic—a representational logic of symbolic or instrumental representations of women, minorities, etc. Though, to me, it was clear that the absence of women (and its effects) went way beyond a mere lack of representation, at the time I was not capable of articulating a satisfying argument—neither to my fellow editorial members nor to myself. Was it really a choice between tokenism and a more homogenous, male-dominated politics? Are these the only terms we have to judge and value difference and the deliberate effort to include diverse subjects in movement spaces?

These personal experiences are just two examples of a problem that many of us can probably relate to in various ambits of our own lives, perhaps most centrally in our experiences of politics. I delineate them here, however, because I believe the persistence and nature of such experiences force us to ask some very serious questions of our movements and ourselves: questions, on the one hand, about the actual significance of difference, about the relationships between theory / practice, potentiality / actuality, and about the nature of democracy, or 'good' politics, and, on the other, about the effects of our 'new' theories of horizontality, affinity, fluidity, critical of more traditional modes of organisation.

For example: Does it matter if we have a fabulously astute and sensitive notion of what 'good' politics would, or should, look like—democratic, non-representational[17]—if we cannot involve more people in the conversation? That is, is it of any use to have a great (theoretical) notion of the politics we want when the very subjects we are claiming to be inspired by—that is, those who have traditionally been othered, marginalised, excluded—are still not present to participate in the discussion? What does it mean to see oneself as part of a movement governed by feminist and minoritarian logics when, in so many of the most visible spaces, the voices and language of women continue to be less than audible? Are difference, diversity, and inclusiveness merely instrumental, with no value beyond allowing us to make symbolic claims to greater democracy?

Moreover, is it inevitable that our 'new' horizontal, antiauthoritarian politics that claim to work according to logics of openness, affect, affinity, and non-identity—as opposed to hierarchical organisations with traditional notions of membership, ideology, identity, and leadership—become secluded, homogeneous spaces with little diversity? Does the fact that we formally profess these values make it more difficult for us to see and confront the lived contradictions—even though inherent to them is a notion of critical reflexivity? Could it be that, at least in part, our inability to address these imbalances and absences is an unintended consequence of these supposedly 'new' theories—inspired by the theoretical practice or ideals of feminism but purely theoretically to such an extent that they have few mechanisms for holding us accountable, acknowledging, or even recognising when the original goals of these ideals are betrayed?

I am convinced that part of the problem stems from the fact that the terms and theories we generally use to deal with inclusion / exclusion and difference are rather limited. They remain trapped in an instrumentalist and molar notion of the political in which difference is either treated as a problem to be worked through in the service of greater unity or as a matter of quantitative inclusion.[18] Moreover, they tend to belong to a very abstract and rational kind of political theory. That said, in dealing with the absence of different voices we are always walking a fine line, because insisting on the importance of inclusion is often automatically read as calling for a return to a simple representational politics, ie, liberal multiculturalism, premised on the belief that the deliberate presence of diverse subjects will be sufficient to constitute actual democracy or a 'better' politics.

A large problem with this approach, however, is that it tends to be essentialist at different levels. One, it assumes that certain subjects—biological females, or people of colour—have an essential similarity to other minorities, as well as essential differences from the dominant—that is, white males. Two, these 'minoritarian' figures are not only considered *essentially* similar but also as having a greater disposition to progressive political positions, simply by virtue of being 'minorities'. This logic is extremely problematic not least because it is difficult to deny that many women are as guilty of masculinist, retrograde politics as men, and that there are as many differences among people of colour and women as there are similarities. (Just think of Margaret Thatcher, Hillary Clinton, Clarence Thomas, and countless others.)

While this is not the time or place to get into the fine distinctions between essentialism and other approaches to privileging difference, it is critical to point out that there are significant differences between *valuing* difference and inclusion and believing in the *reality* of essentialism.[19] For, despite the risk of being accused of essentialism or representationalism (if such an ism exists!), my own experiences and observations have made clear to me that the *absence* of diverse subjects—especially those who have been othered, excluded, and oppressed in myriad ways—does have detrimental effects. And that, conversely, when such subjects *are present* and actually participating—when there is diversity—there is *something* positive and qualitatively special that does happen. So this 'something' is not only a matter of being more inclusive or augmenting the size and unity of our movements; it is about creating a qualitatively different and more effective form of progressive politics. As such, and fully critical of both essentialism and representational logics, I want to claim that there is *something* absolutely crucial about the actual presence and participation of diverse subjects. The questions to ask then are: How can one advocate the importance of diversity and inclusion outside essentialist or representational theoretical frameworks? How does that link to the potentiality of our movements?

This is no simple matter precisely because this 'something' is not easily measured nor rationally explained through the political or philosophical theories we are used to, but rather makes itself understood at a much more visceral, affective, and conjunctural register—through particular experiences and the lived messiness of political life. It is, however, key to understanding the gender problem, perhaps also to addressing it. As such, and taking my cue from this theoretical practice tempered by the messiness of life, I think that rather than try to *explain* this argument, I will point to some experiences that demonstrate it.

Experiential versus Abstract Theory

Towards the end of September 2006 I attended a four-day gathering in the north of Spain. The space was beautiful: an old church with a great deal of unused land, now home to the Espacio Social Colectivo para la Autogestion, la Diversidad y la Autonomia ('Collective Social Space for Self-Organisation, Diversity, and Autonomy'—Escanda), a live experiment in sustainable collective living—an effort to turn the ideas that have been promoted and experimented with at various counter-summits, social forums, *encuentros* ('encounters'), and myriad other sites of anti-capitalist activist networks into a lasting and ongoing project where the difficulties and complexities of actually living such a politics can be confronted. It seems fitting then that true to this spirit of taking on the challenges, complexities, and difficulties we face despite our best-intentioned activist efforts, an international group of women decided to organise a women-only radical (anti-capitalist) gathering. It was, to my knowledge, the first gathering to specifically and deliberately address the 'gender problem' in the radical areas of our movements. In contrast to most women-only or feminist meetings, the gathering self-identified *first* as part of the anti-capitalist / antiauthoritarian / radical-environmental networks that had been quite active in Europe for at least a decade, and only secondarily as feminist. In fact, many of us arrived very critical of separatism and the exclusion of men—both in terms of whether that was good politically and ethically and whether we would like it personally.

As the lengthy and often intense discussions and other activities made apparent, the need for such a space was greatly felt. During a go-around at one of the first sessions, women from different countries[20] indicated that they had come to the gathering primarily because of their persistent experiences of exclusion and marginalisation of two general types: 1) working with men in various organisations or initiatives where men dominated and intentionally or unintentionally diminished and marginalised women; 2) constantly having 'female' issues (birth control / families, women's health, rape and violence, body image, etc), which were almost always considered less urgent or important, relegated to separate spaces that only women put energy into. These are both clearly important, yet quite commonly recognised manifestations of the gender problem.

However, it was only once there, experiencing the event and space first-hand, that we discovered other—unexpected, even unarticulatable—reasons why such a space was so important. Through the gathering we came to better understand that many of us needed / wanted this space because the negative aspects of patriarchy and machismo (always, as we came to agree, inextricably linked to capitalism) were not limited to our problems with men. They affected everything including the tones of our discussions, the dynamics of our groups, and perhaps more importantly our relationships with other women (as well as with ourselves).

One of the most powerful and profound discussions I participated in was about power issues among women. During a workshop dedicated to the question, we spent most of the time recalling and admitting—through some tears and much embarrassment—persistently difficult experiences with women, even friends. These difficulties, we recounted, manifested themselves through jealousy, competitiveness, non-solidarity, and in other subtle and specific ways, at times making our relationships with women, both in activism and in life, more difficult than those with men. It was obvious that this was not an easy conversation for any of us, probably because it forced us to confront the fact that many of the sacred cows underlying women's solidarity were far from given.

Although I had recognised and been troubled by my own experiences of this kind, this was literally the first time I had had a frank discussion about it or recognised this as a problem—one, moreover, that we ourselves were involved in perpetuating—shared by many women. While we did not come up with conclusive solutions, our very ability to name it turned out to not only be power-ful on a personal level; it also had important political effects.

At a very immediate level, it changed the dynamics of the rest of the gath-ering. More significantly, it signalled a rather fundamental shift in our political approaches more generally—both analytically and practically. At an analytical / conceptual level it *demonstrated* (not only postulated) how the mutually reinforc-ing cultures of capitalism and patriarchy functioned not primarily by excluding women and others from hierarchies of power, *but by constituting and producing them as certain kinds of subjects within those hierarchies*. At a more practical level, the way in which such a complex, emotional, and guilt-soaked issue could be engaged so productively gave us a hopeful, yet still difficult to define, sense that we were discovering what a 'good' political modality might be.

In fact, throughout the meeting, and not even directly related to this one dis-cussion, many of us were struck by how different the dynamics of this space were from other activist spaces we were familiar with. It was not that it was devoid of power dynamics, differences, or conflicts; it was the fact that there was *something* to the sensibility of the space, something that encouraged a conscientious and deliberate engagement with those conflicts and problems. Moreover, in contrast with other political settings where difficult questions with no easy answers often become fodder in the political game of winning more people to one side or stance, in this space we were able to engage difficult problems that had no easy solutions, without pretending to resolve them. This was significant in and of itself.[21]

What was that something? That enigmatic, 'hard to put into theoretical or political language' something? Why was it so politically powerful? What did it have to do with the fact that this was a women-only space, created explicitly to address the gender problem/s in our movements?

These questions bring us back to those I led off with. They are in many ways the opposite side of the same coin. For rather than point to the problem, the fact that 'something' is missing or lacking when certain subjects are absent, this moment illustrates that something is gained when they are present. Difficult to name or explain in rational language precisely because it is accessible in its lived and experiential form, this 'something'—an ethos and ability of becoming—is precisely what hints at a possibility for different forms of articulating the desires and theories that guide political practice.

Feminism: Conflict and Problems at Their Best

Despite my own scepticism about coming to a women-only gathering, the event turned out to be one of the most significant experiences I had had in years. It changed me at both a political and human level. However, only in the process of thinking through the complexities of the gender problem in other areas of the movement was I able to begin to articulate why it had been so important. As this paper has shown, gender dynamics within our movements are a constant source of distress and concern. Until Escanda I had mainly experienced the problematic in the negative—as something to be addressed and resolved (that is, eliminated). I had not, however, had many positive examples of not only what a space addressing the problem might be like, but also how potent, empowering even, both such an experience and such a space could be.

There, for once, I felt like I really understood the significance of feminism. That is, I understood it at a visceral and tangible level, rather than a rational or political one. At the same time, the reasons feminism had become a source of inspiration and aspiration for so many contemporary movements, *as well as* what made the gap between its potential versus actual instantiations so frustrating, became clearer.

For who can deny that while feminism hasn't ushered in an age of equality or the end of patriarchy, machismo, or capitalism, it has profoundly transformed our social relations, our cultural norms, our very ways of being and seeing in the world? Whatever our gripes with its multigenerational manifestations, there was / is something about the feminist movement that has made it effective in truly widespread, durable, and still dynamic ways.[22] So, while I am not claiming that other movements like civil rights, labour, environmental, etc haven't had important effects, I do think feminism as movement—as an ethic and sensibility that forces people to consciously and continuously challenge dominant norms—has been quite unique, in both its content and form.

Key to this has been the fact that feminism itself has been rife with conflicts, rifts, and problems. Open conflicts have taken place between and among women from different economic and cultural backgrounds, of different sexual and gender identities, and from and within different global regions: it is / was continuously the object of critique. However understanding these conflicts as wholly negative is partly a problem of how we read conflict and critique. Arguably, one of the reasons feminism has been so significant despite its most problematic manifestations is precisely because it has managed (or been forced) to really engage the conflicts and complexities that have traversed it throughout its history: conflicts between universalism and difference, questions of cultural values and rights, differences between the North and the South, etc; and because the multiple and at times contradictory elements that comprised it have subsequently worked to transform the discursive and lived spaces of feminist articulation to both everyday life and politics. Some of the most important insights about organising across differences came as a result of the fact that women of colour, queer women, anarchist women, and women from the Global South (among others) critiqued, seceded, and worked to change what they perceived as a hegemonic feminism. While there is no doubt that the critiques must continue and the conflicts still exist, it is also undeniable that they have been extremely productive, if not constitutive of some of feminism's most important contributions and insights into the nature of power and social change.[23]

This ethos and ability—the experience—of engaging the intersectional complexities of life despite, or even with and through, conflicts and differences without falling apart or disbanding was a large part of what made the Escanda gathering so powerful. In the end it did not feel like we left the space with a 'women's programme' to take to the places where we lived and worked, but rather, a set of tools, insights, and capacities—subtleties not usually recognisable in politics, including a different capacity or way of knowing and engaging with problems and each other—that in emerging from a space so attentive to the most hard to articulate problems in our movements and politics offered a great deal for all of our activist endeavours.

Towards a Conclusion

I would understand if at this point readers were a bit confused. What does this dramatic description of an event among a relatively small group of women have to do with my initial concerns about the gap between our potentials and practices and the related but far from identical problem of diversity and inclusion? Why did I have to spend so much time in detailing such a specific and small-scale event?

The answer might seem a bit banal, one that you might say I could have just come out and stated much earlier: it is, at a very basic level, a matter of opposing experiential theoretical production and political desire against the far more common abstract and philosophical forms of politics and theory. This is a straightforward enough statement, and in itself it might seem both obvious and not necessarily politically important. However, in practice—both theoretical and political—it is neither that simple nor, I would argue, inconsequential in terms of (potential) political effects. For, as might have become obvious in my own descriptions of the experience at Escanda or my difficulty in adequately and politically delineating the problem of *Turbulence* and so many other moments—that 'something', either missing or gained, is, on the one hand, difficult to explain and articulate, but, on the other, extremely vital and productive.

At the very heart of this 'something' is the difference between the political knowledge/s obtained through messy, subjective, and visceral experiences—experiences that are in and of themselves dynamic and never 100 per cent reproducible, even if repeatable, and whose political effects and significance are not fully legible in more traditional ideas of political outcomes and effects, which tend to have more immediate and macro-temporalities and spatialities—and the more rational and intellectual forms of theory production. Moreover, I suggest that it is within this 'something' and the related creation of critical and affected subjectivities and ways of knowing that this 'new' possibility of politics lives: a more effective politics characterised by the logics of problematics and engagement, rather than the more typical modality of dogmatism and polemics.[24]

This unpredictable and experiential something does not, however, mean that there is no place for theorising or for making clear arguments, say, on the importance of the presence of women, minorities, and other groups that have been historically marginalised. To the contrary, it is an argument for different standards for verifying the utility or worth of such theories, always in an ongoing and reflexive temporality. Returning to the fear of, or weariness with, essentialism, which most arguments for necessary inclusion must face: the reason 'better'— more egalitarian, reflexive, astute, etc—politics are more likely when women and minorities are actually present has little to do with essentialist notions about the nature of certain people. Instead, it has everything to do with the ways in which subjectivities constituted by material-historical conditions and experiences of exclusion, marginalisation, and difference—*in strong contrast with those who have a theoretical, even if heartfelt, commitment to inclusion and diversity*—know and engage with the world and political problems. Subjectivities that, because of their historical experience, tend to be more privy to or aware of the complex, often contradictory, nature and difference between ideals and reality.

As such, when we try to make sense of how or why there can be such stark contradictions between the theories we espouse and the realities we live—how people can claim to promote a feminist or minoritarian politics but have few mechanisms of accountability or redress when women continue to be marginalised, and where political modalities stay the same—I think we need to more seriously and profoundly consider this difference between abstract and experiential theory.

I think that by paying attention to this difference we would also find that, at least in part, our inability to address the contradictions mentioned above is actually an unintended consequence of the fact that we have embraced these 'new' theories—inspired by the theoretical practice and ideals of feminism and tending to see affinity, fluidity, horizontality, and lack of identity as their defining logics—without the concomitant recognition or visceral knowledge that these theoretical ideals emerged from historical, lived, and complex experiences, and that those experiences more often than not involved conflicts and encounters with difference that made problems visible through critique and engagement that was not just intellectual or rational but often passionate, personal, and dynamic.

Recalling the quotation by Braidotti cited in the introduction to this essay and the difference between a philosophical project and a "far reaching project . . . seeking to unite life and thought" by activating counter-memories, counter-subjectivities also help clarify what is at stake in this difference: fundamentally different temporalities and registers for assessing and seeing the 'political' such that, rather than looking for political outcomes in quantitative or measurable realms, we become more attuned to the subjective, affective, and epistemological as sites of 'real' political change and action.

Ultimately, one of the most important lessons of feminism for our new politics, as well as of Zapatismo and other sources of inspiration, is that the most important insights come from lived and unexpected experiences, including lived encounters with difference, and lived experiences of the limitations of certain political models and ideologies. If we only talk and theorise among ourselves we are very unlikely to come across encounters that disrupt our ways of doing and thinking, disruptions that are themselves the key to maintaining the subversive or critical side of any politics. If we don't look to the subjective, to the experiential, to those bodies that live in the worlds and movements being theorised, chances are there will be little difference between the old-school political approaches and their demographics and the new.

The 'movement of movements' is a term I have been using as a sort of catchall to refer to the new politics or the potential for new politics that the contemporary phase of struggle has offered. I think that at its best this movement has the potential to have similar lived lessons emerge from encounters and even clashes among our different elements; we have already had many. It is this potential that people sense when they refer to the movement as woman, as new, as exciting—as becoming. But the politics articulated in discourse, ideals, and potentialities is itself precarious if not tempered by a conscious commitment and understanding of some of the dynamics I have tried to lay out here.

References

Sonia Alvarez, Nalu Faria, and Miriam Nobre, 2004—'Another (also feminist) world is possible: Constructing transnational spaces and global alternatives from the movement', in Jai Sen, Anita Anand, Arturo Escobar and Peter Waterman, eds, 2004—*World Social Forum: Challenging Empires*. New Delhi: Viveka Foundation

Gloria Anzaldúa, ed, 1990—*Making Face, Making Soul—Haciendo Caras: Creative and Critical Perspectives by Women of Color*. San Francisco: Aunt Lute Foundation Books

Emma Bircham and John Charlton, eds, 2001—*Anticapitalism: A Guide to the Movement*, second edition. London: Bookmarks

Rosi Braidotti, 1996—'Nomadism with a difference: Deleuze's legacy in a feminist perspective', in *Man and World*, vol 29, pp 305–14

Janet Conway, 2007—'Reinventing emancipation: The World Social Forum as a site for movement-based knowledge production'. Unpublished paper, talk presented at UNC Chapel Hill, Social Movement Working Group Symposium, March 9 2007

Gilles Deleuze and Felix Guattari, 1987—*A Thousand Plateaus: Capitalism and Schizophrenia*. Translated by Brian Massumi. Minnesota: University of Minnesota Press

Catherine Eschle, 2005—'"Skeleton Women": Feminism and the Antiglobalization Movement', in *Signs: Journal of Women in Culture and Society*, vol 30 no 3, pp 1741–69

Catherine Eschle and Bice Maiguashca, 2007—'Rethinking Globalised Resistance: Feminist Activism and Critical Theorising in International Relations', in *The British Journal of Politics and International Relations*, vol 9, pp 284–301

Michel Foucault, interviewed by Paul Rabinow, 1984—'Polemics, Politics, and Problematizations', May 1984, at https://foucault.info/doc/foucault/interview-html (Accessed August 30 2017)

J K Gibson-Graham, 1996—*The End of Capitalism (as We Knew It): A Feminist Critique of Political Economy*. Cambridge, Mass: Blackwell Publishers

J K Gibson-Graham, 2004—'The Violence of Development: Two political imaginaries', in *Development*, vol 47 no 1, pp 27–34

J K Gibson-Graham, 2006—*A Postcapitalist Politics*. Minneapolis: University of Minnesota Press

Global Project, Invisibili, and Ya Basta, 2004—'Is it Cause I'm Cool? A Discussion After London for the Autonomous Movement Networks About the ESF and the N/ Europa Challenge', at http://dev.autonomedia.org/node/3643 (Accessed August 30 2017)

Felix Guattari, 1996—*Soft Subversions*. Edited by Sylvere Lotringer. New York: Semiotext(e)

Donna J Haraway, 1991—'Situated Knowledges: The Science Question in Feminism and the Privilege of Partial Perspective', in Donna J Haraway, 1991—*Simians, Cyborgs, and Women: The Reinvention of Nature*. London and New York: Routledge

Emilie Hayes, 2017—'Open Space in Movement: Reading Three Waves of Feminism', in Jai Sen, ed, 2017—*The Movements of Movements, Part 1: What Makes Us Move?*. Volume 4 in the *Challenging Empires* series. New Delhi: OpenWord, and Oakland, CA: PM Press

John Holloway and Eloína Peláez, eds, 1998—*Zapatista! Reinventing Revolution in Mexico*. London, and Sterling, VA: Pluto Press

Mary E John, 2005—'Feminist Interventions', in Jai Sen and Mayuri Saini, eds, 2005—*Are Other Worlds Possible? Talking New Politics*. New Delhi: Zubaan, pp 96–103

Laura Roskos and Patricia Willis, 2007—'Women's Bodies, Gender Analysis, and Feminist Politics at the Fórum Social Mundial', in *Journal of International Women's Studies*, vol 8, no 3, April 2007

Subcomandante Marcos, 2000—*Our Word is Our Weapon: Selected Writings*. Edited by Juana Ponce de León. New York: Seven Stories Press

Tom Mertes, ed, 2004—*A Movement of Movements: Is Another World Really Possible?* London and New York: Verso

Cherríe Moraga and Gloria Anzaldúa, eds, 1981—*This Bridge Called My Back: Writings by Radical Women of Color*. Watertown, Mass: Persephone Press

Notes from Nowhere, 2003—*We Are Everywhere: The Irresistible Rise of Global Anticapitalism*. London and New York: Verso

Michal Osterweil, 2005—'Place Based Globalism: Locating Women in Italy's Alterglobalization Movement', in Wendy Harcourt and Arturo Escobar, eds, 2005—*Women and the Politics of Place*. West Hartford, CT: Kumarian Press

Michal Osterweil, 2008—'A Different (Kind of) Politics is Possible: Conflict and Problem(s) at the USSF', in Judith Blau and Marina Karides, eds, 2008—*The World and US Social Forums: A Better World is Possible and Necessary*. Leiden: Brill

Amory Starr, 2005—*Global Revolt: A Guide to the Movements Against Globalization.*
London and New York: Zed Books
Simon Tormey, 2005—'From Utopian Worlds to Utopian Spaces: Reflections on the
Contemporary Radical Imaginary and the Social Forum Process', in *ephemera*, vol 5
no 2, pp 394–408
Simon Tormey, 2006—'"Not in My Name": Deleuze, Zapatismo and the Critique of
Representation', in *Parliamentary Affairs*, vol 59 no 1, pp 138–54

Notes

1.   Deleuze and Guattari 1987, p 277.
2.   Global Project, Invisibili, and Ya Basta 2004.
3.   Italian male no-global activist 2002.
4.   Gibson-Graham 2004, p 32.
5.   Braidotti 1994, p 312.
6.   By 'movement of movements' and alterglobalisation movement, I am referring rather broadly to the diverse set of actors, networks, and organisations that are most commonly affiliated with transnational protest or global days of action against the IMF, World Bank, NAFTA, and other aspects of neoliberal globalisation, but which also includes movements and spaces such as the Zapatistas and the World Social Forum movement, which are as much about developing new forms of politics as they are about opposing neoliberalism. The term 'movement of movements' distinguishes itself from the notion of a singular movement and posits the potential for another kind of movement ready to deal with fragmentation and impasse that has characterised the left in recent years. For more books about this mosaic of movements, see Notes from Nowhere 2003; Mertes 2004; Bircham and Charlton 2001; Starr 2005.
7.   As above, in endnote 6.
8.   For more on this, see Holloway and Peláez 1998; Marcos 2001; Guattari 1996; Anzaldúa 1981 and 1990.
9.   I have to acknowledge that as I write this I am trying to negotiate between delineating a general tendency I have observed to be central to the 'movement of movements" potential for producing something akin to a new politics and my own recognition that it is by no means possible to argue that all, or even most, contemporary movements involved in the alterglobalisation movement have actually embraced or recognised these tendencies. The best I can do, then, is suggest that, qualitatively, these new aspects are what give us hope and possibility for a new kind of politics—so these are the tendencies that get narrated and described, not only by academics or observers but among and between movement organisations and networks.
10.   See, for example, Alvarez 2004; Eschle 2004 and 2005; and several articles in a special issue of *The Journal of International Women's Studies* 2007. See also Gibson-Graham 2006. Notably, while activists have begun to speak a lot about feminism and women's issues, there is a real scarcity of more activist-oriented documents on this topic.
11.   See also Osterweil 2005.
12.   Since 2002, I have been fortunate enough to be able to conduct research towards my PhD. This allows me time and space to engage the alter-globalisation movement

that I am personally very sympathetic to, and even consider myself part of. Most of my research has taken place in Italy, but also at various social forums and other transnational events and moments of visibility.

13. See Conway 2007; Alvarez 2004.

14. http://www.ipsterraviva.net/tv/wsf2005/viewstory.asp?idnews=153 (Inactive August 30 2017).

15. I wrote an earlier version of this piece for the first issue of *Turbulence*, specifically to try to articulate and address the problem. See www.turbulence.org.uk/becoming-woman.html (Inactive August 30 2017).

16. In addition to having few pieces by women published in the final publication, far fewer women than men submitted in the first place (although some did and were not accepted)—partly because fewer women were solicited. Clearly, the problem is complicated, with many layers of causality.

17. For more on this critique of representational logics in politics, see Tormey 2005 and 2006.

18. For more on this distinction, see a sister article: Osterweil 2008.

19. The discussion about "situated knowledges" and standpoint theory within feminism is also very helpful here, and my argument, while born of concrete experiences, is certainly helped by their more theoretical explanations. As Haraway writes: "Many currents in feminism attempt to theorise grounds for trusting especially the vantage points of the subjugated; there is good reason to believe vision is better from below.... But here lies a serious danger of romanticising and / or appropriating the vision of the less powerful while claiming to see from their positions. To see from below is neither easily learned nor unproblematic, even if 'we' 'naturally' inhabit the great underground terrain of subjugated knowledges. The positionings of the subjugated are not exempt from critical re-examination, decoding, deconstruction, and interpretation" (Haraway 1991, pp 188–90; quoted in Conway, 2007). Janet Conway's unpublished manuscript brilliantly describes the politics of difference in the World Social Forum.

20. The women were mostly European, the majority from England and Spain, but others from France, Switzerland, the US, and elsewhere.

21. I have actually written another article that is, in many ways, the sister to, or extension of, this piece. In it, I spend more time elaborating this argument on the difference between traditional political modalities and those that, through real engagement with difference and complexities posit different political outcomes. See Osterweil 2008.

22. At least in the Global North, but from what I have read, this is a pretty global phenomenon; see John 2005.

23. Ed: For an exploration of this ground, see the essay by Emilie Hayes in the companion volume to this book, *The Movements of Movements, Part 1: What Makes Us Move?* (Hayes 2017).

24. I pick up this distinction between a politics of polemics versus one of problematics from a short interview by Paul Rabinow with Foucault in May 1984, titled 'Polemics, Politics and Problematizations' (Foucault, with Rabinow, 1984).

The Asymmetry of Revolution[1]
John Holloway

It is an honour and an excitement to be here in a different world, a strange world of artists. When I was trying to think what I could possibly say about art to artists, I remembered that a few months ago, someone described me as the poet of the *altermundista* (alter-globalisation) movement. I do not know why he said that, but I was very flattered, even though I knew that the person who said it intended it as an insult, or at least a disqualification. He meant it as an insult because he was saying that revolutionary theory should not be confused with poetry. Poetry is dangerous because it has to do with a beautiful but unreal world, whereas revolutionary theory is about the real world of hard struggle. In this real world of struggle, poetry and art and beauty do not play an important role: revolutionary struggle confronts ugliness with ugliness, guns with guns, brutality with brutality. There will be time for poetry and beauty and art after the revolution.

I do not agree with this argument. On the contrary, I want to argue that revolutionary theory and practice must be beautiful or else it is not revolutionary; and also that beauty must be revolutionary in order to be beautiful. The ugliness of capitalism must be confronted with the beauty of dignity: the struggle for another world is essentially asymmetrical.

Famously, Adorno said that after Auschwitz it was impossible to write poetry.[2] We do not have to think back the sixty years to Auschwitz to understand what he meant. We have enough horrors closer at hand, perhaps especially here in Colombia, especially here in Latin America, especially in the world of today (Abu Ghraib, Guantánamo). In this world, to think of creating something beautiful seems a terrible insensitivity, almost a mockery of those who, at this very moment, are being tortured, brutalised, raped, killed. How can we write poetry or paint pictures or give talks when we know what is happening around us?

But then what? Ugliness against ugliness, violence against violence, power against power is no revolution. Revolution, the radical transformation of the world cannot be symmetrical: if it is, there is no transformation, simply the reproduction of the same thing with different faces. Asymmetry is the key to revolutionary thought and practice. If we are struggling to create something different, then our struggle too must be something different.

Asymmetry is all-important because what we are fighting against is not a group of people but a way of doing things, a form of organising the world. Capital is a social relation, a form in which people relate to one another. Capital is the enemy, but this means that the enemy is a certain form of social relations, a form of social organisation based on the suppression of our determination of our own doing, on the objectification of the subject, on exploitation. Our struggle for a different world has to mean opposing different social relations to the ones that we are fighting against. If we struggle symmetrically, if we accept the methods and forms of organisation of the enemy in our struggle, then all we are doing is reproducing capital within our opposition to it. If we fight on the terrain of capital, then we lose, even if we win.

But what is this asymmetry, this otherness, that we oppose to capital?

In the first place, asymmetry means refusal, the refusal of capital and its forms. No, we do not accept. No, we do not accept that the world should be driven by profit. No, we refuse to subordinate our lives to money. No, we shall not fight on your terrain, we shall not do what you expect us to do. No!

Our 'No' is a threshold. It opens to another world, to a world of other doing. No, we shall not shape our lives according to the requirements of capital, we shall do what we consider necessary or desirable. We shall not labour under the command of capital, we shall do something else. To one type of activity we oppose a very different type of activity. Marx referred to the contrast between these two types of activity as the "twofold character of labour" and he insisted that this two-fold character of labour is "the pivot on which a comprehension of political economy turns"—and therefore of capitalism.[3] He refers to the two sides of labour as "abstract labour", on the one hand, and "concrete or useful labour", on the other. Abstract labour refers to the abstraction that the market imposes on the act of creation: it is emptied of all concreteness, abstracted from its particular characteristics, so that one labour is just the same as another. It is alienated labour, labour that is alienated or abstracted or separated from the people who perform it. (The concept of abstract labour has nothing to do with the material or immaterial nature of the labour.) Concrete or useful labour refers to the creative activity that exists in a particular social context in an unalienated way, free from alien determination. To make the distinction a bit more clear, we shall speak of abstract labour, on the one hand, and useful-creative doing, on the other.

Our 'No' opens the door to a world of useful-creative doing, a world based on use value not on value (or its visible manifestation, money), a world of a doing that pushes towards self-determination. Where is this world? Orthodox Marxist theory tells us that it exists in the future, after the revolution, but this is not true. It exists here and now, but it exists in the cracks, in the shadows, on the edge of impossibility. Its core is useful-creative doing, the push towards self-determination that exists in, against, and beyond abstract labour. It exists *in* abstract labour in the daily activity of all of us who sell our labour power in order to survive; *against* in the constant revolt against abstract labour both from within employment and in the refusal to enter into employment; and it exists *beyond* abstract labour in the attempts of millions and millions of people all over the world to dedicate their lives, individually or collectively, to what they consider necessary or desirable.

All Cracked Up

If capitalism is understood as a system of command, then these attempts, these doings that go against and beyond abstract labour, can be understood as cracks in the system. It is people saying, individually, collectively, sometimes massively: no, we shall not do what money commands. We, in this place, at this moment, shall do what we consider to be necessary or desirable, and we shall create the social relations that we want to have.

These cracks may be so small that nobody sees them (the decision of a painter, say, to devote her life to painting, whatever the consequences) or they may be bigger (the creation of an alternative school, or this conference, for example) or they may be huge (the revolt of the Zapatistas in Mexico or the *piqueteros* in Argentina or the Indigenous in Bolivia). These cracks are always contradictory (they can never be pure non-capitalist spaces in a capitalist world), and they always exist on the brink of impossibility, because they are standing out against the dominant flow of the world. As artists know perhaps better than anybody, it is difficult to exist on passion alone. And yet that is what many artists do: in spite of the difficulties, they put their creative doing before abstract labour, they put use value before value, they refuse to accept the logic of money and try to live. Not all—but many.

Despite the fact that they stand against the logic of the world, these cracks exist all over the place, and the more we focus on them, the more we see that the world is full of cracks, full of people refusing to conform, refusing to subordinate their lives. To speak of cracks has nothing to do with marginality: there is nothing more common than being anti-capitalist. Revolution is quite simply the recognition, creation, expansion, and multiplication of these cracks.

I speak of cracks rather than autonomies to emphasise three points: first, that they are ruptures which are rooted in negation, that they go against the dominant flow; second, that they are ruptures in movement—cracks run, they expand or are filled; and third, that a world of cracks is a fragmented world, a world of particularities in which the cracks tend to join up but do not necessarily tend towards unity.

Our vision of the world changes as we enter into another world, a world based not on abstract labour but on useful-creative doing, not on value but on use value. This is the world of communism, but it is not (or not only) in the future but is a world that already exists here and now, in the cracks, as movement.[4] The world of capitalism appears to be one-dimensional, but it is not. There is never a total flattening of alternatives. There is always another dimension, a dimension of resistance, of otherness—the world of communism that exists in the cracks, in the shadows, a subterranean world.

This half invisible world is a world of pain but not of suffering. It is a world of pain because the other world, the world of abstract labour, sits on top of it, suppresses and represses it. The world of abstract labour is a world of money, of things, of fetishised social relations, of the objectification of human subjects, objectification to the point of murder, rape, and torture. Pain is at the centre of our world, but not suffering. Suffering implies the acceptance of objectification. But our world is the world of the subject struggling against her objectification, of the creator struggling against the negation of her creativity. Our pain is not the pain of suffering but the pain of an anguished scream, the pain of hurt and rage, the pain that moves us to act.

Our pain is the pain of dignity.

> In our heart there was so much pain, so much death and hurt, that it no longer fitted, brothers, in this world that our grandparents gave us to carry on living and struggling. So great was the pain and the hurt that it no longer fitted in the heart of a few people and it overflowed and filled other hearts with pain and hurt, and the hearts of the oldest and wisest of our peoples were filled, and the hearts of the young men and women, all of them brave, were filled, and the hearts of the children, even the smallest, were filled, and the hearts of the animals and plants were filled with hurt and pain, and the heart of the stones, and all our world was filled with hurt and pain, and the wind and the sun felt the hurt and the pain, and the earth was in hurt and pain. All was hurt and pain, all was silence.
>
> Then that suffering that united us made us speak, and we recognised that in our words there was truth, we knew that not only pain and suffering lived in our tongue, we recognised that there is hope still in our hearts. We spoke with ourselves, we looked inside ourselves and we looked at our history: we saw our most ancient fathers suffering and struggling, we saw our grandfathers struggling, we saw our fathers with fury in their hands, we saw that not everything had been taken away from us, that we had the most valuable, that which made us live, that which made our step rise above plants and animals, that which made the stone be beneath our feet, and we saw, brothers, that all that we had was *dignity*, and we saw that great was the shame of having forgotten it, and we saw that *dignity* was good for men to be men again, and dignity returned to live in our hearts, and we were new again, and the dead, our dead, saw that we were new again and they called us again, to dignity, to struggle.[5]

Dignity

Our world is not just a world of pain but of dignity. Dignity is the refusal inside us, the refusal to submit, the refusal to be an object, and therefore it is more than mere refusal. If I refuse to be an object, then I assert that in spite of everything that reduces me to the level of an object, I am still a subject and I create, I create differently. Dignity is the affirmation of useful-creative doing against the abstraction of labour, here and now, not in the future. Dignity is the refusal to be like them, the refusal to fall into the logic of capital. Dignity is asymmetrical struggle. Whereas in a war one army is much the same as another, in the struggle for a different world it is essential that we do not act like them, organise like them, speak like them.

Dignity is the affirmation that we are not victims. We are exploited, humiliated, repressed, tortured: but we are not victims. Why? Because in spite of everything, we still have that "which made our step rise above plants and animals":[6] we still have something that goes beyond, something that overflows our humiliation, our objectification. There is a world of difference between a politics of dignity and a politics of the poor victim. Victims are the downtrodden masses. They need leaders, hierarchical structures. The world of victims is a world of power, a world that dovetails neatly with the structures of the state, the world of the party, the world of the monologue. But if we start from dignity, if we start from the subject that exists against and beyond her objectification, this takes us to a very different politics, a politics of dialogue not of monologue, of listening not of talking, a politics not of parties and hierarchical structures but of assemblies or councils, forms of organisation that seek to articulate equally all the voices of dignity in revolt, a politics that seeks not to win the power-over symbolised by the state but to strengthen the power-to-do that comes from below.[7] A politics, too, of doing not complaining. Victims complain, dignity does.

Dignity means not only refusal and useful-creative doing but also the recognition that we are self-divided, each and all of us. Dignity is a self-antagonism within us, a self-antagonism inseparable from living in a self-antagonistic society, a turning not only against capitalism but also against ourselves. We submit, but we do not. We allow ourselves to be treated as objects, but then raise our heads and say no, we are creative subjects. Breaking capital, we break ourselves.

Dignity is an ec-stasy within us, ecstasy in the literal sense of 'standing out', a standing out against and beyond. We would be victims if we did not have this ec-static dignity within us that keeps the stones beneath our feet. The stones are beneath our feet because they have no dignity. If we tread upon them, they remain trodden upon. Stones are identities: they are. Our ec-static dignity is our non-identity, or, better, our anti-identity, our refusal to simply be. Capital imposes an identity, tells us what we are. Our dignity replies that no, we are not: we are not, because we do, we create and, in doing so, we negate and create ourselves. We overflow all identities, all the roles and personifications and character masks that capital imposes upon us. We overflow all classifications. Capital imposes classifications upon us, divides us into classes. Our struggle is a class struggle not to strengthen our class identity but to break it, to dissolve classes, to free us from all classification. This is important because, among other things, it makes sectarianism impossible. Sectarianism is based upon identitarian thought: it labels, conceives of people as fitting neatly within a classification. When our starting point is dignity, it signifies the acceptance that we and others are contradictory, self-antagonistic, overflowing, unclassifiable.

Overflowing identity, we overflow time itself, identitarian time, clock time. Our world of pain and dignity, our shadowy world of doing against and beyond abstract labour is a world of the 'dead not dead', of the 'born not yet born'. Our dead are not dead, they are waiting. As both the Zapatistas and Walter Benjamin make clear, the dead are awaiting their redemption.[8] We saw our fathers with fury in their hands, and now it is up to us to redeem them. The world of dignity that our ancestors fought for is a world that does not yet exist, but that means that it exists not yet, as Ernst Bloch tells us.[9] If the struggles of the past exist in the present of our world, so too does the future possible. It really exists not yet, in the cracks, in our dreams, in our struggles, in our breaks from the dominant world, in our creations that prefigure another world, in the always fragile existence of the possible future in the present.

Fragile, shadowy, half invisible, teetering on the brink of impossibility: that is the world in which we live, poor mad rebels who have no certainties but one—our scream of 'No' against capitalism, against this world that is destroying us and destroying all humanity. Sometimes it all seems hopeless. Our dignity is there all the time, but sometimes it seems to sleep, drugged by money, labour, or fear. Our ec-stasy is always there, but sometimes it seems crushed under the weight of routine. Our nonidentity is there, but sometimes it seems totally imprisoned within the iron cage of identity. The not yet is there, but sometimes it seems tightly bound to the hands of the clock that go tick-tock, no-hope, no-hope.

How does our dignity wake? How does it touch other dignities? How do our dignities speak to one other? We are the "*sin voz*" (the "without voice"), as the Zapatistas put it. This is not just because we have no access to the radio and television, but also for a deeper reason. Our struggle, being anti-identitarian in the sense that it goes against and beyond identities, is also anti-conceptual in the same sense, a struggle that breaks through and beyond concepts, that pushes beyond the language of conceptuality. The concept identifies, encloses, and therefore is unable to capture that which breaks beyond identity. The language of dignity must be conceptual (to understand and to criticise what we are doing), but also it must go beyond the conceptual, must explore other forms of expression. Revolutionary theory, then, must be both rigorous and poetic.

Our world is a world in search of a language, not just now but constantly, in part because the other world, that of abstract labour, steals our language all the time, but also because we are always inventing new doings and new forms of struggle. Social theory, art, and poetry are all part of this constant search.

It is probably the Zapatistas who have understood this search and the unity of aesthetics and revolution better than any other group. I refer not only to the language of the communiqués but to their profound sense of theatre and symbolism.

When they rose up on the first of January 1994, they not only expressed their own dignity but brought our dignities to life. "As more and more rebel communiqués were issued, we realised that in reality the revolt came from the depths of ourselves", Antonio García de León has commented.[10] The dignity of the Zapatistas in Chiapas resonated with our slumbering dignities and awoke them.

A politics of dignity is a politics of resonance. We recognise the dignity in the people around us, in the seat next to us, in the street, in the supermarket, and try to find a way to resonate with it. It is not a question of educating the masses or bringing consciousness to them, it is a question of recognising the rebelliousness that is inseparable from oppression, the rebelliousness that is inside all of us, and of trying to find its wavelength, of trying to engage it in a meeting of dignities. It is not necessarily a question of convincing whole peoples but of touching something within them. This is surely the question that should be behind all anti-capitalist political action: How do we resonate with the dignities around us? This question easily gets lost when we adopt closed, identitarian conceptions of our struggle.

How do we resonate with the dignities that surround us?

We need a sharp sensitivity to recognise the many forms of rebelliousness against oppression, and thence the rejection of all dogmatism. We have to hear the inaudible, see the invisible.

A world of dignity cannot be a world of 'I know, you don't know'. It is a world of shared not knowing. What unites us is that we know that we must change the world, but we do not know how to do it. This means a politics of asking-listening, but it also means constant experimentation. We do not know how to touch the dignities that surround us, so let's experiment.

Let's experiment, bearing in mind that the only art that makes sense and the only social theory that makes sense is an art (or social theory) that understands itself as part of the struggle to break capitalism, to overcome present society. This means understanding what we are doing as a revolt, an insubordination, a subversion, a crack in capitalist domination. And always with the central principle of asymmetry. We do not want to be them, we do not want to be like them.

Asking we walk.

References

Theodor W Adorno, 1990—*Negative Dialectics*. London: Routledge

Walter Benjamin, 1969—*Illuminations*. New York: Schocken Books

Ernst Bloch, 1986—*The Principle of Hope* (3 vols). Oxford: Blackwell

EZLN, 1994a—*La Palabra de los armados de verdad y fuego* ['The Word of Those Who are Armed with Truth and Fire', in Spanish]. Mexico City: Editorial Fuenteovejuna

EZLN, 1994b—*Documentos y Comunicados: 1º de enero / 8 de agosto de 1994* ['Documents and Communiqués: 1 January / 8 August 1994', in Spanish]. Mexico City: Ediciones Era

John Holloway, 2002—*Change the World Without Taking Power*. London: Pluto
John Holloway, 2010—*Crack Capitalism*. London: Pluto
Karl Marx, 1965—*Capital*, Vol 1. Moscow: Progress

Notes

1. Talk given in the Primera Cátedra Latinoamericana de Historia y Teoría del Arte Alberto Urdaneta ['Alberto Urdaneta First Latin American Chair of History and Theory of Art', in Spanish], Museo de Arte Universidad Nacional, Bogotá, Colombia, September 17 2007. Ed: I warmly thank the author for making available the manuscript for publication in this book.
2. A comment that he later qualified; see Adorno 1990, p 363.
3. Marx 1965, p 41.
4. For a development of the argument that communism is the emancipation of useful-creative doing from abstract labour, see my book *Crack Capitalism* (London: Pluto, 2010).
5. Letter from the Clandestine Revolutionary Insurgent Committee of the EZLN (EZLN 1994a).
6. Ibid.
7. On the concept of power-to-do, see Holloway 2002.
8. See Walter Benjamin's 'Theses on the Philosophy of History', in Benjamin 1969, pp 253ff.
9. See Bloch 1986.
10. Antonio García de León in his prologue to an edition of the Zapatista communiqués (EZLN 1994b, pp 14).

OpenWord

The Shock of Victory[1]
David Graeber

Introduction

The biggest problem facing direct action movements is that we don't know how to handle victory.

This might seem an odd thing to say because a lot of us haven't been feeling particularly victorious of late.[2] Most anarchists today feel the global justice movement was kind of a blip: certainly inspiring while it lasted but not a movement that succeeded either in putting down lasting organisational roots or transforming the contours of power in the world. The anti-war movement was even more frustrating, since anarchists and anarchist tactics were largely marginalised. The war will end, of course, but that's just because wars always do. No one is feeling they contributed much to it.

I want to suggest an alternative interpretation. Let me lay out three initial propositions here:

1. Odd though it may seem, the ruling classes live in fear of us. They appear haunted by the possibility that if average US Americans really get wind of what they're up to they might all end up hanging from trees. I know this seems implausible, but it's hard to come up with any other explanation for the way they go into panic mode the moment there is any sign of mass mobilisation, and especially mass direct action, and usually try to distract attention by starting some kind of war.

2. In a way this panic is justified. Mass direct action—especially when organised on democratic lines—is incredibly effective. Over the last thirty years in the US, there have been only two instances of mass action of this sort: the antinuclear movement in the late '70s and the so-called 'antiglobalisation' movement from roughly 1999–2001. In each case, the main political goals were reached far more quickly than almost anyone involved imagined possible.

3. The real problem such movements face is that they always get surprised by the speed of their initial success. We are never prepared for victory. It throws us into confusion. We start fighting each other. The racheting of repression and appeals to nationalism that inevitably accompanies some new round of war mobilisation then plays into the hands of authoritarians on every side of the political spectrum. As a result, by the time the full impact of our initial victory becomes clear, we're usually too busy feeling like failures to notice.

Let me take the two most prominent examples, case by case: the anti-nuclear movement and the global justice movement.

The Anti-Nuclear Movement

The anti-nuclear movement of the late '70s marked the first appearance in North America of what we now consider standard anarchist tactics and forms of organisation: mass actions, affinity groups, spokescouncils, consensus process, jail solidarity, and the very principle of decentralised direct democracy. It was all somewhat primitive compared to now, and there were significant differences—notably much stricter, Gandhian-style conceptions of non-violence—but all the elements were there, and for the first time they had come together as a package. For two years the movement grew with amazing speed and showed every sign of becoming a nationwide phenomenon. Then, almost as quickly, it disintegrated.

It all began when, in 1974, some veteran peaceniks turned organic farmers in New England successfully blocked construction of a proposed nuclear power plant in Montague, Massachusetts. In 1976, they joined with other New England activists, inspired by the success of a year-long plant occupation in Germany, to create the Clamshell Alliance. Clamshell's immediate goal was to stop construction of a proposed nuclear power plant in Seabrook, New Hampshire. While the alliance never managed an occupation, more a series of dramatic mass arrests, combined with jail solidarity, their actions—involving, at peak, tens of thousands of people organised on directly democratic lines—succeeded in throwing the very idea of nuclear power into question in an unprecedented way. Similar coalitions sprang up across the country: the Palmetto Alliance in South Carolina, Oystershell in Maryland, Sunflower in Kansas, and, most famous of all, the Abalone Alliance in California, reacting originally to the completely insane plan of building a nuclear power plant at Diablo Canyon, almost directly on top of a major geographic fault line.

Clamshell's first three mass actions in 1976 and 1977 were wildly successful. But it soon fell into crisis over questions of democratic process. In May 1978, a newly created Coordinating Committee violated process to accept a last-minute government offer for a three-day legal rally at Seabrook, instead of a planned fourth occupation (the excuse was reluctance to alienate the surrounding community). Acrimonious debates began about consensus and community relations, which then expanded to the role of non-violence (even cutting through fences or defensive measures like gas masks were originally forbidden), gender bias, and so on. By 1979, the alliance split into two contending and increasingly ineffective factions; and after many delays the Seabrook plant (or half of it anyway) did go into operation. The Abalone Alliance lasted longer, until 1985, in part because of its strong core of anarcha-feminists, but in the end Diablo Canyon too got its license and went into operation in December 1988.

On the surface this doesn't sound too inspiring. But what was the movement really trying to achieve? It might be helpful here to map out its full range of goals:

- Short-Term Goals: to block construction of the particular nuclear plant in question (Seabrook, Diablo Canyon . . .).
- Medium-Term Goals: to block construction of all new nuclear plants, delegitimise the very idea of nuclear power and begin moving towards conservation and green power and legitimise new forms of non-violent resistance and feminist-inspired direct democracy.
- Long-Term Goals (at least for the more radical elements): smash the state and destroy capitalism.

If so, the results are clear. Short-term goals were almost never reached. Despite numerous tactical victories (delays, utility company bankruptcies, legal injunctions) the plants that became the focus of mass action all ultimately went on line. Governments simply cannot allow themselves to be seen losing such battles. Long-term goals were also obviously not obtained. But one reason they weren't is that the medium-term goals were all reached almost immediately. The actions did delegitimise the very idea of nuclear power—raising public awareness to the point that when Three Mile Island melted down in 1979, it doomed the industry forever. While plans for Seabrook and Diablo Canyon were not cancelled, just about every other pending plan to build a nuclear reactor was, and no new ones have been proposed for a quarter century. There was indeed a move towards conservation, green power, and a legitimising of new democratic organising techniques. All this happened much more quickly than anyone had anticipated.

In retrospect, it's easy to see most subsequent problems emerged directly from the very speed of the movement's success. Radicals had hoped to make links between the nuclear industry and the very nature of the capitalist system that created it. As it turns out, the capitalist system proved more than willing to jettison the nuclear industry the moment it became a liability. Once giant utility companies began claiming they too wanted to promote green energy, effectively inviting what we'd now call the NGO types to a place at the table, there was an enormous temptation to jump ship—especially because many only allied with more radical groups to win a place at the table to begin with.

The inevitable result was a series of heated strategic debates. But it's impossible to understand this without first understanding that strategic debates, within directly democratic movements, are rarely conducted as such. They almost always take the form of debates about something else. Take for instance the question of capitalism. Anti-capitalists are usually more than happy to discuss their position on the subject. Liberals, on the other hand, really don't like to have to say, "Actually, I am in favour of maintaining capitalism", and whenever possible they try to change the subject. So debates that are actually about whether or not to directly challenge capitalism usually end up as short-term debates about tactics and non-violence. Authoritarian socialists or others who are suspicious of democracy itself don't like to make that an issue either and prefer to discuss the need to create the broadest possible coalitions. Those who do like democracy but feel a group is taking the wrong strategic direction often find it much more effective (or convenient) to challenge its decision-making process rather than its actual decisions.

Another factor here is even less noted but equally important. Everyone knows that faced with a broad and potentially revolutionary coalition, any government's first move will be to try to split in it. Making concessions to placate the moderates while selectively criminalising the radicals—this is Art of Governance 101. The US government, though, is in possession of a global empire constantly mobilised for war, and this gives it another option that most governments do not have. Those running it can, pretty much any time they like, decide to ratchet up the level of violence overseas (either by sending US troops into combat, creating proxy wars, nuclear sabre-rattling, or some combination of the three). This has proved a remarkably effective way to defuse social movements founded around domestic concerns. It seems no coincidence that the Civil Rights Movement was followed by major political concessions and a rapid escalation of the war in Vietnam; that the anti-nuclear movement was followed by the abandonment of nuclear power and a ramping up of the Cold War, with Star Wars programmes and proxy wars in Afghanistan and Central America; that the global justice movement was followed by the collapse of the Washington Consensus and the War on Terror. As a result, the early Students for a Democratic Society (SDS) had to put aside its initial emphasis on participatory democracy to become a mere anti-war movement; the anti-nuclear movement morphed into a nuclear freeze movement; the horizontal structures of the Direct Action Networks (DANs) and People's Global Action (PGA) gave way to top-down mass organisations like Act Now to Stop War and End Racism (ANSWER) and United for Peace and Justice (UFPJ).

From the government's point of view, the military solution does have its risks. The whole thing can blow up in one's face, as it did in Vietnam (hence the obsession, at least since the first Gulf War—or, so it has seemed from the protesters' perspective—to design a war that is effectively protest-proof). There is also always the small risk that some miscalculation will accidentally trigger a nuclear Armageddon and destroy the planet. But these are risks politicians faced with civil unrest appear to have been more than willing to take—if only because directly democratic movements genuinely scare them, while anti-war movements are their preferred adversary. States are ultimately, after all, forms of violence.

For them, changing the argument to one about violence is taking things back to their home turf. Organisations designed either to wage or oppose wars will always tend to be more hierarchical than those designed with almost anything else in mind. This is certainly what happened in the case of the anti-nuclear movement. While the anti-war mobilisations of the '80s turned out far larger numbers than Clamshell or Abalone ever did, they also marked a return to marching with signs, permitted rallies, and abandoning experiments with new forms of direct democracy.

The Global Justice Movement

I'll assume our gentle reader is broadly familiar with the actions at Seattle in 1999, the IMF-World Bank blockades six months later in Washington at A16, and so on that began the 'anti-globalisation' movement.[3]

In the US, the movement flared up so quickly and dramatically even the media could not dismiss it completely. It was also quick to start eating itself. DANs were founded in almost every major US city. While some of these (notably Seattle and LA DAN) were reformist, anti-corporate, and fans of strict non-violence codes, most (like New York and Chicago DAN) were overwhelmingly anarchist and anti-capitalist and dedicated to diversity of tactics. Other cities (Montréal, Washington, DC) created even more explicitly anarchist Anti-Capitalist Convergences. The anti-corporate DANs dissolved almost immediately, but even most of the anti-capitalist ones fell apart in the two years after 9/11. There were endless, bitter debates: about non-violence, about summit-hopping, about racism and privilege issues, about the viability of the network model. Then there was 9/11, followed by a huge increase in the level of repression and resultant paranoia and the panicked flight of almost all our former allies among unions and NGOs. By the time of the protests against 2003 Free Trade Agreement of the Americas (FTAA) Summit in Miami, it seemed like we'd been put to rout, and a paralysis swept over the movement from which we've only recently started to recover.

September 11 was such a catastrophe that it makes it almost impossible for us to perceive anything else around it. In its immediate aftermath, almost all the structures created in the anti-globalisation movement collapsed. But one reason it was so easy for them to collapse was not just that war seemed such an immediately more pressing concern, but that once again, in most of our immediate objectives, we'd already, unexpectedly, won.

I joined NYC DAN right around the time of A16. At the time DAN as a whole saw itself as a group with two major objectives. One was to help coordinate the North American wing of a vast global movement against neoliberalism and what was then called the Washington Consensus; to destroy the hegemony of neoliberal ideas, stop all the new big trade agreements (WTO, FTAA); and to discredit and eventually destroy organisations like the IMF. The other was to disseminate a (very much anarchist-inspired) model of direct democracy: decentralised affinity-group structures, consensus process, and the replacement of old-fashioned activist organising styles with their steering committees and ideological squabbles. At the time we sometimes called it 'contaminationism', the idea that all people really needed was to be exposed to the experience of direct action and direct democracy and they would want to start imitating it all by themselves. There was a general feeling that we weren't trying to build a permanent structure; DAN was just a means to this end. When it had served its purpose, several founding members explained to me, there would be no further need for it. On the other hand, these were pretty ambitious goals, so we also assumed that even if we did attain them, it would probably take at least a decade.

As it turned out it took about a year and a half.

Obviously we failed to spark a social revolution. But one reason we never got to the point of inspiring hundreds of thousands of people to rise up was that we again achieved our other goals so quickly. Take the question of organisation. While the anti-war coalitions still operate like top-down popular front groups, as anti-war coalitions always do, almost every small-scale radical group that isn't dominated by Marxist sectarians of one sort or another—and this includes anything from organisations of Syrian immigrants in Montréal to community gardens in Detroit—now operates on largely anarchist principles. The contaminators themselves might not know it, but contaminationism worked.

Alternately, take the domain of ideas. The Washington Consensus lies in ruins. So much so it's hard now to remember what public discourse in the US was even like before Seattle. Rarely have the media and political classes been so completely unanimous about anything. That 'free trade', 'free markets', and no-holds-barred supercharged capitalism was the only possible direction for human history, the only possible solution for any problem, was so completely assumed that anyone who cast doubt on the proposition was treated as literally insane. Global justice activists, when they first forced themselves to the attention of CNN or *Newsweek* were immediately written off as reactionary lunatics. A year or two later, CNN and *Newsweek* were saying we'd won the argument.

Usually when I make this point in front of anarchist crowds someone immediately objects: "Well, sure, the rhetoric has changed, but the policies remain the same".

This is true in a manner of speaking. That is to say, it's true that we didn't destroy capitalism. But we (taking the 'we' here as the horizontalist, direct-action-oriented wing of the planetary movement against neoliberalism) did arguably deal it a bigger blow in just two years than anyone since, say, the Russian Revolution.

Let me take this point by point:

Free trade agreements

All the ambitious free trade treaties planned since 1998 have failed. The Multilateral Agreement on Investment (MAI) was routed; the FTAA, the focus of our actions in Québec City and Miami, stopped dead in its tracks. Most of us remember the 2003 FTAA summit mainly for introducing the 'Miami model' of extreme police repression against obviously non-violent civil resistance. It was that. But we forget this was more than anything the enraged flailing of a pack of extremely sore losers—Miami was the meeting where the FTAA was definitively killed. Now no one is even talking about broad, ambitious treaties of that scale. The US is reduced to pushing for minor country-to-country trade pacts with traditional allies like South Korea and Peru or, at best, deals like Central American Free Trade Agreement (CAFTA), uniting its remaining client states in Central America—and it's not even clear it will manage to pull that off.

The World Trade Organization

After the catastrophe (for them) in Seattle, WTO organisers moved their next meeting to the Persian Gulf island of Doha, apparently deciding they would rather run the risk of being blown up by Osama bin Laden than face another DAN blockade. For six years they hammered away at the Doha Round. The problem was that, emboldened by the protest movement, Southern governments began insisting they would no longer agree to open their borders to agricultural imports from rich countries unless those rich countries at least stopped pouring billions of dollars of subsidies at their own farmers, thus ensuring Southern farmers couldn't possibly compete. Since the US, in particular, had no intention of making any of the sacrifices it demanded of the rest of the world, all deals were off. In July 2006, Pierre Lamy, head of the WTO, declared the Doha round dead; at this point no one is even talking about another WTO negotiation for at least two years—when the organisation might very possibly not exist.

The International Monetary Fund and World Bank

This is the most amazing story of all. The IMF is rapidly approaching bankruptcy as a direct result of the worldwide mobilisation against it. To put the matter bluntly: we destroyed it. The World Bank is not doing all that much better. But, by the time the full effects were felt, we weren't even paying attention.

This last story is worth telling in some detail, so let me leave this section for a moment and continue with the main text.

The Fall of the IMF and the World Bank

The IMF was always the arch-villain of the struggle. It is the most powerful, most arrogant, most pitiless instrument through which neoliberal policies have, for the last twenty-five years, been imposed on the poorer countries of the Global South, basically by manipulating debt. In exchange for emergency refinancing, the IMF would demand structural adjustment programmes (SAPs) that forced massive cuts in health, education, and price supports on food, as well as endless privatisation schemes that allowed foreign capitalists to buy up local resources at fire sale prices. Structural adjustment somehow never worked to get countries back on their feet economically, which meant they remained in crisis, and the solution was always to insist on yet another round of structural adjustment.

The IMF had another less celebrated role: global enforcer. It was its job to ensure that no country (no matter how poor) could ever default on loans to Western bankers (no matter how foolish). Even if a banker were to offer a corrupt dictator a billion-dollar loan and that dictator placed it directly in his Swiss bank account and fled the country, the IMF would ensure that a billion dollars (plus generous interest) was extracted from his former victims. If a country did default, for any reason, the IMF could impose a credit boycott, with economic effects roughly comparable to that of a nuclear bomb. (All this flies in the face of even elementary economic theory, whereby those lending money are supposed to accept a certain degree of risk; but in the world of international politics, economic laws are only binding on the poor.) This role was its downfall.

What happened was that Argentina defaulted and got away with it. In the '90s, Argentina was the IMF's star pupil in Latin America—they literally privatised every public facility except the customs bureau. Then, in 2002, the economy crashed. The immediate results we all know: battles in the streets, popular assemblies, the overthrow of three governments in one month, road blockades, occupied factories.... 'Horizontalism'—broadly anarchist principles—was at the core of popular resistance. The political class was so completely discredited that politicians were obliged to put on wigs and phoney moustaches to eat in restaurants without being physically attacked. When Néstor Kirchner, a moderate social democrat, took power in 2003, he knew he had to do something dramatic in order to get most of the population to accept even the idea of having a government, let alone his. So he did. He did, in fact, the one thing no one in that position is ever supposed to do. He defaulted on Argentina's foreign debt.

Actually Kirchner was quite clever about it. He did not default on his IMF loans. He defaulted on Argentina's private debt, announcing that for all outstanding loans, he would only pay 25 cents on the dollar. Citibank and Chase went, of course, to the IMF, their accustomed enforcer, to demand punishment. But, for the first time in its history, the IMF balked. First of all, with Argentina's economy already in ruins, even the economic equivalent of a nuclear bomb would do little more than make the rubble bounce. Second, just about everyone was aware that it was the IMF's disastrous advice that set the stage for Argentina's crash in the first place. Third and most decisively, this was at the very height of the impact of the global justice movement: the IMF was already the most hated institution on the planet, and wilfully destroying what little remained of Argentina's middle class would have been pushing things just a little bit too far.

So Argentina was allowed to get away with it. After that, everything changed. Brazil and Argentina together arranged to pay back their outstanding debt to the IMF itself. With a little help from Chávez, so did the rest of the continent. In 2003, Latin American IMF debt stood at $49 billion. Now, in 2007, it's $694 million. That's a decline of 98.6 per cent. For every thousand dollars owed four years ago, Latin America now owes fourteen bucks. Asia followed. China and India both now have no outstanding debt to the IMF and refuse to take new loans. The boycott includes Korea, Thailand, Indonesia, Malaysia, the Philippines, and pretty much every other significant regional economy. Also Russia. The Fund is reduced to lording it over the economies of Africa and maybe some parts of the Middle East and the former Soviet sphere (basically those without oil). As a result its revenues have plummeted by 80 per cent in four years.

In the irony of all possible ironies, it's increasingly looking like the IMF will go bankrupt if it can't find someone willing to bail it out. Neither is it clear that anyone particularly wants to. With its reputation as fiscal enforcer in tatters, the IMF no longer serves any obvious purpose, even for capitalists. There have been a number of proposals at recent G8 meetings to make up a new mission for the organisation—a kind of international bankruptcy court, perhaps—but each proposal got torpedoed for one reason or another. Even if the IMF does survive, it has already been reduced to a cardboard cut-out of its former self.

The World Bank, which early on assumed the role of good cop, is in somewhat better shape. But emphasis here must be placed on the word 'somewhat'—its revenue has only fallen by sixty per cent, not eighty per cent, and there are few actual boycotts. On the other hand, the Bank is currently being kept alive largely by the fact that India and China are still willing to deal with it, and both sides know that, so it is no longer in much of a position to dictate terms.

Obviously, this does not mean that all the monsters have been slain. In Latin America, neoliberalism might be on the run, but China and India are carrying out devastating 'reforms' within their own countries, European social protections are under attack, and most of Africa, despite much hypocritical posturing on the part of the Bonos and rich countries of the world, is still locked in debt and now also facing a new colonisation by China. The US, its economic power retreating in most of the world, is frantically trying to redouble its grip over Mexico and Central America. We're not living in utopia. But we already knew that. The question is why we never noticed our victories.

Olivier de Marcellus, a PGA activist from Switzerland, points out one reason: whenever some element of the capitalist system takes a hit, whether it's the nuclear industry or the IMF, some leftist journal will start explaining to us that, really, this is all part of their plan—or maybe an effect of the inexorable working out of 'the internal contradictions of capital'—but certainly nothing for which we ourselves are in any way responsible.

Even more important, perhaps, is our reluctance to even say the word 'we'. The Argentine default, wasn't that really engineered by Néstor Kirchner? What does he have to do with the globalisation movement? I mean, it's not as if his hands were forced by thousands of citizens rising up, smashing banks, and replacing the government with popular assemblies coordinated by the Independent Media Center (IMC). Or, well, okay, maybe it was. Well, in that case, those citizens were People of Colour in the Global South. How can "we" take responsibility for their actions? Never mind that they mostly saw themselves as part of the same global justice movement as us, espoused similar ideas, wore similar clothes, used similar tactics, in many cases even belonged to the same confederacies or organisations. Saying 'we' would imply the primal sin of speaking for others.

Myself, I think it's reasonable for a global movement (usually traced back to the Zapatista uprising in 1994 and a series of *Encuentros* that followed, leading to the creation of networks like PGA whose prime movers were the peasant movements of Brazil and India) to consider its accomplishments in global terms. These are not inconsiderable. Yet just as with the anti-nuclear movement, they were almost all focused on the middle term. Let me map out a similar hierarchy of goals:

- Short-Term Goals: blockade and shut down particular summit meetings (IMF, WTO, G8, etc).
- Medium-Term Goals: destroy the 'Washington Consensus' around neoliberalism; block all new trade pacts; delegitimise and ultimately shut down institutions like the WTO, IMF, and World Bank; disseminate new models of direct democracy.
- Long-Term Goals (at least for the more radical elements): smash the state and destroy capitalism.

Here again, we find the same pattern. After the miracle of Seattle, short-term—tactical—goals were rarely achieved. But this was mainly because when faced with such a movement governments tend to dig in their heels and make it a matter of principle that they shouldn't be achieved. This was usually considered much more important, in fact, than the success of the summit in question. Most activists do not seem aware that in a lot of cases—the 2001 and 2002 IMF and World Bank meetings, for example—police ended up enforcing security arrangements so elaborate that they came very close to shutting down the meetings themselves, ensuring that many events were cancelled, ceremonies were ruined, and nobody really had a chance to talk to each other. But the point was not whether trade officials got to meet or not. The point was that the protesters could not be seen to win.

Here too the medium-term goals were achieved so quickly that it actually made the longer-term goals more difficult. NGOs, labour unions, authoritarian Marxists, and similar allies jumped ship almost immediately. Strategic debates ensued, but they were carried out, as always, indirectly, as arguments about race, privilege, tactics, almost anything except actual strategic debates. Here too everything was made infinitely more difficult by the state's recourse to war.

It is hard for anarchists to take much direct responsibility for the inevitable end of the war in Iraq, or even to the very bloody nose the empire has already acquired there. But a case could well be made for indirect responsibility. Since the '60s and the catastrophe of Vietnam, the US government has not abandoned its policy of answering any threat of democratic mass mobilising by a return to war. But it has had to be much more careful. Essentially, it has to design wars to be protest-proof. There is very good reason to believe that the first Gulf War was explicitly designed with this in mind. The approach taken to the invasion of Iraq—the insistence on a smaller, high-tech army, the extreme reliance on indiscriminate firepower, even against civilians, to protect against Vietnam-like levels of US casualties—appears to have been developed, again, more with a mind to heading off any potential peace movement at home than a focus on military effectiveness. This would help explain why the most powerful army in the world has ended up being tied down and even defeated by an almost unimaginably ragtag group of guerrillas with negligible access to outside safe areas, little funding, and limited military support. As in the trade summits, the government is so obsessed with ensuring that forces of civil resistance not be seen to win the battle at home that they would prefer to lose the actual war.

Perspectives (with a Brief Flashback to the '30s in Spain)

How, then, to cope with the perils of victory? I can't claim to have any simple answers. I wrote this essay more to start a conversation, to put the problem on the table—to inspire strategic debate.

Still, some implications are pretty obvious. The next time we plan a major action campaign, I think we would do well to at least take into account the possibility that we might obtain our mid-range strategic goals very quickly, and that when that happens many of our allies will fall away.

Second, we have to recognise strategic debates for what they are, even when they seem to be about something else. Take one famous example: arguments about property destruction after Seattle. Most of these, I think, were really arguments about capitalism. Those who decried window breaking did so mainly because they wished to appeal to middle-class consumers to move towards global exchange style green consumerism, to ally with labour bureaucracies and social democrats abroad. This was not a path designed to create a direct confrontation with capitalism, and most of those who urged us to take this route were, at least, sceptical about the possibility that capitalism could ever really be defeated. Those who did break windows didn't care if they were offending suburban homeowners, because they didn't see them as a potential element in a revolutionary anti-capitalist coalition. They were trying, in effect, to hijack the media to send a message that the system was vulnerable—hoping to inspire similar insurrectionary acts on the part of those who might be considering entering a genuinely revolutionary alliance: alienated teenagers, oppressed people of colour, rank-and-file labourers impatient with union bureaucrats, the homeless, the criminalised, the radically discontent. If a militant anti-capitalist movement was to begin in the US, it would have to start with people like these; people who don't need to be convinced that the system is rotten, only that there's something they can do about it. At any rate, even if it were possible to have an anti-capitalist revolution without gun battles on the streets—which most of us are hoping for; let's face it, if we come up against the US army, we will lose—there's no possible way we could have an anti-capitalist revolution while also scrupulously respecting property rights.

The latter actually leads to an interesting question. What would it mean to win not just our medium-term goals but also our long-term goals? At the moment no one is even clear how that would come about, because none of us have much faith remaining in *the* revolution in the old nineteenth- or twentieth-century sense of the term. After all, the total view of revolution whereby there will be a single mass insurrection or general strike and then all walls will come tumbling down is entirely premised on the old fantasy of capturing the state. That's the only way victory could possibly be that absolute and complete—at least if we are speaking of a whole country or meaningful territory.

By way of illustration, consider this: What would it have meant for the Spanish anarchists to have actually 'won' 1937? It's amazing how rarely we ask ourselves such questions. We just imagine it would have been something like the Russian Revolution, which began in a similar way, with the melting away of the old army, the spontaneous creation of workers' soviets. But that was in the major cities. The Russian Revolution was followed by years of civil war in which the Red Army gradually imposed the new state's control on every part of the old Russian Empire, whether the communities in question wanted it or not. Let us imagine that anarchist militias in Spain had routed the fascist army, which then completely dissolved, and kicked the socialist Republican government out of its offices in Barcelona and Madrid. That would certainly have been victory by anybody's standards. But what would have happened next? Would they have established Spain as a non-republic, an anti-state existing within the exact same international borders? Would they have imposed a regime of popular councils in every single village and municipality in the territory of what had formerly been Spain? How exactly?

We have to bear in mind here that there were many villages, towns, even regions of Spain where anarchists were almost non-existent. In some, just about the entire population was conservative Catholic or monarchist; in others (say the Basque Country), there was a militant and well-organised working class, one that was overwhelmingly socialist or communist. Even at the height of revolutionary fervour, most of these would stay true to their old values and ideas. If the victorious Federación Anarquista Ibérica ('Iberian Anarchist Federation', FAI) attempted to exterminate them all—a task which would have required killing millions of people—or chase them out of the country or forcibly relocate them into anarchist communities or send them off to re-education camps—they would not only have been guilty of world-class atrocities, they would have had to give up on being anarchists. Democratic organisations simply cannot commit atrocities on that systematic scale; for that, you need communist- or fascist-style top-down organisation, since you can't actually get thousands of human beings to systematically massacre helpless women and children and old people, destroy communities, or chase families from their ancestral homes unless they can at least say they were only following orders. There appear to have been only two possible solutions to the problem:

1. Let the Republic continue as the de facto government controlled by the socialists; let them impose government control over right-wing majority areas and get some kind of deal out of them to leave the anarchist-majority cities, towns, and villages alone to organise themselves as they wish to and hope that they kept the deal (this might be considered the 'good luck' option).
2. Declare that everyone was free to form their own local popular assemblies, and let them decide on their own mode of self-organisation.

The latter seems more fitting with anarchist principles, but the results wouldn't have been very different. After all if the inhabitants of, say, Bilbao overwhelmingly desired to create a local government, how exactly would one have stopped them? Municipalities where the Church or landlords still commanded popular support would presumably put the same old right-wing authorities in charge; socialist or communist municipalities would put socialist or communist party bureaucrats in charge; right and left statists would then each form rival confederations that, even though they controlled only a fraction of the former Spanish territory, would each declare themselves the legitimate government of Spain. Foreign governments would recognise one or the other—since none would be willing to exchange ambassadors with a non-government like the FAI, even assuming the FAI wished to exchange ambassadors with them, which it wouldn't.

In other words, the actual shooting war might end, but the political struggle would continue, and large parts of Spain would presumably end up looking like contemporary Chiapas, with each district or community divided between anarchist and anti-anarchist factions. Ultimate victory would have to be a long and arduous process.

The only way to really win over the statist enclaves would be to win over their children, which could be accomplished by creating an obviously freer, more pleasurable, more beautiful, secure, relaxed, fulfilling life in the stateless sections. Foreign capitalist powers, on the other hand, even if they did not intervene militarily, would do everything possible to head off the notorious 'threat of a good example' by economic boycotts and subversion, and by pouring resources into the statist zones. In the end, everything would probably depend on the degree to which anarchist victories in Spain inspired similar insurrections elsewhere.

The real point of this imaginative exercise is just to point out that there are no clean breaks in history. The flip side of the old idea of the clean break, the one moment when the state falls and capitalism is defeated, is that anything short of that is not really a victory at all. If capitalism is left standing, if it begins to market your once-subversive ideas, it shows that the capitalists really won. You've lost; you've been co-opted.

To me, this is absurd. Can we say that feminism lost, that it achieved nothing, just because corporate culture felt obliged to pay lip service to condemning sexism, and capitalist firms began marketing feminist books, movies, and other products? Of course not: unless you've managed to destroy capitalism and patriarchy in one fell blow, this is one of the clearest signs that you've gotten somewhere. Presumably any effective road to revolution will involve endless moments of co-optation, endless victorious campaigns, endless little insurrectionary moments, or moments of flight and covert autonomy. I hesitate to even speculate what it might really be like. But to start in that direction, the first thing we need to do is to recognise that we do, in fact, win some. Actually, recently, we've been winning quite a few. The question is how to break the cycle of exaltation and despair and come up with some strategic visions (the more the merrier) about how these victories build on each other to create a cumulative movement towards a new society.

References[4]

Joe Bandy and Jackie Smith, eds, 2004—*Coalitions across Borders: Transnational Protest and the Neoliberal Order*. Oxford: Rowman & Littlefield

Pierre Beaudet, Raul Canet, and Marie-Josée Massicotte, eds, 2010—*L'Altermondialisme: Forums sociaux, résistances et nouvelle culture politique* ['Alter-globalisation: Social Forums, Resistance, and New Political Culture', in French]. Montréal, QC: Les Éditions Écosociété

Big Noise Films et al, 1999—*Showdown in Seattle*, at https://vimeo.com/223772965 (Accessed August 30 2017)

Jeremy Brecher, Tim Costello, and Brendan Smith, 2000—*Globalization from Below: The Power of Solidarity*. A Book from Commonwork: A Resource and Strategy Project for Globalization from Below. Cambridge, MA: South End Press

Kevin Danaher and Roger Burbach, eds, 2000—*Globalize This! The Battle Against the World Trade Organization and Corporate Rule*. Monroe, ME: Common Courage Press

Richard Day, 2005—*Gramsci Is Dead: Anarchist Currents in the Newest Social Movements*. London: Pluto Press / Toronto: Between the Lines / Ann Arbor: University of Michigan Press

Marianne Maeckelbergh, 2009—*The Will of the Many: How the Alterglobalisation Movement is Changing the Face of Democracy*. London: Pluto Press

Elizabeth Betita Martínez, March 2000—'Where Was The Color in Seattle? Looking for reasons why the Great Battle was so white', in *ColorLines*, vol 3 no 1, March 2000, at http://colorlines.com/archives/2000/03/where_was_the_color_in_seattlelooking_for_reasons_why_the_great_battle_was_so_white.html (Accessed August 30 2017)

Tom Mertes, ed, 2004—*A Movement of Movements: Is Another World Really Possible?*. London: Verso

Notes from Nowhere, eds, 2003—*We are Everywhere: The Irresistible Rise of Global Anti-Capitalism*. London / New York: Verso, at http://artactivism.members.gn.apc.org/stories.htm (Accessed August 30 2017)

Geoffrey Pleyers, 2010—*Alter-Globalization: Becoming Actors in the Global Age*. Foreword by Alain Touraine. London: Polity Press

José Seoane and Emilio Taddei, 2002—'From Seattle to Porto Alegre: The Anti-Neoliberal Globalization Movement', in *Current Sociology*, vol 50 no 1, pp 99–122

Jackie Smith, 2008—*Social Movements for Global Democracy*. Baltimore: The Johns Hopkins University Press

Jackie Smith, Christopher Chase-Dunn, Donatella della Porta et al, 2007—*Global Democracy and the World Social Forums*. Boulder, CO: Paradigm Publishers

David Solnit, 2011—'Seattle WTO Shutdown '99 to Occupy: Organizing to Win 12 Years Later', on *The Indypendent*, December 5 2011, at http://www.indypendent.org/2011/12/05/seattle-wto-shutdown-99-to-occupy/ (Accessed August 30 2017)

David Solnit, 2014—'The Roots Of Global Revolt: The 20th Anniversary of NAFTA and the Zapatistas', at https://dorsetchiapassolidarity.wordpress.com/2014/01/08/the-roots-of-global-revolt-the-20th-anniversary-of-nafta-and-the-zapatistas/ (Accessed August 30 2017)

Sidney Tarrow, 2005—*The New Transnational Activism*. New York: Cambridge University Press

Notes

1. This essay was first published on *Infoshop News*, October 12 2007, at http://www.infoshop.org/inews/article.php?story=2007graeber-victory (Inactive August 30 2017). Ed: My thanks to the author for his prompt permission to include this essay in this collection.

2. Ed: When reading this essay, keep in mind that the original version was published in October 2007, a time when—as he discusses—the 'global justice and solidarity movement' of the early 2000s seemed to be in decline / dormant, three years and more before Tahrir Square irrupted, and four years before Occupy Wall Street (with which, incidentally, the author was closely involved). It could well be said, this essay looks ahead to . . .

3. Ed: For those not familiar with this history, the following might be useful: Bandy and Smith, eds, 2004; Beaudet, Canet, and Massicotte, eds, 2010; Big Noise Films et al 1999; Brecher, Costello, and Smith 2000; Danaher and Burbach, eds, 2000; Day 2005; Maeckelbergh 2009; Martínez, March 2000; Mertes, ed, 2004; Notes from Nowhere, eds, 2003; Solnit, December 2011; Solnit, January 2014; Tarrow 2005.

4. Ed: I have added all of these references to make this provocative essay more accessible to readers who are less familiar with 'the "antiglobalization" movement' or, more generally, the recent history of world movement.

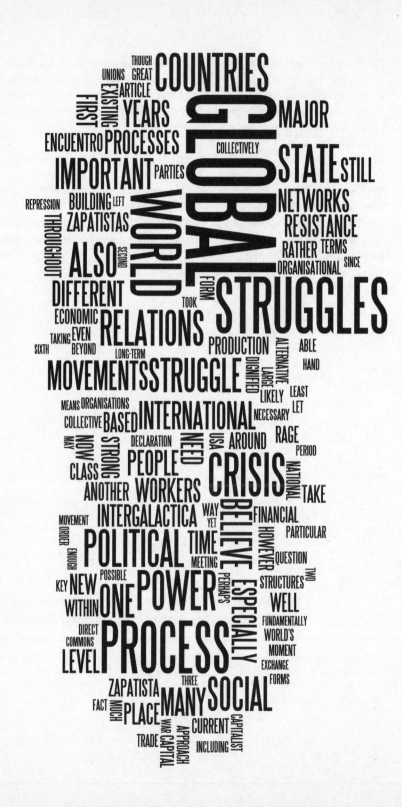

OpenWord

Gathering Our Dignified Rage
Building New Autonomous Global Relations of Production, Livelihood, and Exchange[1]
Kolya Abramsky

Introductory note by the author, August 2018:
This article, 'Gathering Our Dignified Rage', is being published here nearly ten years after it was originally written. When recently discussing with the editor of this book whether or not to include the article, I was very torn. On the one hand, I feel that the piece is still of interest and raises important issues. Many of the issues are even more relevant now than when it was written, and other things that the article anticipated have to a considerable degree come about.

Yet on the other hand, in other areas I find the text extremely inadequate for the current situation. In many respects it has been completely left behind by the course of events in the last few years. There have simply been too many key global developments, and the world is a different place than it was seven years ago. I told the editor that I was very reluctant to have my article published in its current form, that it was simply too out of date. Furthermore, I argued that my own thinking had changed too much in the intervening years. I felt it would be sloppy and unprofessional, as well as politically unconstructive, to include an article that had been written very much as a 'real time' intervention in a very current political debate in a very specific moment, and that the arguments did not stand the test of time. After much haggling and toing and froing, we came to the agreement that my article would be included as it was originally written, but that I would have a chance to write a few accompanying words with my concerns and updated thoughts.

***

Firstly, I believe that in relation to the current juncture at a world level, my 2008 article is too orientated towards the global Zapatista process alone, and concretely towards two particular moments in it, the World's Festival of Dignified Rage and a new Intergaláctica meeting. These moments are now very far away in movement history, nearly ten years ago. Since then, the global Zapatista process has gone in a very different way from anticipated at the time, opting for more targeted interventions (such as the Zapatista *Escuelitas*, 'Little Schools') rather than larger international gatherings. Personally, I have not been involved in these processes for many years and have not followed developments closely.

Second, and perhaps my main concern, is that the article as it was written is strongly rooted in the concept of trying to revive global networks of resistance. At

411

the time of writing, in 2008, I believed this was a key and realistic task. Now this task seems to me to be a less realistic (though still necessary) proposition, as several of the global networks that were still at least somewhat relevant in 2008 (such as Peoples' Global Action [PGA], the World Social Forum, and Indymedia) have now either completely collapsed or are less and less relevant globally. Somewhat paradoxically, these organisational forms have become less and less relevant just at the time that the global financial-economic (and increasingly political) crisis that erupted in 2008 made such global organisational processes of struggle ever more necessary. Yet these organisations have not shown themselves to be strong enough to maintain their relevance in the context of this crisis.

On the level of basic 'events and facts', there are also a number of key changes in the global landscape that have occurred since this article was written, and which I believe need to be taken into account when reading it. Each, in its own way, makes the article inadequate for understanding, preparing for, strategising, and organising the struggles that are ahead of us. These are:

1. The deepening of the global financial-economic-political, and (I would argue, increasingly geopolitical) crisis.
2. The emergence of new political party orientated resistances in response to this, such as Syriza in Greece and Podemos in Spain.
3. The full development of the Obama presidency as a fundamentally 'business as usual' US presidential administration, despite some progressive and positive elements.
4. The development of the BRICS process, including establishing the BRICS Development Bank.
5. The further shift to the right of several leftist governments in Latin America, especially in Brazil, but also arguably in Bolivia, Ecuador, and to a lesser degree in Venezuela (the latter has also been heavily impacted by falling global oil prices).
6. The election of Narendra Modi of the right-wing BJP party as Prime Minister of India.
7. The strengthening of the far right in the European Union, especially in France, Greece, and the UK.
8. The rise of racial dimensions to class conflict in the USA.
9. The major economic and military tensions developing between the USA and Russia.
10. The massive increase in so-called 'clash of civilisations', through the rise of ISIS.
11. The deepening of the Eurozone crisis, including an increasing French-German tension.
12. The major failure of Syriza to stand up to the demands of the Euro and its implementation of austerity measures.

I believe that these global developments present enormous challenges to movements and struggles around the world, and that the next years are likely to involve some very difficult and harsh struggles, struggles that most of us find ourselves very ill-prepared to engage in. While the article that follows was written in a spirit of hope and inspired by others in struggle, frankly, today I find it far too optimistic and nostalgic for something upbeat. In the current situation, I do not believe that such a reading of events and the balance of class forces on a global level is being honest about the very daunting struggles ahead of us, struggles which unfortunately there is a very large chance we will lose.

Although I do still believe that globally coordinated struggle is extremely necessary, perhaps even more necessary than it was before, I also believe that it is not just coincidental that most of the global organisational forms that were once greatly relevant are now no longer useful. I believe this is because they lack a material base adequate to the tasks at hand. In the past, global networks were useful, and they still are, for a task that was predominantly about exposing, denouncing, and protesting capitalist relations and the global nature of these processes and the institutions that protect them. I believe the global networks that emerged during the early 2000s were at one point strong enough for these tasks and, in their own terms, were extremely successful. However, both through their own success and the development of the global crisis itself, the next phase of struggle has now been pushed onto the agenda. It is no longer enough just to denounce and protest; rather, it is becoming ever more urgent to actually construct (and defend) new relations of production, distribution, and livelihood. It is precisely these tasks that the existing global networks were not strong enough for. My original essay— which follows this Introductory Note—does point to the urgency of these tasks, and to the fact that the then-existing networks were already having difficulty making this transition from denunciation to constructing (and defending) new relations of production, distribution, and livelihood. However, I believe that the developments which have occurred since the article was written further reveal the sheer inadequacy of these networks and organisations, not just in the detail of their practice but in their fundamental organisational form and strategies.

I believe that this inadequacy is closely related to the fact that the key struggle in the current moment is a national level class struggle, at a juncture where 'the crisis' is manifesting itself as an extremely hardcore class war from the side of capital. Virtually *every single* national government in the world today is *complicit* in waging this war at the national level and is complying with the demands of capital at the global level.

There are only a very few exceptions in the form of a small number of leftist governments who are themselves desperately struggling to keep afloat and to avoid either being toppled from power and / or pushed to the right. As such, the struggle in the current and coming period is a class struggle that has to be waged primarily at the national level and not at the global level. As such, I believe it is unlikely that global networks can become relevant again until struggles are stronger at a national level in many countries of the world.

However, there is also a need to carefully assess what the terrain of this national level of struggle is and what its goals are. I believe that the crisis in the Eurozone, and, more broadly, the global crisis, has moved from a financial to an economic crisis and is now fundamentally a political crisis—ie, *the struggle for who resolves the crisis and on whose terms.*

This is still *fundamentally a class question.* The political aspects of this crisis are more advanced in some countries where there is already massive political instability (eg, Greece) than in others that, at least for the time being, appear stable (eg, Germany). Nonetheless, despite the varying levels of intensity and visibility of this political crisis, the crisis has thrown the issue of state power (at the national level) back onto the agenda of emancipatory struggles, whether we like it or not. If we fail in the years ahead, things will move more and more to the authoritarian right wing. A guiding force of many of the antiauthoritarian global anti-capitalist processes of the late 1990s and early 2000s was the argument that globalisation and the apparent shift of locus from national state power to global capitalist relations and their institutions meant that there was no longer a "Winter Palace" to storm, à la Soviet Union (neither metaphorically nor literally). I believe the deepening political crisis makes this argument no longer valid. Instead, the slogan of the Argentinean struggles *Que Se Vayan Todos* ('They All Must Go') has become more and more urgent.

This is not to say that struggles must limit themselves to this; it is certainly not sufficient to work at the national level alone or to work in relation to state power alone. However, *it is nonetheless a necessary part of the struggle to move beyond where we currently are that cannot be ignored or bypassed.* This is not to say that the struggles against global capital and its institutions are no longer relevant. Far from it, this remains an essential terrain of struggle, but—I believe, and suggest—will only have a strong basis as the class struggle advances at the nation-state level.

Consequently, I believe the next phase for movements needs to be developing national mass-based political parties (including, but not necessarily, electoral parties), and the next phase in international networking will be an international process around these political parties. Should this happen, it would mark a change from recent movement practice. Until recently, and notwithstanding the importance of the Brazilian Workers' Party (PT) in the formation and early life of the World Social Forum, a major, perhaps dominant, feature of much of the international networking of the 1990s and the first decade of the 2000s was a strong level of criticism and even outright rejection of political parties, and at some moments—such as in the WSF—their deliberate exclusion, at least in formal terms. This approach of giving priority to non-party organisational forms perhaps reached a high point with many of the anti-austerity protests in Europe in the early years of the post-2008 crisis, which specifically defined themselves as 'non-political'. I believe, however, that this approach is no longer useful, is actually a hindrance, as it results in movements shying away from even attempting to understand the question of state power, let alone engaging in a struggle for it. Potentially, this also massively feeds into a right-wing agenda.

Without a shift towards building new (or perhaps, in some cases, rebuilding old) political parties, I think it is very likely that many movements will become politically irrelevant, and along with this and as a consequence, we will allow the right wing to win all over the world. At a personal level, I admit that this flies in the face of many of the things that I wrote some years ago, including the article that is printed in this book. Nonetheless, this is my reading at this juncture of deepening capitalist crisis.

In relation to this, there are a number of interesting developments in recent years and months that are worth highlighting. On the one hand, for better or for worse and not without their own contradictions, large strands of the 'non-political' movements against austerity in Greece and Spain have clearly revised their strategy, opting to devote energy to building political parties that seek to gain power through the electoral process, namely Syriza and Podemos, parties which within a limited space of time have massively grown in both membership and influence.

On the other hand, an example that is surely interesting—and very necessary—to look at is India, a country that is widely heralded as having some of the most numerous, most mass-based, and most democratic social movements in the world, including both rural and urban movements. Yet despite this, and even if the movements are managing to restrain the government in some areas—such as land—they spectacularly failed to prevent the extreme right-winger Modi and the BJP Party from coming to power through elections in 2014. What are the causes and implications of this in terms of movement strategies?

Another interesting example in this regard is related to developments in Brazil. In 2013, in the face of emerging political protests related to austerity and other issues, the major trade unions and peasant movements were very strongly critical of the 'non-political' approaches that some strands of the movement adopted. Currently, the right wing that both fuelled and took advantage of these is increasingly using the destabilisation of established legitimacy structures in Brazil to present an extremely anti–working class and popular agenda that favours traditional elites and is calling for the military to again impose itself over democratic political forms.

Finally, it is worth mentioning two different examples, this time relating to efforts to 'reclaim' existing social democratic parties that have moved ever more neoliberal in recent decades. In the UK, there has been a very unexpected 'palace coup' in the leadership of the Labour Party, a party that has been at the vanguard of the global process of neoliberalisation of workers and social democratic parties, by a very strong left-wing team led by Jeremy Corbyn. A similar process unfolded in the USA, as a self-proclaimed socialist Bernie Sanders threatened to depose the favourite contender for leadership of the Democratic Party, Hillary Clinton.

In this context, a fundamental question is how to struggle for state power and what this means. Is it about merely taking over the existing state apparatus through elections and replacing one government with another (as has, to some degree, happened in several countries now, perhaps most especially in Latin America)? Or is it about going deeper than merely changing governments—and about destroying old political and economic relations?

This is not a question that can be settled in the abstract. It will only be resolved in struggle, in different ways in different countries and contexts. I believe that there is almost certain to be a resurgence of what can broadly (and very imprecisely) be labelled as 'progressive leftist' electoral parties, which, although not very radical and confrontational, are at least 'broadly progressive'. We are already seeing this occurring, such as with Podemos in Spain or Syriza in Greece (both of which emerged out of, or at least in close dialogue with, certain strands within mass movements). Furthermore, I believe that we are likely to see such parties presenting serious electoral challenges and getting voted into power in several countries, as has been the case in Greece, and in Spain where Podemos won 20 per cent of the vote and sixty-nine seats in Congress.

Such governments may well offer very real possibilities for the movement to buy time, as they may slightly slow down the disintegration of existing power relations and the ongoing assault from capital, while at the same time allowing struggles to consolidate themselves and strengthen their organisational capacity for the battles that almost certainly lie ahead. As such, I believe it is important to support these parties. However, I believe that we are reaching the limits of what such 'progressive' electoral parties will be able to achieve, as they will either not be able to defend themselves and will be forced out of power by capital, or they will be allowed to stay in power on the condition that they abandon their progressive demands and sing to the tune of capital. Again, the example of Syriza's trajectory during this past year is a case in point.[2]

However, for me, the failure of Syriza to implement a durable progressive agenda (let alone a more radical anti-capitalist one) does not indicate that left-wing political parties and socialism are dead. Rather, it is illustrative of the very serious danger of a 'soft left' that is simply unable to deal with the level of confrontation required by the current conjuncture and the balance of class forces, and which fails to address fundamental ownership issues and class power. A soft left that merely seeks to change governmental practice and policy, rather than destroying or fundamentally changing the existing state structures, and in no way seeks to suppress capital. Perhaps, in crude and definitely over-simplistic terms, it is possible to characterise such efforts as being a sincere voice of conscience, mainly motivated by idealism rather than the material capacity to suppress and to replace the existing order.

What is crucial to recognise is that it is not possible to implement far-reaching political alternatives unless there is a far-reaching economic alternative to back it up, and at the same time, it is equally impossible to implement far-reaching economic alternatives unless there is a far-reaching political alternative to back it up. I believe that this is one of the fundamental paradoxes of political struggle in the current moment, if not *the* fundamental paradox. In other words, I believe there is *still* the need to take over—and to decommodify—key means of production and reproduction, and there is still a need to do this without offering capital any compensation. Furthermore, there is *still* the need to impose these changes on capital and to suppress it, as capital cannot be wished away or convinced out of existence. There is also *still* the need to learn how to defend our gains in power; otherwise they will be rolled back in counterrevolution. And arguably, and though beyond the scope of this article to explore in any depth, given that the limits of the twentieth-century Keynesian reformist deal have almost certainly been reached in most of the world (with the possible exception of China), the need for all of this is more urgent now than it ever has been (and perhaps even more difficult? . . . Or, conversely and somewhat strangely, perhaps even more realistic?).

Another important limitation of electoral parties and politics in the current period, which I believe struggles are likely to come up against much more acutely and visibly in the years ahead, is the fact that state structures do not collapse in neat accordance with predetermined electoral cycles of four or five years, but rather do so in moments of extreme and rapid declining legitimacy and the unravelling of existing class coalitions that are in power. In general, or at least in periods of political stability, state structures do not collapse very frequently, as legitimacy structures are usually strong enough to hold ruling coalitions together for durable lengths of time. However, we are currently in a historical moment characterised by the breakdown of existing class power blocs and the consequent massive and accelerating crises of legitimacy in an increasing number of countries throughout the world, caused by the global crisis. This means that the collapse of state structures is likely to become more frequent than it has been in the recent past throughout large parts of the world—a process which is already underway to a limited degree. Consequently, movements—and also governing and opposition political parties—that are accustomed to operating in periods of relative political stability, now have to be also prepared for such moments of instability and state collapse. It cannot be overemphasised that in many respects they are getting overwhelmed by the rapid and somewhat inexorable nature of these changes.

This means that the question of 'Dual Power' is very much back on the agenda, as a twin process in which the collective power to confront established power relations strengthens and simultaneously so does the collective power to self-govern, until at some point new alternative power structures of self-governance are able to substantially or completely replace the existing power structures. This in turn starkly raises the question of both the commons and trade unions. The commons, despite being a concept that means many things to different people, are significant as a form of collective autonomous self-governance over specific resources and territories by certain defined communities, and trade unions are significant as the dominant form in which workers, defining themselves as workers, organise in the workplace (or, in the case of the unemployed, in the non-workplace). Both the commons and trade unions have major potentials for confronting, breaking down, and suppressing existing power structures and for building and defending alternative power structures. However, they both also have some major limitations.

First, the commons. I believe that a resistance based in the commons is vital, but it is important to recognise that this also has some limitations. Many autonomist thinkers and organisations tend to view the commons as an end in its own right. I believe this essentially ignores the key question of politics—which is still fundamentally a question of class power—and this in turn is still fundamentally a question of state power at the national level. As such, a commons-based approach is unlikely to be strong enough to defend itself in the face of capitalist counter-revolution. On the other hand, if the commons are seen as being an organisational form that acts as a stepping stone for simultaneously building collective and democratic social, political, and economic counter-power with which to strengthen people's capacities to survive, defend themselves in the face of capital's worsening assaults, and further struggle to destroy both existing state power and existing relations of production, as well as to prepare for taking state power in the future, then I believe that the commons approach can be very strong.

In this respect, there are some important parallels with what happened in the Civil War that preceded the establishment of the People's Republic of China. During this period, and under the leadership of the Communist Party, people built strong collective social, political, and economic counter-power that was able to implement land reforms and democratise rural ownership structures, as well as decision-making structures, thus destroying feudal structures as *necessary steps* along the road to taking state power. In the particular historical case of China, the democratic revolution was a necessary stage along the road to the socialist revolution. It is certainly not coincidental that the Zapatistas, a much cited example of a successful commons, started as and have remained an armed organisation, consistently, categorically, and explicitly refusing to disarm themselves, despite concentrating on building collective social and economic power from below.

While they do not currently seek to take state power, only time will tell for how long they will continue with this strategy.

It is equally important to look critically at the question of trade unions. The problems of trade unions throughout the world are well documented. Some analysts and activists are even of the opinion that these problems are so acute and so insurmountable that unions are a largely irrelevant organisational form belonging to the dustbin of history. Some of the major problems are as follows: a) falling membership in some of the countries where historically they have been strong, such as in Western Europe and North America; b) an obsession with social dialogue that is based around sitting at a table with capitalists, and which is no longer possible due to the uneven balance of class forces, which is currently skewed heavily in capital's favour; c) the exclusive focus on workers as workers and the lack of a political approach that involves taking into account other sectors of the population and wider political and social relations; d) an insistence on regulating companies (especially multinational companies) instead of seeking to change the relations of ownership and control; e) failure to cope well with the changing composition of the global workforce, including informal, temporary, precarious, and self-employed workers (many of whom are women), or with migrant workers (many of whom are undocumented and / or non-citizen workers); f) the failure to cope well with unemployed workers; g) the fact that unionised workers are just a small percentage of those in formal waged employment, let alone those who are not in such employment; h) being too stuck in the model of protecting and demanding 'jobs' and waged employment, rather than in protecting and demanding other forms of livelihoods that are based in the commons; and, finally, i) the ongoing existence of the Cold War division between the two major global trade union federations, the International Trade Union Confederation (ITUC) and the World Federation of Trade Unions (WFTU).[3]

All these problems are undeniably very real and difficult to overcome. Nonetheless, it is important to realise that many of the above critiques are over-simplistic and overgeneralised. For instance, in many countries (often corresponding to global geographical shifts in the world division of labour) union numbers and union density are not falling but are actually growing, such as in Brazil or India. In some countries, the approach to ownership of key means of production is more political than in others, such as in South Africa. Difficult though these obstacles are, I do believe that they urgently need overcoming, and that this should be seen as a pressing task for emancipatory movements in the coming years. Trade unions are *still* the only organisational form that can mobilise large numbers at the point of production (and increasingly also at the point of distribution, such as workers in the global logistics sector). As such, they *still* offer strategic possibilities for major disruption of capital's global circuits of production and distribution. And they *still* offer serious possibilities for major processes of reconstruction, based on forms of collective and democratic ownership and control of society's key assets and also their decommodification (perhaps in some sectors, such as fossil fuels, even collectively and democratically planning and implementing for their long-term phase out).

As such, I believe that dismissing unions as no longer relevant as an organisational form and viewing the commons as the only viable organisational approach is an extremely unhelpful contribution to struggle, and if emancipatory social and political transformation is our objective, this is frankly a naive understanding of the key levers of change in production relations. If trade unions are understood to be an anachronistic irrelevance, then which other formations have the economic, political, and mobilising power at the point of production to achieve this?

Without serious involvement from workers and trade unions, most talk of developing alternative relations of production and distribution, as well as forms of political power, is likely to remain empty dreaming and dangerous sloganeering. Rather, linking a strong trade union approach with a strong commons approach has enormous potential for rebuilding the concept of worker-peasant alliances on a global level, a concept that has been of the utmost significance in most historical revolutions.

Finally, a few words about the need to seriously re-enter historical debates about the development of capitalism and revolution. It is common to hear the argument that the state-based route to emancipation has failed, and that consequently the traditional left or socialist approaches are no longer relevant. I believe that this is a fundamentally flawed and over-simplistic discourse. The state-based route has not failed. Rather, what has failed is that movements struggling for this route simply gave up on this strategy in the core capitalist countries, especially in the USA, Germany, and the UK, and so the route to taking over state power was not actually given the chance to be tested in these countries. This was for several reasons: a) the struggles were able to get very real and positive results through reformist approaches, based on some form or another of social democracy and welfare state, so many movements consciously opted not to pursue struggles for more fundamental change; b) the repression against movements seeking to take over state power in these countries was simply too harsh; and c) it was simply too difficult a task to overthrow and / or smash the existing state.

I do believe that in a very sincere attempt to distance ourselves from the real horrors of so-called twentieth-century socialism much of the post-Stalinist left, especially younger generations, is very uninformed on the history of 'really existing socialism' (beyond the generalities)[4] and has a discourse that is almost (though perhaps not quite) equivalent to the Cold War right-wing approach to history (ie, in somewhat crude terms, "thank fuck the Soviet Union is over, we can now forget about it. Good riddance to bad rubbish. We don't even need to learn about it in any detail"). For me this approach to the 'old left' is fundamentally unsatisfying, and inadequate. The distinction between the 'socialism of the twentieth century' and the 'socialism of the twenty-first century' is a somewhat spurious distinction, and we can neither choose, deny, nor kill our forbearers in struggle, despite some of their undeniable errors, crimes, and atrocities.

I believe there is still a very real and urgent need to study the so-called old left in power, and to reopen some of the key debates associated with it, especially those pertaining to the class nature of the Soviet Union and China (as well as the socialist bloc more generally, including the international socialist division of labour under COMECON), as well as about the causes and outcome of the Sino-Soviet rift that took place in the late 1950s and 1960s. I believe this is one of the most serious international relations 'events' of the twentieth century, short of the two World Wars. Yet it is hardly understood or studied by people in contemporary left-wing processes. As these processes become more and more in the distant past and more and more of the direct protagonists are dying off, there is an ever-greater need to study them carefully. Furthermore, I believe that some of these questions can only be answered looking back in time, including understanding the changes that have occurred in global class relations since the break-up of the Soviet Union and the introduction of market reforms in China. It is hard not to conclude that this has been a period in which the balance of class forces fundamentally shifted in capital's favour. The recent hundredth anniversary of the Russian Revolution, in 2017, reminds us of the need for some serious collective reflection on all these issues. Such a reopening of old histories and old debates is far from an empty, academic discussion and has the potential to contribute to major organisational advances in the coming period of struggles.

Coming back to my article, 'Gathering our Dignified Rage': despite all my concerns raised in this introductory note, I do nonetheless believe that there is an urgent need for globally coordinated struggle. I believe that the next phase of 'the' global crisis will almost certainly be a phase of major geopolitical shifts and alliances. The way in which these shifts occur will not be determined by chance, but rather will be determined, at least to a large extent, by how the national level of class struggle develops in different countries. In turn, the way in which class struggles within particular countries evolve in the coming years will also be greatly influenced by the changing geopolitical relations at regional and global levels. In particular, an important factor will be whether struggles ally with each other in an internationalist process of class struggle or new and exclusive national protectionist deals are made between sectors of the world's working class and sectors of capital. All of this will have a great impact in determining whether major state powers cooperate with each other in the years ahead or go to war with each other, a question that can no longer be ignored by movements.

As such, I believe that there is a need to strengthen internationalist struggles at the national level. I believe we need to see a resurgence of strong global processes of resistance, characterised around three fundamental aspects: (a) a political struggle for state power (b) that is geared towards building lasting alternative economic relations and (c) that resists the drive to war. Whether or not any of this happens is anyone's guess and will at least partially depend on the collective decisions and actions that people undertake. However, there is certainly no room for triumphalism or for getting lost in 'inspiring stories.'

***

> Up there, they intend to repeat their history.
> They once again want to impose on us their calendar of death, their geography of destruction.
> Down here we are being left with nothing.
> Except rage.
> And dignity.
> There is no ear for our pain, except that of the people like us.
> We are no one.
> We are alone, and just with our dignity and our rage.
> Rage and dignity are our bridges, our languages.
> Let us listen to each other then, let us know each other.
> Let our rage grow and become hope.
> Let our dignity take root again and breed another world.
> If this world doesn't have a place for us, then another world must be made.
> With no other tool than our rage, no other material than our dignity.[5]

It has been three and a half years since the Zapatistas[6] issued their 'Sixth Declaration of the Lacandon Jungle'.[7,8] The declaration, issued through collective discussion in the Zapatista communities in the summer of 2005, called for a Third Intergaláctica to take place "from below and to the left". Since the declaration was issued, much has happened. The developments of both global capitalism and global resistance described so eloquently and humorously in the call have come into clearer definition. Dynamics have accelerated, and the stakes have increased. And now, with the capitalist world-economy seemingly unravelling before our eyes, the Zapatistas are seeking to usher in the next stage in the process. People in struggle throughout the world have been invited to Mexico to participate in the 'World's First Festival of Dignified Rage', which will take place at the end of 2008.[9] Let us dare to seize this glimmer of hope that has been so generously and boldly offered in order to come together in such a way as to collectively shape the world that emerges from the current crisis, ensuring that it is centred around respect and nourishment of human life and not destruction, suffering, and despair. Though the abyss appears near, the moment is ripe for action, for hope, and for long-term strategic visions.

A Movement not for Complacency

The call for a Third Intergaláctica followed two previous Zapatista Intergalácticas, self-organised international gatherings of several thousand people aimed at weaving a global network of grassroots struggles. The invitations to participate in these meetings were humorously extended to participants throughout the galaxy, hence the name.[10] The first took place in 1996 in Chiapas, and the second in the Spanish state the following year. These first two Intergalácticas had a profound effect on inspiring, galvanising, and even giving some organisational form to a major new circulation of global struggles witnessed in the subsequent decade.[11] There are many good reasons to believe that the new process of global convergence and resistance called for by the 'Sixth Declaration' could have a similarly important inspirational and catalytic effect in creating a space in which the next stages of global resistance can take shape and collectively organise themselves.

The Call Came at a Moment when It Was Urgently Needed

In a nutshell, the Call for a Third Intergaláctica came at a moment when existing global processes of struggle were beginning to run up against their own limitations. After a rapid and far-reaching success, they were starting to get stuck in the difficult process of collectively defining and moving into the next phase of resistance.

Let us first briefly describe these global processes and recall their stunning success. The ten years preceding the call saw a marked rise in the global networking of struggles. A number of highly active, imaginative, visible, and above all effective organisational processes came into existence. In particular, the following organisational processes stand out: Peoples' Global Action, the World Social Forum, the Via Campesina, and Indymedia, though these are merely the tip of the organisational iceberg. These initiatives had a very rapid and far-reaching twofold success.[12]

On the one hand, they played an enormous role in strengthening communication and the process of building common political perspectives between large numbers of different and fragmented social struggles in many different countries. There has been a great flourishing of self-organised efforts to question and resist power structures, frequently based on a confrontational approach to capitalism rather than lobbying. Importantly, great attention is paid in these efforts to principles of autonomy, diversity, and non-hierarchical organising. At times, global networks have worked extraordinarily well. In a remarkably short time period these networks have become excellent at organising large global meetings, conferences, global days of action on common themes, calling for emergency solidarity actions in support of particular local struggles, as well as swiftly translating and circulating up to date and accurate information and news throughout the world. Indeed, these communication flows, which simply did not exist fifteen years ago, have become so regular that they are frequently taken for granted and hardly noticed any more.

On the other hand, these global networks also did the seemingly impossible. In the midst of triumphalist post–Cold War capitalist rhetoric, they dared to denounce capitalism and were so successful that they rapidly plunged the system and its major global institutions into a crisis of legitimacy. Institutions such as the World Bank, International Monetary Fund (IMF), World Trade Organization (WTO), World Economic Forum, or G8 are increasingly unable to hold their summits without facing major protests and riots, immense security costs, and harsh media critique. Similarly with summits relating to multilateral and bilateral free-trade agreements. These institutions are not just facing a crisis of legitimacy but also deep existential crises. Frequently negotiations are stalled (most notably the WTO and the Free Trade Area of the Americas), as conflicts of interest shift from the protests in the streets to the negotiating corridors themselves. The World Bank and IMF are increasingly unable to meet their budgetary requirements or to maintain their clients. And when the USA launched its War on Terror, the global networks were able to respond in such a way as to plunge the US state and its military apparatus into a legitimacy crisis, both beyond and within the US. While nation-states still retain considerable legitimacy, there has nonetheless been a profound questioning of states, their electoral systems, and political parties. Many of these developments were, seemingly, unthinkable just fifteen years ago.

And yet, this global convergence process also had major limitations and had reached an impasse. Despite their immense success in certain areas (namely denunciation, delegitimation, and building communication channels between struggles), the movements seemed incapable of actually slowing and reversing the rapid lurch towards an authoritarian global politics based on fear, coercion, militarism, racism, and religious fundamentalism. More worryingly, such political developments could not be attributed simply to the whims of maniacal leaders the world over, but rather to their undeniable mass appeal. Importantly, such mass politics is at the expense of and in direct competition with the mass appeal of the more emancipatory visions of social change based on the autonomy, diversity, and self-organisation that global resistance networks are based on.

Faced with these challenges, it seemed as if a form of at least temporary paralysis and routinisation had set in with the existing global processes. This was true both in terms of immediate visible activities at the global level and in terms of being able to open up wider long-term strategic approaches.

It Was on the Lips of Many, but Few Dared to Say It Explicitly

Movements seemed unable to build on their success in order to deepen and expand existing networks to make them functional enough to create alternative social relations, rather than just denouncing existing relations of power. At this moment, the Sixth Declaration implicitly recognised the potential of these struggles, but also their extreme limitations, and dared to seek to offer a possible way out or at least an invitation for people to collectively explore and chart new paths in this direction.

The Rise of Resistance and Movement

For years the brutality of the global financial regime has been apparent to all who bore its brunt, and to the rest who cared to look. And now, surprisingly or not, depending on how you may view these things, its sheer fragility has also been revealed in no uncertain terms to people throughout the world. It is no longer possible to label the critics as doomsayers when major banks, markets, and car companies are hurtling into the void. Governments around the world have responded as headless chickens before a crisis of their own making. Now, the very policymakers who have led the world to the abyss are claiming to be its saviours in the making. With bailouts galore, governments have been quick to attempt to rescue failing financial infrastructures and industrial sectors. They have produced vast quantities of money seemingly out of nowhere, perhaps pulling it from out of their arses, in a move that literally mortgages the futures of several generations of waged and unwaged workers throughout the world. Yet the bailouts are hardly 'working', even in their own terms. Markets stabilise for a few days, then plunge again. While there is much talk of 'pulling together', 'common sacrifice', and above all of 'bipartisan' solutions, it is crystal clear that important interstate tensions are emerging, especially between the EU, China, and the USA, and also within the EU itself, as economic and political forces pull Germany in one direction and Britain, France, and Italy in another. The US political system has been split internally, first over the large bailout of the banks, and more recently (and ongoing as this article is being written), over the bailout of the historic Detroit car industry.

At the same time, in a state of confused semi-incredulity at the demand that they and their unborn children should shoulder the burden of the crisis, people throughout the world are slowly but surely breaking out from the constraints imposed by the appeals to trust the world's leaders in sailing a bi-partisan-ship to the distant shores of salvation.

In the USA there is a slowly reawakening resistance on foreclosures, ranging from political lobbying to collectively negotiating rescheduling of bank loans to direct action and community-based resistance to eviction to squatting. While nowhere near the scale of anti-eviction resistance during the 1930s Great Depression, there are nonetheless encouraging signs underway.[13] Of great significance is the grassroots, predominantly Latino, worker occupation of the Republic Windows and Doors factory in Chicago over severance pay and other benefits owed to them by Bank of America, having been laid off when the factory was suddenly closed down. The occupation took place under the leadership of UE Local 1110 (the United Electrical, Radio and Machine Workers of America, a union with a history of important struggles).[14] The factory occupation, which lasted six days, was supported by solidarity actions in numerous cities throughout the US and around the world and was ultimately victorious.[15] It was an important victory in the US, showing once again the people's determination and creativity in times of crisis. A week of action calling for a 'People's Bailout' has been called by Jobs With Justice, for December.[16]

People in Europe have responded particularly strongly and quickly to the crisis, especially in its southern peripheries of Italy, Spain, and Greece. In Italy repeated waves of strikes, tending towards general strikes, have mobilised literally millions of workers throughout the country. In Spain, a country where the speculative housing and construction boom is rapidly unravelling causing great social dislocation, there was a major day of protest in many places throughout the country on November 15 2008, in response to the G20 meeting which took place in Washington with the aim of shoring up the international financial system. Bank workers have also staged an occupation of the main branch of the BBVA Bank, the second largest bank in Spain. And within days of Lehman Brothers going under, a man named Enric Duran, calling himself 'Robin Bank' (after Robin Hood), announced that he had stolen close to half a million euros from thirty-nine Spanish Banks in order to give the money to emancipatory social movements.[17] In Greece, mass riots and protests were triggered by the police murder of a teenager, coinciding with a strike that had been called previously by two major unions. This has turned into a many-day major social uprising in a country where youth unemployment was as high as 70 per cent in some places, even prior to the effects of the world-economic crisis being felt. Importantly, in all three of these countries, a common slogan has emerged in a very short space of time: "We will not pay for your crisis".

Yet processes of globally coordinated resistance in the face of the crisis have been slow to emerge, though a number of interesting, if entirely embryonic, initiatives are underway. A wide-ranging statement combining demands and a programme of action for a "transitional programme for radical economic transformation" to a radical economy was issued by participants in an international meeting of social movements that took place at the Asia-Europe People's Forum in Beijing in October 2008.[18] There were some attempts to have globally coordinated protests during the G20 meeting in November 2008, including a meeting of the Latin American Continental Social Alliance that took place in Ecuador, though this emergency meeting was held so swiftly that it was impossible for any major global coordination of protests to occur. One interesting feature was a statement put out by ALBA (Bolivarian Alternative of the Americas) countries saying that G20 was not the appropriate space to resolve the crisis. It is expected that preparation for protests during the next G20 meeting in April 2009 in London might be more impactful.[19] An international NGO meeting to discuss the crisis and responses has also been called in Paris in January 2009. On the level of direct action, groups in Spain and in the USA have come together to call for a global debtors strike and boycott of banks.[20]

As a side note, it is also worth mentioning two other global processes of resistance that are intimately related, though not explicitly connected, to the financial crisis. The first is the food and fuel riots that rocked more than thirty countries in early 2008, a rapid and spontaneous reaction to food and fuel inflation. These took place even before the banking crisis became fully developed. The bailouts are likely to generate a period of major inflation, thus making such protests and riots increasingly common occurrences. The second important process is the international mobilisations that are underway to protest the Copenhagen UNFCCC (United Nations Framework Convention on Climate Change) talks, which will take place in December 2009, exactly ten years to the day since the WTO was routed in Seattle in 1999.

And yet, while offering some hope, all of these responses are still very much embryonic, and there is a long way to go before we will collectively be strong enough to change the course through which the crisis is to be resolved. This crisis is merely an extension of the permanent crises that many throughout the world have already been living through for centuries, and it makes increasingly clear the tasks that lie ahead of us. Furthermore, if we are to avoid greater human suffering and barbarities, we are faced with a paradox. While we need to take the time to do it right, we also need to speed up and do it right simultaneously, since neither doing it wrong nor doing it slow is an option. Now is a time not for empty discussion but for discussion through which we can collectively transform ourselves and our ability to create something new together. Yes, let's take the time to draw a deep and celebratory breath at the fact that the George Bush presidency is in its last days and to celebrate the first African American to enter the White House, proudly acknowledging within minutes of his victory that "Native American, gay, straight, disabled, and not disabled" had contributed to his win.[21] While voting for Obama may or may not have been the answer, his victory surely represents more than a victory of one particular politician, but rather a mass-based process that is yearning and searching for a radical change of direction in the face of deep crisis.

For sure, it is hard not to be happy on hearing Obama speak out in favour of the Chicago factory occupiers. Yet despite all this, are we really to believe that Obama represents anything more than a concerted effort to shore up capitalism in its disastrous entry into the twenty-first century, the West's belated answer to Mikhail Gorbachev, upon whom history bestowed the correspondingly unfortunate task of shoring up a failing state communist model in its moment of terminal crisis? And is there not a certain ironic ring to the rallying call: "Let's turn Obama into the West's Gorbachev!"?[22]

Above all, now is not a moment for complacency but one for acting in order to win strong reforms in the immediate term, avoiding co-optation and preparing seriously for revolution in the medium term. . . . *It is a moment for gathering the combined powers of our Dignified Rage.*

Dignity

Dignified and Undignified Ways Out of a Crisis: Negotiating the Space between Repression, Divisions, and Co-optation

Not to be outsmarted or left behind by global dynamics in the financial sphere, *the same day* that Lehman Brothers, one of the world's largest investment banks, went under, the Zapatistas issued their invitation to the wonderfully named 'World's First Festival of Dignified Rage'.[23] This timing may or may not have been a coincidence, but the current moment is both a time of great urgency and of great possibility and openness to major changes in social relations. Above all, it is crucial that we keep at the forefront of our minds the prescience of the call's emphasis on *Dignified* Rage. For the dangers which almost certainly lie ahead should we follow a path of each to their own *un*dignified rage are almost unimaginable, as demonstrated in the recent horrendous multiple attacks in Mumbai. The Nazi Holocaust is a clear reminder of the extents of horror that can be unleashed by undignified rage in the face of a worldwide financial crisis.

The current situation is likely to open up all kinds of calls for financial and monetary reform, some new, some rehashes of old schemes. The Tobin Tax, designed as an international mechanism to simultaneously curb financial flows and raise revenue for desirable purposes[24] is one such example. Already much of the mainstream press in the USA and Western Europe are quick to condemn 'greedy finance capital' and call for its regulation, while simultaneously celebrating and attempting to prop up the 'good industrial capitalism'. Noble 'Main Street' is pitted against heinous 'Wall Street'. However, the debate about monetary and financial reform is not new. It has surfaced repeatedly, with more or less energy, at different moments of financial crisis. The debate was central to the development of the 1848 European (and other) revolutions which followed close on the heels of a major financial crisis in 1847, forming the central component of Marx's critique of different proposed 'alternatives', which he famously debated with the French anarchist Proudhon in *The Poverty of Philosophy*. More recently, the attempt to curb 'finance capitalism' while shoring up 'industrial productive capitalism' was closely related to the rise of corporatism, fascism, and Hitler in the Great Depression of the 1930s. In contrast, in 2001, when Argentina's banks went under, there was a twin process of factory occupation and the creation of local alternative currencies, which for a period sustained literally millions of people who simply could not afford to use the official currency.

Yet a simplistic focus on reforming the monetary and financial system in isolation presents an enormous threat to current emancipatory struggles. On the one hand, it is likely to be largely ineffective, while, on the other, it may open up a big space for scapegoating and ensuring the conditions for a renewed round of capitalist accumulation. Such a focus attempts to solve problems on one level, namely the financial and monetary, while in fact these problems originate on another level, namely the existing worldwide *relations of production and reproduction.* As such, the World's First Festival of Dignified Rage is one more step towards creating a global process of resistance and the construction of alternative relations that is called for in the Sixth Declaration, and which the proposed Intergaláctica would seek to contribute to. It remains unclear what form the Intergaláctica will take, should it indeed occur, and whether it will be a one-off international event or an ongoing long-term process of constructing alternatives. For that matter, it also remains an open question whether what emerges is actually called the Intergaláctica or whether it goes by another name. However, for the moment, and for the purposes of this text, I will assume that something called an 'Intergaláctica' is still on the agenda.

What is more important than the name is that the process of resistance and transformation which emerges be based on a broad and meaningful participation of globally networked struggles in order to effectively move into a higher phase of struggle. Despite certain very important successes, these global processes are still very limited, and it is important to acknowledge and confront these limitations head on. It is one thing to bring activists from many different countries and struggles together for a face-to-face meeting or protest that takes place over a very short and specific time period, normally lasting a few days. It is quite another thing to build long-term deep social relations between struggles at the global level, relations that create fundamentally different relations of production, reproduction of livelihoods, and exchange, and that go beyond the nation-state and market as forms of organising social relations. Until now most global relations between struggles in different parts of the world have been quite ephemeral and highly superficial, often relying on small numbers of specific individuals rather than being appropriated by larger numbers in the respective movements. At this stage of the young networks' lives, this state of affairs is not especially surprising, due to many different barriers such as resources for travel, regular computer-based communication, foreign language skills, detailed knowledge of the world-economy, the ability to take time away from local struggles and immediate day-to-day concerns, etc. While these limitations have not presented a major barrier to networking, protest, and denunciation, they do seem to present a *major* bottleneck to the *far* bigger task of collectively creating lasting new social relations based on diversity, autonomy, and decentralisation.

This bottleneck, though not often acknowledged openly and collectively, has meant that global networking processes are not nearly decentralised enough, especially in relation to their own rhetoric of extreme decentralisation; nor are they deep enough in terms of their ability to sustain meaningful exchange and mutual support processes, especially between movements in Southern countries. Furthermore, their reliance on small numbers of individuals makes them extremely vulnerable, both to the inactivity of specific individuals and to co-optation and repression (individuals are easier to kill, imprison, and buy off than broader collective processes). Above all, global movements are still a very long way from constructing social relations that go beyond both the nation-state and the world market, and, in many cases (especially in the imperialist countries with a strong social welfare state), there is still great dependency on state structures, and as the current crisis has shown clearly, financial structures such as the banking and pension systems.

While the construction of alternative relations of production and repro-duction of livelihoods and exchange is frequently at the centre of specific local struggles (especially land-related struggles in Southern countries), these relations almost never extend to the regional or global level, and where they do (such as direct exchange coffee or the occasional solidarity project related to building infrastructure, such as health clinics or renewable energy installations), they still have a very small reach and are limited to specific products (often artisanal). In general, global resistance networks are still far better at spreading news and coor-dinating protests in different parts of the world than they are at spreading prod-ucts, people, skills, and financial and technical support. (Though this latter set of activities does occur frequently, for the most part it occurs within the context of fairly paternalistic NGO activity that is based around the premise of reform and integration into existing power relations rather than around a horizontal politics rooted in autonomy, solidarity, diversity, and a confrontational approach to pow-er.) At the level of 'resisting states', there have been important regional integration processes in Latin America, most notably the ALBA, spearheaded by Chávez, or the Hemispheric Integration of the Peoples, spearheaded by Evo Morales. These states have been able to embark on more extensive and long-term cooperation processes, such as in health, energy, communication, and finance. However, for the most part, such cooperation has taken place within the framework of na-tion-states, rather than building direct movement to movement relationships.

Overcoming these bottlenecks in global networking processes would take horizontal autonomous self-organisation to new levels in terms of a collective ability to build far-reaching and lasting global alternatives that go beyond both the nation-state and the market.

There is an urgent need for movements to tackle these difficult tasks. If these bottlenecks are not overcome very rapidly to enable a serious and accelerated worldwide process of constructing alternative relations, there is a danger that everything that has been built up in the last years will be lost.

It is in this context that the Zapatista call for another Intergaláctica must be understood. For the Intergaláctica to contribute to a long-term process of building new social relations at the global level, it will be important that it be a participatory process, driven forward by struggles across the world, constructed through a process of dialogue and exchange. The Zapatistas have set the ball rolling with a direct invitation. This invitation is based on the Zapatistas' own awareness that they themselves have fought a long social struggle in the laborious and painstaking process of constructing long-term autonomous social relations. This process has been based on collectively taking over land, one of the fundamental means of production and reproduction of people's livelihoods. However, the Intergaláctica is not just the responsibility of the Zapatistas but of all those who identify with it throughout the world. Active rather than passive participation from these different struggles will be what give the process real depth and meaning. This includes the need for a collective global discussion process based in decentralisation and autonomous self-organisation to define what kind of a process the Intergaláctica should be. What are its goals, contents, and methods? Who will participate in it, and through what kind of process and what forms of participation? And if it is to involve large international meetings or *Encuentros* along the way, *where* would they take place and *when*? However, before discussing possible ways forward for creating such a global process, let us look more closely at the *undignified* ways of resolving crisis.

Indignities in the Face of Resistance

Historically, capital and state power have responded to popular resistance through the combined use of three major strategies: dividing struggles, integrating them through partial reforms, and repression. These three strategies have not been employed in isolation from one another but in careful combination. They have been implemented with varying degrees of success (from the point of view of capital and state power) but never permanently. In the current context of global resistance we are already in the whirlwind of these three responses. Having slowly brewed over the last several years, these dynamics are likely to be greatly intensified and accelerated by the current economic crisis and the election of Obama. The degree to which we are able to anticipate, prepare for, and confront this three-pronged response will greatly determine how successful movements are in defining the terms of debate and terrain of struggle in order to expand the space from which to go about building viable long-term emancipatory social relations and moving beyond their current impasse. It will also be crucially important not to lose sight of history. Let us look at the three prongs—division, integration, and repression—one by one.

The continued existence of the capitalist world economy has relied on its ability to *divide* populations from one another, both within countries and between countries, in order to prevent unity of struggle within the worldwide division of labour. Especially important has been capital's ability to prevent global circulation of struggles by maintaining a world system divided into nation-states. The worldwide division of labour has been hierarchically structured, based on imposed (and continually reimposed) divisions around (especially but not exclusively) race, ethnicity, and gender hierarchies, as well as those between waged and unwaged labour. When considering the global division of labour, certain (minority) sections of the world's population have been implicated in the exploitation and discrimination of certain other (majority) sections of the world's population, due to gaining direct or indirect material rewards from their position in the hierarchy. In particular, the imperial expansion of the late nineteenth century (the 'Scramble for Africa', etc) and the consequent subjugation of workers in the colonies enabled often quite substantial partial reforms to be granted in response to the growing strength of workers' struggles in capital's core sites, Europe and the USA.

Another crucial divide throughout history has been the citizen / non-citizen divide or, taken to its worst racist extreme, the 'human' / 'non-human' divide, as epitomised in the twentieth century by the genocidal social deal offered to 'pure German' workers in the Germany of the Hitler period.[25] Last but not least, let us not forget the so-called post–World War Two 'welfare state' model which has provided large sections of the populations in the capitalist centres (especially but not exclusively white male unionised workers) with greatly improved material standards of living and political freedoms at the expense of the great majority in peripheral countries, as well as of people of colour and unwaged (especially women) workers within the core capitalist countries themselves.

The second major strategy employed in response to social struggle has been *integration* and *co-optation*. This has worked to integrate struggles by partially giving in to certain demands for social, economic, and political reforms, while not substantially challenging private ownership, profit relations, political decision-making, and labour control mechanisms that have defined capitalist (and imperialist, patriarchal, racist . . .) social relations. In the first half of the twentieth century, the Keynesian welfare state was widely introduced in core capitalist countries in response to the fear of the Russian Revolution inspiring and supporting similar processes throughout the world. In the second half of the century, in response to the 1949 triumph of the Chinese Revolution, developmentalism combined with formal political independence was introduced into the erstwhile colonies. The Keynesian deal which linked productivity to high wages was so ingenious that not only was it able to buy off social struggle but also to actually harness it to such an extent that, safely channelled, demands for higher wages actually contributed to economic growth.

Last but not least has been *state repression*. Those resistances which could not easily be integrated or bought off with reform have simply been crushed and intimidated out of existence, involving mass imprisonments, torture, and political murder, as well as war. Of crucial importance in terms of developments in the twentieth century was the repression of the revolutionary wave which circulated much of the world in the wake of World War One and the Russian Revolution, the fascist destruction of movements in Europe, Stalin's repression of worker resistance in both the USSR and satellite states, repression by the US and its allies in Third World countries such as Vietnam or Indonesia, and the fierce repression of African-American struggles in the USA, especially in the late 1960s and the '70s, among many other examples.

Worldwide Unity against Division:
An Indispensable Basis for a Dignified Way Out of the Crisis

Bearing this in mind, perhaps one of the most important tasks facing emancipatory struggles in the coming years will be to maintain and deepen levels of internationalism and inclusivity of global networks across the hierarchies, old and new, which divide people from one another. The inclusive nature of the term 'Intergalactic' (fortunately, broad enough to include 'aliens'!) is apt. Unity is understood here to be a decentralised unity based on a diversity of autonomous forms of self-organisation from which different struggles can communicate and cooperate with each other, not only to break free from the domination of capital over their lives but also to break down hierarchies and divisions that exist within the division of labour itself. Thus, it is of central importance that relevant movements and struggles are aware of the implications of the Intergaláctica process and are actively participating in giving it shape.

A key question that needs to be addressed before any other is: *Who* will take part in this process and on what basis? For a long-term and transformatory global process such as the Intergaláctica to come to fruition, it is especially important that people from as many countries and as many different struggles of exploited, oppressed, and marginal social groupings as possible are able to participate in its construction. Yet beyond such general and vague niceties is the particular need for overcoming divisions that are currently being fostered within the world economy itself. Unless intentionally addressed by emancipatory struggles these divisions are likely to be reproduced within global networks themselves. In particular, four types of 'global' divisions currently stand out, divisions which are likely to become much deeper and more damaging in the near future.

The so-called 'Clash of Civilisations' is a process which could turn out to have similar divisive effects on global struggle as the Cold War did, in which (on a greatly uneven and hierarchical basis) people from 'the West' and 'the Arab world' are trained to fear, distrust, and hate one another and are divided by ignorance and encouraged to align themselves to one or the other side of absolute religious and cultural divides based around 'good' and 'evil'. The recent attacks in Mumbai together with Obama's hardline approach to the war in Afghanistan do not bode well for the near future. Crucially, until now, 'the Arab world' has hardly been involved in the (contemporary) secular global networks of anti-capitalist struggles mentioned above.[26] Furthermore, these global networks still remain largely ignorant of and isolated from struggles in the Arab world, though the situation in Palestine, Iraq, and Afghanistan is changing this slowly, and some interesting links between movements have been made, such as the International Solidarity Movement in relation to Palestine, and links between migrant worker struggles in the USA and UK and Iraqi oil workers' unions. Most recent are the amazingly successful and hopeful efforts of the Free Gaza Movement to break the Israeli siege of Gaza by entering the territory in ships. Especially as energy and climate change becomes increasingly central to world political and economic debates, there is great need for global movements to be wide enough to include on their own terms the important struggles of oil workers in Arab countries. As people sitting on some of the most important energy reserves in the world, they surely have an invaluable contribution to make in the imagining and building of a new world.

Second, Africa has been exploited and marginalised to the lowest levels of the hierarchical world economy. Unfortunately, these processes of marginalisation have sometimes also been reproduced in global anti-capitalist networking processes. As the world economy becomes increasingly multipolar, a process surely greatly advanced by the current crisis, Africa will almost certainly have even less of a share of the global surplus than it had in the last years. Food and energy inflation are likely to have a particularly strong impact on Africa, hitting women, the young, and the elderly particularly hard. It is not unlikely that Zimbabwe, a country with seemingly limitless skyrocketing inflation and fierce internal political struggle and repression, presents a grim warning of things to come. It is also becoming increasingly apparent that struggles over control of Africa's oil are going to have a major global impact. The fact that the last two World Social Forums have taken place in Africa (Nairobi and Bamako, the latter as part of the 2006 Polycentric Forum) and the Forum for Food Sovereignty took place in Mali last year has perhaps slightly improved this situation.[27]

Despite this, however, African struggles are still highly marginalised within many global anti-capitalist networking processes. The multiple wars in Africa have had very little prominence within global networks; a discussion of reparations for slavery for Africans and their diaspora is still very low on the agenda of most global networks; and most discussion around debt is still based in the language of pleading for 'debt forgiveness', rather than demanding non-payment of illegitimate debts. These discussions, especially in relation to reparations, need to be central in any global debate on resistance in the face of crisis.

Third, the *citizen / non-citizen divide*, despite sparking a vast amount of self-organised struggles throughout the world, especially in North America and Western Europe, makes it incredibly difficult if not impossible for undocumented migrants to travel to international meetings, gatherings, and protests, and to make any form of direct exchanges with movements in other countries. Any form of contact with struggles in other countries must, by necessity, always be indirect, either through the web, texts, videos, radio, etc, or through intermediary (documented) supporters, who may or may not be mandated by the undocumented people concerned. This reliance on indirect and mediated communication presents profound challenges to self-organisation and unmediated self-representation. Movements will have to think of creative ways to overcome this division.

Fourth, *imperialist or rival power blocs*. Rivalries between regional power blocs have increased in recent years and are likely to continue doing so in the future, especially along the lines of tension between the USA, China, and EU countries but also with other countries, including India, Brazil, Russia, Japan, and the Koreas, and the alignments that these latter countries' governments and capitals choose in relation to the former countries.[28] Currently it is still fairly easy for information and people to circulate between these regions. However, regional and national protectionism (as well as military tensions) could emerge to make such contact more difficult in the future. Importantly, until now, Chinese struggles, which are accelerating rapidly in parallel to China's growth as an economic power, have been more or less entirely absent from global anti-capitalist networking processes. However, in recent years there have been some intentional outreach efforts towards Chinese struggles, driven by people active in a range of different global networks, most prominently the World Social Forum and most recently the Asia-Europe People's Forum in Beijing in October 2008. The fact that the last major WTO summit took place in Hong Kong also provided an important moment for connections to be made between different struggles, but there is still a great deal of work to be done in this area. The global economic crisis makes this task even more urgent. The US bailout effectively mortgages generations of workers, in particular Chinese workers, since the Chinese economy is the only real guarantee of these loans. In other words, the bailout is based on the highly spurious assumption that workers in China will actually be prepared to shoulder the burden of propping up the world economy. The crisis is hitting Chinese export factories particularly hard, especially migrant workers, and it remains to be seen what type of responses emerge.[29] There is great danger that interstate competition, rivalry, and conflict can increase as different powerful states seek to find 'national' solutions to the crisis through offering protections to workers.

Global resistance efforts, such as the Intergaláctica or whatever global process emerges from the international process kickstarted by the Zapatistas, will have to acknowledge, anticipate, and overcome these divisions to strengthen the global unity of emancipatory struggles. The attempts of capital and state power to divide the global circulation of struggles and peoples are almost certain to intensify in the coming years. However, high levels of participation in the Intergaláctica from certain regions, countries, and sectors are very *unlikely* to happen spontaneously and may in fact require an *intentional* and *targeted* preparation process that seeks out contacts and collaboration, trying to build new relationships where currently none exist and to overcome obstacles such as language and access to funds.

Building the Intergaláctica Slowly but Surely: A Review of Events from the Sixth Declaration to the World's First Festival of Dignified Rage

The global process outlined in the Sixth Declaration has got off to a seemingly solid start. Since 2005, the Zapatistas have convened three large-scale international gatherings—or *Encuentros*—as well as a continental meeting (convened together with other organisations) and an international caravan. A fourth international gathering, the World's First Festival of Dignified Rage, is about to take place as this is being written (December 2008). So far, the process has been predominantly driven forward by the Zapatistas, with a strong response coming from different groups around the world. The fact that the Intergaláctica itself has been slow to take shape (and in fact has scarcely been mentioned in Zapatista communiqués since the Sixth Declaration was issued) does not detract from the fact than an important international process is slowly getting underway. Arguably, given that it will be desirable to build a deep long-term process, rather than a superficial one-off glitzy meeting, the slow pace of building the Intergaláctica is in fact a wise move and is hopefully laying a sound basis for accelerating the process in the near future.

To date, the process outlined in the Sixth Declaration has passed through a number of stages.[30] The Other Campaign within Mexico, an initiative aimed at building a strong countrywide *non-electoral* political process from below and to the left, has gone through various phases.[31] The first and second 'Encuentros of the Zapatista Peoples with the Peoples of the World' (December 2006–January 2007 and July 2007) paralleled a period of consultation in which struggles around the world were able to make proposals for the Intergaláctica. In October 2007, an '*Encuentro* of the Indigenous Peoples of the Americas' was convened by eight Indigenous organisations, including the Zapatistas, in Sonora, Mexico. In December 2007–January 2008, there was an international women's *Encuentro* dedicated to Comandanta Ramona, who died in 2006. In response to the ongoing escalation of repression directed against the Zapatistas, an international Observation and Solidarity Caravan took place in Zapatista territories, Chiapas, in the summer of 2008. All of these events have been important events in their own right. However, none of them are the Intergaláctica proposed in the Sixth Declaration. Rather, they can all be understood as steps along the way to building an ongoing and long-term global process, one that may take the name Intergaláctica or some other. And now the Zapatistas are marking their twenty-fifth anniversary by holding the World's First Festival of Dignified Rage.[32]

Let us briefly review the international aspects of this process. *Narconews*, one of the main English language websites following developments since the Sixth Declaration was issued, has links to Other Campaign–related materials in eight languages, interestingly, including Farsi. Even before the first *Encuentro* took place in Chiapas in December 2007–January 2008, a decentralised process of preparatory meetings and other activities had taken shape throughout much of Europe and South, Central, and North America in response to the Zapatista call. Between July 2005 and July 2006 (the period of consultation), nineteen different activities were reported in sixteen cities in nine countries. Importantly, this included several within the USA, involving close overlap with those involved in the powerful migrant struggles that are erupting there. Many of them are Chicanos (Mexican Americans) and Mexican migrants involved in the Other Campaign within the USA, which has been dubbed the 'Other Campaign on the Other Side'.

Whilst most of these meetings and initiatives have been fairly conventional processes of one-way solidarity with what is occurring in Mexico, some of them have gone further, employing the language and perspectives of the Other Campaign to engage in activities relating to local issues. Important examples of this are the local struggles organised by an immigrant organisation called the Movement for Justice in El Barrio, in Spanish Harlem, New York, and two different border camps against the US and Mexican border, as well as the complementary, although not explicitly linked, 'Another Politics is Possible' track at the US Social Forum in Atlanta. From these meetings and activities, a number of proposals have emerged for how the future Intergalactic *Encuentro* should be organised and what its contents should be, which will be addressed later in this article. Although not without its limitations, it is clear that there is a strong international process emerging around the Intergaláctica.

The two Zapatista *Encuentros* drew several thousand people to the autonomous Zapatista *Caracoles*[33] in Chiapas, about half from Mexico and the other half from close to fifty countries around the world. The first meeting was held in one of the *Caracoles*, Oventic, over four days, and the second was held in three *Caracoles* (Oventic, La Morelia, and La Realidad) over nine days. The two meetings were opportunities for the Zapatistas to present their grassroots achievements of autonomy and self-government to people in struggle from different parts of the world, as well as for the Zapatistas to learn about struggles in other countries.

In the first *Encuentro*, members of the Juntas de Buen Gobierno (Good Government Councils) presented Zapatista experiences in the following areas: autonomy and other forms of government; the other education; the other health; women; communication, art, culture, and the other commerce; and land and territory. The final session of the first *Encuentro* was devoted to hearing proposals from around the world as to how, when, and where to build the Intergalactic *Encuentro*, proposals from the period of international consultation opened by the Zapatistas. Interestingly, the strongest participation from outside Mexico probably came from the USA and Canada, including a large number of Indigenous and First Nations organisations from these countries, as well as organisations active in the Other Campaign on the Other Side.

The second *Encuentro* built on the first *Encuentro*, going into greater depth about the nuts and bolts of autonomous organising, with presentations by promoters and other community activists from each municipality around the themes of autonomy, collective work, health, education, and women. A very impressive delegation of Via Campesina representatives from major peasant organisations worldwide, from Brazil, Bolivia, Honduras, Dominican Republic, USA, Canada, Québec, Basque Country, India, Thailand, Korea, and Indonesia participated in this *Encuentro*. Unfortunately the one African representative, from Madagascar, was denied a visa. One day was devoted to speeches from most of the Via Campesina delegates. The second *Encuentro* did not have a session devoted to the Intergaláctica, and in fact there was almost no mention of the Intergaláctica, clearly a deliberate decision on the part of the Zapatistas. On the other hand, there was an important, unofficial, and self-organised side meeting involving around fifty people living in the US. One of the major themes of discussion was the need to have a movement similar to the Other Campaign within the USA, which would aim to start a form of long-term grassroots political process that goes beyond electoral politics. Mexicans and non-Mexicans alike were proposing this.

In addition to a more in-depth presentation of how the Zapatistas have organised over the last years, the second *Encuentro* was a space for greater participation from different Zapatista communities, with people representing each municipality, in three different *Caracoles* instead of only one. This was an important space to give large numbers of Zapatistas direct experience with international meetings, with the many different forms of participation that this involved, from speaking on a panel before thousands of people to preparing cultural events to organising the logistical side of large international gatherings to international *baile popular* (popular dance). Perhaps the most important deepening of the process could be seen in the Via Campesina participation, giving the *Encuentro* the international scope and presence of mass-based grassroots organisations that the first *Encuentro* had lacked to a degree (in the first *Encuentro* there were few, if any, participants from Asia and none from Africa). This process of building specific sectoral alliances along the road to the Intergaláctica has been developing over time, with Via Campesina distributing Zapatista corn at the World Forum for Food Sovereignty in Mali in early 2008. The decision to hold the Indigenous Peoples' *Encuentro* and a women's *Encuentro* later in the same year was a further step in building important sectoral links and taking the time necessary to ensure that the process being constructed is firmly anchored in real struggles before moving on to the Intergaláctica itself.

The third *Encuentro* was a women's encounter, of 'Zapatista Women with Women of the World'.[34] It took place from December 28 2007 to January 1 2008. Why a women's encounter? "Because it was time", repeated the Zapatista voices, who had implemented the Revolutionary Law for Women in the very early stages of the Zapatista uprising. Over 3,000 people came together to listen, observe, celebrate, and build stronger resistances with these rebellious Tzetzal, Tzotzil, Chol, and Tojolabal Zapatista women. The days were filled with talk of the concrete measures Zapatista women and girls have taken to organise for self-determination, liberty, democracy, and justice in their own communities. Through a long process of struggle, Zapatista women have gained many advances in their communities, ranging from the outlawing of alcohol and drugs to curbing domestic violence to taking ever more positions of representation and responsibility as education and health promoters in the Good Government Councils, as comandantas of the EZLN, and in artisan cooperatives, to choosing their own partners. For the days of the *Encuentro*, men were given a secondary role. They were not allowed to represent or translate, or even sit inside the auditorium. Signs had been hung around the *Caracol* reading: "In this gathering, men cannot participate as note-takers, translators, presenters, spokesmen, or representatives [of an organisation]. Men can only work making food, sweeping and cleaning the *Caracol* and the latrines, taking care of the children, and carrying firewood". Thus women's voices were heard directly and not spoken over or marginalised, while at the same time they emphasised that the movement included their brothers, husbands, children, elders . . . everyone in the community.

The First American Indigenous Peoples' *Encuentro* was held in Yaqui tribal territory on October 11–12 2007, in Vicam, Sonora, Mexico. The gathering brought together Indigenous groups from all over the continent, communities in resistance for 515 years, to tell their stories of "pain and dignified rebellion" and to share "experience and wisdom" in order for "the continent to recover its voice".[35] In particular there was strong participation from the settler countries known throughout the world as 'Canada' and the 'United States', including from the Kanien'keha:ka (Mohawk), the Mik'maq, the Denen nations, the Haudenosaunee nation, and the Anishinaabe. A number of years ago the CIA issued a report saying its greatest fear was that the continent's Indigenous People could form an alliance of resistance. Well . . . it seems that this is indeed happening.

The latest event in this marathon process of globally orientated resistance is the World's First Festival of Dignified Rage, which will take place at the end of December 2008.[36] The Zapatistas are hosting this festival on the basis of their listening and reading of the different proposals and discussions generated in the course of the events described above which have occurred in the three years since the Sixth Declaration was issued. The festival will consist of different thematic exhibitions and discussions in which invited organisations, collectives, and individuals will present themselves in their own terms. After a strong process in which the Zapatistas have used the international gatherings to present in great detail their experiences at transforming social relations in Chiapas, the festival now offers a space for people from everywhere to learn from one another. Importantly, the list of participating organisations includes workers' organisations from Iran.

An important feature of this whole process has been the progressive deepening of the revolutionary discourse and how this is markedly different from most other international networking processes. In the first *Encuentro* the speeches repeatedly stressed the need for resistance to find ways of self-organising in order to come together in common struggle. The emphasis was on the need to *organise* resistance that is already occurring throughout the world. The second *Encuentro* started with a pre-*Encuentro* event the night before, which in no uncertain way laid out the terms of struggle, setting the scene for the main *Encuentro*. The Zapatistas recognise that there are three main ways of embarking on anti-capitalist struggle: establishing alternative consumption patterns, establishing alternative trade patterns, or establishing alternative production relations. They have chosen the third, namely collectively taking over the means of production. Having taken over the land, they stressed the importance of rural and urban unity in struggle, so that in addition to taking over land it will become possible to take over factories in the future. Whilst respectful of the other methods of trying to create non-capitalist relations, taking over the means of production is, in their opinion, the most direct way of struggling against capitalism and creating alternative social relations. Related to this is their experience of basing autonomy on a process of disengaging from reliance on the state, creating their own self-managed systems in place of the very limited and distorted health, education, and other state support systems and mechanisms.

For an Intergaláctica coming 'from below and to the left', such a shift in rhetoric is a very important challenge to global movements, which seem very timid around discussing (and above all acting on) the question of means of production. It is an especially challenging discourse for struggles in the core capitalist countries, where that idea was largely abandoned years ago in favour of some form of social democratic welfarism. Yet another important challenge that has been thrown out by the Zapatistas, if not explicitly then at least through the language used by them, is the need to fundamentally challenge the concept of expanded citizenship as an emancipatory route. Neither the Sixth Declaration nor the spoken Zapatista word at the *Encuentros* have contained any trace of lobbying around this or of defining people in relation to the state. The word 'citizen' is refreshingly absent. 'Citizens' have existed throughout history only in relation to non-citizens, people defined to be of unequal status. The concept of citizenship is intimately bound up with the concept of the nation-state, and the struggle for alternatives that go beyond the nation-state must also point to a conception of the human being that goes beyond citizens and citizenship.

No Time to Lose!
Accelerating the Construction of New Autonomous Global Relations of Production, Livelihoods, and Exchange

So what are the long-term strategic and short-term organisational concerns that lie ahead? In a nutshell, there is the need for a global process that seeks to both *expand* and *deepen* global networks, on the one hand, to include geographical (as well as sectoral) areas that are scarcely part of global networks and to avoid 'national' solutions to the crisis, and, on the other hand, to increase the functional strength of existing networks so that they can move beyond exchange of information and coordination of protest towards an accelerated process of building long-term autonomous and decentralised modes of self-organisation based on collective relations of production, exchange, and consumption that are based on dignified livelihoods.

Expanding the geographical and sectoral reach of global networks will entail a particular effort to reach out to struggles in Arab countries, China, and Africa, so that they can participate actively in defining the global process of struggle that develops in the future. This is likely to require going beyond existing contacts and making special efforts at both linguistic and political / cultural translation. It will also be important to continue developing creative ways that allow for as unmediated and direct a participation as possible of migrant struggles, many of whose members lack the legal (let alone financial) possibility to travel internationally. Crucially, this is not just about expanding networks for the sake of it but to keep struggles internationalist and not nationalist in orientation, to ensure that our struggles do not inadvertently result in one section of the world's population winning reforms that can only be offered on the backs of another section of the world's population, as was the case with the nationally oriented reforms offered by Keynesianism. This is especially crucial when it comes to the Western welfare states. Particularly challenging in this regard is how to meet the demands of refugee and migrant populations in these countries in a way that avoids integrating them as new privileged layers into an already unequal and hierarchically organised worldwide division of labour. It will be important to find ways of meeting these demands while simultaneously undermining the global hierarchy.

Deepening the functionality of global networks will entail strengthening the capacity of direct exchanges between movements (especially South-South) so that they are really able to learn from each other and to dialogue with one another in order to build common analyses, perspectives, and above all common agendas for creative and constructive actions, both short- and long-term. In particular, this might include exchange of experiences on how to avoid, prepare for, and respond to repression; exchange of experiences on how to avoid co-optation—especially new forms of protectionism and racist deals, dangers of regional integration, reforms that do not challenge the global market, etc; exchange of experiences about differing approaches to the state in order to avoid falling into dogmatic approaches towards taking state power or not and about a discussion process that addresses what actually works, how organisations make decisions about how to approach the state, factors to take into account, compromises to make, etc. It could also include very practical exchanges of all the concrete skills and knowledges necessary for autonomous self-management, such as language training, agricultural techniques, renewable energies, self-managed health, to name a few examples. It would be important to build such a participatory process on the basis of the delegates mandated from organisations and movements, not just individuals, including developing the financial basis to make these expensive processes viable.

These are some short-term activities that could provide a basis for long-term strategies that seek to fundamentally change the global social relations that currently exist. The financial crisis reveals the urgently necessary but enormously difficult task of massively reducing people's dependence on the money economy and financial institutions, so that we can collectively disengage from them and leave them behind. This is an especially difficult task in the core capitalist countries, where people's daily lives are so intertwined with this world. It will only be possible if we are able to build major capacity in the key non-commercial and mutual support–based areas to satisfy our basic needs (eg, food, shelter, energy, health, education, pensions, etc), in order to reduce our dependency on waged labour. It will be necessary to reach a far greater capacity than currently exists. Paradoxically, for this to happen movements will have to be able to access large sums of money, infrastructure, skills, and knowledge, as well as many other sources of wealth, again on a far greater scale than movements are currently able to muster.

It will require a concerted worldwide effort to acquire key means of generating wealth and sustaining life.

Faced with a worsening world economic crisis, a two-pronged approach is called for. On the one hand, there is the need to demand vast sums of money from the state, in the form of public funds and an increasing share of public wealth, and access to interest-free and unconditional loans that could enable movements to buy collectively controlled and non-commercial sources of wealth generation such as those described above. It will also be necessary to create levels of mobilisation and pressure on national governments and international institutions so that they are unable to avoid making these concessions, especially in relation to the new Obama government, while at the same time maintaining autonomy and avoiding co-optation.

On the other hand, it will be necessary to once again place at the heart of revolutionary strategies the seizure *without compensation* of the key means of production (and reproduction).

Again, this is a monumental task, one that will not occur without strong social mobilisation and struggle, but it is a process made much more possible and realistic by the massive bankruptcies and devaluation of capital that the crisis entails, leaving a trail of abandoned buildings, companies, and other pools of social wealth that are deemed 'non-competitive' and hence useless. Crucially, if they are not taken over and collectivised, they will be bought up on the cheap and will fuel a new round of socially and ecologically disastrous capital accumulation.

Entire corporations, and even countries, are simply waiting to be taken over and collectivised and defended for common use outside of the realm of profit, not least General Motors, Ford, and the USA itself!

And so, the Zapatistas have invited people throughout the world:

Let our dignity take root again and breed another world.
If this world doesn't have a place for us, then another world must be made.
With no other tool than our rage, no other material than our dignity.

References

Kolya Abramsky, 2008 [2007]—'The Bamako Appeal and the Zapatista Sixth Declaration—From Reorganising the Existing World to Creating New Ones', CE1 in the *Critical Engagement* series from CACIM. New Delhi: CACIM

Chris Carlsson, 2018—'Effective Politics or Feeling Effective?', in Jai Sen, ed, 2018—*The Movements of Movements, Part 2: Rethinking Our Dance*. Volume 5 in the *Challenging Empires* series. New Delhi: OpenWord, and Oakland, CA: PM Press

David Graeber, 2018—'The Shock of Victory', in Jai Sen, ed, 2018—*The Movements of Movements, Part 2: Rethinking Our Dance*. Volume 5 in the *Challenging Empires* series. New Delhi: OpenWord, and Oakland, CA: PM Press

Alex Khasnabish, 2017—'Forward Dreaming: Zapatismo and the Radical Imagination', in Jai Sen, ed, 2017—*The Movements of Movements, Part 1: What Makes Us Move?*. Volume 4 in the *Challenging Empires* series. New Delhi: OpenWord, and Oakland, CA: PM Press

Xochitl Leyva Solano and Christopher Gunderson, 2017—'The Tapestry of Neo-Zapatismo: Origins and Development', in Jai Sen, ed, 2017—*The Movements of Movements, Part 1: What Makes Us Move?*. Volume 4 in the *Challenging Empires* series.
New Delhi: OpenWord, and Oakland, CA: PM Press

Rush Limbaugh, June 2009—'Obama Tears Down US Economy, Mikhail Gorbachev
Endorses Plan', on *Free Republic*, June 8 2009, at http://www.freerepublic.com/
focus/news/2267622/posts (Accessed August 31 2017)

Subcomandante Insurgente Marcos (for the Indigenous Revolutionary Clandestine Committee—General Command of the Zapatista Army for National Liberation—EZLN),
2008—'Zapatistas Call for Worldwide Festival of Dignified Rage', on *white light black
light*, at http://www.pscelebrities.com/whitelightblacklight/2008/10/zapatistas-
call-for-worldwide-festival.htm (Accessed August 31 2017)

Subcomandante Insurgente Marcos (EZLN's Sixth Commission) and Teniente Coronel
Insurgente Moisés (EZLN's Intergalactic Commission), 2008—'Zapatistas: The First
World Festival of Dignified Rage / Digna Rabia', at https://floweroftheword.wordpress
.com/tag/first-global-festival-of-dignified-rage/ (Accessed August 31 2017)

Nde/Apache Cultural Historical Organization, Tierra y Libertad / Chicana Indigenous
Zapatistas: The First World Festival of Dignified Rage / Digna Rabia' Organization,
Native and Immigrant Indigenous Development Organization, Michelle Cook (Dene
/ Navajo Nation), Tohono O'Odham Nation, Mexico—United States, Traditional
Authorities of Vicam Community, Yaqui Tribe, National Indigenous Congress, and
Clandestine Revolutionary Committee, General Command of the Zapatista National
Liberation Army (EZLN), 2007—'Call for a Gathering of The Indigenous People of
The Americas', at https://intercontinentalcry.org/gathering-of-indigenous-
people-of-the-americas-spread-widely/ (Accessed August 31 2017)

Barak Obama, 2008—'Obama Victory Speech—VIDEO, TEXT', on *Huffington Post*, at
http://www.huffingtonpost.ca/entry/obama-victory-speech_n_141194 (Accessed
August 31 2017)

Anand Teltumbde, 2017—'Dalits, Anti-Imperialism, and the Annihilation of Caste', in
Jai Sen, ed, 2017—*The Movements of Movements, Part 1: What Makes Us Move?*.
Volume 4 in the *Challenging Empires* series. New Delhi: OpenWord, and Oakland,
CA: PM Press

Zapatista Army of National Liberation (EZLN), 1996—'Invitation-summons to the
Intercontinental Encounter for Humanity and Against Neoliberalism, Mexico, May
of 1996', at http://www.nadir.org/nadir/initiativ/agp/chiapas1996/en/invite.html
(Accessed August 31 2017)

Zapatista Army of National Liberation (EZLN), 1997—'To the Second International
Encounter for Humanity and against Neoliberalism', July 1997, at http://struggle.ws/
mexico/ezln/1997/encounter_come.html (Accessed August 31 2017)

Zapatista Army of National Liberation (EZLN), nd—*Primer Festival Mundial de la
Digna Rabia* ['First World Festival of Justified Rage', in Spanish], at http://dignarabia
.ezln.org.mx/ (Accessed August 31 2017)

Notes

1. Ed: This essay was originally written for an earlier version of this book in late 2008. I've chosen to leave the essay largely as it was written—especially the tenses referring to the immediate present and to the future—primarily to emphasise the extraordinary prescience of this essay in terms of anticipating the wide range of movements that irrupted in 2011, and indeed, not only in terms of praxis but also of location (the so-called 'Arab Spring', the *indignados* movement in Spain, Occupy Wall Street in New York, and Occupy more generally in North America and in Europe, the student strikes, such as in Québec, and so much else). As we finally came closer to publication, the author felt strongly that several major developments have taken place at a world level in this intervening period that demanded a critical introduction to his essay. After discussion and after seeing early drafts for his intro, I came around to agreeing—and indeed feeling that his equally major introduction adds very substantially to this book, and more generally to our book project. I warmly thank the author both for writing the original essay and for more recently preparing the introduction.

2. As this introduction is being completed, Syriza have just won the latest election in Greece (September 20 2015). Time will tell what the implications of this will be.

3. During the Cold War, ITUC's predecessor, the International Confederation of Free Trade Unions (ICFTU), was closely associated with 'the West' and with social democratic parties, while the WFTU was closely associated with 'the East'—especially the Soviet Union—and with communist parties outside of the communist bloc.

4. Ed: This is the term used in Europe. In some other parts of the world, it is called 'actually existing socialism'.

5. Communiqué announcing the World's First Festival of Dignified Rage, September 15–16 2008.

6. It is important to stress that that this article deals with the global resistance process the Zapatistas have launched with their Sixth Declaration. However, it is not a discussion about the Zapatistas themselves, nor is it an attempt at analysing the internal political developments within Chiapas or Mexico. Ed: For discussions of the Zapatista movement as such, see the essays by Xochitl Leyva Solano and Alex Khasnabish in the companion volume, Sen, ed, 2017 (Leyva Solano and Gunderson 2017; Khasnabish 2017).

7. Ed: As his essay was originally written in 2008, and then subsequently mildly revised in the course of editing, I have decided to leave the time location as it was.

8. For a detailed discussion of the global dimensions of the Zapatistas' 'Sixth Declaration of the Lacandon Jungle', and for a comprehensive reference to related links, etc, see Abramsky, August 2008 [April 2007].

9. The invitation to the World's First Festival of Dignified Rage, together with information about participants and programme, can be found at http://enlacezapatista.ezln. org.mx/ (Accessed August 31 2017).

10. Zapatista Army of National Liberation (EZLN), May 1996 and 1997. Ed: In the first two invitations / 'summons', the geographic term used was 'intercontinental' not intergalactic; but among participants, "the meetings were definitely referred to as Intergalácticas while they took place. Maybe the invitations were not yet thinking in

such broad terms ... [but] they have definitely come to be known as Intergalácticas, even if not originally framed in those terms". The author, Kolya Abramsky, in personal correspondence, September 21 2010.

11. Ed: For a discussion of the global resonance of the Zapatista movement, see the essay by Alex Khasnabish in the companion volume, Sen, ed 2017 (Khasnabish 2017).

12. Ed: For a comparable discussion, see the essay by David Graeber in this volume (Graeber 2018); for a detailed and almost ethnographic reflection by a participant on one action during those times, see the essay by Chris Carlsson, also in this book (Carlsson 2018).

13. An interesting organisation to have emerged in this respect is Take Back the Land. See http://takebacktheland.org/ (Accessed August 31 2017).

14. For instance, it was one of eleven trade unions that during the early days of the Cold War were persecuted and thrown out of the major US labour federation, the Congress of Industrial Organisations, for their unwillingness to persecute radicals within these unions.

15. For a series of reports, see http://chicago.indymedia.org/newswire/display/84882/index.php (Accessed August 31 2017).

16. See www.jwj.org/bailout (Inactive August 31 2017).

17. The 'confession' can be found at http://www.17-s.info/en/i-have-robbed-492000-euros-whom-most-rob-us-order-denounce-them-and-build-some-alternatives-society (Inactive August 31 2017).

18. The statement and discussion around it can be found at http://casinocrash.org/?p=235, http://casinocrash.org/ (Inactive August 31 2017).

19. See 'UK seminar: A coherent civil society response to the financial crisis', on *Bretton Woods Project*, December 18 2008, at http://www.brettonwoodsproject.org/art-562842 (Accessed August 31 2017).

20. The portal to the call in several different languages can be found at http://www.17-s.info (Inactive August 31 2017) The US side of the process can be found at http://www.bankstrike.net/?q=node/1 (Inactive August 31 2017).

21. Huffington Post, December 2008.

22. Ed: The only live citation we've found is, ironically, a commentary from the hard right in the US; Limbaugh, June 2009.

23. Marcos, September 2008, and Marcos and Moisés, November 2008.

24. The main international civil society organisation promoting the Tobin Tax is ATTAC (Association for the Taxation of Financial Transactions to Aid Citizens). Information about the organisation and the proposal for a Tobin Tax can be found at www.attac.org (Accessed August 31 2017).

25. Ed: Or to the Dalits by the caste system in South Asia; see the essay by Anand Teltumbde in the companion volume, *The Movements of Movements, Part 1: What Makes Us Move?* (Teltumbde 2017).

26. Ed: This situation has dramatically changed since about December 2010–January 2011, with the irruption of the so-called 'Arab Spring', or Arab *intifada*, starting in Tunisia, then spreading to Egypt, and then widely across the Arab world—and deeply resonating with and inspiring similar movements in Europe and North America, subsequently spreading to Turkey, Brazil, Romania, and elsewhere. All

of which is a mark of the prescience of this essay and its historical analysis, as well as an extraordinary exercise of indignant and dignified imagination by its author.

27.   Ed: When this essay was written, the next WSF was to be held in Dakar, Senegal, in January 2011.

28.   Ed: The geopolitical structure of the world has dramatically and substantively changed during the period since this essay was written in precisely the directions anticipated by the author, with the definitive emergence of the BRICS alliance on the world stage (Brazil, Russia, India, China, South Africa) and of ALBA (*Alianza Bolivariana para los Pueblos de Nuestra América*—'Bolivarian Alliance for the Peoples of Our America') in Abya Yala.

29.   For a useful source of information on Chinese labour struggles, see *China Labor Bulletin*, at http://www.clb.org.hk/ (Accessed August 31 2017).

30.   Information and footage from these events and processes can be found at http://zeztainternazional.ezln.org.mx/ and http://enlacezapatista.ezln.org.mx/ (Both accessed August 31 2017).

31.   A discussion about The Other Campaign is beyond the scope of this article, and, in any case, the author is in no way qualified to write such a piece.

32.   The author attended the First and Second *Encuentros* of the Zapatista Peoples with the Peoples of the World. The observations that follow about these gatherings are based on this direct experience. However, the descriptions of the other events, which he did not attend, are based on second hand readings from the Zapatista websites, other related sites, and personal conversations with people who did attend, and consequently may be slightly less accurate, updated, and detailed.

33.   *Caracol* is the most important organ of self-governance in the Zapatista construction of autonomy. Its literal translation in English is 'snail', though the word 'conch' is also frequently used.

34.   I was not at this *Encuentro*. English language reports, which form the basis of the following paragraph, can be found at http://zapagringo.blogspot.com/2008/02/womyns-encuentro-reportback.html (Accessed August 31 2017).

35.   Nde / Apache Cultural Historical Organization, Tierra y Libertad / Chicana Indigenous Organization, Zapatista National Liberation Army et al, April 2007.

36.   Ed: See: Zapatista Army of National Liberation (EZLN) nd.

Towards the Autonomy of the People of the World
Need for a New Movement of Movements to Animate People's Alliance Processes[1]
Muto Ichiyo

The Second Wave

My point of departure in imagining 'another world' is that we are in the second historical wave of people's movement against capitalism, the first wave being the nineteenth to twentieth century communist-socialist movement concentrating on the seizure of state as the decisive instrument of social change. Here I can hardly go into a historical assessment of that state-centred paradigm, but it is obvious that that historic movement guided by that paradigm was tested and failed in a big way, leaving global capitalism triumphant, though in a miserable shape. The second wave is there to undermine and overthrow the capitalist regime in new ways—that is, in ways not dedicated to the seizure of the state and establishment of the party-state. I believe that this is the major lesson learned from the failure of the first wave. The second wave struggle certainly requires new practice guided by new visions and using new means to achieve 'another world'. What then should be the visions and strategies of the second wave?

There seems to be a broad consensus among many of us who desire change that the world today is managed and ruled by a composite global power centre to keep extremely destructive capitalism going. Empire or not, this is a de facto global centre of rule consisting of diverse agencies, national and transnational, as well as public and private, an organic formation into which nation-states have become inextricably enmeshed. True, this global power is not monolithic but is divided by clashing interests among its components. Yet they join forces when it comes to the point of defending their basic logic and rule, as well as their interests, against the actual and possible resistance from popular forces. There is in fact no legitimacy for this power nor is there any democracy in the way global affairs are managed. The second wave of anti-capitalism movement therefore has to be a political struggle to resist, undermine, and overthrow this global power structure, a struggle for global democracy of a new type. It is clear that the global democracy we need is not a world government, as a resurrection of the sovereign nation-state on a world scale. We are not struggling for a United States of the World, a universal state vested with the mission of abolishing capitalism from above.

What we envisage as 'another world' must be a self-governance of the people of the world (global autonomy) that manages social and economic systems in non-capitalist ways. If this is to be our perspective, it follows that the key to bringing a change of this nature is the ability of the people of the world to organise themselves into a global democratic autonomy, politically and morally forcing the capitalist power centre and capitalist markets to follow its rules, and finally terminating capitalism. Is such a perspective grounded?

The first step towards answering this question is to recognise that there is as yet no such entity as the 'people of the world' as a potent agency of autonomy. It therefore follows that the possibility of bringing about 'another world' depends on whether and how the people of the world can emerge as a body of global autonomy and, more specifically, whether and how social movements can be instrumental to the emergence of the people of the world exercising autonomy.

A People's Alliance and Transborder Democracy

Let me take a look into this problematic using as a referent some of our pre-WSF experiences, namely, the 'People's Plan 21' (PP21).[2] In hindsight, this programme was a forerunner of 'the movement of movements for another world',[3] projecting visions of global social change beyond the state-oriented perspective. As a chief organiser of the programme, I feel it worthwhile to look back on it from the point of view of historical continuity as a contribution to the ongoing discussion.

It was in August 1989, immediately before the fall of the Berlin Wall, that we, a coalition of movement groups in Japan, took the initiative in organising, together with popular movements and NGO friends from other lands mainly in Asia, a large international programme titled the 'People's Plan for the 21st Century'. It was a multi-issue, multi-sector movement-project-attempt to search for a twenty-first century planned and created by the people themselves, not by big business and elitist bureaucrats. The programme, held in the form of close to twenty thematic and sector-wise international events all over the Japanese archipelago with more than 120,000 Japanese and 300 overseas participants, culminated in a synthesis gathering in Minamata, a place known for mercury pollution that victimised hundreds of thousands of people and for the resulting grassroots struggle against the polluting company.[4] That struggle of the poorest of the poor in a peripheral Japanese locality was launched in the 1950s and culminated in the 1970s, raising environment concerns in Japan and beyond. The purpose of the PP21 programme was to get people's efforts together to bring about *janakashaba*, a 'world that does not stand like this', an original phrase coined by fishing people victimised by pollution and in the midst of the struggle. The synthesis conference adopted the Minamata Declaration, setting the keynote of the programme, and it was agreed that PP21 should be continued as a people's linking process. The second PP21 convergence was held in 1992 in Thailand and the third in South Asia in 1996, culminating in a big mobilisation in Kathmandu.

We were subsequently unable to maintain the momentum, largely due to internal difficulties. In 2002, following the initiation of the World Social Forum process in 2001, the organisers of the PP21 process met and decided to stop holding large multi-issue, multi-sector convergences so as not to duplicate the WSF. But the ideas and linkages created through PP21 have left some imprints in the later movements. Unlike the WSF, PP21 adopted declarations, beginning with the Minamata Declaration in 1989 through the Rajchadamnoen Pledge adopted by the Thai programme in 1992 to the Sagarmatha Declaration adopted in Kathmandu in 1996.[5]

The key concepts we introduced were *transborder participatory democracy* and a *global alliance of the people*, posited as the people constituting themselves to exercise autonomy. Emphasising that our hope for the future hinged on the formation of such a global people's alliance, we called it the 'Alliance of Hope'. We envisioned both a transborder participatory democracy[6] and a people's alliance, not as static institutions or bodies but as dynamic processes of constant formation and renewal. In other words, we adopted these concepts as movement concepts. I believe that these concepts are relevant in designing our global strategies of today.

The State of the Global People

Bound Together in Hostile Relations

In PP21, we chose the word 'people' to designate the body to self-rule but, as pointed out earlier, we were keenly aware that there is no such 'people' as an actually existing body to exercise democracy as self-rule. On the contrary, drawing from my presentation to the PP21 Assembly in 2002,[7] we said that:

> they [the people] are "divided into various groups positioned differently in the global hierarchical structures, divided by gender, ethnic, religious, geographical, class, cultural, and national borders",[8] while the people's identities are not static, but dynamically changing, overlapping, and mutually interacting. As such "these groups are being forced to live together under conditions imposed upon them". We said that "state-supported global capital is organizing all these groups into a system of international and hierarchical division of labor" and that "this order is lauded as the world of interdependence". Read interdependence globalization. "But it is an interdependence forced upon the people and permeated by hostility and division. The dominant system perpetuates itself by organizing internal division, and setting one people's group against another". We had in mind "national chauvinism, machinated communalism, cultural exclusivism, sexism, and the whole varied panoply of radical ethnic prejudices" that "serve the ruling elites well in their efforts to establish a great organization incapable of its own unity".

Currently, capitalist globalisation entails two parallel phenomena. On the one hand, the accelerated development of communication technology and networking beyond borders has created a cosmopolitan arena, in which people, especially the young, from far-flung cultural and political, as well as geographical, locations and milieus are communicating and sharing information, sentiments, and cultures. Actions resisting the capitalist global rule spread fast benefitting from this development. On the other hand, we witness serious divisions ripping the people into antagonistic collectives and causing conflicts among them. People are badly divided, segmented, and set to fight each other, often to the point of violence, even murderous conflicts. The divides run between collectives of various kinds as well as individuals. Inter-people conflicts of various social, historical, and economic origins have often been rekindled and aggravated under the spur of competition for survival most communities are forced into. Religious and other 'fundamentalisms', jingoism, misogyny, racism, other hate campaigns, internal wars, and other forms of violence wielded by common people against one another are now part of the daily life on the surface of the globe. During the Bush war, Empire's exercise of vertical violence bred, aggravated, and exploited horizontal violence among people's collectives. How then can the people across the world autonomously rule themselves?

This perception leads us to the rejection of the notion of a global civil society that sees the world society more or less as an association of homogeneous individuals. The 'civil society' discourse prevalent in the 1990s reflected the rise of NGO culture over social movements as complementary to the neoliberal offensive of capitalism. Similarly, we take exception to the idea advanced by some overoptimistic theorists who argue that the 'multitude' under the hegemony of non-material labour already embodies the 'common' and comes together preserving and benefitting from their singularities.[9] I wish things were like that, but this postulate of predetermined harmony among people's communities is not borne out by people's realities unfurling in front of our eyes.

Building Alliances

The capitalist globalisation regime is dividing people into conflictual situations within the same process that links them up in the unequal global division of labour. The strained inter-people relationships thus formed, not made out of choice and characterised by antagonistic closeness, breed inter-people violence and conflicts. On the other hand, this same process can, as it often does, generate the urge and initiative among some of the people dragged into antagonism to create new mutual relations beyond the externally erected barriers. The two diametrically opposed urges are stimulated by the same capitalist globalisation process.

Alliance-building therefore relates in part to the effort to demolish—from within—the structural and subjective barriers that both separate and link the people's communities. In other words, if members of the groups linked together into external-ly determined relationships begin to interact with one another, find that relationship not fatalistic, and discredit, weaken, and overcome it by creating new relationships of their own making, in which people from both sides find each other different than before, then the process to an alliance gets down to a start. In the PP21 programme, we called it 'inter-people autonomy', meaning that communities self-manage not only their internal affairs but also their mutual relationships. People's alliance—as a step towards people's autonomy on a global scale—emerges as people's collectives and communities create new relationships of their own making.

Here I am talking about very diverse groupings of global people with inter-secting identities. Their diversity, instead of being developed as the richness of human civilisation, is exploited by the capitalist regime as the base of competition useful for capital accumulation. Alliance-building is to give back life to diversity as the wealth of global society.

But what groups of people are we talking about? Global society is articulated into extremely complex, in fact, infinite, sets of relationships, both macro and micro. These are constantly changing, so it would be useless to try to enumerate them. They come to the surface as new resistance occurs asserting certain identi-ties. But some of the macro divisions are historically present, brought forward by major movements of the oppressed people involved. Among such division lines are those relating to North-South, gender, class, urban-rural, national, ethnic, cultural, and religious relationships.

These and numerous other burning issues are now closely intertwined, precluding the likelihood of separate solutions for each of them. Discussing this topic, I presented a sketchy view years ago, which I think may still have some rele-vance though it certainly needs elaboration and updating. Allow me to reproduce some relevant paragraphs from that paper:

> [G]lobalization of capital supported by the global power center has not only made the world smaller, but also has telescoped major events and problems having arisen in the past centuries into the present. This defines the nature of alternatives we are committed to create. In other words, in resolving burning problems of today, we must undo history tracing back to where the problems originated. As it were, we face a single complex of problems. And the problems integrated into this single complex, having arisen at different times and settings in history, not only have been bequeathed to us unresolved, but have been fused in peculiar combinations so that the possibility of resolving those problems sep-arately and one by one is close to precluded. To simplify, the present condenses in its midst at least the following problems and their legacies:
>
> 1. Thousands of years of domination of women by men;

2. Five hundred years of domination of the South by the North; the conquests of the people and their civilizations in the 'new continent' legitimated the notion of conquest in general—the conquest of people by the 'civilized' and the conquest of nature by human beings;

3. Two hundred years of domination of agriculture by industry (industrial revolution);

4. Two hundred years of domination of society by the modern state and inter-state system;

5. Two hundred years of the domination and exploitation of labor by capital;

6. One hundred years of imperialist domination of colonies;

7. Forty years of destruction of nature and diversity (homogenization) in the name of development.[10]

You can add any number of 'current' problems that have survived through history. The point is that none of them has survived in its original shape. These have been brought into a deformed synthesis in diverse combinations. Modern capitalism, for instance, integrates (2) to (5) on the basis of (1), while (7) integrates all the preceding problems. Item (2), mediated by (1), (3), (5), and (6), produces (7) in the form of the widening gap between the North and the South. And so on.

Our alternatives address precisely this problem complex. Given the organic intertwinedness of the problems, the process to overcome it needs be a single process. 'Single' does not mean 'in one fell swoop'. Nor do we anticipate an apocalyptic settlement. It means disentanglement in the same historical time and in interrelatedness. It means that trying to fully resolve any one of the problems as separate from the others cannot, after all is said and done, succeed in resolving even that problem. This is a crucial point. For instance, the environmentalist movement will never succeed in preserving nature if it refuses to consider Southern poverty.

The clue to disentanglement is to begin with alliance-builders siding with the dominated in the above list: women, Indigenous People, other oppressed minorities, the South, agriculture, labour, the civil, nature, and diversity. Already, vigorous voices have been raised and demands presented by or on behalf of them. We have fairly active social movements on all of those issues. The starting point in our search for global alternatives is to exert our full force to work changes on the dominating side in line with the demands of the dominated—on men, conquerors, the North, capital, the state, human exploitation of nature, and homogeneity. Without the prerogative of the dominated, there is no emancipating alternative.

As hard as we might try, we shall find that an alternative world cannot be constituted by a mere mechanical summing up of such efforts. For there is no guarantee that alternatives evolved by different sectors and on diverse issues fall in predetermined harmony into a single picture of an alternative world. Alternatives pressed by urban citizens may collide with those developed by farmers. A feminist perspective may create misgivings among traditional communities. Conflicts are bound to occur.

But the differences and even conflicts can be constructive. They may be a driving force towards weaving comprehensive alternatives. If the conflicts end in antagonism, the current system will survive, capitalising on them. Mere compromise is postponement of antagonism. But if the differences are brought to a higher level of synthesis through dialectical interaction, then we have an Alliance of Hope with ever self-enriching alternative visions and programmes that fully cope with the entirety of the historical problem complex.

Characteristics of Inter-Movement Politics for Inter-People Alliance

Social movement today, in my view, faces this kind of historic challenge. For alliance-building, movement plays a decisive role in helping this process get underway. Boaventura de Sousa Santos, discussing the World Social Forum and the global left, noted that one of the salient contributions of the WSF was "the passage from a movement politics to inter-movement politics".[11] By 'inter-movement politics', he signalled "a politics run by the idea that no single issue social movement can succeed in carrying out its agenda without the cooperation of other movements". I fully agree. Inter-movement politics, however, is not complete in itself. Nor is it merely a matter between issue-based movements. In the people's alliance context, it carries a more general signification. A few important features involved include the following:

- *Inter-people politics:* inter-movement politics, if relevant, must involve inter-people politics. Meaningful social movements are always an organic part of their respective constituencies. Inter-movement politics can have significance only when it is integral to inter-people politics and is not closed within itself. In other words, inter-movement politics is tested by the degree to which it engenders inter-people interactive politics conducive to people-to-people alliance-building.
- *Movement and constituency:* this does not mean, however, that a specific movement 'legitimately' and monopolistically represents one constituency considered more or less homogeneous. The constituency itself is a mobile entity comprising complex identities. The relevance of inter-movement politics should prove itself by the organic relationships it creates and recreates with the community. Inter-movement politics also works within the same constituent community that usually generates plural movement initiatives.

- *Interaction:* interaction between people, as collectives and as individuals, in a positive context is one of the main modes of alliance-building. Interaction in a hostile context would mean escalating hostility, distrust, and clashes, but we have abundant experience that people from usually unfriendly or even hostile groups, meeting in a favourable context, find each other just common human beings and friends.[12]

- *Mediation:* let me call the kind of interaction I sketch out here, 'virtuous interaction'. The other type is a vicious interaction, which aggravates conflicts. For virtuous interaction to take place, mediation is essential. Movement is expected to be an essential element of mediation. Assumptions under the old paradigm were that classes are represented by their parties and class alliances are deemed arranged when the parties representing them come together to sign a joint front agreement. But we know that movements, let alone political parties, do not represent people's collectives. It is the people's groups themselves that interact and enter into alliance processes. And it is in these processes that movements based in their constituencies can play indispensable mediating roles.

- *Bonds:* How can virtuous interaction take place among different communities, even those apparently antagonistic to one another? I cannot go too far into this crucial question here, as that would involve philosophical inquiries. But we know that there are certain bonds that enable human beings to live together in friendly relationships. Despite mounting evidence to the contrary, tempting us to be cynical, we cannot totally deny the working of this deeply seated social characteristic. Christians may call it love, Confucians call it *ren* (*jin* in Japanese; perfect value, or benevolence), Buddhists *karuna* (*jihi* in Japanese; mercy), Hardt and Negri "love as a political concept",[13] and others use other names. I dare not give it a name, though in 1969 we called it "peopleness".[14] At a more practical level, John Brown Childs, theorist and advocate of transcommunality, talks about "general ethics of respect".[15] All these terms seem to point to the ability of the people to make human linkages, displayed in multifaceted actual practices.

- *Internal impacts:* virtuous interaction can cause changes in emancipating directions not only in the relationships between groups but also in the internal power relationships and cultures within the groups involved. Contacts and interactions with others may initially make a community unwelcoming and defensive, but if the contexts in which the interactions take place and the ideas get exchanged are emancipatory, and if the interactions are properly mediated, there emerge people within the group willing to change the dominant structure, if any, of the group itself. This is a very complex process, sometimes leading to impositions, but if the channels of mediation are properly constituted, it can create a virtuous cycle of mutual learning and change processes.

As Childs observes, "These ethics of respect can lead to some transformation of interacting participants", and "this transformation is not a one-sided conversion to a single perspective, but rather involves an opening up to shared understandings".[16]

- *Structural changes:* we have said that under the capitalist regime different communities and collectives of the people are bound together, even despite themselves, in antagonistic relationships, typically of hierarchical formation. Alliance-building therefore would not continue, even if virtuous interaction is constituted, if the oppressing / oppressed, exploiting / exploited, dominating / dominated relationships that exist between collectives are allowed to continue. For alliance-building to continue and develop, this process should entail processes mitigating the structural and subjective inequalities in power relationships, in view of the eventual goal of their abolition. Otherwise, alliance-building will remain mere lip service and be discredited.

- *Alliance and economic articulation:* this aspect of the matter takes us to the broader field of building another world, or another global society. In classical Marxist-Leninist understanding, a worker-peasant alliance was not only the key to the formation of revolutionary power but also the basis for economic articulation between industry and agriculture, or urban and rural, in a new society.[17] The experience of the first wave—mostly negative—should be reassessed from this angle, namely, the economic aspects of class alliances and antagonisms. The people's alliances that we are envisaging here, which embody a far more complex inter-group dynamic than worker-peasant, are pregnant with future economic articulations of another world. This means that people's alliances are not just political partnerships that are likely to collapse the moment the political goals they are aimed at are achieved but constitute rather the embryo of a society yet to come. Alliance-building through interaction and relational transformation will involve processes of changing existing socio-economic patterns of articulation towards a better world.

- *Dialogue with nature:* interaction should take place not only among human beings. The alliance-building process of necessity entails reflection on the whole course of capitalism-driven modern civilisation, particularly its arrogance towards nature, including our bodies. Interaction—or dialogue—with nature will have to be initiated, learning particularly from the wisdom of Indigenous Peoples and redefining development and progress, in order to find ways to undo the self-destruction we have willingly inflicted upon ourselves.

- *Social contracts as steps in an ever-evolving people's charter:* alliance-building through positive and virtuous interaction is a dynamic process, and therefore fluid and changeable. But at each phase of the process, the parties involved must negotiate terms of agreement at a given time on a certain basis. In other words, the permanent process needs times of punctuation. This will represent the formal aspect of alliance-building. This means that we are coming up with inter-people social contracts at diverse levels. Some of them may be written out and signed and others may be accepted as new habits observed and practised. At a time when nation-states still exist, the autonomous agreements may be institutionalised or even made into state laws or written into international covenants. Let me emphasise that these are processes already underway; but they are not necessarily perceived as steps towards alternative world building, as they are usually seen only in the respective issue-based contexts. Thus, in actuality, alliance-building processes are, explicitly or implicitly, social contract processes. The agreements and contracts are also renewable and actually being renewed, reflecting new inter-people relationships. Movements are there as agencies to remake them through inter-movement politics. If these numerous autonomous inter-people contracts and agreements proliferate and are accumulated, linking ever broader segments of global people's activities, and if they begin to guide the course of events, then we approach inter-people autonomy whose shared basis will be a people's charter composite of numerous agreements and in constant process of renewal.

Movement or Space? The WSF as a New Type of Movement

Now I go back to the actual movement, the 'movement of movements' and its important arena, the World Social Forum. I have heard that for some time the question of whether the WSF is a space or a movement has been debated as an issue relevant to its very essence. I have no doubt that the WSF is a movement, but it should consciously be a movement of a new type. Chico Whitaker, probably one of the stronger proponents of the 'space' school of thought, says that "movement and space are completely different things". I disagree with this dichotomy. According to Chico:

A movement *congregates* people—its activists, as the activists of a party—who decide to organise themselves to collectively accomplish certain objectives. Its formation and existence entails the *definition* of strategies to reach these objectives, the *formulation* of action programmes, and the *distribution* of responsibilities among its members—including those concerning the direction of the movement. Those who assume this function will lead the activists of the movement, getting them—through authoritarian or democratic methods, according to the choice made by the founders of the movement—to take responsibility for their commitments in the collective action. Its organisational structure will necessarily be pyramidal, however democratic the internal process of decision-making and the method used to choose those who will occupy different levels of management. On the other hand, its effectiveness will depend on the explicitness and precision of its *specific objectives* and, therefore, of its own boundaries in time and space.[18]

Sure, the WSF should not and cannot be a movement of the type Whitaker has described. True, there may be some people who want to reorganise the WSF in that image. But the rejection of this type of movement does not justify the idea of the WSF being a square rented for free use. In between these two poles is the possibility and necessity of a new type of movement. The WSF, I believe, should develop itself as such a movement—*a movement devoted to generating and mediating interactions among diverse groups of people, deliberately igniting processes to build and develop inter-people alliances based on multilateral agreements that will form the body of the people's charter for global people's self-rule.*

Is such an effort a 'movement'? I think this is exactly what people mean when they use the term a 'movement of movements'. This coinage vaguely implies cooperation among various movements but can be understood as only a temporary, utilitarian cooperation. I think it can mean far more.

The WSF has created excellent possibilities for a new type of movement to emerge. In fact, numerous workshops and other events in the arena offer opportunities for various issue-, sector-, class-, gender-, and otherwise-based movements to meet and develop common platforms and common action. But systematic efforts by the WSF to encourage inter-movement politics, it appears to me, have been absent or minimal. As far as I know, the assemblies of social movements that are held during and / or alongside the WSF as voluntary projects were not intended, nor were they appropriate, as occasions to facilitate serious, patient discussion and negotiation for transborder alliance-building. Setting dates for worldwide action and agreeing on general goals was, it seems, the utmost that social movement gatherings could aim at. It is time for us to clearly recognise inter-movement politics, and for that matter inter-people politics, in their own right as new dimensions of movement. We need to use the WSF, and all other opportunities we get, to do this work.

I think the time is ripe for change. Ironically, the Bush administration gave us a focus—the war—while the WTO gave us another focus, neoliberal globalisation. The WSF functioned as an effective arena where, by the momentum of huge convergences, people emerged as 'another superpower', making their presence felt. But that stimulus is gone with the downfall of Bush, leaving Empire and global capitalism bogged down, so that the hostile global foci that have so far facilitated people's mobilisations have also become less visible. Instead of constituting ourselves chiefly by reacting to the global power, we need to find ways to constitute ourselves among ourselves through the medium of a movement of movements.

References

AMPO, 1990—'Righting A World Turned Upside Down: Steps into the People's Century', in *AMPO* vol 21, nos 2–3 (1990)

AMPO, 1992—'The Rajchdadamnoen Pledge', in *AMPO*, vol 24 no 2

AMPO, 1997—'On the 1989 PP21 Conference', in *AMPO*, vol 21 nos 1–2 ('Steps into People's Century')

Anon, 1998a—'PP21: On the Way to the People's 21st Century', in *AMPO*, vol 20 no 3 (1988)

Anon, 1998b—'Building Human & Spiritual Bonds Across the Pacific—Interview with Lopeti Senituli', in *AMPO*, vol 20 no 3 (1988)

Jeremy Brecher, John Brown Childs, and Jill Cutler, eds, 1993—*Global Visions: Beyond the New World Order*. Boston, MA: South End Press

Michelle Chihara, September 2002—'Naomi Klein Gets Global', interview on *AlterNet*, September 24 2002, at http://www.alternet.org/story/14175/naomi_klein_gets_global (Accessed September 1 2017)

John Brown Childs, 2003—*Transcommunality—From the Politics of Conversion to the Ethics of Respect*. Philadelphia: Temple University Press

John Brown Childs, 2018—'Boundary as Bridge', in Jai Sen, ed, 2018—*The Movements of Movements, Part 2: Rethinking Our Dance*. Volume 5 in the *Challenging Empires* series. New Delhi: OpenWord, and Oakland, CA: PM Press

André C Drainville, 2012—*A History of World Order and Resistance: The Making and Unmaking of Global Subjects*. London and New York: Routledge

André C Drainville, 2017—'Beyond *Altermondialisme*: Anti-Capitalist Dialectic of Presence', in Jai Sen, ed, 2017—*The Movements of Movements, Part 1: What Makes Us Move?*. Volume 4 in the *Challenging Empires* series. New Delhi: OpenWord, and Oakland, CA: PM Press

Michael Hardt and Antonio Negri, 2004—*Multitude: War and Democracy in the Age of Empire*. New York: Penguin Press

François Houtart, 2018—'We Still Exist', in Jai Sen, ed, 2018—*The Movements of Movements, Part 2: Rethinking Our Dance*. Volume 5 in the *Challenging Empires* series. New Delhi: OpenWord, and Oakland, CA: PM Press

Michiko Ishimure, 2003—*Paradise in the Sea of Sorrow: Our Minamata Disease*. Translated by Livia Monnet. Michigan Classics in Japanese Studies, no 25. Ann Arbor: Center for Japanese Studies, University of Michigan

Alex Khasnabish, 2017—'Forward Dreaming: Zapatismo and the Radical Imagination', in Jai Sen, ed, 2017—*The Movements of Movements, Part 1: What Makes Us Move?*. Volume 4 in the *Challenging Empires* series. New Delhi: OpenWord, and Oakland, CA: PM Press

Naomi Klein, 2004—'Reclaiming the Commons', in Tom Mertes, ed, 2004—*A Movement of Movements: Is Another World Really Possible?* London: Verso, pp 219–29

Xochitl Leyva Solano and Christopher Gunderson, 2017—'The Tapestry of Neo-Zapatismo: Origins and Development', in Jai Sen, ed, 2017—*The Movements of Movements, Part 1: What Makes Us Move?*. Volume 4 in the *Challenging Empires* series. New Delhi: OpenWord, and Oakland, CA: PM Press

Muto Ichiyo, 1989—'For an Alliance of Hope', Keynote Speech at the PP21 Conference in Minamata, Japan, 1989, in *AMPO*, vol 21 nos 2–3

Muto Ichiyo, 1993a—'For an Alliance of Hope', Keynote speech to the PP21 Minamata conference, in Jeremy Brecher, John Brown Childs, and Jill Cutler, eds, 1993— *Global Visions*. Boston, MA: South End Press

Muto Ichiyo, 1994—'Alliance of Hope and Challenges of Global Democracy', in *Ecumenical Review*, January 1994. Geneva: World Council of Churches

Muto Ichiyo, August 1996—'Hope in Kathmandu: Third Major PP21 Program in South Asia', in *AMPO: Japan-Asia Quarterly Review*, vol 27 no 2, pp 40–45

Muto Ichiyo, June 2002—'Neo-Liberal Globalization and People's Alliance', Contribution to the People's Plan 21 General Assembly, Rajabhat Institute, Bangkok, June 22–23 2002, on *Europe Solidaires Sans Frontières*, at http://www.europe-solidaire.org/spip.php?article2765 (Accessed September 1 2017)

Muto Ichiyo, November 2009—'Towards the Autonomy of the People of the World: Need for a New Movement of Movements to Animate People's Alliance Processes', on *Europe Solidaires Sans Frontières*, at https://www.europe-solidaire.org/spip.php?article16580 (Accessed September 1 2017)

PARC (Pacific Asia Resource Centre), nd—'AMPO: Japan Asia Quarterly Review Back Issues List', at parc-jp.org/alter/ampo/ampo_backissue_list.pdf (Accessed September 1 2017)

PP21, 1992—On the PP21 Conference in Thailand, in *AMPO*, vol 24 no 3 (sic; no 2)

PP21, August 1996—'The Sagarmatha Declaration', in *AMPO: Japan-Asia Quarterly Review*, vol 27 no 2

Boaventura de Sousa Santos, 2008a—'The World Social Forum and the Global Left', in *Politics & Society*, vol 36 no 2, 2008, pp 247–70

Jai Sen, 2017a—'The Movements of Movements: An Introduction and an Exploration'. Introduction to Jai Sen, ed, 2017—*The Movements of Movements, Part 1: What Makes Us Move?*. Volume 4 in the *Challenging Empires* series. New Delhi: OpenWord, and Oakland, CA: PM Press

Ui Jun, ed, 1992—*Industrial Pollution in Japan*. Tokyo: United Nations University Press

Chico Whitaker, 2004—'The WSF as Open Space', in Jai Sen, Anita Anand, Arturo Escobar, and Peter Waterman, eds, *World Social Forum: Challenging Empires*. New Delhi: Viveka Foundation

World Social Forum Organising Committee and World Social Forum International Council, June 2001—'World Social Forum Charter of Principles', June 10 2001, revised and approved version of original April 2001 Charter, at http://open democracy.typepad.com/wsf/2005/02/previous_posts_.html (Accessed September 1 2017)

Notes

1. Ed: This is an edited and revised version of an essay originally prepared by the author in August 2009 for *ZNet*'s 'Reimagining Society' project, which was published at https://www.europe-solidaire.org/spip.php?article16580 (Accessed September 1 2017) (Muto, November 2009). I would like to warmly thank Muto-san for very substantially revising his arguments for publication in this collection.

2. The contents of the 1989 PP21 programme are covered in *AMPO*, vol 21, nos 1–2 ('Steps into People's Century' see AMPO, 1990); those of the 1992 Thai PP21

in *AMPO*, vol 24 no 3 [Ed: sic; no 2; see AMPO, 1992, and for the issue number correction, see PARC (Pacific Asia Research Centre), nd]; and those of the 1996 programme in *AMPO*, vol 2, no 2 (AMPO 1997; see also Anon, 1998a and Anon 1998b, and Muto, August 1996); available from the Pacific-Asia Resource Center (PARC), Toyo Bldg—3F, 1-7-1 Kanda Awaji-cho, Chiyoda-ku, Tokyo 101-0063 Japan; Phone: +81-3-5209 3455; Fax: +81-3-5209 3453; Email: ampo@parc-jp.org. The keynote address by Muto Ichiyo to the Minamata conference was reprinted in Brecher, Childs, and Cutler 1993 (Muto 1993); major documents and declarations from 1989 through 1996 were published in a book form in Hong Kong in 1997; and all back issues are listed in PARC, nd. Copy availability can be checked with PARC in Tokyo; also for major statements from PP21 convergences, see www.ppjaponesia. org/ (Inactive September 1 2017).

3.   Ed: Canadian author Naomi Klein perhaps first used this term 'the movement of movements' in 2002 to refer to the phenomenon some also call the 'global justice movement' and the 'global justice and solidarity movement'; others seem to use it to refer to just the World Social Forum, because it was at one point seen by some as becoming a convergence of such movements. See Chihara, September 2002; for more discussion of the movement as it emerged, see Klein 2004, Mertes, ed, 2004, Notes from Nowhere, eds, 2003, and Pleyers 2010; and for a very different view on the phenomenon, Drainville 2012, and also André Drainville's essay in the companion volume, Drainville 2017. In addition, see my Introduction to the companion volume, where I critically engage with the term 'the movement of movements', and put forward an argument as to why there is in fact no one 'movement of movements' (and why we should not even think of things in this way), and that it is much more fruitful to look at the 'movements of movements', plural (Sen 2017a).

4.   Ui 1992; Michiko 2003.

5.   Ed: The author is here referring to one of the WSF's hallmarks—as spelled out in Clause 6 of its Charter of Principles: "The meetings of the World Social Forum do not deliberate on behalf of the World Social Forum as a body. No one, therefore, will be authorised, on behalf of any of the editions of the Forum, to express positions claiming to be those of all its participants. The participants in the Forum shall not be called on to take decisions as a body, whether by vote or acclamation, on declarations or proposals for action that would commit all, or the majority, of them and that propose to be taken as establishing positions of the Forum as a body. It thus does not constitute a locus of power to be disputed by the participants in its meetings, nor does it intend to constitute the only option for interrelation and action by the organisations and movements that participate in it" (World Social Forum Organising Committee and World Social Forum International Council, June 2001).

6.   Transborder participatory democracy is: (a) worldwide democracy practised by the people of the world; and (b) the right of the people to participate in any decisions that affect them, regardless of where those decisions are made. This concept was proposed by Ichiyo Muto in the keynote address to the 1989 PP21 Minamata gathering.

7.   Muto's paper to the 2002 PP21 general assembly, at www.ppjaponesia.org (Inactive September 1 2017). Ed: Link is to a page in Japanese; for those who can't read that, see Muto, June 2002.

8. Quotes in this paragraph are from Muto's keynote speech at the PP21 Minamata gathering; see endnotes 2 and 12; Muto 1989; Muto 1993.

9. Hardt and Negri 2004.

10. Muto 1994.

11. Boaventura de Sousa Santos, 'The World Social Forum and the Global Left', at http://www.forumsocialmundial.org (Inactive September 1). Ed: see instead Santos 2008a.

12. Due to the nature of this paper, it is difficult to cite concrete examples of interaction among people's groups causing virtuous internal changes. These occur at both the macro and micro levels. In terms of large-scale interaction, think of the encounters between the Zapatista movement and the Mexican civil society organised by the EZLN (*Ejército Zapatista de Liberación Nacional*, the Zapatista Army of National Liberation). These systematic interactions caused encounters within Mexican civil society as well as intercontinental encounters. Mediated encounters, interactions, and alliance-building efforts are underway at billions of levels from macro to micro, involving interim solutions of all kinds; even 'conflict resolution' processes may contain lessons. It is therefore important for us to study these instances from the perspective of the people's potentials to create and recreate social / political relationships of their own as against imposed mutual relationships. Ed: For details and discussions of the encounters organised by the Zapatistas, see the several essays in Part 1 of this two-part book: Khasnabish 2017, and Leyva Solano and Gunderson 2017; and for a discussion of more recent developments in the Zapatista movement, see the essay in this book, Houtart 2018.

13. Hardt and Negri 2004, p 351.

14. Muto 1989.

15. Ed: Childs 2003, p 22; see also the not unrelated essay by Childs in this book (Childs 2018).

16. Muto 1989.

17. I use 'articulation', adopting but also extending dependency theorist Quentin Meillassoux's concept, referring mainly to articulation of the capitalist and pre-capitalist modes of production.

18. Whitaker 2004, pp 112–13.

Towards the Fifth International?[1]
Samir Amin

Capitalism is a worldwide system; therefore, its victims cannot effectively meet its challenges unless they organise themselves at that same global level. Yet the 'Internationalism of the Peoples' has always had to confront serious difficulties produced by the unequal development associated with the globalisation of capital. Here I propose to identify the origin and nature of the obstacles that impede the construction of a convergence within the variety of class struggles, and dominated, oppressed, and exploited peoples. In common words: Why is it that peoples of the North and the South are so little aware that they are both victims of the same logic of capitalist exploitation? Why is it that, within a country, those who fight for the rights of women or for democracy, for instance, often do not feel interested in the struggles of common labourers for immediate demands and vice-versa?

Objective Reasons for the Diversity within Global Capitalism

Capitalism as an essential mode of production that defines modern times is based on the axial class conflict between labour and capital. The centrality of this concept is at the origin of the proletarian character proclaimed by international organisations of popular classes engaged in anti-capitalist social struggles and in the socialist (or communist) horizons towards which the proletariat in question has defined its liberation. Therefore, I find that it is altogether natural that the proletarian International originated in the advanced centres of the system of global capitalism in Western Europe in the nineteenth century. It should be known that socialist and communists movements among the working classes of industrial Europe did feel the need to organise themselves on an international basis (even if, in fact, restricted to Europe) quite early, as of the second half of the nineteenth century.[2] Yet because of the imperialist character of the global expansion of capitalism, the affirmation of this dominating reality has also contributed to hiding other characteristics of social struggles on the peripheries of the system.

The diversity of social conditions and policies in the states and nations that constitute the global system is a consequence of the nature of the developments that characterise the global capitalist expansion and, specifically:

1. The inherent contrast between centres and peripheries in this development (in other words, the essentially imperialist nature of this expansion in all phases of its history).
2. The multiplicity of centres constituted as historic nation-states, engaged in a permanent competition, positioning one against the other. Despite being subordinated to the demands for accumulation at the centres of this system, social formations on the peripheries have never been marked by the central position of the workers' proletariat in the whole organisation of production. Here the peasant societies and—to varying degrees—many other classes and social groups are also major victims of the system.

During the course of their formation, nations were always marked by their particularities, regardless of whether they were dominating or dominated. The hegemonic blocs of classes and interests that helped capital establish its dominance, as well as the blocs that the victims of the system built or tried to build to meet the challenge, have therefore always been different from one country to another and one era to another.[3] This has created political cultures that articulate value systems and 'traditions' of expression, organisation, and struggle in their own ways. These, and the cultures in which they are expressed, are all objective diversities. Finally, the development of the forces of production through scientific and technological revolutions has led to changes in the organisation of work and to various forms of subordination to capitalist exploitation.

Taken together, these diverse realities make it impossible to reduce political actors to bourgeoisie and proletariat. That simplification might work in polemical rhetoric, but it is useless for the elaboration of an effective policy. Because of its objectivity, diversity segments the working classes and dominated and exploited peoples, weakening their resistance and even their offensive struggles whenever they succeed in changing the relations of force to their own advantage. Moreover, the diversity does not help to bring about a natural convergence of struggles against what only afterwards will be seen as the principal adversary. On the contrary, it causes potentially negative conflicts of interest between, for instance, urban and rural workers (over the price of food products) or between nations (or dominating national blocs).

The dominant powers' strategies of reproduction often successfully exploit the negative effects of this segmentation of interests and struggles. The flexibility of capitalism, often analysed as an expression of its exceptional power (compared to the rigidity—effective or mythical—of other systems), is only the practical consequence of its reproduction as the dominant pole under conditions of diversity and permanent evolution.

Nationalism frequently bolsters the successes of capital's strategies and the hegemonic bloc it leads. At the centres of the imperialist system, this happens by rallying those political forces that benefit from the support of working classes towards the global strategies of dominant classes. Colonisation and imperialist domination were legitimised in this way—yesterday by the discourse of 'civilising missions', today by many who pretend to export democracy and defend human rights everywhere. Socialist parties and social democrats have often practised this alignment and deserved the qualification of social-colonialists (or social-imperialists). This applies also to the social-liberal Atlanticists of contemporary Europe. Further, nationalism has sometimes been aggravated by inter-imperialist conflicts. As we know, working classes (at least the parties that represent them) have rallied behind their respective bourgeoisies in major conflicts, as during World War I.

By contrast, the situation in dominated peripheries typically generates reactions calling for national liberation. These are perfectly legitimate and positive when seen in the long-term perspective of abolishing exploitation and oppression, but they also entail dangers and illusions. Representatives of the exploiting class may become too strong within the liberation front, or later.

This is a major and permanent problem in the globalised system of capitalism. The system, imperialist by nature, produces and reproduces the contrast between imperialist centres and dominated peripheries, and therefore imposes the national struggle as a necessary step towards further social progress.

The Historic Lessons of the Socialist and Communist Internationals

The diverse conditions of the reproduction of the different partners of global capitalism have always constituted a major challenge to the success of struggles conducted by victims of the system. The Internationals of the workers' movement were conceived precisely to surmount this major obstacle. After a century and a half of the history of the Internationals, it would be useful to draw some lessons that may clarify contemporary challenges and options for strategic action.

The First International, called the International Workingmen's Association, was created precisely to surmount the negative effects shown through the national dispersion caused by the European revolutions of 1848. The new social subject, the primary victim of the expansion of capitalism in Western and Central Europe, which had expressed its socialist or communist dreams in the year 1848, ended up broken by the counter-revolution. It called itself the 'proletariat', at that time composed of a minority assembled in the large factories and mines of the era and a majority of handicraft workers. This new class was located exclusively in the Northwest region of Europe (and was spreading to the United States), so the possibility of an intervention by the International made itself felt only within this region.[4]

Despite its limitations, the First International was able to manage the diversity of social and political struggles in a democratic spirit that placed it at the forefront of its generation. The association brought together organisations of varying nature and status—(embryonic) political parties, unions and cooperatives, civic associations, and personalities (like Marx, Proudhon, and Bakunin). Their range of intervention, analyses of challenges, strategies, visions, and mobilising ideologies was diverse—extremely so. The limitations of this generation's ideas are easily enumerated: patriarchal notions of the relations between men and women, ignorance of the rest of the world, etc. We could also thrash out, once again, the nature of the conflicting ideologies (infantile Marxism, anarchism, workers' spontaneity, etc), their relevance and efficacy, and so on, but that is certainly not the objective here. We should keep only this lesson given by the first experience: democratic respect for the principle of diversity. This is an important lesson for us today.

The Second International was conceived on wholly different principles. The accelerated proletarianisation of the epoch had given birth to new forms of workers' parties with relatively impressive numbers of followers and influences on the working classes. The parties differed in many ways, ranging from English labour to Marxist social democrats of Germany and French revolutionary trade unionism. Nevertheless, these parties rallied—at least initially—towards substituting the capitalist order with socialism. However, of greater importance was the principle of *one* single party for each country; *the* party that was to exclusively represent *the* class, seen as the unique historical subject of social transformation; *the* party that potentially bore 'the correct line', regardless of whether it opted for—as history would later show—moderate reform or revolution. Engels and the first Marxist leaders (Kautsky, Labriola, and others) certainly considered these options as proof of progress vis-à-vis the First International, as they probably were, at least in part.

The new generation of leaders of the International did not always ignore the dangers of the main options of the time, as some have too hastily observed. Still, the limits to democratic practices in the political and social movements inspired by the parties of the Second International stemmed from these original, fundamental options.

On the whole, these parties drifted towards imperialism and nationalism. The Second International rarely addressed the colonial question and imperialist expansion. It often legitimised imperialism by claiming that its consequences were 'objectively' positive (in that it forced retarded people towards capitalist modernity). This historical perspective was, however, refuted by the imperialist nature inherent in the global expansion of capitalism. 'Social imperialist' is an apt description of this alignment of social democratic parties with linear bourgeois economism (which I maintain Marxism has nothing in common with) and continued to be one of its features up until after World War II, with its rallying to Atlanticism and subsequently social liberalism.

The drift towards imperialism reinforced the chances of a parallel alignment with the nationalistic visions of the leaders of capitalism, at least regarding international relations. As is well known, the parties of the Second International floundered in the chauvinism produced by World War I. The Third International was created to correct this drift, as it partially did. It did, in fact, make its presence felt globally, supporting the creation of communist parties in all the world's peripheries and proclaiming the strategic character of the alliance of the Workers of the West with the Peasants of the East. Maoism expressed this development when it expanded the call for internationalism to include the "oppressed peoples" at the side of the "workers of the world". Later, the alliance between the Third International (which had become Comintern), the Non-Aligned Movement following Bandung (1955), and the Tricontinental (1966) reinforced the ideas and practices of the globalisation of anti-capitalist struggles on a truly global scale.

Even so, the Third International not only conserved the organisational options of the Second, but also reinforced its traits: one 'single' party per country, bearing the one and only 'correct' line and catalyst of all the demands; trade unions and mass organisations considered 'transmission belts'. In addition, the Third International found itself in a situation unknown to the First or Second: it had to protect the first socialist state, and later the camp of socialist states. How this necessity evolved and what (negative) effects it had in relation to the evolution of the Soviet system itself are not objects of this paper.

The Fourth International, which reacted against this evolution, did not innovate on the forms of organisation initiated by the Third. It only wanted to return to the origins of its forerunner. It is well known that the Trotskyite leaders of the Fourth International never questioned the choices of Lenin and Trotsky and considered the Third International to have been 'right' from 1917 to 1927, until Stalin 'betrayed' it! They never questioned the reasons of this 'treason'.

Bandung and the First Globalisation of Struggles (1955–1980)

In 1955, the governments and the people of Asia and Africa proclaimed in Bandung their desire to reconstruct the global system on the basis of recognising the rights of nations that, until then, were dominated. The 'right to development' set the foundation for a pattern of globalisation that was to be realised through multipolar negotiations, compelling imperialism to adjust itself to new demands. The success of Bandung—and not its failure, as often thoughtlessly proclaimed— is at the origin of the enormous leaps forward made by the people of the South in the domains of education and health, in constructing the modern State and reducing social inequalities, and moving into the era of industrialisation. Of course, the limitations of these gains, especially the democratic deficit of the national populist regimes that 'gave to the peoples' but never allowed them to organise themselves, must be considered seriously in the balance sheet of the epoch.

The Bandung system related itself to two other characteristic systems of the period following World War II: the Soviet (and Maoist) system and the welfare state of Western social democrats. These systems were certainly in competition and even in conflict (although conflicts were not allowed to escalate beyond certain local limits), but they were also complementary. In this situation, it makes sense to talk about global struggles since, for the first time in the history of capitalism, struggles took place across the planet, within all nations, and interacted. The proof of the struggles' interdependence, and of historic compromises assuring stability in the management of concerned societies, came with developments that followed the erosion of the potential in the three systems. The collapse of the Soviet system sparked real social advances in the social democratic model, which were the only possible way of facing the 'communist challenge'. The echo of the Chinese Cultural Revolution in Europe, in 1968, should also be remembered.

The progress of industrialisation beginning in the Bandung era was not a result of the unfolding of imperialism but was imposed by the victories of the peoples of the South. Without doubt this progress fed the illusion of a 'catching up', but imperialism, which had to adjust itself to the development of the peripheries, in reality rebuilt itself around new forms of domination. The old dichotomy between imperialist / dominated countries, a synonym for industrialised / non-industrialised countries, was slowly replaced by a new dichotomy founded on "the five new monopolies"[5] of the imperialist centres: the control of new technology, natural resources, financial flows, information, and weapons of mass destruction.

The accomplishments and limits of the period take us back to the central question of the future of the bourgeoisie and capitalism at the system's peripheries. This is an enduring question in as much as the global unfolding of capitalism, by the polarising effects due to its imperialist nature, leads to a basic inequality between the centre and the periphery with respect to potential bourgeois and capitalist development. In other words: Is the bourgeoisie of the peripheries constrained to subject itself to the requirements of this unequal development? Is it necessarily a comprador bourgeoisie? Is the capitalist road, in these conditions, necessarily a dead end? Or does the margin of autonomy the bourgeoisie has in certain circumstances (a margin that needs to be specified) allow a national capitalist development that is autonomous and able to advance towards 'catching up'? Where are the limits of these possibilities? At what point do these limits force us to qualify the capitalist option as illusory?

Several doctrinaire and one-sided responses to these questions were offered, first in one and then the opposite direction, but in the end they were always adjusting to evolutions that had not been foreseen correctly by either dominating forces or popular classes. In the aftermath of World War II the communism of the Third International qualified all the bourgeoisies of the South as comprador, and Maoism proclaimed that the road to liberation could only be opened by socialist revolution, which advanced in stages directed by the proletariat and its allies (the rural working classes in particular), and especially by their avant-garde, the Communist Party.

Bandung set out to prove that this judgment was hasty, and that under the direction of the bourgeoisie a hegemonic national populist bloc was capable of bringing about some of the desired development. However, once the neoliberal offensive of the oligopolies of the imperialist centre (the Triad: the US, Europe, Japan) put an end to the Bandung era in the 1980s, the bourgeoisies of the South appeared again ready to adopt a subordinate comprador role and to accept unilateral adjustment. (This adjustment of the peripheries to the centre is in a way the inverse of the adjustment of the centres to the peripheries during the Bandung era.) But this reversal of tendency had barely occurred before a new window of opportunity for the national capitalist option again seemed to open in the so-called 'emerging countries', especially China, but also others such as India and Brazil. Without a deepened analysis of these potential advances and their contradictions and limits it will not be possible to build effective strategies for the convergence of local and global struggles.

New Era, New Challenges?

The era of the Internationals and Bandung has ended. The three dominating systems of the period following World War II no longer exist. This has paved the way for a triumphant capitalist offensive. Capitalism and imperialism have entered a new phase with qualitatively new features. The task of identifying these transformations and their significance should be at the centre of our debate.

Let me recall some central theses I have advanced concerning these transformations:[6]

- The transformation of the organisation of work and of the stratification of classes and social groups in relation to the technological revolution in progress (information, genetic, space, nuclear) and to accelerated industrialisation in emerging peripheries has resulted in a set of multiple social and political actors, articulated in a new manner in their possible conflicts and alliances. The precise identification of these new subjects of social transformation, of their interests and aspirations, of their visions of the challenges and the responses they have brought, of the conflicts that separate them and obstruct their convergence in diversity, is the first condition for a fruitful debate on local and global strategy.

- The centre / periphery opposition is no longer a synonym for the dichotomy of industrialised / non-industrialised countries. The polarisation of centres / peripheries that gave the expansion of global capitalism its imperialistic character continues and even deepens because of the "five new monopolies" enjoyed by imperialist centres. Under these conditions, projects for accelerated development, undertaken with immediate and indisputable success in the emerging peripheries (in China mainly, but also in other countries of the South), cannot abolish imperialist domination. These projects contribute to the establishment of a new centre / periphery dichotomy but do not surpass it.
- The noun 'imperialism' is no longer to be conjugated in the plural like it used to be in previous historical periods. From now on it is a 'collective imperialism' of the Triad (US, Europe, Japan). This means that the common interests of the oligopolies based in the Triad are stronger than their eventual conflicting ('commercial') interests. This collective nature of imperialism expresses itself through the use of common instruments by the Triad in the management of the global system: at the economic level, the WTO (Colonial Ministry), the IMF (Colonial Monetary Agency), the World Bank (Propaganda Ministry), the OECD, and the European Union (conceived to prevent Europe abandoning liberalism); at the political level, the G7 / G8, the US Army and its instrument NATO (the marginalisation / domestication of the UN completes the picture).
- The hegemonic project of the US, which operates through a programme of military control over the planet (which, among other things, implies the abrogation of international law and the self-proclaimed right of Washington to wage preventive wars whenever it wants to), articulates itself in the collective imperialism and gives the US leadership the means to overcompensate for its economic weaknesses.

I would also like to mention the main conclusions of some further reflections on these ongoing transformations of capitalism:

- It is said that the scientific revolution will lead to the replacement of types of work done under vertical hierarchies of command with 'network organisations' of free individuals. In this new, science-dominated mode of production, the individual is thought to become the real subject of history, taking over the tasks of previous historic subjects, such as classes and nations.
- Furthermore, it is maintained that the imperialist era has ended and that in the present post-imperialist globalisation system the "centre is everywhere and nowhere".[7] In accordance with this idea, confrontations between multiple economic and social powers have replaced those between states, which earlier constituted the framework for relatively stable blocs of hegemonic power.

- Emphasis is being put on the 'financialisation' of the management of a new 'patrimonial' capitalism, not analysed in terms of specific conjunctural phenomena belonging to the present moment of 'transition' (a transition that leads to a new system whose nature is therefore in itself an object of discussion) but as stable features of the new system being built.

I am not hiding the fact that I, for my part, have strong reservations with regard to these theses. What I present below is not a thorough discussion of these questions—indisputably necessary—but only some observations concerning the political method needed to make these debates serve the positive construction of an alternative based on the principle of convergence in diversity.

How to 'Do Politics'?

Following the end of the twentieth century, a new generation of militants and movements definitely rejected the way of doing politics that had characterised earlier critical movements of the left (particularly the Second, Third, and Fourth Internationals). The traditional way is justly reproached for the less than democratic practices on which it was built: the refusal of diversity, the pretence of one or another to hold the secret of a 'correct line', deduced by way of 'scientific' (and thus impeccable) analysis, the excessive centralisation of organisation and power of decision (in parties, unions, and associated movements), and the ensuing fatal bureaucratic and doctrinaire deviations. The concept of the 'avant-garde', or 'vanguard', is considered dangerous and, consequently, rejected by many of the leaders of social movements who meet in the World Social Forums.

This criticism should be taken seriously and accepted in its essential parts. In this sense, the principle of opting for diversity and for a democratic way of handling diversity—which is at the origin of the convergence of 'social movements' at the global, regional, and national 'social forums'—should be strictly respected.

The diversity in question is multidimensional, and concerns theory and practice. Diversity of explicit or implicit analysis is not only present in the wide range of contemporary movements but also very often within particular movements. In order to have an idea of this diversity, one may examine the extreme positions prevalent on the relation between theory and practice.

At one extreme we find those who put forward a (probably simplified) Leninist thesis, affirming that 'theory' (which must be as 'scientific', that is, true, as possible) must be conveyed to the movement from 'the outside'. Others substitute or associate theory with a dream world of a creative utopia. At the other extreme are those who state that the future can only be the natural and almost spontaneous result of a movement free from concerns about systematic formulations.

Accepting this diversity means tolerating a whole range of opinions, which means adopting the perspective that the future is produced both by means of pre-formulated concepts and by the movement. For my part, I define the objective—which I will continue to call socialism / communism—as the simultaneous product of theory and practice, of their gradual convergence. This proposal does not imply a theory that has been ordained 'correct' a priori or any predefined vision of the final goal. I will go even further and propose that we admit that the diversity concerns both visions of the future itself and its ethical and cultural foundations. 'Marxism' (in the singular or plural), 'radical reformism', 'liberation theology', 'anarchism', 'radical ecologism', and 'radical feminism' all have their place in the effort necessary to build a convergence in diversity.

This being so, organising the convergence while respecting diversity does not exclude debate between opposing points of view but implies it, on condition that the aim of the confrontation is not to cast miscreants out.

Having reached this point, I should like to formulate my own propositions. In itself and in its spontaneity, the movement cannot produce any desirable future; it does not provide an exit from chaos. All the more so if the movement declares itself apolitical. We know that, for perfectly respectable ethical reasons and because history provides real examples of how 'power corrupts', part of the movement rejects the idea that it should 'come to power'. The enthusiasm for the Neo-Zapatism of Subcomandante Marcos stemmed, for a good part, from this position—undoubtedly sometimes justifiable. However, it cannot form the basis of a general rule that may be applied in the future (or even in the present). More generally, the apolitical option which Hardt and Negri[8] have formulated (together with—not accidentally—their 'post-imperialist' thesis) is naive at best; at worst it signals that they accept the notion of an apolitical civil society within a reactionary US political culture.

The way of doing politics that I believe is needed to challenge the present capitalistic / imperialistic system and to produce a positive alternative consists of treating diversity like the First International did, not like the Second, Third, and Fourth Internationals. Indeed, I find that the debates of the First International[9] are strikingly analogous with those within the WSF.

Objectives and Means of a Strategy for Convergence in Diversity

My starting point is that the system in place (capitalism in the era of the collective imperialism of a Triad led by the US, supported by subordinate bourgeoisies of the South) is unsustainable. Capitalism has reached a stage where its victim (its adversary) is no longer exclusively the class of proletarians whose work it exploits; rather, it is all of humanity whose survival is threatened. At this stage the system deserves to be called senile, and its only future is to cede its place to 'another world', for better or worse.

From now on, the further accumulation of capital requires the destruction of peasant societies (half of humanity) through a policy of 'enclosures' to be implemented on a planetary scale. Yet the system does not have the capacity to absorb the peasants it has chased from the fields into industrial activities. It also leads to rapid exhaustion of non-renewable resources, to accelerated destruction of biodiversity, and to exacerbating the threat to the present ecological balance essential for reproducing life on earth. A consequence of the devaluation of the labour force is that a greater contribution is demanded from the women who do care work. We could continue the list of areas where the destructive consequences of capitalist expansion vastly predominate its creative effects. The pursuit of capital accumulation has become an obstacle to the production of wealth made possible by the development of science and technology.

This evolution signifies that the historic subject that bears the desired transformation must henceforth be conceived in the plural. Movements of resistance and protest are intervening in a growing number of areas. But this plurality of anti-capitalistic subjects, this expression of a potentially invincible power of social movements, is simultaneously the manifestation of the immediate weakness of those same movements. The sum of their demands—however legitimate, and they are legitimate—and of the struggles conceived in their name do not constitute the efficient alternative needed to unleash a series of successive advances.

The challenge is serious and will only be surpassed on condition that a victorious coalition, an alternative hegemonic bloc, is formed. The challenge is such that those who want to act efficiently can hardly satisfy with immediate and partial responses (in order to achieve 'capitalism with a human face'), without a perspective that goes 'beyond' capitalism. Without doubt every strategy of the real struggles must include objectives for the short and the long term, in order to identify the steps in the movement's progression. The mere affirmation of a far off objective (for example, 'socialism') is not only insufficient but may also be discouraging. Immediate goals must be set up and action organised to guarantee that militant mobilisations achieve victories. But this is not sufficient. It is ever more necessary to re-establish the legitimacy and the credibility of a long perspective, that of socialism / communism.

In the aftermath of the collapse of the Soviet system, China abandoned Maoism to engage in the path we know, and when the populist regimes of the Bandung era went off course, even the term socialism lost all credibility and legitimacy. The regimes that had emerged from revolutions made in socialism's name and the state powers that had been established by victorious national liberation movements gradually engaged in disgraceful and sometimes criminal activities. They lived in the midst of lies and crooked, repetitive rhetoric. These regimes and states are responsible for the collapse of hope, which capitalism immediately profited on. No wonder the re-emerging 'movement' of the 1990s accepted capitalism as the impassable horizon of the foreseeable future (if not the end of history) and chose to ignore imperialism's violations of the rights of nations.

But it is time to understand that this moment should be transcended. It is time to be radical. It is time to comprehend that the savage neoliberal offensive only reveals the true face of capitalism and imperialism.

In this frame the issue of the European institutions poses a central challenge to Europe. These institutions were conceived to set Europe on the road to economic liberalism and political Atlanticism forever, and the European Commission is, in this sense, the perfect guarantor of the durability of the power of European reaction. The call for 'another Europe' or a 'social Europe' is a pure incantation as long as this institutional construct is not seriously questioned.

The European institution annihilated state sovereignty, without which democracy turns into a surreal farce. State sovereignty has not been substituted by federal power or confederation, the necessary conditions for that are lacking anyway. It reduced the real Europe to a European dimension of the American political project (Atlanticism and the decisive role of NATO, led by Washington, in the foreign policy of Europe). As long as the action of the collective imperialism of the Triad continues alongside present liberal globalisation, the European institution will serve as one of its instruments.

The 'plural left', as it is called in Europe, is certainly not the means whereby the peoples of this continent can reach the end of the tunnel. It is built on the principle of 'alternation' with the right, within limits imposed by liberal and Atlanticist European institutions (and therefore it is not an alternative). The reconstruction of 'another left' is a condition without which it is difficult to imagine Europe ruled by Europeans.

Will contradictions between 'Europe' and the US manifest themselves with growing force? Some find economic conflicts of interest between the dominant firms in the two countries / regions highly probable. I am not persuaded by this argument. I believe that the contradiction lies elsewhere, in the contrast between the political culture of Europe and that of the US, which will lead to a political conflict of which the first manifestations are already visible.[10] In my opinion, the new upsurge of European political cultures, which are threatened by 'Americanisation', can result in the rebirth of a left up to the challenge—an anti-liberal and anti-Atlanticist left.

On the other hand, the peoples of three continents (Asia, Africa, Latin America) are today confronted with a system in many respects analogous with that in place at the end of World War II: a colonial system that does not recognise their sovereign rights and imposes an economic system that suits the expansion of the oligopolies of imperialist centres and corresponding political systems. The expansion of the so-called 'neoliberal global imperialist system' is nothing less than the construction of 'apartheid on a global scale'.

At Bandung, the nations and states of Asia and Africa responded to this challenge. Those states came into existence after the victory of revolutions made under the banner of socialism or powerful liberation movements, and therefore benefited from an established legitimacy. The coalitions that constituted the revolutionary blocs and the national liberation movements always included important bourgeois segments aspiring to become rulers of new society, even if they could not rule alone. This bourgeois dimension of Bandung, which manifested itself in a vision of economic development typical of the time, rehabilitated the 'national bourgeoisie', whose historic role appeared to have ended in the early post-war period. The Bandung era was deeply marked by the tension between the ambitions of these bourgeois elements and the aspirations of popular classes.

The new imperialist order will be challenged. Who will challenge it? What will be the result? These are the questions that states and peoples of the periphery will have to answer.

The Reconstruction of the Front of the Peoples of the South

The ruling classes of the South have largely accepted the role of subordinate comprador. They are not capable of questioning the dominating reality. The peoples, engaged in the daily struggle for survival, also seem ready to accept their lot or, worse, swallow new illusions that the ruling classes are feeding them (political Islam is the most dramatic example). On the other side, the mobilisation of movements of resistance and the struggles against capitalism and imperialism across the three continents, the successes and electoral victories of the new lefts in Latin America (whatever limits those victories may have), the progressive radicalisation of many of these movements, the critical positions that the governments of the South are beginning to take in the WTO, all prove that 'another world', better than the present one, is becoming possible.

An offensive strategy is needed for the reconstruction of the front of the peoples of the South. This requires a radicalisation of social resistance to imperialist capital. It requires politicisation of the resistance, the capacity to make the struggles of peasants, women, workers, the unemployed, the 'informals', and democratic intellectuals converge and assign to the entire popular movement objectives for democratisation and social progress (these are indissolubly associated) that are possible in the present and in the long term. It requires that the values that give this movement legitimacy be applicable universally (in a socialist perspective), therefore surpassing cleavages that posit peoples of the South against each other (Muslims and Hindus, for example). Parareligious or para-ethnic 'culturalisms' (for instance political Islam, political Hinduism) cannot be allies in the fight for an alternative to imperialism. In fact, in spite of their postures as anti-West / anti-imperialist, these movements position the oppressed peoples of the South against each other instead of calling them to unite against the common imperialist enemy. They operate in the frame of the so-called clash of civilisations, a strategy pursued by imperialists, whom they serve.[11]

It is possible that the mobilisation and advances of popular struggles will affect the policies of the powers in place in the South, and even change these powers for the better. Such inflections are beginning to show in, for instance, the formation of the G20 and the G99 within the WTO, even if this crystallisation of diverse (converging or diverging) interests may entail ambiguities.

The ruling classes of certain countries of the South, however, have visibly opted for another strategy—neither one of passive submission to dominant forces in the global system nor one of declared opposition; but one of active interventions followed by hope for accelerated development in their countries.

China was better equipped than others to make this choice and has achieved incontestably brilliant results. China benefited from the solidity of its nation as a result of the revolution and Maoism, from the decision to keep control over its currency and its capital flows, and from its refusal to abandon state ownership of land (the main acquisition of the peasant revolution). Can this experience be continued? And what are its limits? Analysis of the contradictions of this option brings me to the conclusion that the project of a national capitalism capable of imposing itself as an equal with the major powers of the global system is largely built on illusions. The objective conditions inherent in its history do not permit a historic social compromise between capital, workers, and peasants that would guarantee the stability of the system. The system will necessarily slide towards the right (and will therefore confront a growing social movement of the popular classes), or evolve towards the left, building a 'market socialism' as one step in the long transition towards socialism.

The apparently analogous choices of ruling classes in other 'emergent' countries are even more fragile. Neither Brazil nor India is capable of resisting with enough force the combination of imperialism and local reactionary classes, because they have not had a radical revolution like China. That WTO made these two governments side with liberal globalisation (in Hong Kong, December 2005) incontestably helped imperialism avoid the disaster awaiting it and dealt a hard blow to the emerging front of the South. This supreme error—if it was not something worse—only serves the interests of the most reactionary local classes (the Brazilian and Indian big landowners!), who are imperialism's natural allies and sworn enemies of the popular classes in these countries. The hope that a part of the historic left of Latin America invested in the social democratic model is founded on a major error of assessment: European social democracy was able to make its achievements because it could turn social-imperialist. That is not a viable option for Brazil and other countries of the South.

Towards a Fifth International?

The globalisation of capitalism's strategies creates the need for a counter-strategy for its victims. Should we conclude that a new International is needed to assure the convergence of the struggles of the people against capital?

I do not hesitate to give a positive answer to this question, on condition that the envisioned new International is conceived in the same way as the First. It should be a socialist / communist International, open to all who want to act together to create convergence in diversity. Socialism and communism have to be the products of the movements and struggles of the peoples themselves. They cannot be imposed from above according to a pre-given definition. This proposition does not exclude the formulation of theoretical concepts for the society to come. Instead, it evokes precise formulations of such concepts and excludes the monopoly of one concept over the right way and phases of transition.

It is certainly difficult to achieve these fundamental democratic principles. The exercise of democracy is always difficult. We should draw 'limits', accept that defining strategic objectives implies making choices, and recognize that there is no predetermined way of handling the relation of a majority to one or more minorities.

In order not to go against the principles that I just formulated, I shall not try to answer these questions. I shall only propose some major strategic goals for the battle ahead, arranging them in three sections:

1. Roll back liberalism at all levels, nationally and globally. To this end, a number of immediate goals can be formulated, for instance, the exclusion of agriculture from the WTO's agenda; the abrogation of decisions by imperialist powers on intellectual and technological property rights; the abrogation of decisions that hamper the development of non-commercial management of natural resources and public services; the abrogation of bans on the regulation of capital flows; the proclamation of the right of states to cancel debts that, after audit, are proved to be immoral or despicable, etc.

2. Dismantle the programme of military control over the planet by the military forces of the US and / or NATO. The repudiation of international law by the US and the 'authorisation' it gives itself to conduct preventive wars must be condemned without reservation. The functions of the UN must be restored. There must be an unconditional and immediate withdrawal of the occupying army stationed in Iraq and of the Israeli administration of occupied Palestine. All military bases of the US dispersed across the continents must be dismantled.

As long as this project to control the planet is not morally, diplomatically, politically, and militarily defeated, any democratic and social advances of the people will remain vulnerable and under threat of being bombed by the US Air Force.

3. Repeal the liberal and Atlanticist conceptions upon which the institutions of the European Union are based. This implies reconsidering the whole European institutional framework and the dissolution of NATO.

Initiatives aiming at formulating a strategy of convergence corresponding to the general vision proposed here have already been taken. In Bamako, Mali, on January 18 2006, on the eve of the Polycentric World Social Forum (P-WSF) that was to take place there, one full day was dedicated to debates on the strategy and construction of convergence in diversity.[12] The fact that this meeting could be held and that it produced interesting results shows that the global social movement is already moving in this direction.

The Fifth International that I have sketched out here, or—more modestly— the strategic actions proposed in the Bamako Appeal, which I am here referring to, should contribute to the construction of the internationalism of the peoples. It should embrace all peoples from North to South, not only the proletariat but all social classes and popular strata that are victims of the system, and thus all of humankind, whose survival is threatened. The proposed internationalism should strengthen and complete 'another internationalism', namely the solidarity between the peoples of Asia, Africa, and Latin America against the Triad's aggressive imperialism. The solidarity of the people from the North and the South cannot be based on charity but on common action against imperialism.

The reinforcement of the internationalism of the peoples will facilitate advancements in three directions that, taken together, form the alternative: social progress, democratisation, and strengthening national autonomy through negotiated globalisation.

Who will subscribe to this perspective? At this point we must return to the question of 'limits'. The Fifth International should not be an assembly for political parties alone; it should welcome all organisations and resistance movements of the people and guarantee both voluntary participation in the construction of common strategies and independence of decision-making. Thus political parties (or their fractions) should certainly not be excluded. Whether we like it or not, the parties remain important gathering points for civic action.

The fundamental principles may be formulated in the following two complimentary sentences:

1. No socialism without democracy (and therefore no progress towards socialism without democratic practices);

2. No democratic progress without social progress.

Thus it becomes understandable that not just a few small groups of political extremists and some goodwilled NGOs will join this perspective. Many big movements of struggle (trade unions, peasant associations, women's organisations, citizens' movements) know from experience that 'there is strength in numbers'. The parties of the Third and Fourth Internationals will also find themselves a place if they stop being self-proclaimed avant-gardes! Many democratic, social, and anti-imperialist parties of the peripheries will certainly understand the advantages of coordinated anti-imperialist struggles. Unfortunately, parties of the Second International that side with liberalism and Atlanticism have excluded themselves from this prospect. This is not the place to go further into the issue of the 'conditions' for membership (analogous with the famous twenty-one conditions drafted by Lenin in 1919, to be fulfilled by members of the Third International). Serious debates on these principles and the statutes of the International are indispensable. We only ask that we start reflecting on these issues.

The WSF will certainly count among friends of this International if it comes into existence. The fundamental democratic principle of the WSF—that everybody who accepts its Charter is welcomed without reservation—makes it possible for members of the new International to co-exist with organisations that contribute to convergence in diversity, even if they do not adhere to a socialist perspective, as well as with organisations that decide not to participate in the formulation of common strategies. This diversity gives strength to the movement and should be preserved.

Nevertheless the idea of a Fifth International has its adversaries, and their number will increase if it becomes a reality. There are already those who wish to maintain the WSF in a state of maximal impotence. The ideologies by which they want to legitimise the inactivity are well known.[13] One of their propositions is the pretended equivalence of the diversity of the Forum with that of the self-proclaimed 'plural left' (in Europe, principally). Another is the thesis of the 'apolitical civil society' (or even 'anti-political civil society'). This thesis, which has always been typical of the political culture of the US, has attracted a number of NGOs over the past decades.

Their goal is to turn the WSF into a complement to the Davos Forum. In other words, instead of questioning the principles of liberalism, capitalism, and imperialist globalisation, they are giving these principles new legitimacy through minimum 'social demands' (like the 'struggle against poverty'). Associations (as apolitical as possible) of the so-called 'civil society' are considered instrumental in the formulation of such demands.

There are already a number of such adverse initiatives supported by the Davos establishment, the G7, the big foundations in the US, and the institutions of the EU. The Mediterranean Forum (the so-called 'Barcelona Initiative' promoted by the EU), and the Arab Democracy Forum (later called the 'Future Forum') promoted by US agencies, the coalitions of hand-picked NGOs formed on the initiative of international institutions (principally the UN and the World Bank) in order to 'follow' the big conferences organised by the institutions of the system (WTO and others) are probably meant to divide the social forums, or maybe to make them break down, or at least stop their potential development, growth, and radicalisation.

All these adverse initiatives must be combated and the popular movements convinced through patient discussions that they simply serve the strategies of dominant capitalist / imperialist reactionaries. It is only through such long and patient persuasive efforts that the vision of creating a Fifth International will finally become credible and felt as an objective need for the success of popular struggles towards another and better world.

References

Samir Amin, 1980—*Class and Nation*. New York: Monthly Review Press

Samir Amin, 2004—*The Liberal Virus*. London: Pluto

Samir Amin, 2006a—*Beyond US Hegemony: Assessing the Prospects for a Multipolar World*. London: Zed

Samir Amin, 2006b—*Pour la Cinquième Internationale* ['Towards the Fifth International', in French]. Paris: Le Temps des Cerises

Forum pour un Autre Mali, Forum Mondial des Alternatives (France), Forum du Tiers Monde (Sénégal), ENDA (Sénégal) et al, February 2006—'The Bamako Appeal', January 18 2006. Text as circulated by Samir Amin, President of the World Forum for Alternatives, at http://www.openspaceforum.net/twiki/tiki-read_article.php?articleId=66 and http://mrzine.monthlyreview.org/bamako.html (Both accessed September 1 2017)

Michael Hardt and Antonio Negri, 2000—*Empire*, Cambridge, MA: Harvard University Press

Notes

1. This essay summarises a longer work, Samir Amin, 2006—*Pour la Cinquième Internationale* ['Towards the Fifth International', in French] (Paris: Le Temps des Cerises). Many of the issues suggested in this essay are more fully explored in the book. Ed: This article first appeared in this form as Chapter 9.1 in Jai Sen and Madhuresh Kumar, compilers, with Patrick Bond and Peter Waterman, January 2007—*A Political Programme for the World Social Forum? Democracy, Substance, and Debate in the Bamako Appeal and the Global Justice Movements—A Reader* (New Delhi: CACIM, and Durban: University of KwaZulu-Natal Centre for Civil Society) pp 399–418. This 2007 essay was an edited version of the original essay of the same title published in Katarina Sehm Patomäki and Marko Ulvila, August 2006—'Democratic Politics Globally: Elements for a Dialogue on Global Political

Party Formations', NIGD Working Paper 1/2006, NIGD (Helsinki: Network Institute for Global Democratisation), pp 121–44. The original was translated by Mikael Böök. I would like to warmly thank the author for agreeing that this essay be included in this collection.

2. Amin 2006b.
3. 'Nation' is considered here in the broad sense of the people living in a country, without necessarily referring to a 'theory of nationhood', which I have discussed, elsewhere, see Samir Amin, *Class and Nation*, (New York: Monthly Review Press, 1980).
4. It was, therefore, not actually 'international' but only 'European' at the time, yet with a view to becoming 'international'.
5. For details, see Amin 2006a.
6. Amin 2006b.
7. Hardt and Negri 2000.
8. Ibid.
9. For details, see Amin 2006b.
10. This idea is developed in Amin 2004.
11. For details, see Amin 2006a.
12. See Forum pour un Autre Mali, Forum Mondial des Alternatives (France), Forum du Tiers Monde (Sénégal), ENDA (Sénégal) et al, February 2006.
13. Amin 2006b.

OpenWord

The Lessons of 2011
Three Theses on Organisation[1]
Rodrigo Nunes

The year 2011 was exceptional, one which could—hopefully—come to be remembered in the same breath as 1968 and 1848. That being so will depend on whether the coming years will fulfil its promise, making it appear retrospectively as the start of something. Understanding the nature of that promise and the means by which it can be fulfilled, therefore, are part and parcel of making that happen. A key challenge in this regard is to strip what happened in 2011, as much as possible, from false representations, both negative and positive, created by media coverage and the sometimes misleading reflections of protesters. To try, in other words, to stay as close as possible to what people were and are doing, rather than what they said or were said to be doing.

Negri's dictum on Lenin—'organisation is spontaneity reflecting on itself'—suggests spontaneity is never simply formless but always already belying *some kind* of organisation.[2] It is a long-standing mistake of the 'organisation' debate that it takes place as if one should choose between absolute formlessness ('spontaneous' movement) and form (the Party). As much as a party, however tightly controlled, will always have some degree of porosity and anomalous deviation, what seems formless always contains its own form, even if mutable and open. The three theses that follow aim to both draw out some of the lessons already implicit in the last year and a half's struggles and to get closer to what is characteristic of their underlying forms.[3]

1. It Is Possible to Have a Mass Movement without Mass Organisations
This lesson is not particularly new; it has been known since at least 1968, or since the late 1990s if we are to eschew the classical references. It is nonetheless both worth repeating and phrasing in this way, since attempting to translate the questions thrown up by the present into the language of older debates can offer more of a grip on them than merely insisting on their absolute novelty.

What matters here is not only the extent to which mass organisations (parties, unions—notable exceptions being the strikes in Egypt, and local support by unions in Tunisia) were seen as 'part of the problem' or simply not invited but also the extent to which they were questioned *as mass organisations*. In the face of a large, heterogeneous, developing, living movement, their mobilising capacity seemed limited by comparison—and the *quality* of their representation too stale, too ossified, too much of a *representation* to matter. When masses of people rose up against the representative system and the dearth of real options it offered, unions and parties were widely regarded as representing that system itself, rather than those they notionally represent.

To say this, of course, does not tell us anything about the staying power of the movements that appeared in 2011—whether a choice not to form mass organisations will entail a progressive loss of momentum, or whether forming them will simply be divisive without bringing any gains—nor does it say anything about whether mass organisations *as such* are an outdated proposition.[4] But it does say something about the state of *existing* mass organisations, and the potentials that reside in the encounter between widespread discontent and access to technological tools that allow for mass, multipolar communication. It is, thus, evidently good news: mass organisations are in crisis everywhere (and this includes Latin America, from where I presently write); it is good to know that it is possible to bypass them in order to produce political effects.

It also says something about the crisis of representation and how it will be a long time until it is solved. Some were quick to point out the 'failure' of movements in Tunisia, Egypt, and Spain, in the sense that the forces that eventually came to power were not much better than those that were removed. There is a truly bizarre logic in this: if these movements started out by decrying how all essential decisions were outside the scope of representative democracy and all the available options were different shades of the same, to expect to prove them wrong by pointing out that what they got was ultimately a different shade of the same is essentially to corroborate their assertion. This argument can only make sense if one has already accepted the premise these movements reject—that there is no alternative to the 'there is no alternative' that they oppose. It fails to acknowledge how they have, from the start, set their sights on a much longer game than can be measured by electoral cycles (and which will demand a lot more from them to be achieved).[5]

In regard to the political system as a whole, these movements are exercising—and that is perhaps all they can do at present—what Colectivo Situaciones have called *poder destituyente*, de-instituent power.[6] They undoubtedly also possess a constituent power whose future and direction is as yet impossible to predict. It may result in new political forms, new mechanisms of representation, new institutions or, at the very least, new organisations. It may result in all of those at once, as was the case in Bolivia in the aftermath of the neoliberal crisis.[7] But right now, their main achievable goal is probably that of flushing the system; and not only can this not be done overnight, the sharpening of contradictions in the short term—Spain now [in 2012] has a right-wing government elected by 30 per cent of the population, while polls indicate that around 70 per cent agree with the *indignados*, who the new government are on a declared collision course with—may lead to just that in the longer run.

2. Organisation Has Not Disappeared but Changed

Many have observed how the obvious similarities between 2011 and the alter-globalisation moment went oddly unnoticed among the commentariat.[8] In what concerns organisation, there is a double irony in this invisibilisation. On the one hand, the alter-globalisation moment marked the first attempt to elaborate the transformations to organisational practice brought about by new communication technologies, the Internet above all. On the other, it already manifested the same tabula rasa, new dawn attitude that some adopt today: new technological conditions have changed the way we organise forever; it is all about connected individuals now, the time of hierarchical organisational forms is over. Therein lies, of course, a third irony: as is often the case with the modern attitude of announcing the present as a total break with the past, it appears retrospectively as an anticipation of something then still to come. The 'new technological conditions' of ten years ago—mailing lists, cameraless phones, and Indymedia!—pale in comparison to the access to the means of production of information that we see today; conversely, today's 'total break' has already been around in some form for ten years.

The problem is that different things tend to get mixed up in the discussion, and activist practices associated with older organisational forms—such as 'factory floor' or 'door to door' community organising—are lumped in with the organisational form itself. As a consequence, the argument flits from claiming that 'some organisational forms are no longer necessary' to 'some forms of activism have become superfluous' and ends up producing a falsified picture of how social media have actually been put to political use.

In a well received article from late 2010 that went on to seem thoroughly debunked by ensuing events, Malcolm Gladwell drew on Mark Granovetter's groundbreaking work in social network theory to suggest that social media are fabulous tools when it comes to spreading information and fostering low involvement forms of action ('share', 'like', 'retweet', 'donate') but are not as good when it comes to developing dependable relations, commitment, and what it sometimes takes to really get an action or campaign off the ground. One of that text's strongest conclusions was that "Facebook activism succeeds not by motivating people to make a real sacrifice, but by motivating them to do the things that people do when they are not motivated enough to make a real sacrifice".[9] In other words, social media are an excellent medium for weak tie activism but the development of strong ties requires greater organisational consistency than 'clicktivism'.[10] As anyone who's ever organised anything will know, it is sadly not as simple as 'tweet it and they will come'.[11]

My hypothesis is that, rather than contradicting this conclusion, the political use of social media in 2011 highlights a possibility underestimated by Gladwell: under certain special conditions, the *quantity* of connections enabled by social media can indeed produce the *quality* of stronger ones—a marginal effect that weak ties always possess that is intensified by favourable circumstances, and which we could describe as a general lowering of each individual's participation threshold.

If one pays attention to how events unfolded, the myth of isolated individuals coming together on the randomly picked date of a Facebook event becomes shaky. Even the instance seemingly closest to the 'spontaneous uprising' narrative, Tunisia, is arguably best described as starting with strong ties. Mohamed Bouazizi's shocking act of self-immolation first galvanised a small circle of friends and family who tried to make sure the information about his death and the protests that followed got out of the town of Sidi Bouzid. The story was picked up by *Al Jazeera*, there was support from the local trade union branch and student groups, and longer-term activists and media critics of the government began to speak (and act) out.[12]

The movement, in other words, was not simply from weak ties to strong ties, isolated individuals to strong commitments, the Internet to the streets; but (small scale) strong ties to weak ties (more people hearing about what had happened) to strong ties (activist groups and individuals becoming involved on a larger scale) to a broader fringe of weak ties becoming strong ties as things gathered momentum. This is illustrated in the geographical spread—from the countryside to *Al Jazeera*, then from social media and YouTube to the capital and abroad, where each relay produced not only a greater number of informed people but also people who became active. And it is not too much to imagine that communication among individuals was taking place not only through media, social or otherwise, but also through meetings and nascent or pre-existing organisations of different kinds.

Equally, and in relation to the movement that irrupted in Egypt in January 2011, it is well known that, for years, activist groups there had had their attempts to channel mass opposition to the Mubarak regime frustrated and repressed. Then the events in Tunisia and the viral spread of information and availability of online mobilising tools provided them with an opportunity that they seized. It is true, someone did create a Facebook event calling for the January 25 'Day of Anger'; this someone, however, was no random 'concerned citizen', but the admin of a Facebook page ('We are all Khaled Said') with over 400,000 followers that had existed for half a year. That admin, the now famous Wael Ghonim, attributes the idea to his collaborator AbdelRahman Mansour and the final decision to a brainstorming session over a month earlier with Ahmed Maher of the April 6 Youth Movement, in which they agreed that the Facebook page would spearhead the call, while the activist group would take care of logistics.[13] (April 6 had already mobilised for that date—Police Day—in the past.) And as the idea of a protest on that and subsequent dates caught on, it was worked out and made operational by several other already existing and then sprouting organisations and affinity groups.

The communication that enabled the Arab Spring in Tunisia, Egypt, and then elsewhere in 2011 (or 15M and Occupy) did not simply spread from one individual to the next via social media; in each case, what happened was always a much more complex relay between already established hubs—either 'strong tie' groups or communication nodes with a large following and credibility—and a long tail of ties with decreasing intensity, in a sort of ripple effect with many epicentres. If there can be mass movements without mass organisations, it is because social media amplify exponentially the effects of relatively isolated initiatives. But that they do so is not a miraculous phenomenon that can magically bypass quality by producing quantity out of nothing; it requires the relay through hubs and strong tie groups and clusters that can begin to operationally translate 'chatter' into action. As that happens, under propitious conditions, the spread of information also aids the development of strong ties down the long tail: once a friend or family member goes to a demo or you see stirring images of one, you are more likely to go, and so on. So we can only speak of 'spontaneity' if we understand the new flows of information and decision-making as also being necessarily routed by previously existing networks and organisations and more tightly knit affinities, and thus along the lines of previously given structures that no doubt were transformed in the process; certainly not in the sense of an ideal 'association of individuals' who previously existed as individuals only. This is even more explicit in those cases, such as 15M and Occupy, where there was an open, overground organising process prior to things 'kicking off'.[14]

Finally, it is interesting to speculate on how the beginnings of both the Tunisian and Egyptian revolutions are tied to death and sacrifice, of Mohamed Bouazizi and Khaled Said above all. There is no greater test of commitment or of the strength of ties than being ready to die. The relation between years of police abuse and violence, and then the irrepressible resolve demonstrated by protesters in those countries seems clear—the way in which the risk of taking action being the highest was turned into the most fundamental 'strengthener' of ties: the disposition to die together if necessary and the solidarity that it creates.

3. The Primary Organisational Form of 2011 Was Not the Assembly

At the most evident level, the primary organisational form employed by movements in 2011 was the camp. From the extraordinary example set by Tahrir Square, the model spread to Wisconsin, Israel, Spain (where, however, it was an unplanned outcome of the 15 May demonstration), and then, after Occupy Wall Street (initially devised as a camp) and the 15 October day of global action, to the rest of the world. It was the most powerful meme, which is unsurprising seeing as it provided the most stirring images and, with Egypt, the most captivating victory.

Yet it is important to bear in mind the precise connection between form and goal that made Tahrir into a victorious symbol. Far more than simply a meme, it was a tactic that consisted in concentrating the movement in one place with a very concrete, if negative, demand: that Mubarak step down. Even then, it is clear that it would not have managed to achieve its goal had the regime not realised they were losing control of several other parts of the country.

As the camp became a meme, this connection was lost. It is remarkable that in the case of the *indignados* movement, for instance, the first tweet from @acampadasol—the first Twitter account of the first 'spontaneous' (ie, moving from strong ties to developing strong ties along the weaker intensity long tail) camp in Spain, at Puerta del Sol, Madrid—stated that 'we shall stay here until we reach an agreement'. Who the 'we' was and with whom agreement was to be reached were things left unstated in the micro-blogging website's peculiar syntax. By the time it got to the various worldwide 'Occupy' actions that sprang up after October 15, this tie was lost. The same can be said about other related memes, such as the 'human mic', which started out as a practical solution to a ban on amplification at Zucotti Park in New York and went on to become a marker of a certain 'Occupy' way of doing politics, even where the original impediment that had elicited it did not exist.

This is not to say that subsequent iterations of the camp meme were in no way tactical; they were, except the tactic was different. In the absence of the clear-cut negative demands that existed in Egypt and Wisconsin, what they were doing was not trying to enforce a collectively shared will but attempting to create the political space in which a collectively shared will *could* be constructed, so that a social force capable of effecting change through 'contamination' and / or enforcement of its will could appear. In this sense, if their 'diminishing tactical returns' resembles what happened to the counter-summit cycle of the alter-globalisation movement, to criticise them without recognising the other crucial function they exercise—like Badiou, for example, did back in 2003 in regard to counter-summits—amounts to missing what people *actually* do by virtue of focusing on what they (or the media) *say* they do.[15]

The strength of camps such as the ones seen in Spain, Israel, and several Occupy sites lay in their provision of a focal point for widespread dissent. They were moments when already existing virtual and non-virtual social networks collided with one another, were reshuffled and given greater consistency by direct contact and co-presence. More than that, they provided a space in principle accessible to all, regardless of any previous experience of activism or insertion into the social networks in which the process had initiated. Finally, they did so while also exposing people to the challenge of sharing a space and its running, which, if it can be rather testing, can lead to the development of stronger ties. In other words, what these later camps did was to act on the *conditions of possibility* of politics: in the context of profound disempowerment and a severe crisis impacting on highly atomised societies, they functioned as a space where the fabric of relations that one calls 'the political' could, at least for those who were there, be partially (re)constituted.

The whole difficulty was that, while they did this, both outsiders and insiders also expected from them concerted political action and clear positions. They had to *grow up in public*. All this in a situation whose tactical coordinates were not time bound, with no obvious idea of what that holding on indefinitely entailed, and facing the Herculean (maybe Sisyphean) task of deciding it on the spot with very large numbers of very diverse people.

Much was made of the general assemblies, which is no surprise considering how at once impressive and quaint they looked (cue the de rigueur journalistic remark on hand gestures), but also how they seemed to address the widespread experience of a democratic deficit. One of the most typical comments made by participants speaks of everyone's ostensible gladness to be given a voice in front of others. And if virtual networks were the original medium for affective spread and contagion, the 'reshuffling' enabled by open mic spaces where people could exchange points of view, begin new relationships, and get into other networks— let alone the sheer power of discovering commonalities with people one would otherwise never meet—cannot be underestimated.

Yet the very difference in intensity in moving 'from the Internet to the streets' can produce an overvaluation of the assembly in the face of everything else. During the Arab Spring, Christian Marazzi compared the logics of contagion proper to financial markets and to the events taking place in the Mahgreb.[16] In the former, it is the deficit of information that leads to mimetic behaviour that, in the frantic heights of a speculative bubble, becomes entirely self-referential and incapable of observing any dynamics outside of itself; instead it assumes some (market Big) Other knows something 'we do not know'. In the latter, an excess of information produces an 'imitation of oneself' whose material referent is the very social body. In these terms, the risk that assemblies carry with them could be described as a *fetish of presence*—of restricting the imitable 'oneself' to the assembly itself, losing sight of non-presential affects as well as the 'others' of that experience, which in turn is made into a less inclusive, less connected 'you just had to be there'. This mistakes the immediate, *visible* body of the mo(ve)ment for the whole of its real one—which is mediate as well as immediate, virtual as well as actual, diffuse as well as concentrated, variable as well as given, and dependent at all times on a complex assemblage of bodies, technological interfaces, words, affects, and ideas.

This dynamic can be intensified by the very tendency of the media to represent assemblies as the movement's core. If, however, we take a step back from the most visible to apprehend the entire process that enabled it and kept it alive, what becomes apparent is that this movement's key organisational form, while in its own way also open and horizontal, is *not* the assembly.

We could call it *distributed leadership*: the possibility, even for previously 'uncharted' individuals and groups, to temporarily take on the role of moving things forward by virtue of coming up with courses of action that provide provisional focal points for activity. (I have previously referred to this as 'diffuse vanguardism', defining it as the power 'to ignite large scale effects without any sort of [previously existing or at a proportionally large-scale] decision-making procedure.')[17] It applies equally both to the first outliers, groups or individuals who started networking towards the mass actions that then developed into camps and assemblies, and to all those whose initiatives, by example more than persuasion, by contagion more than argument, managed to cut through deadlocks in decision-making processes progressively reduced to the assembly form.

What makes this form of leadership different is the fact that it does not require a previously established 'leader' or 'vanguard' status (membership numbers, political trajectory, reputation). In fact, one of the key things that appears to work in favour of an initiative in the present environment is *precisely* its being 'anonymous' or (to put it in sports language) 'unseeded'. It is only natural that the present crisis being to a great extent one of representation there should be suspicion towards 'representative' names.

At the same time, producing an initiative that resonates and gains traction with others usually demands more than just 'throwing an idea out there'. It implies setting an example to be followed, and thus depends on it being embodied in a group of people who 'make it happen'. Such seems to be the case with arguably the most important development to take place after the camps—the focus on anti-eviction actions and occupations with a view to providing housing for foreclosure victims. Again, a mediation takes place between strong and weak ties, producing strong ties in the process. But even at times when the participation threshold is lower, successful new initiatives are likely to be those that offer relatively low entry levels, perhaps increasing in commitment and militancy with time.[18]

The logic of distributed leadership characteristic of 2011 struggles is that of the 'leader of the pack' as described by Deleuze and Guattari in their *A Thousand Plateaus*; and yet, if we read Hegel minus the teleology (the only way to do it today), we will find it is not too distinct from those *Werkzeuge* of world history, 'world-historical individuals'. In Catherine Malabou's felicitous phrase, what we have here is the movement of a changing body / border precipitated by the occurrence of singular initiatives 'as the cutting edge of excess / overrunning (*comme bord de débordement*)'.[19] Interestingly, more optimistic readings of today's movements, while ostensibly predicated on something like 'collective intelligence' rather than history (or Spirit), appear to rely on a surreptitious teleology according to which this intelligence, rather than responding to conjunctural problems with the resources at its disposal at any given time, is in the long run 'working out' the solutions for all crises faced today.[20] In a somewhat extreme case of presence fetishism, assemblies and working groups figure as stand-ins for humankind as a whole.

But it would be naïve to think that such leadership, while distributed, is done so evenly. What visualisations of the social media networks behind the likes of Occupy and 15M[21] illustrate is that these networks, like the social ones behind them, possess what is called a 'scale-free' structure.[22] That is, their characteristic distribution consists of a large number (or 'long tail') of less connected nodes and a small number of hubs with a greater number of both more connected and further removed nodes. As such, any simplistic 'levelling' conceptualisation of horizontality as absolute equality is contradicted by all the available knowledge, mathematical and intuitive, on the structure of this kind of network. (Was this not a variation on the liberal theme of a naturally righteous free association of individuals, at any rate?)

Yet this does not make these movements 'undemocratic' either. First, it must be noted that the majority of the most important Twitter accounts in these visual representations did not exist just over a year ago. If they acquired their present relevance it was through being relevant at the time when new connections and a particular kind of traffic among them boomed. This argument can no doubt be extended beyond social media. Second, while it is obvious that there is something self-confirming about being a hub—those who have more connections will automatically be heard more—this very self-confirming loop entails dependence on a process of constant legitimation. That is, while distributed leadership is not an ideal 'free market' of information, analysis, and initiative but subject to preferential attachment, a hub's 'stock' also fluctuates according to the quality of traffic that it routes and initiatives that it proposes or backs.[23] Furthermore, that something is routed by a 'strong' source does not necessarily make it 'catch on'; for every successful initiative there are hundreds that do not 'take off'. At the same time, one of the things that make a source strong is the fact that it can draw attention to smaller, less connected nodes, and thus contribute to increasing their visibility and connectivity. Finally, the more connected and excitable the 'machine-body' of a networked movement—at peak moments in the mobilisation of bodies, affects, and virtual connections—the likelier it is for traffic from less connected nodes to be picked up, the quicker and easier the movement from weak to strong ties that an initiative requires to be made effective, and the faster traffic can be rerouted in general.[24]

Thus, however counter-intuitive, we could speak of a 'vanguard' of these movements, if we understand it as an 'immanent vanguard' endowed with a power of immanent command. Its capacity to 'lead' has to be proven each time, or rather, its status fluctuates much more rapidly. It is only a vanguard to the extent that it 'works'—and when it does not, it does not, maybe even in ways that will damage its power to 'work' in the future.[25] It is a cause that inheres in its effects. Now, it could be argued that this was the only sense in which vanguards ever actually existed historically. But to make this point is tantamount to suggesting that there is no *objective* ballast to vanguard status—the identification of one having long been the chimera of different strains of Marxism—beyond the effectiveness of its (temporary, localisable, though potentially much wider than its initial context) 'leadership'.

References

Kurt Andersen, December 2011—'The Protester', in *Time*, December 14 2011, at http://content.time.com/time/specials/packages/article/0,28804,2101745_2102132,00.html (Accessed September 2 2017)

Alain Badiou, 2003—'Beyond Formalisation: An Interview', with Peter Hallward and Bruno Bosteels, translated by Bruno Bosteels and Alberto Toscano, in *Angelaki: Journal of the Theoretical Humanities*, vol 8 no 2, 2003, p 120, at https://www.scribd.com/doc/56190920/Badiou-Interview-Angelaki (Accessed September 2 2017)

Albert-László Barabási and Albert Réka, 1999—'Emergence of Scaling in Random Networks', in *Science* vol 286, pp 509–12, at https://www.sciencemag.org/content/286/5439/509.full (Accessed September 2 2017)

Judith Butler, 2012—'So, What Are the Demands?', in *Occupy Theory, Occupy Strategy* 2, 2012, pp 8–11, at https://www.scribd.com/doc/86333441/Butler-Judith-So-What-Are-the-Demands-Occupy-Wall-Street (Accessed September 2 2017)

Colectivo Situaciones, 2009—'Disquiet In the Impasse', in *Turbulence* 5, 2009, at http://www.turbulence.org.uk/turbulence-5/disquiet-in-the-impasse/index.html (Accessed September 2 2017)

Colectivo Situaciones, 2011—*19 & 20, Notes for a New Social Protagonism: An 18th Brumaire for the 21st Century—Militant Research on the December 19th and 21st 2001 Uprisings in Argentina*. Translated by Nate Holdren and Sebastien Touza. New York / Wivenhoe: Minor Compositions, with Common Notions and Autonomedia

Gilles Deleuze and Felix Guattari, 1980—*Mille plateaux* ['A Thousand Plateaus', in French]. Paris: Minuit

Guillermo Delgado-P, 2017—'Refounding Bolivia: Exploring the Possibility and Paradox of a Social Movements State', in Jai Sen, ed, 2017—*The Movements of Movements, Part 1: What Makes Us Move?*. Volume 4 in the *Challenging Empires* series. New Delhi: OpenWord, and Oakland, CA: PM Press

DRY-CR, April 2012—'*La 'Asociación Democracia real Ya' no es Democracia Real Ya*' ['The 'Democracia Real Ya' Association is not Real Democracy', in Spanish], on *¡Democracia Real Ya!*, at http://www.democraciarealya.es/blog/2012/04/22/la-asociacion-democracia-real-ya-no-es-democracia-real-ya/ (Accessed September 2 2017)

EFE, April 2012—'*Democracia Real Ya se constituye como asociación*' ['Real Democracy is constituted as an association', in Spanish], in *El País*, April 22 2012, at http://politica.elpais.com/politica/2012/04/22/actualidad/1335113954_554411.html (Accessed September 2 2017)

The Free Association, 2011—'On Fairy Dust and Rupture', on *The Free Association*, May 2011, at http://freelyassociating.org/on-fairy-dust-and-rupture/ (Accessed September 2 2017)

Wael Ghonim, 2012—*Revolution 2.0: A Memoir*. London: Fourth Estate

Malcolm Gladwell, October 2010—'Small Change: Why the Revolution Will Not Be Tweeted', in *New Yorker*, October 4 2010, at http://www.newyorker.com/magazine/2010/10/04/small-change-malcolm-gladwell (Accessed September 2 2017)

Mark S Granovetter, 1973—'The Strength of Weak Ties', in *American Journal of Sociology*, vol 78 no 6, pp 1360–80

Philip N Howard, Aiden Duffy, Deen Freelon, Muzammil Hussain, Will Mari, and Marwa Mazaid, 2011—'Opening Closed Regimes: What was the role of social media in the Arab Spring?'. Working paper of the Project on Information Technology and Political Islam, 2011, at http://pitpi.org/index.php/2011/09/11/opening-closed-regimes-what-was-the-role-of-social-media-during-the-arab-spring/ (Inactive September 2 2017)

Andy Kroll, October 2011—'How Occupy Wall Street Really Got Started', on *Mother Jones*, October 17 2011, at http://www.motherjones.com/politics/2011/10/occupy-wall-street-international-origins (Accessed September 2 2017)

Vladimir Ilyich Lenin, 1993—*'Left Wing' Communism: An Infantile Disorder*. London: Bookmarks

Manuel Lucas, 2012—*'A quién seguir esta primavera? Un estudio en Twitter sobre la Spanish Revolution'* ['Who to follow this spring? A study on Twitter on the Spanish Revolution', in Spanish], at http://www.manuelalucas.com/?p=53 (Accessed September 2 2017)

Catherine Malabou, 1996—'Who's Afraid of Hegelian Wolves?', in Paul Patton, ed, 1996—*Deleuze: A Critical Reader*. London: Wiley-Blackwell

Christian Marazzi, 2011—*'Mahgreb e mercati finanziari: La logica del contagio'* ['Maghreb and financial markets: The logic of contagion', in Italian], in *UniNomade*, 2011, at http://www.uninomade.org/maghreb-e-mercati-finanziari-la-logica-del-contagio/ (Accessed September 2 2017)

Oscar Marín Miró, Alejandro González, Ruben Abad, Marco Martínez, Leonardo Menezes, and Roberto Maestre, December 2011—'15 Octubre 2011: Mapas de la revolución global en Twitter' ['October 15 2011: Map of the global revolution on Twitter', in Spanish], on *ParadigmaLabs*, at http://www.paradigmatecnologico.com/blog/15-octubre-2011-mapas-de-la-revolucion-global-en-twitter/ (Accessed September 2 2017)

Antonio Negri, 2004—*Trentatre lezioni su Lenin* ['Thirty-three lessons of Lenin', in Italian]. Rome: Manifestolibri

Rodrigo Nunes, August 2009—'Dictionary of Received Ideas (In the Interest of Passing Them On)', on *ZNet*, at http://zcomm.org/znetarticle/dictionary-of-received-ideas-in-the-interest-of-passing-them-on-by-rodrigo-nunes/ (Accessed September 2 2017)

Rodrigo Nunes, January–February 2010—'The Global Moment: Seattle, Ten Years On', in *Radical Philosophy*, January–February 2010, at https://www.radicalphilosophy.com/commentary/the-global-movement (Accessed September 2 2017)

Rodrigo Nunes, 2018b—'The Global Moment: Seattle, Ten Years On', in Jai Sen, ed, 2018—*The Movements of Movements, Part 2: Rethinking Our Dance*. Volume 5 in the *Challenging Empires* series. New Delhi: OpenWord, and Oakland, CA: PM Press

G Pór, 2012—'How Revolution Carries Itself Forward by the Working Groups of Occupy', on *The Future of Occupy*, at thefutureofoccupy.org (Inactive September 2 2017)

Pablo Rodríguez, 2011—*'Como se gestó el 15M?'* ['How was 15M conceived?', in Spanish], at https://storify.com/pablobuentes/que-es-y-como-se-gesto-el-movimiento-15M (Accessed September 2 2017)

Yasmine Ryan, January 2011—'How Tunisia's Revolution Began', on *Al Jazeera*, 2011, at http://www.aljazeera.com/indepth/features/2011/01/2011126121815985483.html (Accessed September 2 2017)

Raúl Sánchez Cedillo, 2012—'*El 15M como insurrección del cuerpo-máquina*' ['The 15M as an insurrection of the body-machine', in Spanish], on Uni*NomadE*, at http://www.uninomade.org/el-15m-como-insurreccion-del-cuerpo%C2%ADmaquina/ (Accessed September 2 2017)

Juliette Simont, 1997—*Essai sur la quantité, la qualité, la relation chez Kant, Hegel, Deleuze* ['Essay on the quantity, quality, relation between Kant, Hegel, Deleuze', in French]. Paris: L'Harmattan

Matt Sledge, October 2011—'Reawakening the Radical Imagination: The Origins of Occupy Wall Street', on *Huffington Post*, October 11 2011, at http://www.huffingtonpost.com/2011/11/10/occupy-wall-street-origins_n_1083977.html (Accessed September 2 2017)

Notes

1. Ed: This essay was first published on *Mute*, June 7 2012, at http://www.metamute.org/editorial/articles/lessons-2011-three-theses-organisation (Accessed September 2 2017). Thanks to both the author and the publisher for being open to republication.

2. Negri, 2004, p 42. He continues: "Otherwise, it is impotence and defeat trying to justify themselves".

3. Ed: This article was written and published in 2012. I have left the tense used by the author as it was, to allow the article to stand and represent / reflect a moment in the larger unfolding of world movement at that juncture.

4. Just recently, in fact, a group of founding members of Democracia Real Ya decided to start a non-profit association of the same name, allegedly to bypass decision-making paralysis in order to exercise 'coordinated pressure' on institutions. See, EFE, April 2012. The move was denounced in an official statement that insisted on the original conception of a 'leaderless coordinated network of individuals that neither can nor should conform to a legal framework'. See, DRY-CR, April 2012—*La 'Asociación Democracia Real Ya' no es Democracia Real Ya*, http://www.democraciarealya.es/blog/2012/04/22/la-asociacion-democracia-real-ya-no-es-democracia-real-ya/ (Accessed September 2 2017).

5. The same argument can be made about the tiresome discussion on lack of demands: to make demands that can be met means, precisely, that one remains within the scope of the present system; so any 'real' demands, ie, dealing with the real choices foreclosed by the system, will inevitably seem impossible or nonsensical. This does evidently not mean that there cannot be concrete local demands, defensive or offensive, which will be useful focal points, precipitating fights which work as stepping stones for movements—eg, anti-foreclosure legislation. One should always be careful not to mistake the "subjective 'rejection'" of institutions for their 'actual destruction'. See Lenin 1993, p 73. On demands, see Butler 2012, pp 8–11.

6. See Colectivo Situaciones 2009 and 2011.

7. Ed: For a discussion of the unfolding of social movement in Bolivia over the recent past, see the essay by Guillermo Delgado-P in Part 1 to this book, *The Movements of Movements: Struggles for Other Worlds*, Part I (Delgado-P 2017).

8. On the choice of referring to it as 'moment' rather than 'movement', see my 'The Global Moment: Seattle, Ten Years On', January–February 2010; also in this volume in slightly edited form (Nunes 2018b).

9.   Gladwell, October 2010.

10.   Granovetter defines the strength of a tie as "a (probably linear) combination of the amount of time, the emotional intensity, the intimacy (mutual confiding), and the reciprocal services which characterize the tie" (Granovetter 1973, p 1361).

11.   Not that such widely available intuitive knowledge prevented Kurt Andersen from claiming just that. See Andersen, December 2011.

12.   See, for example, the narratives of how the 'Jasmine Revolution' unfolded in Ryan, January 2011, and Howard, Duffy, Freelon et al 2011.

13.   Ghonim 2012, p 225.

14.   A step-by-step explanation of the 15M's organising process between February and May 2011 was provided by P Rodríguez. Good accounts of Occupy Wall Street's lead-up to Zucotti Park include: Sledge, October 2011; Kroll, October 2011. As the former summarises it: "The movement didn't get that big simply because AdBusters . . . sent out a flashy email promoting it, or because the hacker collective Anonymous flicked out a few tweets. Instead, it took a group of about 200 committed activists forty-seven days to outline the ground rules that have allowed the protest to flourish".

15.   Badiou 2003.

16.   Marazzi 2011.

17.   See my 'Dictionary of Received Ideas (In the Interest of Passing Them On)', on *ZNet*, at http://zcomm.org/znetarticle/dictionary-of-received-ideas-in-the-interest-of-passing-them-on-by-rodrigo-nunes/ (Accessed September 2 2017).

18.   In this regard, see The Free Association 2011.

19.   Malabou 1996, p 221. As both Malabou and Juliette Simont have argued, the distance between Deleuze (and Guattari) and Hegel can often be smaller than the former would like to see transpire. See Simont 1997.

20.   Pór 2012.

21.   Lucas 2012; and Miró, González, Abad et al 2011.

22.   The scale-free model was introduced by physicist Albert-László Barabási, among others, to refer to the power-law distribution of nodes (and consequent hub / long tail structure) characteristic of most complex networks known to us. See Barabási and Albert Réka 1999.

23.   Growth (the addition of new nodes over time) and preferential attachment (the tendency of more connected nodes to attract more nodes) are the two basic laws governing the formation of scale-free networks in the model advanced by Barabási and his team.

24.   Sánchez Cedillo 2012.

25.   In Deleuze and Guattari 1980, pp 46–47: "No doubt there is no more equality, no less hierarchy in packs than in masses, but they are not of the same kind. The leader of a pack or band plays move by move, must risk everything in each move, whereas the leader of a group or mass consolidates and capitalises on past gains".

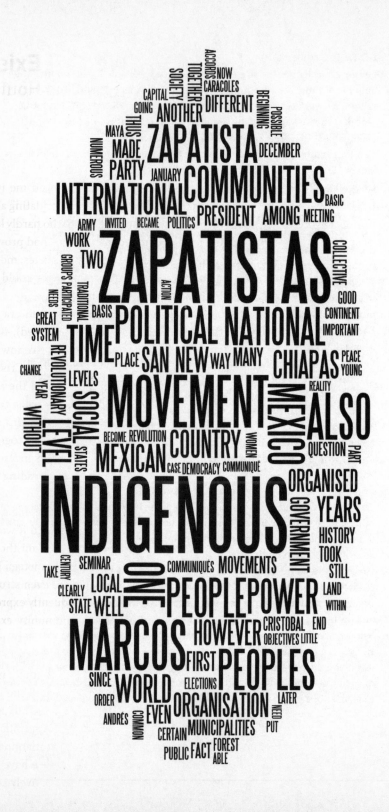

'We Still Exist'[1]
François Houtart

When I arrived in Mexico at the end of 2012, many people asked me if the Zapatistas still existed. There were so many rumours that were circulating about them. Hardly anyone talked about them, which meant, for those who hardly knew them, that they had disappeared. In fact, Subcomandante Marcos had provided the media with such an enormous amount of texts, declarations, stories, more or less symbolic narratives, that the silence of this great communicator could only mean withdrawal or, worse still, admission of defeat.

On December 21 that year, the day of the change in the Mayan era (and not the end of the world, as the sensational world press had proclaimed), 40,000 people wearing the Zapatista balaclava paraded in silence through five towns in the state of Chiapas, 20,000 of them in the historic state capital, San Cristóbal de las Casas. They had come from the mountains of the centre and the north of the state and from the Lacandon Forest to the east of San Cristóbal, a region as large as Belgium, and they took everyone by surprise. One can imagine what was involved in preparing such an operation: collecting the vehicles together, mobilising the people with everyone's agreement, taking to the roads in a region of uncertain security, covering scores of kilometres and peacefully parading in an orderly manner in the five towns. It was completely unexpected.

The way the demonstration took place was most impressive: no one spoke, no banners, no slogans, no final speeches—people just walking—and it was the response to the opening question above. The message was clear: you thought we were in decline, but we still exist and are as strong as we were nineteen years ago, when we took several of these same towns by arms. We are even stronger because we are now taking them without arms. Our silence eloquently expresses the reinforcement of our local organisation and the many community experiences under way, as opposed to the current disaster of Mexican society, mired in a drug-trafficking war, the twists and turns of dirty politics, the systematic use of torture, the rigging of elections, and the beginning of an economic recession. We don't want to give lessons to anyone but in this new era of the Maya people, we want to confirm that we exist and that, in spite of all the talk about our disappearance, we are very much alive, in a territory where drug trafficking and alcoholism—typical of the Indigenous societies that have been marginalised since the nineteenth century—have virtually disappeared, where we have been able to set up many basic schools over the last decade. We are collectively active, declaring the human values of solidarity, conviviality, and shared responsibilities. The short communiqué issued after the march declared: "Did you hear? It is the sound of your world collapsing. It is that of ours rising anew".[2]

It was a strong message and it had a considerable impact on Mexican opinion. It had repercussions all over the continent and even beyond Latin America. How could these Indigenous communities proclaim their existence so publicly when they were living in poverty, isolated from all official support (the communities, the municipalities and the five Good Government Councils at the regional level, sited in the *Caracoles*,[3] receive no assistance at all from the state, either for their administration or for health or education), fought by the public authorities, attacked by paramilitary groups, and subject to monitoring by outposts of the government army? In truth, no one had expected it—but the surprises did not stop there.

Some Historical Background

Five years ago,[4] I spent several days at the Earth University in Chiapas, which had become an important base for the Zapatistas to train young people from the communities in agriculture, the local economy, cooperatives, and social and political analysis, as well as on how to organise international meetings. It is situated on the outskirts of San Cristóbal. I was there for a colloquium that had been organised in homage to André Aubry, a Frenchman who had been a worker-priest and who had come to work with the bishop of San Cristóbal, Monsignor Samuel Ruiz. Aubry had also worked closely with the Zapatista movement. When the journal *Alternatives Sud* was launched in 1994, it featured a number of articles on the Zapatistas, and he had collaborated with us at CETRI.[5] Tragically, Aubry then lost his life in a car accident in 2007. Subcomandante Marcos participated in the seminar, which brought together over a thousand participants, and other invitees included Pablo González Casanova, the former rector of the National Autonomous University of Mexico (UNAM), Naomi Klein, the Canadian journalist, and Immanuel Wallerstein, the North American sociologist. I too had been invited to speak.

With his usual sense of humour, Marcos started to pay tribute to Aubry, referring to him as Don Durito of the Lacandona (a character and a literary device in Marcos's writings, who is a beetle from the forest who thought of himself as Don Quixote and whose squire was Marcos himself), by saying "The problem with reality is that it knows nothing about theory".[6] Coming, however, from a member of an old guerrilla movement inspired by Guevarism that had been formed in 1968, after the massacre of the students in Tlatelolco Square in the federal capital, and that at the beginning of the 1980s had made its base in the Lacandon forest in Chiapas, such an opening could have seemed strange. The reality however was that after spending years with the Indigenous communities, the Zapatista National Liberation Army (EZLN—*Ejército Zapatista de Liberación Nacional*) had learned a lot of things. Marcos himself, who had been a professor in communication sciences at the UNAM, had soon cast aside his great ideas of being 'an avant-garde that had come to announce to the masses the path that was to be followed to make the revolution'. He came to realise both that knowledge was something to be shared and that the Indigenous People were imbued with profound wisdom, honed by over 500 years of resistance to oppression without losing their identity.

Of course, the reference in their name to Emiliano Zapata, who at the beginning of the twentieth century had started agrarian reform in Mexico in order to extricate the country from a feudalism inherited from colonisation, was a sign that we were no longer living in precolonial times. It was important to look to the future. But instead of bringing 'the truth' from outside, the neo-Zapatistas understood that they had to discover it from the inside. It was in the same spirit that Joseph Cardijn, the founder of the Jeunesse Ouvrière Chrétienne (JOC) in Belgium in 1925, encouraged the young workers themselves to look, think, and change the conditions of the workers using the method '*Voir, Juger, Agir*' ['See, Judge, Act']—or that Paulo Freire in Brazil, with his *Pedagogy of the Oppressed*, did, using existing popular wisdom to gradually build up people's perspectives and knowledge.[7] Similarly, Marcos went to the school of the autochthonous peoples and lived with them to make the necessary changes in his thinking.

It was not that Marcos despised theory. As an intellectual and a student of Rosa Luxemburg (who said "there is no revolution without theory"),[8] he could not do so, but he reorganised his thinking. He added, when introducing his interventions to the 2007 colloquium: "I think that I might be permitted to explain the rudiments of this theory, which is so different to the one practised".[9] The 'Sub' in his title is of course a critique of modernity, but he does not go in for the excesses of certain postmodernists whose refusal of systems, structures, theories, organisation, and history transforms them into the best ideologues of neoliberalism. In fact, neoliberalism has a great need to spread ignorance about the systemic organisation of the material bases of capitalism and its characteristic power relationships, and post-modernism plays a useful role in doing this.

The uprising of the different Maya Peoples on January 1 1994, which was supported by the EZLN, was thus no chance happening, nor was it a simple explosion of spontaneity. It was the outcome of a cross-fertilisation between a group of revolutionaries who were well versed in Marxist analysis and the Indigenous communities who were marked by their long history of repressed struggle and who knew better than anyone what active solidarity at the service of a common cause is. They prepared themselves for an insurrection of some kind as the very basis of their survival was being affected.[10] A decade of coexistence culminated in the former losing their revolutionary arrogance and discovering that 'one learns by walking,'[11] and in turn the ancestral struggle of the latter became part of the struggle of peoples all over the world against an economic system of dispossession and death.[12]

The contemporary struggles of the Mayas did not start with the Zapatistas in 1994. In neighbouring Guatemala—which is equally the home of the Mayas—there had been many, very bloody revolts by the Indigenous People. In fact, the Indigenous victims of Guatemala can be counted in hundreds of thousands as they fought for land and autonomy and were massacred by political and military regimes that were all supported by the United States. At the time, the latter saw the struggles as the prelude to a Sovietisation of Central America. Using Honduras as a base, they intervened in 1954 to overthrow the regime of President Jacobo Árbenz, because he was promoting agrarian reform and social-democratic reforms. Equally, a movement like the JOC, which was deeply rooted among the young workers in the towns and the countryside in the Third World has, since the 1960s, also paid a heavy price for its contribution to social struggles. A number of its leaders, whom I knew personally, have been assassinated.

In 1981, the annual meeting of the progressive bishops of the continent took place at Tehuantepec, in Oaxaca state, which is next door to Chiapas, near the Pacific Ocean and close to the frontier with Guatemala. Among the Mexicans were San Cristóbal bishop Samuel Ruiz and Don Sergio Méndez Arceo, bishop of Cuernavaca. They had invited me too, in order to present the socio-religious analyses that I had carried out. One afternoon, a Guatemalan nun, accompanied by a young Indigenous girl, asked to be received urgently by the group. She explained that massacres of the Indigenous Peoples were being carried out in Guatemala and that she had just crossed the border. She presented as a witness the young girl, who spoke in her own language. She knew hardly any Spanish, so the nun translated for her. Her father had just been assassinated in the Spanish Embassy, which had been taken by assault by a group that wanted to attract international attention about the situation of the autochthonous peoples. Its community was the object of reprisals. She spoke for a good half-hour, her voice almost inaudible, typical of the way the Indigenous women speak. We listened to her without interruption as we were shattered by what she said. We then asked for more specific details in order to pass them on to the groups who were defending human rights. This young girl was called Rigoberta Menchú and some years later she was to receive the Nobel Peace Prize.

As for the Zapatista revolt, the date January 1 1994—the day on which the Zapatistas army came out of the forests—had also not been chosen by chance. This was no symbolic reference to the Mayan calendar, as there was to be twenty years afterwards. Rather, it was the date when the North American Free Trade Agreement (NAFTA), the treaty between Mexico, the United States, and Canada, was to come into force, and thus for the Zapatistas symbolised neoliberalism. This agreement, which would turn out to be so disastrous for Mexican agriculture, favoured certain elitist sectors of the country, but above all the interests of agribusiness and some industries of the United States. It was a case, as in all similar ones, of a 'treaty between a shark and sardines'. Within a few years, Mexico—which had historically been a major exporter of maize—instead became one of the largest importers of North American maize, while more than four million small farmers had lost their work. The latter exercised such migratory pressure that the United States in turn constructed a 'Wall of Shame' on their southern frontier, where four times more people lost their lives each year over the subsequent years than during the entire existence of the Berlin Wall. And where in Mexico, NAFTA had been preceded and heralded, in 1992, by the abolition of Article 27 of the Constitution, which dealt with agrarian reform, thus preparing the country for new land concentration and ending the dream of Emiliano Zapata.

By occupying the towns of Chiapas with a disciplined army and a well-conceived military strategy, the Zapatistas did not intend to go on to take Los Pinos (the presidential residence in Mexico City), but rather to create a shock to arouse the social forces of the country, particularly the Indigenous Peoples, in order to start a process of economic and social transformation.

A year earlier, in the night of December 31 1993–January 1 1994, they had proclaimed the First Declaration of the Lacandon Jungle, specifying their demands: land, dwellings, education, freedom, democracy, justice, and peace—and the resignation of President Salinas de Gortari. In fact, the region was one of the most depressed areas of the country and, unfortunately, twenty years later, the situation has hardly changed. According to an article in *La Jornada* of 4 January 2013, of the 7 million inhabitants of Chiapas, 2.7 million were living in extreme poverty—in other words, 40 per cent. Needless to add, they were almost all Indigenous People. Illiteracy affected 25.4 per cent of the population, as opposed to 10 per cent in the country as a whole, and 32.2 per cent have no access to health care.

The reaction of the government to the Zapatista uprising was violent. There was fighting and there were victims. After twelve days, the authorities proposed a ceasefire and the opening of negotiations. The Zapatistas accepted this, since their aim—which had been to attract the attention of the nation and the rest of the world to an intolerable situation—had been achieved, and in any case the power differential made other solutions impossible.

A person who played an important role in this peace process was Monsignor Samuel Ruiz, and this was not by chance. In fact, for many years he had inspired the base communities among the Indigenous populations. He had also been very active during the Second Vatican Council and was a member of the group 'the Church of the Poor', which met regularly in the Belgian College of Rome with the aim of expressing active solidarity with the world's oppressed. He had put these principles into practice in his Chiapas diocese and was a worthy successor of the first bishop of San Cristóbal, the Dominican Bartolomé de Las Casas, who in the sixteenth century defended the Indigenous Peoples of Chiapas against the owners of the Spanish haciendas.

In the Medellín Conference of 1968, which brought together the bishops of the continent to apply the Council's decisions to Latin America, he was one of those who supported liberation theology. He organised a catechism to involve the communities and an Indigenous deaconship to inspire the Christian communities. In sum, it was another way of being for the Church, not vertical and authoritarian but popular and sharing. Need it be said that in the restoration wave that swept through the continent in reaction to the reforms of the Second Vatican Council, he was a target for the Holy See, which sent him an apostolic visitor, imposed on him an auxiliary bishop with right of succession, and finally demanded his resignation. This demand was announced to him by telephone during a meeting of the progressive bishops of Latin America held on the outskirts of São Paulo in Brazil (to which I had also been invited as a participant).

Monsignor Samuel Ruiz had sown the seeds of a participatory religious organisation, giving the Indigenous communities a sense of their responsibility in building another society more in line with the values of the Gospel. It was in no way an amalgam, but it could be said, in the religious field, that an affinity had been created between the new Christian vision and what the Indigenous organisations were to become as a result of the Zapatista insurrection, as well as what, after the end of the fighting, was going to develop into the Zapatista municipalities.

The negotiations with the government opened in February 1994 in the cathedral of San Cristóbal. In spite of this, in 1995 President Ernesto Zedillo launched a military offensive, trying to capture Subcomandante Marcos. But it was a failure. Discussions continued over several months. There were two other personages who were important in the history of this process, the sociologist Pablo González Casanova and Miguel Álvarez, a collaborator of Monsignor Samuel Ruiz and coordinator of the support movement with the Indigenous Peoples. The result was the Peace Accords of San Andrés (a small town near San Cristóbal) on the rights of the Indigenous communities. They were signed by the EZLN and the government on February 16 1994, but President Zedillo later refused to allow the vote for the constitutional reform that would transform them into legal norms.

The Zapatistas' actions also took place at the national and international level. In 1996, it organised an 'encounter', or conference, entitled—by Marcos— 'Intergalactic', against neoliberalism.[13] The event attracted thousands of people and was a kind of forerunner of the World Social Forum. The same year, the National Indigenous Congress was founded in Mexico to bring together the forces of the autochthonous peoples of the country in a common action. In 1998, the

Zapatistas organised a national consultation to promote the application of the San Andrés Peace Accords, collecting huge numbers of signatures in the public squares throughout the country. At the same time, also in the Mexican capital, there was a meeting of a group studying social change, in which Samir Amin and Danielle Mitterand (the wife of French President François Mitterand) participated. I was also among the participants, and we were invited to meet with a Zapatista delegation in the suburbs of the town, at Xochimilco, at the bottom of a little sacred hill whose rocks still bore the traces of the Aztec calendar, where the Zapatistas celebrated the Spring solstice. They came down from the mountain, while the members of our group started to climb up it. Their spokesperson addressed us and I had to translate his speech. He started by expressing the satisfaction of the movement in saluting 'Mme Françoise Mitterand'.[14] I was rather taken aback but happily everyone else seemed to have understood what he meant.

A little later, in the large park nearby, which had been reconquered and was administered by the local people, we were invited to make a tour of the lake in a boat. To our amazement, another boat crossed ours, full of Zapatistas with their balaclavas. Truly, only in Mexico could a revolutionary movement allow itself to be so eccentric! And yet, there was a logic to it. There was a ceasefire, at that time respected by both parties, and the Zapatistas were carrying out a political action.

In 2001, they organised the 'Earth-Coloured March' to claim the rights of the Indigenous Peoples. This took them to the Zócalo, the main square of Mexico City, and they were also received by Parliament. Marcos asked an Indigenous commander to address the Assembly. However, that same year, after the refusal of the president in 1995 to implement the San Andrés Accords, it was now the turn of the parliament do so. It passed a unanimous vote by all the large parties against putting the Accords into practice.

As I happened to be in Mexico City that day for a seminar at the UNAM, together with Pablo González Casanova and Miguel Álvarez I participated in a protest demonstration in front of Parliament. The Zapatistas felt betrayed, including this time by a party of the left, the PRD (the Party of the Democratic Revolution), founded by Cuauhtémoc Cárdenas, son of the great reforming president of the twentieth century. (This party was basically a grouping of frustrated members of the PRI [Institutional Revolutionary Party], rather than a real left-wing party.)

On the other hand, the impact of Zapatism on Mexican society turned out to be real. By now, a large part of the Mexican intelligentsia was sympathetic to the Zapatistas, and the appeal of the movement created a favourable climate for a democratic advance. There was a regrouping of the Indigenous Peoples of Mexico, and the Zapatistas organised a popular consultation on the need for democratic participation in the country.

The Zapatistas also went on with their internal organisation in spite of increasingly violent attacks, the use of paramilitaries to try and retake the land that had been recovered during the insurrection, and the internal divisions among the Indigenous communities encouraged from outside, as well as the demoralising activities of certain Pentecostal religious movements. Several of them were condemned to long prison sentences, including Alberto Patish Tán, member of the Other Campaign and his companions who, in 2013, are still imprisoned. In 2003, they started the Good Government Councils in the *Caracoles*. The same year they organised a symbolic takeover of the old capital of Chiapas. In 2005, they launched the 'Sixth Declaration of Lacandon Jungle', which took up again the basic orientations of their struggle,[15] and, in 2007, they organised an international conference of women for a dignified life and another development.

However, on the political level the situation remained blocked. Although the Zapatistas had initially supported the PRD, they later separated from it. For the 2006 elections, between January and June, they organised Another Campaign throughout the country, advocating a regrouping of the antisystemic social organisations and collectives at the margin of the electoral battle, which they considered to be hostile to their objectives. They formed alliances, not only with the other Indigenous movements but also with numerous marginalised and subaltern groups, excluding the classic left, ie, those parties participating or having participated in power and the main union movements. They also associated with NGOs and intellectuals who were critical of the powers in place at all levels, national and local.

It was the PAN (National Action Party) that won the elections by a small margin, and it imposed a reactionary right-wing policy and alignment with the United States. In 2007, during the colloquium organised in memory of André Aubry, I asked Subcomandante Marcos, at the beginning of my speech, whether it was appropriate to advocate abstention at the national level, as this could only favour the right. It was a delicate question, and probably naive and out of place. Marcos, however, was not offended and he replied, first in French and then in Spanish: "How can you ask us to vote for our executioners?"

The governor of Chiapas at the time, Juan Salinas Sabines, son of another governor, Jaime Salinas Sabines, was a member of the PRD and he had been one of the most vicious persecutors of the Zapatistas. They had also been victims of attacks at Zinacantan by the PRD municipal authorities. Massacres had already occurred when the PRI was in power (notably, in 1997, when forty-five Tzotzils—an ethnic subgroup of the Maya—mainly women and children, were killed in a church at Acteal). Paramilitaries had been used to do the dirty work. Again, the authorities tried to sow dissension between the different Indigenous groups. The old landowners recovered their land and were supported by the forces of law and order. This resulted in displaced populations and caused numerous victims. Marcos was right, the power in place at Chiapas had been disastrous for the Indigenous movement.

And yet, at the national level, Andrés Manuel López Obrador (AMLO, as he was called), the new president of the PRD, did not promote a reactionary programme. Before the electoral campaign in 2005, he had been prevented by the government in power from presenting himself as a candidate for the elections. This caused the largest demonstration that Mexico had ever known: more than a million people in the streets of the capital demanded democracy. Having arrived from Europe that very night for a seminar at UNAM, I was able to participate and see the meaning of this demand, which some years later was going to erupt in the Arab world.[16] It was not the political destiny of a personality that was at stake but a whole system that had stolen sovereignty from the people. It was a question of principle and of dignity and, while it was true that numerous placards bore the name of AMLO, most of them expressed the desire to make democracy function, fragile as it was, in this case.

Andrés Manuel López Obrador however lost the elections. He rightly denounced the results but in vain. Four years later, in 2010, he was on the campaign beat again, travelling to all the municipalities in the country. At the time of the World Social Forum in January of that year, I found myself on a panel with him, in a tent that had been put up in the Zócalo in Mexico City. In the same square a group of trade unionists from the electricity sector were carrying out a fast against its privatisation. The theme of our panel was the economic system. Rather disappointingly, AMLO avoided the subject and concentrated on his election campaign, explaining how, from village to village, he had made contact with the rural world of Mexico. Certainly, this was a good strategy, but what was the content of his programme? He hardly explained this at all. As his campaign developed, he specified his objectives, but they were less ambitious than even the most prudent positions of the 'progressive' regimes of the rest of Latin America.

This time around, the Zapatista made no announcement, and this was widely interpreted as a sign of weakness. It is true that their call for abstention during the preceding national elections had disappointed part of the Mexican left, particularly many intellectuals, who distanced themselves from Zapatism in the belief that, while certainly there were reasons to be critical, it had overlooked the political logic at the national level and fallen back on local positions. For the Zapatistas, the silence they adopted in 2012, six years after having advocated nominal abstention, was probably the expression of a disavowal of existing political practices, while awaiting and discreetly preparing for new strategies.

The Sense and Meaning of Democratic Participation: A Society Needs to Be Built on a Basis Other than Capitalism

Up until now we have concentrated on the general context of the development of the Zapatista movement, but what about its internal practices? As we saw, Chiapas is one of the poorest regions of Mexico, where the land tenure system has excluded and marginalised the Indigenous populations, pushing them into the mountains and the forests. They receive no benefit from the oil revenues or the large plantations, particularly those producing agro-fuels. Natural wealth benefits Mexican private and international interests. Tourist activities form an economic enclave, while the 'development projects' and the construction of infrastructures are part of counter-insurrection strategies. Meanwhile, as we have seen, the levels of infant mortality and illiteracy remain high. Health and educational facilities are lacking. Numerous Indigenous Peoples rub shoulders with each other but they seldom really mix. Their languages are despised and their traditional beliefs folklorised. It is true that they are juridically recognised as being human beings, but what does that mean in actual fact?

It is clear for the Zapatistas that the capitalist organisation of the economy is socially perverse. They understand clearly that it has destroyed the very foundations of life in common, favouring individual property over common needs and transforming the country and its various regions into 'domains' of international capital. The movement has evoked the long history of the Indigenous Peoples and a return to the collective memory of how the original peoples of the continent had been reduced to slavery as from the end of the fifteenth century. They were forced to produce the precious metals that were to serve as a base for the primitive accumulation of European capital. They also had to work as agricultural labour in the plantations until they became almost extinct and the survivors were obliged to take refuge in the mountains and the forests. The independence movements of the nineteenth century promised by the creole elites never recognised the history and identity of the autochthonous peoples while the expansion of agrarian capitalism transformed them into cheap agricultural labour.

In Mexico, in spite of the revolutionary efforts at the beginning of the twentieth century, which had reconstituted the collective land of the Indigenous Peoples (the *ejidos*) and recognised part of their traditional social organisation, the original populations were unable to make their presence felt as a constitutive part of Mexican society. It is important to know this to understand the meaning of the Zapatista revolt. Neoliberalism, which has been dominant since the end of the 1970s, has succeeded in sweeping away the conquests of the revolutionary past. Little by little, the whole country has become embroiled in the logic of a deregulated market, external debt is groaning under the weight of interest payments, the oil income has been monopolised by a minority, unequal relations with the economies of the North have grown, and finally the last vestiges of agrarian reform have been suppressed. The PRI, the party that emerged from the revolution, has gradually put it itself at the service of the capitalist project and, deeply corrupt as it is, organises its political reproduction through election after election.

The ceremonies organised in 1992 for the 500th anniversary of the 'Encounter between Civilisations', as the Spanish government called it, or 'The Conquest', as most Latin American peoples see it, heightened the awareness of the Indigenous Peoples all over the continent. It was an opportunity to come out of clandestinity, to affirm their cultures as a way of life, to make the structure of their collective organisation known, as well as their traditional leaders, the value of their religions and their cosmovision. Gradually an identity was revealed which, although it had been repressed, had never completely disappeared. In various places, as in Ecuador, Bolivia, and even in Guatemala from the 1980s, it has turned out to be a political force.

And yet, in Mexico as elsewhere, the awakening of the Indigenous Peoples never appeared as separatism. In Chiapas, the different Maya Peoples clearly state that they are Mexicans. What they are demanding is their place in the national society. In the Zapatista municipalities and in the *Caracoles*, all public functions take place under the national Mexican flag. The 'separatist danger' of the Indigenous movements was once a slogan of the Mexican urban bourgeoisie who were evidently afraid of losing their hegemony over the political system. It analysed the movement in cultural and political terms and did not realise that the Chiapas 'indigenism' was gradually becoming a socio-economic force that, while obviously criticising the political system as the institutional guarantee of the economic system, never questioned the national identity. That there are still nostalgic desires for a return to a past that has been idealised among the original peoples is more than probable, but this is the last reproach to be levelled against the Zapatistas, who have succeeded in making a synthesis between the affirmed Indigenous identity and the critique of capitalism as a system of exclusion within Mexican society.

The challenge therefore consisted in putting the declared principles into action. According to their original orientation, the Zapatistas have acted at the level they were able to control, that is the local, their territories. Reorganising production of the material basis of human existence (the economy) outside the logic of accumulation was one of their first objectives. For this it was necessary to abolish private property of the land as the basis of agricultural production. Thus, recovering the collective lands of the Indigenous communities was undertaken, together with the democratic organisation of their exploitation. Cooperatives have been organised for the production and marketing of products and the surplus utilised to finance equipment for common usage. Other cooperatives have been set up that, among other things, contributed to mobilising so many people for the demonstrations of December 21 2012.

In the first of three communiqués issued at the beginning of January 2013, Subcomandante Marcos, in the name of the Clandestine Revolutionary Indigenous Committee and the Zapatista National Liberation Army, emphasised that the manner in which they had responded to the needs of the communities had had positive results over the last nineteen years.[17] Agricultural productivity (strictly organic, ie, without using chemical or transgenic products) has been greater in the Zapatista groups than in other communities. According to local witnesses, this is especially the case of coffee destined for export. This has made it possible to finance common services, in spite of the absence of any public subventions and violent and recurrent attacks. (Between 1995 and 1999, there had been many attacks and forced displacements of people; in June 2012, there were numerous victims in the mountains in the centre of the country.)

Returning to Marcos's communiqué, he said that in some areas non-Zapatistas came to use the movement's health services, considering them more efficient. It should also be added that international solidarity had played a not negligible role by financing part of these services. However the crisis being what it is and the fact that the Zapatista experience has been going on for nearly two decades, it was logical that this assistance would diminish. Thus, it has had to be compensated for by local efforts.

The production initiatives, as in all collective social and political organisation, need appropriate forms for the basic philosophy of the movement, that is, the participation of everyone, or direct democracy. Of course, the traditional social practices of the Indigenous Peoples could be a source of inspiration. But they too were not exempt from 'caciquismo' [clique dominance] and 'machismo'. It was therefore necessary to redefine the exercise of power and this was one of the fundamental tasks of the movement, as the writings of the subcomandante bear abundant witness.

To avoid power becoming an objective in itself, thus losing its function of serving an end, the communities are constantly consulting among themselves, for example, selecting those to be responsible for the management of various degrees of power, while those holding responsibilities for municipal tasks and the Councils are elected by the communities as a whole. There is also consultation, in the case of important decisions, to obtain the views of the grassroots. The regular presentation of the management accounts by all those responsible became systematic and, to avoid the institutionalisation of power, a rotation system was set up. In the Caracoles, for example, this is done every fortnight and the service is voluntary, with no payment. The basic needs (food, lodging) of those designated by the communities and the municipalities are taken care of—at a simple level. Thus it is not a privilege. Equality of the sexes is strictly respected.

All this could seem to be somewhat utopian or, as Bernard Duterme has written, inspired by a 'libertarian spirit',[18] and it is well that it is so. However, this experience has been going on for over twenty years. There is no doubt that it is a question of 'learning by walking', as the Zapatistas say,[19] and one should not idealise a social organisation of collective management as though it is above reproach or as though they were "people born before original sin" (as Franz Hinkelammert, the philosopher of German origin, once said with such sympathy, when referring to Nicaragua).[20] Fidelity to participatory and direct democracy comes at a price: nothing is done quickly. This also connects up with the traditional Indigenous conception of time, which is cyclical and not linear. The symbols of the *Caracol* and the spiral, with their unfolding character, embody this perfectly. But what is constructed is built on solid ground.

Achieving the equality of sexes in exercising the collective tasks is also a principle that sometimes seems to work against efficiency because the behaviour of the women has been affected by so many centuries of submission. Having participated in numerous meetings in municipalities and the *Caracoles*, I could not help noticing it. Even if the numbers of men and women are mathematically the same, the former leave little time for the latter to speak, while the latter are not always very keen to come forward. The heavy weight of culture cannot be corrected by decrees. It is true that the *Popol Vuh*, the great Maya mystical narrative, described creation as the result of the joint action by a double divinity, male and female, and that the categories opposing so-called 'Occidental'[21] thinking are expressed in terms of complementarity. But in all societies, myths stem more from theory or utopia than from reality.

Some people have concluded that the Zapatistas despise power, arguing that their attitude towards national politics reinforces this belief. In turn, the idea has developed that the Zapatistas are faithful disciples of John Holloway, who, in the book of his that became famous, put forward the idea that it was possible to change society without taking power.[22] Nothing could be further from the Zapatista position, as has been shown by authors such as Carlos Antonio Aguirre Rojas,[23] Jérôme Baschet,[24] and Bernard Duterme.[25] There is in fact no contempt at all for politics among the Zapatistas who exercise power; their interest is to 'do politics in another way'. For them, the question is: How useful is it to govern, dispossessing the population of their capacity to act in order to concentrate power in the hands of interests who are not concerned about the people? They thus believe it is necessary to reconstruct society from below, taking whatever time this requires.

For instance, the Sixth Declaration of the Lacandon Jungle clearly states: "Do we say that politics are of no use? No, we say that it is *this kind of* politics that is useless. And this is so because it does not take the people into account, it does not listen or take any notice of them, only contacting them at elections. . . . [For this reason] we are trying to construct, or reconstruct, another way of doing politics".[26]

For the Zapatistas, the basis of the organisation of power is therefore self-government. This functions at the levels of the communities, the municipalities, and even the Good Government groups within the *Caracoles*. But what will be the relationships with the Mexican states, not to mention with the national Mexican federation? Is the geographic and demographic dimension not a factor that changes the very quality of the exercise of power?

Obviously, the Zapatistas have not yet been able to experiment in the field, and their practical attitude in this respect has been to reject the existing forms— this seems to bring them close to anarchist theses. But looking more closely, and not excluding a certain sympathy for these positions, one can see that they have a dose of realism which does not exclude the possibility of a political formation at the service of the people at the national level that is not corrupt but effective. However, it is clear that in the present circumstances, the movement wants to concentrate on building up another power where it is possible to do so, namely at the local level.

As the Zapatista municipalities spread out to join with others over half the territory of the state of Chiapas, a question also arises about the relationships between such different bodies. The former are all self-governed but without any support at all from the regional or federal authorities, so they must create their own tax base. The latter receive official contributions and subsidies, but they are strictly controlled: it is essential that they remain within the tutelage of the state for the political project of counterweight to the Zapatistas, the attraction being better services. The two jurisdictions co-exist in the municipalities, and in the case of the small town of San Andrés, for example, this works out fairly well. An agreement was reached to share certain tasks: the Zapatistas are responsible for rubbish collection and public hygiene.

On the other hand, there is no possibility of establishing a modus vivendi—a way of living and working together—between the two different systems in fields such as health and education, because the basic philosophy is very different. Preventive health care is the organisational basis of the Zapatistas, while the content of their education, at different levels, has been adapted to the basic needs of the communities, their history, their situation in the country and in the world. And this is valid both for the primary schools, which have multiplied over the last few years, and for the secondary schools whose pupils are sent and financially supported by the communities. The Earth University (CIDECI-Unitierra) is no exception, in spite of its autonomous status. It is situated in the Colonia Nueva Maravilla, located on the outskirts of San Cristóbal de las Casas, and was built entirely by Zapatista volunteers. Its buildings stretch right to the foothills of the mountain and the main auditorium can hold over 1,000 people in simple conditions. It teaches both technical and humanist knowledge. Its director, Dr Raymundo of the Gregorian University of Rome, keeps a discreet but authoritative control over the whole establishment. His office is situated in the centre of the campus and it emits classical music all day, which inspires his work and thoughts.

The municipalities, and above all the Good Government Councils at the level of the *Caracoles*, also resort to traditional justice. This is one of the demands of all the Indigenous Peoples of the continent. They believe that certain causes are best defended at this level because they are not taken into consideration by modern law, particularly in the field of land tenure. hey also think that the compensation penalties (to work for the family of the victim or for the community) are much more effective socially speaking than punishments like prison or fines.

The Dialectic of Sub-Leadership

We have already referred to Marcos and the trajectory of his life. He is a high-level intellectual, with mastery over a range of knowledge. A philosopher by training, he has taught communication, which led him to become a virtuoso in writing and speaking. His training in critical and revolutionary thinking gave him a sound basis in socio-economic analysis, while his gift in direct human relations helped him understand the culture of others and become familiar with the mentality of the original peoples. His realism drove him into renouncing dogmatism and to seek the paths of a power that had to be fundamentally reformed—hence his title of Subcomandante (Sub-Commander). However, in a leadership tradition that is very Latin American, he cannot be ignored, which risks complicating the institutionalisation of the political movement and its long-term reproduction. There is no doubt that personal charisma is a real advantage, but it is not enough. The 'Sub' understood this very well at the grassroots level, but did he question Elias Contreras[27] about the 'colour' of power, when its principal representative, who is also a mere mortal, starts out on a path that will transform him into an immortal?

Marcos's sense of humour—which is evident in his literary work, his communiqués, and his instructions—has made him a very attractive personage, although he is sometimes carried away in a logic of style to the point of almost becoming a prisoner of it. The pedagogical value of his writings however, cannot be disputed—except, perhaps when he allows himself to be swept along by the 'communication sciences' demon. At that moment, one needs to be a connoisseur of Greek mythology to be able to follow the labyrinths of his thinking. One even needs to be able to decode the esotericisms of postmodern thought, which specialises in the destruction of dogmas, systems, structures, and theories—in sum, of the 'great narratives'—and where the form becomes the message. There is no doubt that Marcos knows how to navigate through all these reefs, but ordinary mortals can find themselves somewhat lost, and, as far as communication is concerned, it is somewhat like asking a wood beetle (for example, Marcos's Don Durito) to imagine he is a dragonfly.

Thus, while he always sticks to the same pipe, the different 'balaclavas' that are worn by the 'Sub' make him into a multiple personage. He is, at one and the same time, the promoter of a guerrilla warfare that has marked Mexican history, the inspirer of a political formula that redefines the basis of power, the supporter of the revolt and then the organisation of the Maya peoples of Chiapas, as well as being a man of letters. In 2005, the very day when at the University of Guadalajara

I was participating in the jury to examine the thesis of a Cuban sociologist on the sociology of religion, Marcos was presenting his most recent novel at the language and literature department of the same university. Some people thought that this was rather strange for a revolutionary leader. Others felt that there was no reason why such a person could not be a writer as well.

In February 2013, at the inauguration of the Havana Book Fair, I met a Cuban historian who had been a military attaché in Mexico and who presented a specialised work in that field. We talked about Zapatism. He asked me if Marcos had returned to Chiapas. Somewhat astonished at the question, I said that very probably he had done so as his most recent communiqués were sent from 'the mountains of southeast Mexico'. According to the Cuban, however, Marcos had in fact stayed a long time in the capital. He added that the president of the Republic had also played a nasty trick on him during this time, authorising him to hold a public meeting on the very evening when a great concert of the two best musical groups of the country was to be held in the city.

One cannot help wondering sometimes about the attitude of Marcos to Cuba. His revolutionary movement broke out thirty-five years after the Cuban Revolution, a little after the fall of the Berlin Wall, in the midst of the contestation of the 'really existing socialism' regimes. His movement did not aim at taking power at the national level. That seemed to distance him from the Cuban Revolution at the level of both objectives and methods. A number of intellectuals and social movements in different parts of the world like to emphasise these differences, considering them as support for their own critical views of Cuba, as the island was felt to be the vestige of a past that had difficulty in dying.

In 2003, during a constitutive meeting of the movement 'For the defence of humanity' in Mexico, I was able to hear the message of Marcos. He had sent a video, very professionally produced, to welcome the birth of this movement whose originator was Pablo González Casanova, one of his friends. The two hundred participants included intellectuals, artists, journalists, and social movement leaders. Among them was Evo Morales, at that time leading the *cocaleros* (coca leaf growers) movement in Bolivia, and who has been president of the country since 2005, Abel Prieto, minister of culture in Cuba, and Carmen Bohórquez, Venezuelan historian who was to become the executive secretary of the movement and whose main headquarters would be in Caracas. Marcos gave an illustrated history of the Cuban Revolution. He affirmed that if it had not happened it would not have been possible for the social and political movements in the other countries of the continent to develop as they had. He eulogised Fidel Castro. In sum, it was a clear position that impressed the audience. Marcos knew how to read history: without doubt, Cuba was no paradise, but the country had profoundly transformed the collective objectives of a society, in spite of all the obstacles imposed by the United States, which is very close to their shores.

"If your revolution doesn't know how to dance, don't invite me!" (Marcos)

On December 31 2012, the *Caracol* Oventic invited a number of people to an international seminar to be held at the Earth University in order to participate in the ceremony for the New Year. They were mostly those who had given presentations and a few foreigners. Since 1995, this body has functioned under the name of Aguascalientes 2 (the first had been destroyed under orders from President Zedillo). In 2003, it became a *Caracol* because the Zapatistas had no wish for it to become a tourist attraction. That day the seminar ended its work towards 9:00 p.m. There was just time to snatch a bite to eat before the invitees were gathered into cars and minibuses to take us to the *Caracol*. One of the minibuses lacked petrol and went around the town seeking a fill-up. But try finding it at 10:00 p.m. on the eve of the New Year, when everyone is getting ready to celebrate and already the first fireworks were exploding everywhere! While we waited for the minibus, the other vehicles collected outside the town, because it was safer to travel as a convoy. After waiting for an hour, we got under way, climbing up a mountain road, the curves of which made me feel quite sick.[28]

We arrived about a quarter to midnight. An incongruous collection of hundreds of vehicles were parked alongside the road. The bars protecting the *Caracol* were closed and guarded by Zapatistas in their balaclavas. We could hear the noise of a crowd several hundred metres further down. It was extremely cold. The full moon made it possible to see the main outlines of the countryside, like an Impressionist painting, and thousands of stars were shining in the sky. It was evident that the Zapatistas had been waiting for us to arrive much earlier and that those in charge had joined the ceremonies that we could hear from below. We discerned the notes of the Mexican national hymn on the stroke of midnight, the invocations of the shamans, the speeches of the community chiefs.

All the while we were talking with the guardians. They explained that they did not have the mandate to open the doors for us and that they had to consult those who were responsible. Four of them very kindly agreed to go down the hill, at the slow pace of mountain dwellers, to the courtyard of the secondary school where the ceremony was taking place. We were going to learn, physically, the meaning of direct democracy and the notion of circular time. After quite a while we saw their silhouettes outlined against the mountain path: the return up was slower than the descent. They had sheets of paper in their hands and they said we could enter but that we would have to fill in our names, nationalities, dates of birth, professions, and passport numbers. It all took a good quarter of an hour and the four companions set off again, always at the same rhythm, for verification by those responsible. Finally they came up again and opened the bars for us to enter.

All this took an hour and a quarter and we waited in the cold, without being able to sit but fascinated by the experience. No one complained. On the contrary, there on the mountainside we felt involved, happy that things were going well, and were meeting increasing numbers of women, men, and children, all hooded in their balaclavas. The ceremony had just finished and the dances were about to begin. Two musical groups alternated during the event one playing *mariachis*— traditional Mexican music—and the other more local popular songs, all under a huge Mexican flag. Hundreds of Zapatistas began to dance, shifting from one leg to another in time to the rhythm of the orchestras and almost without stopping. My stomach, somewhat upset by the journey, prevented me from giving a brilliant performance, but invigorated by the atmosphere, I participated as best I could.

Coming together from all parts of the territory of the *Caracol*, these Indigenous and peasant communities were breaking with their everyday activities to be together and celebrate the anniversary of the 1994 uprising and, at the same time, the beginning of the solar calendar. The latter was not part of their tradition but dated back to the time in history when they were conquered, a calendar however that they made their own. The festivities were still in full force when we decided to return to our vehicles to take the road back to San Cristóbal. It was three o'clock in the morning. Our return took a long time and we remembered that the seminar was continuing on the morning of the 1st of January.

The Socio-Political Organisation

The Zapatista institutions function at three levels. The first is that of the communities, based on the traditional structures and roles, both for exercising organisational tasks and at the symbolic level. The basic principles are autonomy and direct democracy. The second level (*marez*) is constituted by the autonomous communes and the municipalities, with the authorities elected by the communities. They correspond to the local administrative bodies introduced by colonisation and reproduced by independence, while transforming and transcending them. As such, they carry out classic administrative tasks and share the territory with non-Zapatistas.

The Good Government Councils, organised since 2003 in the form of *Caracoles*, form the third level, coordinating the two other levels. This is where the common services of administration, health, education, and justice operate when they cannot be dealt with by the two lower levels. All the decisions of these Councils have, however, to be approved at the grass roots, by the communities, in accordance with the principle 'lead by obeying' (*mandar obedeciendo*). A collective that exists at three levels makes it possible to ensure a constant flow of information. All this enabled the Zapatistas to claim, in their communiqué of December 30 2012 (of which more, later): "Not without many mistakes and numerous difficulties, we already have another way of doing politics".[29]

The Zapatista National Liberation Army (EZLN) has its own particular structure. It was created in the Lacandon Jungle during the 1980s, is run by Marcos, and is composed essentially of Indigenous People from different Maya nationalities up to the highest levels. It was the EZLN that launched the operations in 1994 that occupied the main towns of Chiapas. Since the ceasefire, they have withdrawn to the forest in the southeast of the state and no longer undertake military actions, although they have not disbanded and will not do so until the San Andrés Peace Accords have been applied. To keep it operational, each community annually provides a certain number of young men and women to do their military service. The army is above all composed of permanent *insurgents* and reservists who have to update their training from time to time.

The New Communiqués at the End of 2012: 'We Still Exist'

On December 30 2012, during the Third International Seminar for Reflection and Analysis, Subcomandante Marcos made the three communiqués public after a long silence. They were dated end December 2012, the first one issued jointly by the Indigenous Revolutionary Clandestine Committee and the General Command of the Zapatista National Liberation Army,[30] while the other two by the EZLN only. The first was the most meaningful. As well as reminding us that the Zapatistas had not disappeared and that they had even improved their situation quantitatively and qualitatively, the main proposal was to demand the application of the San Andrés Peace Accords that recognise the rights of the Indigenous Peoples and that, before being denounced by the president at that time, had been signed by the federal government run by the same party (the PRI), which has now retaken the government of the country.

In their own characteristic style, the Zapatistas from the beginning said, "They [the politicians] do not need us to suffer a defeat. We do not need them to survive". It is necessary to remember that the elections had, however dubiously, brought the PRI back into power, after two presidential mandates of the PAN, the right-wing party, and following the constitution of a new party on its left, the PRD. Thus, for the Zapatistas, the new era of the Maya calendar had coincided with a new political configuration of the country.

The communiqué also announced new initiatives to consolidate the National Indigenous Congress and to reconstruct the links with the social movements at the national and international levels. It reaffirmed a criticism of the political milieu and all the political parties that have exercised power.

The other two communiqués were more specific. One was entitled 'Do we not know you yet?'[31] It listed the names of the new politicians in power, asking sarcastically whether the list had not been issued on the wrong date (December 24), as it should have been on December 28 (the day of the Innocents)? One after the other, their political histories were evoked, those of the governors and those of the ministers, reciting their crimes: massacres, imprisonments, corruption.

The third communiqué was a letter addressed to Luis Hector Álvarez of the PAN about the defeat of his party, citing particularly President Felipe Calderón, under whom Mexico experienced the bloodiest period of its history.[32] Álvarez had just published a book of memoirs (*Corazón indígena* ['The Indigenous Heart']). He had been a member of the Parliamentary Commission for Concord and Pacification (COCOPA) and Marcos had appreciated his attitude at that time. He was then nominated by President Fox (PAN) as Commissioner for Peace in Chiapas, and thereafter placed in charge of the Commission for the Development of the Indigenous Peoples, where he had played a very negative role. Marcos invited him to abandon his party and to return to the path he had followed earlier on.

(As always, these communiqués start out with literary references, in this case especially to Mario Benedetti. For the non-initiated this can seem rather disconcerting, even the result of a certain '*déformation professionnelle*' ['professional deformation']. But, there it is, it's Marcos's style and he has probably reached the age when it is difficult for him to change.)

The proposal of the 'Sub' that the government legally recognise the San Andrés Accords was received favourably among part of public opinion and even amidst certain political circles. The new governor of Chiapas, of the Ecological Green Party of Mexico (created by Salinas de Gortari), reacted positively to returning to the dialogue. He liberated two sympathisers of the Zapatista movement who had been imprisoned since June 2012. In Parliament there was a vote along the same lines by the Permanent Commission of the Union Council. The proposal was made by Dolores Padima of the PRD, but she also received support from parliamentarians in the PRI and the Ecological Green Party of Mexico. However, three months after Marcos's intervention, no concrete action had been taken.

Even within the Mexican left, there is reticence. Some cannot forget the Other Campaign, or the fact that the Zapatistas then put all the political parties in the same basket. A few—and this information was given to me in Cuba by the former vice president of the Mexican Senate[33]—said that if Marcos wants to insist on the implementation of the San Andrés Accords, he should change his attitude and also 'stop monopolising the international assistance destined for the communities'. In sum, these are accusations that can discredit the Zapatista leadership, even if they were put forward without evidence.

The International Dimension

From the beginning, Subcomandante Marcos has stressed the international—and supra-national—dimension of the Zapatista action. The Zapatistas have always clearly spelt out the antisystemic character of their movement ('capitalism is a reality that is not only local'). And their opposition to neoliberalism has been central in the objectives of the resistance. The 'Intergalactic' meeting of 1996 was a particularly striking example of this, and the presence of numerous nationalities among the participants, including personalities like Alain Touraine, emphasised its importance. In 2007, they organised an 'International meeting of women for dignity'; in 2009, on the 15th anniversary of the insurrection, they organised a World Festival of Dignified Rage, always showing the same concern to open up perspectives and reiterating that "The world we want is one where many worlds fit".[34] Likewise, there were a number of international seminars organised between 2007 and 2012.

International solidarity plays an important role in supporting the movement. Thousands of people have crossed the seas, above all young people, attracted by the objectives and methods of the Zapatistas. Many have mobilised to provide material aid. The international peasant movement Via Campesina is close to the Zapatistas because of their rural character and the methods of organic cultivation that they advocate. They have delegated a permanent representative to the movement.[35]

The Zapatistas' experience of interaction with the World Social Forum, which was held for the first time at Porto Alegre in Brazil in 2001, was, however, not very fruitful. On the one hand, the Zapatistas were afraid of losing their freedom of initiative by participating in such a forum, and, on the other, the principles spelt out by the WSF in its Charter excluded the organisation of 'political' activities within the Forum, not only by political parties but also by movements of armed resistance.[36] The reality is that in 1994 the Zapatista revolt used arms, and also that by the early 2000s when the WSF took shape the EZLN had still not disbanded—it is also a fact that they had not undertaken any military operations since then. If there had been genuine goodwill on both sides, it is possible that it would have been a way to find a solution, for example, through a non-governmental organisation, as several political parties had done. But this did not happen.

The announcement in the first communiqué at the end of 2012 that they were going to take new initiatives at the international level has clearly created interest, evoked for instance by the title of the Third International Seminar (December 30–31 2012 and January 1–2 2013), 'Planet Earth and Anti-Systemic Movements'. Various Indigenous movements participated in this meeting, from the Qom of Argentina to the Mapuches of Chile, as well as CONAIE (the Confederation of Indigenous Nationalities of Ecuador) and, obviously, the Zapatistas and numerous members of the National Indigenous Congress of Mexico. Also present was a former leader of the Black Panthers in the United States, a representative of the Movement for Justice in New York's El Barrio, an important movement of peasants from Argentina, and intellectuals from Mexico and Europe. There is no doubt that the discussions in the Seminar reflected the direction desired by the movement, in relation to its antisystemic tradition and its defence of Mother Earth, but the communiqué gave little information about the kind of new international initiative that was to be proposed.

All this gradually became more specific in the communiqués subsequently issued, now no longer from the mountains of southeast Mexico but—as the Zapatistas phrase it—from "any corner around the world". During the first months of 2013, they clearly put the emphasis on the unity between national and international struggles. A few years before, the EZLN's Sixth Declaration had already defined the movement as being a network of anticapitalist struggle.[37] They spelled out their objectives clearly: "Moving from anticapitalism to the world we want to build—but what kind of world? With whom? And how?"[38] As for the continuity of the movement, this was notably clarified by the designation of a second Subcomandante, Moises, a Tseltal who up until then had been Marcos's lieutenant and who now came to be responsible for organising some of the new initiatives.[39]

What Can Be Made of the Experience and the 'Rebirth' of Zapatism?

In concluding, I venture some thoughts in this area.

First of all, it is clear that the Indigenous basis of the movement is an essential element for its continuity. Zapatism is, of course, not uniquely Indigenous, and all the Zapatistas are not Indigenous People, but the expression of the struggle to recover the dignity and identity of the autochthonous peoples is fundamental to the movement. This can serve as a reference for other societies and countries where plurinationality is a reality.

A second observation is the antisystemic character of the movement, as it is aware of the need to formulate another paradigm for human life on Mother Earth. This requires an overall vision, including relationships with nature, the material production of the bases of life, collective organisation and culture for interpreting reality, and building a social ethic. This can be interpreted in different ways, such as the 'buen vivir' and the Common Good of Humanity.

The third is the conception of the exercise of power, remaining faithful to basic democracy. This is another philosophy of public service, which functions at the local level and can serve as an example, even if it remains fragile and difficult to put into practice. The great question for the future is clearly the application of these principles at the regional and national levels.

A fourth question concerns the 'decolonisation of the mind', which is particularly relevant to the content of education, whether by reference to the past or to the construction of the future. Social and economic transformations cannot be made without cultural change.

Finally, charismatic leadership, which is usually a characteristic of revolutionary movements, but also of peasant and Indigenous revolts, has proved very useful for launching and building the movement, but it is perhaps problematic for its continuity—and the Zapatistas seem to be well aware of this.

The Zapatistas have given and continue to provide a great lesson for rethinking and for reconstructing socialism. They do it at their own level, with their experience, but also with a vision that goes beyond their immediate horizon. At a moment when they are posing questions about what a post-capitalist world could be, it is time to give them a place within the alternative world movement and international sociopolitical construction—on the condition, however, as Don Durito (the beetle in the forest) would say, that their own calendar and their own geography (or in other words, their philosophy and their will) allows them to do so.

References

Kolya Abramsky, 2018—'Gathering Our Dignified Rage: Building New Autonomous Global Relations of Production, Livelihood, and Exchange', in Jai Sen, ed, 2018—*The Movements of Movements, Part 2: Rethinking Our Dance*. Volume 5 in the *Challenging Empires* series. New Delhi: OpenWord, and Oakland, CA: PM Press

Carlos Antonio Aguirre Rojas, 2010—*Chiapas, Planeta Tierra* ['Chiapas: Planet Earth', in Spanish]. Mexico City: Ediciones Contrahistorias

Jérôme Baschet, 2005—*La rébellion zapatiste: Insurrection indienne et résistance planétaire* ['The Zapatista Rebellion: Indian insurrection or planetary resistance', in French]. Paris: Champ-Flammarion

Jérôme Baschet, March 2013—"Les zapatistes sont toujours la!', ['The Zapatistas Are Still There', in French] *Revue du CQFD* no. 109, March 2013, at http://cqfd-journal.org/Les-zapatistes-sont-toujours-la

Bernard Duterme, 1998—*Indiens et Zapatistes* ['Indians and Zapatistas', in French]. Brussels: Editions Luc Pire

Bernard Duterme, October 2009—'*Passés de Mode, les Zapatistes?*' ['Old fashioned, the Zapatistas?', in French], in *Le Monde Diplomatique*, October 2009, p 9

Bernard Duterme, April 2011—'*Retour sur la rébellion zapatiste: enjeux, limites et portée*' ['Back to the Zapatista rebellion: Challenges, limitations, and scope' in French]. Interview by Renaud Duterme, in *A Voix Autre*, April 22 2011, on CETRI, at http://www.cetri.be/spip.php?article2176&lang=fr (Accessed September 2 2017)

Paulo Freire, 1970—*Pedagogy of the Oppressed*. New York: Continuum

Franz Hinkelammert, 1987—'*La Teologia del Imperio*' ['The Theology of Empire', in Spanish], in *Amanacer*, no 53, pp 20–26

John Holloway, 2002—*Change the World Without Taking Power*. London: Pluto Press

Alex Khasnabish, 2017—'Forward Dreaming: Zapatismo and the Radical Imagination', in Jai Sen, ed, 2017—*The Movements of Movements, Part 1: What Makes Us Move?*. Volume 4 in the *Challenging Empires* series. New Delhi: OpenWord, and Oakland, CA: PM Press

Yvon Le Bot, 1997—*Subcomandante Marcos: El sueño Zapatista* ['Subcomandante Marcos: The Zapatista Dream', in Spanish]. Mexico City: Plaza y Janés

Xochitl Leyva Solano and Christopher Gunderson, 2017—'The Tapestry of Neo-Zapatismo: Origins and Development', in Jai Sen, ed, 2017—*The Movements of Movements, Part 1: What Makes Us Move?*. Volume 4 in the *Challenging Empires* series. New Delhi: OpenWord, and Oakland, CA: PM Press

Rosa Luxemburg, 1898—'Reform or revolution', in *Leipziger Volkszeitung* (1898), as cited by Peter Hudis and Kevin B Anderson, eds, 2004—*The Rosa Luxemburg Reader*. New York: Monthly Review Press, p 44

Subcomandante Insurgente Marcos, on behalf of the Indigenous Revolutionary Clandestine Committee and the General Command of the EZLN, December 2012—'¿ *Eschucaron? Es el sonido de su mundo. Es el del nuestro resurgiendo*' ['Did You Hear? It is the sound of your world collapsing. It is that of ours rising anew', in Spanish]. Translated by Leonidas Oikonomakis. Mexico, December 2012, at http://roarmag.org/2012/12/subcomandante-marcos-declaration-ezln/ (Accessed September 2 2017)

Subcomandante Insurgente Marcos, on behalf of the Indigenous Revolutionary Clandestine Committee and the General Command of the Zapatista Army of National Liberation, December 2012–January 2013—'EZLN Announces The Following Steps: Communiqué from the Indigenous Revolutionary Clandestine Committee—General Command of the Zapatista Army of National Liberation of December 30, 2012', at http://enlacezapatista.ezln.org.mx/2013/01/02/ezln-announces-the-following-steps-communique-of-december-30-2012/ and at http://roarmag.org/2013/01/ezln-zapatista-subcomandante-marcos-communique/ (Both accessed September 2 2017)

Subcomandante Insurgente Marcos (EZLN's Sixth Commission) and Teniente Coronel Insurgente Moisés (EZLN's Intergalactic Commission), November 2008—'Zapatistas: The First World Festival of Dignified Rage / *Digna Rabia*', at https://flowerofthe word.wordpress.com/tag/first-global-festival-of-dignified-rage/ (Accessed September 2 2017)

World Social Forum Organising Committee and World Social Forum International Council, June 2001—'World Social Forum Charter of Principles', June 10 2001. Revised and approved version of original April 2001 Charter, at http://opendemocracy .typepad.com/wsf/2005/02/previous_posts_.html (Accessed September 2 2017)

Zapatista Army of National Liberation (EZLN), May 1996—'Invitation-summons to the Intercontinental Encounter for Humanity and Against Neoliberalism, Mexico, May of 1996', at http://www.nadir.org/nadir/initiativ/agp/chiapas1996/en/invite.html (Accessed September 2 2017)

Zapatista Army of National Liberation (EZLN), July 2005—'Sixth Declaration of the Selva Lacandona', July 1 2005 [originally published in June 2005 in Spanish by the EZLN], at http://www.anarkismo.net/newswire.php?story_id=805 (Accessed September 2 2017)

Zapatista Army of National Liberation (EZLN), November–December 2012—'Letter to Luis Héctor Álvarez Álvarez', at http://enlacezapatista.ezln.org.mx/2013/01/08/letter-to-luis-hector-alvarez-alvarez1/ (Accessed September 2 2017)

Zapatista Army of National Liberation (EZLN), December 2012—'We Don't Know You Yet?', December 29 2012, at http://enlacezapatista.ezln.org.mx/2013/01/07/we-don%C2%B4t-know-you-yet/ (Accessed September 2 2017)

Notes

1. Ed: I warmly thank François Houtart for sending me the original version of this wonderful essay when he wrote it, and for then also so readily giving me permission to include it in this book. That however was in mid-2013, and since it has taken some time to get this book out, and there were others who were also interested in publishing it at the time, I assume that it is already out, perhaps in different languages. Notwithstanding this, and especially since we have changed the title (from the original 'The Zapatistas Still Exist') and edited the essay somewhat—and added and / or completed many references, I consider this as a kind of first publication and once again thank the author for the privilege. Translation from the original French by Victoria Bawtree, with some modifications by Jai Sen.

    Note December 2017: The author of this extraordinary essay and another great essay in Part 1, François Houtart, walked on in June 2017. As mentioned in my Introduction to this book, it is my great privilege to have known him quite well, and I feel honoured to have essays by him in both these books; and though he was also a normal human being with human frailties, I salute the dignity and rage with which he conducted his life.

2. Marcos, on behalf of the Clandestine Revolutionary Indigenous Committee— General Command of the EZLN, December 2012.

3. The name of the large shell that serves as a trumpet in Indigenous ceremonies; also a symbol of cyclical not linear time and of the social organization and the exercise of power which was given by the Zapatistas to the administrative unit of government, above the municipalities, also including the health centre and the secondary school.

4. Ed: This essay was written in 2013.

5. The Centre Tricontinental, founded in 1976 at Louvain-la-Neuve in Belgium, publishes this quarterly periodical.

6. Baschet 2005, p 47. Jérôme Baschet has put together a number of writings by Subcomandante Marcos, with an introduction in which he gives a very complete picture of the significance of the Zapatista movement in Mexican society. I thank the author for having contributed his specific knowledge to this essay.

7. Freire 1970.

8. Luxemburg 1898.

9. Baschet 2005, p 47.

10. Le Bot 1997.

11. Ed: Referring here to a Zapatista formulation of movement praxis that has come to be well-known, '*preguntando caminamos*' ('asking, we walk').

12. Ed: While this detailed and very personal narration by François Houtart of course stands witness to the history and prehistory of the Zapatista movement, for a detailed discussion of the prehistory of the Zapatista outbreak in January 1994, see the essay in in the companion volume, *The Movements of Movements, Part 1: What Makes Us Move?*, 'The Tapestry of Neo-Zapatismo: Origins and Development' (Leyva Solano and Gunderson, 2017), and for a discussion of the international resonance of the Zapatista movement, see the essay in the companion volume by Alex Khasnabish (Khasnabish 2017) and in this book by Kolya Abramsky (Abramsky 2018).

13. Zapatista Army of National Liberation (EZLN), May 1996. Ed: Initially called an 'Intercontinental Encounter', Marcos came to later refer to it as 'Intergalactic'.

14. Ed: The feminine version of then French president's Christian name, François.
15. Zapatista Army of National Liberation (EZLN), July 2005.
16. Ed: The author is here referring to the so-called 'Arab Spring' during 2010–2011, which irrupted first in Tunisia and Egypt, and then across North Africa.
17. Marcos, December 2012–January 2013.
18. Duterme 2011.
19. Ed: As in endnote 12: 'asking, we walk'.
20. Ed: We have not been able to determine the precise citation for this quote, possibly Franz Hinkelammert, 1987—'La Teologia del Imperio', in Amanacer, no 53, pp 20–26.
21. Apropos this term, which betrays its European origin, Marcos says that we suffer from problems of geography.
22. Holloway 2002. John Holloway's thinking is obviously more nuanced than the simplified title of his book. He distinguishes between 'power-over' and 'power-of' and he also insists on the importance of social movements in the transformation of societies.
23. Aguirre Rojas 2010, pp 181–84.
24. Baschet 2005, p 31.
25. Duterme 2009.
26. Cited by Aguirre Rojas 2010, p 177.
27. Elias Contreras is responsible for investigating the Zapatista army and is always ready, according to Subcomandante Marcos, to resolve complex problems.
28. Ed: When reading this, keep in mind that the author was a young 87 when he made this trip.
29. Or, as translated in the version cited, "Here, not without many mistakes and many difficulties, another form of doing politics is already a reality". (Marcos, December 2012–January 2013).
30. Ibid.
31. Zapatista Army of National Liberation (EZLN), December 2012.
32. Zapatista Army of National Liberation (EZLN), November–December 2012.
33. Yeidckol Polevnsky, an independent senator in Mexico, along with other Mexican legislators, attended the 'Second International Conference on the Equilibrium of the World', in Havana, Cuba, in 2008, and presented to the conference a book on José Marti by Alfonso Herrera Franyutti titled Martí en Mexico: Recuerdos de una época ['Martí in Mexico: Memories of an era', in Spanish], which was particularly appreciated. Ed: José Martí, 1853–1895, is a Cuban national hero and an important figure in Latin American literature.
34. Ed: See Zapatista Army of National Liberation (EZLN), July 2005—'Sixth Declaration of the Selva Lacandona'. See also the essay in this book by Kolya Abramsky on the Festival of Dignified Rage (Abramsky 2018).
35. Ed: For discussion of the international resonance of the Zapatista movement, see the essays in this book by Kolya Abramsky (Abramsky 2018) and in Part 1 by Alex Khasnabish (Khasnabish 2017).
36. See Clause 9 of the WSF's Charter of Principles: "The World Social Forum will always be a forum open to pluralism and to the diversity of activities and ways of engaging of the organisations and movements that decide to participate in it, as well

as the diversity of genders, ethnicities, cultures, generations and physical capacities, providing they abide by this Charter of Principles. Neither party representations nor military organisations shall participate in the Forum. Government leaders and members of legislatures who accept the commitments of this Charter may be invited to participate in a personal capacity" (World Social Forum Organising Committee and World Social Forum International Council, June 2001).

37. Zapatista Army of National Liberation (EZLN), July 2005.
38. Baschet 2013.
39. Ed: As was already evident in 2008 in the joint authorship of the key EZLN document issued that year, 'Zapatistas: The First World Festival of Dignified Rage / *Digna Rabia*' (Marcos [EZLN's Sixth Commission] and Moisés [EZLN's Intergalactic Commission], November 2008).

Afterword

Another World Is Inevitable . . . but which Other World?

Lee Cormie

Just now, the peoples of the world have embarked, some willingly and some not, on an arduous, wrenching, perilous, mind-exhaustingly complicated process of learning how to live as one indivisibly connected species on our one small, endangered planet.
—Jonathan Schell[1]

Conceptions about the world, about life, and about the relationship between nature and the cosmos have been shaken, forcing us to rethink all the theoretical structures with which we have organized our own visions.
—Ana Esther Ceceña[2]

If the catastrophe that is coming can be avoided and humanity is to have another opportunity, it will because these others, below and to the left, not only resist, but are also already drawing the profile of something else.
—Subcomandante Insurgente Marcos[3]

The cascading irruptions and expanding range of 'progressive' / 'left' movements around the world over the last half-century—from the postcolonial, antiracist, feminist, ecological, Indigenous, LGBTQ 'liberation' struggles in the 1960s to the 'antiglobalisation' protests, Arab uprisings, Occupy Wall Street, and European anti-austerity movements, Idle No More, Black Lives Matter in the 1990s, 2000s, and 2010s—have radically transformed the ways we see the world and the debates and struggles over the future: the range and diversity of voices and numbers of social actors, centres of power, axes of debate, modes of action, sites of struggle, and horizons of possible futures. They have transformed what we know and how we know, introducing new voices, standpoints, and perspectives, establishing communities and movements as centres of knowledge, incorporating broader ranges of traditions, exposing endless entanglements of power and authority, confirming the continuing (expanding?) significance of mystery, ignorance, and uncertainty, remapping the boundaries of the known and the unknown, reframing 'theory' and 'practice', thinking and doing. They have repeatedly confirmed that less and less of the world is simply God-given or natural, inevitable, and good, and that more and more of life is shaped—and misshaped—by human agency. They have transformed the social bases of personal and collective identities, every 'I' and every 'we',

527

remapped the boundaries of self-interest and solidarity. They have greatly expanded the range of choices we face in ordering our lives individually and collectively, at every scale from the most intimate and local to planetary and beyond. They have also immensely complicated scholarly and political debates, enriching our understanding both of ideological orthodoxies and rigged eco-social systems, on the one hand, and of the limits, contradictions, and absences of existing progressive / left critical discourses and politics, on the other. Moreover, they have repeatedly confirmed that there is no single critical discourse, no single cause, no single community, organisation, or movement, no single vision of another world that incorporates all these concerns. Confusion and paralysis are not the only responses, however. For in the chaos of cascading planetary social / ecological catastrophes, and beyond both illusory unity in dogmas or grand theories ('*pensamiento único*') and 'postmodern' relativism, there are signs of another kind of hope and politics in proliferating activisms, movements, networks, coalitions, and campaigns.

This Afterword—written in relation both to this book and to its accompanying volume *The Movements of Movements, Part 1: What Makes Us Move?*[4]—is an invitation to readers, from your own contexts, standpoints, traditions, and struggles, to join the contributors to both books in these dialogues about new social actors, new media of communication and organisation, new modes of action and logics of transformation, expanding horizons of reality and possibility, widening circles of solidarity, and deepening hopes for 'a world where many worlds fit.'

Introduction

As the compiler and editor of these two books Jai Sen insists, "there is no question that deep-rooted ferment has broken out across much of the world—in the North as well as the South".[5]

In many ways the essays in these two volumes of *The Movements of Movements* testify to these developments, in their insights into particular debates and struggles and in their frequent points of overlap and convergence demonstrating increasingly broader bases of dialogue, solidarity, and collaboration. There have been so many successes in different struggles.[6] And recognising them, educating people about them, and celebrating them are essential in distilling a fuller sense of emergent trends and shifting horizons, and in expanding circles of activism and support.[7]

At the same time though, there are many developments contributing to confusion, paralysis, even despair. There are too many concentrations of colossal wealth and unaccountable power, too many truths denied, too much growing suffering, too many unnecessary deaths, too much surveillance, torture, imprisonment, too many executions, too many eco-social catastrophes, too many defeats of progressive movements and reforms. While appreciation is deepening for the wisdom and inspiration of earlier decades—even centuries—of progressive movements, there is also a growing awareness of limits of recent progressive discourses and politics and calls for 'reinventing politics', as reflected, for example, in the Zapatistas' 'Intergalactic *Encuentros*' and in the World Social Forum process around the world since 2001.[8,9] Moreover, as these movements, and the commentaries in these books, repeatedly confirm, there is no single critical discourse which is adequate to all the concerns and issues, no single cause which—above all others—determines the future, no single movement which—above all others—holds the key to the future, no single widely embraced vision of an alternative world, no single path forward.

And, as Sen argues in his Introduction to the first volume of *The Movements of Movements*, there is no single, grand, encompassing movement either.[10] As Kalouche and Mielants point out in the first book, "Agents are no longer participating in 'one' movement; instead they were participating in as many commitments as their social consciousness called for". Accordingly, it is "impossible to outline contemporary movements based on their 'identity', 'adversary', or 'social goal'".[11] Similarly, Nunes argues in this book that it is only possible to speak of the global 'movement' metaphorically, "calling a whole what is really only a collection: something whose only criteria for membership would be existence on the same globe, something that could never be totalized or given any kind of unitary shape or direction—a 'wild' in-itself, never to be fully appropriated for-itself".[12]

The collection of essays in these two books faithfully reproduces—and also itself embodies—the complex and chaotic character and multiple dimensions of these dialogues, in their diverse expressions in different places, their increasingly dynamic, frequently jagged, at times conflicting, always incomplete character, the ever-expanding and ever more complex dynamics of producing culture and knowledge, the proliferating challenges to conversion arising from the 'new' voices of so many 'others' on so many fronts, the scope and pace of changes transforming the world.

Yet there are also signs of a convergence on a number of critical points. It is increasingly difficult to avoid the sense that the 'world' as we have known it is changing in many fundamental ways. Or that dominant—including 'critical'—ways of seeing it and framing options have (in different ways in different contexts, traditions, and conjunctures) blinded people to important dimensions and dynamics of this world. Or that previously marginalised traditions offer many deep insights and wisdom. Or that anyone can avoid making fundamental, far-reaching choices about the future, as individuals and as members of groups. Or that, whatever our tradition or context, we all need broader, more inclusive 'planetary' images of the world in order to locate ourselves vis-à-vis all the 'others' and the expanding global dynamics that are shaping all our realities today (while at the same time rejecting the notion of any single, uniquely privileged, authoritative, dominant, or hegemonic vision). Or that historically marginalised peoples, groups, and causes (like ecology and peace) must be—and are today—central in every process of forging promising alternatives. Or that virtually everywhere, decision-making priorities, frameworks, and processes must be radically transformed.[13]

Perhaps, then, the many-faceted, complex, partial, unfinished character of dialogues across movements is not a sign of weakness, but rather a sign of a new stage in the emergence of planetary dialogues, solidarity, and collaboration. Perhaps, in their coming together across so many diversities and discovering commonalities, movements are again pushing beyond the limits of existing scholarly and political frameworks and horizons, drawing on a far wider array of traditions for alternative perspectives and insights, addressing a far broader range of issues, with far wider popular participation, addressing far more complex processes of order and change, nurturing post-imperial (*'pensamiento único'*, or 'one right way of thinking') modes of knowledge, ethics, and politics, contributing to far deeper understandings of history and far more realistic readings of the world as it is, and imagining far more plausible and more widely shared hopes for different—and 'better'—futures.

In this essay, I suggest that there are five interwoven threads running through the tapestries of contemporary progressive social movements around the world. From my standpoint, though, these are a series of 'observations', less than arguments (and much less than one single argument), and certainly not deductions from an overarching theory; they are perhaps elements of an emergent 'new common sense'[14] increasingly shared across many differences around the world:

1. The historically unprecedented irruptions of social justice and eco-justice movements around the world and their increasing significance in the struggles over emergent global civilisation and the future of life on earth;
2. The associated knowledge revolutions, the deepening awareness of the limits of positivist science, a turn to other traditions of knowledge and wisdom, and emergent 'epistemologies of the South';
3. The encompassing, multifaceted, and global character of neoliberal globalisation, and of capitalist projects since the dawn of 'modernity' more generally, along with the limits of economistic discourses of 'the economy', both mainstream and critical;
4. Beyond the destructive impacts of the project of 'neoliberal globalisation', the vast array of changes sweeping the world, and emergent but widely divergent possible futures, from techno-utopian posthumanity to eco-social catastrophes; and—
5. More inclusive, more modest, more plausible, and more promising visions of other ethics, other politics, and other worlds.

Of course, from different standpoints in different social worlds and drawing on different traditions, the world looks different and history unfolds differently.

This Afterword is thus an invitation to readers, from your own standpoints, traditions, struggles, and conjunctures, to join the contributors to the two volumes of *The Movements of Movements* in further widening these dialogues about the expanding horizons of reality and possibility, the different places in it for different movements, the cross-cutting challenges they confront, the common grounds they are discovering, and their contributions to increasingly shared struggles for "a world where many worlds fit".[15]

Locating Myself

Born in the US in 1943 and educated in Canada and the US, I have been a researcher / teacher / writer and sometime activist concerning social justice movements and coalitions since the 1970s. In addition to publishing many articles on Christian liberation theologies and social movements, I have also been involved in major church-based social justice initiatives: in the US with Theology in the Americas in the 1970s and 1980s, an historic initiative in nurturing dialogue and collaboration across diverse 'liberation' movements organised around the antagonisms of class, race, ethnicity, and gender, and of a 'developed' 'First World' with an 'underdeveloped' 'Third World'; on occasion with colleagues in the Ecumenical Association of Third World Theologians, one of the first sustained efforts to nurture Africa-Asia-Latin America dialogue—launched in Tanzania in 1976—and in Canada (where I eventually also became a citizen) with the Canadian Ecumenical Jubilee Initiative, which in the late 1990s, with colleagues in Jubilee South and other Jubilee 2000 movements, nurtured collaboration with a broad range of groups (both church-based and secular) in campaigns calling attention to 'social debt', 'ecological debt', and more generally 'illegitimate and odious debt', and demanding the cancellation of Third World debts. I have also been a participant / observer in World Social Forum events since 2002, and a member of the International Committee of the World Forum on Theology and Liberation since its inception in 2005. Currently I am a professor emeritus of theology and interdisciplinary studies in the Faculty of Theology, the University of St Michael's College and the Toronto School of Theology, in Toronto, Canada. Recently, as my contribution to the companion volume to this book indicates,[16] I have been focusing on the presence of faith-based groups in social justice coalitions, on the grave inadequacies of secularist scholarly and political discourses so profoundly distorting our understanding not only of religious traditions, communities, and concerns but also of 'culture', 'politics', and 'the economy' more generally, and on expanding appreciation for other traditions of knowledges, hopes, and faiths in new 'ecologies of knowledges'.[17]

Most importantly, in terms of my formation and continuing education, I have often been blessed and endlessly amazed by the generosity, courage, and humour of 'poor' and marginalised people I have encountered over many years, who have welcomed me, even in the most appalling conditions of extreme poverty and great risk from dictatorships and death squads. Over the years they and their activist and scholarly allies and friends, some of whom also became my dear friends, have shaped my deepest sensibilities concerning suffering and hope and the struggles to change the world.

And now I am also deeply indebted to the contributors, and especially to Jai Sen, friend and editor of *The Movements of Movements*, for providing such rich, enlightening, provocative, often challenging insights, expanding my horizons and provoking new questions on the twisting path of my own ongoing (re-)education. Taken together in various combinations of two or three or more, these essays often converge and overlap, suggesting new synergies; at other points they diverge on important issues, pointing to many differences and to possible tensions and clashes. At the same time, though, they reflect an increasingly shared awareness that, as Nunes says, "the capacity to exchange and cooperate" with others around the world is expanding.[18] And, beyond purely abstract and false universalisms, these contributions push me, and I trust you readers too, to read across contexts and movements, looking for cross-cutting experiences and insights, points of reference, wider solidarities, and expanding horizons on possible futures.

Of course, with many others, I have also become convinced that there is no 'God's eye view' (or at least no one on earth can indisputably see through God's eyes!), and that there is no one right standpoint, perspective, or reading of history.[19] Yet I also believe deeply that authentic hope for the future—if there is indeed to be a future for us—must be widely shared, collaboratively witnessed to in campaigns and movements, celebrated, and continuously renewed. And in this spirit, repeatedly encountered in these books, I offer the following reflections.

Makers of History Too

Mainstream discourses have long centred on great ideas or theories or cultures or ideologies, and on great men (saints and religious leaders, explorers and conquerors, generals, scientists, entrepreneurs) as the movers of history. And the rest, the great majorities of peoples and cultures, have been simply marginalised or forgotten altogether or ridiculed as 'primitive', 'backward', 'pre-modern', 'irrational' obstacles to 'progress'. But, with the worldwide irruptions of social movements in the 1960s (sometimes referred to as the 'world revolution')[20] and the subsequent proliferation of movements over the subsequent decades, this picture is increasingly found only in the dustbins of history.

Over the last half-century, cascading eruptions of progressive social movements—labour, liberationist and postcolonial, social justice, feminist, environmental, Indigenous, anti-racist, peace, food, LGBTQ, Dalit, animal rights, etc—have radically transformed the debates and struggles over reality and possibility. And new movements continue to irrupt. By the early 2000s, according to one guesstimate there were "over one—and maybe even two—million organisations working towards ecological sustainability and social justice" around the world.[21] Some commentators argue that when seen collectively, the phenomenon constitutes "the largest social movement in all of human history".[22] Indeed, irruptions have become major features in societies around the world to the extent that even the mainstream *Time Magazine* was compelled to select 'the protester' as its 'person of the year' for 2011.[23] And it has become increasingly difficult to avoid the conclusion that long marginalised and forgotten, poor and excluded peoples, other species, and the earth are actors, too, and have become increasingly powerful features of twenty-first-century societies around the world.[24] Moreover, there is no end in sight, as more and more of the world's historically silenced and marginalised 'others' irrupt, like Idle No More and Black Lives Matter.

Meanwhile, frustration with the limitations, failures, and absences of established forms of critical scholarship, movements and parties grew throughout the 1980s, 1990s, and 2000s to the present. As Meyer and Alidou noted in their essay in this book:

> Our words have failed to adequately describe the world we want to see.
> From Kiswahili to Gujarati to Mandarin and Spanish—from French and most especially including the imperial polyglot known as English—we have not always succeeded in communicating our messages in consistently coherent and inspiring ways. The workers of the world have not united; too many still live in mental and physical chains. At least some of the responsibility for this fact must be faced as an internal weakness: the international left has not been able to consistently 'speak' to 'the people'.[25]

Equally, in his essay here Adamovsky observes simply: "the people do not trust in the left, and they have very good reasons not to".[26]

At the same time though, and as the contributors to *The Movements of Movements* repeatedly confirm, there are many signs of renewal and increasing momentum, especially in the intersections and cross-fertilisations of these movements, in the Intergalactic *Encuentros* of the Zapatistas from the mid-1990s, in the World Social Forum gatherings since 2001, and in countless other 'crossroads' and 'squares' from Tahrir Square in Cairo to Zucotti Park in New York in 2011 to Taksim Gezi Park in Istanbul in 2013.

Perhaps it is even fair to say, as one commentator did in 2003, observing irruptions of peace movements around the world in opposition to the US-led war in Iraq, that a new 'superpower' has emerged.[27] But if so, this is a new, fundamentally different kind of superpower: more open, more decentralised, more diverse, more participatory, more inclusive, more transparent, more accountable, more modest, more realistic, with more promising visions of the future for all.

We are still learning how to recognise 'success', though, which depends on our frameworks for viewing 'nature', 'society', and 'history'—burning issues in a world of knowledge explosions, new technologies, new modes of social organisation, and vastly expanding human capacities to act. And yet, while many questions remain about how to see more clearly, there is also a growing sense in many circles of successes, locally, regionally, internationally, some small and others 'historic', perhaps even 'epic'.[28]

And at the same time, our views of history are becoming more inclusive, complex, and dynamic, including understanding it in terms of chaos and of non-linear dimensions and dynamics.[29] This emerging perception allows space for recognition of the key roles of movements, their successes (as well as detours and defeats), of unexpected new openings and possibilities. Indeed, in many quarters older notions of 'revolution' are disappearing. 'Success' is being redefined.[30] And hopes are being radically reimagined.

Knowledge Revolutions

As the experience of movements around the world repeatedly confirms, and as is clearly echoed in these books, the central axes of social life revealed by these movements—class, gender, race, place, national origin, world-system, nature / civilisation, sexual orientation, violence, disabilities, etc—remain central. However, this experience also affirms that no single critical discourse is adequate to all these concerns and issues. One response to this new understanding has been to create ever-growing lists of oppressions, of '-isms' (classism, racism, sexism, etc). As Drainville points out in his essay in this collection, however, "analyses of transnational doings often do little more than assemble . . . a list, putting side by side everything is sight and labelling the lot 'anti-globalisation', or 'globalisation from below'". And he goes on to warn, "listing is not theorising".[31] And it is increasingly clear that the cumulative effects of developments in social movement politics and in the critical scholarship inspired by them add up to far more than growing lists of oppressions. Far beyond mere lists, they are pointing to vast expansions of our horizons on the world (past, present, and possible futures), to radical questioning of basic categories and theoretical frameworks, to deepening suspicions concerning the epistemological foundations of modern science and expertise, and to quests for alternative epistemologies, ontologies, and cosmovisions. And where it is increasingly clear that struggles over ways of seeing the world—'knowledge'—are in fact pivotal in the struggles over the future.[32]

Information Explosions and Knowledge Revolutions

Many anthropologists and historians define human nature specifically in terms of knowledge, of capacities—to learn, to communicate through various forms of culture, to store information, and to share it across distance and time.[33] From the beginning human history has turned on key developments in the history of data gathering, information processing, storage, and communication, from the inventions of rituals, myths, and cosmovisions, sagas and epic poetry and writing to the establishment of priesthoods and schools of philosophy and metaphysics to the invention of the printing press—and in our times, to the creation of the Internet. Certainly 'knowledge' has been central in the organisation and development of 'modern' societies. And by the end of the nineteenth century Europeans, at the centre of the colonial / modern world-system, had established the modern social sciences (including economics and history) as the central authoritative discourses for analysing problems, projecting possible futures, making choices, planning, accounting costs and benefits, managing, policing, etc in this world-system. Indeed, modern academic disciplines are constitutive features of modern institutions and societies, built into their organisation and functioning.

Moreover, there are many indications today that 'knowledge' is becoming even more central, with the vast expansions of knowledge production in schools and universities, libraries, scholarly associations, conferences, publishers, journals, newsletters, corporate research departments, government departments, all of which are now exponentially expanding with new technologies and channels of data gathering and processing like the Internet (for instance, Wikipedia, and blogs, Facebook, and Twitter).[34] Areas of study and specialisation and their applications in new technologies are proliferating and contributing to the exponential expansions of human agency (more accurately, the agency of some humans) in every direction, from nanoscale to planetary scales and, since the launch of Sputnik in 1957, into the heavens above.[35] Moreover, in the process, the "nature of scientific inquiry and its application to the great challenges facing mankind [sic]" are also changing[36]—for example, in the collection, processing, and application of insights from 'big data'. Some commentators are even heralding the dawn of a new 'digital age' with 'knowledge' increasingly transforming all of life, including an 'information economy' centred on and driven by 'knowledge' and 'knowledge industries'.[37] And many commentators, including many critics, continue to hinge their hopes for the future on the expanding human capacities for knowledge and reason.[38]

However, as the recent histories of progressive social movements also repeatedly confirm, the prevailing forms of 'knowledge' are also, and equally, central parts of the problem. New waves of critical histories of science are revealing other darker dimensions of modern knowledge and epistemology, pointing to other more promising ways of knowing and other possibilities for the future.[39]

'Modernity', 'Development', and Beyond

Critical rereadings inspired by social movements are radically transforming our understanding of modern European history, marked by many twists and turns in the shifting matrices of expanding knowledge, new technologies, expanding nation-states, colonies and empires, industrial, cultural and political revolutions and wars, and waves of 'globalisation'. And they are helping us to see the larger patterns of thought dominating mainstream scholarship and politics since the nineteenth century. For example, as Lander notes, "In recent debates about hegemonic knowledge in the modern world, a number of basic assumptions have emerged that allow us to characterize the dominant conception of knowledge as Eurocentric".[40]

In the course of trying to understand the dynamic and rapidly changing world since the sixteenth century, European thinkers elaborated a doctrine of 'progress', centring on key insights concerning knowledge, technologies, modes and scales of social organisation, and progressively expanding human agency. This doctrine emerged in efforts to collect, order, and synthesise in-rushing data and reports from around the world from missionaries, conquerors, traders, and immigrants, and from expanding industries seeking to understand and exploit more of nature. These thinkers forged a host of new scientific disciplines to organise these processes of knowledge production, to deepen and systematise knowledge. And as a framework for ordering the avalanches of data concerning nature, human nature, and the course of history, they formulated their own creation story, a modern myth that they framed in evolutionary terms, with Europe at the forefront leading the way at every stage. And they built this outlook into the foundations and cultures of what are today called the modern natural sciences, the social sciences, and the humanities, and also into the organisation into disciplines and departments of modern universities, which, though under assault from within and without in the early decades of the twenty-first century, remain dominant.[41]

In this perspective, 'others' around the world—including European peasants and workers—were and still are mired in backward religions and cultures, ignorance, irrationality and superstitions, internecine conflicts and wars, and 'poverty'. However, 'progress' was and is argued to be potentially in their future too. For, these scholars insisted, the 'laws' of development are necessarily 'universal'. In its most ambitious expressions, this is thus a social evolutionary worldview, in which, resonating with Darwin's view of biological evolution, all the basic dimensions of human life—consciousness, reason, and society—are evolving in a linear direction from the 'primitive', 'ignorant', 'backward', and 'poverty-ridden' past to the enlightened and rational, modern, peace-loving, and wealthy societies allegedly evident in modern Europe. In addition to claiming to sum up all that could reliably be known about the earth and the human condition, this doctrine of European superiority also legitimised the 'white man's burden' of civilising the 'others' even against their own wills, for the long-term interests of coming generations, if not of the current generation still mired in ignorance and superstition.

Of course, as critical voices have helped us to see, many important parts of the story, not only around the rest of the world but also in Europe were omitted, such as the increasing concentrations of wealth and power, the gaps between rich and poor, the endless wars of conquest and colonisation, expanding environmental havoc, etc. Moreover, prominent scholarly and political voices managed to minimise, or suppress altogether, the many contributions of 'traditional' communities (like many Indigenous communities) and progressive social movements— Marxist, labour, social democratic, first-wave feminist, anti-colonial and postcolonial, environmental, peace—in moderating the excesses of colonial / capitalist exploitation and war at home and abroad.[42] But the unprecedented violence and destruction unleashed in World War I and World War II at the heart of the 'most advanced' societies in history plunged their political and scholarly establishments into crisis, along with their doctrines of 'modernity' and 'progress'.

Still, as influential idolatries and ideologies always do, this doctrine also captured some important 'truths' of new developments in the 'modern' world: pointing to the transformative effects of information explosions and knowledge revolutions, cascading new technologies, new modes and scales of social organisation (nation-states, colonies, empires, world-system, 'globalisation'), and the sweeping transformations of social life and 'nature' accompanying them. Indeed, even Marxist critics, so deeply critical of central aspects of this class-divided 'modern' world, also appropriated this Eurocentric evolutionary framework in plotting the history of science, technology, 'capitalism', and the still-to-come 'communism'.[43]

Meanwhile, freed at home from the massive domestic destruction resulting from the wars in Europe, North Africa, and the Pacific, US elites resurrected and recentred the original Eurocentric doctrine of 'progress' as they wrestled with the challenges and possibilities confronting what had suddenly become the most powerful nation on earth.[44] In the turmoil and uncertainty following World War II, US scholars and political leaders drew on these traditions in forging a new, vastly expanded myth of 'development', along with expanded apparatus for its implementation around the world (and for the 'containment' of all opponents). This was a revised and expanded version of progress, with the US replacing Europe as the global leader, and it encompassed far more than 'the economy', indeed the whole of modern life: culturally, psychologically, socially, politically, religiously, as well as economically.[45]

In the rapidly expanding university system, these experts articulated a new, interdisciplinary discourse of 'modernisation',[46] as a project far exceeding the imperial reach of the past, and for the first time in history encompassing the whole world (with the temporary exception of the Second 'communist' world, which however needed to be 'contained'—by covert wars and brutal dictatorships if necessary—until its internal failures and contradictions became obvious and it collapsed). They pictured an encompassing vision of scientific breakthroughs, technological innovations, expanding markets and economic growth, increasing prosperity, and greater freedom—colloquially, the 'American Dream'. They legitimated this vision as 'science'—(allegedly) value-free, neutral, objective, and universally relevant. And, alongside economics and the other social sciences, they created new disciplines (such as 'development studies', 'area studies', 'international relations', and 'Sovietology')[47] and new institutions with global reach for implementing this global project: for analysing the sources of 'backwardness' and 'underdevelopment', identifying the levers of change, developing expertise for assisting policymakers, and creating new technologies—'aid' and 'development programmes'—promising to transform national cultures and the psychologies of their peoples and leaders and to quickly lift 'static and backward' nations (and peoples) from 'backwardness' and 'poverty' (and with the infusion of massive military and police 'aid' to 'contain' critics).

Moreover, they popularised this vision around the world via the new media of television and the dissemination of school and university curricula and textbooks, a process strategically supported by the CIA and other government agencies in the writing, publication, and dissemination of key texts.[48] They enshrined this project in new global institutions like the World Bank and the International Monetary Fund, as centres for 'educating' the world's leaders and policymakers, for promoting via loans and aid programmes the often radical transformation of 'traditional' forms of political and economic organisation and replacing them with standardised 'modern' approaches to 'development', and for the global structuring of economic relations.[49] And with the advent of air travel a whole new globetrotting generation of consultants and advisors was born.

Indeed, by the early 1960s US scholars and commentators were so confident in their scientific methods and their understanding of 'modernisation' and 'development' that they triumphantly announced the 'end of ideology', of debates about the course of history, dynamics of order and change, and of all other future possibilities, simply casting socialists, communists, and other critics into the dustbin of history (or sentencing them to be 'sacrificed'—tortured and executed in the jails of dictators—if they could not be contained long enough for the magic of 'progress' to work).[50] Prominent experts even worried that, bored by endless technological innovations, capitalist growth, and affluence "man" [sic] would fall into a "secular spiritual stagnation" and a desperate search for stimulation, perhaps even opting "to conduct wars with just enough violence to be good sport—and to accelerate capital depreciation—without blowing up the planet!"[51]

Countermovements and Proliferating Critical Discourses

Imagine the shock of these esteemed scholars and experts at the exploding waves of critical social movements that erupted around the world just then, at the dawn of the 1960s![52]

Of course, there were many antecedents—in traditional Indigenous communities, and in labour, Marxist, social democratic, first-wave feminist, anti-colonial and postcolonial, environmental, peace, etc movements—but these contributions were largely effaced in public discourse. So the new irruptions appeared like bolts from heaven. Suddenly clouds of new critical actors and discourses irrupted, revealing how many peoples and groups are simply 'disappeared' (made invisible), how many voices are distorted or simply silenced, how many great gaps and inequalities remain unnoticed from on high, how often 'science' and expertise are used against the victims, how many victims are blamed for their sufferings and their 'sacrifices', rationalised as 'necessary', how much violence is routinely deployed in establishing and maintaining 'peace' and 'order', how the balance sheets of 'progress' depend on the externalisation of so many costs to so many people and to life on earth.[53]

Beginning in the 1960s, with a deepening awareness of the inadequacies of prevailing political and scholarly frameworks concerning 'society' in all its dimensions (including the study of social movements), activists and sympathetic scholars launched a whole series of new critical lines of inquiry: updated Marxist, neo- and post-Marxist, dependency, feminist, critical race, world-system, Indigenous, ecological, poststructural, postcolonial, subaltern, critical postmodern, LGBTQ, critical geography, critical migration, and animal rights—among others. The authors of each sought to formulate a perspective on central aspects of each community's or constituency's experience in ways which gave them and their movements leverage in contested and shifting intellectual and political landscapes. Each revealed a dynamic at the heart of their experience: 'class', 'colonialism', 'racism', 'patriarchy' or 'sexism', 'dependency', 'world-system', 'caste', 'anthropocentrism' (centred on the human, marginalising concern for other creatures and the earth), 'heteronormativity', and 'coloniality of power'. And coming together in antiglobalisation movements and elsewhere, as Cho Hee-Yeon points out in his essay in these books, they established a new broader base for knowledge, requiring an 'epistemological revolution'[54] or series of revolutions. Suddenly, with 'new' voices drawing on their own experiences and traditions, an expanding range of new lenses was available for 'seeing the world in technicolour'. And movements carried these new ways of seeing into struggles over the organisation of virtually every corner of social life around the world.

Of course, as long-time activists and sympathetic scholars know, these diverse lenses, like the movements they are a part of, did not all develop at the same time, in the same terms, or in the same places. They did not immediately fit together so well either. There were seemingly endless clashes between 'old' and 'new' lenses over 'base' and 'superstructure', 'primary' and 'secondary' contradictions, over the allegedly universal concern of 'Marxists' with 'systemic' issues and allegedly narrower focus of so-called 'identity politics' on women, or racism, or the environment, etc. In India, for example, in their essay in these books Roma and Ashok Choudhary point to "a false divide between preservation / environmental groups and forest dwellers",[55] a divide which has been widely echoed elsewhere. And, more generally, the continuing inability—in critical theories and movement practices—to fully incorporate the concerns of 'others' contributed to a growing sense by the end of the 1990s of the limits of these critical discourses and movements, and to the urgent need for expanding dialogue across 'differences' and for theoretical and political 'reinventions'.

From the beginning, though, there had also been many signs of openness and dialogue across differences. As Tariq Ali says of the 1960s in his essay, "All the movements learnt from each other. The advances of the civil rights, women and gay movements, now taken for granted, had to be fought for on the streets against enemies who were fighting the 'war on horror'".[56] And this cross-learning has continued, with recent waves of critical scholarship and political thinking, like feminist intersectional approaches[57] and Latin American decolonial approaches,[58] explicitly attempting to build on and incorporate the experience and insights of preceding movements and scholarly traditions in formulating still more inclusive perspectives and agendas for change.[59]

Thus, Andean Indigenous groups are proposing to reframe the multiple crises sweeping their communities and the world beyond simply 'economic' or 'environmental', as a *crisis civilizatoria* ['civilisational crisis'] which encompasses every aspect—social, economic, political, cultural, ecological—of life, generating "a global disorder of historic magnitude". And the Forest Peoples and Forest Workers in India echo this insight in a recent Declaration:

> This is no ordinary crisis. Not merely a climate crisis—or in your words, this magnified, self-created monster of a financial crisis. We believe it is a Crisis of Civilisations. It's no ordinary clash but a fundamental clash between our knowledge systems; of being, of nature and your wisdom, technology, and demonic tendencies. Your world rests on ideas of power, territories, boundaries, profit, exploitation and oppression and you try to own everything, including Mother Nature. . . . If you want to include us in your world by 'civilising' us, we will happily choose to remain uncivilised. Call us savages, we do not care! We have learnt amidst these trees, this water, this air, and other forest beings—a life of freedom, of being without boundaries, and yet never forgetting the boundaries of nature.[60]

In these and many other admixtures, old and new traditions are rapidly developing.[61]

And expanding openness to other perspectives and dialogues with / across other-than-modern ('transmodern') traditions also points to further flowering of whole new families of critical (and utopian) discourses. Indeed, some are already evident in rapidly proliferating Indigenous, aboriginal, Maori perspectives and politics[62] and new waves of critical discourses from other civilisational traditions (Asian,[63] African,[64] and Latin American)—each with incredible internal diversity, each and all evolving in dialogue with many 'others'.[65]

Specifically, in terms of the relationship between sympathetic scholarship and activist practice, with widening participation by 'poor' and 'marginal' peoples, Leyva Solano points to profound shifts:

> Modern science (and therefore the social sciences) are the offspring of capitalism and have always depended on it. Without denying this connection, it is important to add that today, at the beginning of the twenty-first century, new social relations are emerging in the interstices between committed academics, flexible activisms, and indigenous as well as anti-systemic movements. This allows us to affirm that new forms of knowledge production are in process. This new knowledge can no longer be labelled as exclusively activist or academic.[66]

And it is no longer exclusively by and for elites!

Looking through these proliferating critical lenses, the world is constantly growing larger, more multifaceted, dynamic, and complex.

'Science', Secularism, and Beyond

Modernism's claims to authority centre on its 'scientific' character. If in certain religious traditions God alone sees and knows all, the architects of the modern scientific revolutions in the sixteenth to the nineteenth centuries in Europe forged a substitute 'God's eye view' via positivist scientific methods which (allegedly) screen out the effects of social location and perspectives, values and self-interests, promising to reveal, if not the whole truth all at once, progressively more with each advance of 'science'.[67] In this view, after millennia of ignorance and superstition marking earlier stages of human history, modern 'science' is finally revealing the 'truth' about the 'laws of nature', including human nature and society, and offering 'neutral' expert advice to opinion makers and officials in every field, pointing the way 'forward'. Scientific advances, new technologies, expert policy-making, industrial revolutions, economic growth, and democracy will bring expanding personal freedom and prosperity to millions of people, peace too, and technological solutions to problems still plaguing humanity.

In this framework, 'tradition' is more or less equivalent to 'religion'. Indeed, the doctrine of 'secularism' lies at the very heart of 'modernity', predicting the disappearance of religion in the modern world as the progress of science pushes back the darkness of ignorance and superstition, the realms of human agency expand, and 'man' takes the reigns of destiny into his own hands. This positivist spirit infuses the secular definitions of the natural sciences, social sciences, and humanities, and the organisation of disciplines and departments in 'modern' universities around the world, with 'religious' matters relegated to private life at best, and theological faculties relegated to the disciplinary margins or excluded altogether. This outlook has deeply shaped 'modern'—liberal, progressive, and radical—political discourses too.[68]

Secularist tendencies in and across critical discourses have been immensely costly: inhibiting dialogues with most of the world's 'others' in their own terms and the recognition of their agency in resisting domination and sustaining hopes for another world, in the past and present; underestimating the limits of 'modern' science and rationality; arrogantly rejecting other traditions as resources in forging alternatives; hindering respectful dialogue across traditions in nurturing broader solidarities, coalitions, and campaigns.[69] In these volumes, for example, Daulatzai strongly criticises the dominant expressions of feminism at the World Social Forum in Mumbai for perpetuating positivist images of knowledge as "neutral, value-free, and uncharged with historical contingency". And she insists that "the imperative of a politics of resistance free from religious sentiments will fail to address the needs of vast majorities of the planet's inhabitants as well as continue to provide opportunities for more fundamental and violent alternatives to flourish".[70]

However, this secularist edifice is rapidly crumbling, as many contributions to these books also confirm.[71] For example, Toth—in his essay in these volumes— points to the importance of 'religion' in understanding modern Muslim societies:

> In Muslim societies where outright secularists still constitute a minority and where the eighteenth-century Enlightenment separation of religion and politics became a colonially-imposed doctrine, Islam still strongly colours the beliefs, actions, and perceptions of movement activists. . . . As with so many social movements, then, purely economic or sociological analyses are necessary, but insufficient. The doctrines and cultural beliefs, too, must be examined to fully understand how local movements erupt into global campaigns, and why.[72]

Religious traditions are vibrant and politically significant in other contexts too. Indeed, while some, like Daulatzai above, are condemning secularist tendencies in the WSF, others are pointing to the massive and largely unrecognised presence of religious people, cultures and ethics, and organisations and movements in left and progressive movements. Levy, for example, argues that the progressive Catholic Church—and Latin American 'liberation theology' in particular—deeply "influenced the conception, mission, organisation, content, and evolution of the WSF", and indeed that the progressive Church in Brazil was "the single most important social actor in the formative years of contemporary Brazilian civil society, creating, nurturing, and supporting modern social movements across Brazil in both urban centres and the countryside".[73]

So secularist blindness continues to exist uneasily with continuing, powerful, but largely unrecognised ('underground') religious influences. And from many directions there are calls for transcending the 'sacred' / 'secular', 'faith' / 'science' binary altogether, opening up new possibilities for drawing on other traditions with alternatives to modern categories and new disciplinary boundaries for re-reading the past and imagining the future.[74]

At the same time, doubts about the alleged certainties of Western modes of natural and social science, including economics, are spreading like wildfire.[75] Indeed, announcements of disciplines in decline, even 'disciplines in ruins',[76] are proliferating, along with deep crises in universities, which have been their home.

And epistemological revolutions are underway around the world, with growing awareness of the limitations, partiality, and incompleteness of all knowledge (including 'science'), growing openness to 'other' traditions, and—in a world with many fundamental and still unanswered questions about the future—new epistemological spaces for 'hope' and 'faith' as other modalities of engaging the shifting boundaries between the known and the unknown, reality and possibility.

Resurgent Religious / Philosophical / Cosmological Questions

Of course, there is no room for religious triumphalism. Indeed, popular forms of triumphalist 'conservatism' and 'fundamentalism' are also deeply modernist, forged in Europe and in the US in the eighteenth to twentieth centuries in reaction to the changing world system and to modern 'liberalism', and carrying within them many of the flaws of other modern traditions, notably an insistence on 'one right way' of thinking, a hostility to 'radicalism' (often portrayed as 'heresy'), and a despair over the prospects of change for the better in history. On the other hand, other more deeply 'non-Western' traditions escape many sins of modern 'liberalisms' and 'conservatisms', offering other ways of seeing and organising life. But virtually all have been profoundly impacted by 'Western' influences; they also have had their own dynamics of creativity and growth, stasis, decadence, decline, and (sometimes) renewal. Thus, for example, in their essay in these books Leyva Solano and Gunderson point to the complex processes between the early 1950s and the 1994 eruption of the Zapatistas, processes of religious awakening—perhaps more adequately, 'reawakening and renewal'—and of accompanying political radicalisation and organisation.[77] Other articles in this collection address the roots of contemporary Islamic social justice renewal and militancy in the writings of Muhammad Abduh, Hasan al-Banna, and Sayyid Qutb.[78]

As every religious activist knows, every tradition is marked by intense debates over interpretations of sacred texts, the history of the tradition, status vis-à-vis other religious traditions, 'modern' religious / cultural traditions in particular, forms of leadership and communal organisation, ethics, the religious significance of currently pressing problems like global climate change (which more and more religious groups are defining as 'matters of faith!'),[79] and prospects for the future.[80] Moreover, every existing 'tradition' is rooted in earlier expressions of the tradition forged in different times and places addressing other constellations of reality and possibility. From the beginning, then, each tradition is marked internally by controversies and conflicts, and each is also confronted by changing contexts—in our times, in historically unprecedented and far-reaching ways by developments in science, technologies, new modes and scales of social organisation, and shifting relationships with (the rest of) nature, which are again transforming the world, humanity's place in it, and the horizons of possible futures.

In these changed and changing circumstances, no religious tradition contains—in any simple sense—'answers' to all the important questions of this new context. On the contrary, in addition to whatever limitations and sins of the past for which they must repent, all face fundamental challenges. For the whirlwinds of historical transition are reopening the classic religious / philosophical questions concerning 'creation' (or 'nature'), along with humanity's and other species' places in it. No one can today escape making choices, if not in theory, certainly in practice, as we—individually and collectively—scramble to reorder our lives together, with one another, with other-than-humans, and with the earth.[81] Existing communities and their traditions of knowledge, hope, and faith, forged in different worlds, are today also fundamentally challenged, to reorientation, conversion, and renewal or to extinction.

'Globalisation' and Beyond: Some Questions

Dawn of a Post-Neoliberal Era?

By the end of the 1990s, diverse groups and movements around the world were discovering common ground in targeting 'globalisation' as the cause of much of their suffering, for instance, in the cross-fertilisation and convergence of widely diverse movements in the 'antiglobalisation' demonstrations that broke out in Seattle in 1999 protesting the World Trade Organization's (WTO) agenda, which then quickly spread across North America, Europe, and elsewhere. (More accurately, 'neoliberal globalisation' was the target and 'alter-globalisation' the goal, since many 'globalising' developments—for example, communication and cross-cultural interactions—are welcomed in progressive circles.) 'Neoliberalism' or 'neoliberal globalisation', often referred to simply as 'globalisation' (as if it were a single, natural, coherent, non-contradictory, uncontested, linear—and 'good'—process), was increasingly identified as central to the problems confronting many movements with their different contexts and causes around the world.

In many respects these movements were amazingly successful, for instance in derailing the World Trade Organization's plans, discrediting the International Monetary Fund, and promoting widespread defections from neoliberal orthodoxy in the wake of the 2008 financial meltdown ('we're all Keynesians now'). Some commentators even dared to announce the 'end of neoliberalism'[82]

In the wake of Occupy Wall Street and of the Arab uprisings in 2011, though, it has again become transparently clear that ideological victories in the battles over public opinion do not automatically sweep away or transform the centres of political and economic power, like corporate offices, banks, government departments, military headquarters and bases, think tanks, and political parties. These remain in the hands of elites, and their supporters—abetted by often uneducated and systematically misinformed 'publics'—are often successfully and very rapidly mobilised by elites to avoid punishment, to reformulate their project for the post-crisis period, to reassert their power and authority, to organise new coalitions, and to (re)mobilise support.

While there are many signs of crisis in neoliberal projects around the world, and of growing resistance, there are also too many signs of expanding concentrations of power, massively increased surveillance,[83] reasserted neoliberal projects like the Trans-Pacific Partnership (TPP),[84] continuing control and distortion of mainstream media fuelling widespread ignorance and confusion, continuing mind-boggling US military power and expanding conflicts,[85] alongside increasing confusion among elites, deepening irrationality, desperation, and fanaticism, above all in the Republican Party in the US.[86]

What about 'Capitalism'?

There has been much less agreement across movements on this question. And everything depends on the definition.

Certainly there is little dispute that economic struggles over land and labour and capital and markets have been central in the modern world (and for much longer), and that vastly expanding production of goods and services have radically—though unequally—transformed societies everywhere. And for one hundred and fifty years since the consolidation of European empires around the world (or for five hundred years since Columbus launched the European project of globalising conquest and colonialism), despite crisis after crisis, the architects of 'modern' projects of expanding private property and markets, colonies, and empires have asserted that 'progress'—in science, technology, and markets—is the central law of human history and promoting 'capitalist' values and culture and ideologies, institutions, and structures is the key to endlessly expanding markets, technological breakthroughs, prosperity, affluence, individual freedoms, and peace. After every crisis—like the linked crises marking the first half of the twentieth century: World War I, the Great Depression, and World War II—reformed coalitions of elites and their supporters have drawn on these cultural and intellectual traditions, concentrations of wealth, formal and informal networks, administrative and governance architectures, and residual institutional power in various centres (like Wall Street) in reasserting their 'leadership' and forging a renewed capitalist project reflecting their interests in changed conditions.

In response to the cascading economic and political crises of the 1970s,[87] in the US and Britain especially, neoliberals and their neoconservative allies led the way in formulating revised projects for preserving their status, wealth, and power in a changing, increasingly globalised world. They mobilised massive media resources in preaching this doctrine far and wide. And they succeeded once again in turning this latest version of 'capitalism' into common sense (the so-called Washington Consensus)[88] in the centres of power around the world, in the curricula of economics departments treating it as natural and good (no longer requiring definition, criticism, or debate),[89] in the headquarters of corporations and political parties, in the legal systems of governments, in the agendas of international financial institutions like the World Trade Organization, the World Bank, and the International Monetary Fund, in expanding webs of 'free-trade' agreements. This has been a truly extraordinary development.

Indeed, at each transition, they have expanded their claims, in terms both of geographical reach—after the collapse in 1989 of the Soviet Union, extending to the whole world—and, even more fundamentally, also of the domains of life itself, now including the transmutation of culture and knowledge into 'intellectual property', citizens into stakeholders, democracy into 'governance', and the 'commodification' of culture and religion, even of biology and basic life processes.[90] These projects are consistently branded as 'capitalist' by their architects and supporters and have put a capitalist stamp on culture, institutions, and structures around the world. And the high priests of this global orthodoxy brand their critics as 'anti-capitalist'. Not surprisingly, many critics adopt this 'anti-capitalist' label too.

There are many reasons, though, for questioning this essentialising of 'capitalism' for obscuring the magnitude of resistance, the agency of its opponents, their impacts, the depths of crises in the past and currently, and the range of open questions concerning the future. Indeed, some, like Nunes in this book, insist that the problem with 'capitalism' is that it is "a name given *a posteriori* to a historical development that is still in motion". In his view, "we do not even know what capitalism is, [so] how can we know what its overcoming is?"[91]

Beyond 'the Economy'?

Indeed, for many people, criticism of 'neoliberal capitalism' does not rule out appreciation of other forms of capitalism. In their view, it is not 'capitalism' as such that is the problem but 'unfettered' or 'unregulated' capitalism, (supposedly) like that which existed before the welfare state capitalism and developmentalism of the immediate post-World War II years, and like that which re-emerged in the 'neoclassical' capitalism of Thatcher and Reagan at the end of the 1970s. In this view, the solution is a more 'regulated' capitalism, like the post–World War II Keynesian welfare state in the North and 'development' in the South.[92]

A host of other critics, though, point to the Keynesian welfare state and the global developmentalist project as the results of an unique confluence of extraordinary developments: the enormous technological and economic impetus of World War II (including the development of increasingly global communications and transportation), the propaganda and politics of 'total war' and its follow-up in the Cold War, with its threat of a 'socialist' or 'communist' alternative (along with the growing strength of the labour movement), the unprecedented military, economic, and political power of the US, and the readiness of US elites (after intense internal debates and compromises among various factions) to pick up the mantle of global hegemon in the wake of the enormous losses suffered by Britain and other European powers during the war.[93] They also describe the rise of 'social democratic' European states in similar historically specific terms.

But many other critics question whether continuing 'developmentalist welfare-state capitalist projects' was even possible in the 1970s and 1980s. For the world had already changed so profoundly between the end of World War II and the 1970s[94]—a claim that the emerging neoliberal / neoconservative movement made central to its call for 'radical' cultural, political, and economic change. Since then the scope, scale, and pace of changes have intensified, such as the increasing globalisation of commodity chains, the defeat of the USSR, the emergence of BRICS (Brazil, Russia, India, China, South Africa), and the weakening (at least relatively) of US economic and political (but not military) power.[95] In this view, there is no going back, and even if, miraculously, the capitalist faithful could be persuaded that relinquishment of some small portion of their immense wealth— and power, especially—would be in their own interests too.

In addition, many of these discussions of 'the economy' and of reforming 'capitalism' proceed with little reference to the monumental concentrations of wealth and power that have taken place in this time, and their role in obstructing change. They also tend to overlook 'other' issues like climate change, proliferating resource wars, and the resulting global surges of refugees and immigrants,[96] etc, as if all this is somehow separate from the functioning of 'the economy'.

Moreover, expanding studies of capitalist development in diverse times and places are convincing many historians that 'capitalism' has changed so often and so fundamentally that reliance on the single term obscures the range and magnitude of fundamental changes that have occurred, as well as the dynamics of continuity, crisis, and change in the past and in the present.

Furthermore, even among those who view 'capitalism' as a problem, there are many who do not view it as *the* problem. As noted above, alongside economic justice movements, other critical discourses have emerged identifying the heart of the issues in terms of sexism or patriarchy or heteropatriarchy, racism, technocratic rationality, colonialism or empire, 'modernity', 'Eurocentrism' or 'Western civilisation' (or even 'civilisation' itself), caste, and anthropocentrism. And for many with these concerns, even critical discourses of 'capitalism' still fail to grasp these fundamental dimensions of their lives.

Indeed, there is a growing sense in many circles that capitalist projects have in fact never been only 'economic',[97] that economistic tendencies in both mainstream and critical discourses of 'economics' obscure other important actors, dimensions, and dynamics of eco-social worlds, and that they oversimplify and too narrowly restrict visions of future possibilities.[98] In this view, the actual functioning of institutions and structures like markets incorporates and depends on countless religious, cultural, political, as well as economic, processes and choices.[99] So 'economism' fundamentally distorts 'the economy'. Moreover, portraying 'capitalism' as a steamroller distracts attention from the specific features of specific conjunctures, the tensions and contradictions in reigning policies, the tensions and conflicts among different factions of ruling elites and their supporters, shifting configurations of interests, and real crises versus the manufactured crises that elites manipulate to scare people into supporting them.[100] It also (re)marginalises the agency of all the non-capitalist 'others' (including 'nature' and workers) struggling to live according to other logics and fans the flames of despair over ever being able to derail such a monster.[101]

'Capitalism' versus 'Socialism' and Beyond?
Given the confusion around 'capitalism', many wish that the term would be abolished altogether.[102]

At the same time, suspicions proliferate over 'capitalist' approaches to problems, which presume: the allegedly separate sphere of 'the free market', which operates by morally and politically neutral and universal economic 'laws' that must be insulated from outside 'intervention' by governments, workers, communities; the unlimited privileges and powers accorded to the owners and managers of 'capital'; human beings who are driven primarily by individual economic self-interest, whose selfishness is magically transformed by an 'invisible hand' into the common good; accounting frameworks which conveniently externalise the costs to workers, communities, societies, other species, and the biosphere; and the gospel of 'growth' at all costs, as the only path to resolving all major social and ecological problems. Of course, in many contexts modified versions of capitalist policies may be the only ones with any hope of being implemented. Still, there is a growing sense on many fronts that many current crises require, as Klein insists concerning the climate crisis, "that we break every rule in the free-market playbook—and that we do so with great urgency".[103] As the contributions to these volumes confirm, struggles for 'another world' concern 'the economy' and so much more.

For example, in his essay in these volumes Corntassel urges strategies of "sustainable self-determination" for Indigenous Peoples of Turtle Island, an Indigenous-centred discourse rooted in their own local communities, spiritual traditions, and practices, "rather than seeking state-based solutions that are disconnected from indigenous community relationships and the natural world". Overcoming some Western epistemological biases with strategies "to decolonise and restore indigenous relationships that have long been severed", he proposes forging more holistic, flexible, and dynamic frameworks that include ecological, medicinal, food, and other cultural factors. These would be locally (re)centred projects, "[at] the community level as a process to perpetuate indigenous livelihoods locally via the regeneration of family, clan, and individual roles and responsibilities to their homelands". At the same time, they have broader links and implications with "the potential to re-establish larger regional trading networks with each other to promote formidable alliances and sustainable futures". Thus:

> Sustainable self-determination offers a new global benchmark for the praxis of indigenous livelihoods, food security, community governance, and relationships to the natural world and ceremonial life that enables the transmission of these cultural practices to future generations.[104]

In a similar spirit, Philip McMichael points to lessons learned from food sovereignty movements like Via Campesina concerning the 'global' implications of such movements:

> While Via Campesina recognizes the jurisdictional authority of the state, it also seeks to transform that authority, by challenging the state to enable states to have the right and the obligation to sovereignty, to define, without external conditions, their own agrarian, agricultural, fishing and food policies in such a way as to guarantee the right to food and the other economic, social and cultural rights of the entire population.[105]

And thus:

> In advocating an alternative modernity, including 're-territorialization' of, and among, states, the food sovereignty movement fundamentally challenges the institutional relations of neoliberal capitalism that contribute to mass dispossession—paradoxically reproducing the peasantry as an 'unthinkable' social force [long defined by liberals and radicals alike as hopelessly 'backward'], as a condition for its emergence as a radical world-historical subject.[106]

A similar spirit inspires many urban movements too. This was made especially clear to me in the US Social Forum in Detroit in 2010. Only fifty years ago, Detroit was the leading edge of high technology mass production consumer capitalism, centred on the auto industry. And, as faith-based activist Lydia Wylie-Kellerman pointed out in preparing for the Forum, "the auto in large part created the American middle class", along with well-paid working-class jobs, expressways, and suburbs of 'the American dream'. In remarkably short order, though, this dream turned into a nightmare, as neoliberal globalisation promoted the flight of factories abroad and massive deindustrialisation, assaults on unions, largely white flight to the suburbs, drastically shrinking population, empty houses (18 per cent of all homes vacant or abandoned), rising crime, and the tearing down of houses, leaving 30 per cent vacant.[107] From being the icon of a wonderful new world, Detroit rapidly went to being the icon of urban apocalypse, the end of the world. And many see Detroit's story as the larger story of the US. As Lydia's father, pastor and activist Bill Wylie-Kellerman says: "For decades, Detroiters have known the economic collapse that the whole US has begun to feel in the last two years". But there is also good news: "Amid signs of death, urban resurrection is afoot. In all these things are the opening and spaces for a whole new way of life".[108] There are proposals to 'green' what's left of the auto industry in Detroit, but this would require "repenting the idolatry of the automobile" and a renewal of "corporate vocations to serve human life rather than growth (or now mere survival), let alone market share or even profit. Is that possible?" On the margins, another more modest "economy of creativity and self-reliance" is budding, in urban agriculture and alternative media (basement sound studios and community-oriented broadcasting)—inspired in part by the way Cubans met the shock accompanying the cessation of foreign aid with the fall of the USSR in the 'special period' (1989–end of 1990s). "Another city is possible in the shell of the old", Bill Wylie-Kellerman affirms. Indeed, "For those with eyes to see, it's actually happening".[109]

More generally, more inclusive perspectives drawing on the insights of broader ranges of progressive movements and scholarship point beyond 'capitalism' towards other definitions of 'reformist' and 'radical', and towards other strategies besides frontal assaults on 'the system' and its centres of power; strategies which are more widely participatory, immediately practical, manageable locally, and—their supporters say—simultaneously realistic and hopeful.[110]

Capitalist Techno-Utopias and Apocalyptic Eco-Social Catastrophes

Beyond particular constituencies, issues, and movements, the sheer range and diversity of movements that are taking place across the world today, and of their agendas, point to much deeper, broader, and more far-reaching processes of change under way on earth. And the expanding horizons of human agency being probed and experimented with in these movements are at the heart of this story. For they are confirming, repeatedly, that less and less of life (but not nothing) is simply God-given or natural and inevitable, and that more and more of life (but not everything) is shaped—and misshaped—by human agency. So established categories, frameworks, and horizons are increasingly inadequate not only because they are being challenged by other ideas but because the world is changing in fundamental ways, including the most 'material'.[111] The plate tectonics of personal, social, and natural worlds are shifting. And established traditions of seeing and ordering the world are increasingly inadequate in enabling us to engage this new, rapidly changing world.

This is perhaps the weakest front in most critical discourses. Repeated insistence today on key insights from the past concerning particular axes of oppression and exploitation (class, gender, race, ecology, colony / empire, etc), while still absolutely central, can also contribute to a sense of an eternally unchanging present—and to obscuring the many successes in progressive movements in many struggles around the world and the broader scope of changes sweeping the world, which are also transforming (not necessarily reducing, and in some cases intensifying) previously established dynamics of class, race, gender, ecology, etc.[112]

And it is impossible to escape these broader changes, the challenges they pose, or—in the swift-moving currents of epochal change—making choices. Here I want to underline the importance of addressing these crosscutting issues and broader horizons. For the failure to see the connections among issues limits their appeal and reinforces the perception of seemingly endless list of competing 'identities' and 'special interests'. It abandons the broader fields of public discourse to mainstream believers in 'progress', on the one hand, and right-wing nightmares of 'apocalypse', on the other, both with deeply flawed interpretations of the past, leaving only the simplistic binary of utterly false hope for techno-utopian salvation versus utterly despairing visions of end times, with no escape.

In my contribution to the companion volume of this book,[113] I sketched two poles in the widely different discourses of the future. Both reflect certain concrete experiences and powerful historical trends: at one pole, great leaps forward in an unfolding market-centred techno-utopian future and, at the other, cascading eco-social apocalypses. The prophets of the techno-utopian future ecstatically announce it in universal terms, as the destiny of all. But, of course, this cannot be true.

There is no doubt that some people—especially in the 1% and in the expanding 'middle classes' around the world—anticipate wonderful new possibilities for themselves and their children, lives of prosperity, dramatically enhanced and rapidly expanding personal choices in every area, indeed substantially longer lifetimes. Moreover, advances in bio-technology, pharmo-technologies, information technologies, cognitive technologies, and human-machine interfaces, globally linked in a world brain, point to expanding capacities to address inherited deficiencies, illnesses, injuries, along with social and ecological problems—and even more, to enhanced human capacities in every area, even to 'improved' post-human and transhuman successor species!

But this, of course, is not the future for the great majorities. For there is no 'deus ex machina', no god in the machine who will magically appear and solve the problems confronting humanity, no social, scientific, or technological breakthroughs which are magically going to fill in the yawning chasm between rich and poor, magically affirm the dignity of all the 'others' and their traditions, magically redistribute wealth, magically transmute ecosystem costs into benefits, magically convert hyperconsuming middle classes and elites to radically constrained lifestyles and smaller ecological footprints.[114] Indeed, the ecological costs of 'middle class' lifestyles alone have already overwhelmed the carrying capacity of the earth.[115] And technologically enhanced lives of even greater consumption will be even more wasteful, socially disruptive, and environmentally devastating. Moreover, throughout the history of civilisation, technological advances have typically been appropriated by elites for their own enjoyment, and for managing and policing social order, further deepening the chasms between rich and poor. And today in the midst of knowledge revolutions, cascading new technologies, and expanding human agency, mind-boggling concentrations of wealth, power, and paranoia are fuelling the false hopes and distorted faith (in theological terms, 'idolatry') of global elites, their gross distortions of public debate, their rigging of institutions and social structures, their deafness to the cries of so many victims, and their blindness to the darkening storms of ecological-social apocalypses.[116]

And expanding choruses of voices are warning of deepening turmoil, cascading eco-social catastrophes, perhaps even a "war of global civilization".[117] Some commentators like James Lovelock, formulator of the Gaia hypothesis, are even warning about the end of civilisation as we know it: "[B]efore this century is over, billions of us will die and the few breeding pairs of people that survive will be in the Arctic where the climate remains tolerable".[118] Indeed, thousands of insect, plant, amphibian, and animal species are disappearing in what is already the sixth mass extinction event in the history of life on earth.[119] Some commentators even insist that human extinction ('humanicide') is becoming plausible, perhaps with cosmic implications if life is rare in the universe and consciousness even rarer, with God knows what implications for the evolution of the cosmos.[120]

At this juncture in the history of life on earth, then, the contributors to these volumes are telling us that hope for another world, for mitigating the worst effects of current constellations of power and for avoiding endlessly cascading catastrophes crucially depends on continuing and expanding eruptions of progressive social movements and their supporters.

Moreover, some are convinced that genuine hope requires the utmost realism. Apart from the true believers in 'capitalism' with their techno-utopian visions of the future, many analysts anticipate as the most plausible—and the most *hopeful*—vision of the future an uneven series of catastrophes, with hard lessons only being learned gradually and haltingly after each crisis. Gradually, more and more people will undergo deep conversions in values and outlooks and develop capacities for making difficult choices and 'sacrifices'. Only then, in this view, will a more profound historical transformation be possible, emphasising "the quality of life and material sufficiency, human solidarity and global equity, and affinity with nature and environmental sustainability".[121]

Realistic and Hopeful: Reinventing Politics

As the two volumes of *The Movements of Movements* confirm, with the fading illusions of *pensamiento único* (one right way of thinking) and of a single big movement, activists and their supporters around the world are searching for signs of convergence *across* movements in forging more inclusive identities and solidarities, shared values and hopes, expanding agency, and more effective collaboration in campaigns transforming the world. At the risk of repeating points addressed above, it is worth considering them again as regular features in social movement convergences across differences and distances. From my perspective, there are at least seven points of convergence.

Partiality and Incompleteness

The great and flowing diversity of progressive social movements pushes us towards more complex pictures of the world, of the past, of the actually existing world ('the system'), of the swirling currents of change already transforming it, and of widely divergent possible futures. It pushes us towards different understandings of current social dynamics and social actors, different views of self-interest and the 'common good', different perceptions of history, different visions of 'another world', and different strategies for moving ahead.[122] It also pushes us to more complex pictures of progressive movements themselves—old and new, profuse, multifaceted, multicentred, diffuse, uneven, operating on different scales, in different contexts, with different temporalities, at different stages of development, frequently overlapping with other movements, sometimes in tension and conflict, frequently collaborating in campaigns, evolving through successes and failures, confronting changing contexts and new challenges, forging broader networks and coalitions, transforming the horizons of possibility.

For example, Sader points to the tumultuous and chaotic history of progressive movements in Latin America since the 1960s, a "series of upswings and downswings, triumphs, and setbacks" testifying to "the continent's instability, and its poor capacities for consolidating alternative programs". But, he insists, it is also "a sign of the left's astounding ability to recover from its defeats, no matter how crushing these seem to be—Che's murder, the coup in Chile, the rout of the Sandinistas, or the tightening grip of neoliberal processes". Nevertheless, survivors of dictatorships and defeats continued struggling in the margins. And by the 2000s progressive movements were instrumental in transforming electoral politics and pressuring governments in Cuba, Venezuela, Bolivia, and Ecuador especially to resist neoliberal globalisation and "defy North American imperial hegemony".[123] These were historic accomplishments, which helped to change realities on the ground throughout Latin America, with ripple effects around the world. Nevertheless, in the fast-moving currents of historical transition, the ground has shifted again dramatically, in part reflecting the fruits of recent successes but also raising new issues which are destabilising movements and coalitions and the governments they helped to shape and plunging the region into new rounds of debate and struggle.[124] To survive in changing circumstances, movements have to change too, often in fundamental ways.

Meanwhile, the epistemological earthquakes at the heart of social movement struggles are also becoming clearer. More and more people are turning away from the supposedly eternal truths of grand orthodoxies, theories, scientific laws, ideologies, and overarching political programmes ('systemic alternatives') to more pragmatic approaches to 'truth' and politics. In these larger more complex pictures of knowledge, every formulation of truth is 'partial' and 'provisional'. But this stance is far from endless 'postmodern relativism'. Postmodernist perspectives do capture the insights that the claims from one perspective can always be challenged by claims from other perspectives, and that, with expanding media and expanding participation of formerly marginalised / 'silent' others, the spheres of contentious public debates are also expanding. But postmodernists also project the image of eternally continuing debate, as if no issue is ever 'settled', an academic illusion which misses the central fact that life in the concrete world—even for elite ivory tower intellectuals!—involves inescapable choices confronting individuals and groups on the central issues of the times, like climate change, growing polarisation between rich and poor, and the epistemological turmoil destabilising universities too. In these debates positions formulated around certain insights become crystallised by different social actors as 'truths' on which the future depends. And there is no escape; people cannot avoid choosing, in the process making great leaps of faith beyond reasonably certain knowledge and anticipated outcomes, and staking our lives, our communities and societies, even the world, on the outcome. And in different ways these choices become realities, and we live—or die—with the results . . . until experience, changing context, and new insights inspire us—or our descendants—to new conversions and revisions of inherited ways of thinking.

So, there is no one big theory. Rather, movements depend less and less on grand theories, and more and more on "a prudent, finite knowledge that keeps the scale of actions as much as possible on a level with the scale of consequences".[125]

And there is no one big movement. At the same time, though, across the immeasurable complexities of contexts and eco-justice and social justice struggles around the world, there is a growing sense, as Nunes says, of "concrete universalism" in which:

> every struggle appears as neither exclusively local nor exclusively global: all struggles communicate on different levels, while no struggle can in practice subsume all others. There are no partial, 'local' solutions that can stand in isolation, and there is no 'global' solution unless this is understood as a certain possible configuration of local ones.[126]

Thus, what is often labelled *the* antiglobalisation or alter-globalisation movement is in reality

> nothing but the tip of the iceberg: the convergences produced by a much wider and deeper weft of connections, both direct (as when groups engaged in communication and coordination with each other) and indirect (when struggles resonated and reinforced each other without any coordination), among initiatives that were sometimes very local, sometimes very different, sometimes even contradictory.[127]

And around the world social movements and critical scholars are confronting the challenges of reframing themselves in these concrete, partial, incomplete—and increasingly linked—terms.

Irreducible Centrality of the 'Other(s)'
In a world of increasing awareness of great hierarchies of wealth and power (Occupy Wall Street's "the 1% versus the 99%"), there is also a growing sense that poor and marginalised peoples and groups have a right to speak for themselves, to be respected and taken seriously (which does not always mean agreement), to participate in decision-making, and to equitable shares of benefits as well as costs of collective choices. At the heart of this dynamic is the priority on nurturing people's dignity and an appreciation for their own traditions and capacities to speak for themselves and to participate fully in public debates and decision-making. This requires confronting mainstream discourses formulated from the perspective of ruling groups—and many perspectives aspiring to be 'critical' and 'progressive', even 'radical' too—in terms of all the 'others'' experiences, problems, and aspirations.

In this respect, it is important to keep in mind the limitations of the dominant social movement theories themselves, and the uneven process of transcending them. Bayat, for example, notes that the prevailing frameworks draw exclusively on Western experience; and he questions the extent to which "they can help us understand the process of solidarity building or the collectivities of disjointed yet parallel practices of non-collective actors in the non-Western politically closed and technologically limited settings" of the Middle East in particular. So he is compelled to coin a new phrase, "social nonmovements", to capture the agency of 'ordinary people'. And through this lens he detects that "the urban disenfranchised, through their quiet and unassuming daily struggles" are involved in refiguring "new life and communities for themselves and different urban realities on the ground in Middle Eastern cities".[128]

Moreover, as movement histories repeatedly confirm, understanding evolving social movement horizons requires recognition that often 'newer' groups not only introduce new standpoints and concerns but also—the fruits of many years, decades, even centuries of resistance below the radar of mainstream media and the established left—new proposals for moving forward in more inclusive ways. Thus, for example, Teltumbde notes that Dalits in India have long been perplexed by the traditional 'left' "who swear by anti-imperialism [but] are apathetic to their [Dalit] struggle", leaving Dalits not very enthusiastic about the "anti-imperialist movement" either: "The persistent neglect [by the Left] of the caste oppression suffered by them has made them suspicious of it".[129] Perhaps, then, it should not have been a surprise that at the World Social Forum in Mumbai in 2004 Dalit activists led the way in organising a 'World Dignity Forum' as a step beyond this and other impasses among left and progressive groups, where they called for

> the modernization and globalisation of previous radical traditions of social justice, preserving their vision of social change while updating their analysis and language and consequent prescription. We . . . believe that the term dignity and the forums like World Dignity Forum can provide a new axis for a radical and social mobilisation, locally, regionally, globally . . . a new politics and new global alliance of the marginal, excluded and struggling population. . . . The familiar questions of dignity, inclusion, discrimination and exclusion were given new significance with new alliances; new ones emerged. Dignity, social inclusion and social justice became more vocal and visible, at least in some settings of Asia, Latin America and Europe.[130]

In a similar spirit, in his essay in these books Khasnabish refers to the Zapatistas in Mexico as "teachers to political movements and activists elsewhere . . . teaching not a series of lessons on 'how to make a revolution' but rather broader and more foundational lessons in political horizons, ethics, and possibilities".[131] Nothing is more basic, for all our thinking, organising, and action than the 'others', in all their wonderful—and perplexing—diversity.[132]

And, as McNally proclaims, "Hope rises up with each revolt of the downtrodden".[133]

Heterarchy, Diversity, Pluriversality, and Nonlinearity

As suggested above, looking through the proliferating lenses of the world's others, the world is growing larger, more multifaceted, dynamic, complex, and chaotic. Social movements and critical discourses reflect this world too, displaying ever-greater diversity, in the range of contexts, movements, causes, critical discourses, and modes of commentary. And the recognition of 'diversity' is increasingly central in contemporary movement discourses, as confirmed in many contributions to *The Movements of Movements*. This is evident, for example, as suggested above in reference to recent writings of Latin American decolonial thinkers combining the gains of earlier traditions of 'political economy' (Marxisms, dependency, world-system) with the gains of 'cultural' discourses concerning gender, racism, and anthropocentrism (feminist, subaltern, antiracist, postcolonial). In this expanded and more complex perspective, the old Marxist paradigm of infrastructure and superstructure, and its emphasis on 'systems' and 'structures' more generally, are replaced by historical-heterogeneous approaches to structure, or 'heterarchy': "[A]n entangled articulation of multiple hierarchies, in which subjectivity and the social imaginary is not derivative but constitutive of the structures of the world-system".[134] This opens space for recognising the roles of 'subjectivity' and the agency of diverse marginalised majorities, as well as of elites, in the always-contested construction of culture, structures, and systems and their reproduction over time. It also introduces 'religion' and 'culture' in all their diversity into analyses of 'structures' and 'systems'. And it includes 'nature'. In this sense, Childs in this book points to "social, cultural, and political heterogeneity as a potential basis for, rather than a barrier to, cooperation and mutual understandings", and calls for "great flexibility for [recognising] the wide varieties which the spirit of freedom and justice takes among the many diverse peoples of the world".[135]

In a similar spirit, Escobar argues that the most promising discourses of historical transition

> link together aspects of reality that have remained separate in previous imaginings of social transformation: ontological, cultural, politicoeconomic, ecological, and spiritual. These are brought together by a profound concern with human suffering and with the fate of life itself. By 'life' I mean the unending ensemble of forms and entities that make up the pluriverse—from the biophysical to the human to the supernatural—and the processes by which they come into being. This clearly goes beyond a concern with nature, even if most . . . [transition discourses] are traversed by ecological issues; it could not be otherwise, given that they are triggered by, and respond to, the interrelated crises of energy, food, climate, and poverty.[136]

And as our understanding of social worlds becomes more complex and dynamic, so also does our understanding of social movements. Indeed, as Löwy notes in his essay here, "one would search in vain for a common project, a consensual reformist or revolutionary programme". Rather, the *altermundialista* utopia is reflected in the sharing of certain values, like the dignity of the human being, participatory democracy, the defence of the environment, solidarity, pluralism. In this light, "The plurality of languages, cultures, music, food, and life forms is an immense wealth which one must learn to cultivate".[137]

Moreover, it is also increasingly clear that history is not simply linear, never mind carefully planned and precisely managed. Indeed, Bayat doubts that

> revolutions can ever be planned. Even though revolutionaries do engage in plotting and preparing, revolutions do not necessarily result from prior schemes. Rather, they often follow their own intriguing logic, subject to a highly complex mix of structural, international, coincidental, and psychological factors. . . . [R]evolutions are never predictable.[138]

On the other hand, he does think that "having or not having an idea about revolutions will have a marked impact on the aftermath", in the ways different constituencies mobilise and frame options (or fail to) in the subsequent play of events.[139]

Translation and Interculturality

Multiple developments are pushing 'translation' to the centre of religious / cultural dynamics and political struggles around the world: expanding and increasingly intensive communications technologies are shrinking distance around the world and proliferating avenues of participation; expanding transportation networks and travel; increasing immigration and refugee flows bringing 'others' to neighbourhoods, workplaces, schools, houses of worship, and playing fields. Moreover, in progressive scholarly and political circles especially, the deepening recognition of the centrality of 'culture' in social systems, of the great diversity of cultures and languages, and of many incommensurabilities (the impossibility of completely translating experiences, sensibilities, ideas) among them, is leading to more attention to translation in mobilising strategies and in movement cultures and institutional dynamics too.

For example, the centrality of translation has been evident in World Social Forum organising processes from the beginning. Babels is an international network of volunteer interpreters and translators that emerged to support the social forums. In the process of developing a proposal after their experience at WSF IV in Mumbai in 2004, and while preparing for WSF V in Porto Alegre, they noted that "translation is not a mere logistical or technical issue. It is an essential part of the process itself. It helps building the Forum in an open and inclusive way". In the Mumbai WSF, the goal was to make interpretation available at least in some major events in each of fourteen official languages! As the Babels report says:

[B]y restricting the number of languages allowed to take part into the venue, we're restricting the number of cultures represented. Restricting the number of languages compels the participants to master one of the mainstream languages of the venue, thus shaping and moulding their very presence and political activity. Allowing more languages to be represented within the Forum makes it so that more people can take part in the event.[140]

For many reasons, this high point has not been replicated in various WSF events. But the challenge remains. And there are signs that 'translation' is becoming increasingly significant, not only for big events but also in the everyday lives of communities and organisations.[141] Concretely this means a new priority on providing substantial resources in developing personal and organisational skills and capacities for two-way / multi-way, on-going translation at the heart of political work.[142]

In this process however, 'translation' involves—and means—far more than translating words and sentences. As the Babels group points out: "[T]he same idea in a 'foreign language' and in your 'mother tongue' will never sound the same or relate to the same political and social contexts; one word or one concept may not have the same meaning and impact from one language to another, from one culture to another".[143]

For example, in his essay in these books Corntassel points, in contrast to usual Western usage, to the radically different understanding in Indigenous communities of 'health' ("much deeper than just the absence of disease or injury") and 'politics' ("Indigenous political actions emanate from our spiritual commitments").[144] Thus, many 'translators' prefer the term 'interpreters' to convey this fuller sense of translating across cultures. They also call attention to incommensurabilities, which limit understanding at any point in time and mark each dialogue as unfinished. And they underline the great diversity of the world's cultures and languages—by one count over 6,900![145]—and point to the vast uncharted territories still to be explored.

The challenges of conversion and translation concern organisational cultures and processes as well. Mac Sheoin and Yeates point to "the rich and growing panoply of organisational forms and instruments" being employed in progressive movements,[146] which many find inspiring. But many (including me!) have learned the hard way that organisational forms, procedures, and tactics cannot simply be abstracted from one historical context and imported elsewhere, and that organising across cultural differences inevitably involves many radical challenges.

For example, this lesson clearly emerged in the two-and-a-half-year organising process for a Northwest Social Forum in North America during 2002–2004. The organisers aimed to gather movements from Alaska, Idaho, Montana, Oregon, and Washington in the US, and from British Columbia in Canada. Indeed, they mobilised about one hundred and fifty groups to plan and participate in this event, scheduled for October 2004. But just nine days before the event the organisers cancelled it. Readers with experience in organising coalitions and processes of encounter like the WSF will recognise the range of reasons identified in a follow-up analysis: "a combination of organisational issues, decision-making process, race relations, use of technology, difficulties with funding, geographic dispersion and a tight timeline".[147]

In particular though, the cancellation was triggered by the withdrawal of the Indigenous Programming Committee (and subsequently two other committees) over differences between mainstream and Indigenous organising cultures, commitments, protocols, procedures, and timelines. Indigenous planners, representing and accountable to their villages and communities, concluded that unclear decision-making processes and tight timelines violated their own internal processes and timelines and their understanding of the original movement-to-movement protocol.[148] They withdrew; two other groups withdrew as well; and the planners, with little consultation and under great pressure since the event was only nine days away, postponed the event, which no group has since restarted.

For at least some non-Indigenous participants, though, it became clear that deeper dialogue and collaboration across these cultural differences required a cultural shift on their part, extended engagements with Indigenous communities and movements, and much longer timelines.[149] It also required appreciation for the needs of particular communities and movements, some of which may, at particular times, choose to continue separately in order to focus on their own internal development, requesting (at least implicitly), in the words of Indigenous activist and scholar Vine Deloria, Jr, "a cultural leave-us-alone agreement" for a while from friends and potential allies.[150]

Similar 'cultural' dynamics are also evident in many other cross-cultural and cross-class encounters. And these experiences have contributed to relativising and decentring Western modes of 'general theory' and 'ideology', tight organisational structures, and planning. As Santos argues, "translation is the procedure that allows for mutual intelligibility among experiences of the world without jeopardising their identity and autonomy—without, in other words, reducing them to homogeneous entities".[151] In other words, 'translation' is central to the processes of nurturing broader dialogues across differences and collaboration in reinventing 'culture(s)' and 'politics'.

Many examples of these challenges are provided by the contributors to these volumes. For example, Abramsky acknowledges the serious limits of 'global' organising today and insists that expanding the geographical and sectoral reach of global networks requires a particular effort to reach out to groups so far underrepresented in progressive and left organising struggles, eg, in Arab countries, China, Africa, Central and Eastern Europe, "so that they can participate actively in defining the global process of struggle that develops in the future".[152] Similarly, in her essay in this book Hayes points to developments within transnational feminisms of strategies "ensuring open space to facilitate dialogue across linguistic and cultural differences, address power relations between participants, and enable the poorest to participate".[153]

Practice and Prefiguration

As suggested above, the priority in expanding circles of critical scholarship and politics is shifting from theory, worldview, and ideology. The goal is not a new theory, metanarrative, or worldview, though these continue to be important, but new, expanded, more complex horizons of dialogue across multiple ways of seeing and centres of debate and struggle.[154] Vargas notes, for example, that "in the new millennium, feminists are experiencing fundamental modifications in their ways of thinking and acting, and are becoming more complex and diverse".[155] In particular, she points to the disintegration of old paradigms, and of the "messianic, universal narratives of past movements", and insists that "the transformation of the world depends on the 'transformation of vision'" and the emergence of a "new political culture".[156]

Relatedly, as noted above, Leyva Solano points to the new modes of knowledge that are emerging in "the interstices between committed academics, flexible activisms, and Indigenous as well as anti-systemic movements".[157] In this perspective, theory is not neglected, but is rather de-centred and directly related to personal / communal experiences.[158] And there is a priority on practice, first of all in the places where we have some influence, perhaps even power, in our own families, neighbourhoods, organisations, and institutions. As Adamovsky says, "Our institutions of a new type need to be 'anticipatory', that is, they must embody in their own shape and forms the values of the society we are striving to build".[159]

This emphasis is especially evident, for example, in Indigenous struggles with land bases that make immediate experiments in alternatives possible without waiting for state support.[160] It is also evident in the horizontal decision-making and direct action of Occupy Wall Street activists, peace activists, and others.[161] At the same time, though, as important as prefiguration is, it is also important to recognise that some goals require collaboration and organisation on much larger scales, over much longer time frames. So far there are no widely convincing formulas for balancing local short-term prefigurative goals and long-term larger scale goals.[162]

Thus, as Juris and Pleyers point out in this book, spaces like the WSF Youth Camps are "laboratories where alter-activists experiment with new ideas, practices, and forms of social action".[163] And the Free Association coins a new word for this process, 'worlding': "By envisaging a different world, and by acting in a different world, we actually call forth that world". Indeed, they insist, "It is only because we have, at least partially, moved out of what makes 'sense' in the old world that another world can start to make its own sense".[164]

Openness to Conversion

Implicit in the discussions above of the limits of science, partiality of all knowledge, and transcultural dialogues in mutual respect is openness to conversion(s)—not in the narrow sense of simply stepping from one already-established doctrinal tradition into another but in the deeper and broader sense of transformation, even of fundamental recreation, which ultimately moves all participants (in quite different ways depending on starting points and contexts) in often unexpected directions.[165]

This is clear in the histories of critical discourses at the level of categories and theoretical frameworks. As Bhambra points out:

> reinterpretations of history are not just different interpretations of the same facts; they also bring into being new facts. These new facts should cause us to rethink our accepted frameworks of explanation, which have often been established on the basis of much narrower histories. In so doing, they also transform the meaning of pre-established facts whose status as facts (and also for whom they are facts) is brought to light.[166]

And, while there are experiences of great insights, even euphoria when breakthroughs occur, the paths moving out of old familiar categorical and theoretical landscapes are rarely smooth and straightforward. As Manzo points out:

> [E]ven the most radically critical discourse easily slips into the form, the logic, and the implicit postulations of precisely what it seeks to contest, for it can never step completely outside of a heritage from which it must borrow its tools—its history, its language—in its attempt to destroy that heritage itself.[167]

Conversion is also a deeply personal process. As Smith insists, "Political projects of transformation necessarily involve a fundamental reconstitution of ourselves as well".[168] Indeed, as Che Guevara proclaimed—and subsequently was martyred for—"At the risk of seeming ridiculous, let me say that the true revolutionary is guided by great feelings of love".[169] In a similar spirit, Poo testifies to the life-transforming effects of activist organising:

> Great organizing campaigns are like great love affairs. You begin to see life through a different lens. You change in unexpected ways. You lose sleep, but you also feel boundless energy. You develop new relationships and new interests. Your skin becomes more open to the world around you. Life feels different, and it's almost like you've been reborn. And, most importantly, you begin to feel things that you previously couldn't have even imagined are possible.[170]

McNally also confesses, "To make history—to change the actual course of world events—is intoxicating, inspiring, and life-transforming".[171]

And more generally, as Osterweil notes, at stake in dialogues across differences are

> also fundamentally different temporalities and registers for assessing and seeing the 'political' such that, rather than looking for political outcomes in quantitative or measurable terms, we are more attuned to the subjective, affective, and epistemological as sites of 'real' change and action.[172]

Conversion has communal dimensions too. As Smith testifies from the point of view of scholarship and organising with US Indigenous communities:

> Communities that have suffered from years of colonial and racist violence cannot reasonably be expected to have remained unscarred by the experience. Ironically, we often feel that the only way to publicly confirm our status as victims of such violence is to deny vociferously the effects of our victimization. In doing so, however, we not only burden ourselves with an unfair (not to mention impossible) standard of prelapsarian innocence, but we also set ourselves up for failure: knowledge of our problems cannot remain with our communities; inevitably, our shortcomings will be known.[173]

Thus, as Alfred and Corntassel note, "The battle is a spiritual and physical one fought against the political manipulation of the people's own innate fears and the embedding of complacency, that metastasising weakness, into their psyches".[174]

In addition to the very different challenges to conversion confronting privileged communities, organisations, and individuals, organising within 'marginalised' communities also involves processes of personal and communal conversion and renewal. As Vargas points out, feminists organised panels at various World Social Forums bringing together "trade unionists, 'untouchables', peasants, homosexuals, lesbians, and transsexuals into dialogue with one another to discuss their differences but also to share reflections on how to expand each group's perspective on transformation and their enrich their common ground for action".[175]

More generally, as Escobar notes, none of the participating movements in the antiglobalisation movement "can by itself tackle the entire 'system' or the global situation (not even understand it as a whole)". Indeed, no "single movement can 'see the whole'",[176] Therefore, encountering others in the course of struggling to change the world sooner or later involves shocks to existing ways of seeing and thinking about the shape of the world, our 'responsibilities'—including newly recognised 'responsibility' for benefitting from some of the bad fruits of the rigged system inherited from our predecessors—and the choices before us. And challenges to conversion are becoming 'normal'.

In narrower political terms of organising cultures, institutions, and procedures, challenges to conversion(s) are also inescapable. This is clear in the example of the aborted Northwest Social Forum above. It is also clear in Ho's description of positive developments among queer movements and their allies in Asia:

> Internal struggle has never been absent from the gay community as mainstreaming gays and militant queers diverge on strategies and issues. Yet one is also encouraged by the fact that at the December 2005 WTO ministerial meeting in Hong Kong, queer groups from quite a few East Asian states lined up with other social movement groups (labour, farmer, women, sex worker) in fierce protest against WTO policies. Such collaboration has proven to be both educational and solidarity-building.[177]

And Houtart points to the eventual conversions from 'revolutionary arrogance' by Marxists in southern Mexico after more than a decade of solidarity with Indigenous Peoples.[178] Indeed, Khasnabish argues that "the encounter of the two groups resulted not in the 'revolutionising' of the indigenous communities but rather in the 'defeat' of Marxist dogma at the hands of these indigenous realities". This 'defeat' was central in forging the path leading to the Zapatista uprising.[179]

And, finally, as these examples confirm, in the worldwide irruptions of progressive / left social movements 'conversion' is seldom singular and complete for individuals, communities, or organisations and movements. Rather, as Muto points out concerning the Alliance of Hope in Japan in the 1990s, it was organised "not as static institutions or bodies but as dynamic processes of constant formation and renewal".[180] Similarly, Walsh describes decolonial projects in Latin America as "simultaneous and continuous processes of transformation and creation, the construction of radically distinct social imaginaries, conditions, and relations of power, knowledge".[181] Holloway suggests that we live in "a world of not knowing" in which "What unites us is that we know that we must change the world, but we do not know how to do it . . . [which] means a politics of asking-listening . . . [and] constant experimentation".[182] And, Santos, drawing on experience in WSF processes, points to the impact of expanding contact with other movements from other contexts, sooner or later requiring them "to question their very identity and autonomy as they have been conceived of so far". Inevitably, in addressing simultaneously the broad range of different movements—ecological, pacifist, Indigenous, feminist, workers, etc—this requires profound "respect for the identity of every movement, [and] an enormous effort of mutual recognition, dialogue and debate",[183] and, it goes without saying, many 'conversions' on all sides.

This dynamic of multiple and ongoing conversions may sound chaotic, and in the experience of many it often is.[184] As De Angelis urges in his essay, "we must abandon linear thinking, since social transformation emerges out of our actions, subjectivities, desires, organisational capability, ingenuity, and struggles in unpredictable ways".[185] And our editor Sen speaks of "the dance and the music of worlds in movement";[186] indeed, he subtitled this book, the second volume of *The Movements of Movements*, "Rethinking Our Dance", suggesting the emergence of new modes of communication and organisational dynamics far beyond the old. And Wallerstein turns to chaos theory for an image to grasp the new dynamics of movements in a radically changing world: "We learned in the last half-century that every fluttering of a butterfly's wings changes the world climate. In this transition to a new world order, we are all little butterflies".[187]

At the same time, though, as suggested above, many activists testify that openness to dialogues and conversion does not mean that there are no stable centres of knowledge and action. Rather, as Smith suggests, it means that "there should be a stable centre [eg, in the ongoing life of the community or movement]—but [also] that . . . re-centring is a continual process".[188] Indeed in many places there are possibilities for agreement with others on specific issues and concrete collaboration in campaigns. Indeed, Bensaïd warns of the dangers that even good slogans can become abstract and empty, even the WSF's 'another world is possible'; and he points to the importance of concrete proposals: "We need, now, to be specific about what the other 'possible' world is and—above all—to explore how to get there".[189]

In various ways, then, these dynamics are evident in coalition politics everywhere, though attention is only beginning to be paid to the magnitude of the challenges, the range of fronts, and the depth of the processes of conversion, and their implications for our epistemologies and politics.

Generosity and Capacity for Sacrifice

Of course, people of affluence and privilege, including many of us in the 'middle classes' of the world, not to mention the upper classes, have no business preaching constraint and sacrifice to the poor and marginalised of the world.[190] And indeed discourses of 'necessary sacrifice' are constantly mobilised against the demands of popular movements. Still, struggling people everywhere also know very well that survival, not to mention hope for a better world, involves great juggling and many sacrifices, as individuals and communities: of one priority over another, of short-term versus long-term, of one constituency's priorities over another's (at least in the short run). As Delgado-P notes in his essay on movements in Bolivia under the Morales government, many have not yet seen their demands fulfilled, but they see themselves as involved in "a slow but sure process of redefinition . . . that requires postponing specific demands where, ultimately, the stake is to ensure that Bolivia is refounded".[191]

And the conviction is growing that, as was evident in the climate change negotiations at COP21 in Paris in 2015, major 'sacrifices' are absolutely essential to hope for 'another world'—especially for the middle and upper classes of the world. For these societies have been and continue to be the major sources of greenhouse gases (along with China, which has recently joined this group) and have also enjoyed the 'benefits', aided and abetted by accounting systems that externalise many costs of GDP growth and consumer lifestyles. In this framework, not surprisingly, many Northern environmental movements have ignored these connections between consumerism and climate change (and other ecological costs); as North and Featherstone note in their essay, "Debates around climate change alone . . . have frequently isolated processes like carbon emissions and global warming from the wider, unequal social and environmental relations upon which neoliberal globalisation rests".[192] In recent years, though, this separation is increasingly being criticised, along with affluent 'middle class' hyperconsumption lifestyles. And the conviction grows that climate justice requires radically shrinking middle-class consumerism and its immense ecological footprints.

Furthermore, marginalised peoples, like Andean Indigenous groups, have other traditions, and other aspirations for the 'good life'—'*sumak kawsay*' in Quechua[193] and '*buen vivir*' in Spanish—that stress relationships with all of Mother Earth. In such a worldview, 'self-interest' and its supposed opposite 'altruism' are defined and framed very differently. Instead of a simple binary relationship, complementarity, reciprocity, and the well-being of the community as a whole are central.[194] And in this perspective, 'living well' is a radical alternative to 'having more', as the ideology of growth and consumerism. Moreover, as Dávalos points out:

> [T]here are literally thousands of millions of human beings, completely and radically outside the figure of the consumer and free and competitive markets. Human beings different from the ontology of the consumer and commercialization. Human beings whose life coordinates are established from other categories, standards and ethics. Human beings who live in communities with an atavistic memory of ancestral relations that have nothing to do with modern individuality, nor with the dominant liberal reasoning.[195]

A major exception to the generalised neglect in critical scholarship and politics of middle-class overconsumption and any need to consider 'cutting back' is the largely European degrowth movement. This movement stresses an equitable downscaling of production and consumption, along with a deepening of democracy, more equitable distribution of wealth, defence of ecosystems, and "a voluntary, smooth and equitable transition to a regime of lower production and consumption".[196] Of course, above all, this requires a 'decolonisation of minds', a renewed capacity to imagine a 'convivial utopia', a revitalisation of the local, and a rich variety of experiments in reducing ecological footprints in ways appropriate for different contexts.[197]

Conclusion

The contributors to *The Movements of Movements* expand our horizons in every direction. The range of issues being addressed by progressive social movements today is mind-boggling. Among other factors, the wide range of new social knowledges that social movements are constantly producing—and that they are also stimulating scholars to produce—is making it ever clearer that we are witnessing the end of the local worlds we have known and can only dimly see a future that will be so fundamentally different in so many ways. Indeed, so many commentators today are searching for appropriate analogies to grasp the magnitude of changes shaking the world: in civilisational terms comparable to the development of agriculture 10,000 years ago, or to 'axial' shifts associated with the inventions of civilisation 5,000 years ago, or to the fall of the western Roman empire 1500 years ago, or to the rise of colonial capitalist modernity in the last 500 years, with its accompanying devastation of 'non-Western' cultures and civilisations; in ecological terms, 'climate change', habitat destruction, and 'biodiversity crisis'; and in geological and evolutionary terms, 'epochal', comparable to the transition marked by the extinction of the dinosaurs and thousands of other species 65 million years ago and the dawn of a new geological and evolutionary era, the Anthropocene, in which one species alone, *homo sapiens*, is responsible for such massive planetary change and destruction, indeed for changing the dynamics not only of human history but of the evolution of life on the planet.[198]

We are today witnesses to and actors in the emergence of a very different kind of world, with whole new dimensions of existence (eg, cyberspace); new modes of ignorance and knowledge, hope and faith; new dynamics of identity and solidarity; new eco-social relations; new (and old) social actors, centres of power, and calculus of social order and change; and with new scales of action, new possibilities, and new risks on previously unimaginable scales.

In this tumultuous world, progressive social movements and their supporters and allies are 'reinventing' ways of seeing the world and generating new knowledges. They are envisioning alternative futures and modes of acting, locally, regionally, internationally, and increasingly globally. In all their diversity, they are increasingly central to hope for a future that is more inclusive, more realistic, and more promising for countless poor and marginalised peoples and societies, and ultimately for the human species as a whole and for thousands of other species, for the future of life on earth, perhaps even in the cosmos.

Indeed, as critical rereadings of history proliferate, the conviction grows that 'marginal' communities, classes, and movements have often (always?) been central actors in sustaining life in hierarchically organised civilisations, especially for the majorities, meeting basic needs and supporting victims, restraining some of the worst excesses of ruling classes and policymakers, recovering from their extravagant excesses and disasters.[199] And, most importantly, often against impossible odds, they have kept alive hope that 'another world is possible'.

As the contributors to *The Movements of Movements* repeatedly testify, the 'others' are doing so again. In all their diversity there is also growing recognition of commonalities in suffering and hope across the South and the North too.[200] And around the world there are many signs of the birth of a new "world where many worlds fit". As the faith-based organisers of a conference in São Paulo in 2012 on the international financial architecture affirmed:

> Persons living in poverty and deprivation as a result of neoliberal financial systems have demonstrated that alternative life-giving economies are alive, impacting millions of indigenous and grassroots people. It is to these initiatives that we must turn for criteria that truly speak to an alternative. Throughout the world, people's movements resist the temptation to surrender to a death-dealing economic system. At the same time, many poor and marginalised people survive through a variety of systems which, even though not recognised by big business, governments and mainstream economies, nevertheless keep them alive and nurture hope. . . . [N]umerous alternatives have already been established by people all over the world . . . that serve as signposts of change.[201]

And as Leyva Solano insists, "many other worlds are already in the process of planetary construction".[202]

Most often, the poets and songwriters should have the first and last words. Thus, as Shailja Patel writes in the proem to volume one of *The Movements of Movements*:

> Some moments, life asks of us:
> What do you hope?[203]

And we are left trembling in awareness . . . we are actors in epochal transitions . . . we cannot escape choices . . . our responses involve many great uncertainties . . . and leaps of faith which can contribute to tipping the balance among divergent possible futures.

And then, surprisingly:

> Some mornings life wakes us up
> sets our hearts beating
> sets our nerves thrumming
> warns us
> we're about to leap
> into our iciest fear

our largest growth

our most piercing joy.

Some mornings,

We take a huge breath, say

Yes

to it all.[204]

References

Kolya Abramsky, 2018—'Gathering Our Dignified Rage: Building New Autonomous Global Relations of Production, Livelihood, and Exchange', in Jai Sen, ed, 2018—*The Movements of Movements, Part 2: Rethinking Our Dance*. Volume 5 in the *Challenging Empires* series. New Delhi: OpenWord, and Oakland, CA: PM Press

Alberto Acosta, 2013—'Ecuador: Building a Good Life—*Sumak Kawsay*', in *Upside Down World*, January 24 2013, at http://upsidedownworld.org/main/index.php?option=com_content&view=article&id=4087:ecuador-building-a-good-life-sumak-kawsay&catid=25: ecuador&Itemid=49 (Accessed September 4 2017)

Ezequiel Adamovsky, 2018—'Autonomous Politics and its Problems: Thinking the Passage from the Social to Political', in Jai Sen, ed, 2018—*The Movements of Movements, Part 2: Rethinking Our Dance*. Volume 5 in the *Challenging Empires* series. New Delhi: OpenWord, and Oakland, CA: PM Press

Taiaiake Alfred and Jeff Corntassel, 2017—'Being Indigenous: Resurgences against Contemporary Colonialism', in Jai Sen, ed, 2017—*The Movements of Movements, Part 1: What Makes Us Move?*. Volume 4 in the *Challenging Empires* series. New Delhi: OpenWord, and Oakland, CA: PM Press

Tariq Ali, 2017—'Storming Heaven: Where Has The Rage Gone?', in Jai Sen, ed, 2017—*The Movements of Movements, Part 1: What Makes Us Move?*. Volume 4 in the *Challenging Empires* series. New Delhi: OpenWord, and Oakland, CA: PM Press

Samir Amin, 2018—'Towards a Fifth International?', in Jai Sen, ed, 2018—*The Movements of Movements, Part 2: Rethinking Our Dance*. Volume 5 in the *Challenging Empires* series. New Delhi: OpenWord, and Oakland, CA: PM Press

Amnesty International. 2015—*The Global Refugee Crisis: A Conspiracy of Neglect*. London, UK: Amnesty International Ltd, at https://www.amnesty.org/en/documents/pol40/1796/2015/en/ (Accessed September 4 2017)

Kurt Andersen, 2011—'The Protester', in *Time Magazine*, December 14 2011, at http://content.time.com/time/specials/packages/article/0,28804,2101745_2102132,00.html (Accessed September 4 2017)

Stephen Anderson, 2010—How Many Languages Are There in the World?', on *Linguistic Society of America* (2010), at http://www.linguisticsociety.org/content/how-many-languages-are-there-world (Accessed September 4 2017)

Arjun Appadurai, 2000—'Grassroots Globalization and the Research Imagination', in *Public Culture*, vol 12 no 1, pp 1–19

Giovanni Arrighi and Beverly Silver, 1999—'Conclusion', in Giovanni Arrighi, Beverly J Silver, Iftikhar Ahmad, Kenneth Barr, Shuji Hisaeda, Po-keung Hui, Krishnendu Ray, Thomas Ehrlich Reifer, Miin-wen Shih, and Eric Slater, 1999—*Chaos and Governance in the Modern World System*. Minneapolis: University of Minnesota Press, pp 271–89

Yilidz Atasoy, 2008—'The Islamic Ethic and the Spirit of Turkish Capitalism Today', in Leo Panitch and Colin Leys, eds, 2008—*Global Flashpoints: Reactions to Imperialism and Neoliberalism*, Socialist Register 2008. New York, NY: Monthly Review Press, pp 121–40

Babels, April 2004—'Assessing the Language Issue for the WSF 2005 in Porto Alegre', April 20 2004, on *Babels*, at http://www.babels.org/spip.php?article65 (Accessed September 4 2017)

César Augusto Baldi, 2013—'*Sumak Kawsay*, Interculturality, and Decolonialization', on *Critical Legal Thinking*, April 15 2013, at http://criticallegalthinking. com/2013/04/15/sumak-kawsay-interculturality-and-decolonialization/ (Accessed September 4 2017)

Pedro Barreto Jimeno, SJ, Rev Dr Olav Fykse Tveit, Nduna John et al, 2015—'Statement of Faith and Spiritual Leaders on the Upcoming United Nations Climate Change Conference, COP 21 in Paris in December 2015', on *The Forum on Religion and Ecology Yale*, at http://fore.yale.edu/climate-change/statements-from-world-religions/ interfaith/ (Accessed September 4 2017)

Asef Bayat, 2013a—*Life as Politics: How Ordinary People Change the Middle East*, second edition. Stanford, CA: Stanford University Press

Asef Bayat, 2013b—'The Arab Spring and Its Surprises', in *Development and Change*, vol 44 no 3 (2013), pp 587–601

Michel Beaud, 2004—*A History of Capitalism 1500–2000*, fifth edition. Translated by Tom Dickman and Anny Lefebvre. Delhi: Aakar Books

Bret Benjamin, 2007—*Invested Interests: Capital, Culture, and the World Bank*. Minneapolis: University of Minnesota Press

Daniel Bensaïd, 2017—'The Return of Strategy', in Jai-Sen, ed, 2017a,—*The Movements of Movements, Part 1: What Makes Us Move?*. Volume 4 in the Challenging Empires series. New Delhi: OpenWord, and Oakland, CA: PM Press

Gurminder Bhambra, June 2011—'Historical Sociology, Modernity, and Postcolonial Critique', in *The American Historical Review*, vol 116 no 3, pp 653–62

Fred Block, 2005—'Towards a New Understanding of Economic Modernity', in Christian Joerges, Bo Straith, and Peter Wagner, eds, 2005—*The Economy as a Polity: The Political Constitution of Contemporary Capitalism*. London, UK: University College London, pp 3–16

Manuela Boatcă, 2015—*Global Inequalities Beyond Occidentalism*. Burlington, VT: Ashgate

Howard Brick, 2006—*Transcending Capitalism: Visions of a New Society in Modern American Thought*. Ithaca, NY: Cornell University Press

Neil Brooks, 1995—*Left Vs Right: Why the Left is Right and the Right is Wrong*. Ottawa, ON: Canadian Centre for Policy Alternatives

Michael Burawoy, 2010—'Forging Global Sociology from Below', in Sujata Patel, ed, 2010—*The ISA Handbook of Diverse Sociological Traditions*. Thousand Oaks, CA: SAGE Publications, pp 52–66

David Calleo, 1996—'Restarting the Marxist Clock? The Economic Fragility of the West', in *World Policy Journal*, vol 13 no 2, pp 57–64

Chris Carlsson, 2018—'Effective Politics or Feeling Effective?', in Jai Sen, ed, 2018—*The Movements of Movements, Part 2: Rethinking Our Dance*. Volume 5 in the Challenging Empires series. New Delhi: OpenWord, and Oakland, CA: PM Press

Manuel Castells, João Caraça, and Gustavo Cardoso, 2012—'The Cultures of Economic Crisis: An Introduction', in Manuel Castells, João Caraça, and Gustavo Cardoso, eds, 2012—*Aftermath: The Cultures of the Economic Crisis*. Oxford: Oxford University Press

Ana Esther Ceceña, 2012—'On the Complex Relation Between Knowledges and Emancipations', in *South Atlantic Quarterly*, vol 113 no 1, pp 111–32

Dipesh Chakrabarty, 2009—'The Climate of History: Four Theses', in *Critical Inquiry*, vol 35, Winter 2009, pp 197–222

Lucas Chancel and Thomas Piketty, 2015—'Carbon and Inequality: From Kyoto to Paris', in *Vox*, December 1 2015, at http://www.voxeu.org/article/carbon-and-inequality-kyoto-paris (Accessed September 4 2017)

Ha-Joon Chang and Ilene Grabel, 2014—'Beginning of the End of the Neoliberal Approach to Development?', in *CounterPunch*, March 21–23 2014, at http://www. counterpunch.org/2014/03/21/beginning-of-the-end-of-the-neoliberal-approach-to-development/ (Accessed September 4 2017)

John Brown Childs, 2018—'Boundary as Bridge', in Jai Sen, ed, 2018—*The Movements of Movements, Part 2: Rethinking Our Dance*. Volume 5 in the *Challenging Empires* series. New Delhi: OpenWord, and Oakland, CA: PM Press

Cho Hee-Yeon, 2017—'From Anti-Imperialist to Anti-Empire: The Crystallisation of the Anti-Globalisation Movement in South Korea', in Jai Sen, ed, 2017a—*The Movements of Movements, Part 1: What Makes Us Move?*. Volume 4 in the *Challenging Empires* series. New Delhi: OpenWord, and Oakland, CA: PM Press

David Christian, 2005—*Maps of Time: An Introduction to Big History*. Berkeley, CA: University of California Press

Stephen Cohen, 1985—*Rethinking the Soviet Experience*. New York, NY: Oxford University Press

Committee on Issues in the Transborder Flow of Scientific Data, US National Committee for CODATA, and Mathematics Commission on Physical Sciences, and Applications, 1997—*Bits of Power: Issues in Global Access to Scientific Data*. Washington, DC: National Academy Press

Raewyn Connell, 2007—*Southern Theory: The Global Dynamics of Knowledge in Social Science*. Sydney, Australia: Allen & Unwin

Christopher Connery, 2006—'The Asian Sixties: An Unfinished Project', in *Inter-Asia Cultural Studies*, vol 7 no 4, December 2006, pp 546–53

Janet Conway, 2011—'Cosmopolitan or Colonial? The World Social Forum as 'Contact Zone'', in *Third World Quarterly*, vol 32 no 2, pp 217–36

Lee Cormie, 1980—'The Sociology of National Development and Salvation History', in Gregory Baum, ed, 1980—*Sociology and Human Destiny*. New York, NY: Seabury Press, pp 56–85

Lee Cormie, 2017—'Re-Creating The World: Communities of Faith in the Struggles For Other Possible Worlds', in Jai Sen, ed, 2017—*The Movements of Movements, Part 1: What Makes Us Move?*. Volume 4 in the *Challenging Empires* series. New Delhi: OpenWord, and Oakland, CA: PM Press

Jeff Corntassel, 2017—'Rethinking Self-Determination: Lessons from the Indigenous-Rights Discourse', in Jai Sen, ed, 2017a—*The Movements of Movements, Part 1: What Makes Us Move?*. Volume 4 in the *Challenging Empires* series. New Delhi: OpenWord, and Oakland, CA: PM Press

Laurence Cox and Alf Gunvald Nilsen, 2014—'We Are the Authors and Actors of Our Own History', in *Roar Magazine*, September 10 2014, at http://roarmag. org/2014/09/cox-nilsen-we-make-our-own-history/ (Accessed September 4 2017)

Anila Daulatzai, 2018—'Believing in Exclusion: The Problem of Secularism in Progressive Politics', in Jai Sen, ed, 2018—*The Movements of Movements, Part 2: Rethinking Our Dance*. Volume 5 in the *Challenging Empires* series. New Delhi: OpenWord, and Oakland, CA: PM Press

Pablo Dávalos, 2008—'Reflections on *Sumak Kawsay* (Good Living) and Theories of Development', in *América Latina en Movimiento*, August 5 2008, at https://www.alainet.org/en/articulo/136929 (Accessed September 4 2017)

Massimo De Angelis, 2018—'PR like PRocess! Strategy from the Bottom Up', in Jai Sen, ed, 2018—*The Movements of Movements, Part 2: Rethinking Our Dance*. Volume 5 in the *Challenging Empires* series. New Delhi: OpenWord, and Oakland, CA: PM Press

Olivier de Marcellus, August 2006—'Biggest victory yet over WTO and "free" trade. Celebrate it!', on *InterActivist Info Exchange*, at http://interactivist.autonomedia.org/node/5349 (Accessed April 13 2011, inactive September 4 2017)

Guillermo Delgado-P, 2017—'Refounding Bolivia: Exploring the Possibility and Paradox of a Social Movements State', in Jai Sen, ed, 2017a—*The Movements of Movements, Part 1: What Makes Us Move?*. Volume 4 in the *Challenging Empires* series. New Delhi: OpenWord, and Oakland, CA: PM Press

Sharon Doetsch-Kidder, 2012—*Social Change and Intersectional Activism: The Spirit of Social Movement*. The Politics of Intersectionality. New York, NY: Palgrave Macmillan

André C Drainville, 2017—'Beyond *Altermondialisme*: Anti-Capitalist Dialectic of Presence', in Jai Sen, ed, 2017—*The Movements of Movements, Part 1: What Makes Us Move?*. Volume 4 in the *Challenging Empires* series. New Delhi: OpenWord, and Oakland, CA: PM Press

Enrique Dussel, 2000—'Europe, Modernity, and Eurocentrism', in *Nepantla: Views from the South*, vol 1 no 3, pp 465–78

Lynn Eden, Robert Rosner, Rod Ewing, Lawrence M Krauss, Sivan Kartha, Thomas R Pickering, Raymond T Pierrehumbert, Ramamurti Rajaraman, Jennifer Sims, Richard C J Somerville, Sharon Squassoni, and David Titley, January 2016a—'It's Still Three Minutes to Midnight', in *Bulletin of the Atomic Scientists*, January 22 2016, at http://thebulletin.org/it-still-three-minutes-midnight9107 (Accessed September 4 2017)

Lynn Eden, Robert Rosner, Rod Ewing, Lawrence M Krauss, Sivan Kartha, Thomas R Pickering, Raymond T Pierrehumbert, Ramamurti Rajaraman, Jennifer Sims, Richard C J Somerville, Sharon Squassoni, and David Titley, January 2016b—'Overview', in *Bulletin of the Atomic Scientists*, January 22 2016, at http://thebulletin.org/overview (Accessed September 4 2017)

Niles Eldredge, 2001—'The Sixth Extinction', in *ActionBioscience*, June 2001, at http://www.actionbioscience.org/evolution/eldredge2.html (Accessed September 4 2017)

Arturo Escobar, 2004—'Other Worlds Are (Already) Possible: Self-Organisation, Complexity, and Post-Capitalist Cultures', in Jai Sen, Anita Anand, Arturo Escobar, and Peter Waterman, eds, 2004—*World Social Forum: Challenging Empires*. New Delhi: Viveka, pp 349–58, at http://www.choike.org/nuevo_eng/informes/1557.html and http://www.openspaceforum.net/twiki/tiki-index.php?page=WSFChallenging Empires2004 (Both accessed September 4 2017)

Arturo Escobar, 2007—'Worlds and Knowledges Otherwise: The Latin American Modernity/Coloniality Research Paradigm', in *Cultural Studies*, vol 21 nos 2/3, March 2007, pp 179–210

Arturo Escobar, 2009—'Latin America at a Crossroads: Alternative Modernizations, Postliberalism, or Postdevelopment', on *Society for International Development Blog*, July 27 2009, at http://www.tandfonline.com/doi/abs/10.1080/09502380903424208 (Accessed September 4 2017)

Arturo Escobar, 2012—'Preface' to *Encountering Development*. Princeton, NJ: Princeton University Press, pp vii–xliii

Arturo Escobar, 2015—'Degrowth, Postdevelopment, and Transitions: A Preliminary Conversation', in *Sustainability Science* vol 10 no 3, April 2015, pp 451–62, at http://www.degrowth.org/wp-content/uploads/2015/07/ESCOBARDegrowth-postdevelopment-and-transitions_Escobar-2015.pdf (Accessed September 4 2017)

The Free Association, 2018—'Worlds in Motion: Movements, Problematics, and the Creation of New Worlds', in Jai Sen, ed, 2018—*The Movements of Movements, Part 2: Rethinking Our Dance*. Volume 5 in the *Challenging Empires* series. New Delhi: OpenWord, and Oakland, CA: PM Press

Harriet Friedmann and Amber McNair, 2008—'Whose Rules Rule? Contested Projects to Certify Local Production for Distant Consumers', in Saturnino M Borras, Jr, Marc Edelman, and Cristóbal Kay, 2008—*Transnational Agrarian Movements Confronting Globalization*. Malden, MA: Wiley-Blackwell, pp 239–66

James K Galbraith, 2014—*The End of Normal: The Great Crisis and the Future of Growth*. New York, NY: Simon & Schuster

Lori Gallegos, 2015—'Sketch of a Decolonial Environmentalism: Challenging the Colonial Conception of Nature Through the Biocultural Perspective', in *Inter-American Journal of Philosophy* vol 6 no 1, May 2015, pp 32–47, at https://www.academia.edu/9375053/Sketch_of_a_Decolonial_Environmentalism_Challenging_the_Colonial_Conception_of_Nature_through_the_Biocultural_Perspective (Accessed September 4 2017)

General Command of the Zapatista Army of National Liberation—Clandestine Revolutionary Indigenous Committee, 2001—'Words of the EZLN in Puebla', at http://www.csuchico.edu/zapatist/HTML/Archive/Communiques/ccri_puebla_feb.html (Accessed September 4 2017)

J K Gibson-Graham, 2002—'A Diverse Economy: Rethinking Economy and Economic Representation', at http://avery.wellesley.edu/Economics/jmatthaei/transformationcentral/solidarity/solidaritydocuments/diverseeconomies.pdf (Accessed September 4 2017)

J K Gibson-Graham, Stephen Resnick, and Richard Wolff, 2001—'Toward a Poststructuralist Political Economy', in J K Gibson-Graham, Stephen A Resnick, and Richard D Wolff, eds, 2001—*Re/Presenting Class: Essays in Postmodern Marxism*. Durham, NC: Duke University Press, pp 1–22

Global Ecumenical Conference, 2012—'The São Paulo Statement: International Financial Transformation for the Economy of Life', from Conference on 'A New International Financial and Economic Architecture', São Paulo, Brazil. Sponsored by the World Council of Churches, the World Communion of Reformed Churches, and the Council of World Mission, at http://wcrc.ch/uncategorized/sao-paulo-statement-presented-to-latin-american-governments (Accessed September 4 2017)

David Graeber, 2007—'The Shock of Victory', in *Infoshop News*, October 12 2007, at https://theanarchistlibrary.org/library/david-graeber-the-shock-of-victory (Accessed September 4 2017)

David Graeber, 2012—'Revolution at the Level of Common Sense', in Federico Campagna and Emanuele Campiglio, eds, 2012—*What We Are Fighting for: A Radical Collective Manifesto*. London: Pluto, pp 165–75

David Graeber, 2018—'The Shock of Victory', in Jai Sen, ed, 2018—*The Movements of Movements, Part 2: Rethinking Our Dance*. Volume 5 in the *Challenging Empires* series. New Delhi: OpenWord, and Oakland, CA: PM Press

Greg Grandin, 2015—'The TPP Will Finish What Chile's Dictatorship Started', in *The Nation*, September 11 2015, at http://www.thenation.com/article/the-tpp-will-finish-what-chiles-dictatorship-started/ (Accessed September 4 2017)

Ramón Grosfoguel, 2005—'The Implications of Subaltern Epistemologies for Global Capitalism: Transmodernity, Border Thinking, and Global Coloniality', in Richard

Applebaum and William Robinson, eds, 2005—*Critical Globalization Studies*. New York, NY: Routledge, pp 283–92

Ramón Grosfoguel, 2006—'World-System Analysis in the Context of Transmodernity, Border Thinking, and Global Coloniality', in *Review* vol 2 no 2, pp 167–87

Ramón Grosfoguel, 2007—The Epistemic Decolonial Turn: Beyond Political-Economy Paradigms', in *Cultural Studies* vol 21 nos 2/3, March 2007, pp 211–23

Ernesto Che Guevara, 2005 [1965]—'From Algiers (Letter to the Editor of *Marcha* [Montevideo, Uruguay], 12 March 1965)', in David Deutschmann, ed, 2005—*The Che Reader: Writings on Politics & Revolution*. North Melbourne, Victoria, Australia: Ocean Press, at https://www.marxists.org/archive/guevara/1965/03/man-socialism.htm (Accessed September 4 2017)

Jacob Darwin Hamblin, 2013—*Arming Mother Nature: The Birth of Catastrophic Environmentalism*. Oxford, UK: Oxford University Press

Ange-Marie Hancock and Nira Yuval-Davis, 2012—'The Politics of Intersectionality: Series Editors' Introduction', in Sharon Doetsch-Kidder, ed, 2012—*Social Change and Intersectional Activism: The Spirit of Social Movement*. New York, NY: Palgrave Macmillan, pp ix–xiv

Donna Haraway, 1988—'Situated Knowledges: The Science Question in Feminism and the Privilege of Partial Perspective', in *Feminist Studies* vol 14 no 3, pp 575–99

Michael Harrington, 1962—*The Other America: Poverty in the United States*. New York, NY: Macmillan

Paul Hawken, 2007—*Blessed Unrest: How the Largest Movement in the World Came Into Being, and Why No One Saw It Coming*. New York, NY: Viking

Emilie Hayes, 2017—'Open Space in Movement: Reading Three Waves of Feminism', in Jai Sen, ed, 2017—*The Movements of Movements, Part 1: What Makes Us Move?*. Volume 4 in the *Challenging Empires* series. New Delhi: OpenWord, and Oakland, CA: PM Press

Robert Heilbroner, 1998—'The 'Disappearance' of Capitalism', in *World Policy Journal*, vol 15 no 2, pp 1–7

Eric Helleiner, 2003—'Economic liberalism and its critics: The past as prologue?', in *Review of International Political Economy*, vol 10 no 4, pp 685–96

Doug Henwood, August 2011—'Headless Chickens', in *Left Business Observer*, no 133, August 21 2011

Josephine Ho, 2018—'Is Global Governance Bad for East Asian Queers?', in Jai Sen, ed, 2018—*The Movements of Movements, Part 2: Rethinking Our Dance*. Volume 5 in the *Challenging Empires* series. New Delhi: OpenWord, and Oakland, CA: PM Press

Eric Hobsbawm, 1995—*Age of Extremes: The Short Twentieth Century 1914–1991*. London, England: Abacus

John Holloway, 2018—'The Asymmetry of Revolution', in Jai Sen, ed, 2018—*The Movements of Movements, Part 2: Rethinking Our Dance*. Volume 5 in the *Challenging Empires* series. New Delhi: OpenWord, and Oakland, CA: PM Press

Alf Hornborg, 2011—'How We Have Been Mystified by Technology', interview by Adam Robbert and JP Hayes, on *Kickitover.org*, July 14 2011, at http://kickitover.org/2011/07/14/interview-alf-hornborg (Accessed October 19 2011, inactive September 4 2017)

François Houtart, 2018—'We Still Exist', in Jai Sen, ed, 2018—*The Movements of Movements, Part 2: Rethinking Our Dance*. Volume 5 in the *Challenging Empires* series. New Delhi: OpenWord, and Oakland, CA: PM Press

'Information Society', on Wikipedia, at https://en.wikipedia.org/wiki/Information_society (Accessed September 4 2017)

International Planning Committee for Food Sovereignty, 2006—'*Sovranita Alimentare*' ['Food Sovereignty', in Spanish]. Final Declaration For a New Agrarian Reform Based on Food Sovereignty, March 9 2006, at http://movimientos.org/cloc/fororeforma-graria/show_text.ph (Accessed January 31 2008, inactive September 4 2017)

Jeffrey S Juris and Geoffrey Pleyers, 2018—'Incorporating Youth or Transforming Politics? Alter-Activism as an Emerging Mode of Praxis among Young Global Justice Activists', in Jai Sen, ed, 2018—*The Movements of Movements, Part 2: Rethinking Our Dance*. Volume 5 in the *Challenging Empires* series. New Delhi: OpenWord, and Oakland, CA: PM Press

Fouad Kalouche and Eric Mielants, 2017—'Antisystemic Movements and Transforma-tions of the World-System, 1968–1989', in Jai Sen, ed, 2017—*The Movements of Movements, Part 1: What Makes Us Move?*. Volume 4 in the *Challenging Empires* series. New Delhi: OpenWord, and Oakland, CA: PM Press

Alex Khasnabish, 2017—'Forward Dreaming: Zapatismo and the Radical Imagination', in Jai Sen, ed, 2017—*The Movements of Movements, Part 1: What Makes Us Move?*. Volume 4 in the *Challenging Empires* series. New Delhi: OpenWord, and Oakland, CA: PM Press

Michael Klare, 2015—'Delusionary Washington: The Desperate Plight of a Declining Superpower', in *Truthdig*, May 28 2015, at https://www.truthdig.com/articles/delusionary-washington-the-desperate-plight-of-a-declining-superpower/ (Accessed September 4 2017)

Naomi Klein, 2013—'Overcoming "Overburden": The Climate Crisis and a Unified Left Agenda', Remarks at the founding convention of UNIFOR, a new mega union created by the Canadian Autoworkers and the Canadian Energy and Paper Workers Union, in *Common Dreams*, September 4 2013, at https://www.commondreams.org/view/2013/09/04 (Accessed September 4 2017)

Vinay Lal, 2002—'The Disciplines in Ruins: History, the Social Sciences, and Their Cate-gories in the "New Millennium"', in *Emergences: Journal for the Study of Media and Composite Cultures*, vol 12 no 1, pp 139–55

Edgardo Lander, 2002—'Eurocentrism, modern knowledges, and the "natural" order of global capital', in *Nepantla: Views from the South*, vol 3 no 2, pp 245–68

Edgardo Lander, 2007—'Dominant Tendencies of Our Days: Is Our Time Running Out?', in *Worlds and Knowledges Otherwise 2, Dossier 1*, Fall 2007, pp 41–63, at https://www.tni.org/en/article/dominant-tendencies-of-our-days-is-our-time-running-out (Accessed September 4 2017)

Serge Latouche, 2006—'How Do We Learn to Want Less: The Globe Downshifted', in *Le Monde Diplomatique* (English edition), January 2006, at http://mondediplo.com/2006/01/13degrowth (Accessed September 4 2017)

Sarah Lazare, 2016—'Noam Chomsky: Why the Republican Party is a Threat to Human Survival', on *Alternet*, January 26 2016, at http://www.alternet.org/election-2016/noam-chomsky-why-republican-party-threat-human-survival (Accessed September 4 2017)

Michael Leon Guerrero, Tammy Bang Luu, and Cindy Wiesner, 2009—'The Road to Atlanta', in Jai Sen and Peter Waterman, eds, 2009—*World Social Forum: Challeng-ing Empires*, second edition. Montreal: Black Rose Books, pp 315–31

Daniel Lerner, 1958—*The Passing of Traditional Society: Modernization in the Middle East*. New York, NY: The Free Press

Penny Lernoux, 1989a—'The Papal Spiderweb I: Opus Dei and the "Perfect Soci-ety"', in *The Nation*, no 248, April 10 1989, at https://www.highbeam.com/doc/1G1-7477837.html (Accessed September 4 2017)

Penny Lernoux, 1989b—'The Papal Spiderweb II: A Reverence for Fundamentalism', in *The Nation*, no 248 (April 17 1989), pp 513–16, at https://www.highbeam.com/doc/1G1-7490473.html (Accessed September 4 2017)

Charmain Levy, 2012—'Influence and Contribution: Liberation Theology, the Progressive Church in Brazil, and the World Social Forum', in Jai Sen and Peter Waterman, eds, 2012—*World Social Forum: Critical Explorations*. Volume 3 in the *Challenging Empires* series. New Delhi: OpenWord

Xochitl Leyva Solano, 2017—'Geopolitics of Knowledge and the Neo-Zapatista Social Movement Networks', in Jai Sen, ed, 2017a—*The Movements of Movements, Part 1: What Makes Us Move?*. Volume 4 in the *Challenging Empires* series. New Delhi: OpenWord, and Oakland, CA: PM Press

Xochitl Leyva Solano and Christopher Gunderson, 2017—'The Tapestry of Neo-Zapatismo: Origins and Development', in Jai Sen, ed, 2017a—*The Movements of Movements, Part 1: What Makes Us Move?*. Volume 4 in the *Challenging Empires* series. New Delhi: OpenWord, and Oakland, CA: PM Press

James Lovelock, 2006—'The Earth is About to Catch a Morbid Fever That May Last as Long as 100,000 Years', in *The Independent*, January 16 2006, at http://www.independent.co.uk/voices/commentators/james-lovelock-the-earth-is-about-to-catch-a-morbid-fever-that-may-last-as-long-as-100000-years-5336856.html (Accessed September 4 2017)

Michael Löwy, 2018—Negativity and Utopia in the Global Justice Movement, Jai Sen, ed, 2018—*The Movements of Movements, Part 2: Rethinking Our Dance*. Volume 5 in the *Challenging Empires* series. New Delhi: OpenWord, and Oakland, CA: PM Press

Maria Lugones, 2008—'The Coloniality of Gender', in *Worlds and Knowledges Otherwise 2 (Dossier 2)*, Fall 2008, at https://globalstudies.trinity.duke.edu/wp-content/themes/cgsh/materials/WKO/v2d2_Lugones.pdf (Accessed September 4 2017)

Tomás Mac Sheoin and Nicola Yeates, 2018—'The Anti-Globalisation Movement: Coalition and Division', in Jai Sen, ed, 2018—*The Movements of Movements, Part 2: Rethinking Our Dance*. Volume 5 in the *Challenging Empires* series. New Delhi: OpenWord, and Oakland, CA: PM Press

Nelson Maldonado-Torres, 2009—'*El Pensamiento Filosófico del 'Giro Descolonizador'*' ['The Philosophical Thinking of the 'Decolonization Giro''', in Spanish], in Enrique Dussel, Eduardo Mendieta, and Carmen Bohórquez, eds, 2009—*El Pensamiento Filosófico Latinoamericano, del Caribe y 'Latino' (1300–2000): Historias, Corrientes, Temas Filosóficos* ['Latin American, Caribbean and "Latino" Philosophical Thought (1300–2000): Stories, Currents, Philosophical Issues', in Spanish]. México DF: Siglo Veintiuno

Firoze Manji, 2012—'African Awakenings: The Courage to Invent the Future', in Firoze Manji and Sokari Ekine, eds, 2012—*Africa Awakening: The Emerging Revolutions*. Cape Town: Pambazuka Press, pp 1–18

Firoze Manji and Sokari Ekine, eds, 2012—*Africa Awakening: The Emerging Revolutions*. Cape Town: Pambazuka Press

Kate Manzo, 1991—'Modernist discourse in the crisis of development theory', in *Studies in Comparative International Development*, vol 26 no 2, pp 3–36

Subcomandante Insurgente Marcos (for the Indigenous Revolutionary Clandestine Committee—General Command of the Zapatista Army for National Liberation—EZLN), September 2008—'Zapatistas Call for Worldwide Festival of Dignified Rage', at www.openspaceforum.net/twiki/tiki-download_file.php?fileId=181 (Accessed September 4 2017)

Paul Mason, 2013—*Why It's Still Kicking Off Everywhere: The New Global Revolutions*, second edition. London, UK: Verso

David McClelland, 1966—'The Impulse to Modernization', in Myron Weiner, ed, 1966—
Modernization: The Dynamics of Growth. New York: Basic Books, pp 28–39

Anthony J McMichael, 1993—*Planetary Overload: Global Environmental Change and the Health of the Human Species*. New York, NY: Cambridge University Press

Philip McMichael, 1996—'Globalization: Myths and realities', in *Rural Sociology*, vol 61 no 1, pp 25–55

Philip McMichael, 2008—'Peasants Make Their Own History, but Not Just as They Please', in Saturnino M Borras, Jr, Marc Edelman, and Cristóbal Kay, eds, 2008— *Transnational Agrarian Movements Confronting Globalization*. Malden, MA: Wiley-Blackwell, pp 37–60

David McNally, 2017—'From the Mountains of Chiapas to the Streets of Seattle: This is What Democracy Looks Like', in Jai Sen, ed, 2017—*The Movements of Movements, Part 1: What Makes Us Move?*. Volume 4 in the *Challenging Empires* series. New Delhi: OpenWord, and Oakland, CA: PM Press

Roel Meijer, 2017—'Fighting for Another World: Yusuf al-'Uyairi's Conceptualisation of Praxis and Permanent Revolution', in Jai Sen, ed, 2017—*The Movements of Movements, Part 1: What Makes Us Move?*. Volume 4 in the *Challenging Empires* series. New Delhi: OpenWord, and Oakland, CA: PM Press

Breny Mendoza, 2012—'*La Epistemología del sur, la Colonialidad del Género y el Feminismo Latinoamericano*' ['Epistemology of the South: The Coloniality of Gender and Latin American Feminism', in Spanish], in *Aproximaciones Críticas a las Prácticas Teórico-Políticas del Feminimo Lationamericano* ['Critical Approaches to the Political Theory and Practice of Latin American Feminism', in Spanish]. Bogotá: Centro de Estudios e Investigación Simón Rodríguez, pp 19–36, at http://funceisimonrodriguez. blogspot.ca/2012/10/la-epistemologia-del-sur-la.html (Accessed September 4 2017)

Matt Meyer and Ousseina Alidou, 2018—'The Power of Words: Reclaiming and Reimagining Revolution and Nonviolence', in Jai Sen, ed, 2018—*The Movements of Movements, Part 2: Rethinking Our Dance*. Volume 5 in the *Challenging Empires* series. New Delhi: OpenWord, and Oakland, CA: PM Press

Walter Mignolo, 2011—*The Darker Side of Western Modernity: Global Futures, Decolonial Options*. Durham, NC: Duke University Press

Walter Mignolo, 2013—'On Pluriversality', on *waltermignolo.com*, October 20 2013, at http://waltermignolo.com/on-pluriversality/ (Accessed September 4 2017)

Walter Mignolo and Freya Schiwy, 2007—'Transculturation and the Colonial Difference: Double Translation', in *Revista Científica de Información y Comunicación* ['Scientific Journal of Information and Communication', in Spanish], no 4, pp 12–34, at https:// idus.us.es/xmlui/bitstream/handle/11441/33514/Transculturacion%20y%20la%20 diferencia%20colonial.pdf?sequence=1 (Accessed September 4 2017)

Mark S Mizruchi, 2013—*The Fracturing of the American Corporate Elite*. Cambridge, MA: Harvard University Press

President Evo Morales, 2008—'Save the Planet from Capitalism', open letter on Climate Change from Bolivian President Evo Morales in anticipation of the Poznan Climate Conference. Buenos Aires: Jubileo Sur / Americas, at http://www.zmag.org/znet/ viewArticle/19911 (Accessed January 11 2009, inactive September 4 2017)

Muto Ichiyo, 2018—'Towards the Autonomy of the People of the World: Need for a New Movement of Movements to Animate People's Alliance Processes', in Jai Sen, ed, 2018—*The Movements of Movements, Part 2: Rethinking Our Dance*. Volume 5 in the *Challenging Empires* series. New Delhi: OpenWord, and Oakland, CA: PM Press

NFFPFW (National Forum of Forest People and Forest Workers), June 2009—'Dehradun Declaration', [Declaration by the Indigenous and Forest Peoples of India, taken at the Second National Conference, held in Dehra Dun, India, June 10–12 2009], on *World Rainforest Movement*, at http://www.wrm.org.uy/countries/India/Dehradun.html, (Accessed September 4 2017)

National Intelligence Council, 2012—*Global Trends 2030: Alternative Worlds*. Washington, DC: National Intelligence Council, at https://globaltrends2030.files.wordpress.com/2012/11/global-trends-2030-november2012.pdf (Accessed September 4 2017)

Peter North and David Featherstone, 2017—'Localisation as radical praxis and the new politics of climate change', in Jai Sen, ed, 2017a—*The Movements of Movements, Part 1: What Makes Us Move?*. Volume 4 in the *Challenging Empires* series. New Delhi: OpenWord, and Oakland, CA: PM Press

Gabriela Nouzeilles and Walter Mignolo, 2003—'An Other Globalization: Toward a Critical Cosmopolitanism', in *Nepantla: Views from the South*, vol 4 no 1, pp 1–4

Rodrigo Nunes, 2018a—'Nothing Is What Democracy Looks Like: Openness, Horizontality, and the Movement of Movements', in Jai Sen, ed, 2018—*The Movements of Movements, Part 2: Rethinking Our Dance*. Volume 5 in the *Challenging Empires* series. New Delhi: OpenWord, and Oakland, CA: PM Press

Rodrigo Nunes, 2018b—'The Global Moment: Seattle, Ten Years On', in Jai Sen, ed, 2018—*The Movements of Movements, Part 2: Rethinking Our Dance*. Volume 5 in the *Challenging Empires* series. New Delhi: OpenWord, and Oakland, CA: PM Press

Naomi Oreskes and John Krige, eds, 2014—*Science and Technology in the Global Cold War*. Cambridge, MA: MIT Press

Michal Osterweil, 2018—'Becoming-Woman?' Between Theory, Practice, and Potentiality', in Jai Sen, ed, 2018—*The Movements of Movements, Part 2: Rethinking Our Dance*. Volume 5 in the *Challenging Empires* series. New Delhi: OpenWord, and Oakland, CA: PM Press

Talcott Parsons, 1964—'Evolutionary Universals in Society', in *American Sociological Review*, vol 29 no 3, pp 339–57

Shailja Patel, 2017—'What Moves Us', 'Proem' to Jai Sen, ed, 2017—*The Movements of Movements, Part 1: What Makes Us Move?*. Volume 4 in the *Challenging Empires* series. New Delhi: OpenWord, and Oakland, CA: PM Press

Sujata Patel, 2010—'Diversities of Sociological Traditions', in Sujata Patel, ed, 2010—*The ISA Handbook of Diverse Sociological Traditions*. Thousand Oaks, CA: SAGE Publications, pp 1–18

James Petras, 1999—'The CIA and the Cultural Cold War Revisited'. Review of Frances Stonor Saunders, 2000—*Who Paid the Piper: The CIA and the Cultural Cold War*. London, UK: Granta Books, in *Monthly Review*, vol 51 no 6, November 1999, pp 47–56, at http://monthlyreview.org/1999/11/01/the-cia-and-the-cultural-cold-war-revisited/ (Accessed September 4 2017)

Marie-Emmanuelle Pommerolle and Johanna Simeant, 2010—'African Voices and Activists at the WSF in Nairobi: The Uncertain Ways of Transnational African Activism', in *Journal of World Systems Research* vol 16 no 1 (2010), pp 82–93, at http://jwsr.pitt.edu/ojs/index.php/jwsr/article/view/464 (Accessed September 4 2017)

Poo Ai-jen, December 2010—'Organizing with Love: Lessons from the New York Domestic Workers Bill of Rights Campaign', on *The Progressive*, December 1 2010, at http://www.leftturn.org/Organizing-with-Love (Accessed September 4 2017)

Vijay Prashad, 2014—*The Poorer Nations: A Possible History of the Global South*. Foreword by Boutros Boutros-Ghali. New York, NY: Verso

Aníbal Quijano, March 2007—'Coloniality and Modernity/Rationality', in *Cultural Studies* vol 21 nos 2/3, pp 168–78, at https://www.researchgate.net/publication/233029271_Coloniality_and_ModernityRationality (Accessed September 4 2017)

Radio Free Europe, 2015—'EU Ministers to Hold Emergency Meeting on Migrant Crisis, 2015', September 15 2015, at http://www.rferl.org/content/migrant-crisis-eu-emergency-meeting/27250227.html (Accessed September 4 2017)

Paul Raskin, Tariq Banuri, Gilberto Gallopín, Pablo Gutman, Al Hammond, Robert Kates, and Rob Swart, 2002—*Great Transition: The Promise and Lure of the Times Ahead*. A Report of the Global Scenario Group. Stockholm, Sweden and Boston, MA: Stockholm Environment Institute / Global Scenario Group and Tellus Institute, at http://greattransition.org/documents/Great_Transition.pdf (Accessed September 4 2017)

Bill Readings, 1997—'Dwelling in the Ruins', in *University of Toronto Quarterly*, vol 66 no 4, pp 583–92

Martin J Rees, 2003—*Our Final Hour—A Scientist's Warning: How Terror, Error, and Environmental Disaster Threaten Humankind's Future in This Century—on Earth and Beyond*. New York, NY: Basic Books

Alvaro Reyes, 2012—'Revolutions in the Revolutions: A Post-Counter-Hegemonic Moment for Latin America', in *South Atlantic Quarterly*, vol 111 no 1 (2012)

António Sousa Ribeiro, 2004—'The Reason of Borders or a Border Reason: Translation as a Metaphor for Our Times', in *Eurozine*, January 8 2004, at http://www.eurozine.com/the-reason-of-borders-or-a-border-reason/ (Accessed September 4 2017)

Dani Rodrik, 2008—'The End of the Globalization Consensus is Upon Us', in *The Daily Star* [Beirut, Lebanon], July 22 2008, at http://www.dailystar.com.lb/Opinion/Commentary/2008/Jul-22/115693-the-end-of-the-globalization-consensus-is-up-on-us.ashx (Accessed September 4 2017)

Roma and Ashok Choudhary, 2017—'Ecological Justice and Forest Right Movements in India: State and Militancy—New Challenges', in Jai Sen, ed, 2017a—*The Movements of Movements, Part 1: What Makes Us Move?*. Volume 4 in the *Challenging Empires* series. New Delhi: OpenWord, and Oakland, CA: PM Press

Stephanie Ross, 2017—'The Strategic Implications of Anti-Statism in the Global Justice Movement', in Jai Sen, ed, 2017b—*The Movements of Movements, Part 2: Rethinking Our Dance*. Volume 5 in the *Challenging Empires* series. New Delhi: OpenWord, and Oakland, CA: PM Press

Walt Whitman Rostow, 1960—*The Stages of Economic Growth: A Non-Communist Manifesto*. New York, NY: Cambridge University Press

Jonathan Rowe, 2013—*Our Common Wealth: The Hidden Economy That Makes Everything Else Work*. San Francisco, CA: Berrett-Koehler Publishers

Emir Sader, 2017—'The Weakest Link? Neoliberalism in Latin America', in Jai Sen, ed, 2017a—*The Movements of Movements, Part 1: What Makes Us Move?*. Volume 4 in the *Challenging Empires* series. New Delhi: OpenWord, and Oakland, CA: PM Press

Joel Samoff, 1992—'The Intellectual/Financial Complex of Foreign Aid', in *Review of African Political Economy*, no 53, pp 60–75

Boaventura de Sousa Santos, 1999—'On Oppositional Postmodernism', in Ronaldo Munck and Denis O'Hearn, eds, 1999—*Critical Development Theory: Contributions to a New Paradigm*. New York, NY: Zed Books, pp 29–43

Boaventura de Sousa Santos, 2004—'A Critique of Lazy Reason: Against the Waste of Experience', in Immanuel Wallerstein, ed, 2004—*The Modern World-System in the Longue Durée*. Boulder, CO: Paradigm Publishers, pp 157–98, at http://www.ces.fe.uc.pt/bss/documentos/A%20critique%20of%20lazy%20reason.pdf (Accessed September 4 2017)

Boaventura Santos, 2006—*The Rise of the Global Left: The World Social Forum and Beyond*. New York, NY: Zed Books

Boaventura de Sousa Santos, 2007—'Beyond Abyssal Thinking: From Global Lines to Ecologies of Knowledges', in *Eurozine*, June 29 2007, pp 1–33, at http://www. boaventuradesousasantos.pt/media/pdfs/Beyond_Abyssal_Thinking_Review_2007. PDF (Accessed September 4 2017)

Boaventura de Sousa Santos, 2012—'A Left of the Future: The WSF and Beyond', in Jai Sen and Peter Waterman, eds, 2012—*World Social Forum: Critical Explorations*. Volume 3 in the *Challenging Empires* series. New Delhi: OpenWord

Boaventura de Sousa Santos, João Arriscado Nunes, and Maria Paula Meneses, 2007—'Introduction: Opening up the Canon of Knowledge and Recognition of Difference', in Boaventura de Sousa Santos, ed, 2007—*Another Knowledge is Possible: Beyond Northern Epistemologies*. London, UK: Verso, pp xix–lxii

Ziauddin Sardar, 2005—'The Struggle for Islam's Soul', in *New Statesman*, July 18 2005, at http://www.newstatesman.com/node/162468 (Accessed September 4 2017)

Saskia Sassen, 2013—'Expelled: Humans in Capitalism's Deepening Crisis', in *Journal of World Systems Research*, vol 19 no 2, Summer 2013, pp 198–201, at http://jwsr.pitt. edu/ojs/index.php/jwsr/article/view/495 (Accessed September 4 2017)

Saskia Sassen, 2014—*Expulsions: Brutality and Complexity in the Global Economy*. Cambridge, MA: The Belknap Press of Harvard University Press

Jonathan Schell, 2004—'The Empire Backfires', in *The Nation*, March 29 2004, at https:// www.thenation.com/article/empire-backfires/ (Accessed September 4 2017)

François Schneider, Giorgos Kallis, and Joan Martinez-Alier, 2010—'Crisis or Opportunity? Economic Degrowth for Social Equity and Ecological Sustainability', in *Journal for Cleaner Production*, vol 18 no 6, April 2010, pp 511–18

Peer Schouten, 2008—'Immanuel Wallerstein on World-Systems, the Imminent End of Capitalism and Unifying Social Science', in *Theory Talk* no 13, August 4 2008, at http:// www.theory-talks.org/2008/08/theory-talk-13.html (Accessed September 4 2017)

Science and Security Board of the Bulletin of the Atomic Scientists, January 2016—'Overview', in *Bulletin of the Atomic Scientists*, January 22 2016, at http:// thebulletin.org/overview (Accessed September 4 2017)

Felipe Seligman and Annalena Oeffner, January 2005—'United by Dream of World Without Discrimination', in *Terraviva*, January 31 2005

Jai Sen, 2017a—'The Movements of Movements: An Introduction and an Exploration'. Introduction to Jai Sen, ed, 2017—*The Movements of Movements, Part 1: What Makes Us Move?*. Volume 4 in the *Challenging Empires* series. New Delhi: Open-Word, and Oakland, CA: PM Press

Jai Sen, ed, 2017—*The Movements of Movements, Part 1: What Makes Us Move?*. Volume 4 in the *Challenging Empires* series. New Delhi: OpenWord, and Oakland, CA: PM Press

Jai Sen, Anita Anand, Arturo Escobar, and Peter Waterman, eds, 2004—*World Social Forum: Challenging Empires*. New Delhi: Viveka. Slightly abridged version at http:// www.openspaceforum.net/twiki/tiki-index.php?page=WSFChallengingEmpires 2004 and http://www.choike.org/nuevo_eng/informes/1557.html (Both accessed September 4 2017)

Jai Sen and Peter Waterman, eds, 2009—*World Social Forum: Challenging Empires*, updated second edition, Montreal: Black Rose

Jai Sen and Peter Waterman, eds, 2012—*World Social Forum: Critical Explorations*. Volume 3 in the *Challenging Empires* series. New Delhi: OpenWord

Jon Shefner and Patricia Fernández-Kelly, 2011—'Introduction: Hegemons, States, and Alternatives', in Jon Shefner and Patricia Fernandez-Kelly, eds, 2011—*Globalization and Beyond: New Examinations of Global Power and Its Alternatives*. University of Pennsylvania Press, pp 1–22

Mukul Sharma, 2005—'The World Dignity Forum'. World Social Forum V, Porto Alegre, RS, Brazil

Mukul Sharma and Ashok Bharti, eds, 2004—*The Making of the World Dignity Forum*. New Delhi, India: World Dignity Forum, in association with the Heinrich Böll Foundation and the National Conference of Dalit Organisations

Christopher Simpson, 1998—'Universities, Empire, and the Production of Knowledge: An Introduction', in Christopher Simpson, ed, 1998—*Universities and Empire: Money and Politics in the Social Sciences During the Cold War*. New York, NY: New Press, pp xi–xxxiv

Jakeet Singh, 2015—'Religious Agency and the Limits of Intersectionality', in *Hypatia* vol 10 no 10, pp 1–18

Andrea Smith, November 2005—'Decolonizing Theology', in *Union Seminary Quarterly Review*, vol 59 nos 1–2, November 2005, pp 63–78

Andrea Smith, August 2013—'The Problem with Privilege', on *Andrea366 Blog*, August 14 2013, at https:/andrea366.wordpress.com/2013/08/14/the-problem-with-privilege-by-andrea-smith/ (Accessed September 4 2017)

Andrea Smith, 2017—'Indigenous Feminism and the Heteropatriachal State', in Jai Sen, ed, 2017—*The Movements of Movements, Part 1: What Makes Us Move?*. Volume 4 in the *Challenging Empires* series. New Delhi: OpenWord, and Oakland, CA: PM Press

Edward Snowden, 2013—'Surveillance of Whole Populations Threatens to Be the Greatest Human Right Challenge of Our Time', on *AlterNet*, October 1 2013, at http://www.alternet.org/edward-snowden-surveillance-whole-populations-threatens-be-greatest-human-rights-challenge-our-time (Accessed September 4 2017)

Rebecca Solnit, 2005—'Acts of Hope: Challenging Empire on the World Stage', in *Mother Jones*, June 14 2005, at http://www.motherjones.com/commentary/columns/2005/06/acts_of_hope.html (Accessed September 4 2017)

Rebecca Solnit, September 2014—'What to Do When You're Running Out of Time', on *AlterNet*, September 18 2014, at http://www.alternet.org/environment/what-do-when-youre-running-out-time (Accessed September 4 2017)

Robert Stam and Ella Shohat, 2005—'Traveling Multiculturalism: A Trinational Debate in Translation', in Ania Loomba, Suvir Kaul, Matti Bunzi, Antoinette Burton, and Jed Esty, eds, 2005—*Postcolonial Studies and Beyond*. Durham, NC: Duke University Press, pp 293–316

Robert Stam and Ella Shohat, 2012—'Whence and Whither Postcolonial Theory?', in *New Literary History*, vol 43, pp 371–90

Chris Stewart, 2005—'Humanicide: From Myth to Risk', in *Journal of Futures Studies* vol 9 no 4, May 2005, pp 15–28, at http://www.jfs.tku.edu.tw/9.4.15.pdf (Accessed September 4 2017)

Kathleen Stewart and Susan Harding, 1999—'Bad Endings: American Apocalypsis', in *Annual Review of Anthropology* vol 28 no 1, October 1999 pp 285–310, at http://arjournals.annualreviews.org/doi/abs/10.1146/annurev.anthro.28.1.285?cookieSet=1 (Accessed September 4 2017)

Joseph Tainter and Carole Crumley, 2007—'Climate, Complexity, and Problem Solving in the Roman Empire', in Robert Costanza, Lisa Graumlich, and Will Steffen, eds, 2007—*Sustainability or Collapse? An Integrated History and Future of People on Earth*. Cambridge, MA: MIT Press, pp 62–75

Tricia Talbert, ed, 2015—'NASA's New Horizons Team Selects Potential Kuiper Belt Flyby Target', in *NASA News*, August 28 2015, issue on 'New Horizons: NASA's Mission to Pluto', at http://www.nasa.gov/feature/nasa-s-new-horizons-team-selects-potential-kuiper-belt-flyby-target (Accessed September 4 2017)

Patrick Tayler, 2003—'A New Power in the Streets' in *New York Times*, February 17 2003, at http://www.nytimes.com/2003/02/17/international/middleeast/17ASSE. html?pagewanted=print&position=top (Accessed September 4 2017)

Anand Teltumbde, 2017—'Dalits, Anti-Imperialism, and the Annihilation of Caste', in Jai Sen, ed, 2017—*The Movements of Movements, Part 1: What Makes Us Move?*. Volume 4 in the *Challenging Empires* series. New Delhi: OpenWord, and Oakland, CA: PM Press

Alvin Toffler and Heidi Toffler, 2006—*Revolutionary Wealth*. New York, NY: Currency / Doubleday

Amoshaun Toft, Nancy Van Leuven, W Lance Bennett, Jonathan Towhave, Mary Lynn Veden, Chris Wells, and Lea Lerbel, 2007—'Which Way for the Northwest Social Forum? A Dialogue on Cross-Issue Organizing'. Seattle, WA: Center for Communication and Civic Engagement, University of Washington, 2007, at http://depts. washington.edu/ccce/assets/documents/NWSFReport.pdf (Accessed September 4 2017)

James Toth, 2017—'Local Islam Gone Global: The Roots of Religious Militancy in Egypt and its Transnational Transformation', in Jai Sen, ed, 2017—*The Movements of Movements, Part 1: What Makes Us Move?*. Volume 4 in the *Challenging Empires* series. New Delhi: OpenWord, and Oakland, CA: PM Press

John Trumpbour, ed, 1989—*How Harvard Rules: Reason in the Service of Empire*. Boston, MA: South End Press

Jean-Claude Usunier and Jörg Stolz, eds, 2014—*Religions as Brands: New Perspectives on the Marketization of Religion and Spirituality*. Burlington, VT: Ashgate

Virginia Vargas, 2017—'International Feminisms: New Syntheses, New Directions', in Jai Sen, ed, 2017—*The Movements of Movements, Part 1: What Makes Us Move?*. Volume 4 in the *Challenging Empires* series. New Delhi: OpenWord, and Oakland, CA: PM Press

David Vine, 2015—'Garrisoning the Globe: How US Military Bases Abroad Undermine National Security and Harm Us All', on *Huffington Post*, September 13 2015, at http://www.huffingtonpost.com/david-vine/us-military-bases-abroad_b_8131402. html (Accessed September 4 2017)

Immanuel Wallerstein, 1999—'Uncertainty and Historical Progress', on *Fernand Braudel Center Commentary*, at http://fbc.binghamton.edu/iwposb.htm (Inactive September 4 2017)

Immanuel Wallerstein, 2014—'Antisystemic Movements, Yesterday and Today', in Journal of World-Systems Research vol 20 no 2 (2014), pp 158–172, at http://jwsr.pitt. edu/ojs/index.php/jwsr/article/view/593 (Accessed September 4 2017)

Catherine Walsh, 2012—'"Other" Knowledges, "Other" Critiques: Reflections on the Politics and Practices of Philosophy and Decoloniality in the "Other" America', in *Transmodernity: Journal of Peripheral Cultural Production of the Luso-Hispanic World*, vol 1 no 3, pp 1–17

Peter Waterman, 2017—'The Networked Internationalism of Labour's Others', in Jai Sen, ed, 2017—*The Movements of Movements, Part 1: What Makes Us Move?*. Volume 4 in the *Challenging Empires* series. New Delhi: OpenWord, and Oakland, CA: PM Press

Chaim Waxman, ed, 1968—*The End of Ideology Debate*. New York, NY: Funk & Wagnalls

Hans Weiler, 2004—'Challenging the Orthodoxies of Knowledge: Epistemological, Structural, and Political Implications for Higher Education'. Paper for Colloquium on Research and Higher Education Policy of the UNESCO Forum on Higher Education, Research, and Knowledge, Paris, France, at https://web.stanford.edu/~weiler/ Unesco_Paper_124.pdf (Accessed September 4 2017)

Eve S Weinbaum, 2004—*To Move a Mountain: Fighting the Global Economy in Appalachia*. New York, NY: New Press

John Williamson, 1994—'In Search of a Manual for Technopolis', in John Williamson, ed, 1994—*The Political Economy of Policy Reform*. Washington, DC: Institute for International Economics, pp 9–28

World Economic Forum, 2015—*The Global Risks Report 2015*. Geneva: The World Economic Forum, at http://www3.weforum.org/docs/WEF_Global_Risks_2015_Report15.pdf (Accessed September 4 2017)

Bill Wylie-Kellermann, 2009—'Resurrection City', in *Sojourners Magazine*, May 2009, at https://sojo.net/magazine/may-2009/resurrection-city (Accessed September 4 2017)

Lydia Wylie-Kellerman, 2010—'What's Good for Detroit', in *Sojourners Magazine*, July 2010, at https://sojo.net/magazine/july-2010/whats-good-detroit (Accessed September 4 2017)

Jan Zalasiewicz, Mark Williams, Will Steffen, and Paul Crutzen, 2010—'The New World of the Anthropocene', in *Environmental Science & Technology*, vol 44, February 25 2010, at http://pubs.acs.org/doi/abs/10.1021/es903118j?prevSearch=anthropocene &searchHistoryKey= (Accessed September 4 2017)

Notes

1. Schell 2004.
2. Ceceña 2012, p 111.
3. Marcos 2008.
4. Sen, ed, 2017.
5. Sen 2017a. Long lists like those attached to manifestos and WSF social movements assemblies confirm expanding participation and sense of coming together. And nothing is more important. But it is also important to note that there is no widely accepted list of these movements or set of categories for describing and classifying them (as 'left' or 'progressive', 'right' or 'conservative'). For example, as Santos points out concerning World Social Forum events, "The large majority of movements and organizations that have dynamized the WSF consider themselves to be on the left, even though . . . they very much disagree on what it means to be on the left" (Santos 2006, p 160). And sooner or later, as these volumes confirm, these disagreements involve the most fundamental issues concerning how to describe the 'world' and 'nature' and 'society', 'system', and 'civilisation', indeed over what constitutes a 'movement', and over what constitutes 'progressive' or 'left' alternatives. As a starting point here, I adopt a broad description of 'left' or 'progressive' movements, including, as Maldonado-Torres says: "every movement, every revolution, every intellectual endeavour that has attempted to restore the humanity of the dehumanized, without taking the humanity of the modern colonizer as normative, and promoting generosity and joint action among the dehumanized themselves and their allies" (Maldonado-Torres 2009, p 687). Even this description, though, needs to be expanded to include 'other-than-human' beings and concerns, including the earth, other species, and peace. Also see the section below on 'Irreducible Centrality of the "Other(s)"'. For another perspective on the 'seismic shift' in critical scholarship provoked by these movements, see Stam and Shohat 2012.
6. For example, Abramsky insists that antiglobalisation movements "dared to denounce capitalism and were so successful that they rapidly plunged the system and its major global institutions into a crisis of legitimacy" (Abramsky 2018).

7.   As de Marcellus points out: "it's a strange but frequent phenomenon—when movements finally win them, they often go unnoticed. Partly, because many people have already become discouraged or have moved on to new struggles; partly because the media and dominant ideology avoid recognising popular victories as such and partly because, within the movement itself, a mistaken sort of pseudo-Marxism always immediately revises history to try and show that whatever happened HAD to happen for material, economic reasons and is somehow or another always in the interests of capital! For example, when we arrived in Seattle in 1999, no one imagined that the negotiations could fail. Two weeks after, the US Socialist Workers Party (who had totally missed the rendezvous) and others published all kinds of subtle analyses to show that Clinton actually wanted the WTO to fail" (de Marcellus, August 2006). Indeed, many worry that unrecognised success radically distorts our views of social order, past history, and prospects for change, and, is a major obstacle in social movement organising. Thus, Graeber insists that "The biggest problem facing direct action movements is that we don't know how to handle victory" (Graeber 2007, also 2018). And recognising and celebrating victories—even 'successful failures' (Weinbaum 2004, p 267)—is essential to maintaining and expanding movements. As Carlsson argues in this book: "Our protests and creative alternatives have to inspire even our enemies to join us. . . . Revolution is not something to be imposed but, rather, should be an irresistibly compelling invitation" (Carlsson 2018).

8.   Waterman echoes the questions of many from the 'old' left: "Could it be that the notion of an emancipatory internationalism, if not the song itself, has migrated to other categories of the popular sectors, historically less incorporated into twentieth century capitalism? Could it be that these are the new bearers of the old internationalism, or the popular bearers of a new internationalism within the Global Justice and Solidarity Movement?" (Waterman 2017).

9.   Ed: For those not familiar with the Zapatistas, see Houtart 2018 and Abramsky 2018 in this book, and in the companion volume, *The Movements of Movements, Part 1: What Makes Us Move?* (Sen, ed, 2017), see Leyva Solano 2017, Leyva Solano and Gunderson 2017, and Khasnabish 2017. And on the WSF, see Sen, Anand, Escobar, and Waterman, eds, 2004, Sen and Waterman, eds, 2009, and Sen and Waterman, eds, 2012.

10.   Sen 2017a.

11.   Kalouche and Mielants 2017.

12.   Nunes 2018b.

13.   There is a growing sense of shared challenges and prospects and a need for developing 'planetary' perspectives. For example, Nouzeilles and Mignolo argue: "It is not enough to oppose neoliberal globalization. Since the world is growing increasingly and irreversibly interconnected, we must envision alternative global world orders. The myriad grassroots organizations acting (internationally and locally) all over the world are part of the struggle for another globalization: one that is plural and diverse rather than homogenous, one that does not look at the world according to a fixed set of rules and principles, but rather embraces a world composed of many worlds" (Nouzeilles and Mignolo 2003, p 1). Similarly, Connell insists that "only knowledge produced on a planetary scale is adequate to support the self-understanding of societies now being forcibly reshaped on a planetary scale" (Connell 2007, p vii). At the same time, as critics become increasingly aware of the powerful hold of established orthodoxies on our imaginations, they are also becoming increasingly aware of the impossibility of transcending these frameworks all at once. Chakrabarty, for example, points to still existing tensions between familiar critical discourses and the looming sense of shared 'planetary' challenges and possibilities: "all my readings in theories of

globalization, Marxist analysis of capital, subaltern studies, and postcolonial criticism over the last twenty-five years, while enormously useful in studying globalization, had not really prepared me for making sense of this planetary conjuncture within which humanity finds itself today.... [C]limate change poses for us a question of a human collectivity, an us, pointing to a figure of the universal that escapes our capacity to experience the world. It is more like a universal that arises from a shared sense of a catastrophe. It calls for a global approach to politics without the myth of a global identity, for, unlike a Hegelian universal, it cannot subsume particularities. We may provisionally call it a 'negative universal history'" (Chakrabarty 2009, pp 199, 222).

14.   As Graeber notes, citing Wallerstein, "revolutions transform what might be called political common sense: our most basic assumptions about what politics is, how it is conducted, and what its stakes and purposes are". Moreover, he continues, "we are at an historical moment when the battle over common sense is more strategically important that it has ever been" (Graeber 2012, p 167).

15.   General Command of the Zapatista Army of National Liberation–Clandestine Revolutionary Indigenous Committee 2001.

16.   Cormie 2017.

17.   See, for example, Santos 2007.

18.   Nunes 2018b.

19.   And in the course of writing this essay I became even more conscious of just how deeply my perspective is US- and Canada-centred, also deeply influenced by decades of dialogue with Latin Americans especially, but with much less—though increasing?—interaction with so many 'others': Africans, Asians, Central Europeans, Eastern Europeans, Pacific Islanders, etc.

20.   Ali points to the "glorious decade (1965–75)" when movements were challenging "the power structures north and south, east and west. Countries in each continent were infected with the desire for change. Hope reigned supreme" (Ali 2017). Similarly, Wallerstein argues that: "the world revolution of 1968 [was] ... a fundamental transformative event ... more important than 1917 (the Russian Revolution), 1939–1945 (the Second World War), or 1989 (the collapse of the Communisms in east-central Europe and the Soviet Union), years people usually point out as the crucial events. These other events were simply less transformative than the world revolution of 1968". (Wallerstein, quoted in Schouten 2008). For a perspective on Asian expressions of the 1960s' 'world revolution', see Connery 2006.

21.   Hawken 2007, p 2; see also Mason 2013 and Cox and Nilsen 2014.

22.   Hawken 2007, p 4.

23.   Andersen 2011.

24.   On the basis of their analysis of past history, Arrighi and Silver anticipated the increasing significance of social movements in the struggles over social order: "This pressure from below has widened and deepened from transition to transition [in the capitalist world-system], leading to enlarged social blocks with each new hegemony. Thus, we can expect social contradictions to play a far more decisive role than ever before in shaping both the unfolding transition and whatever new world order eventually emerges out of the impending systemic chaos" (Arrighi and Silver 1999, p 289).

25.   Meyer and Alidou 2018.

26.   Adamovsky 2018. See also Amin: "Following the end of the twentieth century, a new generation of militants and movements definitely rejected the way of doing politics that had characterized earlier critical movements of the left (particularly the Second, Third and Fourth Internationals)" (Amin 2018).

27.   Tayler 2003.

28. Delgado-P points, for example, to the unexpected "leap on to the stage of history" by Indigenous movements and their allies in Bolivia in recent decades (Delgado-P 2017). Ed: See also the essay by David Graeber in this book (Graeber 2018).

29. As Escobar notes, "Our hopes and politics are largely the result of a given framework" (Escobar 2004, p 350).

30. As Graeber argues in his essay in this book: "there are no clean breaks in history. The flip-side of the old idea of the clean break, the one moment when the state falls and capitalism is defeated, is that anything short of that is not really a victory at all. If capitalism is left standing, if it begins to market your once-subversive ideas, it shows that the capitalists really won. You've lost; you've been co-opted. To me this is absurd. Can we say that feminism lost, that it achieved nothing, just because corporate culture felt obliged to pay lip service to condemning sexism and capitalist firms began marketing feminist books, movies, and other products? Of course not: unless you've managed to destroy capitalism and patriarchy in one fell blow, this is one of the clearest signs that you've gotten somewhere. Presumably any effective road to revolution will involve endless moments of co-optation, endless victorious campaigns, endless little insurrectionary moments or moments of flight and covert autonomy. I hesitate to even speculate what it might really be like. But to start in that direction, the first thing we need to do is to recognize that we do, in fact, win some. Actually, recently, we've been winning quite a lot" (Graeber 2018).

31. Drainville 2017.

32. Indeed, Lal's insistence that "Some of the most intense battles in the 21st century will be fought over the shape of knowledge" (Lal 2002, p 139) is being repeatedly confirmed.

33. For example, Anthony McMichael suggests that while "each species is an experiment of Nature . . . [o]nly one such experiment, *Homo sapiens*, has evolved in a way that has enabled its biological adaptation to be complemented by a capacity for cumulative cultural adaptation" (McMichael 1993, p 33).

34. In their essay in these volumes, Kalouche and Mielants point to the "transformations at work in the structures of knowledge across the world-system, and the new technological advances and informational and communicational possibilities . . . [providing] for imaginary significations that undermine linear and determinate 'realities' for more complex multiple ones". They point too to the resulting "more complicated and diverse 'social consciousness' of social actors" (Kalouche and Mielants 2017).

35. Concerning the US National Aeronautics and Space Administration satellite's recent fly-by of Pluto, see Talbert 2015.

36. Committee on Issues in the Transborder Flow of Scientific Data and Commission on Physical Sciences 1997, p 16.

37. As Hobsbawm pointed out at the end of the twentieth century, even before the cascading impacts of cell phones, the internet, social media, and big data: "science, through the technology-saturated fabric of human life, demonstrates its miracles daily to the late twentieth-century world. It is as indispensable and omnipresent—for even the remoter corners of humanity know the transistor radio and electronic calculator—as Allah is to the pious Moslem" (Hobsbawm 1995, p 529). For a popular expression of far-reaching claims about the ways information or 'knowledge' is fundamentally transforming the whole of our lives, from traditional economic activities to time and space, leisure, and geopolitics, see Toffler and Toffler 2006. For a quick overview of critical perspectives on 'knowledge society', 'information society', 'digital economy', 'network society', 'informational capitalism', 'postindustrial society', 'postmodern society', etc, see Wikipedia.

38. For example, British Marxist historian Hobsbawm, even while acknowledging that "during the Short Century more human beings had been killed or allowed to die by human decision than ever before in history", concludes that, because of science, "the twentieth century will be remembered as an age of human progress and not primarily of human tragedy" (Hobsbawm 1995, p 557). In a similar spirit, US historian David Christian acknowledges both that, as on Rapa Nui (Easter Island), whole societies have been destroyed due to the uncontrolled exploitation of natural resources and that today we also "appear incapable of stopping processes that threaten the future of our children and grandchildren". Nevertheless, despite this track record and the immense obstacles to positive change, he hopes for a different ending of the story this time, placing his faith in the progress of knowledge magically translated into technological, social, political and economic reforms: "The most important reason for hope may be that collective learning now operates on a larger scale and more efficiently than ever. If there are solutions to be found, both for humans and for the biosphere as a whole, the global information networks of modern humans can surely find them" (Christian 2005, p 475).

39. As Appadurai points out: "social exclusion is ever more tied to epistemological exclusion and concern that the discourses of expertise that are setting the rules for global transactions, even in the progressive parts of the international system, have left ordinary people outside and behind" (Appadurai 2000, p 2). See also Oreskes and Krige, eds, 2014 and Hamblin 2013.

40. Lander 2002, p 245.

41. As Lal has pointed out: "The academic disciplines have so disciplined the world— one has only to think of the extraordinary legitimacy granted to 'economic science' and the role of economists as the pundits of our times, whose very word, when dispensed through such conduits of the imperial financial architecture as the World Bank and the International Monetary Fund, is law to beleaguered developing coun- tries—that any intellectual, social, cultural, or economic intervention outside the framework of modern knowledge appears to be regressive, a species of indigenism, the mark of obdurate primitives, and certainly futile" (Lal 2002, pp 139–40).

42. Indeed, some historians like Hobsbawm argue that the Russian Revolution in 1917 saved global capitalism: "It is one of the ironies of this strange century that the most lasting results of the October revolution, whose object was the global overthrow of capitalism, was to save its antagonist, both in war and in peace—that is to say, by providing it with the incentive, fear, to reform itself after the Second World War, and, by establishing the popularity of economic planning, furnishing it with some of the procedures for its reform" (Hobsbawm 1995, pp 7–8).

43. Indeed, in this respect, Wallerstein argues: "By their very ideology of inevitable progress, the antisystemic movements served as a conservatizing force on the world's oppressed strata" (Wallerstein 1999).

44. See the work of the most influential US sociologist of the mid-twentieth century, Talcott Parsons, who was central in forging the developmentalist perspective which became enshrined in US policy-making, the World Bank and International Monetary Fund, etc (Parsons 1964). Indeed, as Brick argues, according to Parsons and colleagues, post-War trends in the US and Europe were rapidly resolving the problems and contradictions of earlier capitalist development, catapulting the US and soon-to-follow other nations to nothing less than a new 'postcapitalist' society (Brick 2006).

45. See, for example Lerner 1958; Rostow 1960; McClelland 1966.

46. See Trumpbour 1989.

47. See Cohen 1985.
48. See Petras 1999, for example, concerning the massive role of CIA programmes in (mis)shaping scholarly and artistic horizons in the service of the post-World War II US 'anti-communist' agenda. More generally, see Simpson 1998.
49. See Samoff 1992. Concerning the World Bank in particular, Benjamin argues that: "the Bank was never only, never even primarily, a bank. In its aspirations towards global management, and particularly in its stranglehold over development as both the theoretical principle of modernity and a set of lending practices that have effectively remapped the globe along an increasingly stark grid of economic coordinates, the World Bank has been, and remains today, one of the most influential global-cultural actors of the postwar era". Indeed, he points out, "the World Bank has been instrumental in shaping the very idea of culture as we have come to understand it today" (Benjamin 2007, p xii).
50. See Waxman 1968 and Cormie 1980.
51. Rostow 1960, p 91.
52. Indeed, in mainstream social science and politics, 'poverty' in the US also had to be 'rediscovered'? See Harrington 1962.
53. As Stewart and Harding point out: "The horrors of modern warfare, economic depression, the Holocaust, experimentation on humans, and the atomic bomb were all, in part, precipitated by the application of rationality, science, and the offspring of science, technology, and effected in the name of liberty and equality' (Stewart and Harding 1999).
54. Cho 2017.
55. Roma and Choudhary 2017.
56. Ali 2017.
57. As Vargas points out: "feminists seek to understand and draw attention to the interpretive frameworks used by other social movements, but also to engage them in dialogue to raise issues that are insufficiently incorporated into their transformational agendas" (Vargas 2017). For example, intersectional analysis calls attention to "the intersections of race, class and gender as mutually reinforcing sites of power relations". This perspective initially emerged among black and other racialised women in the US who were critical of mainstream, middle class, white feminism for essentialising women and obscuring the differences among them. As with other fundamental insights into the changing human condition, however, similar approaches were emerging elsewhere too: "intersectionality was an idea whose time had come precisely because of the plethora of authors working independently across the globe to make vastly similar sets of claims" (Doetsch-Kidder 2012, p ix).
58. 'Colonial / modernity', a term coined by Aníbal Quijano, reflects the conclusion that, since the sixteenth century (symbolically coinciding with Columbus's 'discovery' of 'America') 'coloniality' and 'modernity' have been two sides of a single project of constructing 'a new world order', involving, centrally, the suppression—and attempted annihilation—of other modes of knowing (see Quijano, March 2007). And beyond criticising Eurocentric modes of knowledge and organisation, 'decolonising' involves respectful dialogue with these 'other' cultures and traditions. In their expressions in Andean Indigenous and Afro-descendant projects for example, these projects, as Catherine Walsh of the Universidad Andina Simon Bolivar in Quito, Ecuador notes, far exceed 'Western' and conventionally 'radical' notions of theory and politics, aiming at nothing less than the "radical reconstruction of knowledge, power, being, and life itself" (Walsh 2012, p 1). See also Dussel 2000, Escobar 2007, Grosfoguel 2007, Lugones 2008, and Mignolo 2011.

59. Not surprisingly, in light of the recent histories of critical perspectives, efforts to develop intersectional and decolonial perspectives are proceeding unevenly too, with critical voices in various strands of these new traditions pointing to continuing problems. For example, concerning secularist tendencies in intersectional discourses that distort understanding of women's agency and reinscribe narrow 'modern' notions of 'reason' and 'progress', see Singh 2015.

60. NFFPFW (National Forum for Forest Peoples and Forest Workers), 2009.

61. For example, as Escobar has recently pointed out, Latin American decolonial thinking, born in the late 1990s, is already being transformed with a new generation of scholars delving into 'new areas' like 'nature' and the 'over-consumption' of the Latin American middle classes (Escobar 2015). However, as in the past the promoters of new insights can seldom avoid jostling with the authors of earlier waves. Thus, Latin American feminists point to the still underdeveloped dialogue between the first wave of decolonial thinkers and Latin American feminists, which helps to explain the limited understandings of gender and sexuality in decolonial thinking and overall the "new masculine ethos of the epistemology of the south" associated with it (see Mendoza 2012, pp 20–21).

62. Some of the immense diversity and richness of Indigenous perspectives is reflected the contributions in these two volumes, by Alfred and Corntassel 2017, Childs 2018, Houtart 2018, Leyva Solano 2017, Leyva Solano and Gunderson 2017, and Smith 2017.

63. In these books, see Ho 2018, Muto 2018, Roma and Choudhary 2017, and Teltumbde 2017.

64. Sadly missing from these books are contributions from / about African movements, despite many local and regional WSF processes and four major WSFs held in Africa (Nairobi, 2007; Dakar, 2011; Tunis, 2013 and 2015) and the Arab uprisings in North Africa in 2011 (though much of this occurred after most of the material for these volumes had been collected). Concerning the complexities of African participation in the first World Social Forum in Africa (Nairobi, 2007)—"the right to talk about, for, and from, Africa"—which requires also "addressing some of the shortcomings of the sociology of transnational movements", see Pommerolle and Simeant 2010, p 83. More generally, for African perspectives on a rapidly changing Africa and a rapidly changing world, see Manji and Ekine, eds, 2012.

65. As Helleiner has noted, by the early 2000s "the increasingly influential critics of economic liberalism . . . appear to be inspired by ideologies that are a mix of the new and the old. In the 'new camp' we find political movements inspired by green thought, feminist critiques of neoliberalism, and 'civilizational' perspectives [rooted in religious traditions, like Islamic economics]. At the same time, the older critiques of economic liberalism offered by embedded liberals, economic nationalists, and Marxists remain influential, although their ideas and political strategies have often been reformulated in significant ways (Helleiner 2003, p 694).

66. Leyva Solano 2017.

67. Grosfoguel, citing Colombian philosopher Santiago Castro-Gómez, refers to a 'God's eye view' or 'the 'point zero': "The 'point zero' is the point of view that hides and conceals itself as being beyond a particular point of view, that is, the point of view that represents itself as being without a point of view. It is this god's-eye view that always hides its local and particular perspective under a universal perspective. Historically, this has allowed Western man (the gendered terms is intentionally used here) to represent his knowledge as the only knowledge capable of achieving a universal consciousness, and to dismiss non-Western knowledge as particularistic and,

thus, unable to achieve universality" (Grosfoguel 2005, p 284). Similarly, Haraway refers to "the god trick of seeing everything from nowhere" (Haraway 1988, p 581).

68. It is important to note, though, in understanding modern 'conservatism' and its relatives 'neoconservatism' and 'fundamentalism' (in the US especially, the other major coalition partners in creating and sustaining the neoliberal project), that they consistently blame 'secular modernism' for the world's problems. Indeed, 'modernity' is defined by this simple binary opposition: the religious versus the secular, or superstition versus knowledge, faith versus science. In other words, both celebration of religion as the only hope for salvation and condemnation of it as the sure path to hell are equally 'modern'. And the most promising 'postsecularist' alternatives require escaping both poles of this binary.

69. Of course, elites are wrestling with the difficult questions of continued global rule in innovative, interdisciplinary ways, mapping scenarios of multiple possible 'alternative worlds'. And in some respects these perspectives are also 'postsecular', recognising religious communities as major actors and imagining the eclipse of Western secular modernity with the emergence of 'hybrid ideologies' (National Intelligence Council 2012, p 13); see also The World Economic Forum 2015.

70. Daulatzai 2018.

71. Many authors in this collection contribute to rescuing religious traditions, communities, organisations, and movements from the hinterlands of ignorance, backwardness, and irrelevance (which does not mean that they are always 'progressive' or 'left'): see Alfred and Corntassel 2017, Cormie 2017, Daulatzai 2018, Houtart 2017, Kalouche and Mielants 2017, Leyva Solano and Gunderson 2017, Meijer 2017, Toth 2017, and Vargas 2017, and Levy 2012, in a prior volume in the same series. Ho also points to the important role of contemporary right-wing Christian religious movements and NGOs in East Asia, drawing on many 'modern' technologies and techniques, which have indeed "in a perverted way . . . usurped the strategies and energies created by marginal social movements" in obstructing queer movements (Ho 2018).

72. Toth 2017.

73. Levy 2012.

74. In this spirit, Escobar points to more synthetic and comprehensive approaches to 'colonial / modernity': "the combined processes of modernity and coloniality can be seen as projects for the radical reconversion of human and biophysical ecologies world wide. One may speak about a systematic project of cultural, ecological, and economic reconversion along eurocentric lines. Conversely, one may consider the need to build on practices of cultural, ecological, and economic difference for concrete projects of world transformation—for worlds and knowledges otherwise" (Escobar 2007, p 197).

75. See Lal 2002 and Weiler 2004.

76. Readings 1997. As Santos argues, since "social science has been responsible for concealing or discrediting alternatives. . . . [t]o fight against the waste of social experience, there is no point in proposing another kind of social science. Rather, a different model of rationality must be proposed" (Santos 2004, pp 2–3).

77. Leyva Solano and Gunderson 2017.

78. Concerning the Zapatistas, see in these volumes: Abramsky 2018, Holloway 2018, Houtart 2018, Khasnabish 2017, Leyva Solano 2017, Leyva Solano and Gunderson 2017, McNally 2017, and Osterweil 2018. Concerning contemporary Islamic social justice militancy, see Toth 2017, Houtart 2017, Meijer 2017, and Daulatzai 2018.

79. See Barreto Jimeno, Tveit, Fykse, John et al, 2015.

80. Many traditions have 'fundamentalist' currents. For example, as Sardar notes, while Islam is not reducible to 'fundamentalism', there have been 'fundamentalist' currents since the beginning; and they continue today in a 'struggle for Islam's soul' (though Western media focuses almost exclusively on the 'fundamentalist' sides of these conflicts) (Sardar 2005). More and more studies are also confirming that contemporary expressions of 'fundamentalism', despite their appeals to premodern 'religious' traditions and attacks on 'secularism', are also deeply 'modern'. For example, Meijer describes the ways in which the project of "permanent Salafi revolution" of Yusuf al-'Uyairi, the first leader of al-Qaeda in Saudi Arabia, "is thoroughly modernist. It is a total world view that tries to cover all aspects of modern life, framing an ideology for changing reality in all spheres of life" (Meijer 2017). Among Christians, fundamentalist churches are well known, especially in the US. Less recognised though are 'fundamentalist' currents in global Catholicism (see, for example, Lernoux 1989a and Lernoux 1989b). Of course, there are also 'neoliberal' and 'neoconservative' versions of religious traditions; for example, Atasoy describes an Islamic movement in Turkey that embraces many tenets of neoliberal globalisation (Atasoy 2008).

81. Thus, US activist and writer Rebecca Solnit insists: "Right now, we are in a churning sea of change, of climate change, of subtle changes in everyday life, of powerful efforts by elites to serve themselves and damn the rest of us, and of increasingly powerful activist and social-movement campaigns to make a world that benefits more beings, human and otherwise, in the longer term. Every choice you make aligns you with one set of these forces or another. That includes doing nothing, which means aligning yourself with the worst of the status quo dragging us down in that ocean of carbon and consumption. "To make personal changes is to do too little. Only great movements, only collective action can save us now. Only is a scary word, but when the ship is sinking, it can be an encouraging one as well. It can hold out hope. The world has changed again and again in ways that, until they happened, would have been considered improbable by just about everyone on the planet. It is changing now and the direction is up to us" (Solnit, September 2014). Also, see below concerning the Anthropocene.

82. See for example Rodrik 2008 and Chang and Grabel 2014.

83. See Snowden 2013.

84. See Grandin 2015.

85. See Vine 2015.

86. Concerning the fracturing of corporate and political elites in the US in particular, see Mizruchi 2013 and Klare 2015; also see note 118 below.

87. See Prashad 2014, Chapter one, and Galbraith 2014, Chapter two.

88. See Williamson 1994.

89. See Heilbroner 1998.

90. See Usunier and Stolz 2014.

91. Nunes 2018a. On the other hand, many continue to insist that 'capitalism' is the problem, and like Drainville, are convinced that the WSF slogan, 'Another World Is Possible', "advertises the wrong kind of anti-capitalist politics" (Drainville 2017).

92. In these volumes, Cho Hee-Yeon frames South Korean movements in these terms, insisting that "globalisation of capital movement is breaking away from social regulatory mechanisms created through social and class struggles within nation-state boundaries, and integrates all the former fragmented areas into the global free market" (Cho 2017).

93. Calleo argues, for example, that: "the Second World War, with its voracious demand for soldiers and all-out mobilization of production, ended the interwar depression and seemed to bear out Keynes's analysis. And as the war came to a close, fear

of another depression was commonplace. To a considerable extent, as the United States resumed major defense spending, the Cold War continued the Second World War's way of resolving the problem of underconsumption. And in Europe, the Cold War also encouraged 'full employment' and welfare policies to 'humanize' capitalism and give the lie to Marxist propaganda about exploitation. By the 1960s, the United States, while engaged in a military buildup and fighting a colonial war, also adopted neo-Keynesian fiscal policies and developed a welfare state of its own" (Calleo, 1996, p 62).

94.   For example, Galbraith argues that the Vietnam War was a key factor in unravelling the post-World War project: "Economically, the war itself was not such a big thing. Compared with World War II, it was almost negligible. But Vietnam happened in a different time, as Europe and Japan emerged from reconstruction, and the United States was no longer running chronic surpluses in international trade and no longer quite the dominant manufacturing power. Never again would the country's judgment and leadership go unquestioned. Vietnam tipped America towards higher inflation and into trade deficits, and its principle economic consequence was to destabilize, undermine, and ultimately unravel the monetary agreement forged at Bretton Woods" (Galbraith 2014, p 36). Sassen argues that the neoliberal turn of the 1980s represented a "systemic transformation" to a new mode of accumulation harkening back to the early days of the emergence of capitalism in England, of new, technologically complex, globalised dynamics of 'primitive accumulation' marked by 'expulsion' of "growing numbers [who] matter less as workers and consumers than they did in much of the 20th century" (Sassen 2013, p 201); indeed, even "bits of the biosphere [are being expelled] from their life space" (Sassen 2014, p 5). And Philip McMichael argues that beginning in the 1980s "debt management instituted a new organizing principle of 'globalization' as an alternative institutional framework". Indeed, he insists, "in the mid-20th century the foundations of capitalism were reformulated through a massive restructuring of the world order" (McMichael, 1996, pp 26, 30).

95.   In other words, many analysts see fundamental, even 'structural' transformations underway in global relations over recent decades, requiring transformations in critical social theory and politics. For example, Castells, Caraça, and Cardoso argue that another "crisis of global capitalism . . . has unfolded since 2008 [that] is not merely economic. It is structural and multidimensional. . . . [W]e are entering a world with very different social and economic conditions from those that characterized the rise of global, informational capitalism in the preceding three decades" (Castells, Caraça, and Cardoso 2012, p 1). Similarly, Santos, Nunes, and Meneses insist that: "[G]lobal capitalism appears as a civilizational paradigm encompassing all domains of social life. The exclusion, oppression, and discrimination it produces have not only economic, social and political dimensions but also cultural and epistemological ones. Accordingly, to confront this paradigm in all its dimensions is the challenge facing a new critical theory and new emancipatory practices" (Santos, Nunes, and Meneses 2007, p xix).

96.   As this is written, daily headlines feature the colossal waves of Syrian refugees risking their lives to enter Europe—the greatest refugee crisis since World War II—and the immense pressures this is putting on the European Union, exposing unresolved tensions and contradictions, even putting its future in question; see Radio Free Europe, 2015. Concerning refugee and migrant flows more generally, see Amnesty International's report that: "In 2013, for the first time since World War II, the number of those forcibly displaced from their homes exceeded 50 million. Millions more have since been displaced as a result of conflict and crises around the globe" (Amnesty International 2015, p 5).

97.   Benjamin, for example, criticises postcolonial studies for framing the World Bank in essentially economistic terms, which obscure its roles, the scope of resistance it its agenda, and its impacts: "the academic division of labor here described in relation to the Bank unwittingly maintains a similar paradigm. Postcolonial studies finds itself relegated to making localized, ideographic claims about third world tradition and culture, while deferentially heeding social scientific claims about the institutions of international finance and their role in the economic systems of the world economy, claims that, in the absence of critical scrutiny, begin to acquire the universal or eternal weight of nomothetic edict. I am suggesting that the caricatured figure of the Bank as a recurrent trope of postcolonial scholarship naturalizes the institution, and by extension global capitalism, as permanent and inevitable; it cloaks the Bank in a gauzy haze so as to render it visible but ultimately inscrutable to scholars trained to analyze the nuances of culture. And, as a paradigmatic figure of science, technology, rationalism, modernity—those ideologically laden attributes of capitalism and first-world-ness that Pletsch identifies as produced and reproduced by the classifica-tory system of three worlds—the World Bank comes to be understood as a reified abstraction of global capitalism rather than as a powerful political actor engaged in struggle over the modes of production, material resources, and axes of exploitation that define this particular world-historical system of capitalist imperialism—which is to say, hegemonic struggle over the very notion of worlds themselves" (Benjamin 2007, pp xxii-xxiii).

98.   For example, Wallerstein points to the necessity of moving beyond notions of 'economy', 'culture', and 'politics', each operating in its own silo according to its own dynamics. Indeed, he says, "if I knew how to get rid of the separate vocabularies of politics, economics, and culture, I'd be much further ahead" (Wallerstein, in Schouten 2008). In addition, Gibson-Graham warn against "'capitalocentrism', the hegemonic representation of all economic activities in terms of their relationship to capitalism—as the same as, the opposite of, a complement to, or contained within capitalism" (Gibson-Graham 2002, p 2). And they point out that: "a representation of the ECONOMY as essentially CAPITALIST is dependent on the exclusion or suppression of many types of economic activity. Interestingly, the 'excluded others' upon which the seeming coherence of capitalism is based include a range of activ-ities that have been the subject of inquiry by non-economists or non-mainstream economic analysts. We might say that these theorists are constructing an alternative common sense of the economy, one that is growing in influence worldwide. Those we have engaged with include feminist economists who have problematized the household and voluntary sectors, theorists of the informal sector in both the 'third' and 'first' worlds, economic anthropologists who have focused upon indigenous kin-based and 'gift' economies, economic sociologists who have problematized the cultural and social embeddedness of enterprises, those interested in the social economy and its 'alternative' social entrepreneurs, economic networks and orga-nizations, and marxist political economists who have pursued a surplus-oriented economic analysis of different (non-capitalist) enterprises and households, includ-ing worker cooperatives and other communal forms" (Gibson-Graham 2002, p 3).

99.   As Brooks notes: "What conservatives refer to as the free market is in fact comprised of commercial exchanges that are regulated by countless detailed and complex rules of property and contract law. At Osgood Hall Law School [where Brooks teaches], for example, we offer over a dozen courses dealing with the basics of these rules. None of these rules sprang from nature or were ordained by God. They are all the result of legislative outputs shaped by the political process" (Brooks 1995, pp 25–26).

100. Thus, Shefner and Fernández-Kelly point out that: "despite the efforts of neoliberal policymakers, there has been no single neoliberal state. There has instead been a range of state interventions and policies, which are uneven in their allegiance to neoliberalism. The variation in how neoliberalism has been applied by states may be explained by different histories, economic dynamism, indebtedness and subsequent vulnerability, national investment and disinvestment choices, and citizen response. State responses within a wide rubric of neoliberalism help us understand both how hegemony is shifting and how different nations and organized citizens are prepared to manage those changes" (Shefner and Fernández-Kelly 2011, p 10).

101. In this connection, while appreciative of the great contributions of Wallerstein's 'world-system' theory to scholarship and activism since the 1970s, criticism of mainstream social science hegemony, and his support for social scientists in the periphery, Burawoy criticises world-system theory as once again privileging the 'economy'. He also rejects Wallerstein's vision of a unified single social science which would inevitably reinscribe "a unity of the already powerful" (Burawoy 2010, p 53), re-marginalising social scientists in the periphery, not to mention the vast majorities of poor and marginalised peoples. In place of Wallerstein's 'heavenly ideal' of a highly abstract and unified social science, Burawoy proposes bringing Wallerstein "down from heaven to earth": "In direct contrast to the world systems theory, which descends from heaven to earth, here we ascend from earth to heaven. That is to say, we do not set out from an imaginary unity of knowledge, nor from an abstract economic system with natural laws, in order to arrive at sociology in the flesh. Rather, we set out from real existing sociologies, struggling to survive in hostile milieus, and, on the basis of their divisions of labor and their living connections to civil society, we weave the tapestry of international sociology" (Burawoy 2010, p 64).

102. For example, historian Michel Beaud notes that: "Bearing the marks of a complex history—of banks and of industry, of working conditions and of the working world, of worker and union struggles, of repression, of studies by historians and social scientists, of ideological and political debates—the word 'capitalism' carries multiple meanings" (Beaud 2004, p 4). Thus, he acknowledges that: "using the word 'capitalism' remains fraught with difficulty, so heavy are the ideological and political connotations—both positive and negative—which it carries. And of course all this makes it exceedingly difficult to predict how the word will be understood when it is used" (Beaud 2004, p 5). He concludes: "I doubt increasingly whether we may speak of a capitalist system in general" (Beaud 2004, p 6).

103. Klein 2013.

104. Corntassel 2017.

105. McMichael, 2008, p 56, quoting the International Planning Committee for Food Sovereignty 2006.

106. McMichael 2008, p 57.

107. Wylie-Kellerman 2010.

108. Wylie-Kellerman 2009.

109. Wylie-Kellerman 2009. More generally, Friedmann and McNair point to the ways diverse agricultural, slow food, and right to food movements are moving beyond simple 'capitalist' to 'socialist' frameworks: "What matters is that it opens new horizons of possibility. The emerging perspective suggested by *Cojote Rojo* and Local Food Plus, as well as Slow Food, fits within the wide and diverse food sovereignty movement. What distinguishes the Builder movement is that it avoids direct confrontation with capital (at least for the moment) by working with and through markets. Can something so apparently congenial to the dominant system, so apparently subject to appropriation by

governments and corporations, as participation in markets—and pursuit of 'educated pleasure'—actually transform the agrifood system? These projects are on an edge of absorption, co-optation, and the like, and many fall over. Yet others arise and recover. They thus require constant vigilance and self-correction, experimentation and mutual learning. Interstitial social transformation is an idea that invites us to depart from a polar divide between autonomous oppositional movements, on one side, and co-optation by powerful corporations and states, on the other. It is a muddy terrain into which one can sink at any time, yet perhaps also one from which one can renew and redirect the journey as swamps are mapped" (Friedmann and McNair 2008, pp 260–61).

110.   Similarly, Escobar points to the ways initiatives towards self-managed forms of economy in Latin America transcend 'reformist' versus 'radical', 'capitalist' versus 'socialist' binary frameworks: "self-managed forms of economy, even when articulated with the market, are not organized according to liberal principles—implying organizations that are separate from daily life and based on hierarchies, rational planning, and instrumentality—but following communal principles. The resulting array of economic forms could be characterized as a "diverse economy", one in which the multiple relations between types of transaction, forms of labor, and type of organization or enterprise result in the coexistence of capitalist, alternative capitalist, and noncapitalist forms and the suspension of capitalism and the market as an all-determining logic" (Escobar 2009, p 32).

111.   Amin points to a sweeping series of developments: "The transformation of the organisation of work, and of the stratification of classes and social groups, in relation to the technological revolution in progress (information, genetic, space, nuclear) and to accelerated industrialisation in emerging peripheries, has resulted in a set of multiple social and political actors, articulated in a new manner in their possible conflicts and alliances" (Amin 2018).

112.   Thus, Boatcă argues for "A reconceptualisation of the standard dimensions of social inequality in light of the power relations engendered on the colonial side of modernity [which] does not restrict itself to a mere enlargement of the list from class and status to gender, race, ethnicity, sexuality, age, and religious denomination. Focusing instead on processes of othering as systematic and ongoing practices of gendering, racialisation, and ethnicisation allows us to grasp the dynamic, rather than the static aspect of social inequality and stratification" (Boatcă 2015, p 16).

113.   Cormie 2017.

114.   Indeed, Hornborg doubts that "modern technology will be of much use in solving ecological problems", because modern technology involves "shuffling around resources and problems between different social groups"; he points to the example of environmentally destructive sugar cane monocultures in the South producing ethanol for car drivers in the North so that they can reduce their ecological footprints? (Hornborg 2011).

115.   Indeed, as Chancel and Piketty point out, "Global CO_2 emissions remain highly concentrated today: the top 10% emitters contribute to 45% of global emissions, while the bottom 50% contribute to 13% of global emissions" (Chancel and Piketty 2015).

116.   As the Science and Security Board of the *Bulletin of the Atomic Scientists* has recently concluded: "The world situation remains highly threatening to humanity, and decisive action to reduce the danger posed by nuclear weapons and climate change is urgently required" (Eden, Rosner, Ewing et al 2016). They also amplify the list of imminent threats: "climate-changing technologies, emerging biotechnologies, and cybertechnology that could inflict irrevocable harm, whether by intention, miscalculation or by accident, to our way of life and to the planet" (Science and Security

Board of the *Bulletin of the Atomic Scientists*, January 2016). There are many indications that the US 'leads' the world in the irrationality of its elites too. As Henwood points out: "[T]he decay of U.S. society is most advanced at the top. The American ruling class is a rotting formation that is so obsessed with its short-term parochial interests that it's unable to act in the broad interests of systemic stability"—that is, even in their own self-interest? (Henwood 2011, p 6). Indeed, Chomsky views the Republican Party as "a serious danger to human survival" (Lazare 2016).

117. Lander 2007, p 55.

118. Lovelock 2006; Stewart 2005.

119. Eldredge 2001.

120. Rees 2003, p 181.

121. Raskin, Banuri, Gallopín et al 2002, p 15.

122. As Block notes of efforts to reframe earlier histories of modern capitalist development: "this alternative narrative of modernity can be the foundation for new projects of social protection designed to deepen democracy and promote sustainable forms of economic development" (Block 2005). Moreover, in this shift, the 'cultural' dimensions of the debates over 'structures'—concerning visions and values—are central: "the main obstacle to advancing such projects has not been the 'objective' logic of accumulation but rather a colossal failure of imagination. It is an urgent priority to foster a rebirth of social imagination that envisions new forms of political and economic coordination that would operate at different spatial levels" (Block 2005, pp 14–15).

123. Sader 2017.

124. As Reyes has recently pointed out: "Today, from 'Lulismo' in Brazil to 'socialism for the twenty-first century' in Ecuador, Bolivia, and Venezuela, these governments are increasingly facing a new round of discontent—ranging from criticism to open revolt—from the very movements that brought them to power. These new expressions of discontent cannot be understood without the recognition that the cycle of struggles from which they arose not only reconfigured the domestic relations of force in each country and the geopolitical map of the region as a whole, but was in fact the product of an enormous shift in the reconceptualization of the means, ends, and scope of what it means to do politics" (Reyes 2012, pp 1–2).

125. Santos 1999, p 40.

126. Nunes 2018b.

127. Ibid.

128. Bayat 2013a, pp 4–5.

129. Teltumbde 2017. See also Sharma and Bharti, eds, 2004.

130. Sharma 2005. See also Seligman and Oeffner, January 2005.

131. Khasnabish 2017.

132. Thus Escobar advances a standpoint from below, building conceptual inventories, analytical and theoretical frameworks from the bottom up, which "takes as a point of departure the social relations created from below with the goal of survival and then follows the movement, flows, and displacements of this type of society". The result is a transformed view of society: "[W]hat happens below is a veritable society in movement. The implication is that what is seen at play in the wave of insurrections are veritable *sociedades en movimiento* [societies in movement] rather than *movimientos sociales* [social movements]" (Escobar 2009, p 32).

133. McNally 2017.

134. Grosfoguel 2006, p 173. Moreover, he continues: "The old division between culture and political economy as expressed in postcolonial studies and political-economy approaches is overcome. . . . Postcolonial studies conceptualize the capitalist

world-system as constituted primarily by culture, while political economy places the primary determination on economic relations. In the 'coloniality of power' approach, what comes first, culture or the economy, is a false dilemma, a chicken-egg dilemma that obscures the complexity of the capitalist world-system" (Grosfoguel 2006, p 173). Concerning *heterarchy*, see also Tainter and Crumley 2007.

135. Childs 2018.
136. Escobar 2012, p xxi. In Mignolo's terms, 'pluriversality' means recognition of the irreducible differences among cultures, even at the most fundamental level ('ontology' in Western philosophies), while recognising the entanglement of all in colonial / capitalist modernity and affirming diverse decolonial projects of liberation in every sphere and dimension of life. As he says, across the planet, we have "arrived at the end of the era of abstract universals, that is of one universal universality" (Mignolo, 2013).
137. Löwy 2018.
138. Bayat 2013a, p 2.
139. Bayat, 2013b, p 600.
140. Babels, April 2004.
141. See Ribeiro 2004 and Mignolo and Schiwy 2007.
142. Stam and Shohat illustrate this dynamic in critical scholarship, pointing to "the ways debates travel within transnational power formations, resulting in recombinations and recontextualisations as the work becomes filtered through (and clashes with) other historically conditioned schemata, prisms, and grids" (Stam and Shohat 2005, p 313). Of course, efforts to forge ahead cannot avoid reinscribing aspects of the world being left behind; concerning this tendency in World Social Forum processes, see Conway 2011.
143. Babels, April 2004.
144. Corntassel 2017.
145. Anderson 2010.
146. Mac Sheoin and Yeates 2018.
147. Toft, Van Leuven, Bennett et al 2007, p 19.
148. Toft, Van Leuven, Bennett et al 2007, p 10.
149. Ed: For a discussion of this episode and the dynamics involved by the organisers of the US Social Forum that was to follow the Northwest Social Forum, see Leon Guerrero, Luu, and Wiesner 2009.
150. Quoted in Alfred and Corntassel 2017.
151. Santos 2011.
152. Abramsky 2018.
153. Hayes 2017.
154. For example, in terms of global dialogues among different sociological traditions, Patel notes that: "These are diverse because each tradition makes its own assessment and perspective of how it is structured within the global distribution of ideas, scholars and scholarship (whether these are adapted from imports or are stated to be indigenous / endogenous / local / national / provincial), how these relate to its contexts including the culture of teaching and research, institutions, the state and the economy. While these claims are universal, the interpretations of how these are interconnected to the North Atlantic tradition(s) and with each other remain different for each nation-state. Or to put it in other words, what is distinct is how each tradition has contested with the claims of those from the North Atlantic and evolved its own internal assessment of this relationship" (Patel 2010, p 16). In a similar spirit, Mignolo refers to "epistemic diversity (or pluriversality) to understand the limits of abstract-universals that dominated the imaginary of the modern / colonial world from Christianity to liberalism and Marxism" (Mignolo 2011, p 222).

155. Vargas 2017.

156. Ibid.

157. Leyva Solano 2017.

158. As Gibson-Graham, Resnick, and Wolff insist, "Theory is involved in creating terms in and through which subjects come to recognize themselves, to grasp their circumstances and imagine their future" (Gibson-Graham, Resnick, and Wolff 2001, p 19).

159. Adamovsky 2018.

160. In these volumes. see Alfred and Corntassel 2017, Delgado-P 2017, Leyva Solano 2017, and Leyva Solano and Gunderson 2017.

161. Ross points to earlier expressions of these priorities in the movements of the 1960s and 1970s in the US: "New Left social movements, and in particular the feminist, student, environmental, and peace movements of the 1960s and 1970s . . . took up anti-authoritarian themes and practices which continue to inform the anti-statism of contemporary activism. These movements' orientation against centralised institutions is often discussed in terms of their revival of anarchist- and libertarian-inspired internal organisational practices, such as: The valuation of tacit and experiential (rather than expert) knowledge; an emphasis on the prefigurative over instrumental aspects of activism (or at least an insistence that means and ends are organically connected); and the use of consensus-based, dialogical, direct and participatory decision-making processes, rotation of leadership, and horizontal networks of autonomous groups" (Ross 2017). Many authors in these two volumes point to the prefigurative dimensions of increasing numbers of movements, eg, Adamovsky; Childs; Corntassel; Hayes; Holloway; Juris and Pleyers; Leyva Solano; Löwy; Ross; Smith; and The Free Association.

162. As Escobar notes of Latin American movements: "It has been said of today's social movements that one of their defining features is their appeal to the virtual; movements do not exist only as empirical objects 'out there' carrying out 'protests' but in their enunciations and knowledges, as a potentiality of how politics and the world could be, and as a sphere of action in which people can dream of a better world and contribute to enact it. The contemporary wave of movements in Latin America open up again the field of the virtual to other thoughts and other theoretical and political projects; by positing not simply different but radically other codes of existence, they point at unactualized tendencies and capacities, giving expression to an undetermined potential for change. It is in these spaces that new imaginaries and ideas about how to re/assemble the social—and . . . the socio-natural—are not only hatched but experimented with, critiqued, elaborated upon, and so forth" (Escobar 2009, p 13).

163. Juris and Pleyers 2018.

164. The Free Association 2018.

165. As Childs notes in his essay in this book, the ethics of mutual respect "can lead to some transformation of interacting participants", and "this transformation is not a one-sided conversion to a single perspective, but rather involves an opening up to shared understandings" (Childs 2018).

166. Bhambra 2011, p 662.

167. Manzo 1991, p 8.

168. Smith 2013.

169. Guevara 2005 [1965].

170. Poo 2010.

171. McNally 2017.

172. Osterweil 2018.

173. Smith 2005, p 74.

174. Alfred and Corntassel 2017.
175. Vargas 2017.
176. Escobar 2004, p 353.
177. Ho 2018.
178. Houtart 2018.
179. Khasnabish 2017.
180. Muto 2018.
181. Walsh 2012, p 1.
182. Holloway 2018.
183. Santos 2006, p 133.
184. Escobar draws on insights from biology, complexity theory, and network theory to capture the decentralised, self-organised, non-hierarchical character of these movements, and—beyond the capacities of any single movement—emergent expressions of 'macro-intelligence and adaptability'. Indeed, he suggests, "the 'global movement' may . . . develop its life and adapt over a much longer time span than any individual movement that contributes to it (eg, ant colony vs. individual ants)" (Escobar 2004, p 354).
185. De Angelis 2018.
186. Sen 2017b.
187. Wallerstein 2014, p 172.
188. Smith 2017, fn 1.
189. Bensaïd 2017.
190. Indeed, as Smith points out concerning 'confessions of privilege' by many white activists in the US, while claiming to be anti-racist and anti-colonial, they so often metamorphose into "a strategy that helps constitute the settler / white subject" again (Smith 2013).
191. Delgado-P 2017.
192. North and Featherstone 2017.
193. As Acosta explains: "Good Living is a plural concept (it would be better to say, 'good livings' or 'good livings together') that emerges particularly from indigenous communities, without denying the technological advantages of the modern world or possible contributions or knowledge from other cultures that question other assumptions of the dominant modern world. Respect for the sovereignty of communities, for their methods of production and reproduction, and for their territory will provide space for horizontal exchange and interconnectedness that will finally break away from inherited colonial ways of thinking" (Acosta 2013).
194. For a widely discussed vision of 'buen vivir' and its political implications, see Morales 2008. More generally, see Baldi 2013.
195. Dávalos 2008.
196. Schneider, Kallis, and Martinez-Alier 2010.
197. Latouche 2006. For a comparison of Latin American decolonial 'post-development' perspectives and European de-growth perspectives, see Escobar 2015.
198. Scientists across a wide range of disciplines (including botanists, zoologists, atmospheric and ocean scientists, geologists, biologists) are moving towards the conclusion that, since World War II, the world has entered a new geological / biological epoch, the Anthropocene, "a new phase in the history of both humankind and of the Earth, when natural forces and human forces became intertwined, so that the fate of one determines the fate of the other" (Zalasiewicz et al 2010).
199. Indeed, beyond more widely recognised 'victories' of social movements, there are many more unrecognised 'successes' in preventing, inhibiting, or minimising

the violent, short-sighted, and irrational acts of elites and the relentless grinding march of rigged institutions and structures. As Solnit notes concerning these difficult-to-see successes of progressive social movements: "the history of what the larger movements have achieved is largely one of careers undestroyed, ideas uncensored, violence and intimidation uncommitted, injustices unperpetrated, rivers unpoisoned and undammed, bombs undropped, radiation unleaked, poisons unsprayed, wildernesses unviolated, countryside undeveloped, resources unextracted, species unexterminated" (Solnit 2005). In addition, Indigenous communities, environmentalists, and critical scholars have long pointed to the ways in which 'nature' and non-waged workers (women, slaves, informal sector workers) have endlessly 'subsidised' economic development, and have called for new accounting categories and frameworks which recognise these contributions and the also uncounted costs of undermining / destroying them (see Rowe 2013). Concerning an "alternative common sense for the economy" which takes account of a wide range of 'non-market' costs and contributions, see Gibson-Graham in note 99 above.

200. As Manji notes, from an African perspective: "One of the striking features of today's world is the degree to which there is growing recognition across the global South of the commonalities in experience of the dispossessed. Indeed, there is even recognition of those commonalities emerging in the North—as in the recent uprisings in Wisconsin, Spain and Greece. For the first time in many years, we see the potential to create solidarity links with people in struggle based not on charity or pity, but on recognition of the common cause of our dispossession" (Manji 2012, p 15).

201. Global Ecumenical Conference 2012.

202. Leyva Solano 2017.

203. Patel 2017.

204. Ibid.

Notes on the Editor

Jai Sen is an architect by training and first practice, became an activist around the rights of the labouring poor in Kolkata, India, in the mid 1970s, and then moved on to becoming a student of the history and dynamics of movement and of the globalisation of movement in the 1990s. Involved in the organising process of the World Social Forum in India during its first year there, 2002, he has since then been intensively engaged with and taken part in the WSF and world movements through the organisation he is associated with, CACIM (Critical Action: Centre in Movement), including as author, editor, and co-editor of several books and articles on the WSF and as moderator of the listserv WSFDiscuss—now re-incarnated as WSMDiscuss (World Social Movement Discuss). While living in Kolkata from the mid 70s to the late 90s, he was with Unnayan, a social action group, Vice-President of the Chhinnamul Sramajibi Adhikar Samiti ('Organisation for the Rights of Uprooted Labouring People'), and Convenor of the NCHR (National Campaign for Housing Rights) in India; and he also represented Unnayan on the founding Board of the Habitat International Coalition during 1987–91. He is now based in New Delhi, India, and Ottawa, Canada, on unceded Algonquin territory. jai.sen@cacim.net

Notes on the Contributing and Co-Series Editor

The late **Peter Waterman** (1936–2017), after retirement from the Institute of Social Studies, The Hague, in 1998, published various monographs, (co-)edited compilations and numerous academic and political papers—the latter almost all to be found online—and self-published his autobiography (*From Coldwar Communism to the Global Emancipatory Movement: Itinerary of a Long-Distance Internationalist*, available at http://www.into-ebooks.com/download/498/). His work was published in English (UK, USA, Canada, India), Hindi, Italian, Portuguese, German, Spanish, Japanese, and Korean. He had papers posted on the Montevideo-based Choike portal and compilations on the Finland-based Into website, and a blog on UnionBook. He was currently associated with, amongst others, the Programa Democracia y Transformación Global (Lima), with two online journals, *Interface: a Journal for and about Social Movements*, the *Global Labour Journal*, and with the Indian Institute for Critical Action—Centre in Movement (CACIM) in New Delhi. Here he co-edited books on the World Social Forums. After retirement he had invitations for teaching, lectures, and seminars from universities and movement-oriented bodies in Peru, South Africa, Sweden, Finland, Hong Kong, Germany, South Korea, the US, Ireland, and the UK.

Notes on the Contributors

The contributors to this volume are as follows, *listed here alphabetically by* **first name:**

[NB: Please note that the entry for Muto Ichiyo is under M. Although 'Muto' is his surname, per Japanese custom he is commonly referred to as 'Muto-san'.]

Anila Daulatzai, born and raised in Los Angeles, California, completed her PhD in Sociocultural Anthropology at the Johns Hopkins University in the USA. She has taught in the USA at the University of California and the Johns Hopkins University, in Afghanistan at Kabul University and the American University of Afghanistan, and in Switzerland at the University of Zurich. She is currently teaching at the Lahore University of Management Sciences in Pakistan. She has extensive experience of living in the Khyber Pukhtunkhwa region of Pakistan and in Afghanistan—where she primarily worked among refugees and internally displaced people in the Afghan-Pakistani border region in the field of refugee health care and trained Afghan researchers in Afghanistan—and of mobilising for various social justice issues around the world over the past twenty years. She has published articles in various peer-reviewed social science journals and written chapters in books on topics ranging from widows in Afghanistan to a critique of radical progressive politics. She is currently working on her new anthropological research project on heroin users in Pakistan and Afghanistan and is writing an book based on her more than four years of anthropological research in Kabul on the topic of widowhood and care. adaulatzai@gmail.com

Chris Carlsson, director of the multimedia history project Shaping San Francisco, is a writer, publisher, editor, and community organiser. For twenty-five years he has focused on horizontal communications, organic communities, and public space. He was one of the founders, editors, and frequent contributors to the groundbreaking San Francisco magazine *Processed World* and helped launch the monthly bike-ins called Critical Mass. He has edited four books, most recently *The Political Edge* (San Francisco: City Lights Foundation, 2004), and published his first novel, *After The Deluge*, in 2004 (San Francisco: Full Enjoyment Books), and his book *Nowtopia* was published in 2008. He is a member of Media Workers' Union Local 100 in San Francisco and recent board president of CounterPULSE, an arts organisation where he has produced a series of public talks since 2006, and has conducted award-winning bicycle tours for over a decade. http://www.chriscarlsson.com • cc@chriscarlsson.com

David Graeber, currently a Professor of Anthropology at the London School of Economics and formerly an associate professor of anthropology at Goldsmiths College in London, and before that at Yale University in the USA, has worked with the Direct Action Network, People's Global Action, the Planetary Alternatives Network, the IWW, and the Occupy Wall Street movement in New York. His books include *Towards an Anthropological Theory of Value: The False Coin of Our Own Dreams* (New York: Palgrave, 2001), *Fragments of an Anarchist Anthropology* (Cambridge: Prickly Paradigm Press, 2004), *Lost People: Magic and the Legacy of Slavery in Madagascar* (Bloomington: Indiana University Press, 2007), *Possibilities: Essays in Hierarchy, Rebellion,* and *Desire* and *Direct Action: An Ethnography* (both Oakland, CA: AK Press, 2007 and 2009), *Debt: The First 5,000 Years* (Brooklyn: Melville House, 2011), and *The Democracy Project: A History, a Crisis, a Movement* (New York: Spiegel & Grau, 2013). d.graeber@lse.ac.uk

Ezequiel Adamovsky graduated from the University of Buenos Aires, in Argentina, before successfully pursuing a PhD at University College London. He is currently professor at the UBA and researcher at CONICET, Argentina's highest research public body, and has been guest researcher at the CNRS in Paris. He is the author of *Euro-Orientalism* (Oxford: Peter Lang, 2006) and *Historia de la clase media argentina* ['History of middle class Argentina', in Spanish] (Buenos Aires: Planeta de Libros, 2009), among other books. In 2009 he was awarded the James Alexander Robertson Memorial Prize, and in 2013 the Premio Nacional, the highest distinction of the Argentinean state for arts and humanities. As an activist, Ezequiel has been involved in the students' movement and in the Neighbours' Assemblies movement that emerged in Buenos Aires after the rebellion of 2001. He has written extensively on issues of globalisation, anti-capitalism, and leftist politics for websites and journals in several countries and has published *Anticapitalismo para principiantes* ['Anticapitalism for Beginners', in Spanish] (Buenos Aires: Era Naciente, 2003) and *Más allá de la vieja izquierda: Seis ensayos para un nuevo anticapitalismo* ['Beyond The Old Left: Six essays for a new anti-capitalism', in Spanish] (Buenos Aires: Prometeo Libros, 2007). e.adamovsky@gmail.com • http://ezequieladamovsky.blogspot.com.ar/

The late **François Houtart** was a Catholic priest, liberation theologian, and scholar of movements. The last position he held was as Professor at the Instituto de Altos Estudios Nacionales (National Institute of Higher Studies) in Quito, Ecuador. He was closely associated with the Fundación del Pueblo Indio del Ecuador (Foundation of the Indigenous Peoples of Ecuador) and was Vice President of the World Forum for Alternatives. Earlier, he was the founder of CETRI (Centre Tricontinental), a Belgian non-governmental organisation, and Special Representative of the President of the General Assembly of the UN in the

Commission on the Reforms of the Financial and Monetary System, headed by Joseph Stiglitz. He was one of the initiators of the World Social Forum, former chair of the International League for the Liberation of the Peoples, and an expert for the Vatican Council II. As a sociologist, he wrote more than forty books and founded the magazine *Alternatives Sud*.

The Free Association (http://freelyassociating.org/) is an ongoing experiment. We're mainly based in the North of England—although we find ourselves at home nowhere (and everywhere). Sometimes we appear to be tight-knit, acting and thinking in close concert with each other. At other times we're more of a loose network, expanding and contracting as the need arises. A reading group, a writing machine, an affinity group. . . . Our most recent work together is *Moments of Excess: Movements, Protest and Everyday Life* (Oakland, CA: PM Press, 2011). Alex, Brian, David, Keir, Nate, and Nette freely associated to produce this particular essay. info@freelyassociating.org

Geoffrey Pleyers, PhD, EHESS 2006, is FNRS Researcher and a Professor of Sociology at the Université Catholique de Louvain, in Belgium. He teaches social movements and global studies at the University of Louvain and at the École des Hautes Études en Sciences Sociales in Paris, France, and is an invited professor at several universities in Europe and Latin America. He is the 2014–2019 President of the Research Committee 47 on 'Social Movements' of the International Sociological Association, the chair of the Research Network on Social Movements of the French Sociological Association, and a founding member of the coordination committee of the Mexican Research Network on Social Movements. He is also the founding editor of the web journal *Open Movements: For a global and public sociology of social movements*. His publications include *Forums Sociaux Mondiaux et défis de l'altermondialisme* ['World Social Forums and the challenges of alter-globalisation', in French] (Louvain-la-Neuve: Academia, 2007); *Los movimientos sociales* ['Social movements', in Spanish], (Mexico: Anthropos, 2010); *Alter-globalization: Becoming an Actor in the Global Age* (Cambridge: Polity Press, 2010), and *La consummation critique* ['Critical consumption', in French] (Paris: Desclée de Brouwer, 2010). Geoffrey.Pleyers@uclouvain.be • http://uclouvain.academia.edu/GeoffreyPleyers

Jai Sen, see 'Notes on The Editors', p. 601.

Jeffrey S Juris, Associate Professor of Anthropology at Northeastern University, in Boston, has participated extensively as an activist and researcher in the global justice movement, including the WSF and the PGA. He is author of *Networking Futures: The Movements against Corporate Globalization* (Durham, NC: Duke

University Press, 2008), which explores the cultural logic and politics of transnational networking among anti-corporate globalisation activists, a co-author of *Global Democracy and the World Social Forums* (Boulder, CO: Paradigm Press, 2008), and co-editor with Alex Khasnabish of *Insurgent Encounters: Transnational Activism, Ethnography, and the Political* (Durham, NC: Duke University Press, 2013). He has also published numerous articles on this topic, as well as on the relationship between new digital technologies and grassroots social movements. jeffjuris@yahoo.com

John Brown Childs, of mixed African-American and Native American descent, was a Professor of Sociology, at the University of California, Santa Cruz, in the US. Deeply influenced by Haudenosaunee philosophy, he is author of *Transcommunality: From the Politics of Conversion to the Ethics of Respect* (Philadelphia: Temple University Press, 2003), co-editor with Jeremy Brecher and Jill Cutler of *Global Visions, Beyond the New World Order* (Boston, MA: South End Press, 1993), and founder and editor of *Transcommunal Cooperation*, http://transcommunality.org/ • jbchilds@ucsc.edu

John Holloway is a Professor at the Instituto de Ciencias Sociales y Humanidades 'Alfonso Vélez Pliego' in Benemérita Universidad Autónoma de Puebla, Puebla, Mexico. He has published on Marxist theory, on the Zapatista movement, especially *Zapatista*, edited with Eloína Peláez (London: Pluto Press, 1998), and on the new forms of anti-capitalist struggle. His most important books are *Change the World Without Taking Power: The Meaning of Revolution Today* (London: Pluto Press, 2002; revised and expanded edition 2005), and *Crack Capitalism* (London: Pluto Press, 2010). johnholloway@prodigy.net.mx

Josephine Ho, the foremost feminist sex-radical scholar in East Asia, has been writing extensively and provocatively on many cutting-edge issues, spearheading sex-positive views in the region on female sexuality, gender / sexuality education, queer studies, sex-work studies, and transgenderism. She is best-known for her groundbreaking, sex-positive writing on female sexuality, *The Gallant Woman: Feminism and Sex Emancipation*, published in 1994 in the midst of a sex revolution in Taiwan (written in Chinese; ISBN: 978-957-33-1121-6). She founded and continues to head the Center for the Study of Sexualities at National Central University, Taiwan (http://sex.ncu.edu.tw), widely known for its social activism and intellectual stamina. sexenter@cc.ncu.edu.tw

Kolya Abramsky has worked for twenty years as an organiser, educator, researcher, and campaigner on a range of different global justice and anti-capitalist processes. This includes working with a range of different types of organizations, both antiauthoritarian and democratic-centralist. Originally from the UK, he has lived in and worked in a number of countries in Western Europe, in the USA, and more recently in South Africa. He is currently based in the UK, where he is doing freelance work. For the last fifteen years he has worked on the labour, social, and environmental conflicts in the global energy sector and on organisational processes related to an anti-capitalist energy transition. He has worked as the International Energy Officer for the National Union of Metalworkers of South Africa and has also been the coordinator of the World Wind Energy Institute, based in Denmark. He has edited two books, *Sparking a World Wide Energy Revolution: Social Struggles in the Transition to a Post-petrol World* (Oakland, CA: AK Press, 2010) and *Restructuring and Resistance: Diverse Voices of Struggle in Western Europe* (self-published, 2001). He was formerly a Visiting International Scholar and winner of the Manfred-Heindler Award for Energy and Climate Change Research at the Institute of Advanced Studies in Science, Technology and Society, in Graz, Austria. kolyaab@yahoo.co.uk

Laurence Cox co-edits the open-access, activist / academic social movements journal *Interface* (http://interfacejournal.net) and co-directs the MA in Community Education, Equality and Social Activism at the National University of Ireland Maynooth. He has been involved in many different movements and campaigns, in Ireland and internationally, over the past three decades, focussing particularly on building alliances between different movements and communities in pursuit of a more radical vision and practice. As a researcher and writer he has focused particularly on the development of movements' own 'intellectual means of production', in collaboration with activists and popular educators inside and outside academia. He is co-author of *We Make Our Own History: Marxism and Social Movements in the Twilight of Neoliberalism* (Pluto, 2014) and co-editor of *Understanding European Movements: New Social Movements, Global Justice Struggles, Anti-Austerity Protest* (Routledge, 2013); *Marxism and Social Movements* (Brill / Haymarket, 2013); and *Silence Would be Treason: Last Writings of Ken Saro-Wiwa* (Daraja, 2013). laurencecox.wordpress.com • laurence.cox@nuim.ie

Lee Cormie has been a researcher / teacher / writer and sometime activist concerning social justice movements and coalitions since the 1970s. In addition to publishing articles on Christian liberation theologies and social movements, he has been involved in church-based social justice initiatives in the US and Canada, most recently as a participant / observer in World Social Forum events. Over the years he has been especially interested in the debates about grassroots movements and traditions of critical discourse concerning 'liberation theologies' and social movements, 'social systems', 'systemic' injustices, and 'alternatives', translation across cultures and movements, and emerging epistemological diversity in a new ecology of knowledges. He recently retired as a Professor of Theology and Interdisciplinary Studies in the Faculty of Theology, the University of St Michael's College and the Toronto School of Theology, in Toronto, Canada. lee.cormie@utoronto.ca

Massimo De Angelis is a critical political economist working at the University of East London. He is the author of several publications on value theory, the link between capital's globalisation and social struggles, commons and social change, and the political reading of economic narrative. His most recent book is *The Beginning of History: Value Struggle and Global Capital*, (London: Pluto Press, 2007). He edits the web journal *The Commoner* (www.thecommoner.org), where he also keeps a blog. m.deangelis@ntlworld.com • commoning@gmail.com

Matt Meyer is a New York City–based author, educator, and activist who currently serves as coordinator of the War Resisters International Africa Support Network and a UN NGO / ECOSOC representative of the International Peace Research Association. A former draft registration resister and organiser for the Progressive Student Network, Meyer's recent books include the two-volume pan-African peace-building series *Seeds of New Hope* (Trenton, NJ: Africa World Press, 2008) and *Seeds Bearing Fruit* (Trenton, NJ: Africa World Press, 2010), as well as *We Have Not Been Moved: Resisting Racism and Militarism in 21st Century America* (Oakland, CA: PM Press, 2012). Argentine Nobel Peace laureate Adolfo Perez Esquivel has commented that "Meyer is a natural coalition-builder", one who "provides tools for today's activists" in his writings and his work; South African Nobel laureate Archbishop Desmond Tutu, in commenting on Meyer's first book, co-authored with Bill Sutherland, *Guns and Gandhi in Africa* (Trenton, NJ: Africa World Press, 2000) wrote that "Sutherland and Meyer have begun to develop a language which looks at the roots of our humanness". resistanceinbrooklyn.ows@gmail.com

Michael Löwy, Research Director Emeritus in Sociology at the National Centre for Scientific Research, Paris, is a Franco-Brazilian Marxist intellectual. He is a frequent contributor to *New Left Review*, *Socialist Register*, and *International Viewpoint*; his work has been translated into twenty-nine languages. His recent books include *Walter Benjamin: Fire Alarm* (London: Verso, 2001) and *The Theory of Revolution in Young Marx* (Chicago: Haymarket, 2004). lowym@free.fr

Michal Osterweil teaches Global Studies at the University of North Carolina-Chapel Hill, in the USA. Her courses and research focus on social movements and paradigms of social change. She has participated in and written about the 'global justice movement' and related transnational networks, in particular those affiliated with Zapatismo and the World and regional social forums. She is a student of the new ways of 'doing change', ranging from movements like the Zapatistas and the alter-globalisation movement to place-based, environmental, and transformative movements in the US—what she understands as a 'new political imaginary' being simultaneously discovered and created in a variety of spaces and movements. In addition to her academic work she participates in various projects and activist endeavours, including being co-founder of the Carrboro Greenspace (carrborogreenspace.org) and the journal *Turbulence: Ideas for Movement* (www.turbulence.org.uk). mosterweil@mac.com

Muto Ichiyo is an activist-writer on political and social affairs, national and global. Born in 1931 in Tokyo, he joined the student and peace movements in the 1950s; was active in the anti–Vietnam War movement in the 1960s; founded the English journals *AMPO* (1969) and the *Pacific-Asia Resource Center* (1973); initiated the People's Plan 21 in the 1980s, and in the 1990s founded the People's Plan Study Group (PPSG), serving as co-president until 2007; and taught at the Sociology Department of State University of New York at Binghamton, in the US, during the 1980s–90s. mutoi@mrj.biglobe.ne.jp

Nicola Yeates is Professor of Social Policy at The Open University in Milton Keynes, England. She researches global(isation) and regional(isation) processes as they impact on poverty, health, and social welfare. She is a former Editor of *Global Social Policy* and is Chair of the Editorial Board of *Social Policy and Society*. Her publications include *Globalisation and Social Policy* (Thousand Oaks, CA: Sage Publications, 2001), *Globalising Care Economies, Migrating Workers* (New York: Palgrave, 2009), *Understanding Global Social Policy* (Bristol: Policy Press, 2008; second edition 2014), and (with Chris Holden) *The Global Social Policy Reader* (Bristol: Policy Press, 2009). N.Yeates@open.ac.uk

Ousseina Alidou, Director of the Center for African Studies and Distinguished Professor in the Department of African, Middle Eastern, and South Asian Languages and Literature at Rutgers University, is based both in New Jersey and Niamey. A leader in the African Studies Association and the Association of Concerned African Scholars, Dr Alidou is the recipient of numerous academic awards for her writing and research on Muslim women and postcolonial societies. A long-standing activist as well as academic, Alidou has organized both for women's rights and for an end to IMF / World Bank / neoliberal structural adjustment throughout the world. Dr Alidou's current work focuses on post-conflict reconstruction and the development issues needed for lasting peace; she is a Steering Committee member of the Pan African Nonviolence and Peacebuilding Network.

Author of the acclaimed *Engaging Modernity: Muslim Women and the Politics of Agency in Postcolonial Niger* (Madison: University of Wisconsin Press, 2011), Alidou's most recent book is *Muslim Women in Postcolonial Kenya: Leadership, Representation, and Social Change* (Madison: University of Wisconsin Press, 2013). oalidou@scarletmail.rutgers.edu

Rodrigo Nunes is a lecturer in contemporary and modern philosophy at the Catholic University of Rio (PUC-Rio), in Rio de Janeiro, Brazil. He has participated in different community and labour organising projects in both Brazil and the UK, as well as in the organisation of the International Youth Camp and the World Social Forum. He is a member of the editorial collective of *Turbulence* (www.turbulence.org.uk), and his texts have appeared in such publications as *Radical Philosophy*, *Deleuze Studies*, *ephemera*, *Mute*, *Transform*, *Serrote*, *Les Temps Modernes*, *The Guardian*, and *Al Jazeera*, and also in several anthologies. His latest publication is the book *The Organisation of the Organisationless: Collective Action After Networks* (London: Mute, 2014), which attempts to develop a philosophy of political organisation adequate to the networked movements of recent years. rgnunes@yahoo.com

Samir Amin is Director of the Third World Forum, located in Dakar, Senegal, and Chair of the World Forum for Alternatives, based in Cairo, Egypt, and in Louvain, Belgium. An economist and intellectual, he is regarded as one of the foremost thinkers on the changing dynamics of capitalism. Since 2001, he has been actively associated with the World Social Forum as well as the regional forums. Amin has authored many articles and books, including *Accumulation on a World Scale* (New York: Monthly Review Press, 1970), *Transforming the Revolution: Social Movements and the World System* (New York: Monthly Review Press, 1990), *Beyond US Hegemony: Assessing the Prospects for a Multipolar World* (Chicago: University of Chicago Press, 2006), *A Life Looking Forward: Memoirs of An Independent Marxist* (Chicago: University of Chicago Press, 2006), *Ending the Crisis of Capitalism or Ending Capitalism?* (Oxford: Pambazuka Press, 2010); *Global History: A View from the South* (Oxford: Pambazuka Press, 2011), and *The People's Spring: The Future of the Arab Rebellion* (Oxford: Pambazuka Press, 2012); and, with François Houtart, he edited *Mondialisation de resistances: L'état des luttes 2002* ('The Globalisation of Resistance: The State of the Struggles 2002', in French) (Paris: L'Harmattan / Forum Mondial des Alternatives, 2002). Samir.Amin@wanadoo.fr

Shailja Patel is an internationally acclaimed Kenyan poet, writer, and public intellectual. Her first book, *Migritude* (Los Angeles, CA: Kaya Press, 2010), published in Italy, Sweden, and the US, was #1 on Amazon's bestsellers in Asian Poetry and was shortlisted for Italy's Camaiore Poetry Prize. Patel was African Guest Writer at Sweden's Nordic Africa Institute and poet-in-residence at the Tallberg Forum. She has appeared on the BBC World Service, NPR, and Al-Jazeera and has been published by *Le Monde Diplomatique* and *The Africa Report*, among others. Her work has been translated into sixteen languages. Honors include a Sundance Theatre Fellowship, a Creation Fund Award from the National Performance Network, the Fanny-Ann Eddy Poetry Award from IRN-Africa, the Voices of Our Nations Poetry Award, a Lambda Slam Championship, and the Outwrite Poetry Prize. Patel is a founding member of the civil society coalition Kenyans For Peace, Truth and Justice. The African Women's Development Fund named her one of Fifty Inspirational African Feminists for the 100th anniversary of International Women's Day. Poetry Africa honoured her as Letters to Dennis Poet, continuing the legacy of renowned South African anti-apartheid activist Dennis Brutus. She represented Kenya at Poetry Parnassus in the London Cultural Olympiad. shailja@shailja.com • www.shailja.com

Stephanie Ross is Associate Professor of Work and Labour Studies in the Department of Social Science and co-director of the Global Labour Research Centre at York University in Toronto, Canada. Her research and teaching focuses in part on democracy in working-class and social movement organizations. Her 2003 essay in *The Socialist Register*, 'Is This What Democracy Looks Like? The Politics of the Anti-Globalization Movement in North America' has been widely cited by social movement scholars around the world. With Larry Savage, she has edited two books, *Rethinking the Politics of Labour in Canada* (Black Point, NS: Fernwood Publishing, 2012) and *Public Sector Unions in the Age of Austerity* (Black Point, NS: Fernwood Publishing, 2013). She is also president of the Canadian Association for Work and Labour Studies. stephr@yorku.ca

Tomás Mac Sheoin is an independent scholar who writes about the chemical industry and social movements and has long been involved in anti-nuclear and anti-toxic campaigns including in solidarity work around the Bhopal chemical catastrophe since 1985. His most recent book is *Asphyxiating Asia* (Mapusa, Goa: Other India Press, 2003); together with Nicola Yeates, he is also the author of 'Policing Anti-Globalization Protests: Patterns and Variations in State Responses', in Samir Dasgupta and Jan Nederveen Pieterse, eds, *Politics of Globalization* (New Delhi: Sage, 2009); and among other writings, in 2015, he co-edited a special issue of the journal *Social Justice* to mark the thirtieth anniversary of the Bhopal catastrophe. tomas.x@ireland.com

Index

'Passim' (literally 'scattered') indicates intermittent discussion of a topic over a cluster of pages.

618 | The Movements of Movements

A Note on the *Challenging Empires* Series

The *Challenging Empires* series emerged in 2007 from a book produced in 2004 by the editor of the present work, Jai Sen, with Peter Waterman, Arturo Escobar, and Anita Anand. *World Social Forum: Challenging Empires* was an international anthology that critically examined the World Social Forum and the global debates around this emerging phenomenon and located the 2004 edition of the WSF that was held in Mumbai, India, within this larger world. With most chapters of the original English version available online, the book was also translated into German, Hindi, Japanese, and Spanish, and an updated second edition in English was published from Canada in 2008.

The success of this book prompted Jai Sen and the late Peter Waterman to outline a series of volumes—the *Challenging Empires* series—that would critically assess the history and impact of contemporary social movement, including the WSF.

The first subsequent volume in the new series was *World Social Forum: Critical Explorations*, published by OpenWord in 2012.

The two books in the major two-part volume entitled *The Movements of Movements* are the next items. Whereas *Critical Explorations* addressed the World Social Forum alone, these two volumes—*The Movements of Movements, Part 1: What Makes Us Move?*, and its companion volume *The Movements of Movements, Part 2: Rethinking Our Dance*—are about the larger world/s of world movement, and appear at a time when movements for social change and justice are increasingly visible throughout the world. Largely focussed on the period 2006–2010 but also reaching back to 1968 and earlier and forward right up to 2014–15, the books bring together some fifty essays on the epistemological landscape and praxis of world movement. With authors again—as in the earlier volumes in the series —of various ages, races, and persuasions from a wide range of movements, the books attempt to open and deepen conversations between and across movements, drawing readers into those conversations. These volumes (volumes 4 and 5 in the *Challenging Empires* series) go far beyond the WSF, looking at other more spontaneous, structured, and virtual movements.

We are co-publishing *The Movements of Movements* in two parts with an important new actor in international movement publishing, PM Press. The present volume, *Part 1*, lays out and discusses the landscape of contemporary movement and presents and juxtaposes a wide range of movements for change. *Part 2* will directly complement this volume, critically reflecting on movement praxis and on possible futures. Both volumes end with a major essay—appearing as an Afterword—critically locating the collections of essays in our emerging world.

OpenWord and the series editor welcome suggestions and criticism. Send this either to the series editor—see the 'Notes on the Editor' for details—or to OpenWord at www.openword.net.in.

Earlier titles in the *Challenging Empires* series:

World Social Forum: Challenging Empires. Edited by Jai Sen, Anita Anand, Arturo Escobar, and Peter Waterman. Viveka Foundation, New Delhi, India, 2004. (Abridged versions available at http://www.choike.org/nuevo_eng/informes/1557.html and at http://www.openspaceforum.net/twiki/tiki-index.php?page=WSFChallengingEmpires2004)

Volume 2 World Social Forum: Challenging Empires (Revised International Edition) Edited by Jai Sen and Peter Waterman. Black Rose Books, Montreal, Canada, 2009. http://blackrosebooks.net/products/view/WORLD+SOCIAL+FORUM/32439

Volume 3 World Social Forum: Critical Explorations. Edited by Jai Sen and Peter Waterman. OpenWord, New Delhi, India, 2012. http://www.openword.net.in/critical-explorations

OpenWord

OpenWord (http://openword.net.in), the publishing arm of the India Institute for Critical Action: Centre in Movement (www.cacim.net) was founded in 2007 to promote a spirit, culture, and practice of critical openness. It is an expression of the experiences of members and associates and of their attempts to promote critical sociopolitical and cultural action and movement and to contribute to a broader and more effective transformational social power.

OpenWord plans to publish in different fields, looking beyond the boundaries of political, economic, cultural, and academic dogma and privileging authors from the structurally marginalised, with a particular focus on, indigenous peoples, Dalits, and women.

OpenWord seeks to reach young people—students, activists, workers, thinkers, and artists. Commissioning and/or sourcing work from all walks of life and depths of experience, it aims to produce enjoyable publications that challenge us to think beyond accepted boundaries.

OpenWord practises and promotes a culture of open publishing. It critically engages with emerging practices, such as copyleft, open, and non-conventional models of content ownership. **OpenWord** will constantly push existing boundaries to more empowering principles of authorship, ownership, and dissemination of knowledge.

Based in India, **OpenWord** is exploring ways to build a transcultural, global Editorial Collective and to publish material from across the world. It will actively seek to be transnational, transcultural, and transcommunal, thereby contributing to a planetary awareness and consciousness. It will constantly seek both established and new thinking from all parts of the world.

http://www.openword.net.in
openword@openword.net.in
A division of CACIM
R-21 South Extension Part II—Ground floor
New Delhi 110 049
India
cacim@cacim.net

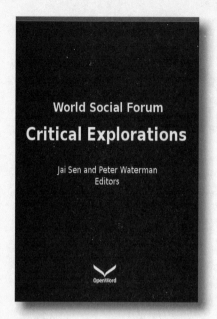

WORLD SOCIAL FORUM
Critical Explorations
Edited by Jai Sen and Peter Waterman

Volume 3 in the *Challenging Empires* series.

This volume brings together 36 essays from around the world—from authors young and old, women and men, black brown and white, and activists, scholars, and those in between, from the South and the North—that enable us all to critically explore and understand the important contemporary phenomenon called the World Social Forum; *and so to better know what kind of world we want to see and to build.* It is a sequel to the widely-acclaimed 2004 book titled *World Social Forum: Challenging Empires.*

Available internationally at http://www.into-ebooks.com/book/world_social_forum/ and in India at http://pothi.com/pothi/book/ebook-jai-sen-world-social-forum-critical-explorations

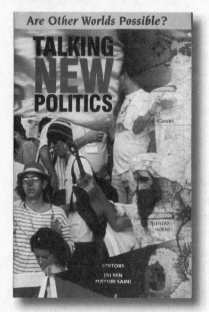

TALKING NEW POLITICS
Edited by Jai Sen and Mayuri Saini

Book 1 in the *Are Other Worlds Possible?* series. Zubaan Books http://www.openword.net.in

This book, the first in a series of three that explore the new ideas generated by the discussions that took place, comprises of chapters based on the presentations made by academics and activists during the seminars, as well as the discussions arising from the presentations. Can the World Social Forum help us to conceptualise and actualise a new politics? Can this new politics be free from violence—of all kinds? Can the experience and knowledge of great movements such as the movement for the environment, and the women's movements, contribute to the creation of a new politics? How can such a politics be sustained?

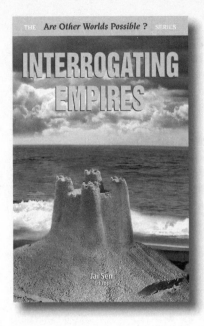

INTERROGATING EMPIRES
Edited by Jai Sen

Book 2 in the *Are Other Worlds Possible?* series. OpenWord and Daanish Books (2011); http://www.openword.net.in

This book is a close look at some of the empires that govern our lives and that we are constantly socialised to believe in and accept, by society, by family, by education, by the market and the media, and by the institutions we are all part of at one point or another in our lives: The empires of patriarchy, casteism, racism, nationalism, and religious communalism—and where each of these is quite aside from what is popularly referred to as "globalisation," even as they interlock with it.

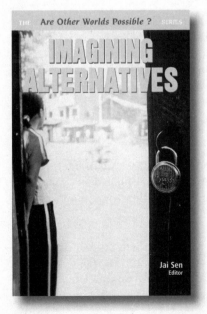

IMAGINING ALTERNATIVES
Edited by Jai Sen

Book 3 in the *Are Other Worlds Possible?* series. OpenWord and Daanish Books (2012); http://www.openword.net.in

People in social and political movements—especially those involved with the World Social Forum—quite commonly say that "Another world is possible"; a world very different from the one we today know. But what do they mean by this? What "other world/s"? Do such worlds only exist in some people's imaginations? And even if they are real, how do we get into these other worlds? And anyway, are such other worlds necessarily more open and more just than the one we know?

This book, the third in the *Are Other World Possible?* book series and preferably read along with the other two (*Talking New Politics* and *Interrogating Empires*), critically explores three of the most important "other worlds" that human beings have so far tried building: Socialism, Cyberspace, and the University.

Also available from PM Press

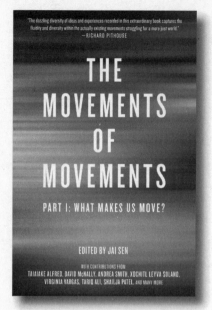

THE MOVEMENTS OF MOVEMENTS
Part 1: What Makes Us Move?
Edited by Jai Sen
$29.95
ISBN: 978-1-62963-240-7

Our world today is not only a world in crisis but also a world in profound movement, with increasingly large numbers of people joining or forming movements: local, national, transnational, and global. The dazzling diversity of ideas and experiences recorded in this collection capture something of the fluidity within campaigns for a more equitable planet. This book, taking internationalism seriously without tired dogmas, provides a bracing window into some of the central ideas to have emerged from within grassroots struggles from 2006 to 2010. The essays here cross borders to look at the politics of caste, class, gender, religion, and indigeneity, and move from the local to the global.

What Makes Us Move?, the first of two volumes, provides a background and foundation for understanding the extraordinary range of uprisings around the world: Tahrir Square in Egypt, Occupy in North America, the indignados in Spain, Gezi Park in Turkey, and many others. It draws on the rich reflection that took place following the huge wave of creative direct actions that had preceded it, from the 1990s through to the early 2000s, including the Zapatistas in Mexico, the Battle of Seattle in the United States, and the accompanying formations such as Peoples' Global Action and the World Social Forum.

Edited by Jai Sen, who has long occupied a central position in an international network of intellectuals and activists, this book will be useful to all who work for egalitarian social change—be they in universities, parties, trade unions, social movements, or religious organisations.

Contributors include Taiaiake Alfred, Tariq Ali, Daniel Bensaid, Hee-Yeon Cho, Ashok Choudhary, Lee Cormie, Jeff Corntassel, Laurence Cox, Guillermo Delgado-P, Andre Drainville, David Featherstone, Christopher Gunderson, Emilie Hayes, Francois Houtart, Fouad Kalouche, Alex Khasnabish, Xochitl Leyva Solano, Roma Malik, David McNally, Roel Meijer, Eric Mielants, Peter North, Shailja Patel, Emir Sader, Andrea Smith, Anand Teltumbde, James Toth, Virginia Vargas, and Peter Waterman.

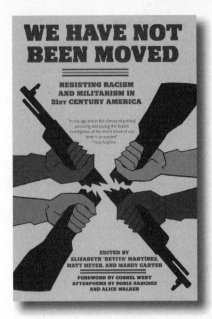

WE HAVE NOT BEEN MOVED
Resisting Racism and Militarism in 21st Century America
Edited by Elizabeth Betita Martínez, Mandy Carter & Matt Meyer
Introduction by Cornel West
Afterwords/poems by Alice Walker and Sonia Sanchez
$29.95
ISBN: 978-1-60486-480-9

We Have Not Been Moved is a compendium addressing the two leading pillars of U.S. Empire. Inspired by the work of Dr. Martin Luther King Jr., who called for a "true revolution of values" against the racism, militarism, and materialism which he saw as the heart of a society "approaching spiritual death," this book recognizes that—for the most part—the traditional peace movement has not been moved far beyond the half-century-old call for a deepening critique of its own prejudices. While reviewing the major points of intersection between white supremacy and the war machine through both historic and contemporary articles from a diverse range of scholars and activists, the editors emphasize what needs to be done now to move forward for lasting social change. Produced in collaboration with the War Resisters League, the book also examines the strategic possibilities of radical transformation through revolutionary nonviolence.

Among the historic texts included are rarely-seen writings by antiracist icons such as Anne Braden, Barbara Deming, and Audre Lorde, as well as a dialogue between Dr. King, revolutionary nationalist Robert F. Williams, Dave Dellinger, and Dorothy Day. Never-before-published pieces appear from civil rights and gay rights organizer Bayard Rustin and from celebrated U.S. pacifist supporter of Puerto Rican sovereignty Ruth Reynolds. Additional articles making their debut in this collection include new essays by and interviews with Fred Ho, Jose Lopez, Joel Kovel, Francesca Fiorentini and Clare Bayard, David McReynolds, Greg Payton, Gwendolyn Zoharah Simmons, Ellen Barfield, Jon Cohen, Suzanne Ross, Sachio Ko-Yin, Edward Hasbrouck, Dean Johnson, and Dan Berger. Other contributions include work by Andrea Dworkin, Mumia Abu-Jamal, Starhawk, Andrea Smith, John Stoltenberg, Vincent Harding, Liz McAlister, Victor Lewis, Matthew Lyons, Tim Wise, Dorothy Cotton, Ruth Wilson Gilmore, Kenyon Farrow, Frida Berrigan, David Gilbert, Chris Crass, and many others. Peppered throughout the anthology are original and new poems by Chrystos, Dylcia Pagan, Malkia M'Buzi Moore, Sarah Husein, Mary Jane Sullivan, Liz Roberts, and the late Marilyn Buck.

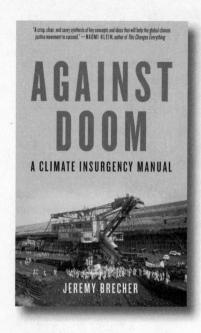

AGAINST DOOM
A Climate Insurgency Manual
Jeremy Brecher
$12.95
ISBN: 978-1-62963-385-5

Before the election of Donald Trump the world was already speeding toward climate catastrophe. Now President Trump has jammed his foot on the global warming accelerator. Is there any way for the rest of us to put on the brakes?

Climate insurgency is a strategy for using people power to realize our common interest in protecting the climate. It uses mass, global, nonviolent action to challenge the legitimacy of public and corporate officials who are perpetrating climate destruction.

A global climate insurgency has already begun. It has the potential to halt and roll back Trump's fossil fuel agenda and the global thrust toward climate destruction.

Against Doom: A Climate Insurgency Manual tells how to put that strategy into action—and how it can succeed. It is a handbook for halting global warming and restoring our climate—a how-to for climate insurgents.

> "Against Doom lays out key elements of a far-reaching, global-scaled, pragmatic, people-powered strategy to topple the power of the fossil fuel industry and the institutions behind it."
> —David Solnit, author of *Globalize Liberation: How to Uproot the System and Build a Better World*

> "A crisp, clear, and savvy synthesis of key concepts and ideas that will help the global climate justice movement to succeed. Brecher outlines many feasible climate solutions that should give all of us hope, despite the odds."
> —Naomi Klein, author of *This Changes Everything: Capitalism vs. the Climate*

———

PM Press was founded at the end of 2007 by a small collection of folks with decades of publishing, media, and organizing experience. PM Press co-conspirators have published and distributed hundreds of books, pamphlets, CDs, and DVDs. Members of PM have founded enduring book fairs, spearheaded victorious tenant organizing campaigns, and worked closely with bookstores, academic conferences, and even rock bands to deliver political and challenging ideas to all walks of life. We're old enough to know what we're doing and young enough to know what's at stake.

We seek to create radical and stimulating fiction and non-fiction books, pamphlets, T-shirts, visual and audio materials to entertain, educate, and inspire you. We aim to distribute these through every available channel with every available technology—whether that means you are seeing anarchist classics at our bookfair stalls; reading our latest vegan cookbook at the café; downloading geeky fiction e-books; or digging new music and timely videos from our website.

PM Press is always on the lookout for talented and skilled volunteers, artists, activists, and writers to work with. If you have a great idea for a project or can contribute in some way, please get in touch.

PM Press
PO Box 23912
Oakland CA 94623
510-658-3906
www.pmpress.org

PM Press in Europe
europe@pmpress.org
www.pmpress.org.uk

FRIENDS OF PM

These are indisputably momentous times—the financial system is melting down globally and the Empire is stumbling. Now more than ever there is a vital need for radical ideas.

In the many years since its founding—and on a mere shoestring—PM Press has risen to the formidable challenge of publishing and distributing knowledge and entertainment for the struggles ahead. With hundreds of releases to date, we have published an impressive and stimulating array of literature, art, music, politics, and culture. Using every available medium, we've succeeded in connecting those hungry for ideas and information to those putting them into practice.

Friends of PM allows you to directly help impact, amplify, and revitalize the discourse and actions of radical writers, filmmakers, and artists. It provides us with a stable foundation from which we can build upon our early successes and provides a much-needed subsidy for the materials that can't necessarily pay their own way. You can help make that happen—and receive every new title automatically delivered to your door once a month—by joining as a Friend of PM Press. And, we'll throw in a free T-shirt when you sign up.

Here are your options:
- $30 a month: Get all books and pamphlets plus 50% discount on all webstore purchases
- $40 a month: Get all PM Press releases (including CDs and DVDs) plus 50% discount on all webstore purchases
- $100 a month: Superstar—Everything plus PM merchandise, free downloads, and 50% discount on all webstore purchases

For those who can't afford $30 or more a month, we have Sustainer Rates at $15, $10, and $5. Sustainers get a free PM Press T-shirt and a 50% discount on all purchases from our website.

Your Visa or Mastercard will be billed once a month, until you tell us to stop. Or until our efforts succeed in bringing the revolution around. Or the financial meltdown of Capital makes plastic redundant. Whichever comes first.